AF516143

Sociology of Health and Medicine

Sociology of Health and Medicine

Madhu Nagla

RAWAT PUBLICATIONS
Jaipur • New Delhi • Bangalore • Guwahati • Kolkata

ISBN 978-81-316-0933-0 (HB)

Reprinted, 2026

Published by
Prem Rawat for **Rawat Publications**
Satyam Apts., Sector 3, Jawahar Nagar, Jaipur - 302 004 (India)
Phones: 0141 265 1748 / 265 7006
E-mail : info@rawatbooks.com
Website: rawatbooks.com

New Delhi Office
4858/24, Ansari Road, Daryaganj, New Delhi 110 002
Phone: 011-23263290

Typeset by Rawat Computers, Jaipur
Printed and bound in India

Contents

SECTION II
Concept and Management in Health Care

SECTION V
Health Policy, Planning and Development

Introduction

Many people think about health in terms of what they eat, how much they exert and are free from disease, but if something goes wrong, the doctors are there to treat and bring them back to normal health. However, health studies goes beyond this narrow thinking of health. Health studies is animated by an understanding that health is more than physical structure, or is only intelligible through the working ideas of mainstream medicine. The idea of health emerges out of a series of diverse social processes and influences, many of these processes operating at levels beyond the physical body with which we experience life in all its states, good or bad. Social structure, culture, politics, emotions, our spiritual selves, and our social and individual perceptions of the world all contribute to what makes us healthy or not. Health studies include the subject matter of sociology, psychology, social policy, social epidemiology, ethics, anthropology, human rights, and social work in an attempt to build the big picture of health. Each discipline possesses its particular strengths in contributing to an overall understanding of health. For example, sociology explores social processes and structures, and so aids in an understanding of how our social class, our gender or our ethnicity influence and shape our health. Psychology investigates the psychological factors that determine health, such as personality, stress and beliefs, and seeks to explain the thought processes that are fundamental to health behaviour. And social policy provides insights into how governments, charities and private companies structure their services and the thinking behind why they do so. Social epidemiologists study about the proportion of people affected by a particular disease at a particular time period. Human rights approach is to study the rights of the people for living a healthy life.

About the Chapters

The textbook is not an end in itself. The outlines of the key assumptions of concepts widely utilized within Health and Medicine studies are presented, and some context for their applications is also provided. However, applying these concepts and theoretical approaches to further understanding of real world health and medicine issues also requires researchers and students to engage in more in-depth readings.

This book is structured into six sections, each of which deals with a specific issue within health, illness and medicine studies, building from the very general philosophical approaches before moving on to concepts that relate to practice and the structuring of health services.

The First Section surveys various concepts that attempt to capture and define health and discusses the scope of health studies. Different approaches of health influence and inform how notions of health care are constructed and maintained within society. It also discusses about the different methodological approaches depending upon the nature of the health studies. This section provides an awareness of what makes health and medicine studies distinct from other approaches to an understanding of health and what insights health and medicine have to offer. It also concentrates on the hospital and social interaction among key players of health delivery mechanism. Hospital is a social system where certain set of roles are expected from doctors and other functionaries. There is an interaction and communication between doctor and patient/client in the clinical situation which has also been looked into the changing perspective.

Section Two deals with social medicine and community medicine at conceptual level and traces its origin from historical to the contemporary time. The distribution of population in terms of morbidity and mortality are dealt within the epidemiological context. It also turns to the notion of health determinants, health promotion and health management. These are the terms which are used for promoting the health among the community and management skills to bring efficiency.

Third Section deals with the plurality of systems of medicine in the health care delivery. The other crucial component in the health care is the role of pharmaceuticals which also traces the dominance of multinationals.

In Section Four we turn our specific attention to health delivery system in India. It mentions about the health delivery in rural and urban situations. It also deals with privatization of health care in India.

State governments are responsible for the well-being in terms of health of their population. They respond to all sections of the society for provisioning of health care through different programmes and policy formulations. Fifth Section also looks at these issues in terms of health inequalities and strategies deployed to counter these outcomes, such as public health programme interventions and policy interventions. The concepts of health rights and ethics are also discussed here. It seeks to explain and contextualize the ways in which health rights are perceived and understood. Ethics of doctors in terms of normative structure are described and how doctors adhere to ethics are analysed in this section.

In Section Six we consider a vital aspect of the reproductive and nutritional issues in health. How women experience their reproductive health in context of gender issues is discussed in this section. Protection agency is responsible for identifying and responding to all sorts of environmental threats and hazards, and for improving our understanding and knowledge of these threats. This section also looks into nutritional issues and health of different sections of people. The role of the insurance companies in providing health care to the community is also discussed in this section. It also discusses and technological issues in health care and finally about the scope of tourism in health care.

Section I

Theories and Methods in Sociology of Health and Medicine

1

Sociology of Health and Medicine

The simplest view of the academic discipline of sociology is that it is somehow concerned with the understanding of human societies. However, this does not take us very far as most people feel that they know a good deal about the society in which they live because they experience it everyday; this can be described as 'common sense' knowledge. Another approach would be to define sociology as a research-based study of society. The best way of defining the contribution of sociology is by looking at the key questions that originally stimulated the development of the academic discipline and which continue to underpin sociological research today:

- What gives social life a sense of stability and order?
- How does social change and development come about?
- What is the nature of the relationship between the individual and society in which they live?
- To what extent does the society into which people are born shape their beliefs, behaviour, and life chances (including health outcomes)?

Sociology of Health and Medicine

Conceptions of health and illness, although not uniform the world over or even in any one society, are of fundamental importance in every society. How health is defined in various societies, how the ill are viewed by the well, how illness is treated, who the healers are, how they are trained, and what their position is in society, the relationships among the religion, class, gender of the ill and their healers, when and how public health policies are inaugurated, the impact of multinational companies and globalization are among the topics which are of interest to the researchers, students and to the health professionals. To cope with the health inequality and increase of medical tourism, the health insurance is becoming a tool for protecting the communities for health care. What are the different sociological approaches and methodologies through which health, illness and medicine aspect can be studied are also well looked in the book. Further, the sociology of health and illness covers sociological pathology (causes of illness and disease), reasons for seeking alternative therapies and compliance and non-compliance with the health care professionals.

It seeks to answer the fundamental issues of the rights of the individual for health care and how ethics are followed in the society while delivering health care. To see the structure and differential impact of health delivery system on rural and urban population various factors are discussed elaborately.

Rampant uses of technology in medicine and effects of environment on health are widely and recently discussed topics.

Sociology of Health and Illness

Disease is a condition defined by doctors and based upon the observation of biological pathology. The conception of disease is 'objective' 'scientific' and based on the bio medical model of pathology which is the basis of modern medical thought. In contrast to the 'objective view of disease, the concept of illness refers to the person's subjective experience of ill health. It goes beyond the biological and physical consequences of disease, affecting the person's subjective well-being and their social functioning. Illness is recognized by departures from the person's normal state of being and by altered feelings which may be diffuse.

To be ill, then, is not simply to be in a physically altered state, but also to be in a society altered condition which is normally disruptive of everyday life and is undesired. Illness is both personal and social. The individuals who feel ill are likely to talk to others in their attempts to make sense of their physical symptoms and feelings of 'disease' and departure from normal functioning. While they may draw upon bio medical ideas and knowledge to make sense of their illness, people also use other ideas which are current in their social groups both to make sense of their illness and to decide what action, if any, should be taken. For example, ideas of what constitute 'flu', how to recognize it, and how to treat it (feed a cold, stare a fever). Such 'lay theories' of illness may be complex and detailed, and provide explanations which link the experiences of illness to the personal and social circumstances of the ill person in ways which may be more consistent and believable to them than professional medical explanations.

Medical sociology centres on the social construction of health and illness – that is, a construction shaped by many elements of the social order and often independent from biomedical phenomena. In this perspective, medical sociology links together and makes sense of the varied manifestations of health and illness: biomedical data, professional practice, institutional structures, social policy, economic and financing, the social epidemiology of disease and death, and the individual experience of health, illness, and medical care. The discipline links the micro-level (self-awareness, individual action, and interpersonal communication), meso-level (hospital and medical education), and macro level (the nation's health status, the structure and political economy of the health care system, and national health policy). The linkages ensure that individual entities are not studies in isolation from their surroundings. (Phil Brown,

'Themes in Medical Sociology', *Journal of Health Politics, Policy and Law*, Vol. 16, No. 3, Fall, 1991).

The political sociology of medicine which explores the relationship between the state and organized interests such as the pharmaceutical industry, changing approaches of the public/patients to maintaining health, managing illness in the context of culture of consumption where health and lifestyle might be seen as commodities, and maintaining a healthy body keeps control over an uncertain and changing world. Consideration of the growth and development of medical pluralism and a discussion of the relationship between structure and agency in the context of social inequalities in health are other areas of the manuscript.

As sociologists published increasingly on health and health care, some began identifying themselves as 'medical sociologists'. These early medical sociologists faced resistance from within sociology itself. Many of their sociological colleagues viewed the emerging speciality of medical sociology with disdain and suspicion, contending it was solely an applied activity, often sponsored by those studying and lacking theoretical substance. Despite the establishment of the subfield, a division began to emerge between those doing 'sociology of medicine' and those doing 'sociology in medicine' (Strauss, 1957).

Sociology of Medicine

Sociology of medicine referred to studies that examined medicine with sociological questions in the forefront, using sociological concepts and theories and is intended largely for a sociological audience. Studies of professions, socialization, and organizations typify this orientation. The sociology of medicine treats the medical world as an object of scientific curiosity. This approach is not geared primarily toward the solution of health problems, but rather toward an explanation of the behaviour of physicians, patients and nurses, and an understanding of the organizational structure in which they interact. Although the social scientists in this posture may illuminate certain topics with important implications for practising health professionals, their chief concern is understanding rather than action. Moreover, the structuring of problems typically derives from a sociological rather than a medical focus. For example, the social scientist sees hospitals as a species of bureaucratic organization or inter-professional role relationships, and compares them with other institutions such as the factory. He is not, in the first instance, devoted to discovering clues to more effective care for patients. It placed the social scientist in the position of relatively detached analyst who studies what goes on in the world of health but is not directly implicated as a participant in the health enterprises.

Sociology in Medicine

In contrast, sociology in medicine included studies that used sociological perspectives and knowledge to investigate medically oriented questions. The primary goals were to solve medical problems and improve medical care. Such research included studies on doctor-patient interaction, social factors affecting the delivery of services and obtaining medical care, and social epidemiology of disease. For many years, sociology in medicine was seen by some sociologists to be of lesser value, because it was an applied rather than a pure use of sociology. Today most researches eschew such distinctions and believe that first-rate sociological research on health can contribute both to the development of medical sociology and to the improvement of health and health care. In fact, in some circles the speciality is no longer called medical sociology but rather the sociology of health and illness. Sociology in medicine is not content to gaze at the behaviour of doctors and patients or at the organization of medical facilities, instead it wishes to inquire, as fellow professionals in health, into the relationships between certain social and psychological factors and a series of medical problems. These problems are of two main varieties: the production of states of illness and the mounting of strategies for coping with them. The two concerns correspond to the major emphases of modern social medicine or social epidemiology. It is interested in discovering where illness occurs in human populations, a prelude to investigating why it should occur in this group and not in that one. Then, in complementary fashion, it wants to explore society's reactions to the facts of ill health. In particular, it seeks knowledge of why people do or do not lend themselves to programmes or prevention or treatment designed by medical professionals. In each of these areas, the main interest will be to assess the ways in which man's social behaviour – his relations to other people and to himself in vital life sectors, such as familial and occupational roles – influences his chances of staying well, becoming ill, or responding to health care. Throughout, it attempts to join peoples' way of life to their ways of health.

The Development of Sociology of Health

Sociology of health, as a speciality within the sociological discipline, began in the post-World War II period. To a large extent, its initial growth was part of the bourgeoning interest in graduate education in all of the social sciences and the efforts within the federal government to support social research in the health sector. Indeed, in many ways, support for social research in health was a means of providing training and research funds for the vitalization of the broader discipline of sociology. It is incorrect, of course, to promote the image that the history of medical sociology began in the 1950s or is solely the US phenomenon.

Interest in the social aspects of health had been present since the 18th century in a variety of disciplines and in a number of countries. Social medicine, social hygiene, and public health developed most notably in France, Germany, and the United Kingdom. The strong growth of sociology of health in the 1950s can be traced to the enthusiasm and farsightedness of a few sociologists who were intent on modernizing sociology. It can also be traced to restless innovators and change agents within medicine who saw the need for a strong social science input into basic medical research, patient care activities, public health, and psychiatry. Well-known sociologists who had made important contributions to the development of theory and research were able to provide support to the emerging speciality of medical sociology (e.g. Merton, 1968; Parsons, 1951). Established leaders in academic medicine, psychiatry, and public health (typically who had some experience collaborating with sociologists) are Hollingshead and Redlich, 1958; Stanton and Schwartz, 1954. In 1950, Donald Young tried to develop the role of social sciences in the development of health science from the sociological perspective. Simultaneously, he also made sure to expand health science in terms of establishing the schools of medicine, public health and nursing schools.

Summing Up

Sociology of medicine referred to studies that examined medicine with sociological questions in the forefront, using sociological concepts and theories that were intended largely for a sociological audience. Studies of professions, socialization, and organizations typify this orientation. In contrast, sociology in medicine included studies that used sociological perspectives and knowledge to investigate medically oriented questions. Sociology of health, as a speciality within the sociological discipline, began in the post-World War II period. Schools of health services administration and programmes in management, public health administration, and health policy train conceptually and methodologically in ways that are commonplace in sociology departments. The concept of illness refers to the person's subjective experience of ill health. It goes beyond the biological and physical consequences of disease, affecting the person's subjective well-being and their social functioning. Illness is recognized by departures from the person's normal state of being and by altered feelings which may be diffuse. To be ill, then, is not simply to be in a physically altered state, but also to be in a society altered condition which is normally disruptive of everyday life and is undesired.

References

Abbot, Andrew (1988), *The System of Professions*, Chicago: University of Chicago Press.

Aiken, L.H., R.J. Blendon, D.E. Rogers and H.E. Freeman (1980), 'Evaluating a Private Foundation's Health Program', *Evaluation Program Planning*, 3(2): 119–29.

Becker, Howard S., Blanche Geer, Everett C. Hughes and Anslem L. Strauss (1961), *Boys in White: Student Culture in Medical School*, Chicago: University of Chicago Press.

Bell, Karen (1988), 'New Reproductive Technologies: Concerns of Feminists and Researchers', *Affilia*, 3(4): 38–50.

Berkanovic, Emil, Carol Telesky and Sharon Reeder (1981), 'Structural and Social Psychological Factors in the Decision to Seek Medical Care for Symptoms', *Medical Care*, 19: 693–709.

Brown, Phil (1991), 'Themes in Medical Sociology', *Journal of Health Politics, Policy and Law*, 16(3): 595–604.

Charmaz, Kathy (1991), *Good Days, Bad Days: The Self in Chronic Illness and Time*, New Brunswick, NJ: Rutgers University Press.

Conrad, Peter (1987), 'The Experience and Management of Chronic Illness', in Julius A. Roth and Peter Conrad (eds), *Research in the Sociology of Health Care*, Greenwich, CT: JAI Press.

Cornwall, J. (1984), *Hard-Earned Lives: Accounts of Health and Illness from East London*, London: Tavistock.

Donovan, J. (1986), *We Do Not Buy Sickness, It Just Comes: Health, Illness and Health Care in the Lives of Black People in London*, Aldershot: Gower.

Fox, Renee C. (1957), 'Training for Uncertainty', in R.K. Merton, G.C. Reader and P.L. Kendall (eds), *The Student-Physician*, Cambridge, MA: Harvard University Press.

Freeman, H.E. and C.E. Lewis (1987), 'The Sexual History-Taking and Counseling Practices of Primary Care Physicians', *Western Journal of Medicine*, 147(2): 165–67.

Freeman, Howard E. and Ozzie G. Simmons (1977), 'Medical Patients in the Community: Family Settings and Performance Levels', in N.J. Smelser and W.T. Smelser (eds), *Personality and Social Systems*, New York: John Wiley.

Freidson, Eliot (1970), *Profession of Medicine*, New York: Dodd, Mead.

Goffman, Erving (1961), *Asylums*, New York: Anchor.

Hewitt, J.P. (1991), *Self and Society: A Symbolic Interactionist Social Psychology*, Boston: Allen and Bacon.

Hollinhshead, August B. and Fredrich C. Redlich (1958), *Social Class and Mental Illness: A Community Study*, New York: John Wiley.

Howard, E. and Sol Levine (eds) (1989), *Handbook of Medical Sociology*, Englewood Cliffs, NJ: Prentice Hall.

Kaplan, G.A. et al. (1987), 'Poverty and Health: Prospective Evidence from the Alameda County Study', *American Journal of Epidemiology*, 125(6): 989–98.

Lemert, E.M. (1972), *Human Deviance, Social Problems and Social Control*, Englewood Cliffs, NJ: Prentice Hall.

Levine, Sol (1987), 'The Changing Terrains in Medical Sociology: Emergent Concern with Quality of Life', *Journal of Health and Social Behaviour*, 28: 1–6.

Levine, Sol, Norman A. Scotch and George J. Vlasak (1969), 'Unravelling Technology and Culture in Public Health', *American Journal of Public Health*, 59: 237–44.

Lorber, Judith (1997), *Gender and the Social Construction of Illness*, Thousand Oaks, CA: Sage Publications.

Mechanic, D., P.D. Cleary and J.R. Greenley (1982), 'Sex Care Differences in Medical Care Utilization: An Empirical Investigation', *Journal of Health and Social Behaviour*, 23(2): 106–19.

Mechanic, David (1962), 'The Concept of Illness Behaviour', *Journal of Chronic Diseases*, 15: 189–94.

Merton, R.K. (1968), *Social Theory and Social Structure*, New York: Free Press.

Mishler, Elliot G., Lorna R. Amara Singhan, Stuart T. Hauser, Ramsay Liem, Samuel D. Osherson and Nancy E. Waxler (1981), *Social Context of Health, Illness and Patient Care*, Cambridge: Cambridge University Press.

Parsons, Talcott (1951), *The Social System*, New York: The Free Press.

Riessman, Catherine Kohler and Constance A. Nathanson (1986), 'The Management of Reproduction: Social Construction of Risk and Responsibility', in Linda Aiken and David Mechanic (eds), *Applications of Social Science to Clinical Medicine and Health Policy*, Princeton, NJ: Robert Wood Johnson Foundation.

Rossi, Peter H. and Howard E. Freeman (1985), *Evaluation: A Systematic Approach*, New York: Sage Publications.

Schur, E.M. (1979), *Interpreting Deviance: A Sociological Perspective*, New York: Harper and Row.

Stanton, Albert H. and Morris S. Schwartz (1954), *The Mental Health Hospital*, New York: Basic Books.

Starr, Paul (1982), *The Social Transformation of American Medicine*, New York: Basic Books.

Straus, Robert (1957), 'The Nature and Status of Medical Sociology', *American Sociological Review*, 22: 200–04.

Zola, Irving K. (1983), *Socio-Medical Inquiries: Recollections, Reflections, and Reconsiderations*, Philadelphia: Temple University Press.

2

Health and its Dimensions

This chapter tells about the health in antiquity. Further it also tells about the concept of health. It also offers the critique of the definition of health given by WHO and synthesis of the debate of subjectivity and objective meaning of health. Further, it presents the new philosophy of health. It also presents the concept of health at global level.

Genesis of Health

Although concerns with health and disease have been a major pre-occupation of humans since antiquity, the use of the word 'health' to describe human 'well-being' is relatively recent. The word 'health' was derived from the old English word 'health', which meant a state of being sound, and was generally used to infer soundness of the body. Prior to the period of the somewhat enigmatic physician known as Hippocrates (460–377 BC, or more appropriately, from around 5 BC), health was perceived as a divine gift. Hippocrates was credited with pioneering the move away from divine notions of health and using observation as a basis for acquiring health knowledge. He was credited with encouraging a focus on environmental sanitation, personal hygiene and, in particular, balanced diets – 'let food be thy medicine; and let thy medicine be food'. He theorized that what we currently regard as 'health' might be defined as the extent of a delicate balance of four fluids: blood, yellow bile, black bile, and phlegm. Ill health, he believed, resulted from an imbalance of these fluids. Nevertheless, a divine view of health persists to this era. For example, Prophet Mohammed's view of health, sickness and death – followed by a high proportion of practising Muslims – may be inferred from the following verse in the holy *Koran:* 'The Lord of the worlds; it is He who heals me when I am sick, and He who would cause me to die and live again' (*Koran*, 26: 80).

With only simple technology, our ancestors could do little to improve health. Hunters and gatherers faced frequent food shortages, which sometimes forced mothers to abandon their children. Those lucky enough to survive infancy were still vulnerable to injury and illness, so half died by the age of 20 and few lived to the age of 40 (Nolan and Lenski, 1999). As societies developed, agriculture and food became more plentiful. Yet social inequality also increased, so that the elites enjoyed better health than the peasants and slaves, who lived in crowded, unsanitary shelters and often were hungry. In the growing cities of medieval Europe, human waste and other refuse piled up in the streets, spreading infectious diseases and plagues that periodically wiped out entire towns (Mumford, 1961).

Debate of Objectivity and Subjectivity for the Concept of Health and Illness

All definitions of health and illness demand consensus on the part of informed observers. The consensus is harder to achieve, however, in areas where 'objective' yardsticks are few and human passions are at stake in the formulation. Each of these qualifications applied to health, medicine has no perfect metre, therefore subjectivity may also come in. Not only does the variety of human behaviour admit many different categories for assigning healthiness or disease but also the question of who (the victim, the physician, the relative, or the formal agent of social control) is perceiving and defining becomes critical.

Here are some basic propositions of social and cultural dimensions of health. The propositions, in turn, are derived from an attempt to specify historically the development of health services and concept of health and disease. The paradigm of clinical medicine which is currently the universally recognized model of medical sciences persists as an individualistic, class-based, and ideological mode of diagnosis, treating and preventing illness. One must distinguish two aspects of scientific knowledge – the degree of exactness with which the science approximated its cognitive object, and the relation of science to reality, which can only be expressed in terms of adequacy, not in objective terms. So the theoretical assumptions on which medicine is based are subjective. This is because science is subjective and medicine is a branch of science.

Both scientific and medical knowledge depend on material production and reflect on social organization of the production, not a historical objectivity. From this proposition follows the theory that contemporary medical definitions of health and disease are inadequate because they are abstractions derived, for specific historical reasons, from the clinical study of the individual. The definitions are inadequate expressions of the relation of medical states (illness) to reality, since individuals are not clinical entities. In reality, the human essence is the product of an ensemble of social relations. The clinical model does not encompass the social relations of the individuals it studies even at its most progressive limits. The clinical paradigm which has been dominating for long time has defined health and diseases from clinical point of view. It takes into consideration the physiological conditions of the individual while ignoring the social conditions of individual. It primarily concentrates on the presence of sickness in one's body. However, in the 19th century, again an elaborated definition of illness was given. The illness is looked in terms of disturbances, exaggeration, dementia and obstacles in the normal functioning of physiological functions. In this definition, the body of the individual is reduced in the machine form and, therefore, its organs can be discretely examined and regulated. The definition latently shows the notion of absence of disease, but at no point of time looks for positive concept of health.

Illich set out a limit to medicine and argued that in the 19th century the strong lobby of medical system was deliberately making the sickness as a focal point. By making sickness as a focal point, naturally the medical system will look forward to mechanical framework to treat the ill person. On the other hand, Foucault (1972), in his analysis of origins of modern medicine, applied the deconstructing approach for understanding illness and health. He argued that contemporary medicine is more concerned with health. The health is to be understood in its qualities of vigour and illness should be understood from the people's point of view.

The proximate source of the clinical paradigm was the hospital base of the medical perception of reality. During the 19th century, the hospital became the place where diseased people were housed, diseases were identified and a census of disease was kept. Along with sickness, health acquired a clinical status, becoming the absence of clinical symptoms (Illich, 1975). Initially, the clinical paradigm appeared in association with disease, but eventually it came to dominate the entire spectrum. One way to approach the spread of the clinical medical paradigm – a phenomenon sometimes referred to as the medicalization of society – is to arrange various medical disciplines on a continuum extending from death at one end to health at the other. The areas of social and preventive health medicine model are basically a social model over a clinical model in the direction of health. The direction of this model basically favours the family and community over an individual. It equally gives importance to its ecological conditions and environment in understanding the health of the community. Environment also includes sanitation which studies the diseases within the epidemiological framework. Epidemiological framework deals with the triad of host, disease and environment. Until and unless these clinical models will not define health by incorporating social model it is hard to find out the definition of health. Thus medicines' failure to develop a positive definition of health results from the individualistic and ideological bias that pervades medical research and medical practice, structures relations between practitioners and patients, shapes the approaches selected for treatment (e.g. chemical or surgical intervention) and the technology employed, and rejects the initiation of collective social action by communities.

Concept of Health and Illness

Physicians have traditionally held a rough, commonsensical view of health as 'the absence of symptoms'. Health, therefore, becomes a residual category, the uninteresting opposite of disease. However useful such a definition may be, separating the treatable and, the classifiable from all others, it clearly begs several questions. It excludes from the category of illness the subtle and latent disturbance that has gone unremarked by the subject or is unapparent to the observer.

A radically different conception of health offered by one physician asserts that health is 'compensated illness'. Here the usual assumption is turned inside out. Instead of positing health as the unusual state of the human being and thinking of all illness as a deviation from some normal condition, this definition assumes that in a sense we are all ill and that our healthiness represents an achievement in counteracting the incursion of disease. Among the attractive features such as conception is its recognition of how pervasive illness, particularly chronic illness, is in cotemporary societies and its implication that health is a process of living rather than a static entity.

The concept of health as functional efficacy enables the analyst to invoke considerations of appropriateness and of fitness for specified activities. That is, it begins to answer the question: health for what? The health of a housewife is presumably quite different in some ways from the health of an actress; what is normally healthy in a 20-year-old sprinter may be a state of functioning both impossible and undesirable in the middle-aged executive. If normal health consists of the ability in an individual to perform adequately, then the criteria of healthiness, still varies as do the styled rights and obligations that form the substance of roles. Health is cherished because of what it enables the person to do, and illness is feared primarily because of its interference with desired behaviours.

But, of course, the problem defining health and illness is not only a question of trying to keep intellectual discourse clean and untrammelled. The concepts we adopt are intimately bound up in medical research, medical care, and eventually, in decisions about what levels of well-being a society will or will not tolerate. One observer has, in fact, argued that the field of public health advances through progressive redefinition of the unacceptable; a tolerable level of population health in 1990 may not have been tolerable in 1970. Judgments about healthiness are therefore laced through the whole social fabric and affect everything from the individual's self-picture to the setting of national policy.

The notion that health and illness are dynamic patterns, changing with time and social circumstances, leads to conclusion that judgments of healthiness must be made many times as the life history unfolds. It also pushes the analyst to reiterate that most evaluations of health are relative, based on a series of perceptions and observations, rather than a unitary standard of measurement. Further, health comes in a dynamic framework to be seen as a continuum of functional ability-disability, finely graded, not as a matter of flat, mutually exclusively categories.

If we take 'dis-ease' literally, as the lack or absence of ease, then we must of course ask: what ease, whose ease? In what context? Such questions seem especially relevant to the chronic illnesses, especially the mental disorders, which have assumed an increasingly important place in the contemporary time. We have to assess functional capacity, and sentiments about the capacity, in the absence of disease and clear-cut syndromes of disorder. Neurosis is different from typhoid fever and rheumatoid arthritis is different from cholera. Therefore, we try to discover who it is that sees the subject as ill, and what purposes govern the act of labelling.

We have noted that in most cases the individual's subjective sense of illness or well-being is consonant with the judgments of health professionals and other concerned observers. The self-rating or number and severity of symptoms, for example, tend to agree quite well with the rating that would be derived from a physician doing a thorough medical history and examination. To a major extent it is fair to say, you are healthy (or ill) if you think you are.

But self-perception does not stand alone and it may in some cases be radically opposed to the way others perceive the subject. Evaluation of health from the outside is usually rooted in either or both of the two kinds of judgment as to function: the non-performance of social roles and the distorted performance of them in a manner disturbing to the partner in relationship or to interested third parties, such as the police or neighbours. Although each of these judgments may also be made by the individual himself, the second (role distortion) may be especially difficult for the subject to assess, and it would be especially vulnerable to varied interpretations on the part of the several participants in evaluation. Here again, the psychological disorders pose the gravest ambiguities of definition. This is partly because of their inherent complexity and partly because of the fact that role fulfilment is seldom present to merit the label of non-performance? How distorted must a given role relationship become before role partners affix the name of illness to the subject's vagaries of behaviour?

Defining Health

Health is a prerequisite of human development and is an essential component for the well-being of the mankind. The health problems of any community are influenced by interplay of various factors including social, economic and political ones. The concepts of health, disease and medicine are largely a product of post-19th century scientific development. Ackerknecht (1942) commented that to 17th century European and American, Indian medicine would not have seemed 'strange primitive' in as much as cupping, bleeding, purging herbal remedies, some forms of surgery and even some exorcism, so also some of the associated beliefs and mystical theories about the causation of illness and the rules of healthy living would have been common to both. In the same vein, we may visualize the concepts of health and diseases etc. of the general unschooled slum people as not significantly different from those of the so-called rural people of India. This is not to deny that some unique conceptions do not characterize the health concepts of individual rural people in different eco-historical cultural zones of India while about the problems encountered in developing satisfactory or adequate concepts, we may have to evolve the medically viable and bio-ecologically feasible indices to define various standards of normality in body temperature, blood pressure and the physiological conditions. The concept of health has remained exclusive and difficult to define. Some people see health as normal condition of the individual while others view it as opposite to illness, while some consider health as well developed and adequately nourished muscular body capable of doing work and able to withstand physical strain. Thus, health can also be considered as the achievement of social and individual usefulness. The definition of health found in medical writings throughout the ages is broadly utopian. Gden on health care in the 2nd century, described health as a 'condition of which we neither suffer pain nor are hindered in the function of daily life', that is when we are 'able to take part in government, bath and drink and eat, and do other things we want'. Health is a state in which one is able to work without any difficulty. When work is hampered, then one will be called or designated as sick. Lieban (1977) said that 'Health and diseases are measures of the effectiveness with which human groups combining biological and cultural resource adopt to their environment. Variations in health are connected with the variations in social circumstances and habit patterns'. Leslie (1976) said that there are some universal perceptions of health and disease and at the same time there are also some perceptions unique to a particular society. Besides the unique socio-cultural systems and perceptions, environmental factors or conditions may also lead to differential spatial distribution of medical concepts. The cognition of health and disease, thus, in a cross-cultural perspective requires not only the biological explanation for the illness but also social, psychological and religious explanation. We all think we know what 'health' is, but it is actually very difficult to define. When discussing health care it is important to realize that what people think as health can vary quite widely.

Health can be defined as the absence of diseases (i.e. negatively), or it can be simply defined as physical fitness. Another way to define health is in terms of what people are able to do (i.e. functionally), thus health may be seen as 'optimal functioning' or the ability to do things. It is customary to distinguish between both negative and positive definitions of health and functional and experimental definitions (Calnan, 1987). The medical view of health – the absence of disease – is clearly negative. By contrast, an example of a positive definition is that offered by the World Health Organization (WHO) (1971) which defines health as 'a state of complete physical, mental and social well-being and not merely the absence of disease and infirmity'. However comprehensive, this has rarely been practicable. well-being is defined as a harmonious relationship between an individual or group and the physical, biological and socio-cultural environment, as also feeling of satisfaction that is associated with this. More recently, WHO (2001) has also indicated that health is a 'cumulative state, to be promoted throughout life in order to ensure that the full benefits are enjoyed in later years'. Good health is vital for maintaining an acceptable quality of life.

A functional definition implies the ability to participate in normal social roles (Parsons, 1979), and this may be contrasted with an experiential definition which takes sense of self into account (Kelman, 1975). Others have stated that health cannot be defined as a state because it is ever changing. Mckenzie et al. (2008) define health as a dynamic state or condition of the human organism that is multidimensional (i.e. physical, emotional, social, intellectual, spiritual and occupational) in nature, a resource for living, and results from a person's interactions with and adaptations to his or her environment. Therefore, it can exist in varying degrees and it's specific to each individual and his or her situation. For example, a person can be healthy while dying, or a person who is a quadriplegic can be healthy in the sense that his or her mental and social well-being are high and physical health is as good as it can be (Hancock and Minkler, 2005). A person's health status is dynamic in part because of the many factors that determine one's health. It is widely accepted that health status is determined by the interaction of five domains: gestational endowments (i.e. genetic makeup), social circumstances (e.g. education, employment, income, poverty, hosing, crime and social cohesion), environmental conditions where people live and work (i.e. toxic agents, microbial agents, and structural hazards), behavioural choices (e.g. diet, physical activity, substance use and abuse), and the availability of quality of care (McGinnis, 2001).

Ultimately, the health fate of each of us is determined by factors acting not mostly in isolation but by our experience where the domains interconnect. Whether a gene is expressed can be determined by environmental exposures or behavioural patterns. The nature and consequences of behavioural choices are affected by social circumstances which in turn affect the health care we receive (McGinnis et al., 2002).

Another approach to defining health is via the examination of people's perceptions of the concept. For example, in a study of elderly people in Aberdeen, Williams (1983) identified three lay concepts of health from his interview data: health as an absence of disease; health as a dimension of strength, weakness and exhaustion; and health as a functional fitness.

These three conceptualizations broadly parallel were deciphered by Herzlich (1973) in her interviews with 80 middle class people living in Paris and rural Normandy a decade earlier. Herzlich identified 'health as a vacuum' – which implies an absence of disease; 'reverse of health' – a biological capacity to resist or cope with illness which increases or decreases over time; and 'equilibrium' which is normal health, rarely attained. Empirical studies have found that people's ideas are likely to incorporate a number of these dimensions. However, there is evidence to suggest some relationships between types of beliefs and social location. For example, d'Houtard and Field (1984), in a study of 4,000 people in France, found that non-manual respondents had more positive and personalized conceptualization of health, whereas manual respondents revealed negative and instrumental definitions. In the UK research, it was found that working-class women are more likely to hold functional conceptualizations of health which may be linked to material constraints and situations in which they have little choice but to fulfil their social obligations. A secondary analysis of Blaxter's data to examine the comparative health beliefs of Asian, Afro-Caribbean and White respondents, Asians were more likely to define health in functional terms and Afro-Caribbeans were more likely to describe health in terms of energy and physical strengths. They were also more likely to attribute illness to bad luck. This supports Donovan's (1986) findings that groups in society with the least power are more likely to hold fatalistic views on illness causation.

The concept of health is difficult to define and measure. Although we associate it with the activities of doctors, it is only indirectly linked to medical treatment. Doctors deal primarily with disease and not with the promotion of health in any positive way. The knowledge of medicine is a catalogue of disorders implying that when none are present people are healthy. But promoting health involves the prevention of disease, not merely its treatment. Given that limited scope exists to restore or repair damaged health, there is little to be learned about health as such in medical literature. So what is health and what are the factors that protect it or put it at risk? At a personal level we all know the answer at least to the first of these questions. We know from personal experience of feeling well and feeling ill how to distinguish health and ill health in subjective terms. But converting subjective knowledge into a standard measure which applies to the whole population is by no means easy. To begin with, not everybody has the same threshold of pain or the same expectations about what counts as abnormal symptoms. Some people go to the doctor for complaints which others may not even notice and yet the latter include people who spend a whole lifetime apparently feeling healthy only to die at an early age of a preventable or treatable condition. The problem is finding a definition for health which covers these variations and permits the measurement of health experience in the population as a whole. WHO has defined health as a state of complete physical, mental and social well-being and not merely the absence of disease and infirmity. This definition was adopted by WHO in its International Conference held at New York in June 1946. The representatives of 61 states conferred to this definition and since then this definition has not been amended.

This definition emphasizes the interdependence of physical and mental welfare stressing that feeling well is not just a physical experience. But how can these different dimensions be converted into a measure which can be used to study the distribution of health in one society or to compare standards of health between societies? In the absence of any universally valid measure, most surveys of health rely on one or other of the health status indicators of morbidity and mortality. The first of these, morbidity, which means quite simply sickness, is an indicator not to health but of its absence. It is measured either through self reported illness in health surveys or from the statistics of time off work. Alternatively it may be constructed from the records of consultation between doctors and patients. The statistics of morbidity in any of these forms represent health negatively as a state of illness at one point in time. As such they tend to convey the impression of ill health in episodic terms as something that happens suddenly and then goes away, rather than as a continuous dimension of experience. They also pose a number of problems of interpretation when applied for the purposes of comparing health experience within a population. Self-reported sickness has the shortcomings already mentioned of being based on subjective judgement. Thus, statistics of absence due to sickness can only present the experience of people at work, while those of medical treatment are as much a measure of availability of, as demand for, services. What of the other health status indicator, mortality? This measure of health is constructed from mortality statistics. It can provide information about risk of death at any age and from any particular cause. Its great limitation is that it only represents forms of ill-health that are ultimately fatal and not all those other forms of pain and suffering that do not result in loss of life. However, it is not influenced by the processes of subjective judgement in the way that morbidity is and, being a more objective judgement it can be used to study changes over time. In fact the incidence of mortality was the only means of studying health in earlier period. Age at death provides a measure of the length of the human lifetime. It indicates, in other words, the durability of the human body, the time it takes to wear out. In this sense mortality is a particularly useful indicator. It captures the positive dimension of health and it avoids the trap of presenting ill-health as an episodic event. Life expectation is the only means of making any sense of what people's health was like in the nineteenth century and before. Health is a unity and harmony within the mind, body and spirit which is unique to each person, and is as defined by that person. The level of wellness or health is, in part, determined by the ability to deal with and defend against stress. Health is on a continuum with movements between a state of optimum well-being and illness which is defined as degrees of disharmony. It is determined by physiological, psychological, socio-cultural, spiritual, and developmental stage variables. An understanding of health is the basis of all health care. Health is not perceived the same way by all members of a community including various professional groups (e.g. biomedical scientists, social science specialists, health administrators, ecologists etc.).

Bourdieu's (1977) anthropological work within France concluded that the working class tended to have an instrumental understanding of their health (the notion of the body as physical capital). By way of contrast, the middle classes/professions were seen to perceive their health in a very different way, as a 'personal project'. Health was perceived as being under their own personal control, and as reflecting the outcome of particular 'lifestyle choices'. This approach reinforces the idea that the notion of 'health' is very much a social and cultural construction reflecting the realities of life for different social groups.

Since society is always in the process of dynamism, the changes in the structures, processes and also modification do occur in the concepts also. The concept of health is also not static. It keeps on changing and new patterns of thought and new philosophy also emerge in the concept of health. We will present below the changing concept of health.

Bio Medical Concept

Earlier the concept of health was viewed in terms of absence of disease and an individual was regarded as healthy. The whole notion of biological concept of health is based on germ theory. Germ theory of disease dominated at the turn of 20th century. Scientists were looking for the causes of diseases in relations to germs and ignoring all the other factors. The medical profession views human body as a machine and points out that failure or obstruction in the machine causes the disease. The task of the doctor is to repair the obstruction or failure of the machine. Thus, this concept of health made the definition of health quite narrow and ultimately left health to the rescue of medicine and health professionals. However, the health viewed in the form of bio medical theory has minimized the role of environmental, social, psychological and cultural determinants of health. The bio medical model of disease which is based on scientific criteria could not find adequate answers in finding the solution for poverty, malnutrition, chronic diseases, mental illnesses, environmental pollution, drug abuse and accidents and population explosion by elaborating the medical technologies.

Developments in medical and social sciences led to the conclusion that the bio medical concept of health was inadequate.

Ecological Concept

The criticism levelled against biomedical concept of health gives birth to the ecological concept of health. Ecologists viewed health in terms of dynamic equilibrium between man and his environment and disease as maladjustment of the human organism to environment. Dubos (1965) defined health in the environmental paradigm and asserted that health implies the relative absence of pain and discomfort and continuous adaptation and adjustment to the environment to ensure optimal function. Human ecological and social-cultural issues are so important that they do determine the occurrence of the disease but, at the same time, also determine the availability and population problem. Ecology is mainly concerned with the two aspects, i.e. man and environment. It can also be explained that if a man is imperfect it means the environment is also imperfect. History is a witness to the argument that improvement in human adaptation to natural environment can lead to longer life expectancies and a better quality of life even in the absence of modern health delivery system (WHO, 1986).

Psychosocial Concept

Continuous development in the social sciences has revealed that health is not only a biomedical phenomenon but it is also influenced by social, political, economic, cultural and psychological factors. Thus, we conclude that health is not only a biological but social phenomenon.

Holistic Concept

The holistic model is the integration of all the above concepts. It gives due importance to social, economic, political and environmental factors for influencing health. It has been defined as an integrated or unified process involving the well-being of a person in relation to his environment. In the ancient time the view was that health means sound mind in a sound body in a sound family in a sound environment. The holistic approach of health recognizes that different sectors of society, namely: agriculture, animal husbandry, water and sanitation, housing, communication, forestry and public works share the concern for health. Thus, overall the emphasis is on the promotion and protection of health.

Critique of Definition of Health

The definition of health given by World Health Organization is also not free from the critical evaluation. The critics argue that this definition is very idealistic and *does provide space means is* not flexible. The critics are also uncomfortable with the word 'complete' as they find it is an imaginative idea that one will be completely free from all worries and without any disease or infirmity. It is unlikely that anyone would be healthy throughout his life. It is also argued that a state of complete state of physical, mental and well-being is closer to happiness than to health (Bircher, 2005). Bircher further argues that words health and happiness show different life experiences, where the relationships are neither fixed or constant. It implies that if one is not able to distinguish between happiness and health and if happiness is not there, then it means these is health problem. Bircher's emphasis is on changing health needs, especially in relation to age, and personal responsibility.

Sarrachi (1996) provides an alternative to the concept of health by including the emerging issues of human rights, equity and justice to the definition of health given by WHO. The definition of health can be modified by adding certain valuable concepts of health emerging in the contemporary society to enrich a more broad definition.

New Philosophy of Health

Health is regarded as a fundamental human right. It is regarded as an essence of productive life and minimizing the expenditure on medical care. Health is not in the isolation rather it is intersectoral and regarded as an essential component of social development. Health is the focal point of quality of life. It is also regarded that health is not only the concern of the individual, but it is also the responsibility of state and international society. The investment in health is investment for society and its development. Health is a worldwide and global phenomenon.

New Public Health

The classical notion of public health, which addressed the structural determinants of health and illness, was somewhat revived by 'new public health' which gives importance to 'social' factors (Baggott, 2004). Addressing the question of ill health of a population, world thus require a political and social intervention rather than biomedical alone. Importance to social and other factors grew out of opposition from various pressure groups, movements and critiques arising from medicine itself which signified that biomedical claims were no longer going to be accepted uncritically by 'lay' persons. In India, Banerji (1971) said that new public health approach was adopted in National Tuberculosis Programme and sociological data was used along with epidemiological details for diagnosis and treatment of the cases to make it a people-oriented technology. On the other hand, there are criticisms about the 'new public health' (NPH) which claims beyond modernist strategies where it distanced itself from hospital-centred curative medicine and focus on multidisciplinary approach. In reality also, NPH distances itself from biomedical approach where an individual is given more importance than social factors. The adoption of broad concept in its understanding includes psychological, physical and social elements. But then, NPH used medical, scientific and epidemiological knowledge for its intervention. Professional expertise like in biomedicine becomes privileged one over lay expertise in guiding the population. This kind of approach increases the surveillance and enhances the power of professionals further as scope of expert surveillances and assessment and also intervention is extended. It is seen as a series of regimes of power and knowledge that are oriented to the regulation and surveillance of individual bodies and the social body as a whole (Peterson and Lupton, 1996). The new public health has given itself into the hand of technology which checks and guides the direction of public health. Technology exercises its power and knowledge by giving greater importance for technological interventions rather than societal aspects in the intervention. Furedi (1977) argued that trust on the experts and institutions were lost due to creation of 'culture of fear' in which professionals with some vested interest risked the individuals. But then Wildavsky (1988) challenged the claim made by the critiques of science regarding the risk of modern society. He believed that risks are exaggerated and the benefits of the technology are not fully appreciated. In order to gain societal approval Giddens proposed the reformed science through social audit, which can clear the misunderstandings and uncertainties. But then one should note that identification and assessment are social processes where society should have a say.

Global Health

Global health is co-terminus with the public health and international health. The concern of global health has originated from the epidemics, hygiene and tropical medicine. We find very scanty material for defining the concept of global health. After searching the concept of global health we find the overlapping of global health with the concept of public health in some form of international health. Now the question arises how should we define global health?

Koplan (2009) has tried to define global health as a notion in which the world is viewed as an aggregate of healthy people who are engaged in research and practice related with certain issues of health. However, there is a need for commonly accepted definition of global health and it should extend beyond semantics. Global health might have some differences at the level of philosophy, strategies, and priorities for action between physicians, researchers, funders, media and the general public. The definition of public health is suggested by Winslow (1920), and it seems that it is closer to the concept of global health. Winslow defines public health as the science and art of preventing diseases, extending life and quality of physical life through organized community efforts. The community efforts are directed towards sanitation and environment for controlling the communicable infections and educating the individuals for personal hygiene. The organizations of medical and nursing teams are needed for early detection and diagnosis, preventive treatment of diseases and the social mechanisms so that every individual is assured of living adequately for the maintenance of health. This will ultimately enhance the longevity and translate into his birthright. The US Institute of Medicine in 1988 in their report on Future Health, described public health in terms of its mission, substance and organizational framework which will translate in tackling the preventive aspect. Community approach is given emphasis over the individual approach. In the dictionary, public health is defined as the efforts to protect, promote and restore the people's health. Public health is the aggregate of sciences, skills and beliefs that is directed to the maintenance and improvement of the health of all people through collective actions and efforts. In the beginning, I mentioned that global health is an overlapping area of public health and international health. These overlapping areas are mentioned below:

- Priority to preventive measures
- More focus on poor, vulnerable and under-served population
- Multifactorial and interdisciplinary approaches
- Priority to health as public good and the importance of systems and structures
- Participation of stakeholders

The above areas of public health and international area show commonalities and thus focus on global health. Hence, global health is affected by transnational determinants like environmental changes, urbanization, epidemics and other health issues. Specifically epidemic issues like AIDS and infectious diseases (dengue, influenza) are global diseases. But before diseases, the global concern is to address tobacco control, micronutrient deficiencies, obesity, injury prevention, and migrant workers' health etc. (Koplan, 2009).

Thus, global health refers to the domestic disparities as well as cross-border issues. Global health also focuses on funding of the underdeveloped nations so that they are treated well. It also incorporates the training and distribution of health care manpower in the underdeveloped society. The analysis of global health also raises the pertinent question that is it directed towards infectious diseases and maternal and child health issues. There is also other side of the concern of the global health that should address the issues of chronic diseases, injuries, mental health and environment. However, in the actual situation the infectious diseases and maternal and child health are the major areas which seek the attention of global health, but it should also direct its efforts for under-nutrition, mal-nutrition, tobacco related diseases and mental health etc. Dietary changes are rapidly taking place and in turn it is giving birth to lifestyle diseases which are also the concern of global health. Lack of physical activity, more dependency on automobiles, smoking, drug abuse, stress are also threats to health, therefore priority should be set. Global health also focuses on the researches done across the cultures and finds out the better prevention module for certain culturally specific diseases. Thus, global health uses the resources, knowledge, and experiences of diverse cultures in addressing the global health challenges throughout the world. To conclude, global health in the true sense is an interdisciplinary approach for prevention, treatment and care of the society as a whole.

Dimensions of Health

The good health or healthy life is composed of many dimensions and these dimensions are discussed.

Physical Dimension of Health

The physical dimension of the health is directly related with the perfect functioning of the body. It is related with the functioning of the body cells and organs at the optimum level. However, there is an ambiguity at the level of defining the optimum level of functioning. Some people view physical health in terms of colour of the skin, height, body weight and other physical features.

There are many sociological studies which have been exclusively done on the conception of health, i.e. how people define health. The conception of health is reflected in the form of fair colour, bright eyes, long, black and silky hair, not too fat, a good appetite, sound sleep, capacity to do hard work and no tiredness even after doing hard work. They also view health in terms of well functioning of the different organs of the body and proper working of sense organs. Physical dimension of health also includes the normal pulse rate, and required level of blood pressure according to age and sex of individual. Young and growing individuals require much more vitality of the organs so that it helps them in their growth of physical body. There is a lot of debate about the optimum level of height and weight. However, man's bio-sociological studies have confirmed that height and weight also vary according to ethnicity, culture and ecological conditions. The studies have concluded that there are number of ethnic communities which are shorter in height but they are equally healthy as other communities are. Thus, we conclude that physical health refers to the state of the body, its composition, development, functions and maintenance of its vital organs. Since health is related with the functioning and maintenance of the body organs, therefore, it is necessary to keep oneself healthy by doing physical exercises, eating nutritious food to keep the body and mind energized. The balance of nutrients in the body is essential for maintaining good health. Besides that as and when the body shows imbalance and results into the symptoms of ill health, it is necessary to go for medical check-up and follow the rules prescribed by the doctors.

Modern medicine has evolved tools and techniques which may be used in various combinations for the assessment of physical health. These include: self-assessment of overall health, inquiry into symptoms of ill health and risk factors, inquiry into medications, inquiry into levels of activity (e.g. number of days of restricted activity within a specified time, degree of fitness), inquiry into use of medical services (e.g. the number of visits to a physician, number of hospitalizations) in the recent past, standardized questionnaire for respiratory diseases, clinical examination, nutrition and dietary assessment and biochemical and laboratory investigations. At the community level, the state of health may be assessed by such indicators as death rate, mortality rate and expectation of life. Ideally, each piece of information should be individually useful and when combined should permit a more complete health profile of individuals and communities.

Mental Dimension

Mental health is not mere absence of mental illness. Good mental health is the ability to respond to the many varied experiences of life with flexibility and a sense of purpose. More recently, mental health has been defined as 'a state of balance between oneself and others, a coexistence between the realities of the self and that of other people and of the environment' (Sartorius, 1983). A few short decades ago, the mind and body were considered independent entities. Recently, however, researchers have discovered that psychological factors can induce all kinds of illness, not simply mental ones. They include conditions such as essential hypertension, peptic ulcer and bronchial asthma (WHO, 1964). Some major illnesses such as depression and schizophrenia have a biological component. The underlying inference is that there is behavioural, psychological or biological dysfunction and that the disturbance in the mental equilibrium is not merely in the relationship between the individual and society. Although mental health is an essential component of health, the scientific foundations of mental health are not yet clear. Therefore, we do not have precise tools to assess the state of mental health unlike physical health. Psychologists have mentioned the following characteristics as attributes of a merely healthy person. A mentally healthy person is free from internal conflicts; he is not at 'war' with himself. He is well adjusted, i.e. he is able to get along well with others. He accepts criticism and does not easily get upset. He searches for identity. He has a strong sense of self-esteem. He knows his needs, problems and goals (this is known as self-actualization). He has good self-control, i.e. balances rationality and emotions. He faces problems and tries to solve them intelligently, i.e. coping with stress and anxiety. Assessment of mental health at the population level may be made by administering mental status questionnaire by trained interviewers.

Social Dimension of Health

Man is a social animal. He is surrounded by a network of social relationships. These relationships are reciprocal and satisfy various needs in the society. Various ideas and interactions take place and, therefore, we also share our emotions. There are diverse cultures in the society and these cultures are regulated by various forms of norms and practices. However these cultures are shared by different community people and cultural diffusion also takes place. The normal individual is a part of all these functions, is capable of sharing the traits of culture and maintains harmony. This sharing process builds the positive image and enhances the interpersonal communicational skills. This is utmost necessary to be involved in the community as well as in the society at large. The more a person is involved in the process of integration, the more he is regarded as a healthy person. Thus, the social dimension of the health includes the level of social skills, social functioning of the individual and one's ability to see oneself as a member of whole society. Overall the social dimension of health is primarily related with an individual as a family member, he is part of society and above all he is member of a larger group. It also focuses on social and economic conditions and well-being of the society which is ultimately related with the network of social relationships. Fillenbaum has pointed out the importance of positive human environment and positive material environment which in turn is related with the social network and financial and material conditions of the individual.

Spiritual Dimension

Besides being a social being, spiritualism is also a necessary part of healthy life. Spiritual life makes one turn towards goals in the life and to achieve these goals one strives for them. A spiritual person sets his own meanings, personal beliefs and his own acceptance or rejection of the creation. Spiritualism is related with one's inner self, therefore, there are no objective meanings attached to it. There are no universal laws which define the meaning to attain the goals, rather it is one's own understanding of existence and creation. This is a new dimension which is important in the present society as life has become very complex. To get released from this complexity one needs to have spiritualism which in turn affects the health. The thought of spiritualism directs the mind to think or reaches out for the constructive meaning of life. Without considering the meaning of life one is worthless. The worth in the life ultimately transcends into good physical well-being and healthy life. This is not an old philosophy of health, rather it has emerged in the contemporary time looking at the complexity of life. To sum up, spiritualism includes integrity, principles, ethics and the purpose in life. It also includes commitment to some higher being.

Emotional Dimension

Emotional dimension of health is the domain under psychology. Since human being is not only a social being but at the same time he is also an emotional being. Therefore, emotional elements are indispensable for a healthy human being. Emotional well-being is the ability in the human beings to adjust and cope with their own and others' feelings. Emotions are present in all human beings in different periods of time, in different situations. They require a course of actions to cope with them. Emotions can be in the pleasant situations as well as in despair situations.

At various times emotions are visible, but at times in the situations of hopelessness, depression, anxiety, etc. they are not easily visible and therefore, can lead to mental illness and ultimately affect health. Therefore, one should be aware of one's weaknesses and strengths which can be helpful in coping with emotionally disturbing situations. It will caution beforehand and one can seek help so that the situation can be altered. Further, it can be altered by building strong cushion of relationships with the family, peer groups and community. There are plenty of researches done on mental health which concludes that absence of emotional security leads to the illness. Emotional health is related to one's feeling whereas mental health can be seen as 'knowing' or 'cognition'.

The people who are working on mental health and emotional health could separate them cognitively. Thus, in the present time, the mental and emotional aspects of human beings should be viewed separately particularly in the context of human health.

Vocational Dimension

Vocational dimension is related with the work one does. Every human being who has come in the world is supposed to do some or other type of work for human existence. It may vary from person to person, but should be adaptable according to human capacity. Work also depends on one's capacity and limitations to perform. The performance of work is directly related with the physical and mental health of the individual. Physical work is related with one's capacity to perform work, while its goal is associated with self-realization of satisfaction and enhanced self-esteem. Its actual potential is realized only when the person is without work or he is out of work or may be retired. This situation immediately affects his health. As people think that vocational dimension is related with the economic aspects or it is valuable in the form of sources of income, but it represents the persons' ability in the form of success to prove his worth in the society and does not become a burden on others.

Intellectual Dimension

Intellectual dimension is related with one's ability to develop skills and knowledge to make life more meaningful. Intellectual capacity gives ability to think rationally and in turn it translates into the idea of creativity and insight in decision-making. Intellectual leanings give ability to plan the things in such a manner that will go a long way and will make life successful. The mind is able to think with openness and act accordingly. It will not be influenced by any subjectivity or other external pressure to influence one's decision. Additionally, positive intellectual thinking will automatically contribute to the good health. It is also helpful in conflicting situation for arriving at rational arguments.

Other Dimensions

A few other dimensions are also important while discussing the health. These are: philosophical, cultural, socio-economic, environmental, educational, nutritional, curative and preventive. A glance at these dimensions shows that there are many non-medical dimensions of health which are equally important for the purpose of health.

Summing Up

Health is not a new phenomenon. The concept of health is a dynamic concept and, therefore, its conception also gets changed. Earlier the health was viewed only in terms of biomedical approach. Over a passage of time many more dimensions have been added in defining the health. Social and preventive concept of health has expanded its boundaries to the community and environmental conditions. Health is defined as complete fitness and being away from diseases. However, this definition has been challenged by the critics and their view is that complete health is a utopian concept and away from the reality. Further, the concepts of public health and international health are co-terminus with the global health. The global health is a broad approach which looks at the world as a single category and hence, concerns various health problems of different cultures and puts forth the prevention, curative and primitive aspects of health care. Global health is a worldwide social goal that encompasses the whole quality of life. This chapter tells about the health and its dimensions.

The good health or healthy life is composed of many dimensions and these dimensions are: physical, mental, social, spiritual, emotional, vocational, and intellectual. These good health parameters are advocated by World Health organization while defining the concept of health and ratified by the participant countries. Mind and body are so closely related with one another that disturbance in one part sends the message and it is exhibited in the form of symptoms. These symptoms are in a way non-functional activity of the bodily organs. There are various procedures to read these symptoms with various instruments as well as with non-performance of activity of organs in the body. Therefore, it is important to understand and read the symptoms of body and to ensure the balance of mind, spirit and body. This integration puts health in the format of multidimensionality. The World Health Organization has only given four dimensions of health and these are: physical, mental, social and spiritual. But with the passage of time many more dimensions have been added in understanding the composite nature of health. The additional dimensions are emotional, vocational, intellectual and political. These dimensions also interact with one another. One can also assume that with the passage of time many more dimensions can be added.

References

Abbot, Andrew (1988), *The System of Professions*, Chicago: University of Chicago Press.

Ackernecht, E.H. (1942), 'Problems of Primitive Medicine', *Bulletin of History of Medicine*, 2: 503–21.

Aiken, Linda H., Robert J. Blendon and David E. Rogers (1980), 'Evaluating a Private Foundation's Health Program', *Evaluation and Program Planning*, 3: 119–29.

Baggott, R. (2004), *Health and Health Care in Britain*, Palgrave: Macmillan.

Banerji, D. (1971), *Family Planning in India: A Critique and a Perspective*, New Delhi: People's Publishing House.

Becker, Howard S., Blanche Geer, Evertt C. Hughes and Anslem L. Strauss (1961), *Boys in White: Student Culture in Medical School*, Chicago: University of Chicago Press.

Becker, M. (1974), *The Health Belief Model and Personal Health Behaviour*, Thorofare, NJ: Slack.

Berkanovic, Emil, Carol Telesky and Sharon Reeder (1981), 'Structural and Social Psychological Factors in the Decision to Seek Medical Care for Symptoms', *Medical Care*, 19: 693–709.

Bernard, C. (1965), *Introduction to the Study of Experimental Medicine*, New York: Collier Books.

Bircher, J. (2005), 'Towards a Dynamic Definition of Health and Disease', *Medical Health Care Philosophy*, 8: 335–41.

Blaxter, M. and L. Peterson (1982), *Mothers and Daughters: A Three Generations Study of Health Attitudes and Behaviour*, London: Heinemann Educational Books.

Bourdieu, P. (1977), *Outline of a Theory of Practice*, Cambridge: Cambridge University Press.

Calnan, M. (1987), *Health and Illness: The Lay Perspective*, London: Tavistock.

Charmaz, Kathy (1991), *Good Days, Bad Days: The Self in Chronic Illness and Time*, New Brunswick, NJ: Rutgers University Press.

d'Houtard, A. and M.G. Field (1984), 'The Image of Health: Variations in Perceptions by Social Class in a French Population', *Sociology of Health and Illness*, 6: 30–60.

Donovan, J.L. (1986), *We Don't Buy Sickness, It Just Comes: Health, Illness and Health Care in the Lives of People in London*, Aldershot: Gower.

Foucault, M. (1972), *Naissance de la Clinique*, Paris: Unniversitaines de France.

Fox, Renee C. (1957), 'Training for Uncertainty', in R.K. Merton, G.C. Reader and P.L. Kendall (eds), *The Student-Physician*, Cambridge, MA: Harvard University Press.

Freeman, Howard E. and Ozzie G. Simmons (1977), 'Medical Patients in the Community: Family Settings and Performance Levels', in N.J. Smelser and W.T. Smelser (eds), *Personality and Social Systems*, New York: John Wiley.

Freeman, Howard E. and Peter H. Rossi (1984), 'Furthering the Applied Side of Sociology', *American Sociological Review*, 22(1): 73–81.

Freeman, Howard E. and Sol Levine (eds) (1989), *Handbook of Medical Sociology*, Englewood Cliffs, NJ: Prentice Hall.

Freeman, Howard E., Edgar F. Borgatta and Natheanie H. Siegel (1975), 'Remarks on the Changing Relationship between Government Support and Graduate Training', in N.J. Demerath, K.F. Schuessler and O. Larsen (eds), *Social Policy and Sociology*, New York: Academic Press.

Freeman, Howard E., K. Jill Kiecolt and Harris M. Allen (1982), 'Community Health Centers: An Initiative of Enduring Utility', *Milbank Memorial Fund Quarterly*, 60: 245–67.

Freidson, Eliot (1970), *Profession of Medicine*, New York: Dodd, Mead.

Furedi, F. (1997), *Population and Development: A Critical Introduction*, New York: Martin Press.

Golub, J.E., S. Bur, W.A. Cromin et al. (2005), 'Patient and Health Care System Delays in Pulmonary Tuberculosis Diagnosis in a Low Incidence State', *International Journal of Tuberculosis and Lung Disease*, 9: 992–98.

Hancock, T. and M. Minler (2005), 'Community Health Assessment or Healthy Community Assessment', in M. Minkler (ed.), *Community Organizing and Community Building for Health*, New Jersey: Rutgers University Press.

Herzlich, C. (1973), *Health and Illness*, London: Academic Press.

Illich, I. (1975), *Medical Nemesis*, London: Calder and Boyars.

Kelman, S. (1975), 'The Social Nature of the Definition Problem in Health', *International Journal of Health Services*, 5: 625–42.

Koplan, J.P. (2009), 'Definition of Global Health', *Lancet*, 373: 1993–95.

Leslie, Charles (1976), *Asian Medical Systems: A Comparative Study*, Berkeley, CA: University of California Press.

Lieban, R.N. (1977), 'The Field of Medical Anthropology', in David Landy (ed.), *Culture, Disease and Healing*, New York: Macmillan.

McGinnis, J.M. (2001), 'United States', in C.K. Koop (ed.), *Critical Issues in Global Health*, San Francisco: Jossey-Bass, 80–90.

McGinnis, J.M. et al. (2002), 'The Case for More Active Policy Attention to Health Promotion', *Health Affairs*, 21(2): 78–93.

McKenzie, James F. (2008), *An Introduction to Community Health*, Canada: Jones and Barlett.

Mumford, Lewis (1961), *The City in History: Its Origin, Its Transformation and Its Prospects*, New York: Harcourt, Brace and World.

Nolan, Patrick and Gerhard Lenski (1999), *Human Services: An Introduction to Macro Sociology*, New York: McGraw-Hill.

Parsons, Talcott (1979), 'Definitions of Health and Illness in the Light of American Values and Social Structure', in E. Jaco and E. Gartley (eds), *Patients, Physicians and Illness: A Source Book in Behavioural Science and Health*, London: Collier-Macmillan.

Petersen, A. and D. Lupton (1996), *The New Public Health: Health and Self in the Age of Risk*, London: Sage Publications.

Sachs, J. (2001), *Macroeconomics and Health: Investing in Health for Economic Development*, Report of the Commission on Macro Economics and Health, Geneva: WHO.

Saracci, R. (1997), 'The World Health Organization Needs to Reconsider Its Definition of Health', *British Medical Journal*, 314: 1409–10.

Üstün, B. and R. Jakob (2005), 'Calling a Spade a Spade: Meaningful Definitions of Health Conditions', *Bulletin of World Health Organization*, 83: 802.

Wildavsky, A.B. (1988), *Searching for Safety*, Vol. 10, New Brunswick, NJ: Transaction Publishers.

Williams, R. (1983), 'Concepts of Health: An Analysis of Lay Logic', *Sociology*, 17: 185–204.

Winslow, C. (1920), 'The Untilled Field of Public Health', *Modern Medicine*, 2: 183–91.

World Health Organization (1971), *WHO Definition of Health*, Geneva: WHO.

—— (1986), *Ottawa Charter for Health Promotion*, Geneva: WHO.

—— (2001), *Men Aging and Health*, http://whqlibdoc.who.int/hq/2001/who-nmh-nph-01.2pdf.

3

Scope of Sociology of Health and Medicine

The human life cannot be understood by physiological science only, it requires to have an understanding of social relationship, culture and human behaviour. Through the process of socialization, we acquire culture and that shapes our way of thinking and acting in the world. For example, if we want to understand the hospital organization, it cannot be understood with the help of scientific or biological factors, we have to develop an understanding of various relationships operating in the hospital. At the same time, sociologists argue that social life is not static rather it has dynamic aspect which goes beyond biological aspects. These dynamic aspects are related with the social, cultural, political and economic milieu.

In the past study on health, disease and illness was the domain of biology. However, with the development of understanding, health, disease and illness have become part of interaction process, social relationships, culture and social structure. One may argue that how sociology is related with health and disease. But it is now very clear that the way biology is indispensable to understand health and diseases, in the same way sociology helps in understanding of occurrence and recovery from diseases. There are some social groups who are more afflicted by certain diseases, while other groups do not suffer within the same locality. The same disease affects different individuals differently. Environment and nutrition are closely related with health which in turn is affected by socio-economic factors. Health and disease are not simply related with natural factors but they are also related with social settings and periods of time.

Scope of Sociology of Health

Health is a subjective and objective reality. We come to know about health problems when the person reports it, behaves differently, or is unable to carry out his/her normal functions. Health and ill health could be understood only in terms of human activity because the differentiation between healthy and unhealthy states depends on the ability to fulfil one's functions and obligations normally. The question then is: how do individuals and groups define the ability to carry out normal functions? It is common knowledge that tolerance to bodily discomfort and pain is not the same for all people. Do social and ethnic groups have different parameters to measure what is normal ability, and what is not, and what is the threshold of pain that is acceptable? Tolerance of ill health also often depends upon access to medical care. Thus, the experience of disease and its detection are deeply embedded in social settings (Sujatha, 2014: 3).

Sociology of health has made several unique contributions. These include: (1) study of medicine as a profession, (2) study of the sick's role and illness experience, (3) history of medicine, social construction of illness and medical knowledge, including medicalization, (4) sociological epidemiology, (5) sociological study of health care services as organizations, (6) social hierarchies and health inequality, (7) doctor-patient communication, (8) significance of market and state organizations in health and medicine, (9) medical education, (10) medical technology, (11) systems of medicine and medical pluralism, (12) mental illness, (13) health rights and ethics in medicine, and (14) health care settings and health transition. In each instance, sociologists have offered a fresh perspective on understanding the issues by examining the impact of power, authority, norms, social inequality, and the distribution of resources. In the following pages, we briefly describe the distinctive sociological stance on each of the aforementioned areas.

Study of Medicine as a Profession

In the 1950s and throughout the 1960s, the dominant activity of sociology of health was to do research on and offer recommendations about health providers which could effectively alter patients' receptivity to advances in medical technology and therapeutic know-how. A major frustration for practitioners then (and now) was the failure of many persons in the community to take advantage of the presumed fruits of medical discoveries, technological developments, and the diagnostic and therapeutic knowledge gained from speciality education.

The study of medical profession has long been a central area of sociology of health and has formed a basis for the sociological study of the professions. As such, sociological concepts of the profession of medicine have provided the very definitions of professional work and the ways in which a profession obtains and maintains control of expertise. Interest in professional authority in general and medicine in particular led to extensive sociological work on medical education and socialization. Early work on the profession included Talcott Parsons' (1951) explanations of professional authority, Renee Fox's (1957) training for uncertainty, Howard Becker and colleagues' (1961) study of medical education and socialization, and Eliot Freidson's (1970) *Profession of Medicine*. These studies examined the power and authority physicians hold as a group, the social and economic privileges associated with the status of medicine, and the ways in which the profession has protected these privileges, both from competing occupations and from women and minorities who had faced restricted access to the profession. In addition, sociologists have examined inter-professional relations between doctors and nurses and other health professionals (including chiropractors, dentists and psychologists). This research has focused on the roles of professionals in the organizations and competition between professions for authority and autonomy. Furthermore, sociological work has contributed to the understanding of the history of medicine as a contested terrain in which physicians first established and then fought to maintain their professional dominance. Physicians' success in these struggles has shaped health care in many years, from doctor-patient interactions to the organization and delivery of care (Starr, 1982; Abbott, 1988).

Sociology of medical profession looks at education and training for professional roles, activities and responsibilities attached to roles and the hierarchy of roles in an organization, referred to as status. The expected and actual role of the medical professional, their professional values, and regulations on medical practice are also critical to the understanding of the medical profession. The conventional focus of sociology of professional approach has been in terms of patient load, time spent with patients, formal relationship among medical specialists (Nagla, 1997), inter-professional rivalry, and the informal cliques among medical professionals (Ahluwalia, 1967). Why a particular caste and ethnic group are not found in nursing profession as much as in medicine are questions about the larger issues pertaining to social identity and the medical profession (Venkatratnam, 1979). Nursing as a profession is also of great over sociological interest. The fact that the number of women who enter the profession is overwhelmingly greater than men raises questions about the gendered nature of nursing roles. Whether it is unpaid work at home or paid work in medical organizations, nurture and caring duties are mostly assigned to women. With the arrival of corporate hospital chains, male nurses are increasingly found in the private sector where the pay scales are higher. With the burgeoning burden of chronic motor dysfunctions, new professions like physiotherapy and radiology are merging in independent roles and the physiotherapists have made their demand public to use the title 'Dr' (Sujatha, 2014). Oommen's (1978) study presents a comparative analysis of doctors and nurses as full-fledged professionals and semi-professionals within organizational context of public hospitals in Delhi. Madan (1980) aimed at examining the relation between doctors and society and the role of professions in modernization. Medical profession also examines some elements of occupational division of labour in medicine, including the proliferation of specialist medical technicians, and a variety of other paraprofessionals who are something more than technicians but less than doctor, yet who both are a function of and contributors to the present complexity of the medical establishment. It also includes midwives, folk practitioners etc.

Study of Social Role and Illness Experience

A second unique contribution of sociology of health has been the study of the sick's role, which expanded into a broader study of illness experience. This area includes the social role of the patient, illness behaviour, illness/patient careers, and the ways that these factors shape and are shaped by doctor-patient interaction. Talcott Parsons' (1951) work on the sick's role laid the foundation for the sociological examination of illness and the expectations placed on those who are ill. Mechanic (1962) has worked on illness behaviour. Whereas medical anthropologists have long studied illness in part as a way to examine the values in a society or group in the face of uncontrollable events, sociologists brought a greater interest in the impact of role expectations, norms, sanctions, and the accommodations or lack thereof for the needs of those with illnesses or disabilities. This work includes rich ethnographic studies of illness experiences (e.g. Roth and Conrad, 1987; Charmaz, 1991), as well as research on factors affecting the decisions to seek care (Berkanovic, Telesky, and Reeder, 1981), and patterns of health care utilization (Mechanic, Cleary, and Greenly, 1982).

Few years ago, black migrants from South Africa to London had been discovered with high rate of throat cancer. While living in South Africa these persons were subjected to the discriminatory apartheid laws, one of which was the prohibition against the consumption of alcohol. But indigenous to their culture was a potent brew that they bootlegged in order to satisfy their thirst. When arriving as immigrants in London, they, as is true of most immigrants to metropolitan centres, were subjected to the ecology and politics of the city and were forced to make their homes in the least desirable sections of London. This happened to be the upper reaches of the Thames estuary, the berthing and distribution centre for crude oil tankers. Carrying with them as they did their culturally acquired taste for their native liquor, they cooked it in discarded petroleum drums. Petroleum being a carcinogenic agent, gave rise to throat cancer. It is a clear example of a link between culture, behaviour and illness.

The women's health movement has encouraged sociological research on illness experience through the movement's criticism of medicine for devaluing women's reports of their own health and well-being and their experiences of illness and medical treatment. As a result, sociological studies of illness experience have evolved into a wide range of quantitative and qualitative work. For example, sociologists' increased emphasis on the patient's perspective fostered the development of what is now known as patient-centred outcomes in health services research. Moreover, medical sociologists have contributed to a rapidly growing body of work on women's experiences with reproductive technologies (Reissman and Nathanson, 1986). These two examples represent areas that have become truly interdisciplinary.

A common trend in the health, culture and structure triad is the study of health-seeking behaviour. The most likely question here is how health seekers in different societies make choices about treatment.

History of Medicine and Social Construction of Illness and Medical Knowledge

A third unique contribution of sociology of health has been the understanding of social history of medicine and the social construction of illness and medical knowledge. This area includes a range of studies from a social constructionist perspective, including those of the sociological history of diseases, medicalization, and the social meaning of illness (e.g. whether particular illnesses are stigmatized). As Judith Lorber (1977) and others have noted, 'what is normal depends on whom is being compared to whom'. In this body of work, sociologists have examined the ways in which new illnesses have been discovered and characterized, the attribution of new medical knowledge, and the myriad ways in which non-medical events and experiences have entered the purview of medicine. Sociologists have also used the constructionist perspective to examine the social processes by which certain constellations of troubles become diseases, such as hypertension, etc. Medicalization and intrusion of medical concerns into everyday life encompasses an ever-expanding list of health behaviours (diet-exercise, risk prevention and preventive care compliance).

Social Epidemiology

One may further ask that why are some conditions like Alzheimer's disease dreaded in the United States and Europe, while it is not seen as a threat in others? How do we understand the global panic created over bird flu, mad cow disease, and other pandemics that led to the killing of millions of birds and animals? Sociologists bring a different theoretical perspective to the health care research by focusing on the multiple ways in which time, space, nativity, social class, etc. contribute to differences in health and by recognizing the persistence of these relationships over time despite ever-changing mechanisms that lead to poorer health among the disadvantaged.

In the wake of migration, displacement and violence, lately epidemiological studies tend to examine independent variables like mobility, war and displacement in relation to disease. The connection between ethnicity and health status has been constantly explored in the context of immigrant communities. Comparative studies of mental health among refugees from different cultures and the social epidemiology of AIDS are frequent topics.

Sociological Study of Health Care Services as Organizations

Sociologists have made a unique contribution to the understanding of health care through research on medical care organization. Just as medicine became the prototype for occupational research on the profession, research on hospitals, medical practices, nursing homes, and other health care organizations has shaped both our understanding of how care is provided and the power and interests that have shaped the provision of health care. Medical sociologists have studied hospitals and mental health institutions as complex organizations designed to meet multiple needs in society, which often involve competing agendas. These organizations are also total institutions with their own norms, roles, actors, and status hierarchies. Goffman's (1962) study of mental asylums as total institutions showed how institutions could totally shape the selfhood of a person. He explained how human behavioural expression is quite diverse, but institutional procedures assign a common protocol to everyone who gets into the mental asylum. In the hospital system, the case sheet is the expert psychiatrist's account of the patient and is an all important reference point for every decision regarding the patient. Foucault (1975) studied the power of medical institutions over the patient.

The concern with the poor, the implementation of government- and foundation-supported social programmes in general, and health initiatives in particular, were accompanied by a need for hard information on the extent to which the efforts were successfully implemented, effective in their outcomes, and efficient from a benefit-to-cost standpoint. Although the assessment of social change efforts and social experiments have a long history, it was the spate of activities in connection with the programmes to reduce poverty and discrimination and to promote more equal access to and use of health and social services that led to the emergence of a new methodological field, generally referred to as 'social programme evaluation' or 'evaluation research' (Rossi and Freeman, 1985).

Sociologists in the health arena and in other social programme areas have been key players in the programmes' evaluation area. Many of the major health care initiatives have been evaluated by teams led or assisted by sociologists. Moreover, the impetus to improve access to and increase use of health services by the poor and other deprived groups to a large extent, required modifying organizational, political, and geographical arrangements for the delivery of health services.

Indeed, the effort to improve health care for the poor and the otherwise disfranchised is one of the impetus for medical sociologists to move into policy research, policy development, macro-planning, and managerial activities. At the same time, it has encouraged health professionals' schools to integrate the concepts of frames and applied research approaches of sociology into their educational programme.

With regard to health policy, there is a need to look at policies as discourses on health, the assumptions they make, and the priorities they set. We have to ask what is the extent of responsibility the government is willing to take up in medical care, and what kind of regulations does it bring and on whom? The health policy studies by social science will have to go beyond the language of the policy statement itself, and will have to examine how it gets translated into action plan for the government machinery at each level, and what the health intervention undertaken means to various actors in the implementation machinery.

Social Hierarchies and Health Inequality

Health varies according to social strata, but the question is: are changes in patterns of inequality leading to changes in health status of specific groups? The concern with the poor entailed a concern with ethnic, caste and class equality. Thus, this was a period in which efforts were made to increase the number of minority health science students and providers. The rationale for this was not only based on concerns for equality but on the belief that persons of minority background would be more effective in dealing with patients of their own ethnic backgrounds. Interest in providing access to care, in creating new types of health care organizational arrangements, and in expanding minority medical education flowered in the 1970s and continued in the 1980s, in part spurred on by the activities of the Robert Wood Johnson Foundation (Aiken, Blendon, Rogers, and Freeman, 1980). In particular, the movement toward Health Maintenance Organizations (HMOs) bloomed, and as a result of their expanded role, increased access to health services and patient care became a major research concern.

Failure of patients to seek out appropriate health care, to communicate fully and reliably symptoms and problems to their providers, to follow through on referrals, to comply with medical regiments, and to engage in appropriate preventive practices bewildered many practitioners and concerned those responsible for medical education and postgraduate training of health providers. The saliency of this issue among health care providers was the basis for a wide range of studies by medical sociologists. Their findings often questioned assumptions made by physicians and other health providers about the motivations of patients, identified cultural and social structural impediments to effective use of the available technology of medicine and clinical acumen of physicians, and drew attention to the discrepancies between the interests of health care providers and the organizations with which they are associated and those of the patients they treat (Levine, Scotch, and Vlasak, 1969).

Women's question with regard to health and medicine highlights the asymmetries and discrimination of women against a larger context of deprivation. It may also be insightful to explore caste-gender situation with regard to health status and health behaviour.

Doctor-Patient Communication

The relationship between the doctor and the patient has always been an important theme of study. The change in this relationship from a personalized to an impersonal one over the years has been an outcome of the change in medicine itself. What kind of professional and personal ethics form the doctor-patient relationship, whether they vary with social background, and how caste, class, ethnicity, race and gender are played out in the relationship, both in the private and public sector, are important areas of enquiry. Self-help association of patients, web group of patients, and support organizations of patients with terminal illnesses supply information that is important for patients.

Certain communities and elder members in the family provided knowledgeable information for health care which is in fact a study of functions of social relationships within medical care. Further, social relationships could have a significant influence on the recovery process. Thus, the significance of family and kinship in the management of ill health cannot be underestimated which needs to be studied.

Over time, health care sociologists subjected medicine and different aspects of the health system to increasingly critical scrutiny in this regard. They challenged the assumptions of biomedical model, questioned the overuse of complex and expensive technology, criticized the asymmetrical features of the doctor-patient relationship, and emphasized the importance of interpersonal, social, and economic considerations in efforts of health promotion and the healing of the sick (Mishler et al., 1981).

Even more, sociologists were at the forefront in documenting that medical decisions 'do not emanate from a routine, scientific calculus but are made by people playing social roles, guided by social values, and located in particular social settings or contexts' (Levine, 1987). The distance that medicine and medical sociology have travelled is evident now in the emergence of quality of life as an overriding social dimension of judging health and illness, as well as a major criterion to evaluate health care in general and technological interventions in particular.

Significance of Market and State Organizations in Health and Medicine

Why is the number of pharmacies growing in cities and small towns though health status, in general, is supposed to be improving? Is health determined by the consumption of medical substances? At the same time community treatment has become vague. Sociologists turned their attention to the study of programmes, organization, politics, and efficacy of community mental health centres, as well as to the actions of their advocates and opponents. Such work, commonplace in the 1970s, is still popular.

In 1960s and the decade that followed marked a period of emphasis on government programmes to improve the lot of the poor. Although health care was originally given low priority, the great society programmes, and those that followed and preceded them, were pressed to include health components (Freeman, Kiecolt, and Allen, 1982). As a result, major efforts were undertaken to improve access to care, including the establishment of neighbourhood, later called community health centres, and of reorganized delivery systems in hospitals. Programmes were also implemented to modify the interpersonal relations of professionals and patients in order to increase utilization and compliance. There also were attempts to increase the supply and to modify the distribution of physicians and other providers in order to relieve the shortages in rural areas and in inner cities.

The 1980s have witnessed a shift in interest, further testifying to the validity of our opening observation about the linkage between the social contexts and the content of scientific and intellectual work. As there has been a shift to a more conservative ideological posture, there has been a dramatic change in emphasis from initiatives related to increased access to health services and interventions directed at improved health status to a concern with the costs of medical care. But cost-containment efforts have their sociological dimensions as well. Key initiatives to decelerate the increase in cost of health services require organizational modifications, redirected professional educational efforts, different criteria for the selection of health care providers, and new strategies for dealing with political consequences of economic containment decisions. Consequently, although the policy issues have changed and the research questions are different, there is no diminution in opportunities for medical sociologists to contribute to work in the health arena and to accrue knowledge of general sociological interest.

Emphasis on the cost of care has brought with it increased interest in the quality of medical care. Efforts at cost containment that limit in one way or another the medical services provided almost automatically provoke concern with their impact on patient outcomes and future well-being. Thus, contemporary topics of sociological interest include studies of the health consequences of patients' membership in different forms of medical care arrangements, from solo practice to health insurance schemes.

The demographic dynamics, the economic considerations, and the continual technical advancements in medicine compel sociological attention to the issue of quality of life. Simply prolonging life in a biological sense may in many cases have little consequences. The key issue, which is a sociological matter, is how decisions – on the use of technology, on the allocation of economic resources for health care, and on the ways services are delivered – affect the quality of life.

Medical Education

Curriculum issues, admission criteria and length of medical education are important aspects of medical education which come in the ambit of sociology of health and medicine. Sociological studies also pertain to examine the social profile of students entering into medical education, their socialization pattern and their selection of particular branch of specialization. Another area of research is to look into the substantive contents and process of medical education. In this sense, medical education has been seen by sociologists as the process by which the novice student, who is a lay person, is socialized into the anatomical view of human body from inside. Sujatha (2014) finds that in case of college education in traditional systems of medicine, the question of socialization into medical view takes on a peculiar form. For instance, students of unani or ayurveda degree courses in India have to learn a non-reductionist medical approach to the body, in the idiom and terminology of biomedicine. Abraham (2013) enquires into the ways in which ayurveda students in south India, who have been socialized in biological sciences in modern schools, get to learn the significance of body through ancient Sanskrit and Malayalam texts in their degree courses.

As regards women and the medical profession, Minocha (1996) shows how entry of women into the modern medical profession in India during the 19th century was facilitated by British women doctors. The recent researches look at the implicit gender bias in medical education and women's choice of specialization.

Medical Technology

Medical care is a function of the interaction between medical technology, professional organization and the social and cultural milieu in which they exist (Rosengren, 1980). Technology in medicine predicts and creates outcomes for health care. Moreover, the capacities of medicine to identify, define, and create its own monopoly over illnesses and instabilities is as much a function of technology as it is of professional organization. Hence, what diseases are given diagnostic and treatment priority are not self-evident. Such disease eminence is a socially produced phenomenon, assisted in its rise by the accepted power and influence of 'technical' definitions and sustained through the professional organization of medicine.

Marxist scholars argue that medicine under capitalism could be irrational and could project technology as a superior option when simpler and cheaper options are available. Whether ultrasound testing at several stages of a normal pregnancy is essential is not entirely a medical decision. The application of diagnostic technologies need not be based on the case at hand but on the idea of risk that is part of medical culture promoted by equipment firms (Lupton, 2003). Recent studies in India and the world over by Anita and Bhatia (1993) show that improved health and longevity do not depend on technology and capital investment (Muraleedharan, 1999).

Systems of Medicine and Medical Pluralism

In every society there is a plurality of systems of medicine. How one system gets patronage over the other system? What is the preference of the people to go for particular system of medicine? What are the parameters on which people prefer one system of medicine over another? Are people more comfortable with the plurality of medicine? These are some of the questions which can be discussed and analysed in the scope of sociology of health and medicine. From the viewpoint of coexisting medical systems like biomedicine, ayurveda, unani and siddha in the public institutions, there are contentious issues about who sets the standard for decision-making and verification of results (Sujatha, 2014: 36). Some studies have also looked into the transformation in the medical content of traditional systems of medicine because they make profuse use of the language and parameters of biomedical classification of disease. The coexistence of several systems of medicine in the public arena with biomedicine as the official system of the government health services is the pattern in most nations' states today. Despite being labelled as 'unscientific', many therapies continue to have popularity among health seekers. Sujatha (2009) pointed out that in the traditional medicine sector, medicinal knowledge is seen as a special gift which may be shared within the village community and sold only to outsiders. Even today, this is a common feature of traditional systems, and studies report how non-bio medical practitioners in Mexico, for instance, are flexible about price and allow voluntary payment (Nigenda et al., 2001). In some places, payment in kind is also accepted. It is important to ask how such arrangements within full-fledged cash economies, and what kinds of changes in the clinical practice of traditional medicines, have come about?

Biomedicine, on the other hand, has almost shifted to the hospital/clinic as the basic unit of medical service. The family doctor no longer visits the house of the sick person as used to be done a couple of decades ago; the clinic has become the place where the sick bodies assemble. Clinics and hospitals are organically linked to the pharmaceutical industry, medical equipment firms, and the government administration at various levels (Sujatha, 2014: 19).

Recent work on the culture of biomedicine in India (Zachariah et al., 2010) points out the crisis of high-cost, technology-centred medicine and the dilemma that it poses for self-conscious physicians. There are several cases of suspicious deaths in contemporary clinical trials on Indian subjects. But the reports have been disregarded in the name of science because the subjects are voiceless and cannot fight legally. The dubious and limited success of biomedicine can hardly justify such a violent method of knowing (Kothari and Mehta, 1988).

Another study of medical pluralism in the Indian context (Ram, 2011) focuses on the role of social class in women's decision about birthing. This ethnographic study of different kinds of hospital spaces in south India shows how the health practices of women who give birth are based on their pre-familiarity, habit, and convenience, which varies with the social strata which they come from. While women from the fishing community drew upon their traditional knowledge to which they were habituated and used biomedical support as a supplement, educated and urban women were more comfortable with the clinic.

Mental Illness

How do we understand spirit possession and mental illness? Healing traditions across the world regard disease as one type in the larger canvas of human suffering. How then do we distinguish something purely as health problem and as a problem of life or misfortune? Questions of this kind may be asked by anybody – a lay person or a physician – when they encounter a crisis in life. But it will be difficult to answer such questions within the experience of particular individuals or particular medical institutions like the hospital, pharmaceutical company, or a healer's site. Social sciences like sociology, anthropology, and history try to answer such questions by examining several situations and experiences in comparative perspective, or by probing few cases in a deeper fashion over a period of time (Sujatha, 2014: 4).

The 1950s also saw literally a revolution in the care of the mentally ill. In part it was a response to the inhuman physical and interpersonal environments of mental hospitals, in part to the widespread adoption of drug therapies, and in part to the influence of psychodynamics thinking and the beginning of the social and community psychiatry movements. Sociologists were key players in the spate of activities that occurred in the decade or so that followed. Field studies of mental hospitals (e.g. Stanton and Schwarts, 1954), studies of patients' and hospital staffs' role behaviour and perspectives (e.g. Goffman, 1962), social epidemiological studies (e.g. Hollingshead and Redlich, 1958) and follow-up surveys of discharged patients (e.g. Freeman and Simmons, 1977) represented an important fund of information that fed into a growing body of knowledge about deviant behaviour and organizational relations.

Today, interest in the consequences of mental illness treatment persists. The aftermath of social psychiatric research and social action efforts during the late 1950s and 1960s was a movement to deinstitutionalize just about everyone. The populations of mental hospitals and facilities for the retarded and developmentally disabled were sharply reduced.

Addlakha (2008) presents an account of mental illness among women as it is managed and explained by the family, the psychiatric institutions, and the patient. Davar (2009) describes the significant role of healing shrines, like *dargahs*, temples, and churches, in providing considerable relief from psychosocial stress. She argues that the issue of human rights violation, often invoked against healing shrines, must be applied equally to the mental hospital as well.

Sudhir Kakkar (1980) examines different kinds of healing traditions of India, in order to find common elements in human pursuits about the self and the world through ayurveda, mysticism/tantricism, and shamanism. Kleinman's (1980) work on mental health, culture, and society adopts a psychiatric approach to Taiwanese healing rituals. Cross-cultural studies in mental health provide rich and deep insights into the relation between mind, body, culture and society.

Health Rights and Ethics in Medicine

Needham et al. (2000) observed that in ancient China, physicians employed by the royal bureaucracy could not receive their salary if people in their jurisdiction fell sick. In the modern institutional set-up of the clinic/hospital, however, payment to the doctor does not depend on whether he/she cures the patient; rather, it is for lending the physicians' expertise. One has to pay for the treatment and consultation even in the event of patient's death.

There is a consumer protection act which also covers the health services. Victim of medical negligence may go to the court and another medical expert has to testify that there has been a mistake if compensation is to be paid. The increasing incidences of attack on doctors by patient's relatives, has opened the door for more transparency of medical procedures. Associations of doctors are also seeking police protection and have put their medical services on hold many times. This brings us to the question: how are medical errors defined and what are the rights of patients when expert procedures cause damages? How are the damages caused by anticipated factors in major medical interventions estimated? Similarly, how is the credibility of mass medical campaigns of the state such as that for immunization maintained despite death and damages to subjects in national programmes?

The cumbersome process of biomedical drug development, and the huge investment it calls for, implies that only multinational giants can succeed in the pharmaceutical sector. The major ethical issue at stake is that the Third World subjects would go through high-risk experimental regimes for drugs not meant for their market; or those that will not be accessible to them when marketed (Sunder Rajan, 2007: 80).

Organ transplantation, stem cell research, surrogate motherhood, amniocentesis, and abortion, all involve key ethics and legal issues; what are their implications to the procedure for various parties is a matter of sociological analysis.

Health Care Settings and Health Transition

Health care received at a large metropolitan medical centre is not the same as that in a small rural community. And even within that category the nature of health care received at a teaching hospital can be very different from that delivered in general hospital. By the same token, treatment in private clinic will be different in comparison to government hospitals. Treatment in a surgical ward is organizationally very different from treatment in a medical ward. Thus, medical care is received in the nexus of some kind of organizational setting, the nature of which is a prime determinant of the care received.

Like any other unit of society keep on changing, the health status of a group also changes over a period of time. Morbidity and causes of mortality are sensitive indicators of social change. Old causes of death are replaced by new causes of death. Likewise, old diseases are eradicated with the advancement in bio medicine, and new forms of diseases emerge. There is a reduction of death rates from infection but increase in death rates due to accidents. Psychiatric and psychosomatic ailments have also increased. The change in accessibility of health care to the certain sections of society also comes into ambit of health transition.

Summing Up

Sociology of health has expanded its scope from the study of medicine as a profession to the studies related to health care settings and health transition. It also studies the sick's role and illness experience and how illness is socially constructed. The study of social hierarchies and health inequality has not only taken in sociology but it is also an important subject matter of economics. The choice to opt a healing system is widely discussed in sociology. Mental illness, health rights and ethical concerns have become a popular theme in the domain of sociology of health. The narratives in doctor-patient communication are regarded as a centre theme in the treatment process.

References

Abbot, Andrew (1988), *The System of Professions*, Chicago: University of Chicago Press.

Abraham, Leena (2013), 'Reproduction of Indigenous Knowledge in Plural Cultures: Ayurveda Education in Contemporary India', in Geetha B. Nambissan and S. Srinivasa Rao (eds), *Sociology of Education in India: Disciplinary Perspectives and Contemporary Concerns*, New Delhi: Oxford University Press.

Addlakha, Renu (2008), *Deconstructing Mental Illness: An Ethnography of Psychiatry, Women and the Family*, New Delhi: Zubaan.

Ahluwali, A. (1967), 'Sociology of Medicine in India: An Approach', *Economic and Political Weekly*, 1(42): 1007–12.

Aiken, Linda H., Robert J. Blendon and David E. Rogers (1980), 'Evaluating a Private Foundation's Health Program', *Evaluation and Program Planning*, 3: 119–29.

Antia, N.H. and K. Bhatia (1993), 'NGO Experiences: Implication for Health Services at the Community Level', in N.H. Antia and K. Bhatia (eds), *People's Health in People's Hand*, Bombay: FRCH, 250–59.

Becker, Howard S., Blanche Geer, Evertt C. Hughes and Anslem L. Strauss (1961), *Boys in White: Student Culture in Medical School*, Chicago: University of Chicago Press.

Berkanovic, Emil, Carol Telesky and Sharon Reeder (1981), 'Structural and Social Psychological Factors in the Decision to Seek Medical Care for Symptoms', *Medical Care*, 19: 693–709.

Charmaz, Kathy (1991), *Good Days, Bad Days: The Self in Chronic Illness and Time*, New Brunswick, NJ: Rutgers University Press.

Davar, Bhargavi (2009), 'Recovering from Psychosocial Trauma: The Place of Dargahs in Maharashtra', *Economic and Political Weekly*, 44(16): 6067.

Foucault, Michel (1975), *The Birth of the Clinic: An Archaeology of Medical Perception*, New York: Vintage Books.

Fox, Renee C. (1957), 'Training for Uncertainty', in R.K. Merton, G.C. Reader and P.L. Kendall (eds), *The Student-Physician*, Cambridge, MA: Harvard University Press.

Freeman, Howard E. and Ozzie G. Simmons (1977), 'Medical Patients in the Community: Family Settings and Performance Levels', in N.J. Smelser and W.T. Smelser (eds), *Personality and Social Systems*, New York: John Wiley.

Freeman, Howard E. and Peter H. Rossi (1984), 'Furthering the Applied Side of Sociology', *American Sociological Review*, 22(1): 73–81.

Freeman, Howard E. and Sol Levine (eds) (1989), *Handbook of Medical Sociology*, Englewood Cliffs, NJ: Prentice Hall.

Freeman, Howard E., Edgar F. Borgatta and Natheanie H. Siegel (1975), 'Remarks on the Changing Relationship between Government Support and Graduate Training', in N.J. Demerath, K.F. Schuessler and O. Larsen (eds), *Social Policy and Sociology*, New York: Academic Press.

Freeman, Howard E., K. Jill Kiecolt and Harris M. Allen (1982), 'Community Health Centers: An Initiative of Enduring Utility', *Milbank Memorial Fund Quarterly*, 60: 245–67.

Freidson, Eliot (1970), *Profession of Medicine*, New York: Dodd, Mead.

Goffman, Erving (1962), *Asylums*, New York: Anchor.

Hollinhshead, August B. and Fredrich C. Redlich (1958), *Social Class and Mental Illness: A Community Study*, New York: John Wiley.

Kakar, Sudhir (1990), *Shamans, Mystics and Doctors: A Psychological Inquiry into India and its Healing Traditions*, New Delhi: Oxford University Press.

Kaplan, Howard B., Robert J. Johnson, Carol A. Bailey and William Simon (1987), 'The Sociological Study of AIDS: A Critical Review of the Literature and Suggested Research Agenda', *Journal of Health and Social Behaviour*, 28(2): 140–58.

Kleinman, Arthur (1980), *Patients and Healers in the Context of Culture*, Berkeley, CA: University of California Press.

Kothari, Manu L. and Lopa A. Mehta (1988), 'Violence in Modern Medicine', in Ashis Nandy (ed.), *Science, Hegemony and Violence*, New Delhi: Oxford University Press, 167–210.

Levine, Sol (1987), 'The Changing Terrains in Medical Sociology: Emergent Concern with Quality of Life', *Journal of Health and Social Behaviour*, 28: 1–6.

Levine, Sol, Norman A. Scotch and George J. Vlasak (1969), 'Unravelling Technology and Culture in Public Health', *American Journal of Public Health*, 59: 237–44.

Lorber, Judith (1997), *Gender and the Social Construction of Illness*, Thousand Oaks, CA: Sage Publications.

Lupton, Deborah (2003), *Medicine as Culture*, London: Sage Publications.

Madan, T.N. (1980), *Doctors and Society*, New Delhi: Vikas Publishing House.

Mechanic, David (1962), 'The Concept of Illness Behaviour', *Journal of Chronic Diseases*, 15: 189–94.

Mechanic, David, Paul D. Cleary and J.R. Greenley (1982), 'Distress Syndromes in Illness Behaviour, Access to Care and Medical Utilization in a Defined Population', *Medical Care*, 20: 361–72.

Merton, R.K., George G. Reader and Patricia L. Kendall (eds) (1957), *The Student-Physician: Introductory Studies in the Sociology of Medical Education*, Cambridge, MA: Harvard University Press.

Minocha, Anita (1996), 'Women in Modern Medicine and Indian Tradition', in A.M. Shah, B.S. Baviskar and E.A. Ramaswamy (eds), *Social Structure and Change: Women in Indian Society*, Vol. 2, New Delhi: Sage Publications, 150–79.

Mishler, Elliot G., Lorna R. Amara Singhan, Stuart T. Hauser, Ramsay Liem, Samuel D. Osherson and Nancy E. Waxler (1981), *Social Context of Health, Illness and Patient Care*, Cambridge: Cambridge University Press.

Muraleedhran, V.R. (1999), 'Technology and the Cost of the Medical Care: Some Emerging Issues and Policy Imperatives', in Barbara Harris White and S. Subramanian (eds), *Illfare in India: Essay's on India's Social Factor*, New Delhi: Oxford University Press.

Nagla, Madhu (1997), *Sociology of Medical Profession: A Study of Medical Organizations and Profession of Medicine in Haryana*, Jaipur: Rawat Publications.

—— (2014), 'Sociology of Health and Medicine', in Yogendera Singh (ed.), *Indian Sociology: Development and Change*, Vol. II, ICSSR Research Surveys and Explorations, Delhi: Oxford Publications.

Needham, Joseph, Lu Gwei-djen and Nathan Sivin (eds) (2000), *Science and Civilization in China- Medicine*, Vol. 6, Cambridge: Cambridge University Press.

Nigeda, G., L. Lockett, C. Manca and G. Mora (2001), 'Non Biomedical Practices in the State of Morelos, Mexico: Analysis of an Emergent Phenomenon', *Sociology of Health and Illness*, 23(1): 3–23.

Oommen, T.K. (1979), *Doctors and Nurses: A Study in Occupational Role Structures*, Delhi: Macmillan.

Parsons, Talcott (1951), *The Social System*, New York: The Free Press.

Ram, Kalpana (2011), 'Culture, Power and Lay Medicine', in Assa Doron and Alex Broom (eds), *Health, Culture and Religion in South Asia*, London: Routledge, 7–20.

Riessman, Catherine Kohler and Constance A. Nathanson (1986), 'The Management of Reproduction: Social Construction of Risk and Responsibility', in Linda Aiken and David Mechanic (eds), *Applications of Social Science to Clinical Medicine and Health Policy*, Princeton, NJ: Robert Wood Johnson Foundation.

Rosengren, William R. (1980), *Sociology of Medicine: Diversity, Conflict and Change*, New York: Harper and Row.

Roth, Julius A. and Peter Conrad (1987), *The Experience and Management of Chronic Illness*, Vol. 6, Greenwich, CT: JAI Press.

Stanton, Albert H. and Morris S. Schwartz (1954), *The Mental Health Hospital*, New York: Basic Books.

Starr, Paul (1982), *The Social Transformation of American Medicine*, New York: Basic Books.

Straus, Robert (1957), 'The Nature and Status of Medical Sociology', *American Sociological Review*, 22: 200–04.

Sujatha, V. (2009), 'Pluralism in Indian Medicine: Medical Lore as a Genre of Medical Knowledge', *Contributions to Indian Sociology*, 41(2): 169–202.

—— (2011), 'Innovation within and between Traditions: Dilemma of Traditional Medicine in Contemporary India', *Science, Technology and Society*, 16(2): 191–213.

—— (2014), *Sociology of Health and Medicine: New Perspectives*, New Delhi: Oxford University Press.

Sujatha, V. and Leena Abraham (2012), *Medical Pluralism in Contemporary India*, Hyderabad: Orient Blackswan.

Sunder Rajan, Kaushik (2007), 'Experimental Values: Indian Clinical Trials and Surplus Health', *New Left Review*, 45: 67–88.

Venkatratnam, R. (1979), *Medical Sociology in an Indian Setting*, Madras: Macmillan.

Zachariah, Anand, R. Srivatsan and Susie Tharu (2010), *Towards a Critical Medical Practice*, New Delhi: Orient Blackswan.

Zola, Irving K. (1983), *Socio-Medical Inquiries: Recollections, Reflections, and Reconsiderations*, Philadelphia: Temple University Press.

4

Approaches in Health and Medicine

The development of the sociology of health and medicine has to be understood in terms of its relation to the dominant paradigms like bio medical model, overmedication and iatrogenesis approach, behavioural model of health, functionalist perspective, political economy perspective, interactionist perspective, labelling perspective and postmodernity and health.

Bio Medical Model

Bio medical approach is to understand the body by the medical professionals. Specifically, it sees the body as similar to machine, which goes wrong if not correctly maintained. The role of medicine is to encourage decent maintenance and to intervene if anything goes wrong. The idea that people's health is predominantly a reflection of science's understanding of the disease process and the development of effective treatments is called a bio medical model of health. In this model:

- Health is the absence of biological abnormality.
- The human body is linked to a machine to be restored to health through treatments of one sort or another which arrest, or reverse, the disease process.
- The health of a society is seen as largely dependent on the state of medical knowledge and the availability of medical resources.

The bio medical model of health underpins the organization and delivery of health care in the modern world. Medical research is predominantly based around understanding the underlying biochemical or genetic disease process with a view to discovering cures. Hospital-based, high technology medicine receives the majority of health care budgets. The general education of most health care professionals revolves around understanding the body and intervening to restore health, and the most prestigious and highly paid members of the health care professions are the experts in curative medicine, the hospital consultants and the leaders of medical research teams.

The origin of this situation can be found in the late 19th and early 20th centuries. During this period, there were great advances in medical science, such as discovery and treatment of bacterial infection, new safer surgical techniques and developments in pharmacology. It was optimistically expected in developed countries after the Second World War that a much greater investment in health care and medical research would quickly be reflected in improvements in health standards. The argument behind such optimism went something like this: scientific medicine has already conquered the diseases that were major killers in the past, such as TB and polio and given time and proper investment, it will overcome the diseases of modern society, such as cancer, heart diseases, arthritis and mental illness.

The rise of dominance of the biomedical model of health is described, with its focus on bodies and disease. The bio medical model developed medical practice as a tool for the rationalization and surveillance of the population. The main assumptions of the model are:

- The germ theory of disease.
- The separation of mind and body, rendering the patient as a sick body.
- That treatment lies in the hands of trained specialists capable of viewing the patient through the medical gaze and not with that of a lay practitioner.

The dominance of the bio medical model is linked with the transformation to modernity and the triumph of science and rationalization. The emergence of nation-states brings the idea of a population to be managed as an economic and military resource. Foucault has been influential in viewing modern medicine as part of a process of regulating and disciplining both individual bodies and the social body. The idea of 'public health' took shape as a way of eradicating pathologies from the social body. A whole range of institutions including hospitals, asylums, prisons, schools and workhouses, developed as a means of regulating and controlling the population.

Bio medicine is potentially the most polarized of all health care models. In its idealized form, biomedicine considers 'professional knowledge' to be expert, rational and scientific. Lay beliefs, by contrast are perceived as ill informed, not rational, unscientific and superstitious, and are thus devalued. According to this theory, lay people have beliefs and doctors have knowledge (Bury, 1997). In the bio medical model, symptoms are promised to the extent that they conform to diagnostic models. The doctor's job is to diagnose relevant symptoms.

In bio medicine the focus is on objective, measurable phenomena, and technology can be used to achieve diagnosis. Advances in medical technology led to a greater ability to localize disease processes within the body, so that sites of pathology could be pinpointed with greater accuracy (Helman, 2001). Although this is of great benefit to users and clinicians, the process 'has also contributed to a narrowing of medical vision – to the reductionism, mind-body dualism and objectification of body so characteristic today of the disease perspective' (Helman, 2001). Normality is established by referring to statistically derived ranges, which do not take account of the individual (for example, a person may always have had 'abnormally low' blood pressure).

Critique of the Bio Medical Model

Despite its dominance, the bio medical model has been subjected to considerable criticism by sociologists. The dramatic decline in the death rate from the middle of the last century was largely due to a fall in deaths from infectious diseases. It was generally believed that the clinical intervention played a major part in this process and, therefore, new developments in treatment would provide further improvements in health. Although this remains the dominant view, it has been questioned by several authorities within medicine. The distinguished immunologist, Macfarlane Burnett (1971), acknowledged the importance of medical intervention in controlling bacterial infection, but suggested that the contribution of laboratory science may have come to an end. He argued that the diseases of modern society are caused by genetic disorders or social problems, such as over-population, which impinge on health. In his view, laboratory research has little to contribute to either of these problems. Other critics have even questioned the contribution of clinical medicine in the past. In a celebrated work, Dubos (1960) argued that patterns of health and disease result from difficulties in adapting to a changed environment. The infectious diseases of 19th century industrial societies were largely a product of urban poverty and filth, and subsequent improvements in health owed much more to public health reforms than to medical intervention. The fact that there were developments in clinical medicine at the same time was incidental. Regarding the weight community gives to the medical contribution, Dubos writes that 'when the tide is receding it is so easy to have the illusion that one can empty the ocean by removing water with a pail' (Dubos, 1960). The question of the role of medicine in the decline of the infectious diseases has been investigated most systematically by McKeown (1979) in *The Role of Medicine*. By tracing the history of specific infectious diseases and seeing how many people were dying from them each year, McKeown was able to show that, in most cases, deaths from infectious diseases were declining long before effective medical treatment was generally available. This can be illustrated by looking at the history of some of the major infectious diseases: TB, scarlet fever, whooping cough and measles. The same pattern, with immunization and treatment playing a relatively minor part in the falling death rate, can be seen in the history of almost all the infectious diseases. The only exceptions being smallpox, diphtheria and more recently polio where immunization was an important factor. Of course, McKeown's observations do not mean that the availability of medical remedies is not important. Programmes of immunization against infection are a safeguard against the spread of certain infections. However, the fact that medical intervention played little part in the decline of the infectious diseases means that it is necessary to look for other explanations.

The public health measures of the 19th century, particularly those heading to cleaner water supplies, had a major part to play in reducing exposure to water and food-borne infections such as cholera. However, that does not explain the decline in deaths from airborne infections, such as TB, which accounted for 40 per cent of the total decline. According to McKeown, the major reason for the declining death rate was that the human organism became stronger and more resistant to disease due to improved living conditions. The reasons for this, in order of importance, were:

- Improved nutrition, resulting from improvements in agricultural production initially due to the introduction of new crops such as potatoes and maize; and later to mechanization and chemical fertilizers.
- Improvements in hygiene, particularly purification of water and sewage disposal and, later, food hygiene. This plays a major part in the decline of water and food-borne infections, which accounted for about a fifth of the total decline.
- Behavioural change, especially contraception and personal hygiene. The reduction in the birth rate not only led to better living standards but also ensured that the benefits of increased agricultural productions were not wiped out by excessive population increase.
- Immunization and therapy had little effect on the reduction of mortality until the introduction of sulphonamides in 1935. Since the 1930 immunization and therapy have been important influences.

All of the above studies demonstrate that the bio medical model of illness does not coincide with how ordinary people understand and explain illness. In addition, people seem to have a clear awareness of the impact of life experiences on health, which is largely absent from the bio medical model.

Criticism also includes that the real causes of improved mortality and morbidity rates are environmental not medical; the patient as a person is negated by becoming a sick body; unscientific may not necessarily mean 'bad', and non-scientific approaches have a contribution to make to health; the medical profession has spread its influence through the medicalization of normal experiences such as pregnancy, sadness and tiredness which is further discussed through the example of use of Ritalin to control hyperactivity in children; and the model has been open to gross political manipulation particularly in the area of 'population policies', the most extreme of which is eugenics. The rapid development of genetic medicine brings these issues to the forefront in contemporary life.

It has also been suggested that bio medicine cannot cope with chronic and stress conditions. Hierarchical medical organization has created long waiting lists and complex referral procedures; concern over the harmful effects of medication and invasive surgery; the asymmetrical power relationship between patient and doctor, and, a religious or philosophical rejection of being treated as a body rather than holistically. Similarly, the expansion of both alternative medicine and complementary medicine is located as a manifestation of the processes of modernization which has promoted the notion of the individual in control as an informed consumer and the conditions which create but cannot cure the illnesses of modernity: insomnia, anxiety, stress and depression.

Overmedication and Iatrogenesis Approach

As health in the past was influenced primarily by environmental change, McKeown argues that the best prospects for improving health in the future life with changing, or at least moderating the effects of, the environmental factors are associated with the diseases of modern society. He suggests that we are misusing our precious health care resources at present by directing most of them into high technology curative medical treatments which have a very limited power to influence patterns of health. Recently, Canada's health care has come under a scathing attack from a book which reached the bestsellers lists (Rachlis and Kushler, 1989). Developing the ideas of McKeown, the authors show that the Canadian health care system, despite being acknowledged as one of the best in the world in terms of access and quality, has had relatively little impact on the health of the Canadian people. They argue that good health has been mistakenly equated with good medical care and advocate a shift in resources from curative to primary health care, with nurse practitioners playing a major role in 'well person' care. Other critics go further than McKeown, arguing that modern medicine's obsession with technology and drug therapy is leading to an epidemic of iatrogenic (i.e. doctor caused) disease. Adverse reactions to prescribed drugs, complications following surgery and the high rates of accidents in hospitals are all examples of iatrogenesis. In a wide-ranging critique, Taylor (1979) claims that medicine has become a 'malignant' technology which is out of control. New technological procedures are now being applied without proper testing regarding both their value and safety. Taylor cites evidence from university teaching hospitals showing that, excluding surgical complications and nursing errors, 20 per cent of patients suffered some form of iatrogenic disease. There is also a 'multiplier' effect with technology breeding technology. For example, induction of labour made premature birth more likely. This resulted in techniques such as ultrasound, x-ray and examination of amniotic fluid to determine foetal age and avoid some of the problems associated with prematurity. Hospitals are not the only source of iatrogenic disease, four out of five visits to General Practitioners now result in the writing of a prescription. Melville and Johnson (1983) estimated that in Britain as many as 10,000 people die each year from (medical) drug-induced deaths, more than are killed on the roads.

Illich (1990) in what is probably the most radical critique, extends the concept to iatrogenesis and argues that the detrimental effects of medicine go beyond direct clinical harm. He further criticizes the 'medical establishments' – by which he means health care professionals, health administrators, pharmaceutical companies, the suppliers of medical equipment and other commercial institutions – of sponsoring sickness by creating unrealistic, health demands which can then only be met by health care services and medical products (social iatrogenesis). Not only are more and more treatments being made available for long-recognized diseases, but more areas of life are being brought under the scrutiny and control of health care professionals. Experiences that were once seen as a normal part of the human condition, such as pregnancy, childbirth, childhood, unhappiness, ageing and dying have now been brought under the medical remit. Illich claims that the result of this increasing 'medicalization' of life is that health professionals have undermined people's ability to manage their own health and to cope with the pain and suffering that are an inevitable part of the human condition (cultural iatrogenesis). He argues that people 'unlearn the acceptance of suffering as an inevitable part of their conscious coping with reality and learn to interpret every ache as an indicator of their need for padding and pampering'. Similarly, as most people now are being treated in hospitals, death is seen less as inevitable and more as a failure of treatment, something that ought not to have happened and which people find more difficult to accept and come to terms with.

Illich argues that the professional dominance of medicine over healing should be broken and that people be encouraged to take more responsibility for their own health. This kind of critique is part of a much wider reaction against the dominance of scientific and technological expertise over ordinary people's lives and this, in turn, is seen as a consequence of the continuing process of industrialization. Navarro (1975) offers an alternative interpretation. He locates the causes of overmedication and iatrogenesis in the capitalist political economy of modern western societies. Capitalist economies produce goods and services largely for profit and people are encouraged to consume and judge their 'success'; in terms of what they have. Capitalist societies are, thus, geared around consumption, and the increasing consumption of health care services and medical goods has to be placed into this context. According to Navarro, health care professionals do not cause overmedication, they merely administer it on behalf of organizations such as private hospitals and pharmaceutical companies, who profit from it.

Critique of Overmedication and Iatrogenesis Approach

The argument that it has been solely the medical professionals who have pushed the boundaries of medicalization into progressively broader areas of social life has been criticized by Moynihan and Smith (2002). They argue that, increasingly, it is the wider population who are demanding to have the illnesses which they believe they suffer from formally recognized. In particular, campaigns have been mounted to ensure that Attention Deficit Hyperactivity Disorder (ADHD), Chronic Fatigue Syndrome and Gulf War Syndrome should all come to have full recognition as diseases. Moynihan and Smith point out that, in these cases, it is the medical professionals who are objecting to the designation of disease status and who are seeking to draw boundaries between what they perceive as 'objective' disease and conditions such as these.

It is important to place these critiques of bio medicine into context. First, rates of medical cure have increased spectacularly in some areas (skin cancer and leukaemia for example). Second, by confining themselves to mortality rates as a 'measure' to health, McKeown and others have underestimated the contribution of clinical medicine to improving the quality of people's lives, by, for example, controlling pain, restoring eyesight, improving mobility and so on. Third, critics of McKeown have questioned the extent to which it is useful to speculate about the control of degenerative diseases from a history of infectious diseases (Lever, 1977). Finally, in respect of Illich's critique, there is not clear evidence that people necessarily give up responsibility for their health as a necessary consequence of medicalization. However, the work of McKeown and others such as McKinlay and McKinlay (1977) who came to the same conclusions about the effect of medicine on American health has demonstrated the links between health and environmental factors beyond reasonable doubt. Most of the major diseases of modern society remain stubbornly resistant to medical cure while the resources for researching and treating them become squeezed in most developed societies (Taylor and Field, 1993).

Functionalist Approach

Functionalist theorists perceive social system as composed of various closely interconnected parts, and they argue that changes, decisions, and definitions made in one part of the system inevitably affect, to some degree, all other parts of the system. Thus, a person's position within the social system subjects him or her to events and stresses originating in remote areas of the system. Behaviour that is adaptive from one's own perspective and peculiar circumstances may be regarded as deviant by society at large. The individual then has the choice of continuing the adaptive behaviour and being defined as deviant or trying to change that behaviour even though the person sees it as necessary for his or her own survival. Many people, not surprisingly, continue the disapproved behaviour and are therefore pressured by society into being deviant. Such people run the risk of confrontation with those authorities, such as psychiatrists, the police, and the courts, charged with controlling or eliminating dysfunctional social processes. Deviance as a social system is, thus, reduced through the application of social sanctions against the offender. These sanctions include the use of jails, prisons, and mental hospitals to remove the deviant from society to ensure social order and cohesion.

Instead of accepting the idea of sickness as a biological concept, Parsons suggested that sickness is a social concept. Parsons (1975) claimed that formal health care performs an important function in modern society by ensuring that ill people are made fit to return to paid work. Accounting to Parsons, when people are ill society tends to release them from normal 'duties' such as going to work. Parsons thought that if too many people claim to be ill it could be dysfunctional for society, not enough work would be completed and a subculture of malingerers, refusing to work could develop. For this reason Parsons argued that a 'sick's role' is of crucial importance to society. People can only be legitimately labelled 'sick' if they conform to the elements of the sick's role. To acquire the sick's role, people must not expect to take care of themselves; want to get better; seek medical advice and comply with the advice given by health professionals. Ensuring that people seek advice and comply with medical instructions, means that patients will get better quickly and return to work. Formal health care is, therefore, functional for both individuals and society. Being ill meant acting in different, deviant ways compared to the norm. Being sick was therefore, a form of social role, with people acting in particular ways according to the culture of society. In modern Western societies, this involves four elements, two of which are rights and two of which are obligations.

Rights of the Sick's Role

1. The sick person has the right to be exempted from normal social obligations, such as attending employment, or fully engaging in family activities. However, the extent to which the person can take on the sick's role and so avoid normal duties depends upon the seriousness of the illness and other people's acceptance that he/she is genuinely ill. For example, employers might reject an employee's claim to be sick and unable to work. They may argue that the person is merely feigning illness. In case like this, medical expert is called upon to decide on the validity of the claim to be sick.
2. The sick role is something that the person can do nothing about and for which they should not be blamed and they therefore have the right to be 'looked after' by others. The sick's role effectively absolves the person from any blame for their social deviance.

Obligations of the Sick's Role

As well as these two rights, there are two related obligations:

1. The sick person must accept that the situation he/she is in is undesirable and that he/she should seek to get well as soon as possible.

2. The sick person must seek professional help and cooperate with the medical profession to get better.

According to Parsons, the rights of the sick role are completely dependent on the sick persons undertaking these obligations; if not, their illness is not regarded as legitimate and they are seen as unfairly appropriating the sick's role.

By suggesting that illness is just one of the number of forms of deviance that could be harmful to society, Parsons expands the idea of illness to include a social dimension. Being ill becomes not just a physical abnormality, but also a social abnormality. Illness is deviant and dangerous to society, and must be controlled. The sick's role provides a way in which society can swiftly deal with the deviance and bring people back to their normal pattern of functioning, which benefits society.

Between 1951 and 1958 Parsons developed the notion of sick role in three major steps. In the same year, an article appeared in the *American Journal of Orthopsychiatry* focusing upon illness and the role of physician, while one year later, together with Renee Fox, he edited an issue of the *Journal of Social Issues* specializing in the sociological analysis of illness and medical care. In the years from 1953 to 1956 he developed the L-I-G-A (Latency-Integration-Goal Attainment- Adaptation) scheme, an idea of social control with occasional references to the sick person's experience when undergoing medical treatment. In 1958, in a contribution to Jaco's (1972) *Patients, Physicians and Illness*, he added the organisms as a fourth system to the hierarchy of culture, society, and personality and he placed illness as a socially legitimate form of withdrawal in the wider framework of cultural definitions of health and illness.

Parsons' perspective of illness is an empirical conceptualization of the norms which regulate social action with regard to illness as a deviance. The problem of health is intimately involved in the functional prerequisites of the social system. In 1978, Parsons introduced the term 'teleonymy' to account for 'healing power of nature ..., a property of living systems ... by virtue of which such systems have a capacity to cope, often without outside intervention'. Such 'teleonymy' accounts for a *vis medicatrix naturae*, and the breakdown of telenomic capacities, namely illness, only needs the *vis medicatrix* where nature does not provide appropriate remedies. That this is not geared towards the so-called somatic illness alone, but, rather, towards psychological and psychiatric disturbances is due to the fact that the normal social roles which the sick individual becomes unable to fulfil are primarily dependent upon mental accomplishments safeguarding interactive reciprocity within the family and work place. It is here that medical sociology has its prime subject matter, maintains Parsons (1958), 'Since it is at the level of role structure that the principal direct interpenetration of social systems and personalities comes to focus, it is as an incapacity to meet the expectations of social roles, that mental illness becomes a problem in social relationships and that criteria of its presence or absence should be formulated'. The sick role is, thus conceptualized as a social 'niche' where the incapacitated have a chance to recover from their weakness, and overcome their urge to withdraw from rather than actively tackle the vicissitudes of the capitalist labour market (Gerhardt, 1979). The doctor's role in this is to provide the legitimation to enter the sick status as well as to spur the urge to leave it. It is in this way that reciprocity between patient and doctor in their sick's role and physician's role make for the former's return to normal rights and duties as a full-fledged member of the work force and other areas of daily concern. Parsons also made it clear that sick role concept could be applied for chronic illness also. The issue is one of the approximation rather than accomplishment of the goal of recovery, and permanently than temporarily being exempted from a partial range of one's duties rather than temporarily being exempted from more or less the total range of one's duties, and so on. In fact, Parsons used the example of his own then mild diabetes to illustrate how the sick role appears differently in individual cases.

Critique of Functionalist Approach

First Parsons (1975) assumed that the health care system was the most effective way of creating a fit and healthy society. However, according to McKeown (1976) it is improved sanitation, sewage disposal, housing and general welfare that has made the most significant contribution to the nation's health.

The concept of the sick's role has been strongly criticized by a number of sociologists.

- The first criticism is that it only applies to acute illness; it is not a useful concept when looking at chronic illness, where people are unwell for a long time with no apparent prospect of improvement and the obligation to get better as soon as possible simply cannot apply. Parsons (1975) responded to this criticism by saying that although complete recovery is not possible, people can 'manage' their illness, carrying on as normal a life as possible.
- The second criticism is that Parsons assumes that the sick's role occurs only when the doctor legitimates the illness. However, according to Eliot Freidson (1970), before consulting the doctor, there is a complete set of lay-referrals, by which he means that ill person will consult others close to him/her as to whether he/she might be ill and the significance of the symptoms. Only after this process will the person go to the doctor.

Freidson argues that other people besides the medical professionals are important in deciding whether a person can occupy the sick's role or not, and that the likelihood that the person will be granted the sick's role can best be understood in terms of legitimacy. Freidson suggests three possible variations of legitimacy. In the first situation, the person is considered to have an illness from which he/she can recover and is granted conditional access to the sick role. This was the model as put forward by Parsons.

In the second situation, where the person simply cannot eat well and suffers from obvious long-term symptoms or even faces death, access to the sick's role is unconditionally legitimate, once granted and so there are no obligations to get better.

The third case is where the illness is stigmatized by others. For example, sexually transmitted diseases may be seen as the fault of the ill person and therefore the sick role may be regarded as illegitimate and it is unlikely that the rights of the sick's role will be granted.

Howard Waitzkin (1971) later applied a modified version of the sick's role to six specific organizational settings: the family, the mental hospital, the totalitarian state, prisons, the armed forces and conscription (when people of certain age are required by law to undertake a period of military service). In each of these settings, he argued that the sick's role provided a way for system to allow a limited amount of deviance, thereby avoiding more serious damage to society. Waitzkin's version of Parson's sick role was intended to show that the basic idea of the sick's role was a useful analytical tool, but that Parsons failed to explore the significance of differences in power and how the sick role could be used to benefit the more powerful in society. This stress on inequality of power leads us to the materialist or political economy perspective on health and illness.

- Parsons' idea of the sick role, where people who are ill are allowed to default on their normal social roles as long as they try to get better by following medical advice, has been criticized because it cannot be applied to disabled people, nor to those with chronic illness.

Conflict Approach

A key assertion of the Marxist perspective is that material production is the most fundamental of all human activities from the production of the most basic of human necessities such as food, shelter and clothing in a subsistence economy, to the mass production of commodities in modern capitalist societies. Whether this production takes place within a modern or a subsistence economy, it involves some sort of organization and the use of appropriate tools; this is termed as the 'forces of production'. Production of any type was recognized by Marx as also involving social relations. In modern capitalist societies, these 'relations of production' lead to the development of a division of labour reflecting in the existence of different social classes. For Marx, it is these forces and relations of production together that constitute the economic base (infrastructure) of society. The superstructure of a society, the political, legal, educational, and health systems and so on, are shaped and determined by the economic base.

The orientation of this approach as applied within health sociology is towards the social origin of disease. Health outcomes for the population are seen as being influenced by the operation of the capitalist economic system at two levels.

First, at the level of the production process, health is affected either directly in terms of industrial diseases and injuries, stress-related ill health, or indirectly through the wider effects of the process of commodity production within modern societies. The production processes produce environmental pollution, whilst the process of consuming the commodities themselves has long-term health consequences such as eating processed foods, chemical additives, car accidents and so on. Second, health is influenced at the level of distribution. Income and wealth are major determinants of people's standard of living like where they live, their access to educational opportunities, their access to health care, their diet, and their recreational opportunities. All of these factors are significant in the social patterning of health.

Critique of Conflict Approach

Alternative medicine is becoming increasingly popular, but so has criticism of it by the medical establishment. Physicians may honestly feel the medical alternatives are inadequate, ineffective, or even dangerous, but they also recognize that the use of these alternatives is financially harmful to their own practices. Eating disorders also illustrate conflict theory's criticism. Many of the women and girls who have eating disorders receive help from a physician, a psychiatrist, a psychologist, or another health care professional. Although this care if often very helpful, the definition of eating disorders as a medical problem nonetheless provides a good source of income for the professionals who treat it and obscures its cultural roots in society's standard of beauty for women (Whitehead and Kurz, 2008). Obstetrical care providers are another example. In most of the human history, midwives or her equivalent were the people who helped pregnant women deliver their babies. In the 19th century, physicians claimed they were better trained than midwives and won legislation giving them authority to deliver babies. They may honestly have felt that midwives were inadequately trained, but they also fully recognized that obstetrical care would be quite lucrative (Ehrenreich and English, 2005).

Political Economy Approach

This perspective is derived mainly from Marxism. In a similar argument to that of the functionalist, political economy writers argue that medicine is closely related to the concept of social control. It is used to define normality, punish deviance and maintain social order. However, the crucial difference is that, unlike functionalism, it sees medicine as operating on behalf of the controlling groups in society.

According to Vicente Navarro (1967), capitalism benefits from medicine in three ways:

1. Medicine ensures that the population remains healthy enough to contribute to the economic system, by working in offices and factories to produce profit for the ruling class. Definitions of health and illness are crucially linked to the ability to produce goods, i.e. a healthy person is one who is productive and therefore profit-making for

capitalism; an unhealthy person is one who produces no wealth. Doctors ensure that people are fit enough to work.

2. Medicine has an ideological function by masking the differences in health by social class, gender and ethnicity, which are caused by differences in wealth, income, and living and working conditions. The medical profession does this by providing an explanation of ill health as the result of bad luck, or of the individual engaging in activities that put health at risk. The wider social factors are, therefore, ignored and any blame for ill health is placed upon the individual.
   Lesley Doyal and Imogen Pennell (1979) have suggested that these wider factors causing ill health are a direct result of capitalism. For example, the role of capitalism in generating pollution which causes a wide range of respiratory diseases and cancers is largely ignored; and only limited controls are placed upon products such as alcohol and tobacco which are known to cause serious ill-health, but which make enormous profit. They also point to more specific conditions of employment under capitalism, which lead both directly and indirectly to ill health through, for example, industrial accidents, high stress levels and alienation.
3. The stress on the biomedical explanations for illness leads to treatments being based upon the use of drugs and advanced technology. In turn, the production of these goods is highly profitable to capitalism. Therefore, not only does capitalism create the conditions for poor health, but it also profits from the attempts to cure the same poor health.

Ellen Annandale (1998) uses the example of the breast implants by a US company. This company began manufacturing breast implants (which increase the size of the bust), made from a type of silicone gel, in 1963. The gel implant was used in over a million transplants. In 1970s, surgeons began to complain that the gel was 'leaking' from the implants in many cases and causing serious medical problems. However, after discussions with the company and representatives of the plastic surgeons using the gel, the controlling authority, the US Federal Drugs Agency, refused to intervene and ban the use of silicone.

This example, according to those supporting the political economy perspective, illustrates the way in which profit dominates approaches to health in capitalism.

Critique of Political Economy Approach

The political economy perspective has been very influential, but it has also received numerous criticisms.

Nicky Hart (1985) has argued that it fails to recognize that capitalism has provided real health care gains as well as increased life expectation for the majority of the population. Bryan Turner (1995) has added the point that capitalist societies have been much more effective in advancing the health of the majority of the population than have socialist societies.

Furthermore, Hart points out that much of the Marxist critique of 'capitalism' is in fact a critique of US health care, where the system is largely privatized and exploitative of the poor. It is far less accurate in its description of British and Northern European health care systems, which are freely available to all without payment, and where there is a large body of law which seeks to limit damage to health by work practices and pollution.

Interactionist Approach

While Durkheim emphasized the influence of the larger society upon the individual, Cooley, Thomas, and Goffman reflect the symbolic interactionist approach to human behaviour, which views human group life from the perspective of the individual. This approach sees the individual as a creative, thinking organism who is able to choose his or her behaviour instead of reacting more or less mechanically to the influence of social processes. It assumes that all behaviour is self-directed on the basis of the symbolic meanings which are shared, communicated, and manipulated by interacting human beings in social situations. Of special relevance to a sociological understanding of stress is Charles H. Cooley's theory of the 'Looking Glass-Self' (1964) which maintains that our self-concepts are the result of social interaction in which we see ourselves reflected in the meanings other people attach to us as social objects. Cooley compares the reflection of ourself in others to our reflections in a looking glass. Cooley's looking glass-self concept has three basic components: (1) we see ourselves in our imagination as we think we appear to the other person; (2) we see in our imagination the other person's judgment of our appearance; and (3) as a result of what we see in our imagination about how we are viewed by the other person, we experience some sort of self-feeling, such as pride or humiliation. The contribution of this theory to an understanding of stress is that an individual's perception of himself or herself as a social object is related to the reaction of other people. Quite obviously stress could result from the failure of the observer to reflect a self-image consistent with that of the subject. Thus, stress can be seen as having a very definite social and personal component based on perception of a social event.

The work of William I. Thomas is also relevant for its understanding of crisis as residing in the individual's 'definition of the situation' (Volkart, 1951). Thomas stated that so long as definitions of a social situation remain relatively constant, behaviour will generally be orderly. However, when rival definitions appear and habitual behaviour becomes disrupted, social disorganization and personal demoralization may be anticipated. The ability of an individual to cope with a crisis situation will be strongly related to socialization experiences that have taught the person how to cope with new events in general. Consequently, Thomas makes two particularly important contributions concerning stress. First, he notes that the same crisis will not produce the same effect uniformly in all people.

Second, he explains that adjustment and control of a crisis situation result from an individuals' ability to compare a present situation with similar ones in the past and to revise judgment and action upon the basis of past experience. The outcome of a particular situation depends, therefore, upon an individual's definition of a situation and upon how that individual comes to terms with that situation. As David Mechanic (1978) stated, 'Thomas' concept of crisis is important because it emphasizes that crises lie not in situation, but rather in the interaction between a situation and a person's capacities to meet it'. Graham and Reeder (1972) add that in Thomas' notion of adaptation 'the individual's repertoire of coping behaviour is a crucial element in understanding the ways in which people come to terms with a given stressful situation'.

Goffman is noted for the dramaturgical or 'life as theatre' approach. The symbolic interactionist orientation is obvious in Goffman's (1959) belief that in order for social interaction to be viable, people need information about the other participants in a joint act. Such information is communicated through: (1) a person's appearance; (2) a person's experience with other similar individuals; (3) the social setting; and (4) most important, the information a person communicates about himself or herself through words and actions. This fourth category of information is decisive because it is subject to control by the individual and represents the impression the person is trying to project which others may come to accept. This information is significant because it helps to define a situation by enabling others to know in advance what a person expects of them and what they may expect of him or her. Goffman calls this process 'impression management'. Goffman says people live in worlds of social encounters in which they act out a line of behaviour, a pattern of verbal and non-verbal acts by which individuals express their view of a situation and their evaluation of the participants, particularly themselves. The positive social value individuals claim for themselves by the line that others assume they have taken during a particular encounter is termed a 'face'. This face is an image of self projected to other people who may share that face. One's face is one's most personal possession and is the centre of security and pleasure, but Goffman is quick to point out that a person's face is only a loan to him or her from society and can be withdrawn if the person conducts himself or herself in a manner others deem as being unworthy. A person may be in the 'wrong face' when information about that person's social worth cannot be integrated into his or her line of behaviour or a person may be 'out of face' when he or she participates in an encounter without the line of behaviour of the type that participants in that particular situation would be expected to take.

Goffman further explains that the maintenance of face is a condition of interaction, not its objective. This is so because one's face is a constant factor taken for granted in interaction. When people engage in 'face-work', they are taking action to make their activities consistent with the face they are projecting. This is important because every member of a social group is expected to have some knowledge of face-work and some experience in its use, such as the exercise of social skills like tact. Goffman sees almost all acts involving other people as being influenced by considerations of face; for example, a person is given a chance to quit a job rather than be fired. A person must be aware of the interpretations that others have placed upon his or her behaviour and the interpretations that he or she should place upon their behaviour. Therefore, Goffman's view of the self is that it has two distinct roles in social interaction: first, the self as an image of a person formed from the flow of events in an encounter; and second, the self as kind of player in a ritual game who copes judgmentally within a situation.

Goffman's principal contribution to our understanding of stress arises from his claim that the self is a sacred object. The self is more important than anything else to us because it is always with us and represents who we are. For someone to challenge the integrity of that self as a social object is an embarrassing situation. Each self is special, and in social relationships that very special self we have tried to nourish and protect for a lifetime is put on display. Goffman has said that role-specific behaviour is based not upon the functional requirements of a particular role, but upon the appearance of having discharged a role's requirements. Thus, stress could be induced when people perceive their chosen face or performance in a given situation to be inconsistent with the concept of self they try to maintain for themselves and others in that situation. Otherwise, people might not be so willing to take such great care that they act out lines of behaviour considered appropriate to their situation.

Critique of Interactionist Approach

Critics fault interactionist approach for implying that no illnesses have objective reality. Many serious health conditions do exist and put people at risk for their health regardless of what they or their society thinks. Interactionist perspectives have been criticized for their over-emphasis upon the individual as the object of sociological study. There tends to be little conception of social structures (other than structures being elaborate fictions we somehow create and sustain). Critics also say the approach neglects the effects of social inequality for health and illness. Day and Day (1977) criticized social interactionist accounts of health and illness for concentrating on the negotiations between medical professionals and patients while ignoring wider social factors such as social inequality, pollution and stress, which provide the actual causes of ill health.

There is little attempt to explain how the social relationships that we create (especially when we live in very large, very complex, social groups) reflect back upon our behaviour to apparently force us into behaving in ways that give us little real choice.

The perspective concentrates too much on the small scale, relatively trivial, aspects of social life. It tends to immerse itself in the minute details of social existence while ignoring the much bigger picture of life at a society-wide level of analysis. The individual, in this respect, is seen to be too small a level of analysis (just as structuralists' are criticized for tending to ignore the role of individual social actors).

By concentrating upon individuals and their common sense, subjective interpretations, all knowledge about the social world is seen to be fundamentally relative (that is, nothing can ever be wholly true and nothing can ever be wholly false). This is significant for a sociological understanding of the social world since it effectively holds that sociology is more or less a pointless exercise. Statements about the social world made by sociologists can be no more reliable or valid than any statements made by non-sociologists. It also, perhaps more importantly, shows how interactionist thought can, at least on this level, be linked to postmodernism.

Interactionist sociology does not adequately address questions of social order and social change. The concepts used by interactionists are not adequately enough to explain, for example, why societies change.

Giddens argues that to understand human behaviour we must examine both social structure and the way individuals see the world, that is, both the way society shapes human behaviour through, say, socialization and the way individuals have choices over their own behaviour. We are capable of making some choices, for example whether to visit a doctor. However, social circumstance such as the cost of the bus fare or the inability to take time off might prevent us from going to doctor. Thus both structure and agency need to be examined.

Sociological Conceptualization of Medical Knowledge and Power: Foucauldian Approach

Science in general and biomedical science in particular can be seen at one level as a proven, reliable, and valid method for developing our understanding of the natural world, including human health and illness. However, such constructions never exist at a purely conceptual level; they are always applied through sets of material practices. The biomedical understanding of human illness and suffering is reflected in the material practices of the medical profession, which for over a period of two centuries has been able to establish its dominance within the evolving organizational systems of health care. It is through such practices that the power of the biomedical discourse of health and illness has become socially embedded. In this sense, medical knowledge and power has long been regarded as defining factors of modern health care systems.

Here we will analyse Foucault's social constructionist analysis of medical discourse. Foucault's work conceptualizes power as the property not of any particular social group, or as something exercised through a structural instrument such as the state, rather it is a relationship which is localized, dispersed, diffused and typically disguised through the social system, operating at a micro, local and covert level through sets of specific (discursive) practices (Turner, 1997). Power is a 'strategy' or set of discursive practices that characterizes the working of modern social systems, summed up by Foucault's much quoted statement that 'power' is a machine that no one owns. Hence, for Foucauldians, traditional forms of governmentality (a conception of which focuses attention on the ways in which power is present at all levels of society, serving to regulate the activities of the population) depend on systems of knowledge and truths that constitute the object of its activity, and hence the roles of experts and their expertise are central.

In case of medicine, power is embodied in and comes with the day-to-day rational scientific practices associated with the work of doctors in the hospital or clinic, which Foucault (1973) termed as the 'clinical gaze'. Such everyday practices contribute to the (social) construction and reproduction of what has been termed the 'biomedical discourse'. For Foucault, the relationship between power and knowledge is an inevitable and inextricable one (he in fact uses the single term knowledge/power), i.e. any extension of power involves an increase in knowledge. Specific forms of power require highly specific formations of knowledge. In this sense, institutions such as medicine (also the law and organized religions) exercise power not through overt coercion but through the moral authority over patients associated with being able to explain individual problems (such as an illness) and then provide solutions (i.e. treatment) for them. As Miller and Rose phrase it, medial 'experts' play a mediating role between 'authorities' and individuals, shaping conduct not through compulsion but through the power of truth, the potency of rationality and the alluring promises of effectivity (Miller and Rose, 1993: 93). In this conceptualization of medical practice, power is essentially relational rather than something that is possessed by individual doctors or the medical profession as a social group. This moral of disciplinary approach means that power is exercised most effectively as the subject of the discourse that 'interiorizes' this gaze. To the point that he is his own overseer, each individual is thus exercising this surveillance, over, and against, himself (Foucault, 1980: 115).

It is in this context that Foucault discusses the place of medicine in the monitoring and administration ('surveillance') of populations and their bodies. This disciplinary form of power is not seen as openly coercive; rather, it might be thought of as a facilitating capacity of resources, a means of bringing into being the subjects 'doctor' and 'patient' and the phenomenon of the patient's illness (Lupton, 1997: 99). Thus whilst there is a recognition of the role of the state in the reproduction of this medical dominance, it does not then follow that the medical profession simply serves the interests of the capitalist state. For example Armstrong's (1993) work, on the 'New Public Health', argues that the public health strategies are purely a contemporary example of medical power exercised through the surveillance of a population's health behaviour. Such an approach would deny that health promotion strategies have emerged directly from a policy process instigated by the British State, which has its own particular sets of interests and goals.

Critique of Foucault's Approach

A central criticism of Foucault's theorization of medicine as discursive practice is that it is overly deterministic. It focuses attention almost exclusively on the ways in which the discourse of medicine (as represented in official texts, medical notes etc.) both subjects and subjugates patients. This is the 'docile body' view of the patient, subject to the conical gaze; there is very little discussion of the ways in which this discourse might be resisted by patients. As Lupton argues, this approach tends to 'present' a consonant vision of a world in which individuals' lives are profoundly experienced and understood through the discourses and practices of medicine and its allied professions (Lupton, 1997: 94). What follows for Lupton is a tendency to neglect examination of the ways in which medical discursive practice is 'negotiated' by the lay population in their avoidance of suffering and in 'maximizing' their health statuses.

Behavioural Model of Health

McKeown has argued that, while nutrition and hygiene were the major influences on health in the past, and remain so in developing world, industrialization and affluences have brought a new set of health problems. There is a growing evidence to suggest that the diseases of modern society are linked to 'behavioural' factors – such as sedentary lifestyles, refined diet and widespread use of drugs such as alcohol and tobacco – all of which are in principle preventable. Health professionals become increasingly interested in the extent to which people in part at least, 'bring about' their own health problems. For example, a report by the Medical Services Study Group of the Royal College of Physicians (1978) investigated 250 cases of people who had died before reaching the age of 50. They concluded that in 98 cases patients had contributed to their own deaths by behaviour such as overeating, drinking, smoking, or not complying with treatment.

Ewles and Simnett (1985) distinguished between primary, secondary and tertiary health education where primary health education is concerned with encouraging people to behave in ways that will help them to avoid disease or injury. Individuals are encouraged for regulating their diets, avoiding misuse of drugs and to take more responsibility for their own health. Secondary health education is concerned with halting or reversing the development of an existing disease or condition. This may include the nurse encouraging high-risk groups to make use of screening services or spotting of disability or developmental delay in children. In tertiary health education nurses aim at helping to prevent further complications where disease already exists so that the best possible level of health may be maintained; for example, giving guidance about diet to diabetic patients or helping patients adjust to irreversible disability.

Social Context Approach

Sociologists emphasize that human behaviour, including health behaviour, has to be understood in terms of the social context from which it emerges. When studied from the point of view of the people concerned, behaviour which may appear to be 'irrational' from a distance may actually have a 'rationality' of its own. Smoking behaviour among working class women provides a good example of this.

In the last two decades smoking has been identified as the major preventable cause of disease in the modern world. In general, people from the working classes have been less responsive to anti-smoking campaigns than the middle classes. Working class women with children have become a priority target for health educationalists, not only for the damage they may be doing to their own health but also because their children are affected directly by 'passive smoking' and indirectly by 'socialization' into smoking behaviour. In a study of women in low income families caring for pre-school children, Graham (1987) argues that smoking must be set in the context of both poverty and motherhood. The women in her study who smoked exhibited more stress symptoms than those who did not and smoking was part of a central strategy by which they were able to maintain their caring role and protect their children when their calm broke down.

Many factors which influence health are outside the direct control of individuals. For example, poor health has been associated with material, or economic factors such as poverty, poor housing, unemployment and manual work (Taylor and Field, 1993). These deprivation factors persist even after controlling for behavioural influences, such as smoking and alcohol consumption (Slater et al., 1985). Research has also consistently linked emotionally stressful life events, the quality of people's social relationships and their health. The search for better health involves more than trying to change individual behaviour. The World Health Organization (1984) has recognized this by defining health promotion as 'the process of enabling people to increase control over their health'. Ziglio (1992) argues that a 'structuralist' or social approach to health promotion involves interventions in the form of the reallocation of resources, community action, government legislation and perhaps more general social change to help produce safer and healthier environments.

Critique of Behavioural Model of Health

Sociologists, while not necessarily disputing the importance of behavioural factors on health, nor the benefits of health education, have questioned over-simplified behavioural theories in a number of ways. Three main types of criticisms have been made. First, that the social context of behaviour is ignored. Second, that many factors affecting health status lie outside the control of individuals. Third, that such programme can become a form of social control.

Labelling Approach

By failing to account for the behavioural variations within the sick's role, the functionalist approach to illness has neglected the various aspects of acting sick. The process of seeking medical care pointed out that two people having much the same symptoms may behave quite differently. One person may become concerned and seek medical treatment, while another person may ignore the symptoms completely. Lipowski (1970) has noted that individual strategies in coping with illness vary from passive cooperation to positive action to get well and from fear at being diagnosed as ill to actual pleasure in anticipation of secondary gains. Several writers, Freidson (1970) in particular, have taken the position that illness as deviant behaviour is relative and must be seen as such; this is the perspective of labelling theory.

Labelling as a sociological construct has been used to inform medical practice since the 1960s in order to draw attention to the view that the experience of 'being sick' has both social as well as physical consequences. Labelling theory is based on the concept that what is regarded as deviant behaviour by one person or social group may not be so regarded by other persons or social groups. Howard Becker (1973), one of the leading proponents of labelling theory, illustrates the concept in his study of marijuana users. His analysis reveals a discrepancy in American society between those people who insist that smoking marijuana is harmful and that use of the drug should be illegal, and those who support a norm favouring marijuana smoking and who believe that use of the drug should be legalized. While the wider society view marijuana smoking as deviant, groups of marijuana smokers view their behaviour as socially acceptable within their own particular group. Becker's position is that deviance is, therefore, created by social groups who make rules or norms. Infractions of these rules or norms constitute deviant behaviour. Accordingly deviance is not a quality of the act a person commits, but instead is a consequence of the definition applied to that act by other people. The critical variable in understanding deviance is the social audience, because the audience determines what is and what is not deviant behaviour.

The applicability of labelling theory as a vehicle for explaining illness behaviour is that while sickness may be a biological state existing independently of human knowledge, illness is a social state created and formed by human perceptions. Thus, as Freidson (1970) has pointed out, when a veterinarian diagnoses a cow's condition as an illness, the diagnosis itself does not change the cow's behaviour. But when a physician diagnoses a human's condition as illness, the diagnosis can, and often does, change the sick person's behaviour. Thus, illness is seen by labelling theorists as a condition created by human beings in accordance with their understanding of the situation.

The labelling approach has not only drawn attention to the construction of illness as a social state, but has also identified the processes through which people come to be formally labelled (or diagnosed) and to accept a deviant identity and lifestyle.

In many cases (e.g. mental illness, epilepsy, multiple sclerosis), the identification of a stigmatizing illness depends on medical diagnosis. The medical model views diagnosis as a neutral scientific process which seeks to identify the nature and cause of disease and disorder through examining its signs and symptoms. This model has, however, been challenged in two ways. First, medical diagnosis can be regarded in some cases as not merely identifying but also as creating a deviant condition. This view has been advanced most frequently in relation to mental illness. However, there is also some evidence to suggest that a formal diagnosis of hypertension can itself produce symptoms of this condition, as well as causing changes in the individual's role and self-conception (Eichorn and Anderson, 1962). Secondly, attention has been drawn to the way in which doctors may differentially label diseases, with the diagnostic process being influenced by the characteristics of the patient's age, sex, social class, race etc. and by the particular circumstances in which the diagnosis is made. For example, the readiness of doctors to diagnose alcoholism has been shown to be influenced by opportunities that exist for formal referral to non-medical agencies that deal with the problem and by the patient's associated condition. In one study, based on a review of hospital case notes, patients who had sustained injuries after they had been drinking and patients who had added some alcohol to an overdose of drugs were more likely to have 'alcoholism' recorded as the primary diagnosis in their case notes than patients who were presented with an ulcer of bronchitis coexisting with alcoholism. Among the latter group, there was also often no reference made to the alcohol problem in the patient's treatment notes or in the summary sent to general practitioners (Blaxter, 1978).

Scheff's (1966) analysis of the labelling of mental illness is important as it incorporates these two critiques of the medical model and draws attention to the social forces which influence both the formal application of the label 'mentally ill' and the way in which the social meanings and responses attached to this label produce a change in the individual's self-concept and behaviour, thus causing secondary deviance. Scheff describes behaviour which may come to be classified as a sign of mental illness as consisting of activities which break the residual rules of society. Residual rules refer to the unspecified rules of conduct which are expected to be followed in a social situation and are, thus, themselves social constructions.

Goffman, in his lifetime, was the major exponent of the dramaturgical perspective premised upon the metaphor of the stage in which actors in everyday life seek to foster and control the impression of self that others have of them. Goffman studied at the University of Chicago with its distinctive version of symbolic interactionism and was considerably influenced by scholars such as Mead, Durkheim, and Simmel. Goffman's contribution to medical sociology is quite considerable. His theoretical perspective of labelling is in the analysis of stigma and its management in everyday life. The Greeks originated the term stigma to refer to bodily signs, cut to the body, which were designed to expose the bearer as a slave, a criminal, or social outcast, someone 'ritually polluted' who was to be avoided, especially in the public places. However, today the term is applied more widely to any condition, attribute, trait, or behaviour that symbolically marks the bearer off as 'culturally unacceptable' or 'inferior' and has as its subjective referent the notion of shame or disgrace. Goffman distinguishes three different types of stigma: stigmas of the body (blemishes or deformities), of character (the mentally ill, the homosexual, or criminal), and of social collectivities (racial or tribal or scheduled castes); all of these are subject to historical and cultural variability. Some of the early Goffman's work links up with the sociology of deviance, especially the labelling perspective as first espoused by Becker, Erikson, and Kitsuse, which draws on the earlier work of Tannenbaum and Lemert. The basic idea of this perspective is that social deviations from some normative framework represent stigmatized roles stemming from a 'process' involving 'primary deviation' (the original infraction), social reaction, and secondary deviation (which involves the person's response to the negative social reaction). Labelling and the symbolic assignment of the normative rule breaker to a deviant/stigmatizing role status, often involving some sort of 'degradation ceremony' are thought to have important consequences for subsequent deviation on the individual's part, and lead to deviant identity formation through an internalization of the externally imputed stereotypical role. The individual's stigma can come to dominate both ego and alter perceptions, and influence in a negative fashion the treatment accorded to the 'deviant' individual. It becomes a 'master status' or 'total identity' and one which is extremely difficult to disavow.

Goffman's sociological definition of stigma runs on a distinction between what he refers to as '*virtual social identity*' – the stereotyped imputations of the attributes and social category of another that we make in routine social interaction, which are transformed into 'normative expectations' as to what the individual ought to be; and '*actual social identity*' – the category and attributes the individual actually possesses. The stigmatized are those who have a deeply discrediting discrepancy between virtual and actual social identity. Those who do not depart negatively from the particular expectations at issue, Goffman terms as 'normals'. As he states: 'What the stranger is present before us, evidence can arise of his possessing an attribute that makes him different from others in the category of persons available for him to be, and of a less desirable kind … . He is, thus, reduced in our minds from a whole and usual person to a tainted, discounted one. Such an attribute is a stigma, especially when its discrediting effect is very extensive; sometimes it is called a failing, a shortcoming, a handicap. It constitutes a special discrepancy between virtual and actual social identity' (Goffman, 1968). A stigma, then, 'is really a special kind of relationship between attribute and stereotype'. That is to say, it is a meaning imposed upon an attribute via images, stereotypes, and attitudes which potentially discredits members of a particular social category. Goffman seems to concur with the labelling theorists when he notes that the attribution of a stigma stems from the definitional working of a society, for before a difference can matter much it must first be conceptualized by society as a whole. Stigma is a societal reaction that 'spoils' normal identity, it is perspective generated in social situations by virtue of unrealized norms that impinge upon the encounter. Scott (1972) has outlined some of the major features of a deviant label and two are pertinent here. First, it carries negative moral connotations, the bearer of the deviant label usually being viewed as 'morally inferior'; and second, deviant labels are 'essentializing labels' in that they carry 'certain implications about character that extend to all areas of personality'. The unhappy consequence of this is that when a deviant label is applied to an individual, he is often demarcated off from the rest of the group and moved to its margins. This fit into Goffman's conception of stigma. Moreover, stigmas 'spread out in waves' from the stigmatized person to his or her close connections, something Goffman terms as a 'courtesy stigma'. However, stigmatized individuals tend to adhere to the same normative beliefs about identity as others do and have a deep-seated sense of being 'normal' human beings, yet because of their adherence to such identity beliefs they are aware of what others regard as their stigma, and at times are likely to agree that they do indeed fall short of what they 'ought' to be. For Goffman, 'shame' becomes a central possibility and the central feature of the stigmatized individual's life. Yet the stigmatized are quite a heterogeneous population of people. One crucial factor is the issue of visibility, namely how well or how badly the stigma functions as a means of communicating the individual's possession of it. Obviously the level of visibility degree is context dependent. For example, the notched teeth of someone displaying one of the Hutchinson's signs connected with congenital syphilis may go unnoticed by those with little knowledge of the condition. Goffman further distinguishes between this aspect of stigma and its 'known-about-ness', referring to the extent to which others know about the attribute; its 'obtrusiveness', meaning the extent to which it actually interferes with the flow of interaction. For example a business man confined to a wheelchair bears a stigma which is relatively unobtrusive around a conference table, yet a man with a stammer finds that he continually violates the tacit code of communication etiquette in spoken encounters; and its 'perceived focus', which refers to the conception others have, not necessarily objective, as to what spheres of life-activity the stigma disqualifies the individual from, like a facial disfigurement may impair acceptance in face-to-face encounters while diabetes may disqualify an individual from certain occupations. These conceptual distinctions are useful because they serve to highlight the contextual dependency of stigmatization (or secondary deviation).

Goffman (1963), like Scheff, viewed stigma bearers as accepting the dominant social values and as a result, 'shame becomes a central possibility, arising from the individual's perception of one of his own attributes as being a defiling thing to possess'. Goffman identified a number of responses by stigma bearers which may take place over a protracted period of time. These include the direct attempt to correct the basis of their failing, which may involve physically deformed people undergoing plastic surgery or mastering areas of activity, such as riding or swimming, ordinarily felt to be closed to a person with his/her condition. Another option is to break with what is called reality and to view one's differences in unconventional ways, and particularly for secondary gain, as when a disability is used as an excuse for a lack of success in areas unconnected with one's condition. Goffman's primary concern was not however with such long-term adjustments, but rather with the way in which stigma bearers interact with normals (the non-stigmatized) when they are in one another's immediate physical presence, 'whether in a conversation like encounter or in the mere co-presence of an unfocused gathering'.

Szasz (1961, 1971) argues that the label of mental illness in a way is a means of coercive social control, or extralegal punishment, and draws a parallel between the use of psychiatric concepts in the modern world and the belief in witchcraft in the Middle Ages. He further argues that the change from religious to medical beliefs and forms of control did not take place because of the realization that persons who were supposed to be heretics were actually mentally sick. Instead, it reflected the wider transformation of a religious ideology into a scientific one. As a result, 'medicine replaced theology, the alienist the inquisitor, and the insane the witch'. Szasz does not deny that people have what he terms 'problems of living'. His main concern is that problems of human conduct may have a moral and political character, which is masked by medical labels. He, thus, advocates that 'real' (i.e. biological) illness should be separated from 'mythical' mental illness and that the disease concept should only apply to 'demonstrable bodily illness' and not to mere deviations in behaviour.

Szasz's views concerning the use of psychiatric labels as a form of social control is regarded as particularly applicable to the involuntary hospitalization of political dissidents. However, Szasz's thesis has been heavily criticized as a general critique of psychiatry and psychiatric concepts.

The question of who exerts control through defining disruptive behaviour as a sign of mental illness is answered by Szasz as being 'society's power holders'. An alternative view is taken by Morgan (1975), who, adopting an interpretive approach, suggests that the labelling of people as mentally ill occurs not because of the exercise of political power but because such people are in fact intelligible to their own friends and families, as well as to the powerful. He suggests the reason for madness being encapsulated as an illness with the public's approval is that unintelligibility is particularly threatening to behaviour thus requiring the powerful antidote of medicine, which represents the embodiment of 20th century scientism.

Critique of Labelling Approach

The most prominent area for testing the theory has been that of mental illness. In what came to be known as the Scheff-Gove debate, a number of studies have continued this old controversy about mental health. Although in the main this field is dominated by genetic and biological thinking, there are some who still argue that stigma and labelling have profound impact on the career of those designated mentally ill.

Becker's definition ignores the defining characteristics of deviancy in favour of suggesting that social interaction is a universal process. Further it might neglect the process of becoming deviant in the first place, or possess only a tacit theory of primary deviance. Becker argues that labels initiate deviant behaviour and that deviant behaviour is ubiquitous in the first place. Some critics argue that (moral) choice is also important.

Other critics point to the social determinism of the approach, which allows for no resistance. This is not usually so, however, not for the work of Goffman, at least, and it does not apply to recent studies which refer to the active seeking of labels (as some sort of badge of honour, perhaps as in Gay pride); these sorts of complex responses are predicted best by symbolic interactionism, in fact.

Labelling theory ignores certain problem areas of deviancy, such as violent crime, physical handicap, or sexual activity. But these are still labelled subsequently, by abstract agencies, and in ways that involve social reaction and self-reaction.

Labelling theory neglects power, especially the power of institutions. This is a dogmatic assertion however, it tends to over-emphasize crime again, especially where there is a political explanation for crime. Many 'deviants', such as blind people, really are powerless.

Labelling theory neglects structure but really, it sees 'structure' in symbolic interactionism terms, and not in Marxist or functionalist ones.

Labelling theory lacks empirical validity but only the crudest versions are tested in works such as that of Gove. Labelling theory allows for much more complexity now, and includes notions of irreversibility of labels, or the positive effects of them.

Postmodernist Approach

Postmodernity means differences and contingency and the disorganized nature of postmodern life means that objectification and rationalization processes lose their ability to affect social control in all spheres. For others the process of 'subjectification' is seen as a totalizing move, from which the individual cannot escape. Authenticity is at best an illusion, as all thoughts and feelings about self and identity are pervasively influenced by discourse of one form or another. Any attempt of resistance can be seen as avoidance or 'denial' and new forms of discourse can always encompass deviant cases. A more pessimistic tone is struck by those who see any attempt to avoid discursive and pastoral power being met with yet another attempt to understand, care and control.

Everyday life itself undergoes a power transformation through rationalizing processes, in which 'docility' in the face of monopolistic professional expertise shifts to an emphasis on active consumerism and lifestyle. Health rather than illness become the watchwords under such conditions, as more and more areas of life become subject to rational calculation and choice. The language of health risks exemplifies this 'reflexive' process, as lay people absorb expert knowledge and reorganize their lives accordingly, being expected to how to 'choose' a healthy lifestyle (Gabe, 1995).

A healthy lifestyle and 'body maintenance' are obviously important in today's culture. Structures concerning smoking, alcohol consumption, drug use (licit and illegal), food and diet, exercise, the proper use of the mind, the ability to deal with stress or traumatic events such as death, together with many other aspects of everyday life, become subject to the public discourses produced by an ever growing array of professionals and semi-professionals.

The change in emphasis, from the examination and specification of disease in terms of pathology, to the widespread calculation of risks to health among 'normal' populations, signifies a broadening of medicine's remit beyond its original 'objectifying' tendency to a new 'postmodern' set of processes. These transform modernity's reliance on expertise and the 'docile' body into a more fragmented and less authoritative scientific voice on the one hand, and a more active and sometimes resistant stance of the lay person on the other. The more the lay person is enjoined to be active in calculating and acting on risk, the more a complicated form of subjectivity comes to the fore.

Advances in medicine and the overall increase in levels of health have created the belief that most people will live long, healthy lives. As a result, there is an increasing emphasis on 'life planning' and 'self-identity' ... as the constraints of life-threatening diseases, early death and insecurity have given way to a more predictable life course, according to Michael Bury (1997). The experience of chronic illness therefore threatens much of what has come to be accepted as normal in contemporary society.

Bury (1997) interviewed patients with rheumatoid arthritis who had only recently been diagnosed with the disease. As a result of these interviews, Bury argued that chronic illness constitutes a major disruptive force in people's lives, undermining the taken for granted assumptions they had about the world and their place in it and forcing them to review their lives, their own bodies and their own identities. He called this process biographical disruption. As a result, people begin to appreciate the tenuous nature of their own lives, and this involves recognition of the worlds of pain and suffering, possibly even death, which are normally only seen as distant possibilities or the plight of others. This in turn leads people to rethink their own lives, in terms of what it has been about and who they really are. There are profound disruptions in explanatory systems normally used by people, such that a fundamental rethinking of the person's biography and self-concept is involved.

Not only does the onset of disease change a person's perception of their life and their body; it also leads to a disruption of relationships, physical activities and economic issues. Arthritis can lead to a physical dependence on others, and this might disturb the balance we all have in terms of giving and receiving help, with the arthritic person unable to give, but only able to receive.

Bury emphasizes that responses to illness are strongly influenced by physical, economic and relationship resources that people have. The more of these they are able to muster, then the more likely they are to maintain a positive body image and be able to live a 'normal' life.

Gareth Williams (1984) interviewed people who had been suffering from rheumatoid arthritis for a considerable time and he calls them 'seasoned professionals'. The aim was to see what the long-term effects of suffering from a chronic illness are. Williams confirms Bury's argument that the diagnosis of serious illness has a 'biographically disruptive' effect on the individual, but he found that over time a process of narrative reconstruction is used by the people to create a sense of coherence and order.

This narrative reconstruction provides an explanation or narrative of how and why one got the disease, as opposed to anyone else or as opposed to any other disease. The individuals construct a narrative that makes sense of the illness and places it in the context of their lives. In doing so, they may well ignore or downgrade the 'correct' medical version of causes; instead, they seek form of meaning for the illness in their lives. The respondents in the study tended to highlight what they saw as significant social events in their lives, such as family death, or a particularly hard employment experience, which they saw as connected to illness. According to Williams, narrative reconstruction is used to 'reconstitute and repair ruptures between body, self and world by linking and interpreting different aspects of biography in order to realign present and past and self and society'.

Postmodern Issues and Health

Postmodernism is characterized by a distrust of science as the 'truth'. The 'age of reason' (enlightenment) allowed people to disbelieve that God had created the universe, but people have also become less trusting of science to provide the truth and more accepting of their own understanding of the world, according to Baudrillard (1988).

We will discuss how postmodernists study health and illness through a series of issues, namely metatheories, discourse, legitimation and resistance, fragmentation, surveillance, and the body.

Metatheories

Postmodernist are sceptical about the way theories such as Marxism provide one single theory (metatheory) to explain the structure of society and human behaviour. In a society there are men and women, different ethnic groups, social classes, different age groups, all living in different locations. These different groups might share experiences or they might have had very different experiences. No single theory, postmodernist claim, can explain such a wide variety of experiences, and too many theories attempt to place people into a limited number of categories rather than recognizing that they might have had very different experiences. For example, many sociologists have explained social class differences in illness and mortality patterns, yet within the working class lie a number of different groups; men and women, age groups, ethnic groups and locations, occupations and educational experiences. Thus, postmodern theories attempt to recognize the fragmented experiences of people. Postmodernists apply their notion that no single theory/metatheory can account for all experiences of the bio medical theory of illness. The bio medical view of illness claims that 'illness' is caused by identifiable factors such as virus or bacteria. Postmodernist do not accept this as the only legitimate view. Theories might be useful in some circumstances yet insufficient in others. Complementary medicine (for example homoeopathy, acupuncture) can therefore exist alongside biomedical knowledge. Postmodernists do not try to state which theory is the best (biomedical or complementary) but are more interested in the way that in the 'battle' between dominant bio medical explanations and complementary medicines each attempts to gain status and power over the other. In other words all theories are simply ideas that compete to become recognized as the truth. In a fragmented world, there are likely to be a number of competing ideas, some of which may be regarded as more legitimate than others.

Discourse

Power is of crucial concern to postmodernist. Power is not necessarily tied to economic control (capitalism) as the Marxist believe, it is more subtle. Power must also be considered to be in language; writers such as Foucault (1963) claim that the way words and phrases are used can affect the way people think. Language that affects thinking is known as 'discourse'. Likewise knowledge about the body confers power; those that have this knowledge must ensure that others believe it to be superior. The possessors of this knowledge can then exercise control over others, that is, doctors can claim to have superior knowledge of the body and dismiss their patients' view. The power of discourse can be illustrated by re-examining a study by Bellaby (1990), who observed the way people in pottery took time off for illness. Medical discourse (for example a doctor's way of understanding the body and phrasing explanations about the body) tends to carry status for many people. In Bellaby's study doctors occasionally 'medicalized' problems to allow some women to have paid time off work. Morning sickness during pregnancy became 'hyperemesis' and the stress brought about by looking after people at home was called an 'anxiety state'. These examples may be viewed as positive (to workers). However, medical discourse has also medicalized human conditions such as being overweight (obesity), being sad (depression) and being worried (anxiety). We might ask what effect the medicalization of these conditions has on individuals who view themselves as obese, anxious or depressed. In addition, Oakley (1993) claims that the medical profession has medicalized childbirth, making it a medical problem rather than a natural process. Women now are encouraged to give birth to their children in hospital rather than at home, as the medical profession is opposed to births taking place outside the traditional hospital's environment. Postmodernism is just a discourse (a kind of language) and provides no truth, because for postmodernist there is no truth, just fabricated knowledge that may or may not gain status.

Legitimation and Resistance

Postmodernists do not place trust in the notion that scientific knowledge is simply created by people or 'fabricated' (made up), with some people managing to impose their views as more legitimate than others. Doctors are generally considered to support the bio medical view of illness, that illness is caused by bacteria, viruses and disease. The view that all illness is caused by abnormalities within the body (biomedicine) is socially created knowledge that has successfully gained status in many Western health care systems. People have started resisting the doctor's claim to possess the truth about human conditions. Patients opting for complementary medicine further illustrate the way dominant medical knowledge can be resisted and challenged. Yates et al. (1993) found that patients were choosing to understand their bodily condition in ways that lay outside medical explanations.

Fragmentation

The rolling back of state services means that people are becoming exposed to a greater variety of services controlled by a greater range of people. Ideas are spread easily across the global media (satellite, TV, international radio, international magazines, computer networks and email), all of which expose many of us to a larger world. People can be informed of a greater range of health views through the media. People's experiences of health services may well be more varied as they choose from a variety of treatments, including conventional medicine and complementary medicine such as acupuncture, herbal medicine and homoeopathy. Consumer society contributes to the fragmentation of health views and health care. If people are generally more used to 'shopping around' and choosing from a range of opportunities, then they might also feel inclined to shop around for the most convincing explanation of their illnesses.

Surveillance

Foucault (1963) discusses the way those in power exercise subtle means of social control simply through the traditional agencies of control (the police, judiciary and army). Technology can be increasingly used to maintain surveillance over people's behaviour (for example via a video camera). For Foucault, surveillance in the postmodern world is not necessarily exercised by others but by individuals themselves through self-surveillance. Glassner (1989) uses the popular discourse in the USA of self-health promotion through exercise and dieting to 'enable', or 'force' individuals to monitor their own body and regulate it so that it 'fits' the dominant view of the way people are persuaded to regulate their own lives rather than leaving it to the state to take responsibility. Self-surveillance might well be a health strategy of the future.

The Body

More attention is being paid to the notion of the body. According to Foucault, the body has been conceptualized as a mere physical entity in which any deviation from its 'normal' state is caused by invading bacteria, viruses or other organic causes, that is, the bio medical view of the body. More recent notions of the body have examined the cultural meanings placed upon it, for example desirable body size, weight and shape. Kirk and Tinning (1994) questioned a sample of Australian adolescent students to examine their perceptions of the body and the way such perceptions affect self-identity (for example self-worth). Consumer society treats the body as a commodity to be displayed in advertisements, films and media programmes, and products are promoted to change the body size through dieting and shape through exercise. The study showed that the students were able to respond critically to these images and ideologies but their effects were still quite powerful. One postmodern view of the body, proposed by Deleuze and Guattari (1984), sees the body not just as a physical entity with bones, skin and organs but as a culturally defined entity about which people hold all sorts of views, for example ideal body shape and size. In this way the body is not just a collection of organs surrounded by skin and supported by bones; the body exists in the abstract, i.e. the concept of a body without organs implies that notions of the body are affected by ideas or discourses that alter the way people view the body.

Critique of Postmodernist Approach

There may not necessarily be disruption as suggested by Bury and Williams. Indeed, a disease could confirm an already existing view of oneself. An example of this is provided by Daniele Carricaburu and Jenine Pierret (1995), who conducted two-hour interviews with 44 HIV positive men, 20 of whom were gay, and 20 of whom were heterosexual haemophiliacs, all living around Paris. Carricaburu and Pierret compared the views of those who were infected through gay sex and haemophiliacs who were infected through blood transfusions. They found that the gay men went through the process of disruption as suggested by Bury, but the haemophiliacs actually engaged in a form of 'biographical reinforcement' as they had already organized their lives and their awareness of themselves as being ill. When they discovered they were HIV positive, it simply reinforced their view of themselves as haemophiliacs who were far more likely to die and who had to live their lives with an expectation of uncertainty.

Carricaburu and Pierret argue that their study indicates that how people respond to disease is not individual, but a reflection of membership of a particular group – in this study, gay men and haemophiliacs – and that this membership has a strong influence on the process of biographical disruption.

Support for the importance of the wider social context in understanding the illness narrative, and, in particular, issues of ethnicity, gender, class and age, has come from a number of researchers.

Pound et al. (1998) explored the experiences of strokes among older, working class people in the East of London and found that these people saw their illness as just another crisis to be faced in their 'hard earned' lives. They had lived in poverty and seen ill health and deprivation all around them throughout their lives, so a stroke was not a 'biographically disruptive' event. Age and class were, therefore, crucial factors in their understanding of illness and in how they coped with it.

Feminist Approach

Although there may be as many types of feminism as feminists, there are certain views that many theorists share. Feminists tend to assume that society is male dominated or patriarchal and thus that men are in control of the key institutions that shape society and individuals, for example men dominate politics, the judiciary and the health services. Why is it important to consider patriarchy? Whilst feminists might use the term in different ways, male domination is an important consideration in health care. In the past men have excluded women from becoming doctors and have attempted to take control of aspects of women's lives such as childbirth, where previously women health workers tended to dominate (Oakley, 1993). Graham (1994) claims that men still make up the majority of consultants and doctors. Men impose their own values on female behaviour, which means more women are viewed as abnormal and are labelled physically or mentally ill. Symptoms reported by females to male doctors may not be treated as serious conditions, but may be simply dismissed as 'women problems'.

Marxist feminists examine women's position within the capitalist system, often viewing women as 'reserve army of labour' to be used in the economy to increase the labour supply and, therefore, reduce wage levels. Women not in paid employment may well be full-time housewives, providing free care to their families and keeping them fit for the labour market. Any increase in emphasis on informal care is likely to impact the traditional female role. Informal care is likely to be seen as a strategy for cutting the cost of formal care provision by passing the workload onto unpaid women. Radical feminists tend to view men, rather than the economic system, as the primary exploiters of women. No matter what is the type of society (capitalist or socialist) in which men and women live, men tend to dominate, shaping society to meet their needs rather than the needs of both males and females. Thus, any health care system in a capitalist or socialist society may still have a stratum of men who control the nature of medical care. There is a case of cross-cultural dimension in sociological research to enable comparison to be made between health care systems in socialist and capitalist societies. In this way sociologists, including feminists, could use empirical evidence to test their claim that men dominate irrespective of the type of economic system.

The strength of the feminist perspective is that it provides an alternative focus on health inequality from the Marxist exploration of class-based inequality. Feminists point out that men dominate in key positions (for example consultants), which might indicate a form of patriarchal control in which men make the key decisions over the health care of women. Oakley's (1993) research, which explores the way men have controlled the management of childbirth in hospitals, is particularly relevant. The radical feminist perspective provides a contrast with that of Marxists, who assume that health care in a capitalist system benefits the bourgeoisie; radical feminists argue that in any economic system the issue of power differences between men and women is of vital importance, and one to which many Marxists, such as Navarro (1976), have paid sufficient attention.

Critique of Feminist Approach

One major problem with the feminist perspective is that it ignores males in society who do not hold power over medical care. The control that male doctors and consultant exercise over the provision of medical care might not only harm women (for example through the side effects of recommended contraceptives such as the pill), but might also fail to meet men's health needs (for example the lack of publicity about screening for prostate and testicular cancer). In this way, both men and women might experience problems with the health care system regardless of the gender of the key health decision-makers.

Summing Up

Health and medicine has to be understood in terms of various theocratical approaches. Bio medical approach has underdone the body similar to machine and therefore require maintenance. However, diseases of modern society are calculated by genetic disorders or social problems. The over medication and its iatrogenic approach explains that more areas of life are being brought under the scrutiny and control of health care professionals and which has undermined people's ability to manage their own health. Ilich has undermined the contribution of clinical medicine in improving the quality of people's lives. From the functionalist perspective sickness is a social concept. Sickness is a social deviance that could be harmful to society and must be controlled. Parsons failed to explore the significance of differences in power and how sick's role could be used to benefit the more powerful in society. Conflict Approach looks at health outcomes for the population as being influenced by the economy of the society. Political economy approach argues that medicine is closely related to the concept of social control. It is used to decline normality, punish deviance and maintain social order. The opponent of this approach argues that capitalism has provided need health care gain and increased quality of life. The contribution of interactions theory to an understanding of stress is that an individual's perception of himself or herself as a social object is related to the reaction of other people. Cities find that many serious health conditions do not exist and put people at risk for their health regardless of what they or their society thinks. Foucauldian approach assumes that in case of medicine, power is embodied in and comes with the day-to-day rational scientific practices associated with the work of doctors in the hospital or clinic which is called, clinical gaze, Foucault's theorization of medicine is overly deterministic. Behavioural model of health suggest that the diseases of modern society are linked to behavioural factors – such as sedentary lifestyles, refined diet and widespread use of drugs, etc.

The labelling approach construct illness as a social state, but also identifies the process through which people came to be formally labelled (or diagnosed) and to accept a deviant identity and lifestyle. Labelling theory ignores problem areas of deviancy, such as violent crime, physical handicap or sexual activity.

Structures concerning smoking, alcohol consumption, drug use, food and diet, exercise, the ability to deal with stress or traumatic events such as death, together with many other aspects of life became subject to the public discourses by an ever growing array of professionals and semi-professionals: The narrative reconstruction that provides an explanation is a part of post modernist approach. However, support for the importance of the wider social context in understanding the illness narrative, and, in particular, issues of ethnicity, gender, class and age is still important. Symptoms reported by females to male doctors may not be regarded as serious becomes the domain of feminist approach.

References

Akhiezer, Naum Il'ich (1990), 'Elements of the Theory of Elliptic Functions', *American Mathematical Society*, 79.

Annandale, Ellen (1988), *The Sociology of Health and Medicine: A Critical Introduction*, Cambridge: Polity Press.
Armstrong, D. (1993), 'Public Health Spaces and the Fabrication of Identity', *Sociology*, 27: 393–410.
Baudrillard, J. (1988), *Selected Writings*, Cambridge: Polity Press.
Becker, Howard S. (1973), *Outsiders: Studies in the Sociology of Deviance*, New York: The Free Press.
Bellaby, P. (1990), 'What is Genuine Sickness? The Relation between the Work-Discipline and the Sick Role in a Pottery Factory', *Sociology of Health and Illness*, 12(1).
Blaxter, M. (1978), 'Disease as a Category and Process', *Social Science and Medicine*, 12: 9–17.
Burnet, Macfarlane (1972), *Potentialities and Limitations of Therapy: Auto-Immunity and Auto-Immune Disease*, Netherlands: Springer, 191–99.
Burnett, M. (1971), *Genes, Dreams and Realities*, Aylesbury, Bucks: Medical and Technical Publishing Company.
Bury, Michael (1997), *Health and Illness in a Changing Society*, London: Routledge.
Carricaburu, D. and J. Pierret (1995), 'From Biographical Disruption to Biographical Reinforcement: The Case of HIV Positive Men', *Sociology of Health and Illness*, 77: 65–88.
Conard, P. (1975), 'The Discovery of Hyperkinesis', *Social Problems*, 23: 12–23.
Cooley, Charles H. (1964), *Human Nature and the Social Order*, New York: Schocken.
Day, Robert and Joanne V. Day (1977), 'A Review of the Current State of Negotiated Order Theory: An Appreciation and a Critique', *Sociological Quarterly*, 18: 126–42.
Deleuze, G. and F. Guattari (1984), *Anti-Oedipus: Capitalism and Schizophrenia*, London: Athlone.
Dennett, Daniel C. (1995), 'Darwin's Dangerous Idea', *The Sciences*, 35(3): 34–40.
Doyal, Lesley and Imogen Pennell (1979), *The Political Economy of Health*, London: Pluto Press.
Dubos, R. (1960), *The Mirage of Health*, London: Allen and Unwin.
Ehrenreich, B. and D. English (2005), *For Her Own Good: Two Centuries of the Experts' Advice to Women*, New York: Anchor Books.
Eichhorn, Robert L. and Ronald M. Andersen (1962), 'Changes in Personal Adjustment to Perceived and Medically Established Heart Disease: A Panel Study', *Journal of Health and Human Behavior*, 3: 242–49.
Ewles, L. and L. Simnett (1985), *Promoting Health: A Practical Guide in Health Education*, Chichester: Wiley.
Foucault, M. (1973a), *The Birth of Clinic: An Archaeology of Medical Perception*, London: Tavistock.
—— (1973b), *The Order of Things: An Archaeology of the Human Sciences*, New York: Random House.
—— (1980), *Power/Knowledge: Selected Interviews and Other Writings 1972–77*, London: Harvester.
Freidson, Eliot (1970), *Profession of Medicine*, New York: Dodd, Mead.
Gabe, J. (1995), 'Health, Medicine and Risk: The Need for a Sociological Approach', in J. Gabe (ed.), *Medicine, Health and Risk: Sociological Approaches*, Oxford: Blackwell.
Gerhardt, U. (1977), 'How Much Parsons?', paper presented to the British Sociological Association's Medical Sociology Group Conference (Unpublished).
—— (1979), 'The Parsonian Paradigm and the Identity of Medical Sociology', *Sociological Review*, 27(2): 229–51.

Glassner, B. (1989), 'Fitness and the Postmodern Self', *Journal of Health and Social Behavior*, 30(2): 180–91.
Goffman, E. (1961), *Asylums: Essays on the Social Situation of Mental Patients and Other Inmates*, New York: Doubleday and Co.
—— (1968), *Stigma: Notes on the Management of Spoiled Identity*, Harmondsworth: Penguin.
—— (1969), *The Presentation of Self in Everyday Life*, Harmondsworth: Penguin.
Graham, H. (1984), *Women, Health and the Family*, Brighton: Wheatsheaf.
—— (1987), 'Women's Smoking and Family Health', *Social Science and Medicine*, 25: 47–57.
Graham, Saxon and Leo G. Reeder (1972), 'Social Factors in the Chronic Illness', in H. Freeman, S. Levome and L. Reeder (eds), *Handbook of Medical Sociology*, Englewood Cliffs, NJ: Prentice Hall.
Hart, Nicky (1985), *The Sociology of Health and Medicine*, Lancs: Causeway Press.
Helman, C. (2001), *Culture, Health and Illness*, London: Arnold.
Illich, I. (1990), *Limits to Medicine: Medical Nemesis: The Expropriation of Health*, London: Penguin.
Jaco, E. (ed.) (1972), *Patients, Physicians and Illness*, New York: Free Press.
Kirk, D. and R. Tinning (1994), 'Embodied Self-Identity, Healthy Lifestyles and School Physical Education', *Sociology of Health and Illness*, 16(5).
Lever, A. (1977), 'Medicine under Challenge', *Lancet*, 1: 353–55.
Lipowski, Z.J. (1970), 'Physical Illness, the Individual and the Coping Process', *Psychiatry in Medicine*, 1: 91–101.
Lupton, D. (1997), 'Foucault and the Medicalisation Critique', in A. Peterson and R. Bunton (eds), *Foucault, Health and Medicine*, London: Routledge.
McKeown, T. (1979), *The Role of Medicine*, Oxford: Blackwell.
McKinlay, J. and S. McKinlay (1977), 'The Questionable Contribution of Medical Measures to the Decline in Mortality in the United States in the Twentieth Century', *Milbank Memorial Fund Quarterly*, 55: 1061–62.
Mechanic, David (1978), *Medical Sociology*, New York: The Free Press.
Melville, A. and C. Johnsons (1983), *Cured to Death*, Seven Oaks: New English Library.
Miller, P. and N. Rose (1993), 'Governing Economic Life', in M. Gane and T. Johnson (eds), *Foucault's New Domains*, London: Routledge.
Morgan, Vincent T. (1975), 'The Overall Convective Heat Transfer from Smooth Circular Cylinders', *Advances in Heat Transfer*, 11: 199–264.
Moynihan, Ray and Richard Smith (2002), 'Too Much Medicine? Almost Certainly', *British Medical Journal*, 324(7342): 859.
Navarro, V. (1975), 'The Industrialization of Fetishism and the Fetishism of Industrialization: A Critique of Ivan Illich', *International Journal of Health Services*, 5: 351–71.
—— (1976), 'Social Class, Political Power and the State and their Implications in Medicine', *Social Science and Medicine*, 10(9): 437–57.
—— (1979), *Medicine under Capitalism*, London: Croom Helm.
Oakley, A. (1993), *Women, Medicine and Health*, Edinburgh: Edinburgh University Press.
Parsons, T. (1951a), *The Social Systems*, Glencoe: Free Press.
—— (1951b), 'Illness and the Role of the Physician', *American Journal of Orthopsychiatry*, 21: 452–60.
—— (1958), 'Definitions of Health and Illness in the Light of American Values and Social Structure', in T. Parsons (ed.), *Social Structure and Personality*, New York: Free Press.

—— (1964), 'Some Theoretical Considerations Bearing on the Field of Medical Sociology', in T. Parsons (ed.), *Social Structure and Personality*, New York: Free Press.

—— (1975), 'The Sick Role and the Role of the Physician Reconsidered', *Millbank Memorial Fund Quarterly: Health and Society*, 53: 257–78.

—— (1978), 'Health and Disease: A Sociological and Action Perspective', in T. Parsons (ed.), *Action Theory and Human Condition*, London: Macmillan.

Pound, P., P. Gompertz and S. Ebrahim (1998), 'A Patient-Centered Study of the Consequences of Stroke', *Clinical Rehabilitation*, 12(3): 255–64.

Punamaki, R. and H. Aschan (1994), 'Self Care and Mastery among Primary Health Care Patients', *Social Science and Medicine*, 39(5).

Rachlis, M. and C. Kushler (1989), *Second Opinion: What is Wrong with Canada's Health Care System and How to Fix it*, Toronto: Harper and Collins.

Scheff, T. (1966), *Being Mentally Ill*, Chicago: Aldine Publishing Co.

—— (1974), 'The Labelling Theory of Mental Illness', *American Sociological Review*, 39: 444–52.

—— (1975), *Labelling Madness*, Englewood Cliffs, NJ: Prentice Hall.

Scott, James C. (1972), *Comparative Political Corruption*, Englewood Cliffs, NJ: Prentice Hall.

Scott, R.A. (1970), 'The Construction of Conceptions of Stigma by Professional Experts', in J.D. Douglas (ed.), *Deviance and Respectability: The Social Construction of Moral Meanings*, New York: Basic Books.

Slater, C. et al. (1985), 'The Independent Contributions of Socio-Economic Status and Health Practices to Health Status', *Preventive Medicine*, 14: 372–78.

Szasz, T. (1961), *The Myth of Mental Illness*, New York: Free Press.

—— (1971), *The Manufacturer of Madness*, London: Routledge and Kegan Paul.

Taylor, Charles (1979), 'What's Wrong with Negative Liberty?', in Alan Ryan (ed.), *The Idea of Liberty*, Oxford: Oxford University Press.

Taylor, R. (1979), *Medicine Out of Control*, Victoria: Sun.

Taylor, S. and David Field (1993), *Sociology of Health and Health Care*, Oxford: Blackwell.

Taylor, S. and N. Tilley (1989), 'Health Visitors and Child Protection: Conflict, Contradictions and Ethical Dilemmas', *Health Visitor*, 62: 273–75.

Turner, Bryan S. (1995), *Medical Power and Social Knowledge*, London: Sage Publications.

—— (1997), 'Foreword: From Governmentality to Risk', in A. Peterson and R. Bunton (eds), *Foucault, Health and Medicine*, London: Routledge.

Volkart, E.H. (1951), *Social Behaviour and Personality*, New York: Social Science Research Council.

Waitzkin, Howard (1979), 'Medicine, Superstructure and Micropolitics', *Social Science and Medicine, Part A: Medical Psychology and Medical Sociology*, 13: 601–09.

Whitehead, K. and T. Kurtz (2008), 'Saints, Sinners and Standards of Femininity: Discursive Constructions of Anorexia Nervosa and Obesity in Women's Magazines', *Journal of Gender Studies*, 17: 345–58.

Williams, G. (1984), 'The Genesis of Chronic Illness: Narrative Re-Construction', *Sociology of Health and Illness*, 6(2): 175–200.

Yates, P. et al. (1993), 'Patients with Terminal Cancer Who Use Alternative Therapies: Their Belief and Practices', *Sociology of Health and Illness*, 15(2).

Ziglio, E. (1992), 'Indicators of Health Promotion Policy: Directions for Research', in B. Badura and I. Kickbusch (eds), *Health Promotion Research*, Geneva: WHO.

5

Methodologies in Health and Medicine

There are several ways in which we can study the social basis of health and medicine. One way is to focus primarily on major trends and institutions; division of labour within and between medical institutions; social hierarchies; and significance of market and state organizations in health and medicine. To study it, one can use the macro perspective. The other approach is to identify smaller and geographically bound units – like communities, tribal groups and aboriginal societies or urban neighbourhoods and organizations – and study their conceptions and practices of health. This can be studied by micro perspectives. At the same time, one can also have the sociological and anthropological perspective to study health and medicine. In the past, there was a distinction between sociology and anthropology, but now in anthropology there are many ethnographic studies on modern culture and institutions. There is also an overlap in studying the urban and industrial societies by sociological and anthropological approaches. There is a lot of cross-utilization of methods of study between the disciplines; medical anthropologists do utilize quantitative data for providing the background, while sociologists use narratives and oral histories. Availability of services, financial, organizational, social and cultural barriers as well as health needs are all components of access to health, and whose evaluation requires a multidisciplinary approach. Assessing various health programmes and policies requires a geomatics, mapping and statistical techniques to case-based approaches and health-seeking behaviour surveys.

In the following pages we will discuss the methodologies for the major health issues.

Methodologies for Impact/Evaluation of Health Policy: Scientific Evaluation Method

Health policy analysis in low and middle-income countries worldwide has increasingly veered towards evidence-based approaches. Assessment of the most optimal – efficient, effective, and affordable – policies and interventions in complex systems encountered across the developing world can be best undertaken with sound knowledge of scientific evaluation methods and techniques.

The tradition and application of impact evaluation in health policy and programme analysis has received a big momentum in recent years with introduction of a number of new programmes and health sector reforms, on the one hand, and greater interest and application of these approaches by leading multilateral development partners such as the World Bank and World Health Organization, on the other. In India, for example new initiatives involving conditional cash-transfer programmes such as the *Janani Suraksha Yojna* (Motherhood Security/ Safe Motherhood Scheme), or cashless hospitalization support-based national insurance under the *Rashitriya Swasthya Bima Yojna* (National Health Insurance Scheme), have led to better understanding and demand for rigorous impact evaluations in order to qualitatively assess benefits accruing to the programme, or, in an alternate way, shortfalls from the expected results.

Methodology for Health Controversies: Multidisciplinary Approach

Since the 1980s, works such as the Centre for Sociology of Innovation, Ecole de Mines or of the Group of Political and Moral Sociology (GPMS) (Boltanski, Thevenot, 2006) reinforced the methodological bases and broadened the theoretical scope of this approach. Multiple research methodologies have thus been developed to study health controversies, whether they be related to HIV/AIDS (Epstein, 1996; Fassin, 2007; Biehl, 2009; Nguyen, 2010), to clinical trials (Petryna, 2009), to the influence of global pharma in shaping psychiatric knowledge (Lakoff, 2006), to the sanitary issues related to genetically modified organisms (Jasanoff, 2005), to nuclear energy or nanotechnologies (Chateauraynaud, 2011), and surrogacy and so forth.

The analysis of scientific and health-related controversies occupies a strategic position within the social sciences, as it studies crucial contemporary issues while using innovative methodological approaches. These include discourse and media analysis, network analysis, the sociology of social movements, the anthropology of laboratory life and public health studies. Such analysis encourages multi-sited approaches to a broad range of field sites among which scientific labs, transnational social movements, regulatory authorities, and public policy administrations occupy a prominent position. In other words, the analysis of health-related controversies fosters a multidisciplinary approach, involving various academic disciplines (sociology, anthropology, political sciences, law studies, and communication sciences), complex objects of study and ground breaking methodologies and theoretical work.

Methodologies for Health and Well-Being: Socio-Historical Approach

'Health is perhaps the most crucial aspect of human well-being', said Amartya Sen. The health of the population is a critical measure of a nation's performance, because the health status of a nation tells us a lot about how its political, economic and social institutions are doing and is hence an inevitable part of public policy and economic analysis of any nation. While measuring health status through standard indicators across geographical, cultural and economic boundaries is one issue, treating women's health status as an indicator of the general is at times found to be at odds with the indicators of social equality, and freedom highlights the need for contextualization of statistical measures. For instance, studies in gender and health often point to the fact that increased income and labour force participation of women in wage labour and blue collar occupations does not necessarily produce better health for them; in fact it may lead to adverse health outcomes for some as in the case of migrant women. Thus, statistical parameters of various phenomena under study may present divergent picture as the existential situation on the ground is more complicated than any one measure can assess. Hence, we need approaches that are sensitive to historical and social context in order to grasp the multiple dimensions of human health and well-being. Also at stake here is the question of how to conceptualize both, health and well-being (the objective and subjective aspects) at the same time and how to assess the relevance of divergent factors associated with them, especially in societies that are undergoing rapid change.

Macro Perspectives of Classical Sociological Traditions

This section includes models, methods and tools followed by the framework for analysis. Models of the subject of sociology have witnessed many different perspectives (micro, macro and synthesis) through time. Prominently, however, the macro perspectives of classical sociological traditions are considered to be still relevant.

Functionalist Perspective: Macro Method

Functionalism begins with the observation that behaviour in society is structured, i.e. relationships between members of society are organized in terms of roles. These relationships, therefore, are patterned and recurrent. The structure of the society can be seen as the sum total of normative behaviour which is governed by norms. Parts of the society such as family, kinship, economy, political system, education, etc. are the major aspects of social structure. An institution can be seen as a structure made up of interconnected roles and interrelated norms. Health as an important part of social structure has to be understood through its interrelated norms or interconnectedness of culture, political and economic institution. Further, the functional analysis turns to a consideration of how a structure functions. This involves the examination of the relationship between different parts of the structure and their relationship to the society as a whole. In simple terms, functions mean effect. Thus, the function of health, as an entity, is the effect it has on the other parts of the social structure and on society as a whole. In practice, the term function is usually used to indicate the contribution that an institution makes to the maintenance and survival of the social system. The function of health as an important entity has to be understood through its contribution to the maintenance of society. This macro functionalist perspective is used as a measuring device to assess the level of health care of the target group who is receiving private health care. The ideal typical formulation of an ideal health care is a mental construct which can, however, be tested in an actual situation. The ideal health care has been constructed with the help of the opinion through a pilot study of few sample respondents.

Methodology for Body and Disease: Foucauldian Medical Discourse

Foucault's (1976) theory of disease was formulated as a discrete phenomenon which was located in the workings of the bodily structures. This conceptualization of disease within the anatomy was the product of what Foucault called the gaze. The gaze implies a 'way of seeing', or indeed smelling and/or touching; it was through the medical gaze that things became visible to the doctor and, once seen, an object formulated as a discrete entity could be observed and analysed. The medical gaze, however, is not a static way of looking; on the contrary, its flexibility constantly permits new objects to come into view. For example contemporary medicine involves increasingly taking patient's interpretations and their experience of their symptoms into account rather than just focusing on their anatomy and physiology. Thus, according to Foucauldian approach, the body, disease and contemporary medical discourse are inseparable.

Foucault used the term power as different from Marx and Weber. Foucault does not think of power as a commodity possessed by an individual or group. Power is conceived as having a local rather than a substantive existence. Power is found solely in its exercise, a body of practical techniques to which knowledge is linked and which are exercised in social relationship.

According to Foucault, the exercise of surveillance in the clinical gaze (the age that knows and decides, and the eyes that governs) constituted a power relationship within the therapeutic encounter.

Understanding Medical Systems: Historical-Anthropological Method

Health is connected to medicine as a profession and the social role and authority of the medical profession could be discerned among other things, from their ability of influence popular conceptions and practices of health. What happens when there is more than one system of medicine in the public arena? How do we assess effectiveness when state sponsored systems of medicine like bio medicine coexist with systems of medicine like homoeopathy, unani, siddha and ayurveda and other local health traditions outside state services but with popular support? Is efficacy a purely clinical phenomenon? These are questions not only of conceptualizing medical care, but also of assessing the efficacy of medicine in a situation of medical pluralism. Drawing upon historical, anthropological research, these questions broaden our understanding of public health policy and take us into the latest and emerging social approaches in the study of medical pluralism.

Physician, Patient and their Interaction Pattern: Illness Narratives Method

The concept of an illness narrative represents the process by which people with a chronic illness construct and make sense of their past, present and future. As the narrative element of the concept implies, this concept is about storytelling, personal biography, interpreting and reinterpreting changes that speaks about the relationships of self, body and society and how chronically ill people create and communicate a presentation of self that is meaningful for both them and for wider society.

Narratives are a product of the practice of medicine enhanced with narrative competence. An important idea is that people who are experiencing illness require physicians who are just medically competent, i.e. physicians who can understand their disease and physicians who can accompany them through their illness, understand their disease and prescribe the appropriate medication and treatment, and empathize with them. Narratives are seen as a vehicle that will allow for authentic engagements.

Narrative is the basic mode of human interaction and a fundamental way of acquiring knowledge. In the rapidly growing field of health communication, narrative approaches are emerging as a promising set of tools for motivating and supporting health-behaviour change.

As Jewson (1976) notes, prior to the development of modern medicine, an essential part of any doctor's interaction with a patient was to gather a personal history and to acknowledge their patient's narrative. The physician would attempt to adduce as much detail as possible about the suffering of the person who was seeking their assistance. As a form of interaction between physician and patient, listening to the patient was considered to be an essential element of the physician's craft (King, 2006). The practice of involving such verbal accounts of the unwell person was related to wider concepts of health in the ancient world and feudal world. In these pre-modern times, health was simply not seen as dysfunction of the physical body. Illness arose, rather, because the whole person, both their mind and body, was regarded as being 'out of balance'. To be healthy, a sick individual required not just intervention on the physical level (often using bloodletting and other approaches that do not sit comfortably with the modern mind) but also to address disturbance and disruption in the mind and body and to reassert balance in those domains. Doing so necessitated eliciting the person's story and their narrative.

The gathering of intimate information in the 16th and 17th centuries was also essential in the diagnosis of illness for other reasons too (Bury, 2001). Without the battery of tests and technology at the disposal of the contemporary doctor there was no other way by which insights into a patient's ill health could be made. In the modern period, however, from the mid-19th century onwards, diagnosis became increasingly informed by scientific and technological methods, and the voice of the patient, their narrative and sense of self featured less and less in medical encounters. It was tests of their blood, or images in X-rays, for example, which indicated the cause of their malaise as opposed to their verbal accounts and interpretations.

The silence of the patient and the denial of their narrative were an enduring feature of early modern medicine as bio medicine asserted its place as the legitimate discourse for all matters connected to health and healing based on its application of rational scientific logic. The perceived illogical and emotional accounts of lay people were seen as irrelevant for the practice of modern scientific medicine (Bury, 2001). Such a situation might have persisted had it not been for changes in wider society and changes in the types of illness that affect contemporary western societies.

Life with a chronic illness often continues for long periods of time and existential concerns about who one is and how one can lead a meaningful life, are an important focus for people with a chronic illness. Illness narratives are therefore, a vital element in this process, the creating, structuring and relating of a sense of self that provides and gives validation of one's identity for both self and society.

Bury's (1991) development of the concept of biographical disruption in relation to the experience of chronic illness was a landmark piece of research in developing and focusing attention on illness narratives. Bury's (2001) work has gone on to identify three different forms of illness narratives. They are contingent narratives; core narratives and moral narratives.

Charon (2001) has identified four central narrative situations in which physicians play a part: physician and patient; physician and self; physician and colleagues; and physician and society.

Physician-patient narratives are to bridge physician and patient, allowing the physician to join the patient in illness. They are told in words, gestures, and silences. Besides being therapeutic, these narratives allow the physician to enter into the world of his patients. Clinical decisions cannot be made algorithmically as each person experiences his illness differently, has very different risk profiles, and is willing to give up different things to continue living.

Physician-self narratives are the reflections and self-examination of contemplative physicians when they attempt to make sense of their own emotional response to patients. Reflections also allow physicians to better understand the patient's story and enable them to have frank and honest conversation with society about the imperfections of the medical system, the limits of medical knowledge and fragility of life.

Physician-colleague narratives are knowledge sharing episodes in which a physician participates with his colleagues who may be other physicians or nurses, social workers, etc. These narratives build social capital and collegiality, and allow physicians to celebrate their role in health care system. In addition, knowledge sharing prevents reinvention of the wheel, spreads best practices, provides opportunities for peer learning, and provides a ready sounding board to air new ideas (Charon, 2001).

Social Context of Health and Illness: Triangulation Method

The vast majority of public health investigations are based on quantitative methods and approaches. Occasionally, these studies offer a qualitative component, for instance, alongside a survey, a few people may be interviewed in greater depth, adding richness and texture to the quantitative statistics. There is an increasing recognition of the value of such evidence, with its sharper focus on both the individual's lived experience and the social context of health/illness.

Hybridity Model to Explain Process of Cross-Cultural Translation of Medical Concepts

The concept of hybridity is rooted in wider notion of a globalized society and within post colonial scholarship, where hybridization is contrasted with homogenization or polarization (Holton, 2000). The term has been generally used in a positive way, to refer to a 'playful combination of various cultural elements in art and literature, and particularly to the forming of an identity in the context of migration' but has only been recently applied to medicine (Frank and Stollberg, 2004). There have been a number of studies applying this theoretical perspective to empirical data on movements of practices across national and cultural boundaries (Obadia, 2012; Reddy, 2002; Santosh, 2013). Hybridity offers a spatial or territorial dimension to analysis giving opportunities to look at how power and knowledge are enacted and re/produced in different geographical and cultural locations. For instance, researchers have considered the process of cross-cultural translation of medical concepts (Garvey, 2011; Kim, 2006; Reddy, 2002; Sagli, 2010) as well as have documented the ways in which transfer, exchange and transformation of knowledge happens (Scheid, 1999, 2002). Khan argues that a simple bio medical dominance model is insufficient to explain the medical system in India and that, 'although the "cultural authority" and hegemony of bio medicine over indigenous science and knowledge were initiated by the colonial state, they were extended by the mainstream national leaderships, and national governments with far more extensive and profound implications and less resistance' (Khan, 2006: 2786). Reddy (2002) explores how Ayurveda in the United States has interacted not only with the American medical culture but also with 'New Age' spiritualities, and Obadia (2007) has described how the religious practice of Buddhism has become 'therapized' in France. The concept of hybridity challenges the empirical basis of both pluralism, which implies little merging of philosophy and practice and can overlook political dimensions (Broom et al., 2009), and dualism, which constructs an illusion of incommensurability (Kesher, 2011; Stevenson, 2004). Hybridity offers an alternative to accounts of integration that tend to stress the 'dominance' of bio medicine and are, therefore, too, blunt to explain empirical data that captures the diversity and creativity of hybrid forms and practices.

Processes of Data Collection, Analysis and Evaluation in Health Studies

Below we will examine some of the processes involved in data collection, analysis and evaluation.

Evidence-based Research

Public health workers are urged to provide evidence of the effectiveness of their work, while planners are required to draw on evidence-based practice to improve the quality of services. So here the question arises, what kind of evidence might best explore health attitudes and explain behaviours? What evidence is needed to show the value of health care work? What type of evidence should service users, providers of health care and policy-makers rely on?

Evidence is defined as the scientific utilizing measurement and quantification. However, can we also include the individual's experience of health care in the analysis? The experiences, opinions, and stories of people all can be captured through the qualitative measures. Therefore, it seems logical to explore the ways in which quantitative and qualitative data can be combined together. We will discuss them in the following paras.

Health Impact Assessment as a Mixed Method

Health Impact Assessment (HIA) is emerging as an important tool for measuring and delivering health public policy. HIA is a combination of procedures, methods and tools that systematically judges the potential and sometimes unintended effects of policy, plan, programme or project on the health of a population, and the distribution of those effects within the population. HIA identifies appropriate actions to manage those effects (WHO and ECHP, 1999). HIA is used to improve health and reduce health inequalities and, more strategically, to inform about policy and programme proposals (Health Development Agency, 2004). Public Health Observatories, 2007 has suggested the process and considerations for the HIA which are as follows:

- Both qualitative and quantitative data.
- The potential effects and impact on the target population of the proposed policy, programme or project.

- The opinions, experience and expectations of the members of the affected community, taking local factors into account.
- Making practical recommendations to aid decision-makers in reaching fully informed decisions and maximizing positive impacts and minimizing negative ones.
- The need for information and recommendations that can be used to continually shape the project or programme in question, provides evidence of both strengths to be developed and weaknesses to be addressed.

Health Care Studies: Qualitative Method

A qualitative investigation aims to explore, describe and/or interpret personal and social experiences, taking into account particular cultural concerns. The approach taken is inductive, exploratory, hypothesis-generating and focused on understanding meanings. This is in contrast to quantitative research, which is deductive and hypothesis-testing, and aims to predict or explain behaviour. In the case of health care, qualitative investigation focuses on individual's everyday meanings, motivations and behaviours related to health. It aims to locate lifestyle risk behaviours within individual's broader life and cultural contexts to examine how social factors impact on health. Some qualitative research will specifically focus on giving a voice to marginalized, vulnerable or disempowered individuals and groups, with a view to empowering them to take control of their own health. For instance, Choudhry et al. (2002) used a method called participatory action research to examine health issues for a group of south Asian immigrant women. In addition to exploring the women's health needs and understandings, the researchers offered various workshops over a three-year period designed to help the women develop knowledge about their own health.

Qualitative research spans quite distinct and specialized approaches. They may be in-depth interviews, focused group interviews, fieldwork observations, etc. In many occasions it may well be desirable to combine quantitative and qualitative methodologies. Sometimes researchers use multiple methods to offset the weakness of one method over another. The triangulation (a commonly used term indicating the use of different points to navigate) is used to enhance the validity of findings. For instance, the evidence base could be seen as strengthened if people report similar things when they are being both surveyed and interviewed. Similarly, when the separate analyses of different researchers are triangulated, the results may be seen to have more trustworthiness or credibility.

While studies routinely combine qualitative methods, there is some debate about how easily qualitative and quantitative methods can and should be combined. Problems can specifically arise when these are combined in the same single study. Research by Steward (2006) is a case in point. She studied the then nature and impact of teleworking (that is, remote or work from home), using a survey to identify teleworkers' views of their work and then in-depth qualitative interviews with the same group to follow up the survey and explore how health, illness and sickness are defined and experienced. She found that, far from providing complementary accounts, the two methodologies clashed. Significantly, she discovered that the survey data was often refuted by participants in follow-up interviews and that participants responded differently depending on whether they were writing down their responses or giving them verbally. For instance, Steward found that asking about 'days off/sick' produced different answers because the meaning teleworkers ascribed to the terms 'off' and 'sick' varied. She concludes that neither approach can be seen as 'right' (although she gained more information and understanding from the qualitative data). 'A mixed methodological approach', she says, 'served to highlight the complexity and ambivalence (of teleworking) ... . It showed how individuals generate information about themselves ... in many often irreconcilable ways' (Steward, 2006: 105). Steward argues that it is impossible to produce a consistent version of the object of study because 'truths' are relative; they vary from one person to another and one person's view may vary depending on the context. The object needs to be seen as socially constructed rather than as a fixed reality.

Processes of Qualitative Method

The actual processes of doing qualitative investigations require certain skills. Three particular stages are discussed here: early planning, collecting data and data analysis. Across all these stages, the skill lies in conducting the research or audit appropriately, ethically, systematically and rigorously.

Early Planning

There is much to decide in the early stages of planning investigations. What precisely is the investigatory focus and question? Who will constitute the participants and how will they be recruited? Are there particular people who need to be approached first? Who controls access to participants? What methods of data collection and analysis will be used? What kind of roles will the researcher and participants play? To what extent will participants be involved in the formulation or validation of findings? How will the participants be briefed in order to give their 'informed consent' and how will they be 'de-briefed'? How will the participants' rights and safety be protected?

Collecting Data

There are natural affinities between methodology and the methods/procedures used to collect and analyse data. The choice of methods generally follows from the choice of methodology (Finlay, 2006). Whichever of the many data collection methods are chosen, the skills lies in being able to carry them off rigorously and sensitively. To illustrate some of the issues and skills involved, consider the case of interviews, focus groups and observation studies, the most frequently employed qualitative methods. Researchers choosing to interview (whether structured or unstructured) need to take care to build a relationship with the participant that ensures that the participant feels listened to, safe and respected. Having enabled the participants to share something of them, the researcher needs to ensure that they are not being forced to disclose information beyond their choice. Focus groups have been used increasingly as a mechanism for accessing health needs and the experiences of service users. Although a good method for accessing a range of different group people, the findings of focus groups must be contextualized and not generalized to the wider population. Hospitals' wards are typical sites for observation studies, where the researcher serves and records whatever is going on. Negotiating access to the research 'field' requires careful planning as often there are gatekeepers who need to be satisfied. For example, studies attempting to explore service users' views and experiences of their treatment could be derailed by a gatekeeper manager who is defensively reluctant to have user complaints by a stranger.

Data Analysis

The analysis of qualitative data is much less concerned with numbers and more concerned with conveying the richness and quality of the data collected. Qualitative investigation can generate large amounts of detailed data. This is strength as well as a drawback. The strength lies in the richness of data; the drawback is in the complexity of the analysis required to interpret and present this in such a way that it does justice to that richness. The task of qualitative analysis is to try to derive some order and meaning out of wealth of data that is collected.

Methodologies for Inequalities in Health

There is a link between caste, class, race, ethnicity, gender and health. Moore (2008) has suggested there can be four different explanations to link social inequality and health on the basis of the following:

1. Statistical Artefact
2. Self-Selection
3. Cultural Differences
4. Material Differences

Statistics, Health and Social Class: The Artefact Explanation

The Black Report and numerous other studies have demonstrated a clear statistical link between mortality, ill health and social class. However, the significance of the link has been disputed by a number of sociologists. Illsley (1986, 1987), in particular, criticized the statistics in the Black

Report for concentrating on the relative inequality between the highest and lowest classes, while neglecting absolute improvements in the health of most people. Illsley explained this apparent contradiction by saying that although the mortality and morbidity rates of the lowest occupational groups were becoming worse relative to the higher occupational groups, the actual numbers of people in the lowest groups were in steep decline.

Another problem with the mortality and morbidity statistics in relation to social class concerns the categorization of people's occupations. Carr-Hill (1987) pointed out that when he examined death certificates, he found that the 'profession' recorded was often incorrectly categorized and this meant that statistics based on death certificates might well be inaccurate. An example of how important this is can be illustrated by the work of Le Grand and Pamuk on health inequalities. Muurinen and Le Grand's (1985) evidence was collected by examining individual death certificates, while Pamuk (1985) collated existing information which distinguished social class groups. The outcome was that Le Grand found smaller differences between groups than what Pamuk did.

From a more radical Marxist perspective, Scambler (2002) criticized the measurement of social class used in the Black and Acheson Reports, as well as that used by the government in its White Paper, *Saving Lives: Our Healthier Nation* (Department of Health, 1999).

Scambler raised the issue of just how accurate the Registrar General's measure of social class and the other classificatory schemes used in the studies is in sociological terms. Scambler argues that by using socio-economic divisions, such as Registrar General's classification, attention is taken away from the ruling class. This has produced a framework in which the debate over health inequalities ignores the massive differences in wealth and power between the ruling class and the majority of the population, a majority which includes professionals in social classes I and II.

Some sociologists, such as Saunders (1993), are doubtful about the usefulness of social class in understanding contemporary society. They suggest that conventional uses of the term 'social class' ignore differences in consumption and other specific lifestyle activities, which have become increasingly important in recent decades. Saunders suggests that by focusing on consumption rather than occupation, more specific factors can be isolated which influence health.

Ill Health and Social Class: The Direction of the Relationship

Illsley (1987) argued that it is perfectly reasonable to assume that fitter, healthier people are more likely to take the higher social positions at the expense of those who suffer from illness or disability, as those who are fit and energetic are more likely to be promoted and to have the opportunity to work hard. In support of this argument, Wadsworth (1986) used information from a national sample of males and found a close relationship between illness in childhood and adult social status. This sort of argument has been rejected by Shaw et al. (2006), who argue that any examination of the evidence will show that those from poorer backgrounds are faced with a range of economic, social and employment factors which combine to create ill health. From this point of view, class position shapes health and not the other way round.

Cultural Explanations

The third type of explanation suggested in the Black Report emphasized cultural factors. This sort of approach suggests that people from lower social classes may be more likely to engage in risky or unhealthy lifestyles, which have an effect upon long-term health, and can lead to early death. The obvious examples are that smoking cigarettes leads to heart disease and various forms of cancer, and eating fatty foods leads to obesity and heart disease. Many studies have shown that working class people are more likely to smoke, eat less fruit and vegetables, consume higher amounts of sugar and have diet with higher levels of fat. All of these things can lead to higher levels of fat. Thus, all of these things can lead to higher levels of morbidity and increased death rates. Consumption of alcohol, too, is higher among working class males.

Research has also shown that there is relationship between levels of exercise and social class. There is also a higher rate of domestic accidents among poorer families.

The key point underlying this approach is that the 'blame' for the high-risk lifestyle can be located either with the individual or with the social milieu in which they live. Those who support this approach argue that the only way to eradicate differences in health between social classes is to provide educational campaigns which persuade people to engage in 'healthier' lifestyles, including changes in diet, exercise regimes and smoking levels.

Critics of this approach argue that working class people are more likely to engage in risky behaviour as a rational response to their circumstances.

A good example of this is Graham's (1993) research on smoking behaviour among low-income mothers. Graham argues that smoking is a way for poorer women to cope with the situation in which they live. It may also be a way of saving money, as smoking cigarettes can be used as a substitute for eating. In later research, Graham and Blackburn (1998) demonstrate that mothers on low income support have much lower levels of 'psycho-social health' than the majority of the population and, for them, smoking provides a means of relief.

Keith Paterson (1981) argues that the cultural approach fails to consider the underlying structure of society, which he believes actually creates these risks. As a result, risks themselves are depoliticized. For example, it is the inequalities and poverty of capitalism which ensures that certain groups in the population are unable to afford 'healthier' foods. Furthermore, capitalism may benefit from the continuation of these differences in lifestyle. Capitalists make profits from selling unhealthy foods, so they continue to advertise and promote unhealthy lifestyles.

Material Explanations

The materialist or structural approach to health argues that the main influences on a person's health can be traced back to the structure of society and the resulting conditions of life which different groups experience. The poorer a person, the less chance they have of good health. However, this should not be explained solely in terms of cultural factors or individual behaviour, but should be seen in the context of wider, political, economic and social structures.

This approach does not deny the differences in behaviour which lead to ill health and high mortality rates among less affluent groups, but argues that the differences are not the real reasons for the higher rates of ill health. Instead, it claims that the way society is organized, it systematically disadvantage certain groups of people, so that they inevitably experience poor health.

Engels (1974) concluded that ill health was a direct outcome of capitalists' pursuit of profit. The dangerous work, long hours and poor pay (leading to under-nourishment) all contributed to the early death of workers. Accident rates are the highest among those in the more dangerous manual occupations, such as factory and building work. Martin et al. (1987) argue that those who live in poorer housing conditions tend to have higher rates of respiratory diseases.

According to Carstairs and Morris (1989), the association between eating habits and ill health can be understood less as cultural choice and more as a response to lack of income to buy better quality foodstuffs. This is illustrated by Lobstein's (2004) study of cost of healthy and unhealthy food in London. In 1988 and 1995, Lobstein compared prices of foodstuffs available in a more affluent part and a poorer part of London. It emerged that healthy food actually cost less in the more affluent areas of London than in the poorer areas, while unhealthy foodstuffs were slightly cheaper in the poorer areas than in the more affluent areas. Poorer people were more likely to have to pay more for healthy food.

Furthermore, the structure and ownership of food outlets have an impact upon the food choices of poorer people. A survey by the Department of Health (1996) found that the total number of food retailers had declined by 35 per cent in the previous 12-year period as a result of the growth in the out-of-town supermarkets and a decline in smaller, local shops. Wrigley (1998) argues that these supermarkets are less available to poorer people without access to cars; and even if they do have transport, the cost of travel will leave them with less money for food. The significance of diet for determining health standards is underlined by Blane et al. (1997), who calculated that 15 per cent of all early deaths are caused by poor diets. Doyal and Pennell (1979) claim that differences in dietary intake by the poorest people are partly a result of differences in income. The poor cannot afford to buy better food; more importantly, the food industry, in its search for profit, produces poor quality, and harmful food, high in chemicals, salts and sugars. Such food causes obesity and ill health.

Summing Up

There are several ways in which we can study health and medicine issues. Impact and evaluation of health policies can be best undertaken with the help of scientific evaluation methods and techniques. Health related controversies fosters a multidisciplinary approach, involving various academic disciplines. The measurement of health and health states is done through standard indicators across geographical, cultural and economic boundaries along with the social and historical context. Macro approach is applied to measure the level of health care of the target population. In the Foucauldian approach, the body, discase and contemporary medical discourse are inseparable. Understanding of medical systems or pluralism in medicine is studied with the help of historical-anthropological method. In the rapidly growing field of health communication, narrative approaches are emerging as a promising set of tools for motivating and supporting health-behaviour change.

The vast majority of public health investigations are based on quantitative and survey methods which is called triangulation method. Hybridily offers an alternative to accounts of integration that tend to stress the dominance of bio-medicine and are, theodor too, blunt to explain empirical data that captures the diversify and creativity of hybrid forms and practices. Evidence-based research is meant for scientific utilizing measurement and quantification. Health Impact Assessment is emerging as an important tool for measuring and delivering health policy. In the case of health care, qualitative investigation focuses on individual's everyday meanings, motivation and behaviours related to health. Health inequalities can be analysed with the help of statistical artefact, and on the basis of cultural and material differences.

References

Ashton, S. and R. Stepney (1982), *Smoking*, London: Tavistock.

Association of Public Health Observatories (2007), 'The HIA Gateway', http://www.apho.org.uk/de fault.aspx?qn=p_hia.

Bailcy, K.V. and A.H. Ferro-Luzzi (1995), 'Use of Body Mass Index of Adults in Assessing Individual and Community Nutritional Status', *Bulletin of the World Health Organization*, 73(5): 673–80.

Beck, U. (1994), *Reflexive Modernization: Politics, Tradition and Aesthetics in the Modern Social Order*, Cambridge: Polity Press.

Becker, M.H. et al. (1977), 'The Health Belief Model and Prediction of Dietary Compliance: A Field Experiment', *Journal of Health and Social Behaviour*, 18: 348–66.

Biehl, Joao (2009), *Will to Live: AIDS Therapies and the Politics of Survival*, Princeton, NJ: Princeton University Press.

Blane, D., M. Bartley and Smith G. Davey (1997), 'Disease Aetiology and Socio-economic Mortality Differentials', *European Journal of Public Health*, 7: 385–91.

Boltanski, Luc and Laurent Thevenot (2006), *On Justification: The Economies of Worth*, Princeton, NJ: Princeton University Press.

Broom, Alex et al. (2009), 'The Inequalities of Medical Pluralism: Hierarchies of Health, the Politics of Tradition and the Economies of Care in Indian Oncology', *Social Science and Medicine*, 69(5): 698–706.

Buchanan, K. (1985), 'Centre and Periphery: Reflections on the Irrelevance of a Billion Human Beings', *Monthly Review*, New York, July/August, 86–97.

Bury, M. (1991), 'The Sociology of Chronic Illness: A Review of Research and Prospects', *Sociology of Health and Illness*, 13(4): 451–68.

—— (2001), 'Illness Narratives: Fact or Fiction', *Sociology of Health and Illness*, 21(3): 263–85.

Carr-Hill, R. (1987), 'The Inequalities in Health Debate: A Critical Review of the Issues', *Journal of Social Policy*, 16(4): 509–42.

Carstairs, V. and R. Morris (1989), 'Deprivation and Mortality: An Alternative to Social Class?', *Journal of Public Health*, 11(3): 210–19.

Charon, R. (2001), 'Narrative Medicine: A Model for Empathy, Reflection, Profession and Trust', *JAMA*, 286: 1897–902.

Chateauraynaud, Francis (2011), *Argumenter dons un champ de forces, Essai de balistique sociologique*, Paris: Editions Petra.

Chomsky, N. (1993), *The Prosperous Few and the Restless Many: Noam Chomsky interviewed by D. Barsamian*, Berkeley, CA: Odonian Press.

Choudhry, U.K. et al. (2002), 'Health Promotion and Participatory Action Research with South Asian Women', *Journal of Nursing Scholarship*, 34(1): 75–81.

Cohen, S. et al. (1986), *Behaviour, Health and Environmental Stress*, New York: Plenum.

De Garine, I. and N. Pollock (eds) (1995), *Social Aspects of Obesity*, South Australia: Gordon and Breach.

Department of Environment, Sport and Territories (1995), *Active and Inactive Australians: Assessing and Understanding Levels of Physical Activity*, Canberra: Commonwealth of Australia.

Department of Health (1999), *Saving Lives: Our Healthier Nation*.

Doyal, L. and I. Pennell (1979), *The Political Economy of Health*, London: Pluto Press.

Ender, N.S. (1988), 'Hassles, Health and Happiness', in M.P. Janisse (ed.), *Individual Differences, Stress, and Health Psychology*, New York: Springer-Verlag, 24–56.

Epstein, Steven (1996), *Impure Science: AIDS, Activism, and the Politics of Knowledge*, Berkeley, CA: University of California Press.

European Centre for Health Policy (1999), 'Health Impact Assessment: Main Concepts and Suggested Approach', *Gothenburg Consensus Paper*, Copenhagen: WHO Regional Office for Europe.

Fassin, Didier (2007), *When Bodies Remember: Experience and Politics of AIDS in South Africa*, Berkeley, CA: University of California Press.

Finlay, L. (2006), 'Mapping Methodology', in L. Finlay and C. Ballinger (eds), *Qualitative Research for Allied Health Professionals: Challenging Choices*, Chichester: Wiley, 9–29.

Foucault, M. (1976), *The History of Sexuality*, Vol. 1, Harmondsworth: Penguin.

Frank, A.G. (1978), *Dependent Accumulation and Underdevelopment*, London: Macmillan.

Frank, Robert and Gunnar Stollberg (2004), 'Conceptualising Hybridization on the Diffusion of Asian Medical Knowledge to Germany', *International Sociology*, 19(1): 71–88.

Gale, Nicola (2014), 'The Sociology of Traditional, Complementary and Alternative Medicine', *Sociology Compass*, 8(6): 805–22.

Garvey, Mary (2011), 'The Transition of Chinese Medicine in Australia', *PORTAL: Journal of Multidisciplinary International Studies*, 8(2).

Graham, H. (1993), *When Life's a Drag: Women, Smoking and Disadvantage*, London: HMSO.

Graham, H. and C. Blackburn (1998), 'The Socio-Economic Patterning of Health and Smoking Behaviour among Mothers with Young Children on Income Support', *Sociology of Health and Illness*, 20(2): 215–40.

Green, Judith and Nicki Thorogood (2014), *Qualitative Methods of Health Research*, London: Sage Publications.

Harpham, T. (1994), 'Urbanization and Mental Health in Developing Countries: A Research Role for Social Scientists, Public Health Professionals and Social Psychiatrists', *Social Science and Medicine*, 39(2): 233–45.

Hart, R.H. et al. (1990), *Integrating Maternal and Child Health Services with Primary Health Care*, Geneva: WHO.

Harter, Lynn M., Phyllis M. Japp and Christina S. Beck (2005), *Narratives, Health and Healing: Communication Theory, Research and Practice*, London: Routledge Communication Series.

Hodge, A. et al. (1996), 'Obesity in Pacific Populations', *Pacific Health Dialog*, 3(1): 77–86.

Hok, Johanna et al. (2007), 'Using Narrative Analysis to Understand the Combined Use of Complementary Therapies and Bio-medically Oriented Health Care', *Social Science and Medicine*, 65(8): 1642–53.

Hollenberg, Daniel and Linda Muzzin (2010), 'Epistemological Challenges to Integrative Medicine: An Anti-Colonial Perspective on the Combination of Complementary/Alternative Medicine with Biomedicine', *Health Sociology Review*, 19(1): 34–56.

Holton, Robert (2000), 'Globalization's Cultural Consequences', *The Annals of the American Academy of Political and Social Science*, 570(1): 140–52.

Hsu, Elisabeth (2000), 'Spirit (Shen), Styles of Knowing, and Authority in Contemporary Chinese Medicine', *Culture, Medicine and Psychiatry*, 24(2): 197–229.

Illsley, R. (1986), 'Occupational Class, Selection and the Production of Inequalities in Health', *Quarterly Journal of Social Affairs*, 2(2): 151–65.

—— (1987), 'Occupational Class, Selection and Inequalities in Health', *Quarterly Journal of Social Affairs*, 3(3): 213–23.

Jasanoff, Sheila (2005), *Designs on Nature: Science and Democracy in Europe and the United States*, Princeton, NJ: Princeton University Press.

Jeffery, Roger and Patricia M. Jeffery (1993), 'Traditional Birth Attendants in Rural North India: The Social Organisation of Childbearing', in Shirley Lindenbaum and Margaret Lock (eds), *Knowledge, Power, and Practice: The Anthropology of Medicine and Everyday Life*, Berkeley, CA: University of California Press, 7–31.

Jewson, N.D. (1976), 'The Disappearance of the Sick-Man from Medical Cosmology', *Sociology*, 10(2): 225–44.

Keshet, Yael (2011), 'Energy Medicine and Hybrid Knowledge Construction: The Formation of New Cultural-Epistemological Rules of Discourse', *Cultural Sociology*, 5(4): 501–18.

Khan, M. et al. (1989), 'Inequalities between Men and Women in Nutrition and Family Welfare Services: An In-Depth Enquiry in an Indian Village', in J.C. Caldwell and G. Santo (eds), *Selected Readings in the Cultural, Social and Behavioural Determinants of Health*, Health Transition Series, No. 1, Canberra, Health Transition Centre, Australian National University, 175–99.

Khan, Shamshad (2006), 'Systems of Medicine and Nationalist Discourse in India: Towards New Horizons in Medical Anthropology and History', *Social Science and Medicine*, 62(1): 2786–97.

Kim, Jongyoung (2006), 'Beyond Paradigm: Making Transcultural Connections in a Scientific Translation of Acupuncture', *Social Science and Medicine*, 62(12): 2960–72.

King, H. (2006), *Greek and Roman Medicine*, Bristol: Bristol Classical Press.

Lakoff, Andrew (2006), *Pharmaceutical Reason: Knowledge and Value in Global Psychiatry*, Cambridge: Cambridge University Press.

Lobstein, T., L. Baur and R. Uauy (2004), 'Obesity in Children and Young People: A Crisis in Public Health', *Obesity Reviews*, 5(2): 4–85.

Manning, W. et al. (1991), *The Costs of Poor Health Habits*, Massachusetts: Harvard University Press.

Martin, C.J., S.D. Platt and S.M. Hunt (1987), 'Housing Conditions and Ill Health', *British Medical Journal*, 294(6580): 1125–27.

McMurray, C. (1995), *Report on the Republic of the Marshall Islands Fertility and Family Planning Survey, November–December*, Unpublished Report, Majuro: Office of Planning and Statistics, Republic of the Marshall Islands.

Mills, S. (ed.) (1988), *Alternatives in Healing: An Open-Minded Approach to Finding the Best Treatment for Your Health Problems*, London: Macmillan.

Moore, Stephen (2008), 'Health, Medicine and the Body', in M. Haralambos and M. Holborn (eds), *Sociology: Themes and Perspectives*, London: Harper Collins

Mull, D.S. (1991), 'Traditional Perceptions of Marasmus in Pakistan', *Social Science and Medicine*, 32(2): 175–91.

Muurinen, J.M. and J. Le Grand (1985), 'The Economic Analysis of Inequalities in Health', *Social Science and Medicine*, 20(10): 1029–35.

Myrdal, G. (1953), *The Political Element in the Development of Economic Theory*, London: Routledge and Kegan Paul.

Nguyen, Vinh-Kim (2010), *The Republic of Therapy: Triage and Sovereignty in West Africa's Time of AIDS*, Durham, NC: Duke University Press.

Nisula, Tapio (2006), 'In the Presence of Biomedicine: Ayurveda, Medical Integration and Health Seeking in Mysore, South India', *Anthropology and Medicine*, 13(3): 207–24.

Obadia, Lionel (2007), 'The Economies of Health in Western Buddhism: A Case Study of a Tibetan Buddhist Group in France', *Research in Economic Anthropology*, 26: 227–59.

—— (2012), 'Globalisation and New Geographies of Religion: New Regimes in the Movement, Circulation, and Territoriality of Cults and Beliefs', *International Social Science Journal*, 63(209–210): 147–57.

Overcash, Janine A. (2003), 'Narrative Research: A Review of Methodology and Relevance to Clinical Practice', *Critical Reviews in Oncology/Hematology*, 48(2): 179–84.

Pamuk, E.R. (1985), 'Social Class Inequality in Mortality from 1921 to 1972 in England and Wales', *Population Studies*, 39(1): 17–31.

Paterson, K. (1981), 'Theoretical Perspectives in Epidemiology: A Critical Appraisal', *Radical Community Medicine*, 2: 23–24.

Petryna, Adriana (2009), *When Experiments Travel: Clinical Trials and the Global Search for Human Subjects*, Princeton, NJ: Princeton University Press.

Ram, Kalpana (2011), 'Culture, Power and Lay Medicine', in Asssa Doron and Alex Broom (eds), *Health, Culture and Religion in South Asia*, London: Routledge, 7–20.

Reddy, Sita (2002), 'Asian Medicine in America: The Ayurvedic Case', *The Annals of the American Academy of Political and Social Science*, 583(1): 97–121.

Robertson, R. (1992), *Globalization, Social Theory and Global Culture*, London: Sage Publications.

Royston, E. and S. Anderson (1989), *Preventing Maternal Deaths*, Geneva: WHO.

Sagli, Gry (2010), 'The Establishing of Chinese Medical Concepts in Norwegian Acupuncture Schools: The Cultural Translation of Jingluo (Circulation Tracts)', *Anthropology and Medicine*, 17(3): 315–26.

Santosh, Romila (2013), *The Practice of Ayurveda in the UK and the Role of Spirituality: A Practitioner Perspective*, Faculty of Humanities and Social Sciences, University of Winchester.

Scambler, G. (2002), *Health and Social Change: A Critical Theory*, Buckingham: Open University Press.

Scheid, Volker (1999), 'The Globalization of Chinese Medicine', *The Lancet*, Special Supplement, 354(10): SIV 10.

—— (2002), *Chinese Medicine in Contemporary China: Plurality and Synthesis*, Durham, NC: Duke University Press.

Sharf, F. Barbara and Marsha L. Vanderford (2008), 'Illness Narratives and Social Construction of Health', in T.L. Thompson et al. (eds), *Handbook of Health Communication*, New York: Routledge.

Sharma, Avi (2011), 'Medicine from the Margins? Naturheilkunde from Medical Heterodoxy to the University of Berlin, 1889–1920', *Social History of Medicine*, 24(2): 334–51.

Shaw, M. (1999), *The Widening Gap: Health Inequalities and Policy in Britain*, Cambridge, MA: MIT Press.

Shaw, M., D. Dorling and G.D. Smith (2006), 'Poverty, Social Exclusion, and Minorities', *Social Determinants of Health*, 2: 196–223.

Simons, J. (1989), 'Cultural Dimensions of the Mother's Contribution to Child Survival', in J.C. Caldwell and G. Santow (eds), *Selected Readings in the Cultural Social and Behavioural Determinants of Health*, Health Transition Series No. 1, Canberra: Health Transition Centre, Australian National University, 132–46.

Skultans, Vieda and Trisha Greenhalgh (2008), *Narrative Research in Health and Illness*, Oxford: Blackwell Publishing.

Spielberger, C.D. et al. (1988), 'The Experience, Expression and Control of Anger', in M.P. Janisse (ed.), *Individual Differences, Stress, and Health Psychology*, New York: Springer-Verlag, 89–108.

Sriratanaban, Pavika (2014), 'Motherhood Fatal Illness Narratives: Death Awareness and Biographical Reinforcement to Restore Continuity', paper presented in ISA Conference at Yokohama, Japan.

Stevenson, Fiona (2004), 'Images of Nature in Relation to Mood Modifying Medicines: A User Perspective', *Health*, 8(2): 241–62.

Steward, B. (2006), 'Investigating Invisible Groups Using Mixed Methodologies', in L. Finlay and C. Ballinger (eds), *Qualitative Research for Allied Health Professionals: Challenging Choices*, Chichester: Wiley, 9–29.

Sujatha, V. (2014), *Sociology of Health and Medicine: New Perspective*, New Delhi: Oxford University Press.

Sujatha, V. and Leena Abraham (eds) (2012), *Medical Pluralism in Contemporary India*, New Delhi: Orient Blackswan.

Tovey, Philip and Alex Broom (2008), 'The Problematic Nature of Conflating Use and Advocacy in CAM Integration: Complexity and Differentiation in UK Cancer Patients' Views', *Health Sociology Review*, 17(4): 384–95.

Van Cleemput, P. et al. (2007), 'Health-Related Beliefs and Experiences of Gypsies and Travellers: A Qualitative Study', *Journal of Epidemiology and Community Health*, 61: 205–10.

Wadsworth, M.E. (1986), 'Serious Illness in Childhood and its Association with Later-Life Achievement', in R.G. Wilkinson (ed.), *Class and Health: Research and Longitudinal Data*, London: Tavistock, 50–74.

Wallerstein, I. and T. Hopkins (1996), *The Age of Transition: Trajectory of the World System, 1945–2025*, London: Zed Books.

Wrigley, N. (1998), 'PPG6 and the Contemporary UK Food Store Development Dynamic', *British Food Journal*, 100(3): 154–61.

Yardley, L. and D.F. Marks (eds) (2004), *Research Methods for Clinical and Health Psychology*, London: Sage Publications.

Zarconi, Joseph, Lura L. Pethtel and Sally A. Missimi (2008), *Narratives in Health Care: Healing Patients, Practitioners, Profession and Community*, Oxford: Radcliffe Publishing.

Zuckerman, M. (1988), 'Sensation Seeking, Risk Taking, and Health', in M.P. Janisse (ed.), *Individual Differences, Stress, and Health Psychology*, New York: Springer-Verlag, 72–88.

Section II

Concept and Management in Health Care

6

Social and Preventive Medicine

Preventive medicine is fairly well understood in the present day, but the meaning, scope and uses of social medicine are not equally clear. The prevailing uncertainties about social medicine seem to be based on two misconceptions: (1) that social medicine is just another name of preventive medicine, as we know it, and (2) that social medicine and socialized or state medicine are synonymous. Social medicine is medicine regarded as a social science which considers the social factors of disease and as an instrument of social policy on which the need for a revolutionary change in general teaching, philosophy and practice is based. The idea that medicine is a social science was first clearly presented by the leaders of the Reform Movement in Germany in 1848 (Virchow) who promulgated the views that the health of the people was a matter of concern to society and that society had an obligation to protect and ensure the health of its members. The broad interconnections between poverty, insanitation, vice, human degradation and diseases were recognized much earlier during the era of sanitation; particularly in England (Sydenham, Chadwick, Farr) but, this was confined to relations between filth and diseases alone; while the need for combined medical, social and administrative action to remove these barriers to social progress is comparatively of recent origin in this century. The usc of bacteriology towards the end of the 19th century, which demonstrated all medical thought and action, checked the development of these ideas from a time, but it was resumed in 1911, when Grotjahn published *Sociale Pathologie*, in which the theoretical basis of social medicine was systematized, and the interconnections among medicine, sociology, anthropology, and economics were defined.

History of Social and Preventivc Medicine

Social medicine has been primarily a European speciality. The seeds that medicine is a social science were sown in the late 19th century by pioneers such as Neumann (1847) and Virchow (1848). But their ideas were far too ahead of their time. The germ theory of disease and discoveries in microbiology checked the development of these ideas. In 1911, the concept of social medicine was revived by Alfred Grotjahn (1869–1931) of Berlin who stressed the importance of social factors in the aetiology of disease, which he called 'social pathology'. Others called it geographical pathology and population pathology. In 1912 Rene Sand had founded the Belgian Social Medicine Association. Developments in the field of social sciences (e.g. sociology, psychology, anthropology) rediscovered that man is not only a biological animal, but also a social being, and disease has social causes, social consequences and social therapy. The ideas of social medicine spread to other countries.

John Ryle and his group in England were influenced by these ideas and visualized social medicine as an evolution of medicine. They promoted the concept of social medicine in England. In England, for a smaller group within the profession, it seemed that both the teaching of medicine and in its practice, the major interest had become focused not upon the prevention of disease and promotion of health but, upon the treatment of diseases states already well-established; not upon the causes of disease but upon its classification; not upon the individual as a person, but on some component part of him that was functioning imperfectly; and not upon the interconnections of disease and society, but upon the immediate effects of disease upon the individual. To the members of this group it seemed that medicine was not rendering to society its greatest possible service, since preventable diseases and ultimately death, which medicine sought to control, were nearly as common as they had even been. They wished to see and participate in a revolutionary change in the interests and objectives of medical thought and action (Crew, 1960). A chair of social medicine was set up at Oxford in 1942 followed by similar others in other universities in England. In 1943, the Interim Report of the Social and Preventive Medicine Committee of the Royal College of Physicians, on teaching of preventive and social medicine and arrangements for social medicine both inside and outside the hospital, recognized that social medicine must be the background of both preventive and curative medicine in the future, and the integration of this, now an important subject, will require considerable revision of the existing curriculum. In 1944, the report of 'Inter-Departmental Committee on Medical Schools' (Goodenough Committee) emphasized that the principles of social medicine should underlay all medical teaching (Crew, 1958).

In the US, preventive medicine has all along been pursuing a very rapid and extensive development, to become very similar indeed to what in the UK had been given the name of social medicine; by the application of epidemiology to search the causal agents of disease in the socio-economic sphere, and was advocating social and political action as much as medical, in the prevention and treatment of disease. The differences in terminology of preventive medicine in the US and social medicine in England are understandable. In the US the emphasis is on individual prevention of disease, for the doctor in his community, while in the UK on community organization, as part of National Health Services, so well organized in that country.

Maternal and Child Health

Preventive care for the special health needs of women and children developed as public concerns in the late 19th century. Public awareness of severe conditions of women's and children's labour grew to include the effects on health and poverty, poor living conditions and general hygiene, home deliveries, lack of prenatal care, and poor nutrition.

Preventive care as a service separate from curative medical services for women and children was initiated in the unsanitary urban slums of industrial cities in the 19th century France in the form of milk stations. One village in France instituted an incentive payment to mothers whose babies lived to 1 year; this resulted in a decline in infant mortality from 300 per 1000 to 200 per 1000 within a few years. The plan was later expanded to a complete child welfare effort, especially promoting breast-feeding and a clean supply of milk to children, which had dramatic effects in reducing infant deaths.

The concept of child health spread to other parts of Europe and the United States with the development of paediatrics as a speciality and an emphasis on appropriate child nutrition. Henry Koplik in 1889 and Nathan Strauss in 1893 promoted centres to provide safe milk to pregnant women and children in the slums of New York City in order to combat summer diarrhoea. The Henry Street Mission, serving poor immigrant areas, developed the model of visiting nurses and public milk stations. The concept of 'milk stations', combined with home visits, was pioneered by Lillian Wald, who coined the term district nurse of public health nurse. This became the basis for public prenatal, postnatal, and child care as well as school health supervision. Visiting Nursing Associations (VNAs) gradually developed throughout the United States to provide such services. Physicians' services in the United States were mainly provided on a fee-for-service basis for those able to pay, with charitable services in large city hospitals. The concept of direct provision of care to those in need by local authorities and by voluntary charitable associations, with separation between preventive and curative services, is still a model of health care in many countries.

In Jerusalem, from 1902, Shaare Zedek Hospital kept cows to provide safe milk for infants and pregnant women. In 1911, two public health nurses came from New York to Jerusalem to establish milk stations ('drop of milk') for poor pregnant women and children. This model became the standard method of Maternal and Child Health (MCH) provision throughout Israel, operating parallel to the Sick Funds which provided medical care. The separation between preventive and curative services persists to the present, and is sustained by the Israeli national government's obligation to assure basic preventive care to all regardless of insurance or ability to pay.

In the Soviet Union, institution of the state health plan in 1918 by Nikolai Alcksandrovich Semashhko gave emphasis to maternal and child health, along with epidemic and communicable disease control. All services were provided free as a state responsibility through an expanding network of polyclinics and other services and prenatal and child care centres, including preventive check-ups, home visits, and vaccinations. Infant mortality declined rapidly even in the Asian republics with previously poor health conditions.

Era of Preventive Medicine

Early in the 20th century, the combined efforts of public health measures concentrating on environmental sanitation and, the bacteriological discoveries leading to vaccines and sera, provided effective measures for both promotion of health as well as prevention of diseases; before and after incidence of infectious diseases. These efforts with general improvements in scientific knowledge in several other fields aided by industrialization, raised the standard of life of communities, and all were responsible for improved public health and private health of such countries in the public and private sectors. This resulted in schools of hygiene and public health everywhere in several countries to teach doctors and, later other auxiliary personnel like sanitary inspectors and nurses in various methods of prevention, and enforcement of public health legislation, which was then enacted starting with compulsory vaccination, general sanitary measures, control of infectious diseases, and pollution of water supplies of foods. As several countries attained higher levels of health and, ships carried infections far and wide with passengers and goods for trade and commerce, they became conscious of inter-country cooperation in health measures. Such are the quarantine regulations applicable to all countries as a two-way traffic in dissemination of diseases, with the responsibility not to export and the right to prevent import of infectious diseases, by quarantine measures and vaccination of ship passengers, as well as restricting or disinfecting goods which are infected or likely to carry infection. Meantime, knowledge of the causation, spread and control of infectious diseases improved and the public demanded that if these can be prevented then why not prevent them; translating to a new adage that prevention is not only better but, cheaper than cure.

Era of Social Medicine

The first half of the 20th century witnessed two world wars: First World War (1914–19) and Second World War (1939–45), which together had several impacts on all countries of the globe, never known in world history. Apart from several epidemics, the permanent socio-economic effects which reflected on the health of the countries all over the world were far more important and did lasting and permanent damage. For example, the First World War which ended in 1919, brought forth during and, as an aftermath several epidemics particularly malaria, relapsing fever, typhus and the world pandemic of influenza (1919–21), which altogether killed and disabled many more than the causalities and wounded people. However, the socio-economic effects of these two World Wars in raising price levels and cutting food supplies, thereby lowering nutritional status, and disruption of millions of families as refugees had far more evil effects on health, than mere cases and deaths from diseases. While communicable diseases could be controlled as noted in the era of preventive medicine, non-communicable diseases such as metabolic, malignant and mental diseases, came to replace the first ranks, originally occupied by infectious diseases. A new outlook on medicine as a social science, which must be taught to the doctor and all his associates in medical schools, and needs be put into practice by the general practitioner as well as those in services and, lastly as an instrument of social policy for governments, came to be realized. Apart from acute diseases which can be either preventive or cured by effective drugs, which came into existence including antibiotic and chemo-therapeutics, the chronic diseases presented different set of problems; like tuberculosis, leprosy and venereal diseases, requiring different strategy and techniques for their control. These are called social diseases as in them sociological factors are as important as biological factors; the soil is even more important than the seeds. Furthermore, studies of health records showed that acute diseases formed a very small minority in the total health of a country, and the vast majority were due to chronic diseases.

Defining Social Medicine

Social medicine has varying meanings attached to its label. By derivation, social medicine is the study of man as a social being in his total environment. Its focus is on the health of the community as a whole. According to Ryle (1943) it was an ideological mission with a political purpose and a social responsibility. It was also the heir apparent to clinical medicine and would change the role of medicine in society by deconstructing medicine at the bedside. Social physicians would practise whole-person medicine in place of technologically determined specialists steeped in the epistemological orthodoxies of experimental science. Doctors trained in social medicine would fulfil their true Hippocratic destiny by becoming naturalist interpreters of health and disease and teachers of a new creed to society. That creed was what Ryle's contemporary Julian Huxley had identified as 'scientific humanism'. For Ryle, the social conscience and scientific intent of social medicine would help to establish scientific humanism as a new secular ethic governing social, economic and political behaviour, and he stressed that 'the ideas and tasks of social medicine may be justly regarded as essential contributors to the developing philosophy of scientific humanism'. Crew (1960) had ably stated that social medicine stands on two pillars – medicine and sociology. Others stated that the maiden sociology married public health and became social medicine. The identity of social medicine as an academic discipline of pure research, as a separate intellectual enterprise from training in the practical art of service administration and management, structured its subsequent institutionalization and professionalization. McKeown and Lowe (1974) have this to say: 'In contemporary usage social medicine has two meanings, one broad and ill defined, the other more restricted and precise. In the broad sense, social medicine is an expression of the humanitarian tradition in medicine and people read into it any interpretation consistent with their own aspirations and interests. Thus, it may be identified with care of patients, prevention of disease, administration of medical services; indeed with almost any subject in the extensive field of health and welfare. But in the more restricted sense, social medicine is concerned with a body of knowledge embodied in epidemiology and the study of the medical needs of medical care of society'. In short, social medicine is not a new branch of medicine but rather a new orientation of medicine to the changing needs of man and society. It emphasizes the strong relationship between medicine and social sciences. The pre-eminent concern of social medicine has unquestionably been the development of epidemiological methods and their application to the investigation of disease. It has entered into a productive relationship with social sciences and statistics to be able to elucidate the role of social factors in disease aetiology (Martin, 1977). These developments represent a forceful bid for the expanding concept of medicine. However, social medicine was criticized because it was virtually isolated from the service world and confined mostly to academic study of health services and chronic disease (Acheson, 1978).

Objectives and Functions of Social Medicine

The objective of social medicine is to secure the health of the population, and its tasks are as follows:

- To assess the health status of population and its development;
- To assess the sanitary conditions of the environment;
- To work out methods and means leading to the promotion of the health of the people and the prevention of disease, disability, and infirmity;
- To organize medical care and rehabilitation for the whole population;
- To control sanitary conditions in the environment; and
- To control the birth rate in order to secure the harmonious development of the population (Kostrzewski, 1970).

Mckeown argued that despite the epidemiological transition from predominantly infectious to chronic diseases in developed countries the 'population approach' remained linked, indeed, it inevitably led medicine to engage with its essential social functions, the organization of socicty's needs regarding the promotion of health and the reduction of sickness. Social function of social medicine was bound to the prosecution of research. Teaching was a secondary concern. The research produced by the discipline would be the persuasive factor not only for establishing intellectual credibility and political force but also for acquiring institutional security.

Aspects of Social Medicine

Social Anatomy

Social medicine is concerned with man in relation to society and with health en masse. It, therefore, requires a complete understanding of the society in which man lives. It involves knowledge of the structure of society or a particular community. This is called social anatomy.

Social Physiology

Anatomy deals with the structure of an organism and physiology deals with the way the organism functions. Social physiology deals with the way society functions as an organized unit.

Social Pathology

Individual pathology deals with quality and effects of disease and assists in diagnosis and treatment. Social pathology deals with the quantity and causes of diseases and assists in prevention. Thus, social pathology may be defined as the systematic study or inquiry into the relationship between human disease and social conditions. It deals with the dysfunction prevailing in the community as a result of such factors as malnutrition, age and sex composition of the population, poverty, accidents, illiteracy, standard of living, etc.

Social Therapy

Social therapy does not consist administration of drugs, but social and political action for the betterment of the conditions of life and the entire lot of man. The doctor who is treating a case of typhoid fever is practising clinical medicine; if he/she also advises the members of the household about safe water supply, food hygiene, control of houseflies and immunization, he/she is practising preventive and social medicine.

Concept of Preventive Medicine

Social medicine is concerned with the social environment and with heredity in so far as these affect health and well-being. Preventive medicine, as its name implies, is a branch of medical practice concerned with the development and employment of measures capable of averting the onset of disease. Using the first part of Winslow's definition of public health, Leavell and Clark (1965) defined preventive medicine as 'the science and art of preventing disease, prolonging life and promoting physical and mental health and efficiency'. In preventive medicine, the focus of attention is on the individual with emphasis on individual responsibility and voluntary cooperation to achieve optimum physical, mental and social well-being whereas in public health, the focus is on groups of individuals who form the community and whose members face common health problems and among whom an organized community effort is essential for their resolution. Preventive medicine is more executive in outlook and comprises the design and direction of measures for the prevention of health and the prevention of disease. The concept of preventive medicine includes both prevention of disease as well as promotion of health; and among diseases includes both communicable and non-communicable diseases, and apart from diseases, several disabilities, deformities and defects, like accidents, alcoholism and allergies and, physical and mentally handicaps. In the promotion of health, the concept of positive health includes physical, mental and social health, which requires considerations of biological, psychological, and sociological factors. Further, with recent changes in priorities, the emphasis has shifted from the epidemic to endemic diseases, and among the latter to socio-economic or social diseases, which contribute by and large, to the country's load of mortality and morbidity rates. The study of natural history of diseases must weigh all these factors: eliciting both initial interceptions of the causes, to later interruption of the progress, finally leading to restoration by rehabilitation. This requires both strategy and tactics – the former where and when provided by preventive medicine, and the latter how, which curative medicine alone can answer. All these require both analysis and synthesis of all known facts and figures, relating to diseases and disabilities by epidemiological and bio-statistical studies, and with such approach we may elicit several epidemiological barriers of prevention.

Preventive medicine has become a growing point in medicine. It is no longer concerned with how it used to be with immunization and personal hygiene, important though they may be. It has branched out into other areas such as screening for disease, population control, and genetic advice, prevention of chronic degenerative and hereditary diseases. Spectacular advances in medical treatment in no way have diminished the need for neither preventive care nor its usefulness. In fact, as medical science advances, it has become more and more preventive in nature.

Preventive Medicine vis-à-vis Social Medicine

The term preventive medicine as such is unsatisfactory at the present time, as it precludes concern with the organization of curative and rehabilitation services; and if it includes, it will be equally misleading, as it encroaches on early diagnosis and treatment. This is the concept of clinical preventive medicine in the US today, but, if applied unadulterated to India, it would lead to final abolition of social medicine in this country (Dakshinamurty, 1962). Social medicine must suit the needs of society of each country, and within it may vary from time to time, dictated by needs of society. Such variations of these terms from country to country are inevitable, as among other reasons, preventive and social medicine have a common epidemiological approach; and enthusiasts have split this again into clinical and field epidemiology: the former for clinical preventive medicine, and the latter for social medicine, which includes within its objectives, organization of health services. The scope of social medicine is to do research on socio-economic conditions prevailing in various social strata of country.

One of the earliest attempts to change the social orientation of medicine in India came through the establishment of departments of social and preventive medicine. For example, in the central provincial health committee meeting of 1948, there was a report on a survey of medical education which revealed that 'the emphasis laid on the teaching of preventive medicine and public health is quite inadequate' (GOI, 1949). Similar sentiments were repeated in speeches and resolutions from the Central Council of Health. A special medical education conference held in Delhi in 1955 called for the strengthening of social and preventive medicine departments as a way of raising the prestige of preventive medicine in health services generally, and these recommendations became regulations of the Medical Council of India in 1961 (Taylor et al., 1976).

The main fallacy in the discussions was the belief that the cause of the low status of preventive work could be traced solely to India's colonial heritage and that its status could be raised by changes of a minor kind within medical curricula, but without changes in career opportunities and rewards for medical practitioners.

Throughout the world, the prestige rankings of medical specializations seem to show a common pattern. General surgery and other surgical specialities are almost always near the top, while public health, social and community medicine and preclinical specializations are usually at the bottom (Taylor et al., 1976). General practice and family medicine have never gained a foothold in Indian medical colleges. Indian medical students surveyed in the 1970s consistently ranked social and preventive medicine at the bottom of a prestige hierarchy, and showed little interest or knowledge in, for example, primary health care (Nichter, 1981; Ramalingaswami and Shyam, 1980). Madan (1980) describes 'the received image of preventive and social medicine as a soft choice', something that only the second-rate medical students specialize in is the view held by most of the doctors he interviewed at the All India Institute of Medical Sciences. Banerji (1974) argues that this is not merely a matter of image; when the new social and preventive medicine departments were created after Independence, the teaching positions were taken by discards, by those who were in senior positions in more prestigious specialities. One indicator of their positions is more prestigious specialities. One indicator of their low status is that in many medical colleges, the posts are held by women, who often find access to medical and surgical specialities more difficult (Bhargava, 1983).

An exaggerated concern for curative specialities, in particular those with the masculine glamour of the 'activist' model of surgery (passive patients in a life or death situation, rescued by dramatic knife work) is not restricted to India. However, it takes on an additional pathos in a context where policy statements by politicians and senior medical bureaucrats repeatedly argue that generalist skills are the most pressing needs. Most doctors at the All India Institute took the view that national concerns might require social and community medicine, but not all doctors should follow that model and that they, in an elite institution, should be the first to be exempted (Madan, 1980).

Social and Preventive Medicine in India

Since World War II, there have been great and rapid changes in the socio-economic set-up and patterns of several countries, which are more pronounced in the under-developed than the developed countries, owing to their lower standards of life. The impact of these socio-economic changes is reflected in the health status of these countries due to three factors viz. first, increased cost of living index with phenomenal increase in price level of food, clothing and housing; second, increasing unplanned urbanization of rural population moving to urban towns which had forestalled industrialization with consequent creation of urban slums endangering their own health as well as health of the permanent town-dwellers; third, changes in the structure and pattern of families with increasing tendency to break the joint-family system and, set up smaller family units with consequent break-up of family-doctor system. These changing patterns have brought in changes in the disciplines gradually from public health to preventive and, now to social medicine which overlap at several stages. To summarize, the three uses of preventive and social medicine are:

- As an academic discipline in the undergraduate course;
- Student today would be doctor tomorrow, therefore it is recognized as a necessary training in the individual clinical practice of a physician, surgeon, etc.; and
- As an instrument of social policy for the administrator, planner or politician in a welfare state, whose goal is socialized medicine in a socialistic pattern of society.

In the analysis, the three uses of preventive and social medicine, considered along with the three socio-economic factors which are responsible for its advent put together, along with political changes to a welfare secular state as in India, has brought about gradual socialization of medicine. This is manifest today in the countrywide coverage of community development projects, catering for all the needs of our rural population, and as an integral part of it, setting up primary health centres, which cater for both curative and preventive health services.

Summing up

The idea that medicine is a social science was first clearly presented by the leaders of the Reform Movement in Germany which promulgated the views that the health of the people was a matter of concern to society and that society had an obligation to protect and ensure the health of its members. Preventive care for the special health needs of women and children developed as a public concern in the late 19th century. Early in the 20th century, the combined efforts of public health measures concentrating on environmental sanitation and, the bacteriological discoveries leading to vaccines and sera, provided effective measures for both promotion of health as well as prevention of diseases.

Social medicine is the study of man as a social being in his total environment. In 1955, strengthening of social and preventive medicine departments were recommended in India by the Medical Council of India.

References

Acheson, R.M. (1978), 'The Definition and Identification of Need for Healthcare', *Journal of Epidemiology and Community Health*, 32: 10–15.

Banerji, D. (1974), 'Anatomy of the Medical Profession in India', *Mimeograph*, New Delhi: Centre for the Study of Social Medicine and Community Health, J.N.U.

Bhargava, G. (1983), 'Sex-stereotyping and Sex-congruency: Components in the Role Definition of Medical Specialties in India', *Social Science and Medicine*, 17(5): 1017–26.

Crew, F.A.E. (1958), 'Preventive and Social Medicine: Its Meaning, Scope and Content', *WHO Medicine and Education Bulletin*, 3(2).

—— (1960), *Medical Education Bulletin*, No. 2, New Delhi: WHO.

Dakshinamurty, Sonti (1962), *Introduction to Preventive and Social Medicine*, Kakinada: Educational Enterprises.

Kostrzewski, J. (1970), *Medical Research: Priorities and Possibilities*, Geneva: WHO.

Leavel, H.R. and E.G. Clark (1965), *Preventive Medicine for the Doctor in His Community*, New York: McGraw Hill.

Madan, T.N. (1980), *Doctors and Society: Three Asian Case Studies*, New Delhi: Vikas.

Martin, F.M. (1977), 'Social Medicine and Its Contribution to Social Policy', *Lancet*, 2(24): 1336.

McKeown, T. and C.R. Lowe (1974), *An Introduction to Social Medicine*, Oxford: Blackwell.

Nichter, M. (1981), 'Toward a Culturally Responsive Rural Health-Care Delivery System in India', in G.R. Gupta (ed.), *The Social and Cultural Context of Medicine in India*, New Delhi: Vikas.

Prasad, B.G. (1972), *Teaching of Community Medicine to Undergraduates in India*, New Delhi: All India Institute of Social Sciences.

Ramalingaswami, P. and A. Shyam (1980), 'Perceptions of Primary Health Care by Medical Students', *Mimeograph*, New Delhi: Centre for the Study of Social Medicine and Community Health, J.N.U.

Rao, K.N. (1967), *Philosophy of Medicine*, Bombay: Current Technical Literature.

Ryle, John A. (1943), 'Social Medicine: Its Meaning and its Scope', *British Medical Journal*, 2: 633–36.

Taylor, C.E. et al. (1976), *Doctors for the Villages*, London: Asia.

7

Public Health

Concepts and Vital Statistics

The development of public health started in the 18th century with the sanitary movement. The concept of contagion was key to this early development, whether from disease (cholera) or ideas (communism). The appalling conditions in the newly industrializing cities demanded a response but there was intense debate about what to do. Many of the discussions at the time resonate with contemporary ones about the balance between the role of the individual, with the feckless poor having only themselves to blame, and that of state in protecting them from danger and enabling them to make health choices.

We then move on the rise of what was called preventive medicine. This emerged in the middle of the 20th century, coinciding with the rise of scientific medicine and optimism about its potential achievements. It was characterized by its focus on the concept of hygiene (not just in relation to infectious disease but, in some countries in the 1930s taking a rather less innocuous form with its emphasis on genetic or racial hygiene, with profound implications for the ability to undertake collective health interventions in the countries concerned even now). Health professionals knew best and played a key role. Education (especially when undertaken by doctors or nurses) was thought sufficient to change behaviour and much disease was avoidable by means of mass activities such as screening.

Later in the 20th century, new ideas began to emerge, rejecting the dominance of the medical model. In 1974, the Canadian Government published the 'Lalonde Report', which proposed the health field concept (Figure 1).

The History of Public Health in India

India has one of the most ancient civilizations in recorded history. Thousands of years before the Christian era, there existed a civilization in the Indus valley, known as Indus Valley Civilization. Mohenjo-daro and Harappa showed relics of planned cities with drainage, house and public baths built of baked bricks suggesting the practices of environmental sanitation, by ancient people as far back as 3,000 BC; India was invaded by

Figure 1
Health Field Concept

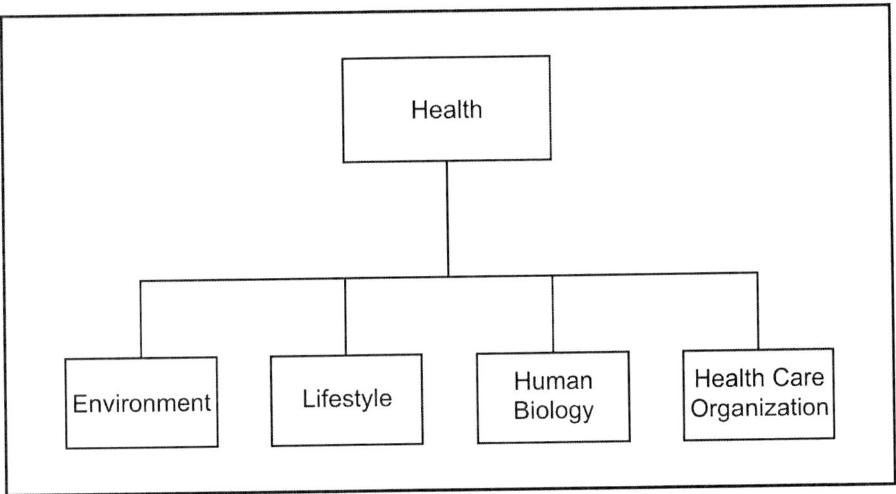

Source: Lalonde, M. (1975), *'A New Perspective on the Health of Canadians: A Working Document'* Ottawa: Information Canada.

Aryans around 1,400 BC. It was probably during this period, the ayurveda and the siddha systems of medicine came into existence. Ayurveda as a science of life developed a comprehensive concept of health. The *Manusmriti* prescribed rules and regulations of personal health, dietetics and hygienic ritual at the time of birth and death, and also emphasized the unity of the physical, mental and spiritual aspects of life (Rao, 1966). The post-Vedic period (600 BC–600 AD) was dominated by the religious teaching of Buddhism and Jainism. Medical education was introduced in the ancient universities of Taxila and Nalanda, leading to the titles of *Pranacharya* and *Pranavishara* (Rao, 1966). A hospital system was developed during the reign of Rahula Sankirtyana (son of Buddha) for men, women and animals and the system was continued and expanded by king Ashoka. The next phase in Indian history (650–1850 AD) witnessed the rise and fall of the Mughal empire. The Muslim rulers introduced unani system of medicine into India around 1000 AD. The origin of unani medicine is traced back to Greek medicine. The unani system since then became part of Indian medicine. With changes in the political conditions in India, the torch which was lighted thousands of years ago by the ancient sages grew dim, medical education and medical services became static, and the ancient universities and hospitals disappeared.

Public Health and Sanitary Policy

By the middle of the 18th century, the British had established their rule in India which lasted till 1947. Before the 1860s, sanitary arrangements for the civilian population were discussed sporadically. For example, in 1810, when some Dacca citizens proposed local improvements, such as the removal of filth, or the repair of wells and drains, the governor-general rejected the proposal out of hand (Ahmed, 1980). By 1823 the governor-general allowed the surplus town taxes to be spent on urban environment; but in Dacca, at least, most effort went into widening roads, draining marshes, and cleaning land for (among other things) a race course (Ahmed, 1980). Efforts depended on the individual officials appointed to improvement committees, all of which were abolished in 1829 as a measure of economy (Ahmed, 1980). More concern was shown for the health of the army; for example, after 1835 medical officers were encouraged to submit details of the climate, geography, and medical statistics of districts in order to guide military campsites and cantonments to healthy places (Ramasubban, 1982). However, one measure of civilian preventive medicine predated the 1860s: vaccination against smallpox was supported with fluctuating energy and attempts were made to eradicate the indigenous practice of inoculation (Arnold, 1985).

In 1859, a Royal Commission was appointed to investigate the causes of the extremely unsatisfactory condition of health in the British Army stationed in India. The Commission recommended the establishment of a Commission of Public Health in each presidency and pointed out the need for the protection of water supplied, construction of drains and prevention of epidemics in the civil population for safeguarding the health of the British Army. The Royal Commission also reported that the health of the army could not be separated from the sanitary condition of the 'native population' close by, and that 'well considered measures of water supply, drainage, paving, cleansing, and general constitution in these towns would be attended with most beneficial results to the health of the troops quartered near them'. All the native towns had some system of cleansing and dealing with human excreta and other nuisances; nonetheless, the commission concluded, there was much more to be done (Sanitary Commission, 1865; Statistical Abstract, 1870). In 1864, Sanitary Commission was appointed in the three major provinces – Bombay, Madras and Bengal. A Public Health Commissioner and a Statistical Officer were appointed with the Government of India. In 1888, the Government of India directed that sanitation should be looked after by the local bodies, but no public health was created to look after sanitation. Sanitary policy was restricted to towns and military areas because the remit of the Commission was to consider improvements for the towns in proximity to military stations (Sanitary Commission, 1865; Statistical Abstract, 1870). A classic example is the Contagious Diseases Prevention Act, designed to protect soldiers from venereal diseases and totally unconcerned with civilian sufferers (Ballhatchet, 1980). For 25 years little was achieved in public health, partly because sanitary officers were subordinated to medical ones, and partly because sanitary concerns were restricted to official circles. In addition, technical disputes about the relationship between sanitary measures and medical science hindered the implementation of policy, especially with respect to the role of clean water in preventing cholera (Farrell, 1973; Jaggi, 1979; Hume, 1984). International criticism arose for the concern of cholera. In 1866, an International Sanitary Conference in Constantinople concluded that India was the source of cholera epidemic, and that the Indian government had failed to control it. The measures proposed to deal with cholera were progressively implemented, for the army and cholera mortality dropped to three deaths per 1,000 in the 1870s. But when medical men came to deal with civilian cholera, they hid behind 'Orientalist' excuses: Indians were inferior, and one sign of their inferiority was their relentless attachment to superstition, which made it impossible to tamper with religious customs such as pilgrimages, which were widely agreed to be a major route of cholera transmission (Ramasubban, 1982).

Sanitary commissioners were expressly excluded from any concern with the cantonments and the European Civil Lines themselves; these remained the responsibility of the army (Harrison, 1980). Increasingly, towns had specific local municipal committees, with some elected members. Initially, these committees focused mainly on conservancy – the removal of faeces from residential areas. In Allahabad in 1870, 280 sweepers were employed to collect sewage and 90 drivers to remove it for burial. In Calcutta in 1867, a municipal railway was built to deal with the transport problem (Harrison, 1980). But the financial limits of these committees prevented them from making such impact on sanitation. Thus, in 1883, when Ranchodlal Chhotalal, the first non-official Indian to be made chair of the Ahmedabad Managing Committee, proposed better water supplies and drainage, better hospitals, and more planning controls over housing, his vehement opponents attacked the increased taxation needed to be paid for the proposed improvements (Gillion, 1968). Eventually, in 1891 an improved water supply scheme was implemented; but it was not until 1903, after the municipality was ordered by the Bombay government to take the advice of experts, that the drainage scheme was completed. Similarly in Allahabad, the water supply scheme first mooted in 1883 was in operation by 1891, but a drainage scheme for the extra supply was not started until 1913 (Harrison, 1980). This delay in providing drainage systems (common throughout Indian towns because of the extra expense involved) meant that introducing clean water supplies actually seems to have increased mortality rates. In six north Indian towns, recorded death rates in the five years following the introduction of filtered water supplied were higher than in the five years before (Klein, 1973). The surplus water probably formed stagnant pools, ideal breeding grounds for mosquitoes, thus increasing the spread of malaria, though deaths due to dysentery, cholera, and diarrhoea probably did decline.

In the late 1880s, Florence Nightingale pressed the Indian government to improve sanitary arrangements in the villages which had been almost totally ignored. No rural agency existed to implement the rules established for village sanitation. Decentralization only reached the provinces in 1872, under Lord Mayo's reforms, and larger towns were given some autonomy in 1882, with the Ripon reforms. A new extension of local government was set in train with acts in Bombay (1889) and other parts of the country designed to promote district authorities for whom sanitary measures would be a primary concern. Training in hygiene and sanitation was expanded, and over the next 10 years, graduates were brought into sanitary work. Activity, however, was severely restricted by the shortage of funds available and by the limitations policy-makers believed were caused by the 'ignorance, prejudices, callousness, and superstitions of the people' (Harvey, 1895). This blaming of the poor and sick for their own conditions may have allowed some doctors to escape the responsibility for eradicating the real causes of high rates of morbidity and mortality. But some doctors advanced more sophisticated arguments, suggesting that European methods of disease control were inapplicable in India, because of social (e.g. caste) and environmental (e.g. the monsoon) barriers (Arnold, 1985). Clearly, medical administrators were uneasy about their record in sanitary work, particularly when challenged in international settings with responsibility for cholera which emanated from Bengal (Jaggi, 1979). However, they were undoubtedly right to argue that implementing sanitary improvements throughout rural India would be beyond the financial limits of Britain, let alone of the Indian government. Funding problems were probably exacerbated by linking sanitary reform to local governments with even less adequate sources of finance than the towns had.

Attempts to intervene in the provision of water, the control of sewage, and other aspects of everyday village life would probably have led to great hostility and little success. Vaccinators had to deal with frequent rumours of the dangers of the treatment and general hostility, partly because they were also trying to eradicate inoculation which was a much more accepted form of smallpox prevention (Arnold, 1985). The response to plague measures after 1896 reinforced this view. Sanitary measures, based on little understanding of village life, would probably have been unsuccessful, though this does not justify the pathetic attempts that were actually made. Expenditures on preventive medicine were always small, relative to overall public or to medical expenditure. Probably only water supplies and some vaccination programmes made marked impact on morbidity and mortality before World War II.

Yet medical administrators appreciated the links between providing sanitation and a population's health, especially in urban areas where collective arrangements for waste disposal, water supply and drainage were major concerns. As in Europe, town planning until 1900 was almost entirely a matter of sanitary provision, fuelled by demands from the wealthy for protection from diseases of the poor. In India this took on a racial form, with attempts to protect Europeans – civilians and the military

– from native diseases. This is obvious in the reports of the sanitary commissioners, but its most notable results lay in the separation of city from cantonment and in other attempts to place physical barriers between Indians and Europeans. The Royal Commission deplored these efforts (Sanitary Commission, 1865), but they accorded with theories of contagion through bad air (Harrison, 1980; King, 1966). Thus, conditions in European areas were much better than in Indian areas; roads were paved and swept, water supply and drainage was quickly improved to a higher standard, and there was definitely less crowding. But sewage removal arrangements in the European areas differed little from those in the rest of the city, at least during the 19th century, and provisions for Indians living there (servants, traders, etc.) were possibly even worse than in the towns (Harrison, 1980; King, 1966).

In 1896, severe epidemic of plague occurred in India which awakened the government to the urgent need of improving public health. The Epidemic Diseases Act was promulgated. After 1900 improvement trusts were established in many larger towns and Patrick Geddes, among others, was asked to advise on the development of urban areas, prompted partly by a concern for the appalling conditions in the slums. The trusts had power to control only new buildings, beyond the city limits. Attempts to improve working-class housing ran into overwhelming opposition from powerful slum landlords as well as the municipal committees, for whom they were too expensive. Despite Geddes' propaganda, it was only in Hyderabad (where the *nizam* gave considerable support) that there was any substantial attack on unsanitary conditions (Meller, 1979).

The other impetus to urban people came from plague epidemics. Plague was probably common in India before the British arrived and its association with rats was known (Anstey, 1936). But it apparently disappeared from India in the early 19th century before being reinforced from China through Bombay in 1896. Since its signs are distinctive and it generated such horror and official inquiry, deaths from plague were probably recorded fairly accurately. So the estimates of some 15 million plague deaths in British India and 18 million in the princely states, between 1896 and 1921, cannot be far off the mark (Census, 1921). The disease spread quickly to most parts of the country, speeded by railways, trade, and commerce. The urban poor suffered most and then, panic stricken, escaped into rural areas, taking the disease with them; Europeans were almost immune. The vital point to note here is that plague reappeared in India when control and prevention measures were understood, and yet the response of the authorities was almost totally ineffective. The Bombay authorities took drastic action; sufferers were compulsorily taken to hospitals, the infected were segregated, premises were evacuated, a sanitary cordon was attempted around affected areas, and travellers were medically inspected. These measures were inadequately explained and few people accepted the rationality of what was proposed. Some resisted openly;

traders rejected bans on exports or the movement of goods, mill owners rejected steam cleansing, while Jains (religious group) and others destroyed rat traps. Others concealed infected people and then dumped their dead bodies anonymously in the street, escaped around cordons, or refused to leave infected areas for fear of theft from their unprotected houses (Klein, 1973). When pushed too far, they rioted.

Western medicine's arrogant self-confidence and its failure to deal with the plague is well exposed by the medical authorities' compromises with Indian opinion. Originally, the authorities wanted all patients to be treated by western doctors, but instead they were forced to accept the use of *hakims* and *vaids* by patients. They also had to deny that plague inoculation would be made compulsory (Arnold, 1985). By 1900, the sanitary commissioner noted that the plague epidemic was treated as a political emergency, noted as a matter of public health, and he argued that this was because the idea of public health was alien to the sympathies and traditions of the people (Annual Report of the Sanitary Commissioner, 1902). Dealing with the threat to trade and social order became paramount, treatment and control measures led to follow behind these imperatives, and the imperial governments withdrew from active attempts to prevent the spread of disease, merely responding to calls for medical services (Klein, 1973).

During 1919, the Montague-Chelmsford Constitutional Reforms led to the transfer of public health, sanitation and vital statistics to the provinces under the control of an elected minister. This was the first step towards decentralization of health administration in India. Municipality and Local Board Acts, containing legal provisions for the advancement of public health, were passed in several provinces. The All India Institute of Hygiene and Public Health, Calcutta, was established with aid from the Rockefeller Foundation. In 1937, the Central Advisory Board of Health was set up with the Public Health Commissioner as Secretary and representatives from the provinces and Indian states as members, to coordinate the public health activities in the country. The Madras Public Health Act was passed in 1939. In this act, the first Rural Health Training Centre was established. Remarkably in 1943, the Health Survey and Development Committee (Bhore Committee) was appointed by the Government of India to survey the existing position in regard to health conditions and health organization in the country, and to make recommendations for the future development. The committee submitted its report in 1946 and gave the recommendations of long-term programme for the attainment of reasonable health services based on the concept of modern health practice.

The public health in pre-Independence India thus has to be seen as a qualified failure. Even in the towns most directly amenable to British influence and action, the conditions of life of most inhabitants remained appalling, with very high mortality and morbidity rates in the worst areas.

Only Europeans' areas enjoyed the benefits of civic concern. This racial distinction and the much more pronounced role taken by the state in Indian towns, provide the main points of difference between the Indian and British experience. Despite having a more centralized, active, and interventionist government than in Britain and one which attempted to draw on British experience, India gained remarkably few benefits. Capitalist development and the rapid unplanned increase of the urban population led to slums, overcrowding, and urban squalor in India just as in Europe (Jeffery, 1988).

India became independent in 1947. Ministries of Health were established at the Centre and States. India joined the World Health Organization as a member state in 1948. The Constituent Assembly adopted the Constitution of India on 26 November. Article 246 of the Constitution of India covers all the health subjects; these have been enumerated in the Seventh Schedule under three lists – Union list, Concurrent list and State list. Article 47 of the Constitution under the Directive Principles of the State Policy states: 'That the State shall regard the raising of the level of nutrition and the standard of living of its people and the improvement of public health as among its primary duties'. The Planning Commission was set up in 1950 and it came out with First Five Year Plan. The Community Development Programme was launched in 1952 which included all round development of rural areas.

In the history of public health, four distinct phases may be demarcated:

Disease Control Phase (1880–1920)

Public health during the 19th century was largely a matter of sanitary legislation and sanitary reforms aimed at the control of man's physical environment, e.g. water supply, sewage disposal, etc. Clearly these measures were not aimed at the control of any specific disease for want of the needed technical knowledge. However, these measures vastly improved the health of the people due to disease and death control.

Health Promotional Phase (1920–1960)

At the beginning of the 20th century, a new concept, the concept of 'health promotion' began to take shape. It was realized that public health had neglected the citizen as an individual, and that the State had a direct responsibility for the health of the individual. Consequently, in addition to disease control activities, one more goal was added to public health, that is, health promotion of individuals. It was initiated as personal health services such as mother and child health services, school health services, industrial health services, mental health and rehabilitation services. Public health nursing was a direct offshoot of this concept. Public health departments began expanding their programmes towards health promotional activities. Winslow, one of the leading figures in the history of public health, in 1920, defined public health as 'the science and art of preventing disease, prolonging life and promoting health and efficiency through organized community effort'. This definition summarizes the philosophy of public health, which remains largely true even today.

Since the State has assumed direct responsibility for the health of the individual, two great movements were initiated for human development during the first half of the present century, namely provision of 'basic health services' through the medium of primary health centres and subcentres is an important development in the history of public health (Roemer, 1978). The concept of health centre was first mooted in 1920 by Lord Dawson in England. In 1931, the League of Nations Health Organization called for establishment of health centres. The Bhore Committee (1946) in India had also recommended the establishment of health centres for providing integrated curative and preventive services. Many developing countries have given the highest priority to the establishment of health centres for providing basic health services. The second great movement was the Community Development Programme to promote village development through the active participation of the whole community and on the initiative of the community. This programme tried to do too much too quickly with inadequate resources. It was a great opportunity lost, because it failed to survive. However, the establishment of primary health centres and subcentres provided the much needed infrastructure of health services especially in the rural areas.

Social Engineering Phase (1960–1980)

With the advances in preventive medicine and practice of public health, the pattern of disease began to change in the developed world. Many of the acute illness problems have been brought under control. However, as old problems were solved, new health problems in the form of chronic diseases began to emerge, e.g. cancer, diabetes, cardiovascular diseases, alcoholism and drug addiction, etc. especially in the affluent societies. These problems could not be tackled by the traditional approaches to public health such as isolation, immunization and disinfection nor could these be explained on the basis of germ theory of disease. A new concept, the concept of 'risk factors' as determinants of these diseases came into existence. The consequences of these diseases, unlike the swift death brought by the acute infectious diseases, was to place a chronic burden on the society that created them. These problems brought new challenges to public health which needed a new phase in the 1960s, described as the 'social engineering' phase. Social and behavioural aspects of diseases and health were given a new priority. Public health moved into the preventive and rehabilitative aspects of chronic diseases and behavioural problems. In this process, the goals of public health and preventive medicine which had already shown considerable overlapping became identical, namely prevention of disease, promotion of health and prolongation of life. In short, although the term 'public health' is still used, its original meaning has changed and in view of its changed meaning and scope, the term 'community health' has been preferred by some leaders in public health as community health incorporates services to the population at large as opposed to preventive or social medicine.

Health for All Phase (1981–2000)

As the centuries have unfolded, the glaring contrasts in the picture of health in the developed and developing countries came into a sharper focus, despite advances in medicine. Most people in the developed countries, and the elite of the developing countries, enjoy all the determinants of good health – adequate income, nutrition, education, sanitation, safe drinking water and comprehensive health care. John Bryant in the introduction to his book, *Health and the Developing World* presented a gloomy picture and a challenge of inequalities in health by saying: 'Large numbers of the world's people perhaps more than half, have no access to health care at all, and for many of the rest the care they receive does not answer the problems they have'. The global conscience was stirred leading to a new awakening that the health gap between rich and poor within countries and between countries should be narrowed and ultimately eliminated. It is concluded that the neglected 80 per cent of the world's population too have an equal claim to health care, to protection from the killer diseases of childhood, to primary health care for mothers and children, to treatment for those ills that mankind has long ago learnt to control, if not to cure (Mahler, 1977). Against this background, in 1981, the members of WHO pledged themselves to an ambitious target to provide 'Health for All' by the year 2000, that is attainment of a level of health that will permit all people 'to lead a socially and economically productive life' (WHO-UNICEF, 1978).

National Health Policy–2002

National Health Policy of 1983, in a spirit of optimistic empathy of the health needs of the people, particularly, the poor and under privileged, had hoped to provide 'Health for All' by the year 2000 through the universal provision of comprehensive primary health care services. In retrospect, it is observed that the financial resources and public health administrative capacity which it was possible to marshal, was far short of that necessary to achieve such an ambitious and holistic goal. Against this backdrop, National Health Policy of 2002 has been announced. Policy has been attempted to maximize the broad-based availability of health services to the citizenry of the country on the basis of realistic considerations of capacity. Equity in health sector is an important goal in the policy. For this marked emphasis has been provided in the policy for expanding and improving the primary health facilities, including the new concept of provisioning of essential drugs through central funding. Further, the policy recognizes the fact that, despite all that may be guaranteed by the central government for assisting public health programmes, public health services would actually need to be delivered by the state administration, NGOs and other institutions of civil society. The attainment of improved health levels would be significantly dependent on population stabilization, as also on complementary efforts from other areas of the social sectors – like improved drinking water supply, basic sanitation, minimum nutrition, etc. – to ensure that the exposure of the populace to health risk is minimized.

This report signaled the beginning of a move away from the medicalization of public health towards one that emphasized the building of healthy public policy. Now there was a focus on intersectoral action, working with sectors such as housing, transport, education and others, enshrined in the World Health Organization's 'Health for All', by the Year 2000 movement. These principles were then set out in the Ottawa Charter in 1986, which called for the following approaches:

- Building healthy public policy.
- Creating supportive environments.
- Strengthening community actions.
- Developing personal skills.
- Reorienting health services.
- Demonstrating commitment to health promotion.

Yet 'Health for All' was effective in catalyzing action at local level, as public health advocates used the fact that their governments had endorsed it to support initiatives such as the 'Healthy Cities' movement, in which local administrations developed wide-ranging programmes to improve health, working through policies on transport, housing and education.

By the mid-1990s, when it became clear that 'Health for All' would not be achieved by the year 2000, the WHO policy strategy was renewed, leading to 'Health 21'. It has a more limited set of targets but, like 'Health for All', it has received relatively little attention.

At the same time, however, a new issue had emerged that was seen, by many, to link closely with issues of health. Concerns about the global environment had forced governments to come together at the Rio Earth Summit. One of the outcomes of that meeting was 'Agenda 21', a plan for sustainable development. Many people who had been working to improve health locally, implementing intersectoral responses, saw this process that they could link with. As a consequence, in many localities there is now a close association between those seeking to enhance health and those working for a sustainable environment.

Health Field Concept

Health field concept is developed by Marc Lalonde. He envisioned environment (e.g. food and water quality), lifestyle (e.g. drug and alcohol use), human biology (e.g. genetics and aging), and health care organization (e.g. accessibility, quality and quantity of services) as the key factors determining health. The health field concept says that health exists when its four components are in balance. It is reasonable to conclude from this model that efforts to improve public health must include programmes aimed at environmental protection and lifestyle management, as well as those directed towards optimizing human functioning and treating diseases.

Vital Health Statistics

Birth Rate

The birth rate is the demographic measure of the rate at which children are born. The most well-known is crude birth rate, which is the number of births that occur each year per 1,000 people in the mid-year population. This rate is called 'crude' because it does not take into account the possible effects of age structure. The birth rate in India has long remained at a high level and continued to remain so till the 1971–81. The sudden decline in birth rate for the 1941–51 decade has been due to difference in methodology adopted for its computation. A clear decline in birth rate is, however, observed since 1981. According to Sample Registration System, the birth rate for the decade 1991–2000 was 27.8 for India.

Death Rate

The death (or mortality) rate is most commonly measured by the crude death rate, which is the annual number of deaths per 1,000 people in the mid-year population. When used to make comparisons, crude death rates are often misleading, because they do not take into account differences in age structure. A population with a relatively large proportion of elderly, for example, will generate a relatively large number of deaths for that reason alone regardless of health conditions. For this reason, crude death rates in some non-industrial, relatively poor societies are worse and death rates are higher at most ages. According to Sample Registration Survey (SRS), crude death in 1981 was 12.5 which came down to 8.7 in 2000 in India.

Infant Mortality Rate

For every 1,000 births in a given year, the infant mortality rate is the number of infants who die before their first birthday. The rate is often calculated in relation to even smaller age spans, such as the neonatal mortality rate which measures deaths during the first 28 days of life. Measures of infant mortality are among the best indicators of general health conditions in a population and often are used to estimate overall morbidity and death rates in countries with poor vital statistics records. According to SRS, the infant mortality in India is 70 per thousand but still it is higher as compared to other developed countries. The developed countries of the world have been able to control their infant mortality rates and have brought it down to almost the lowest possible levels (well below 10 per 1,000 live births), it continues to be very high in India and a majority of other developing countries. In India, still one child in every 14 born alive is not able to see the first birthday.

Specific Death Rate

As different diseases lead to mortality in any population, health planners try to know the extent of mortality in any population because of specified diseases. Death rate due to specific cause is calculated by computing total number of deaths assigned to a particular cause in a given geographical place and year is divided by the mid-year population of that area and multiplied by 10,000. As deaths due to a particular cause among 1,000 persons are not very many, therefore, multiplier is changed from 1,000 to 10,000.

Maternal Mortality Rate

Maternal mortality accounts for the greatest proportion of deaths among women of reproductive age in most of the developing countries. In 1998, the maternal mortality rate had been recorded as high as 407 per 1,00,000 live births.

Life Expectancy

Life expectancy at birth is the average number of years that will be lived by those born alive into a population if the current age specific mortality rates persist. Life expectancy at birth is highly influenced by the infant mortality rate where that is high. Life expectancy at the age of one excludes the influence of infant mortality, and life expectancy at the age of five excludes the influence of child mortality. An increase in the expectation of life is regarded, inferentially, as an improvement in health status. According to Registrar General of India, life expectancy of its population is 64.6 years.

Morbidity Indicators

To describe health in terms of mortality rates only is misleading. This is because mortality indicators do not reveal the burden of ill health in a community, as for example mental illness and rheumatoid arthritis. Therefore, morbidity indicators are used to supplement mortality data to describe the health status of a population. Morbidity is dominated by communicable diseases. According to one estimate, about 17.2 per cent of all deaths and about 20.8 per cent of all illnesses are due to communicable diseases in India. Out of the communicable diseases which have persisted over time, the incidence of malaria staged a resurgence in the 1980 before stabilizing at a fairly high prevalence level during the 1990s. Over the years, an increasing level of insecticide resistance has developed in the malarial vectors in many parts of the country, while the incidence of the more deadly P-Falciparum Malaria has risen to about 50 per cent in the country as a whole. Malaria continues to be a major public health problem with 1.91 million (provisional) cases being reported during 2000. In respect of tuberculosis, the public health scenario has not shown any significant decline in the pool of infection amongst the community, and there has been a distressing trend in the increase of drug resistance to the type of infection prevailing in the country. A new and extremely virulent communicable disease – HIV/AIDS – has emerged. As there is no therapeutic cure or vaccine for this infection, the disease constitutes a serious threat, not merely to public health but also to economic development in the country. The common water-borne infections – gastroenteritis, cholera, and some forms of hepatitis – continue to contribute to a high level of morbidity in the population, even though the mortality rate may be somewhat moderated. Lifestyle diseases – diabetes, cancer and cardiovascular – are continuously on increasing side. Persistent incidence of macro and micro nutrient deficiencies, especially among women and children are also alarming.

Summing Up

The development of public health started in the 18th century with the sanitary movement. With changes in the political conditions in India, the torch which was lighted thousands of years ago by the ancient sages grew dim, medical education and medical services became static, and the ancient universities and hospitals disappeared. In the late 1880s, Florence Nightingale pressed the Indian government to improve sanitary arrangements in the villages which had been almost totally ignored. In 1888, the Government of India directed that sanitation should be looked after by the local bodies, but no public health was created to look after sanitation. Sanitary policy was restricted to towns and military areas because the remit of the Commission was to consider improvements for the towns in proximity to military stations. The Bhore Committee (1946) in India had also recommended the establishment of health centres for providing integrated curative and preventive services. National Health Policy of 1983, in a spirit of optimistic empathy of the health needs of the people, particularly, the poor and under-privileged, had hoped to provide 'Health for All' by the year 2000 through the universal provision of comprehensive primary health care services.

References

Ahmed, S.U. (1980), 'Urban Problems and Government Policies: A Case Study of the City of Dacca, 1810–30', in K. Ballhatchet and J.B. Harrison (eds), *The City in South Asia*, London: Curzon Press.

Annual Abstract of Statistics for East India (1870).

Annual Reports of the Sanitary Commissioner with Government of India (1865).

Anstey, V. (1936), *The Economic Development of India*, London: Longmans.

Arnold, D. (1985), 'Medical Priorities and Practice in Nineteenth Century British India', *South Asia Research*, 5(2): 167–86.

Ballhatchet, K. (1980), *Race, Sex and Class under the Raj*, New Delhi: Vikas.

Census of India (1921), Delhi: Government of India.

Farrell, J.S. (1973), *The Siege of Krishnapur*, London: Penguin.

Fendall, R. (1984), 'We Expect Too Much from Community Health Workers', *World Health Forum*, 5: 300.

Gillion, K.L. (1968), *Ahmedabad: A Study in Indian Urban History*, Berkeley, CA: University of California Press.

Harrison, J.B. (1980), 'Allahabad: A Sanitary History', in K. Ballhatchet and J.B. Harrison (eds), *The City in South Asia*, London: Curzon Press.

Harvey, W. (1895), 'Presidential Address', in *Proceedings of the First Indian Medical Congress*, Calcutta: Indian Medical Gazette.

Hume, J. (1984), 'Colonialism and Sanitary Medicine: The Development of Preventive Health Policy in the Punjab, 1860–1900', *Modern Asian Studies*, 20(4): 703–24.

Jaggi, O.P. (1979), *Western Medicine in India: Medical Education and Research*, Delhi: Atma Ram.

Jeffery, Roger (1988), *The Politics of Health in India*, London: University of California Press.

King, M. (ed.) (1966), *Medical Care in Developing Countries*, Nairobi: Oxford University Press.

Klein, I. (1973), 'Death in India', *Journal of Asian Studies*, 32(4): 639–59.

Lalonde, M. (1975), *A New Perspective on the Health of Canadians: A Working Document*, Ottawa: Information Canada.

Mahler, H. (1977), 'Blueprint for Health of All', *WHO Chronicle*, 31(12): 491–98.

—— (1979), 'Urbanization and the Introduction of Modern Town Planning Ideas in India, 1900–1925', in K.N. Chaudhuri and C.J. Dewey (eds), *Economy and Society*, Oxford: Oxfam.

Morley, David et al. (1984), *Practising Health for All*, New York: Oxford University Press.

Ramasubban, R. (1984), 'Public Health and Medical Research in India: Their Origins under the Impact of British Colonial Policy', *Stockholm: SAREC Report*, No. 4, Swedish Agency for Research Cooperation with Developing Countries.

Rao, K.N. (1966), *The Nation's Health*, Delhi: Publications Division.

Roemer, M.I. (1972), 'Evaluation of Community Health Centres', *Public Health Papers*, No. 48, Geneva: WHO.

Sanitary Commission (1865), *Report of the Commissioner Appointed to Inquire into the Sanitary State of the Army in India*, London: Her Majesty's Stationery Office.

WHO and UNICEF (1978a), *Primary Health Care: Report of the International Conference on Primary Health Care, Alma Ata, USSR*, 6–12 September, Geneva: WHO.

—— (1978b), *Health for All*, Series No. 1, Geneva: WHO.

8

Community Health and Medicine

A person's health status is dynamic in part because of the many factors that determine one's health. It is widely accepted that health status is determined by the interaction of genetics, physical factors, socio-cultural factor, economic factor, and personal health behaviour and health services.

Defining Community

Traditionally, a community has been thought of as a geographic area with specific boundaries, for example, a neighbourhood, city, country, or state. However, in the context of community health, a community is an aggregate of people who share certain common characteristics. Community is also related with certain geographical location, race, ethnicity, age, and occupation who are having common interests for particular problems and having a common bonding. Communities are characterized by following features: membership, i.e. community people have a sense of common identity and belongingness; they share common language, rituals and ceremonies; their values and norms are common; the community members have a mutual influence and are also influenced by each other; their needs are shared and they are committed to meet their common needs; they are also connected by emotions in terms of their common history, experiences and mutual support (Israel et al., 1994). Examples of communities include the people of the city of Delhi (location), the Dravidian community of South India (race), the tribal community of Orissa (ethnicity), seniors in the teaching department (age), the teaching and doctor communities (occupation), the people living in railway tracks of Mumbai (slum people), those living in the orphanages (particular outcome), or local union members (common bond).

A community may be small as the group of people who live in accommodation provided in the hostels at college or university or as large as all the individuals who make up a nation. A healthy community is a place where people provide leadership in assessing their own resources and needs, where public health and social infrastructure and policies support health, and where essential public health services, including quality health care, are available (Institute of Medicine, 2003).

Defining Community Health

Prior to defining the community health, we would like to discuss a similar concept, i.e. public health. The laymen use these two terms interchangeably in various health fields. Most people are referring to the collective health of those in society and the actions or activities taken to obtain and maintain that health. Public health is the most inclusive concept. Whatever we do collectively and when the activity is done publicly to assure the conditions in which people can be healthy is called public health. The public health system, which has been defined as certain actions and activities taken in formal structure by the government, private, voluntary organizations and by individuals (Institute of Medicine, 1988) is an organizational mechanism of providing such conditions. People regard that public health is the responsibility of government like providing sanitation, potable water, vaccination, control and prevention of epidemics etc. Community health refers to the health status of a defined group of people and the actions and conditions to promote, protect, and preserve their health (Mckenzie et al., 2008).

Personal health activities are individual actions and decision-making that affect the health of an individual or his or her immediate family members. These activities may be preventive or curative in nature but seldom directly affect the behaviour of others. Choosing to eat nutritious food, exercise regularly, avoid smoking, etc. are examples of personal health activities. Community health is concerned with the health problems among different groups of population. Such concerns with health problems of population groups lead inevitably to a broad range of interests, i.e. from the cause, prevention and control of diseases, nutritional or otherwise. Thus, community health includes both identification of nutritional and health problems and causes of prevention as well as control of diseases. However, the community health has replaced in some countries, the terms public health, preventive medicine and social medicine. A Euro Symposium in 1966 defined community health as including 'all the personal health and environmental services in any human community, irrespective of whether such services were public or private ones'. In some instances, community health is used as a synonym for 'environmental health'. It is also used to refer to 'community health care'. Therefore, a WHO expert committee in 1973 observed that without further qualification, the term 'community health' is ambiguous, and suggested caution in the use of the term. Community health is defined more broadly and encompasses the entire gamut of community organized efforts for maintaining, protecting and improving the health of the people. It involves motivation of the individual and groups to change the pattern of behaviour. In addition, it also seeks to plan medical care to achieve optimal health of the members of community as a whole.

Previously, the subject of community health was covered in hygiene, public health or preventive and social medicine. In community health, instead of studying individuals as a patient, it is essential to understand that: (i) The patient represents the community, (ii) Diagnosis of disease in the community (referred to as community diagnosis) is essential, and (iii) Planning treatment for the community is the objective. For example, a single case of a cholera patient detected in a village is a danger signal. It shows that the disease is present in the community, there may be many cases of it and unless checked, its spread will grip the whole village. So the appropriate measures for treatment and control of the disease are planned in advance. Since it is a water-borne disease, water sources like river, wells or underground water are examined for infection and accordingly treated. In addition, necessary treatment for the affected people and precautions such as vaccination for vulnerable people is also done. Community diagnosis may require relevant data such as given below. These are collected and interpreted.

(i) Age and sex distribution in the population under study and its distribution in social groups in the community.
(ii) Crude birth rate, infant mortality rate, maternal mortality rate, child death rate, prenatal mortality rate, and neonatal and post-neonatal death rate, etc.
(iii) Incidence and prevalence of certain diseases in the area.

Besides investigating health problems, it is also essential to find out the various social and economic factors in the area influencing the above data. This helps in identifying the basic health needs and health problems faced by the community. After studying all the problems, the priorities are established and community action is planned. This involves a health service system which plans for improvement of water supplies, immunization, health education, control of specific diseases and it requires health legislations. Such health services are planned at individual level, family level and at the level of the community. It is also essential that health care must be planned in such a way that it could be easily utilized by all and encourages people to participate. Another positive feature of community action is that it brings coordination between voluntary organizations and government agencies engaged in overcoming similar problems.

Factors Influencing Community Health

Community health activities are activities that are aimed at protecting or improving the health of a population or community like maintenance of accurate birth and death records, protection of the food and water supply, and participating in vaccination drive, etc. Community health depends on the interplay of a number of complex factors which exert their influence on the lifestyle of the individual. Some of them are beyond the control of the individual, while others are more amenable to personal manipulation. Five major interrelated determinants can be identified. They are: Genetics,

Social and Cultural Factors, Physical Factors, Personal Health Behaviour and Health Services. We will discuss these determinants separately and then we will see their relationship with health.

Genetics

Genetics is a very important determinant of health and it operates in several ways. Certain individuals are born with specific genetic abnormalities, which give rise to particular nutritional problems. It is well known that diabetes shows a familial tendency. Certainly, the children of two diabetic parents have about a one in four chance of developing the disease at some stage of their lives. If only one parent is affected, the chances are reduced to about one in eight. You must have observed that obesity in children is also more common when the parents themselves are over-weight. In this case, environment also has an influence. Environment, lifestyle and nature of occupation may be responsible to predispose the condition of obesity. Heart disease also exhibits familial tendencies. It would be reasonable to suppose that there is an inborn susceptibility to specific diseases and that the manifestation and seriousness of these is a consequence of life experiences. The more negative factors present in the environment or personal behavioural patterns, the more likely the disease will be seen.

Social and Cultural Factors

Social factors are those that arise from the interaction of individuals or groups within the community. For example, who live in the metropolitan cities, where the life is too fast, experience higher rates of stress-related illnesses than those who live in rural societies, where life is simple. Rural areas may not have the same quality of health care facilities which are available to the urban people. Besides those cultural factors also influence the community health. Culture includes the beliefs, traditions and values. There are certain types of health beliefs which are present among the communities and they exercise them. The traditions of specific communities for seeking a particular type of treatment for particular type of health problem depict their health behaviour. Economy of any country or in particular the economy of the community also influences the health of its people and health care facilities. The growth of economy puts its resources towards the health budget and in turn it enhances the health of its people. The national health policy by the government is an important political decision which is directly related to the health of the nation. More coverage of people for providing state health facilities is a government decision and in turn it affects the health of the population. A number of religions have taken a position on health care and health behaviours. For example, some religious communities limit the type of medical treatment their members may receive. Some religious communities do not permit immunization, contraceptions for family planning and certain taboos for certain foods. Some religious communities actively address moral and ethical issues such as abortion, premarital intercourse, and homosexuality. Still other religious communities teach health-promoting codes of living to their members. Obviously, religion can affect a community's health positively or negatively. The influence of social norms can be positive or negative and can change over time. For example, earlier smoking was accepted in the normal routine, however, by making it an offence in the public place, people have started looking down upon a smoker. Thus, the number of smokers in the public places have gone down.

Physical Factors

Physical factors are important in their effects on health. They include the influence of geography, the environment, community size, etc. A community's health problem can be directly influenced by its altitude, latitude, and climate. In tropical country like India, where there is warm and humid temperature, parasitic diseases and infectious diseases are a leading community health problem. Survival from these diseases is made more difficult because poor soil conditions result in inadequate food production and malnutrition. Environmental improvements such as better sanitation and education, and availability of good food, lead to better health and a large proportion of the decline in mortality and morbidity of the country may be attributed to this. In some instances environmental influences have been directly or indirectly detrimental to nutritional status. In case of nutrition, the environment provides a framework within which individual choice can operate. The larger the community, the greater is the range of health problems. Larger population also poses a problem of scarce community resources which leads to the scarcity of food and health care facilities. The ability of a community to effectively plan, organize and utilize its resources can determine whether its size can be used to good advantage.

Personal Health Behaviour

Personal health behaviour denotes the individuals' choice related to health issues. Personal health behaviour is the ultimate decider of the food choices. Individuals will choose whether to smoke or drink, whether to exercise or be immunized and so on. The anti-health effects of personal behaviour can be seen to be manifested as: adoption of undesirable health habits, rejection of health care and non-compliance. Indirectly, a creation of high risk environment and inappropriate behaviour can lead to health problems. Hence, health education is directed as persuading people to act in their own best interests. Socio-economic status is an important consideration in health, whether, a cause or consequence, it is linked with other major detriments. Poor mental capability may lead to reduced progress in education and subsequently restricts job opportunities. Lower income in turn will restrict food choice. Lack of education may affect personal decision-making skills and contribute to underuse of services hence binding more to traditions and beliefs. In order to control this, what is to be done? Should we make an attempt to control environment and services or should we concentrate on influencing personal behaviour?

Health Services

Provision of health services will affect health status. For example, if no nutrition and health education is available, then people are not able to seek help with nutritional problems. It is likely that nutritional problems like Vitamin-A deficiency and other deficiency continue to exist and the nutritional status of the community will be deteriorated. The nature of services whether preventive or curative is also important, otherwise mortality and morbidity rates among vulnerable segments of the community will be on the increasing plane. One of the problems of services is that they are often underutilized by the people who would benefit from them the most. Basing services in the community rather than in the hospital may help to make them more accessible and, therefore, results in increased utilization.

Community Medicine

The term community medicine is a new concept. It is the successor of what has been previously known as public health, preventive medicine, social medicine and community health. Since community medicine is a recent introduction, it has borrowed heavily from the concepts, approaches and methods of public health, preventive medicine and social medicine. The term community medicine means different things in different countries. For example, in most European countries various aspects of community medicine are taught in medical universities under different names, such as general practice, family medicine, community medicine or social medicine. These variations are reflected in the area of the study of health and disease in a population of a particular group or community. The goal of the study is to identify the health problems and needs of particular group or community and then to plan, implement, manage, and finally to evaluate the extent to which health measures can be effectively implemented to meet these needs. The practice of community medicine is related with the community or group not with the individual. Community medicine concept is also used to describe the practice of medicine in the community or group for example by a family physician. The other equivalent term with the family medicine is community medicine. Some other restrict its use to health practice only. In the community, primary health and the integration of medicine with the primary health care of the individual is included. Here the community practitioner or community health team are responsible for health care of the community and also of the individual.

As used in the present context, community medicine is a practice which focuses on the health needs of the community as a whole. The combination of community medicine with 'primary health care' extends the functioning of both elements to health care systems which aims to change the state of health of the community by intervention both at the individual and group level.

Community Diagnosis

The diagnosis of disease in an individual patient is a fundamental idea in medicine. It is based on signs and symptoms and the making of inferences from them. When this is applied to a community, it is known as community diagnosis. The community diagnosis may be defined as the pattern of disease in a community described in terms of the important factors which influence this pattern. The community diagnosis is based on collection and interpretation of the relevant data such as the (a) age and sex distribution of a population or the distribution of population by social groups; (b) vital statistical rates such as the birth rate and death rates; and (c) the incidence and prevalence of the important diseases of the area. In addition, a doctor must be able to find information on a wide variety of social and economic factors that may assist him in making a community diagnosis. The focus is on the identification of the basic health needs and health problems of the community. The needs as felt by the community (some of which may have no connection at all with health) should be next investigated and listed according to priority for community treatment.

Community Treatment: In the community treatment or in community health action, the steps are taken to meet the health needs of the community by integrating the total account of resources available and what the people want in the process of community diagnosis. The actions of the community health are reflected in terms of water supply, immunization, health education, prevention of specific disease, health rights, and health legislations or interventions.

Process of Action for Health at Community Level

Action can be taken at the level of individual, at the level of family and at the level of community. A programme of community action must have the following characteristics: it must utilize all the available resources; it must coordinate the efforts of all other agencies in the community, now termed as inter-sectoral coordination; and it must encourage the full participation of the community in the programme.

Community Responsibility

Health can never be adequately protected by health services without the active understanding and involvement of communities whose health is at stake. Until quite recently throughout the world, the health of people was neglected because of the inadequacy of health resources. They were looked down upon as victims of pathology or as a source of pathology. In the process, they become the target of preventive and therapeutic services. But now, this adverse and apathetic view of people's role in health has changed because of the realization that there are many things which the individual cannot do for himself except through united community effort. The individual and community's responsibility are complimentary, not anti-ethical. Today, it is very necessary to involve communities in a meaningful way. This involves more active participation of families and communities in terms of planning, implementation, utilization, initiation, operation and evaluation of health services. This means that the emphasis has been shifted from health care for the people to health care by the people themselves. There can be three ways in which community can actively participate in the health care:

- Community can provide the facilities of health care.
- Community can share the manpower.
- Community can provide the logistic support and also monetary support.

It also means that the community can be actively involved in planning of health care, the management and also the evaluation of health care process. The most important contribution that can be made by the people is involving themselves in the process of health care and using the health services.

This is particularly true for preventive and protective measures. There can be no universalization pattern of community participation in health services; however, it varies from culture to culture and time to time. There are different economic and social issues which make the differential participation of the community in the health services. The social structure of Indian society includes caste and class as the important elements; therefore, the participation of community also revolves around these elements. Most of the times rigidity of caste-based social structure poses a threat in the smooth participation of community for the health services. Several researchers have attempted to elaborate on the participation of the community in the developmental activities. Cohen and Uphoff (1980) have described the community participation as 'people's involvement in decision-making process about what would be done and how; their involvement in implementing the programmes and decisions by contributing various resources their sharing in the benefits of developmental programmes; and/or their involvement in efforts to evaluate such programmes'. Taken together, these four kinds of involvement appear to encompass most of what would generally be referred to as participation in developmental activities. They further regarded participation as a process in which there is significant involvement of people in situation or actions which ultimately enhance their well-being in terms of security, health or self-esteem. Participation in the developmental processes implies stimulating individuals to take the initiative and mobilizing people to work for the overall social development. United Nations Commission for Social Development Decision defines participation as a process of activities comprising people's involvement in the decision-making, contribution to the development efforts and sharing the benefits delivered from there.

We can summarize the features of the community participation: decentralization in the process of decision-making; participation of the people in setting the goals and their prioritization; sharing of the benefits by masses; development of mechanism of control for assessing the outcome; involvement in the efforts to evaluate the programme; and involvement/self-help for sustaining the programme without external help. The importance of community participation in the developmental activities forms the foundation of the concept of primary health care adopted by the nations of the world at Alma-Ata in 1978, in order to achieve the 'Health for All' by 2000 AD. The conference declaration says: 'Primary health care is very essential at the grass-root level. The health care should be socially acceptable to the community. It should also be universally accessible to the individuals, families in the community. People should actively participate with their complete involvement so that the community and ultimately the country can be benefitted. In this way the country can maintain its development at every stage in terms of self-reliance and self-determination' (WHO-UNICEF, 1978). It is felt that community participation in health care would lead to measure of self-reliance and self-help. The aim is to provide individuals and communities with means to promote their well-being and, in the process, to participate in their own health care. It has been estimated that 65 to 85 per cent of all health care is self-care or is care provided by the family. Therefore, providing means of self-health care would be a great help in achieving the self-reliance in health care. Community participation in health care would also provide an indirect advantage to health personnels by developing continuous dialogue between them and the rest of the community. Such an interaction would enable health personnels to acquire a better understanding of the community's feelings, the level of the aspirations and the pattern of its organization and communication. For their part, people will learn to identify their real health needs, understand the government strategy for primary health care and involve themselves in promoting community action for self-health care. India implemented the Community Health Volunteer or Health Guide Scheme to seek community participation in the primary health care and to cater to the day-to-day health needs of the rural people at their doorstep. Under this scheme, a volunteer is chosen by the village community and is given short-term training (by the health department) in simple medical and basic health care. He is expected to promote the health education, to ensure the ministration of preventive health care measures, to provide the curative services for simple ailments, and to refer complicated cases to the community health centres of hospitals at referral hospitals. This volunteer is also expected to look after the maternal and child health services and work for the acceptance of family planning in the community. The overall philosophy is that the responsibility of health care which had hitherto largely been with the government, now, for the first time, also rests in the hands of the people. The Health Guide being a man of the community is accountable to the community and the community in turn is supposed to supervise his work.

Community Health Programme

The mid-1970s saw the emergence of Community Health Worker Programme (CHWP) stated by non-governmental sector and other voluntary agencies. It was concluded that a group of trained and expert health workers could significantly improve health outcomes in spite of lower literacy levels and educational qualifications. Evaluation of various Community Health Worker Programmes found that there are some important factors which contribute to the success of community health programmes. These are: strong leadership which provides support and training to the other workers; duration of programme must be at least 5–10 years; have a systematic and good quality of referral linkages where higher degree of illness can be handled; and women should also be a part of health care providers. However, the community health programmes which are run by NGOs are dependent on external funding; therefore, they always face the threat of sustainability. On the other side, government programmes fail due to lack of transparency in the recruitment system, poor referral system, overemphasis on curative system and ignoring the preventive aspect. Community Health Care Programmes play a very important role in the health sector reforms. They not only provide primary education and health services rather they are also engaged in bringing awareness for health rights. They are prime movers of health right movements. We need to have Community Health Programmes and simultaneously there is also a need to restructure and strengthen public services.

With the Community Health Programme, Community Health Volunteers (CHVs) are instrumental in carrying out the task of primary prevention of public health efforts. CHVs are the vital links between the community and the health programme. There are both male and female Community Health Volunteers. They are supposed to conduct home visits and respond to various health needs including immunization, preparing slides of malaria, family planning, identifying pregnant and lactating mothers, and also do the disease surveillance. Since they are a part of the community, therefore they are quite familiar with the culture, norms and practices of the community in the various spheres of social and community life. They are also treated as insiders by the community people and not treated as outsiders and thus are close to the people. This establishes their credibility in the community which they serve.

Examples of Community Health Programme: We found one example among the successful stories of the community programmes which are run in different parts of the country. Aga Khan Health Service, India (AKHS, I), implemented the Gujarat Health Project among the rural residents of 54 villages in Junagadh, Patan, and Banaskantha districts of Sidhpur region. Basically the project was targeted for increasing the access to quality of health care series so that the health status of the community can be increased. The health services which are provided to the rural communities are integrated at the first level. Another important aspect is the involvement of local people by giving ownership and required training. This has ultimately enhanced their managerial capabilities and helped in ensuring financial sustainability with the result that incidence of disease and infections are reduced to a considerable extent. It was basically operated at three levels: health centres, diagnostic centres and community volunteers. They also ensured that the benefits reach out to the wider and dispersed rural community.

Summing up

A number of key terms are associated with the study of community health, including, public health and individual health. The factors that affect the health of a community are genetics, social and cultural factors, physical factors, personal health behaviour and health services. Community medicine identifies the health and disease in the population of a defined community or group. And then it plans to meet effectively the needs of community. Community treatment or community action is the total of actions taken for the health needs of the community by taking care of its available resources and the wishes of people which are an outcome of community diagnosis process.

Health can never be adequately protected by health services without the active understanding and involvement of communities whose health is at stake. It requires various community health programmes to improve the health of the people. These programmes include sanitation, drinking water mission, mass vaccination, and rural health programme which are specifically targeted for a particular community to improve its health.

References

Ahmed, S.U. (1980), 'Urban Problems and Government Policies: A Case Study of the City of Dacca, 1810–30', in K. Ballhatchet and J.B. Harrison (eds), *The City in South Asia*, London: Curzon Press.

Annual Abstract of Statistics for East India (1870).

Annual Reports of the Sanitary Commissioner with Government of India (1865).

Anstey, V. (1936), *The Economic Development of India*, London: Longmans.

Arnold, D. (1985), 'Medical Priorities and Practice in Nineteenth Century British India', *South Asia Research*, 5(2): 167–86.

Ballhatchet, K. (1980), *Race, Sex and Class under the Raj*, New Delhi: Vikas.

Census of India (1921), Delhi: Government of India.

Farrell, J.S. (1973), *The Siege of Krishnapur*, London: Penguin.

Fendall, R. (1984), 'We Expect Too Much from Community Health Workers', *World Health Forum*, 5: 300.

Gillion, K.L. (1968), *Ahmedabad: A Study in Indian Urban History*, Berkeley, CA: University of California Press.

Harrison, J.B. (1980), 'Allahabad: A Sanitary History', in K. Ballhatchet and J.B. Harrison (eds), *The City in South Asia*, London: Curzon Press.

Harvey, W. (1895), 'Presidential Address', in *Proceedings of the First Indian Medical Congress*, Calcutta: Indian Medical Gazette.

Hume, J. (1984), 'Colonialism and Sanitary Medicine: The Development of Preventive Health Policy in the Punjab, 1860–1900', *Modern Asian Studies*, 20(4): 703–24.

Jaggi, O.P. (1979), *Western Medicine in India: Medical Education and Research*, Delhi: Atma Ram.

Jeffery, Roger (1988), *The Politics of Health in India*, London: University of California Press.

King, M. (ed.) (1966), *Medical Care in Developing Countries*, Nairobi: Oxford University Press.

Klein, I. (1973), 'Death in India', *Journal of Asian Studies*, 32(4): 639–59.

Lalonde, M. (1975), *A New Perspective on the Health of Canadians: A Working Document*, Ottawa: Information Canada.

Mahler, H. (1977), 'Blueprint for Health of All', *WHO Chronicle*, 31(12): 491–98.

—— (1979), 'Urbanization and the Introduction of Modern Town Planning Ideas in India, 1900–1925', in K.N. Chaudhuri and C.J. Dewey (eds), *Economy and Society*, Oxford: Oxfam.

Morley, David et al. (1984), *Practising Health for All*, New York: Oxford University Press.

Ramasubban, R. (1984), 'Public Health and Medical Research in India: Their Origins under the Impact of British Colonial Policy', *Stockholm: SAREC Report*, No. 4, Swedish Agency for Research Cooperation with Developing Countries.

Rao, K.N. (1966), *The Nation's Health*, Delhi: Publications Division.

Roemer, M.I. (1972), 'Evaluation of Community Health Centres', *Public Health Papers*, No. 48, Geneva: WHO.

Sanitary Commission (1865), *Report of the Commissioner Appointed to Inquire into the Sanitary State of the Army in India*, London: Her Majesty's Stationery Office.

WHO and UNICEF (1978a), *Primary Health Care: Report of the International Conference on Primary Health Care, Alma Ata, USSR*, 6–12 September, Geneva: WHO.

—— (1978b), *Health for All*, Series No. 1, Geneva: WHO.

9

Social Epidemiology

Cause of Diseases and their Changing Patterns

Contemporary approaches favour a multicausal and processual model of the way an individual stays well or becomes ill. The attack is multicausal because the health state of the most compelling interest appears to rest on a concatenation of biological vulnerability, psychological dynamics, and social situational expectations. It is processual because we do not conceive of illness as a single event that impinges on a stationary organism but, instead, as a sequence of malfunctioning phased in and out with the exigencies of experiences as individuals and families move along the arc of life. The current thrust of social epidemiology may be phrased – their total configuration of actions and reactions in social time and space – and health risks to which those populations are vulnerable.

In this chapter we will learn about measures to reduce infectious diseases that have changed over time. We will also introduce you to the changing patterns of infectious diseases and to the factors underlying these changes, and know that these in turn have influenced the way we have tried to contain infectious diseases. Further, we will let you know about the emergence of lifestyle diseases and the underlying causes for the same.

Evolution of Human Diseases

Infectious diseases have afflicted mankind since the dawn of civilization. Understanding the history of interrelationship between the agents responsible and their host provides insights into current trends of infectious diseases, some understanding of how environmental and social changes impact upon disease, and how responses to public health threats were frequently mirrored in the past.

The human race originated in the tropical climate of Africa and was affected by the same parasites as other primates in these areas. As early hunters migrated into more temperate zones, they were exposed to the infections agents. During this period, humans might have been relatively free of infectious diseases. Thereafter, as hunting gave way to agriculture, population grew and stabilized. The development of agriculture, and with it a situation in which domestic animals lived in close proximity to humans, created the opportunity for many infections such as measles to spread to humans. The increase in population size and density provided the ideal conditions for further person-to-person spread of the infectious micro-organisms. Humans, food, and water became established reservoir for many infectious agents.

Before understanding the causal factors of disease, the responses towards diseases were more focused on individual, community, ethnic groups as the originators of disease. The Jewish population in Europe was subjected to severe laws on food preparation, 900 Jews were burnt alive at Strasbourg in 1349, even before the plague arrived. There was a common relationship between the minority population and disease and in turn segregating that population (Coker, Pomerleau and Mckee, 2005: 150).

Control of infectious diseases became possible through the work of Robert Loch and Louis Pasteur. The understanding of the 'germ theory' was first plausibly articulated in the 1870s.

Natural History of Disease

Disease results from a complex interaction between man, an agent (or cause of disease) and the environment. The term natural history of disease is a key concept in epidemiology. It signifies the way in which a disease evolves over time from the earliest stage of its pre-pathogenesis phase to its termination as recovery, disability or death, in the absence of treatment or prevention. Each disease has its own unique natural history, which is not necessarily the same in all individuals; so much so, any general formulation of the natural history of disease is necessarily arbitrary. It is customary to describe the natural history of disease as consisting of two phases: pre-pathogenesis and pathogenesis. Let us consider the events that take place in the natural history of disease, using infectious disease as a principal model (Leavell and Clark, 1965).

Pre-Pathogenesis Phase

This refers to the period preliminary to the onset of disease in man. The disease agent has not yet entered man, but the factors which favour its interaction with the human host already exist in the environment. This situation is frequently referred to as 'man in the midst of disease' or 'man exposed to the risk of disease'. Potentially we are all in the pre-pathogenesis phase of many diseases, both communicable and non-communicable.

The causative factors of disease may be classified as agent, host and environment. These three factors are referred to as epidemiological triad. The mere presence of agent, host and favourable environmental factors in the pre-pathogenesis period is not sufficient to start the disease in man. What is required is an interaction of these three factors to initiate the disease process in man. The agent, host and environment operating in combination determine not only the onset of disease which may range from a single case to epidemics but also the distribution of disease in the community.

Pathogenesis Phase

The pathogenesis phase begins with the entry of the disease 'agent' in the susceptible human host. The further events in the pathogenesis phase are clear-cut in infectious diseases, i.e. the disease agent multiplies and induces tissue and physiologic changes, the disease progresses through a period of incubation and later through early and late pathogenesis. The final outcome of the disease may be recovery, disability or death. The pathogenesis phase may be modified by intervention measures such as immunization and chemotherapy.

It is useful to remember at this stage that the host's reaction to infection with a disease agent is not predictable. That is, the infection may be clinical or sub-clinical; typical or atypical; or the host may become a carrier with or without having developed clinical disease as in the case of diphtheria and poliomyelitis.

In chronic diseases (e.g. coronary heart diseases, hypertension, cancer), the early pathogenesis phase is less dramatic. This phase in chronic diseases is referred to as pre-symptomatic phase. During the pre-symptomatic stage, there is no manifest disease. The pathological changes are essentially below the level of the 'clinical horizon'. The clinical stage begins when recognizable signs or symptoms appear. By the time signs and symptoms appear, the disease phase is already well advanced into the late pathogenesis phase. In many chronic diseases, the agent-host-environmental interactions are not yet well understood.

Agent Factors

The first link in the chain of disease transmission is a disease agent. The disease 'agent' is defined as a substance, living or non-living, or a force, tangible or intangible, the excessive presence or relative lack of which may initiate or perpetuate a disease process. A disease may have a single agent, a number of independent alternative agents or a complex of two or more factors whose combined presence is essential for the growth of the disease.

Disease agents may be classified broadly into the following groups:

Biological Agents

These are living agents of diseases viz. viruses, rickettsiae, fungi, bacteria, protozoa and metazoan. These agents exhibit certain 'host related' biological properties such as (i) infectivity: this is the ability of an infectious agent to invade and multiply (produce infection) in a host; (ii) pathogenicity: this is the ability to induce clinically apparent illness; and (iii) virulence: this is defined as the proportion of clinical cases resulting in severe clinical manifestations (including sequelae). The case fatality rate is one way of measuring virulence (Mausner and Kramer, 1985).

Nutrient Agents

These can be proteins, fats, carbohydrates, vitamins, minerals and water. Any excess or deficiency of the intake of nutritive elements may result in nutritional disorders. Protein energy malnutrition (PEM), anaemia, goitre, obesity and vitamin deficiencies are some of the current nutritional problems in many countries.

Physical Agents

Exposure to excessive heat, cold, humidity, pressure, radiation, electricity, sound, etc. may result in illness.

Chemical Agents

Some of the chemicals may be produced in the body as a result of derangement of function , e.g. urea (uraemia), serum bilirubin (jaundice), ketones (ketosis), uric acid (gout), calcium carbonate (kidney stones, etc.) and results in diseases. These are endogenous in nature. Exogenous agents arising outside of human host are , e.g. allergens, metals, fumes, dust, gases, insecticides, etc. These may be acquired by inhalation, ingestion or inoculation.

Mechanical Agents

Exposure to chronic friction and other mechanical forces may result in crushing, tearing, sprains, dislocations and even death.

Absence or Insufficiency or Excess of a Factor Necessary to Health

These may be (i) chemical factors: e.g. hormones (insulin, oestrogens) and enzymes; (ii) nutrient factors: like protein, fats, minerals, vitamins etc.; (iii) lack of structure: e.g. thymus; (iv) lack of part of structure: e.g. cardiac defects; (v) chromosomal factors: e.g. mongolism, turner syndrome; and (vi) immunological factors: e.g. agammaglobulinaemia.

Social Agents

It is also necessary to consider social agents of disease. These are poverty, smoking, abuse of drugs and alcohol, unhealthy lifestyles, social isolation and maternal deprivation, etc.

Host Factors

In epidemiological terminology, the human host is referred to as 'soil' and the disease agent as 'seed'. In some situations, host factors play a major role in determining the outcome of an individual's exposure to infection (e.g. tuberculosis).

The host factors may be classified as (i) demographic characteristics such as age, sex, ethnicity; (ii) biological characteristics such as genetic factors, biochemical levels of the blood (e.g. cholesterol), blood groups and enzymes, cellular constituents of the blood, immunological factors, and physiological function of different organ systems of the body (e.g. blood pressure, forced expiratory ventilation), etc.; (iii) social and economic characteristics such as socio-economic status, education, occupation, stress, marital status, housing, etc.; and (iv) lifestyle factors such as personality traits, living habits, nutrition, physical exercise, use of alcohol, drugs and smoking, and behavioural patterns, etc. The association of a particular disease with a specific set of host factors frequently provides an insight into the cause of disease.

Environmental Factors

The study of disease is really the study of man and his environment. Hundreds of millions of people are affected by preventable diseases originating in the environment in which they live. For human beings the environment is not limited, as it normally is for plants and animals, to a set of climatic factors. For example, for many social and economic conditions are more important than the mean annual temperature. Thus, the concept of environment is defined as 'all that which is external to the individual human host'. This includes all of man's external surroundings such as air, water, food and housing, etc.

The environment of man has been divided into three components: physical, biological and psychosocial.

The term physical environment is applied to non-living things and physical factors (e.g. air, water, soil, housing, climate, geography, heat, light, noise, debris, radiation, etc.) with which man is in constant interaction. Man's victory over his physical environment has been responsible for most of the improvement in health during the past century. In most developing countries, defective environment (e.g. lack of sanitation) continues to be the main health problem. Man has altered practically everything in his physical environment to his advantage. In doing so, he has created for himself a host of new health problems such as air pollution, water pollution, noise pollution, urbanization, radiation hazards, etc. The increasing use of electrical and electronic devices, including the rapid growth of telecommunication system (e.g. satellite systems), radio broadcasting, television transmitters and radar installations have increased the possibility of human exposure to electromagnetic energy.

The biological environment is the universe of living things which surrounds man, including man himself. The living things are the viruses and other microbial agents, insects, rodents, animals and plants. These are constantly working for their survival, and in this process, some of them act as disease-producing agents, reservoirs of infection, intermediate hosts and vectors of disease. Between the members of the ecological system (which includes man), there is constant adjustment and readjustment. For the most part, the parties try to achieve a harmonious inter-relationship, or a state of peaceful co-existence, even though this may not always be enduring.

It is difficult to define psychosocial environment against the background of the highly varied social, economic and cultural contexts of different countries and their social standards and value systems. It includes a complex of psychosocial factors which are defined as 'those factors affecting personal health, health care and community well-being that stem from the psychosocial make-up of individuals and the structure and functions of social groups' (WHO, 1976). They include cultural values, customs, habits, beliefs, attitudes, morals, religion, education, lifestyles, community life, health services and social and political organization.

In addition to this broad aspect of psychosocial environment, man is in constant interaction with that part of the social environment known as 'people'. He is a member of a social group, the member of a family, of a caste, of a community and of a nation. Between the individual and other members of the group, there can be harmony or disharmony, interests and points of view that are shared or that are in conflict. The behaviour of one individual can affect others more or less directly; conflict and tension between the individual and the group as a whole or between the individual and other members of the group can yield great distress. The law of land, customs, attitudes, beliefs and traditions all regulate the interactions among groups of individuals and families.

Because of the fact that man exists concurrently in so many environmental contexts, it has become customary to speak of man in his 'total environment'. The social environment is so inextricably linked with the physical and biological environments that it is realistic and necessary to view the human environment in whole to promote health in the human environment. A stable and harmonious equilibrium between man and his environment is needed to reduce man's vulnerability to disease and to permit him to lead a more productive and satisfying life.

Defining Disease

Until late in the 19th century, disease had been regarded as resulting from a lack of harmony between the sick person and his environment. Louis Pasteur, Robert Koch, and their followers took a far simpler and more direct view of the problem. They showed by laboratory experiments that disease could be produced at will by the mere artifice of introducing a single factor – a virulent micro-oraganism – into a healthy animal. However, it negates the philosophical view of health as an equilibrium and to render obsolete the traditional art of medicine. In other words, life depends not only upon the reactions through which the individual manages to grow and to reproduce itself but also upon the operation of the control mechanisms which permit the maintenance of individuality. The dual concept of fitness to the external environment and fixity of the internal environment is the modern expression of the Hippocratic dictum that health is a universal sympathy.

It is implicit in the Hippocratic teachings that both health and disease are under the control of natural laws and reflect the influence exerted by the environment and the way of life. Accordingly, health depends upon a state of equilibrium among the various internal factors which govern the operations of the body and the mind; this equilibrium in turn is reached only when man lives in harmony with his external environment.

Rudolf Virchow, inspired by the philosophers of the Enlightenment who believed that poverty was the breeder of the disease, adds that it was the responsibility of physicians to support social reforms that would reconstruct society according to a pattern favourable to the health of man. Thus, according to Virchow, the treatment of individual cases is only a small aspect of medicine. More important is the control of crowd's disease which demand social and, if need be, political action. In this light, medicine is a social science.

Thus, health and disease cannot be defined merely in terms of anatomical, physiological, and mental attributes. Their real measure is the ability of the individual to function in a manner acceptable to himself and to the group of which he is a part.

There have been many attempts to define disease. *Webster* defines disease as 'a condition in which body health is impaired, a departure from a state of health, an alternation of the human body interrupting the performance of vital functions'. The *Oxford English Dictionary* defines disease as 'a condition of the body or some part or organ of the body in which its functions are disrupted or deranged'. From an ecological point of view, disease is defined as 'a maladjustment of the human organism to the environment' (Alan, 1956). From a sociological point of view, disease is considered a social phenomenon, occurring in all societies (Schuman, 1963) and is defined and fought in terms of the particular cultural forces prevalent in the society. The simplest definition is, of course, that disease is just the opposite of health, i.e. any deviation from normal functioning or state of complete physical or mental well-being – since health and disease are mutually exclusive. These definitions are considered inadequate because they do not give a criterion by which to decide when a disease state begins, nor do they lend themselves to measurement of disease.

The WHO has defined health but not disease. This is because disease has many shades ('spectrum of disease') ranging from inapparent (subclinical) cases to severe manifest illness. Some diseases commence acutely (e.g. food poisoning), and some insidiously (e.g. mental illness, rheumatoid arthritis). In some diseases, a 'career' state occurs in which the individual remains outwardly healthy, and is able to infect others (e.g. typhoid fever). In some instances, the same organism may cause more than one clinical manifestation (e.g. streptococcus). In some cases, the same disease may be caused by more than one organism (e.g. diarrhoea). Some diseases have a short course, and some a prolonged course. It is easy to determine illness when the signs and symptoms are manifest, but in many diseases the borderline between normal and abnormal is indistinct as in the case of diabetes, hypertension and mental illness. The end point or final outcome of disease is variable, i.e. recovery, disability or death of the host.

Distinction is also between the words disease, illness and sickness which are not wholly synonymous. The term 'disease' literally means 'without ease' (uneasiness) – disease, the opposite of ease – when something is wrong with bodily function. 'Illness' refers not only to the presence of a specific disease, but also to the individual's perceptions and behaviour in response to the disease, as well as the impact of that disease on the psychosocial environment (Ouslander and Beck, 1982). 'Sickness' refers to a state of social dysfunction. Susser and Watson (1971) have suggested the following usage:

- Disease is a physiological/psychological dysfunction.
- Illness is a subjective state of the person who feels aware of not being well.
- Sickness is a state of social dysfunction, i.e. a role that the individual assumes when ill (sickness role).

The clinician sees people who are ill rather than the diseases which he must diagnose and treat. However, it is possible to be a victim of disease without feeling ill, and to be ill without signs of physical impairment. In short, an adequate definition of disease is yet to be found, a definition that is satisfactory or acceptable to the epidemiologist, clinician, sociologist and the statistician.

Infectious Versus Non-Communicable Diseases

The nature of the disease pattern in any society has important implications as regards the type of health strategy adopted. From the point of view of health planners, there is a crucial difference between infectious and non-communicable diseases. Infectious diseases are spread primarily due to contact with an infected person. The contact may be direct. Such as when an individual comes close or touches an infected person, or indirect, such as when an insect vector or a water source carries infectious material between people. Infectious diseases often occur as epidemics, and although some are associated with a particular age group, most affect people of all ages. A healthy individual may have a better chance of recovery, but will not necessarily be able to avoid contracting an infection unless they have already developed a specific immunity to it. Strategies to control the spread of infectious diseases therefore focus on immunizing populations against specific viruses, isolating infected cases and preventing transmission via water and insect vectors.

In contrast, the risk of developing Non-Communicable Diseases (NCDs) is strongly associated with an individual's physical condition. Factors that increase the propensity to develop NCDs are termed 'lifestyle risk factors', and include lack of exercise, excess body weight, smoking and high rates of alcohol consumption. Individuals of any age whose resistance is weakened by one or more of these risk factors are more likely to develop NCDs than those who are not. In some instances, an infectious disease may increase the risk of developing a specific NCD for example, hepatitis B increases the risk of liver cancer, but more often NCDs occur independently of infection (McMurrary and Smith, 2001).

In addition to above factors, the broader aspects of wealth distribution, in both domestic and international context, are also significant determinants of risk. Lifestyle choice may have been adopted because of limitations in available options. For example, poor diet may be due to unavailability or high market prices of particular foodstuffs. Lack of education may be another factor, and this too could be seen in terms of wealth and availability of educational opportunities.

Whereas the prevention of infectious disease is a relatively centralized activity, which can be tackled with broad-brush public health measures, the reduction of NCDs is largely the responsibility of individual citizens. Health authorities can do little more than provide health education and promote healthy lifestyles. No matter how much effort is put into health education campaigns, their success depends on the extent to which people adopt the healthy practices they are taught. Unfortunately, many factors can intervene to prevent people from adopting healthy lifestyles, even when they are told about the importance of doing so. As a consequence, unhealthy lifestyle habits, including poor diets, insufficient exercise, smoking and heavy drinking, have become major causes of illness and death in most developed countries and also in fast developing countries. Unhealthy lifestyles are costly because they erode the human resource base and the illnesses they cause require expensive treatments. Most developing countries are less able to afford the high costs of investing in health care which in turn is the investment in economic and social development. Lifestyle may, thus, present a significant barrier to economic and social progress.

Emergent and Re-Emergent Infectious Disease

The nature of infectious diseases is changing not only in terms of magnitude and the inability of science to provide all the answers but also for the following reasons. Emerging infectious diseases are those infections in human that have been seen in recent years or are threatening to increase in near future. Most notable are Severe Acute Respiratory Syndrome (SARS), Avian Influenza (Bird Flu), Ebola Hemorrhagic Fever, resulting from apparently new organisms. Ancient diseases such as tuberculosis and diphtheria are re-emerging as serious threats to public health (often having 'disappeared' only in affluent western societies). Novel agents are being implicated in the causation of a number of clinical syndromes (for example, previous human T-Cell lymphotropic viruses I and II, and a number of human herpes viruses) (Coker, Pomerleau and Mckee, 2005: 150).

The spectre of drug resistant organisms, unresponsive to anti-microbial agents, has emerged over the past 65 years. Multi-drug resistance of infectious micro-organisms is a major global health problem. Factors beyond the immediate relationship of microbe and pathogenic host defences influence the growth and spread of infectious diseases. For example, international travel and commerce is known to be associated with the spread of malaria, cholera and pneumococcal pneumonia.

Lifestyle Diseases

Indian economy is robust but, the same cannot be said about the country's workforce. In 2005 alone, the estimated loss to our national income from diseases like heart ailments, stroke and diabetes was a staggering $ 9 billion. And these losses are expected to mount in the near future. Over the next 10 years, India may lose more than $ 200 billion due to employee sickness. Some firms are already losing about 14 per cent of their annual working days – more than 51 days in a year – due to illnesses in its workforce. Not surprising, since the per capita government health expenditure in India is one of the lowest in the world, a dismal $ 7 as against $ 2,548 in the US. In fact, public spending on health has stagnated at 0.9 per cent of the GDP since the mid-1980s. These are some of the findings released by the Indian Council for Research on International Economic Relations (ICRIER) in its study 'Impact of Preventive Health Care on Indian Industry and Economy'. The study based on a survey of disparate companies across 15 states of India, showed that 12 per cent of blue-collar workers were at high risk of getting a debilitating disease compared to 4 per cent of the medium-level and senior-level employees. While blue-collar workers are generally afflicted with acute as well as chronic infectious diseases like tuberculosis and AIDS, senior executives are more prone to lifestyle diseases, owing to lack of exercise and dietary control. ICRIER's survey corroborates what Apollo Hospitals found in its study 'Health and Wellness Survey (2003)'. The study said that more than half of the executives were prone to lifestyle diseases. And nearly 71 per cent of the employees and 82 per cent of the CEOs were overweight. It had also found nearly 48 per cent of the employees and 69 per cent of CEOs were physically unfit. The direct impact of employees' sickness is reflected in man-days lost.

Human insulin (diabetes) and atorvastatin (cholesterol lowering drugs) registered a growth of nearly 40 per cent and 35 per cent respectively during January–December 2007, in value terms. Though the total size of these segments is at present a small proportion of the total industry at nearly ₹ 850 crore, but it is growing at a fast pace. In volume terms too, the growth was 27.75 per cent and 31.25 per cent respectively, according to the lowest data from ORG-IMS. As against this, other major segments, anti-infectives, antibiotics and pain killers, have recorded lower growth rates.

Biocon Chairman and MD Kiran M. Shaw says, 'Diabetes is a global pandemic where insulins occupy the largest share, registering over 30 per cent growth. This segment will only increase in terms of size and opportunity, considering lifestyle is causing juvenile diabetes and people are prone to diabetes at younger ages'.

Studies have estimated that in a little over a decade from now, chronic diseases like diabetes, hypertension, heart attack, cancer and AIDS would account for over 65 per cent of deaths in India compared to 53 per cent in 2005. Also, nearly 11 per cent of Indians urban population above the age of 15 have diabetes.

Similarly, stress both at work and at home is going to take a further toll with the number of people suffering from hypertension estimated to rise 213.5 million in 2025, compared to 118.2 million in 2000 representing an 80 per cent rise.

To prevent cardiovascular diseases (CVD), cholesterol lowering drugs, also called statins, are used extensively for lowering of bad cholesterol (LDL). Says Sanjeev Dani, Senior Vice President of Ranbaxy, 'With the help of cardiologists, Ranbaxy conducts community programmes to encourage lifestyle changes as a first step to control cholesterol, failing which many patients may require prescription of a statin like Atorvastatin, Rosuvastatin or even other lipid lowering drugs like finofibrate. Ranbaxy has been a pioneer in establishing the concept of statins and lipid lowering drugs in India'.

'The awareness about cholesterol among Indians has increased manifold in recent times. The physicians have also appreciated the overwhelming body of evidence of benefits associated with aggressive lowering of lipids', he adds.

Nearly 50 per cent of CVD related deaths in India occur below the age of 70, compared with just 22 per cent in the West. This trend is particularly alarming because of its potential impact on one of Asia's fastest growing economies.

In 2000, for example, India lost more than five times as many years of economically productive life to cardiovascular disease than did the US, where most of those killed by heart disease are above retirement age.

Global Burden of Diseases

In the 'Global Burden of Disease Study 2013' estimated yearly deaths for 188 countries between 1990 and 2013 shows that number of deaths increased from 47.5 million to 54.9 million. Global progress masked variation by age and sex; for children, average absolute differences between countries decreased but relative differences increased. Decomposition of global and regional life expectancy showed the prominent role of reductions in age-standardized death rates for cardiovascular diseases and cancers in high-income regions, and reductions in child deaths from diarrhoea, lower respiratory tract infections, and neonatal causes in low-income regions.

Factors Affecting the Growth and Spread of Infectious Disease

Demographic Changes and Human Behaviour

The world population is growing fast in spite of falling birth rates in developed countries. Overcrowding will increase and this will promote the spread of infectious diseases, including dengue, etc. There is also a link between poverty, malnutrition and infectious disease. Epidemics result from transmission through rapid person-to-person spread amongst susceptible population or through the carriage of vectors. Changes in behaviour, including sexual behaviour and injecting drug use, are associated with changes in the incidence of several infectious diseases.

Technological Development

The development and application of new technologies may have deleterious effects. The epidemic of Bovine Spongiform Encepthalopathy (BSE), which by 2001 had afflicted over 1,79,000 cows in great Britain, has been ascribed to technological changes in the animal and human food chain.

Economic Development

Development projects such as the building of dams, irrigation schemes, hydroelectric power plants, and roads, which are intended to improve social well-being, may have negative effects that include displacement of people, chronic food deficiency, and the development of new and more pernicious forms of poverty.

Climate Changes

Global warming over the next century will result in increase in food productivity in some areas and falls in others. Some low-lying areas will suffer flooding and loss of agricultural land and contamination of fresh water supplies.

Terrorism and Conflict

Wars and conflict environments affect micro-organisms. The movements of large number of people, unhygienic living conditions, malnutrition, and the destruction of public infrastructures encourage diseases and their spread. The pollution of water supplies and catapulting of diseased human corpses into besieged cities are early examples of biological warfare.

Epidemiology of Disease

Epidemiology is the basic science of preventive and social medicine. Although of ancient lineage, it made only slow progress up to the start of this century. Epidemiology has evolved rapidly during the past three decades. Its ramifications cover not only study of disease distribution and causation (and thereby prevention), but also health and health-related events occurring in human populations. Modern epidemiology has entered the most exciting phase of its evolution. By identifying risk factors of chronic disease, evaluating treatment modalities and health services, it has provided new opportunities for prevention, treatment, planning and improving the effectiveness and efficiency of health services.

The foundation of epidemiology was laid in the 19th century, when a few classic studies made a major contribution to the saving of life. Mention is made of an Epidemiological Society in London in 1850s under the presidency of the Earl of Shaftesbury. The Society's main concern was the investigation of infectious diseases. The sudden growth of bacteriology had smothered the development of epidemiology in the universities.

One may define epidemiology as the study of the distribution and determinants of health-related states and events in populations, and the application of this study to control health problems. The diseases included in the subject matter have increased from those which occur in epidemics to include those infectious diseases which are endemic in nature, and more recently chronic diseases, accidents and mental health. Inherent in the definition of epidemiology is measurement of frequency of disease, disability or death, and summary of this information in the form of rates and ratios (e.g. prevalence rate, incidence rate, death rate, etc.). Thus, the basic measures of disease frequency are a rate or ratio. These rates are essential for comparing disease frequency in different populations or subgroups of the same population in relation to suspected causal factors. Such comparisons may yield important clues to disease aetiology.

The best study of mankind is man. This statement emphasizes the importance of making the best use of observations on individuals or populations exposed to suspected factors of disease. Meticulous observations made in Africa by Burkitt led to the eventual incrimination that Epstein-Barr virus has the aetiological factor (possibly conditioned by other factors such as material infection) of the type of cancer known as Burkitt's lymphoma. It was the epidemiological study in New Guinea of 'Kuru' of a hereditary neurological disorder that led to the discovery of slow virus infections as the cause of chronic degenerative neurological disorders in human beings.

Epidemiology and Health Behaviour

Epidemiology has developed an increasingly interdisciplinary focus on human behaviour and its cultural and social influences as causes and prevention of diseases. Research increasingly has aimed at the development of strategies making use of multiple levels of communication for mass intervention in behaviourally-based disease processes. Cardiovascular disease was the first major target of research in most industrialized countries as it is not only the leading cause of death, but is among the first to be linked strongly to socially and culturally influenced behavioural variables. Initial intervention research in Finland during the

1970s has been followed by major demonstration projects in Unites States (California, Minnesota, Rhode Island, and Pennsylvania) and worldwide (Blackburn, 1983). These have been strongly influenced by a variety of fields including social marketing, community analysis, organization, and 'empowerment' strategies as frameworks for the mobilization of communities and the management of social and behavioural change through lifestyle campaigns (Finnegan, Bracht and Viswanath, 1989).

Health Care Facilities and Treatment of Diseases

Many preventable communicable diseases are growing unchecked and under-nutrition linked health problems continue to plague India, with a new set of infectious diseases rearing their ugly heads (HIV/AIDS, drug-resistant TB). Along with it, chronic diseases have begun to rise rapidly and significantly (NCMH, 2005). Although the increase in reporting of ailments in general cannot be considered necessarily as an indicator of deteriorating conditions of population health, the same can be the reflection of two important situations: (a) an increased morbidity burden in the country, and (b) increased health-seeking behaviour of the population in general (Yazbeck and Peters et al., 2002). On both counts, the demand for health care treatment is likely to significantly increase leading to considerable pressure on the existing health care facilities in the country (Selvaraj and Karan, 2009).

Evidence from large household sample surveys (NSSO) suggests that reporting of short duration ailments (based on 15 days recall) has increased almost by four times during the last two decades from approximately 2.4 per cent in 1986–87 to more than 9 per cent in 2004. During the same period, the percentage of population reporting hospitalization has been around 2 to 3 per cent. Since the proportion of non-treated ailments has remained stagnant around 15 to 17 per cent of the total ailing population, it logically follows that health care utilization has risen at the same rate as that of reporting ailments during the same period (Table 1).

Given a considerable rise in the dimensions of the disease burden, concomitant with a significant increase in health care utilization, the population is subjected to inefficient and iniquitous treatment due to inadequate government financing and utter neglect of public provision of health services. During the period under consideration, the role of private sector in health care delivery has witnessed a manifold rise. Evidence from nationally representative large-scale household surveys indicated a diminished role for government health care provision, both on outpatient and inpatient facilities in the last two decades. In 2004, public sector provision of outpatient health care accounted for approximately one-fifth of the total population care as against over one-fourth (26 per cent) in 1987–88 in India (Table 2). As far as hospitalization care is concerned, the share of public provisions, which used to cater to around 60 per cent in

1987–88, had registered a steep decline to approximately 40 per cent in 2004 (Table 3). Altogether, currently public sector provides care to only 26 per cent of the ailing episodes in India.

Table 1

Share (Percentage) of Ailment, Treatment and Hospitalization (1986–87; 1995–96 and 2004)

Particulars of ailment and treatment	*1986–87*	*1995–96*	*2004*
Population reporting ailing (short duration)	2.4	5.5	9.1
Short duration ailment reporting no formal treatment (includes cases of self-treatment)	17.7	15.3	15.7
Population reporting hospitalization	2.6	1.6	2.7

Source: NSSO 42nd Rund (1986–87); NSSO 52nd Round (1995–96) and NSSO 60th Round (2004).

Table 2

Share (Percentage) of Public to Total Short Duration Treated Ailments in Rural and Urban India (1986–1987, 1995–96 and 2004)

Area	*1986–1987*	*1995–96*	*2004*
Rural	25.71	19.71	22.28
Urban	27.21	18.35	19.17

Source: NSSO 42nd Round (1986–1987); NSSO 52nd (1995–1996) and NSSO 60th Round (2004).

As far as outpatient is concerned, it has been widely documented that the majority of private providers in rural areas are fraught with problems of quality and lack of basic amenities at health care centres. A large proportion of these providers are not registered, with an additional 25 per cent only as Ayurveda, Yoga, Unani, Siddha and Homoeopathy (AYUSH) practitioners (Rao et al., 2011). In case of inpatient care, a large number of private health facilities are located in urban areas and are highly expensive. Apart from this, except a few 'five star' providers, variety cost, quality and quantity have been a matter of concern in inpatient care for most of the private providers located in smaller towns and cities.

Table 3

Share (percentage) of Public to Total Hospitalized Episodes in Rural and Urban India Ailing Population (1986–87, 1995–96 and 2004)

Area	*1986–87*	*1995–96*	*2004*
Rural	60.03	45.29	41.61
Urban	60.44	43.07	38.24

Source: NSSO 42nd Round (1998); NSSO 52nd Round (1995–96) and NSSO 60th Round (2004).

Control of Infectious Diseases: The State and Individual Responsibility

The complexity of the interrelationships between variables demands responses that go beyond those that focus on the hosts and organism but encompass socio-economic, cultural, and political imperatives.

Indeed, notions of globalization challenge infectious diseases in ways that are becoming starker. The roles and responsibilities of states and their often limited ability to control infectious diseases that have the potential to cross borders and threaten populations resident in other states is a potential source of tension. The role of WHO is also being redefined by these tensions and challenges. The tension between the individual and society plays out in several arenas when we contemplate responses to infectious diseases. For example, the free movements of people across borders may be inhibited, the quarantine of migrants potentially carrying infectious micro-organisms (for example returning soldiers, economic migrants, refugees from epidemics) – powers to quarantine cities are suggested. Compulsory immunization may be deemed as an appropriate measure in countries where it is not already in place. Likewise, compulsory treatment or isolation of those who pose a threat might be considered where individuals either decline treatment or are untreatable respectively.

Summing Up

At the beginning of the 21st century, infectious diseases remain a major global public health problem. Public health measures both detect and respond to known and unknown risks, linked to the development and monitoring of prevention and control programmes, that are crucial to better health worldwide.

References

Blackburn, H.B. (1983), 'Research and Demonstration Projects in Community Cardiovascular Diseases Prevention', *Journal of Public Health Policy*, 4: 398–421.

Coker, Richard, Joceline Pomerleau and Martin McKee (2005), 'The Changing Nature of Infectious Disease', in Joceline Pomerleau and Martin McKee (eds), *Issues in Public Health*, New Delhi: Tata McGraw-Hill.

Global Burden of Diseases Study (2013), *Global, Regional, and National Prevalence of Overweight and Obesity in Children and Adults during 1980–2013: A Systematic Analysis for the Global Burden of Diseases Study 2013*, Seattle: Institute for Health Metrics and Evaluation.

Gregg, Alan (1956), 'The Future Health Officer's Responsibility: Past, Present and Future', *American Journal of Public Health*, 46: 1384.

Health and Wellness Programme Survey (2003), American Management Association.

Indian Council for Research on International Economic Relations (ICRIER) (2002), *Opportunities and Risks for the Poor in Developing Countries*, New Delhi: India Habitat Centre.

Jinnegan, J.R., Neil L. Bracht and K. Viswanath (1989), 'Community Power and Leadership Analysis in Lifestyle Campaigns', in C.T. Salmon (ed.), *Information Campaigns: Balancing Social Values and Social Change*, Newbury Park: Sage Publications.

Leavell, H.R. and E.G. Clark (1965), *Preventive Medicine for the Doctor in His Community*, New York: McGraw Hill.

'Life Style Diseases Offer Big Bucks for Pharma', *The Times of India*, 17 March 2008.

Mausner, J.S. and S. Kramer (1985), *Epidemiology: An Introductory Test*, Philadelphia: Saunders.

NCMH (2005), *Report of the National Commission on Macro Economics and Health*, New Delhi: Ministry of Health and Family Welfare, Government of India.

NSSO (1996), *India Household Consumer Expenditure*, NSSO 52nd Round, July–June (1995–96), National Sample Survey Organisation, New Delhi: Ministry of Statistics and Programme Implementation, Government of India.

—— (1998), *Household Consumer Expenditure and Employment Situation in India*, National Sample Survey Organisation, New Delhi: Ministry of Statistics and Programme Implementation, Government of India.

—— (2004), *Morbidity, Health Care and the Condition of the Aged*, NSSO 60th Round, January–June, Report No. 507, National Sample Survey Organisation, New Delhi: Ministry of Statistics and Programme Implementation, Government of India.

Ouslander, J.G. and J.C. Beck (1982), 'Defining the Health Problems of the Elderly', *Annual Review of Public Health*, 3: 58.

Peters, D.H., A.S. Yazbeck et al. (2002), *Better Health Systems for India's Poor: Findings, Analysis and Options*, Washington, D.C.: The World Bank.

Rao, M. et al. (2011), 'Human Resources for Health in India', *Lancet*, 377: 587–98.

Selvaraj, Sakthivel and Anup K. Karan (2009), 'Deepening Health Insecurity in India: Evidence from National Sample Surveys Since 1980s', *Economic and Political Weekly*, XLIV(40): 55–60.

Suchman, E.A. (1963), *Sociology and the Field of Public Health*, New York: Russell Sage Foundation.

Susser, M.W. and W. Watson (1971), *Sociology in Medicine*, London: Oxford University Press.

WHO (1976), *Technical Report Series*, No. 587.

—— (1985), *Technical Report Series*, No. 714.

10

Determinants and Promotion of Health

There are many factors which have impact on the ability of individuals, communities and societies to develop and maintain good health and well-being. This chapter throws light on the importance of the social determinants of health.

Determinants of Health

It is recognized that the health and well-being of people is influenced by a range of factors, both within and outside the individual's control (Lalonde, 1974; WHO, 1998). Over the last 45 years, researchers from different disciplines have explained the relative importance of the range of determinants on health and how they impact different sectors of society. These are as follows:

- Marmot et al. (1978) demonstrated gradients in mortality across grades of employment among English civil servants.
- Bartley et al. (1994) have shown that both children and adolescents living in poorer quality housing are more likely to have been of low weight.
- Townsend et al. (1988) have shown that material deprivation (e.g. overcrowding, housing tenure, unemployment) is a predictor of mortality and limiting long-term illness.
- Barker (1998) has shown that the *in utero* experience is linked to the risk of developing diseases later in life.
- Graham (2004) has demonstrated the cumulative effect of social disadvantage over the life course and the contribution of poor early life circumstances.
- McGinnis et al. (2002) have demonstrated the relative impact that various health determinants make on mortality in the USA: 30 per cent due to genetic predisposition, 15 per cent due to social circumstances, 5 per cent due to environmental exposure, 40 per cent due to behavioural patterns and 10 per cent due to shortfalls in health care.

While each of the determinants is important in its own right, health is determined at every stage of life, by complex interactions between social and economic factors, the physical environment and individual behaviour.

The Importance of the Social Determinants of Health

Research efforts over the last 35 years have documented how health is socially patterned (Townsend et al., 1988; Harris et al., 1999). Health status is influenced by individual's characteristics and behaviour (lifestyles) but continues to be significantly determined by different social, economic and environmental circumstances of individuals and populations. Disease prevalence, life expectancy, behavioural risk factors and general well-being all display social gradients related to socio-economic status as well as sex, age and ethnicity. In other words, people living in different socio-economic settings face different risks of ill-health and death. In general, poor have much poorer health than the rich.

The WHO has brought together some of the most influential researches in this area in 2003. They conclude that:

> Even in the most affluent countries, people who are less well off have substantially shorter life expectancies and more illnesses than the rich. Not only these differences in health are an important social injustice, they have also drawn scientific attention to some of the most powerful determinants of health standards in modern societies. They have led in particular to a growing understanding of the remarkable sensitivity of health to the social environment and to what have become known as the social determinants of health.

The report presents what is known about the relationship between the social determinants and health and highlights the policy implications. Table 1 presents the ten topics covered in the report, to illustrate the importance of the social determinants of health.

Table 1

Major Determinants of Health

Topic	*Summary Statement*
Social Gradient	Life expectancy is shorter and most diseases are more common further down the social ladder in each society.
Stress	Stressful circumstances making people feel worried, anxious and unable to cope, are damaging to health and may lead to premature death.
Early Life	A good start in the life means supporting mothers and young children; the health, impact of early development and education lasts a lifetime.
Social Exclusion	Life is short where its quality is poor. Hardship, resentment, poverty, social exclusion and discrimination cost lives.
Work	Stress in the workplace increases the risk of disease. People who have more control over their work have better health.
Unemployment	Job security increases health, well-being and job satisfaction. Higher rates of unemployment cause more illness and premature death.
Social Support	Friendship, good social relations and strong supportive network improve health at home, work and in the community.
Addiction	Individuals turn to alcohol, drugs and tobacco and suffer from their use, but use is influenced by the wider social setting.
Food	Because global market forces control the food supply, healthy food is a political issue.
Transport	Healthy transport means less driving and more walking and cycling, backed up by better public transport.

Source: WHO (2003), Geneva.

HEALTH PROMOTION

What is Health Promotion?

Health promotion is probably the most ethical, effective, efficient and sustainable approach to achieving good health. It was defined initially by the World Health Organization in 1986, but the definition has since been refined to take account of new challenges and a better understanding of the economic, environmental and social determinants of health and disease. The most widely accepted and utilized definition of health promotion is 'the process of enabling people to increase control over the determinants of health and thereby improve their health' (WHO, 1986).

The History of Health Promotion

The term health promotion has a long and complex history. It has its roots in public health movements of 19th century in Europe and North America. The emergence of health promotion is due to infectious disease epidemics which in turn has affected population. Improvements in understanding of the mechanisms for the transmission of infectious disease were matched by the actions of social reformers, such as Chadwick and Simon in the UK and Shattuck in the USA, to influence public opinion and promote political action in the form of legislations and regulation to protect the public. These reforms led to improvement in housing condition, sanitation, food supply and working conditions of the poor people. Basically, these reforms were intended to benefit the entire population. Major improvements in the health and longevity of populations in high-income countries were achieved as consequences of these early public health reforms (McKeown, 1979). This form of societal action has been the cornerstone of public health. Winslow in 1923 provided a scholarly analysis of the origin of public health. According to him education is the key element in the campaign of public health. He stressed on the goals of health education in the context of public health campaign. Thus, the stage was set for the emergence of health education, together with well organized preventive health services, as the major tools for the promotion of public health in the middle of the 20th century.

Promoting Health Education

The lessons learnt in the later half of the 19th century concerning the impact of physical, social and economic environments became somewhat lost during the two decades following the World War II. Countries were busy in reconstruction and development. Governments were also making efforts in providing the availability and accessibility of health care to their people. The public health perspective was lost. Health education, as it existed in the 1950s and 1960s, remained true to the goals advocated by Winslow (1923), being defined primarily in terms of promoting optimal use of health services, particularly preventive services such as mass screening, antenatal and child health services, and immunization programmes.

Investment in health care, whether through private health insurance, publicly funded services or a combination of both grew rapidly in the post-war period. It has resulted in the strengthened role for health education, hence encouraging the appropriate use of health services to reduce demand for services. This contrasted strongly with its established role of promoting use of preventive health services.

Against this background of expansion in medical science and health care, the second half of the 20th century was characterized by growth in the importance of chronic, non-communicable diseases as a cause of premature mortality and morbidity, initially in high-income countries and later in developing and under developed countries.

Efforts to promote optimal use of health services and modification in lifestyle behaviour became the focus to improve public health. Health education was one of the principal tools for focusing the use of preventive health services. The individual and their personal behaviour were the focus for attention, rather than the population and the physical, social and economic environment.

Thus health education was seen not only as offering a solution to the problems of reducing demand for health care but also to a range of emerging threats to individual health. Health education was adopted with enthusiasm and great expectation by governments in countries throughout the world during the 1960s and 1970s. By the end of 1970s, many countries had established a central or national government agency for health education and some form of local infrastructure for the organization and delivery of community-based health programmes.

Model and Theories of Health Promotion

Perceptions of health and the ability of individuals to influence it vary markedly between cultures. Several theories have been developed to explain health-related behaviour. The Health Belief Model argues that health-related behaviour is determined according to industrial evaluations of an outcome, and the expectation that a specific behaviour will produce that outcome (Becker et al., 1977).

Help-Seeking Model

The notion of health as related to social functionality also underpins Zola's (1973) Help-Seeking Model which concluded that the lay public do not seek the help of health professionals or access the formal health care system immediately after they perceive physical symptoms. People were typically found to be initially trying to find ways to accommodate to their symptoms, that is, until they impinge upon, or prevent 'normal role' functioning. It was only at this point of 'crisis' that help would be sought from health care professionals.

Tannahill's Model of Health Promotion

Tannahill's model sees health promotion as comprising of efforts to enhance positive health and prevent ill-health, through the overlapping spheres of health education, prevention and health protection (Downie et al., 1990). Tannahill places health promotion within the framework of the broad range of traditional public health domains (Figure 1), which are united by the principles of health promotion, the nature of which is eclectic and multidisciplinary. The six domains are:

- Preventive services
- Preventive health education
- Health education for preventive health protection
- Positive health education
- Positive health protection
- Health education aimed at positive health protection

There are two basic models for improving health based on medical/behavioural change, educational change or social change. Medical model focuses on the prevention of disease (illness or negative health) and is combined with a philosophy of compliance with professionals' (usually the doctors') diagnosis and prognosis. The educational model is based on the view that the world consists of rational human beings and that to prevent disease and improve health, we merely have to inform or educate people about remedies and healthy lifestyles because, as rational human beings, they will respond accordingly. The social model is based on the view that health is determined by the social,

Figure 1

Model of Health Promotion

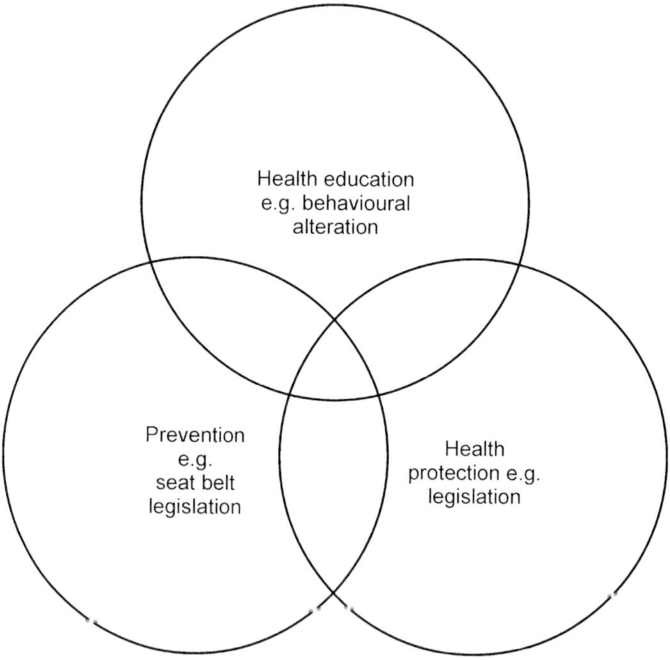

Source: Tannahill, A. (2009), 'Health Promotion: The Tannahill Model Revisited', *Public Health*, 123(5), 397.

cultural and physical environment. In this model, solutions are political and require protecting people from health-disabling environments.

The Tannahill model has been criticized as being clearly within the reductionist, medical model in that it pays insufficient attention to community-based factors. In response to these critiques, Tannahill (2009) proposed a new definition of health promotion as the 'sustainable fostering of positive health and prevention of health through policies, strategies, and activities in the overlapping action areas of (1) social, economic, physical, environmental, and cultural factors; (2) equity and diversity; (3) education and learning; (4) services, amenities, and products; and (5) community-led and community-based activity'.

Attribution Theory

Heider (1958) was the first to propose a psychological theory of attribution, but Weiner and colleagues developed a theoretical framework that has become a major research paradigm of psychology. Attribution theory suggests that the way people attribute causation affects their beliefs about illness, which, in turn, determines their health behaviour (King, 1983). In terms of attribution theory, those who have an external 'locus of control' believe that illness is caused by external forces over which they have little or no control, while those who have an internal 'locus of control' believe that their actions can influence health outcomes (Simons, 1989).

Attribution theory has been used to explain the difference in motivation between high and low achievers. According to attribution theory, high achievers will approach rather than avoid tasks related to succeeding because they believe that success is due to high ability and effort which they are confident of. Failure is thought to be caused by bad luck or a poor performance. Attribution theory is based on three principles:

1. Attribution is a three stage process: (i) behaviour is observed; (ii) behaviour is determined to be deliberate; and (iii) behaviour is attributed to internal or external causes.
2. Achievement can be attributed to effort, ability, level of task difficulty or luck.
3. Causal dimensions of behaviour are: locus of control, stability and controllability.

Studies in many countries have shown that more traditional societies generally have an external locus of control, but with education this changes towards an internal locus of control. Those with an external locus of control commonly attribute illness to factors such as witchcraft, or certain behaviours and foods which have no scientifically proven connection with illness.

Health-related behaviour is also affected by perceptions of beauty, body image and appropriate behaviour. In the most modernized societies the ideal for both men and women is a lean, muscular body. In other countries a certain amount of body fat is considered more attractive, or more appropriate for people of a particular age. For example, traditional values in the Pacific associate obesity with high status (Hodge et al., 1996: 81). While young people are admired for being slender and muscular, and these characteristics are also acceptable in adults, so are heavy bodies (de Garine and Pollock, 1995). Moreover, adults are expected to behave with dignity and decorum. This means slow movement and modest clothing. Activities such as running around in sports clothing are acceptable in children, but are considered inappropriate for adults, especially mature women. As more people are exposed to Western television and film, their perceptions of body image and behaviour are being modified to some extent.

Individual perceptions of ability to treat diseases are influenced not only by beliefs to influence life events. This broader view, which relates to attribution theory and how individuals perceive themselves in relation to the rest of the world, has been termed 'locus of control' (Simons, 1989: 132–146). People who believe in their own ability to take control of events and to solve problems are more likely to seek treatment for illness than those who have a fatalistic view of the world. For example, many studies have shown that mothers with some education are more likely to take sick children to a health centre than mothers with no education. There are various mechanisms through which education affects health behaviour, ranging from a greater control over resources and greater ability to seek care (Caldwell, 1989: 101–111). This effect, however, is that educated mothers are more likely to believe that they can do something to change or control their lives and the lives of their children.

Most cultures have specific images of health and perceptions of the causes of ill-health. They relate to the Health Belief Model and the perceived 'locus of control' as regards ability to treat ill-health. Perceptions vary between cultures, and sometimes also between one region of a country and another or between socio-economic groups.

The Health Belief Model

This is one of the established theoretical model designed to explain health behaviour by understanding people's beliefs about health. The model suggests that the likelihood of an individual taking action for a given health problem is based on the interaction between four types of belief (Figure 2). The model predicts that individuals will take action to protect or promote health if:

- They perceive themselves to be susceptible to a condition or problem.
- They believe it will have potentially serious consequences.
- They believe a course of action is available which will reduce their susceptibility, or minimize the consequences.
- They believe that the benefits of taking action will outweigh the costs or barriers.

The Health Belief Model (HBM) was developed by Irwin Rosenstock in 1966 and has been identified as one of the earliest and most influential

Figure 2
The Health Belief Model

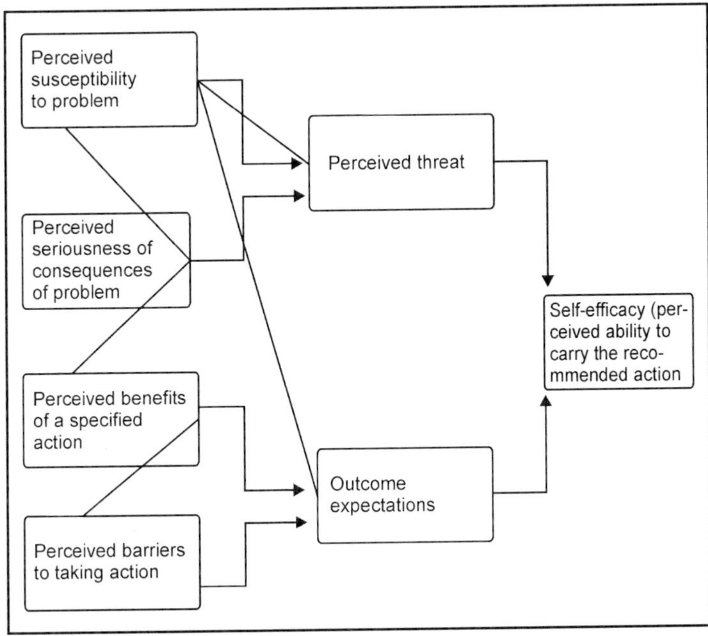

Source: Nutbeam, D. and E. Harris (2004), *Theory in Nutshell: A Practical Guide to Health Promotion Theories,* Mc-Graw-Hill Australia, vii–9.

models in health promotion. It was inspired by a study of reasons people expressed for seeking or declining X-ray examinations for tuberculosis. The Health Belief Model has been found to be the most useful when applied to behaviours for which it was originally developed, particularly prevention strategies such as screening and immunization. Initially the model included four constructs: (1) perceived susceptibility (a person's subjective assessment of risk of getting the condition, as contrasted with the statistical risk), (2) perceived severity (the seriousness of the condition and its consequences), (3) perceived barriers (both those that interfere with and facilitate adoption of behaviour such as side effects, time and inconvenience), and (4) perceived costs of adhering to the proposed intervention. Factors related to motivation were subsumed under susceptibility and fear of the disease (Rosenstock, 1966). It has been less useful in guiding intervention to address long-term, complex and socially determined behaviour such as alcohol and tobacco consumption. The model's advantage is the relatively simple way in which it illustrates the importance of individual beliefs about health and the relative costs and benefits of actions to protect or improve health. Changes in knowledge and beliefs will almost always form part of a health promotion programme and the Health Belief Model provides a reference point in the development of message to improve knowledge and change beliefs, especially messages designed for use by the mass media.

In the 1970s and 1980s, Becker and colleagues modified the Health Belief Model to include people's responses to symptoms and illness, and compliance with medical directives. The model was extended to include illness behaviours, preventative health, and health screening. Demographic variables (age, gender, ethnicity, occupation), socio-physiological variables (socio-economic status, personality, coping strategies), perceived self-efficacy (ability to adopt the desired behaviour), cues to action (factors that instigate preventive health such as information through sought/provided, persuasive communication, and personal experience), health motivation, perceived control, and perceived threat were added to the model (Becker and Maiman, 1975).

Critique of the Health Belief Model has been based on the fact that not all health behaviour is based on rational or conscious choice. It has also been critiqued for focusing on negative factors and ignoring positive motivations that prompt healthy behaviours (Roden, 2002; Rosenstock, 1974). The Health Belief Model also lacks concepts associated with strategies for change. The major complaint has been that the model focuses on individual factors rather that socio-economic and environmental factors and, therefore, encourages victim blaming (Roden, 2004).

The Stages of Change (Transtheoretical) Model

The model was developed to describe and explain the different stages in behaviour change (Prochaska and DiClemente, 1984). The model is based on the premise that behaviour change is a process, not an event, and that individuals have different levels of motivation or readiness to change (Figure 3). Five stages of changes have been identified:

- Precontemplation: this describes individuals who are not even considering changing behaviour or are consciously intending not to change.
- Contemplation: the stage at which a person considers making a change to a specific behaviour.
- Determination or preparation: the stage at which a person makes a serious commitment to change.
- Action: the stage at which behaviour change is initiated.
- Maintenance: sustaining the change and achievement of predictable health gains. Relapse may also be the fifth stage.

From a programme planning perspective, the model is particularly useful in indicating how different processes of change can influence how activities are staged. Several processes have been consistently useful in supporting movement between stages. These processes are more or less applicable at different stages of change. For example, awareness raising may be more useful among pre-contemplators who may not be aware of the threat to health that their behaviour poses, whereas communication of the benefits of change and illustration of the success of others in changing may be important for those contemplating change. Once change has been initiated at action stage, social support and stimulus control (for example,

Figure 3

The Stages of Change (Transtheoretical) Model

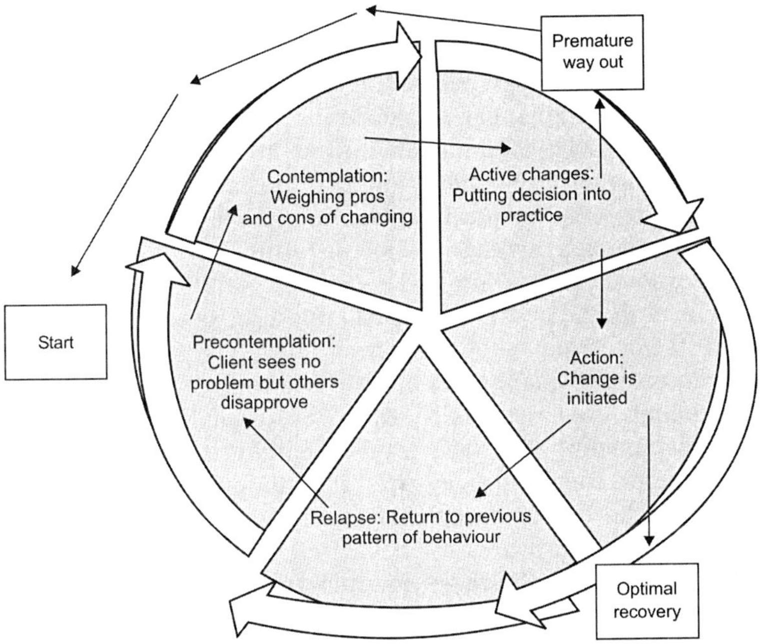

Source: Prochaska and DiClemente (1984).

by avoiding certain situations or having environmental supports in place) are more important. By matching stages of behaviour change with specific processes, the model specifies how interventions could be organized for different populations, with different needs and in different circumstances. The stages of change model stress the need to research the characteristics of the target population, the importance of not assuming that all people are at the same stage, and the need to organize interventions sequentially to address the different stages that will be encountered. The model has been used in workplace programmes to promote regular physical activity, which traditionally has met with limited success (Nutbeam, 2006). The stages of change model have become an important reference point in health promotion interventions because of its obvious advantage in focusing on change process. The model is important in emphasizing the range of needs for an intervention in any given population, the changing needs of different populations and the need for the sequencing of interventions to match different stages of change. It illustrates the importance of tailoring programmes to the real needs and circumstances of individuals, rather than assuming that an intervention will be equally applicable to all.

Ecological Model of Health Promotion

Among the more comprehensive models used in health promotion efforts is the ecological model (McElroy et al., 1988). Developed to be a comprehensive model aimed at a macro level, it has constructs that take into account both the micro and macro issues of the person. The ecological model has four areas for focusing efforts at assisting in behaviour change.

- Individual factors, sometimes called the interpersonal factors, like genetics and individual behaviour.
- Interpersonal factors, like social support and family characteristics.
- Institutional and community environments, which might include work sites, schools, service systems and transportation.
- And finally, broader social, economic and political influences, which could encompass a range of factors from laws and regulations to racism and discrimination.

Each level should be considered as important as others. The first is the individual factor. This emphasizes micro-level issues a person has to overcome in order to change his/her behaviour. This includes knowledge, attitudes, beliefs, and personality traits. Fortunately or unfortunately it also includes genetics. The next level of emphasis within the ecological model is interpersonal relationships. Interactions with family, friends, peers or even the family doctor may determine what a person feels or believes about a given process or behaviour. This can be a double-edged sword, in that sometimes these interactions have a positive effect on behaviours and sometimes they have a negative effect. The community level is considered next, and certainly has a macro level of influence. Social networks, community norms, and standards, whether formal or informal, sometimes determine which health behaviours are acceptable. Institutional factors and public policy or laws are the other factors that influence the health behaviour. Rules at work, such as no smoking policies, affect health, as do seat belts, child safety-restraint laws, and even clean indoor air ordinances that restrict smoking in public places. Taking all of these levels of potential influence into effect can help aid the process of behaviour change. Leaving one or more of these constructs out of any planning process for widespread behaviour change will almost guarantee failure of a health promotion effort.

Ecological model can also be well illustrated with an example for obesity. Here the individual factors could include both genetics and epigenetics (change in gene expression without a modification to the DNA sequence). For example, there is evidence of epigenetic changes associated with obesity that are related to environmental exposures to endocrine disrupting chemicals, and to maternal obesity, exposures early in life that trigger changes in physiological processes that can persist into adulthood. Individual factors also include knowledge, attitudes, and behaviour related to diet and exercise.

The interpersonal level includes cultural factors like food choices, traditions, and cultural meanings of thinness and fatness that are reinforced at the family level as well as the societal level. Other family characteristics that could fall into this category include caregiver behaviour, time pressures affecting the ability to cook and eat together, and the role of food in the context of family relationships.

Institutional factors might include school and workplace food options and opportunities for physical activity, and access to health promoting services like wellness programmes, clinics, or gyms. In the workplace, providing time and space for lactating mothers to pump breast milk may even be a factor. The degree to which breastfeeding reduces the risk of later obesity is still in question.

Theories of Health Behaviour

The range and focus of theories has also expanded over the past decades from a focus on the modification of individual behaviour, to recognition of the need to influence and change a broad range of social, economic and environmental factors that influence health alongside individual behavioural choices. Health promotion operates at several levels: individual, community, organization and nation. Below we will discuss different theories and models.

Social Cognitive Theory of Health Promotion

This is one of the most widely applied theories in health promotion because it addresses both the underlying determinants of health behaviour and the methods of promoting change. The theory was built on an individual and their environment (Bandura, 1955). Social cognitive theory indicates that the relationship between people and their environment is more subtle and complex. For example, in circumstances where a significant number of people are non-smokers and are assertive about their desire to restrict smoking in a given environment, even without formal regulation, it becomes far less rewarding for the individual who smokes. They are then likely to modify their behaviour. In this case, the non-smokers have influenced the smoker's perception of the environment through social influence. This is referred to as reciprocal determinism. It describes the way in which an individual, their environment and behaviour continuously interact and influence each other. An understanding of this interaction and the way in which modification of social norms can impact on behaviour offer an important insight into how behaviour can be modified through health promotion interventions. Added to this basic understanding of the relationship between the individual and the environment, a range of personal cognitive factors form a third part to this relationship, affecting and being affected by specific behaviours and environments. Of these cognitions, these are particularly important. First, the capacity to learn by observing both the behaviours of others and the rewards received for different patterns of behaviour (observational learning). Second, the capacity to anticipate and place value on the outcome of different behavioural patterns (referred to as expectations). Finally, the theory emphasizes the importance of belief in your own ability to successfully perform a behaviour (referred to as self-efficacy). Self-efficacy is proposed as the most important prerequisite for behaviour change and will affect how much effort is put into a task and the outcome of the task. The promotion of self-efficacy is thus an important task in the achievement of behaviour change. It has been proposed that both observational learning and participatory learning (e.g. by supervised practice and repetition) will lead to the development of the knowledge and skills necessary for behaviour change (behaviour capability). These are seen as powerful tools in building self-confidence and self-efficacy.

Community factors include access to, and affordability of, healthy food, recreation facilities, health care services, walkability and the layout of streets, the safety of outdoor spaces, having neighbours who exercise, and community norms related to food choices and accepted weight ranges. Insufficient sleep has been linked to obesity, as it contributes to sleep deficits that prime the body to store more fat.

Other broad factors like broad social policy level could include things like regulations pertaining to school food programmes, agricultural subsidies, exposure to obesogeneic chemicals in food, food packaging, and other products, all of which are affected by the regulatory environment.

Self-Determination Theory

Self-determination theory is a personality theory that includes behavioural factors. It focuses on the motivation behind choices that individuals make. Self-determination theory was inspired by research into intrinsic motivation, which is the idea of engaging in an activity because it is interesting and satisfying rather than being motivated to achieve a goal or receive an external reward such as money. With intrinsic motivation it flourishes if linked with a sense of security and relatedness (Deci and Ryan, 2000). The need for competence, autonomy, and relatedness motivate self-initiated behaviour and allow for optimal function and growth. These needs are not learned, but instead are innate and transcend gender and culture. Competence has to do with being effective in dealing with the environment and producing behavioural outcomes. Negative feedback decreases intrinsic motivation, while positive feedback increases intrinsic motivation. Relatedness involves the desire to interact with, be connected to, and care for others. It involves establishing satisfying relationships with others and society at large. Autonomy is the urge to have agency, initiate action, and regulate one's behaviour. It is undermined by offering external/extrinsic rewards and establishing deadlines, but increasing choices increases autonomy (Deci, 1971). When health care providers offer meaningful and germane rationale for behavioural change, the client's sense of competence increases. According to self-determination theory, there are three ways people orient themselves to the environment and regulate their behaviour, the orientations are autonomous, controlled, and impersonal. Autonomous orientations result from satisfaction of basic needs. Controlled orientations result from satisfaction of competence and relatedness, but not of autonomy needs; and the result is rigid functioning and diminished well-being. Impersonal orientations result from a lack of fulfilling all three needs. Poor functioning and ill-health result when a person has or experiences an impersonal orientation (Deci, 1971).

Theory of Reasoned Action (TRA)

The theory of reasoned action was developed by Martin Fishbein and Icek Ajzen in 1975. An assumption underlying the TRA is that people routinely consider the consequences of their behaviours before engaging in these behaviours. There are three constructs: behavioural intention, attitude, and subjective norms. In this theory, a behavioural intention is a function of the person's attitude about the behaviour and subjective norms. Subjective norms are the perceived expectations of key individuals such as significant others, family members, experts and co-workers. Voluntary behaviour is predicted by one's attitude toward the behaviour and what important people would think if the behaviour was not performed (Fishbein and Ajzen, 1975).

A critique of the TRA is that not all behaviours are under an individual's control, including spontaneous actions, habitual behaviours, and cravings. A second critique is that environmental, economic, and political factors are not part of the theory. The TRA has been tested in a large number of areas including dieting, condom use, and limiting sun exposure, and it has been found to have strong predictive utility.

Theory of Planned Behaviour (TPB)

Ajzen (1985) extended the theory of reasoned action and developed the theory of planned behaviour by adding a perceived behavioural control predictor. The concept of perceived behavioural control came from Bandura's work with self-efficacy, and it is used to account for times when people do not have conscious control over their actions as well as when they intend to carry out behaviour but they do not because they lack confidence or control. Ajzen's work emphasized the role of intention and suggested that the likelihood of behaviour change is dependent on the amount of control a person has over a given behaviour and the strength of their intent to change. The model proposes that intention to engage in behaviour is determined by an individual's attitude towards the behaviour, their perception of the subjective norm, and their perceived behavioural control (PBC). It also proposes that these components are influenced by external variables (personality traits, demographic characteristics, and environmental influences). The 'subjective norm' is a person's beliefs about what important people think they should do in relation to the behaviour. Important people in this context are figures from their social circle whose opinion or respect is valued. A person will be more likely to take up exercise, for example, if they feel that their partner wishes them to do so.

An individual's perceived behavioural control is also sometimes referred to as self-efficacy. The TPB predicts that a person will have a greater intention to exercise if they have a positive attitude towards exercising, if they believe that important people want them to exercise, and if they feel they have the ability to take up exercising. Greater intention is proposed by the model to link to a greater likelihood of the person engaging in the behaviour.

Figure 4
Theory of Planned Behaviour

External variables
Attitude towards the behaviour
Subjective norm
Perceived behavioural control
Intention
Behaviour

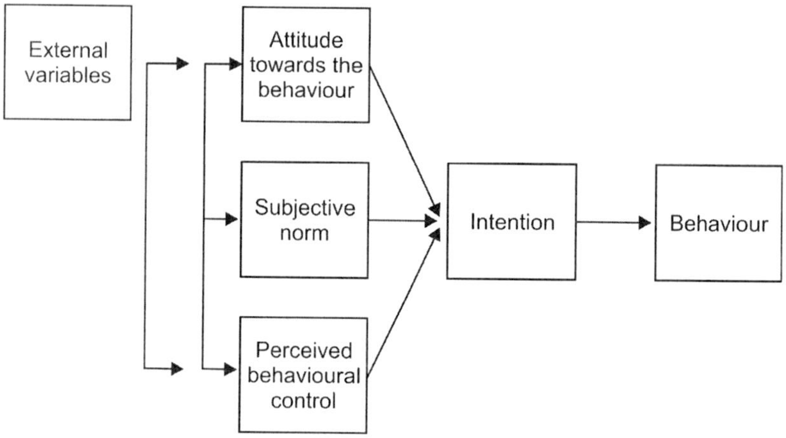

Source: Azjen, I. (1985), From Intention to Action: A Theory of Planned Behaviour, in J. Kuhhl and J. Beckman (eds), *Action Control: From Cognition to Behaviour,* pp. 11–39, Heidelberg: Germany: Springer.

According to TPB, three factors influence intent: (1) the person's attitude toward the behaviour, (2) the person's evaluation of how important significant others such as a partner or co-worker consider the behaviour to be (subjective norms), and (3) the degree of perceived behavioural control or the perceived ease/difficulty associated with the behavioural change. Ajzen suggested that self-efficacy was a major factor in determining how successful a person will be in changing their behaviour, as people who do not believe they have the assets, resources, or ability to change are not likely to do so (Ajzen, 1985). The TPB has been critiqued for focusing on cognitive elements and ignoring the role of emotion in behavioural change. However, it has proven to be an effective theory for predicting health-related behaviour.

Summing Up

Health status is influenced by individual characteristics and behaviour but continues to be significantly determined by different social, economic and environmental circumstances of individuals and populations. To improve the health of the people the organized preventive health services are used for the promotion of public health. Health education was adopted as the major tool throughout the world during 1960s and 1970s. However, there are many models and perspectives for the promotion of health. Tannahill Model of health promotion put efforts in enhancing the positive health and prevent ill-health. The Health Belief Model explains health behaviour by understanding people's belief about health. The different stages of change of health behaviour are well explained by the stages of Change Model. Among the more comprehensive models used in health promotion efforts is the Ecological Model. The most widely applied Social Cognitive Theory in health promotion addresses both the underlying determinants of health behaviour and methods of promoting change. In this theory, a behavioural intention is a function of the person's attitude about the behaviour and subjective norms. Ajzen extended the Theory of Reasoned Action and developed the Theory of Planned Behaviour (TPB) by adding a perceived behavioural control predictor. Thus, these models and theories explained ways of health promotion.

References

Ajzen, I. (1985), 'From Intention to Actions: A Theory of Planned Behaviour', in J. Kuhhl and J. Beckman (eds), *Action Control: From Cognition to Behaviour*, Heidelberg, Germany: Springer, 11–39.

Ashton, S. and R. Stepney (1982), *Smoking*, London: Tavistock.

Bailey, K.V. and A.H. Ferro-Luzzi (1995), 'Use of Body Mass Index of Adults in Assessing Individual and Community Nutritional Status', *Bulletin of the World Health Organization*, 73(5): 673–80.

Bandura, A. (1955), *Self-Efficacy in Changing Societies*, New York: Cambridge University Press.

Barker, D.J.P. (1998), *Mothers, Babies and Disease in Later Life*, Edinburg: Churchill Livingstone.

Bartley, M. et al. (1994), 'Birth Weight and Later Socio-economic Disadvantage: Evidence from the 1958 British Cohort Study', *British Medical Journal*, 309: 1475–78.

Beck, U. (1994), *Reflexive Modernization: Politics, Tradition and Aesthetics in the Modern Social Order*, Cambridge: Polity Press.

Becker, M.H. and L.A. Maiman (1975), 'Socio-Behavioural Determinants of Compliance with Health and Medical Care Recommendations', *Medical Care*, 13: 10–24.

Becker, M.H. et al. (1977), 'The Health Belief Model and Prediction of Dietary Compliance: A Field Experiment', *Journal of Health and Social Behaviour*, 18: 348–66.

Buchanan, K. (1985), 'Centre and Periphery: Reflections on the Irrelevance of a Billion Human Beings', *Monthly Review*, 37(3): 86–97.

Chomsky, N. (1993), *The Prosperous Few and the Restless Many: Noam Chomsky interviewed by D. Barsamian*, Berkeley, CA: Odonian Press.

Cohen, S. et al. (1986), *Behaviour, Health and Environmental Stress*, New York: Plenum.

Deci, E.L. (1971), 'Effects of Externally Mediated Rewards on Intrinsic Motivation', *Journal of Personality and Social Psychology*, 18: 105–11.

DeGarine, I. and N. Pollock (eds) (1995), *Social Aspects of Obesity*, South Australia: Gordon and Breach.

Department of Environment, Sport and Territories (1995), *Active and Inactive Australians: Assessing and Understanding Levels of Physical Activity*, Canberra: Commonwealth of Australia.

Downie, R.S. et al. (1990), *Health Promotion: Models and Values*, Oxford: Oxford Medical Publications.

Ender, N.S. (1988), 'Hassles, Health and Happiness', in M.P. Janisse (ed.), *Individual Differences, Stress, and Health Psychology*, New York: Springer-Verlag, 24–56.

Fishbein, M. and I. Ajzen (1975), *Belief, Attitude, Intention and Behaviour: An Introduction to Theory and Research*, Melno Park, CA: Addison-Wesley.

Frank, A.G. (1978), *Dependent Accumulation and Underdevelopment*, London: Macmillan.

Graham, H. (2004), 'Social Determinants and their Unequal Distribution: Clarifying Policy Understandings', *The Millbank Quarterly*, 82(1): 101–24.

Harpham, T. (1994), 'Urbanization and Mental Health in Developing Countries: A Research Role for Social Scientists, Public Health Professionals and Social Psychiatrists', *Social Science and Medicine*, 39(2): 233–45.

Harris, E. et al. (1999), *Perspective on Health Inequality*, Sydney, NSW: Australian Centre for Health Promotion.

Hart, R.H. et al. (1990), *Integrating Maternal and Child Health Services with Primary Health Care*, Geneva: WHO.

Heider, F. (1958), *The Psychology of Interpersonal Relations*, New York: Wiley.

—— (2013), *The Psychology of Interpersonal Relations*, New York: Psychology Press.

Hodge, A. et al. (1996), 'Obesity in Pacific Populations', *Pacific Health Dialog*, 3(1): 77–86.

Huynen, M.M. et al. (2005), 'The Health Impact of Globalization: A Conceptual Framework', *Globalization and Health*, 1: 14.

Khan, M. et al. (1989), 'Inequalities between Men and Women in Nutrition and Family Welfare Services: An In-Depth Enquiry of an Indian Village', in J.C. Caldwell and G. Santo (eds), *Selected Readings in the Cultural, Social and Behavioural Determinants of Health*, Health Transition Series No. 1, Canberra: Health Transition Centre, Australian National University, 175–99.

King, J.B. (1983), 'Illness Attributions and the Health Belief Model', *Health Education and Behaviour*, 10(3–4): 287–312.

Lalonde, M. (1974), *A New Perspective on Health of Canadians: Working Document*, Ottawa: Government of Canada.

Manning, W. et al. (1991), *The Costs of Poor Health Habits*, Massachusetts: Harvard University Press.

Marmot, M.G. et al. (1978), 'Employment Grade and Coronary Heart Disease in British Civil Servants', *Journal of Epidemiology and Community Health*, 32: 244–49.

McGinnis, J.M. et al. (2002), 'The Case for More Active Policy Attention to Health Promotion', *Health Affairs*, 21(2).

McKeown, T. (1979), *The Role of Medicine: Dream, Mirage or Nemesis*, Princeton, NJ: Princeton University Press.

McLeroy, K.R. et al. (1988), 'An Ecological Perspective on Health Promotion Programming', *Health Edition Quarterly*, 15: 351–57.

McMurray, C. (1995), *Report on the Republic of the Marshall Islands Fertility and Family Planning Survey, November–December*, Unpublished Report, Majuro: Office of Planning and Statistics, Republic of the Marshall Islands.

Mills, S. (ed.) (1988), *Alternatives in Healing: An Open-Minded Approach to Finding the Best Treatment for Your Health Problems*, London: Macmillan.

Mull, D.S. (1991), 'Traditional Perceptions of Marasmus in Pakistan', *Social Science and Medicine*, 32(2): 175–91.

Myrdal, G. (1953), *The Political Element in the Development of Economic Theory*, London: Routledge and Kegan Paul.

Nutbeam, D. (2001), 'Effective Health Promotion Programmes', in D. Pencheon et al. (eds), *Oxford Handbook of Public Health Practice*, Oxford: Oxford University Press.

—— (2006), 'Using Theory to Guide Changing Individual Behaviour', in Maggie Davis and Wendy Macdowall (eds), *Health Promotion Theory*, New Delhi: Tata McGraw Hill.

Nutbeam, D. and E. Harris (2004), *Theory in Nutshell: A Practical Guide to Health Promotion Theories*, Australia: McGraw Hill.

Prochaska, J.O. and C.C. DiClementa (1984), *The Transtheoretical Approach: Towards a Systematic Eclectic Framework*, Homewood, IL: Dow Jones Irwin.

Robertson, R. (1992), *Globalization, Social Theory and Global Culture*, London: Sage Publications.

Roden, J. (2004), 'Revisiting the Health Belief Model: Nurses Applying it to Young Families and Their Health Promotion Needs', *Nursing and Health Sciences*, 6: 1–10.

Rosenstock, I.M. (1966), 'Why People Use Health Services', *The Milbank Memorial Fund Quarterly*, 44: 94–127.

—— (1974), 'Historical Origins of the Health Belief Model', in M.H. Becker (ed.), *The Health Belief Model and Personal Health Behaviour*, Thorofare, NJ: Charles B. Slack.

Royston, E. and S. Anderson (1989), *Preventing Maternal Deaths*, Geneva: WHO.

Ryan, R.M. and E.L. Deci (1991), 'A Motivational Approach to Self: Integration in Personality', in R. Dienstbier (ed.), *Nebraska Symposium on Motivation*, Vol. 38, Lincoln, NE: University of Nebraska, 237–88.

—— (2000), 'Intrinsic and Extrinsic Motivations: Classic Definitions and New Directions', *Contemporary Educational Psychology*, 25(1): 54–67.

Saunders, C. and M. Baines (eds) (1989), *Living with Dying: The Management of Terminal Disease*, New York: Oxford University Press.

Simons, J. (1989), 'Cultural Dimensions of the Mother's Contribution to Child Survival', in J.C. Caldwell and G. Santow (eds), *Selected Readings in the Cultural Social and Behavioural Determinants of Health*, Health Transition Series No. 1, Canberra: Health Transition Centre: Australian National University, 132–46.

Spielberger, C.D. et al. (1988), 'The Experience, Expression and Control of Anger', in M.P. Janisse (ed.), *Individual Differences, Stress, and Health Psychology*, New York: Springer Verlag, 89–108.

Tannahill, A. (2009), 'Health Promotion: The Tannahill Model Revisited', *Public Health*, 123(5): 397.

Townsend, P. et al. (1988), *The Health Divide: Inequalities in Health in the 1980s*, London: Pelican.

Wallerstein, I. and T. Hopkins (1996), *The Age of Transition: Trajectory of the World System, 1945–2025*, London: Zed Books.

Weiner, B. (1986), *An Attributional Theory of Motivation and Emotion*, New York: Springer-Verlag.

WHO (1986), *Ottawa Charter for Health Promotion*, Geneva: WHO.

—— (1998), *Health 21: Health for All in 21st Century*, Copenhagen: WHO Regional Office for Europe.

—— (2003), *The Solid Facts: Social Determinants of Health*, Copenhagen: WHO Regional Office for Europe.

Winslow, C.E.A. (1923), *The Evolution of Significance of the Modern Public Health Campaign*, New Heaven, CT: Yale University Press.

Zola, I. (1973), 'Pathways to the Doctor: From Person to Patient', *Social Science and Medicine*, 7: 677–89.

Zuckerman, M. (1988), 'Sensation Seeking, Risk Taking, and Health', in M.P. Janisse (ed.), *Individual Differences, Stress, and Health Psychology*, New York: Springer-Verlag, 72–88.

11

Risk Management, Perception and Communication in Health Care

Health systems, like other organizations, are dynamic and require continuous management, adjustment, and systems control. Continuous monitoring and feedback, evaluation and revision help to meet individual and community needs.

In this chapter, we will learn about a definition of risk followed by a framework for the management of risk, and an overview of risk perception and the cognitive pitfalls present when dealing with risk. It summarizes with a discussion of culture and communication in health care.

Aim of the chapter:

- Deconstruct risk into its main components.
- Apply management techniques to mitigate the risk.
- Plan how to minimize the risk.
- To understand the relationship between culture and communication and then design strategies to communicate risk situations.

Health Management

Organizations use resources or inputs that are processed to achieve desired results or outputs. The resource inputs are money, personnel, information, and supplied material. Process is the accumulation of all activities taken to achieve the intended results. Output, or outcome, is the product, its marketing, its reputation and quality, and profit. In a service sector such as health, output or impact can be measured in terms of reduced morbidity and/or moratality, improved health, or number of successfully treated and satisfied patients at affordable costs. The management system provides the resources and organizes the process by which it hopes to achieve the established goals. Programme implementation requires systematic feedback for the process to work effectively. When targets are set and strategy defined, resources, whether new or existing, are placed at the service of the new programme. Management is then responsible to use the resources in the best way to achieve the intended targets. The results are the outcome or output measures which are evaluated and fed back to the input and process levels.

Health systems consist of many subsystems, each with an organization, leaders, goals, targets, and internal information systems. Subsystems need to communicate within themselves, with peer organizations, and with the macro (health) system. Leadership style is central to this process. The surgeon as the leader of the team in the operating room is dependent on the support and judgement of other crucial persons on the team, such as the anaesthesiologist, the operating room nurse, pathologist, radiologist, and laboratory services, all of whom lead their own teams. The hospital director cannot function without a creative team approach to quality development of the facility.

Health systems management includes analysis of service policy, budget, decision-making in policy, as well as operation, regulation, supervision, provision, maintenance, ethical standards, and legislation. Policy formulation involves a set of decisions made in pursuit of a course of action for achieving health goals.

Health is a knowledge-based service industry, so that knowledge management and information technology are extremely important parts of health policy, not only in patient care systems, but also in mobilization of evidence and experience in best practices for policies and management decision-making. The gap between information and action is wide and presents an ethical as well as a political challenge. Regions with the most severe health problems lack trained personnel in assessment and exploitation of current state of the art practices and technology in many practical public health fields, including immunization policy and in management of risk factors for stroke.

Knowledge and evidence exists, but the capacity to access and interpret that information is commonly lacking in many countries so that very large number of people die of preventable diseases even when there are, in total, sufficient resources to address the challenges. Adaptation of knowledge to address local problems is essential in a globalized world to prevent international spread of threatened pandemics or, more simply, spread of unhealthful lifestyles to countries in mid-development of a middle class along with a massive poor population.

The management of resources to achieve productivity and measurable success has been characterized and accompanied by development of systems of organizing people to create solutions to problems or to innovate toward defined objectives. Management, like medicine, is both a science and an art. The application of scientific knowledge and technology in medicine involves both theory and practice. Similarly, management practice involves elements of organizational theory, which, in turn, draws on behavioural and social sciences and quantitative methodologies. The application of organizational theory in health care has evolved and become an integral part of training for, and the practice of, health administration. Delegation of responsibilities in health systems, such as in intensive care units, is fundamental to success in patient care with nurse taking increasing responsibility for management of the severely ill patient with multiple system failure.

Management of Patient Behaviour

Human behaviour is individual but takes place in a social context. Changing individual behaviour is needed to reduce risk factors for many diseases. Change can be threatening; it requires alteration, substitution, transformation, methods, or style. Implementation of plans usually requires some change, which often meets resistance. The resistance to change may be professional, technical, psychological, political, emotional, or a mix of all of these. The manager of a health facility or service has to cope with change and gather the support of those involved to participate in creating or implementing the change effectively. Change at the individual level is essential to achieve the goals of the group, whether this is in terms of the functioning of a health care service unit, such as hospital, or whether it is an individual's decision to change from smoking to non-smoking status. The health of the individual and a population both depend on the team member's motivation and experience. The behaviour of the individual is important for his own and community health. Even small steps in the direction of a desirable change in behaviour should be rewarded as soon as possible (i.e. reinforcing positive performance in increments). Change in behaviour is vital in the health field. The health belief model is widely influential in psychology and health promotion. The belief intervention approach involves programmes meant to reduce risk factors or a public health problem. It may require change in organizational behaviour, with involvement and feedback to the people who determine policy, those who manage services, and the community being served.

The concept of empowerment entered the service industries with the rationale that improvement in quality and effectiveness of service require the active physical and emotional participation of the worker. Participation in the decision-making is the key to empowerment. This requires management to adopt new methods that allow the worker, whether professional or manual, to be an active participant. Successful application of the empowerment principles in health care extends to the patient, the family, and the community, emphasizing patients' rights to informed participation in decision affecting their medical care, and the protection of privacy and dignity.

Management involves skills that are not automatically part of a health professional's training. Skilled clinicians often move into positions requiring management skills in order to build and develop the health care infrastructure. Clinical capability does not transfer automatically into management skills to deal with personnel, budgets, and resources. Therefore, training in management is vital for the health professional. The manager needs training for investigations and fact finding as well as the ability to evaluate people, programmes, and issues, and set priorities for dealing with the short-term and long-term issues. Negotiating with staff and outside agencies is a constant activity of the manager, ranging from the trivial to major decisions with wide implications. Perhaps the most crucial skill of the manager is communication; the ability to convey verbal, written, or unwritten messages that are received and understood and to assess the responses as an equal part of the exchange.

Hospital directors in the past were often senior physicians, often called the Superintendent, without training in health management. In India, they are still called Superintendent. The business manager, CEO (Company Executive Officer), has become common in hospital management in the United States. During 1955, when the CEO was called administrator, he or she worked under the direction of a board of trustees who raised funds, set policies, and were often involved in internal administration. Where the CEO was a non-physician, the usual case in some hospitals, often a conflict existed with the clinical staff of the hospital. In some settings, this led to the appointment of a parallel structure with a full-time chief of medical staff with a focus on clinical and qualitative matters. In European hospitals, the CEO is usually a physician, often by law, and the integration of the management function with the role of clinical chief is the prevalent model. Over time, the CEO role has changed to one of a coordinator as the cost and complexity of the health system have increased. The CEO is now more involved in external relations and less in the day-to-day operation of the facility. The CEO is a leader/partner but *premium inter pares*, or first among equals, in a management team that shares information and works to define objectives and solve problems. This de-emphasizes the authoritarian role and stresses the integrative function. The CEO is responsible for the financial management of operational and capital budgets of the facility, which is integral to the planning and future development of the facility. Budget includes four main factors: income, fixed or regular overhead, variable or unpredictable overhead, and capital or development costs, all essential to the survival and development of hospital organization (Tilchinsky and Varavikova, 2009: 455).

Risk Management in Health

Many situations in health promotion can be seen as an example of decision-making in the presence of high risk, involving imperfect information as well as personal preferences, which, at times, can be regarded as inconsistent with rational behaviour.

Risk consists of two parts: an undesirable outcome and the probability of its occurrence. Both have to be seen together, though often the focus is exclusively on outcome.

Risk management can be thought of as going through five steps: identification, analysis, evaluation of actions, implementations and documentations, as seen in Table 1.

Table 1
The Five Steps of Risk Management

1. Risk identification- determining the possible risks faced by a population, company, etc.
2. Risk analysis- determining the importance of the risk, in terms of probability of occurrence and impact, as well as the expected effect of some alternative actions.
3. Action evaluation- determining what can be done to reduce the probability of the event or to mitigate its impact.
4. Implementation- ensuring that responsibility for implementing the decided actions is assigned and the decisions are executed.
5. Documentation- of the analysis performed, the actions taken and the outcomes. This will allow in taking better decisions in the future.

Source: Kunreuther (2002).

Example of the risk situation: A new disease has struck a city with one million inhabitants. Six hundred individuals have been infected. One can adopt emergency programme A, which will save 200 people with certainty or one can adopt emergency programme B, employing a new drug. In the programme B, there is a probability of one-third that all people will be saved and probability of two-third, that all will die. What should one do? (Rosenmoller et al., 2006), (Figure 1).

Figure 1
Example of Decision Analysis

Source: Rosenmoller et al., 2006.

When analysing risk, one has to make a clear distinction between good decisions and good outcomes. Unfortunately, the public often confound the two, particularly in the area of public health. In the example above, a bad decision would be the choice of implementing Programme A or Programme B without previous analysis. A good decision would require a detailed analysis, followed by a value judgement and a choice of Programme A or Programme B. In the presence of uncertainty, the outcome of decision cannot be influenced. Only due to the previous analysis, one can be able to make an informed decision, and thus a good decision.

One has to clearly distinguish between the risk analysis (which can be made by anybody with experience in the field) and the value judgement, which is reserved for the decision-maker (e.g. patient, doctor, health official), based on the previous analysis and set of preferences. It is very important to realize that different people have different risk profiles. That is, the same risk does not mean the same thing to different people; some are more risk-averse, others risk-prone. For example, participating in an experimental drug trial will not be acceptable to a healthy person, while patients with the particular illness to be treated by that drug might exhibit a different preference profile. A curious phenomenon is often present: individuals are risk-seeking when choosing between two losing options but risk-averse when choosing between winning options.

The Figure 1 analysis shows that from the perspective of probability theory, alternatives A and B are equivalent in their expected outcomes, as both have an expected value of people saved equal to 200. This addresses the second point, the value judgement. The risk analysis should never be accepted at face value, it needs to be followed by the decision-maker's value judgement.

Another important element of the risk management is that health officials must be aware of how much risk is there and how the situation is being perceived by the public. There is ample scientific evidence that usually the mapping between actual risks and perceived risks is not congruent. This is primarily due to the cognitive inefficiencies of individuals and people's inability to judge (small) probabilities. Furthermore, a number of psychological effects are involved, leading to misperceptions of risk. Among them one can list voluntary vs. coerced (e.g. working in a nuclear plant vs. living in a nearby village), natural vs. industrial (e.g. sun radiation vs. telephone antennas), familiar vs. not familiar (car driving vs. canoeing), not dreaded vs. dreaded (high blood pressure vs. cancer), chronic vs. catastrophic (car accidents vs. airplane accidents), fair vs. unfair (riding a motorcycle at high speed vs. a pedestrian being hit by the same motorcycle), and so on. Perceived risk is also influenced by imaginability and memorability of hazard (terrorists threats).

Since the late 1970s, a number of publications in scientific journals have dealt with the topic of risk perception. Slovic et al. (1979) give comprehensive accounts of a series of studies and conclude that there are significantly significant differences in the judgements of risk between experts and lay persons, while expert judgements are closer to the truth than those of the public. Once risk is analysed one can move to risk mitigation measure. Risk mitigation generally uses two levers: technology and organization. Technology permits to lower the probability of unwanted outcomes or reduces the severity of unwanted outcomes. Changing standard procedures in the organization allows you to reduce the probability of unwanted outcomes that result from systemic errors in the organization to reduce the negative impact of the unwanted outcome (Pate-Cornell, 1996). Disaster medical services developed in the several nations are an example of organizations' efforts to lessen the effect of unwanted outcomes (e.g. earthquake, flu epidemic).

It also consists of implementing the activities, assigning responsibilities in the implementation of ensuring supervision. Finally, it creates and maintains the proper documentation about the decision process, the assumption made, and the outcomes achieved, and provides the primary source for learning and improving.

Risk Communication

Besides risk assessment and development of control actions, there is another area in risk management that becomes critical when a crisis has already occurred involving numerous stakeholders, i.e. communicating risk to them. Risk communication is very different from risk analysis in the sense that the public tend to focus on outrage and pay less attention to hazard.

When organizations face a crisis with a high degree of uncertainty, communication is difficult because how the situation may evolve and how the public will react to the messages are unknown. In this uncertainty, it is hard to decide what information to reveal or to withhold, whether to speculate or not, and so on. Every crisis is different but at the same time many crises are similar, and one of the similarities is that all crises pose pretty much the same dilemmas of communication policy. Crises experts suggest that institutions should prepare for generic crises before they happen (Mitroff and Anagnos, 2000). The generic crises may include: economic (the sudden collapse of a currency), physical (destruction of a piece of equipment), those related to psychopathic behaviour (product alteration in the market), natural (earthquake), and so on.

Sandman (2002) lists 10 communication dilemmas that managers must deal with when addressing communication with the general public and other stakeholders (See Table 2). Each dilemma can be considered in a continuum from candour, where one has to decide that how much information should be shared and how much information should be hidden (Figure 2).

Table 2

Dilemmas in Risk Communication

Dilemma Extremes	
Candour	Secrecy
Speculation	Refusal to speculate
Tentativeness	Confidence
Being alarming	Being reassuring
Being human	Being professional
Being apologetic	Being defensive
Decentralization	Centralization
Democracy and individual control	Expert decision-making
Planning for denial and misery	Planning for panic
Erring on the side of caution	Taking chances

Source: Sandman (2002).

Figure 2
The Dilemma Continuum

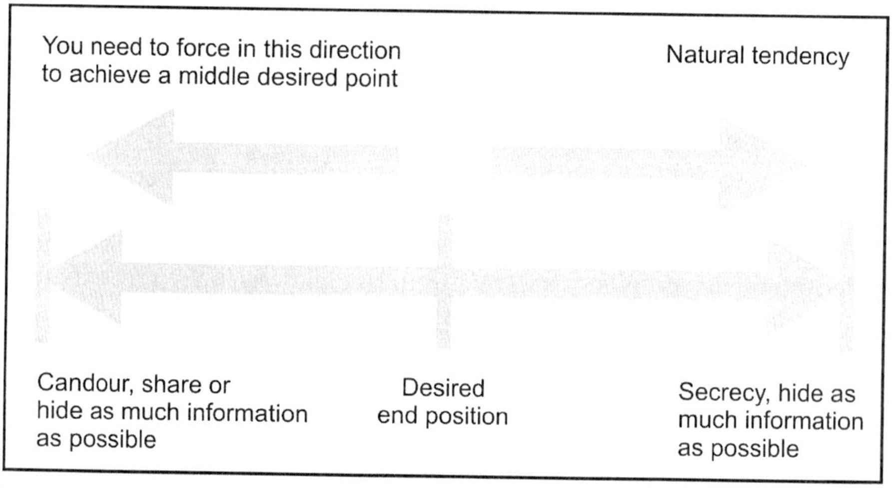

Source: Scheme developed by Jaume Ribera based on Sandman (2002).

Both extremes have clear advantages. In favour of candour would be that people are at their best when collectively facing a difficult situation. The worst is when they find out that they have been misled, then things can get much more unstable, they are more likely to ignore instructions, develop paranoid hypotheses, etc. On the other hand, secrecy might be indicated if the information has not yet been checked. The fear is that people will misunderstand the right information or might panic if they know the whole truth. Another reason would be if opponents take advantage of what is said. Probably the optimal approach is to strike a balance, providing enough information for the communication receiver to be able to act in a positive way, while not disclosing information that is not sufficiently checked and which could mislead the public. However, in all these dilemmas, one may have a natural tendency towards the right, so one ends up in a more moderate situation, i.e. pull towards the left. Becoming aware of these dilemmas is the first step towards handling them better.

Message Mapping

When a crisis appears, perceptions and opinions may have as important a role in determining its resolution as executive actions do. If people do not understand the message directed to them, they will feel irritated and will not follow further advice. On some occasions, people are outraged because they do not understand the risk, and educating the public may work, but in other cases, they do understand the risk and the irritation may be caused by the form of communication (e.g. feeling that the person in charge is withholding information, or receiving what they understand as contradictory versions from different people).

Message mapping is an important tool to assist crisis communication. It aims at achieving message clarity and conciseness and is based on developing a consensus message platform, providing visual aids and road maps for displaying structurally organized responses to anticipated high concern issues, focused at specific stakeholder groups. These are based on widely used mind mapping tools and can be developed manually, or with computer support.

Covello (2002) proposes the following goals of message maps:

- Identifying stakeholders early in the communication process.
- Anticipating stakeholder questions and concerns before they are raised.
- Organized thinking and developing prepared messages in response to anticipated stakeholder questions and concerns.
- Developing key messages and supporting information within a clear, concise, transparent and accessible framework.
- Promoting open dialogue about messages both inside and outside the organization.
- Providing user-friendly guidance to spokespersons.
- Ensuring that the organization has a central repository of consistent messages.
- Encouraging the organization to speak with one voice.

In any crisis it is very helpful to have a message map available, both because of the fact of having them and because of the learning and consensus building involved in producing them. A message map will be developed for a specific stakeholder group and for each main concern that affects this group. Therefore, the first stage in developing the message involves the identification of stakeholder groups and eliciting or discovering their main concerns.

This process can be done in two directions, from the stakeholders to the concerns and vice versa. Some groups prefer a structured 'top-down' approach, first creating a list of stakeholders and then identifying the concerns that they might have. Other groups prefer a 'bottom-up' approach, focusing first on the concerns brought up by crisis and then identifying which stakeholders may be affected by them. In both the cases, what one obtains is a rather extensive list of stakeholders and specific concerns that need to be clustered around stakeholder groups and general concerns, in order to bring the list down to a manageable size. Possible stakeholders in a public health case may include the victims and their families, media, emergency response personnel, law enforcement agencies, hospitals and primary health centres and medical associations. The concerns of each group can be drawn from media reports, web pages of activist groups, meeting records, interviews with group representatives, reviews of complaints received, surveys and focus group meetings.

In the second stage, for each of the main stakeholders and their important concerns, you will need to develop the key messages. One can now concentrate on what they most need to know, what they most want to know and what they are most concerned with. Key messages are generally developed in brainstorming sessions with technical experts, communication specialists, legal advisors and possibly a facilitator. The objective of this phase is to create a set of key messages, addressing a concern of a stakeholder group. A key message may consist of a whole sentence or just two or three keywords, which will later be developed into full messages.

In the third stage, one needs to develop supporting facts and arguments as proof of the messages. Even though one will probably not include these in the primary message, they may be very handy if a particular message is challenged by someone in the audience. As a final stage, before the message is delivered, it is prudent to conduct some testing, presenting the messages to experts and surrogate target audiences, both internal and external.

Health Communication

Health communication is the dissemination and interpretation of health-related messages. The disseminator may be an individual, an organization, or a mass medium. The interpreter may be an individual, a group, an organization, or an indiscriminate mass public. A system is a set of components surrounded by a boundary that regulates the flow of inputs and a transformation into outputs. Below we will look into the interdependence between health care providers and the recipients of that care, as influenced by external structural considerations. Further, the communication system will disseminate health information to a broad general public.

Culture, Communication and Health Promotion

Culture is a system of interrelated values active enough to influence and condition perception, judgment, communication, and behaviour in a given society (Mazrui, 1986: 239). Culture is as much a structure as it is economic and political, and is rooted in institutions such as families and schools as well as in communication industries. 'Culture embodies those moral, ethical and aesthetic values, the set of spiritual eyeglass, through which people come to view themselves and their place in universe. Language as a culture is the collective memory bank of a people's experience in history' (Thiong'O, 1993: 14).

In health promotion and behaviour change programmes, cultural sensitivity refers to the need to develop programmes in ways that are consistent with people's and community's cultural framework, rather than based on the Western paradigm within which most health education, and development programmes are planned, implemented, and evaluated.

Health denotes a process of adaptation. It is the result not of instinct, but of an autonomous yet culturally shaped reaction to socially created reality (Illich, 1976). For example, illness is a socially recognized state, carrying with it certain specific drawbacks, obligations, and privileges, depending on the circumstances (Basch, 1990). Each culture creates its own responses to health and disease.

'To open up to the culture's soul is to allow one to become wet, to become soaked in the cultural and historical waters of those individuals who are involved in the experience' (Freire, 1993: 106). Such involvement and total commitment are transformative for both the interventionists and the target population. The resulting reformation of the curriculum/ programmatic paradigm includes affirmation and encouragement of different languages of expression, health beliefs, and cultural values. For example, binary opposition is unnecessarily constructed between modern information channels that are based on the Western construct and traditional information channels (oral communication). Both systems of communication are effectively functional within their context; in some cases, the two are quite complementary. Unfortunately, many health communication programmes in the past have negated a form of cultural production by ignoring oral communication.

Cultural dynamics such as communication codes, meanings, and context between the storyteller and listener promote knowledge production and acquisition. Thus, oral tradition generally is not only the heritage of the spoken or sung word; it is also the heritage of the ear (Fiske, 1990). Stated differently, people in oral traditional cultures are accustomed to learning by listening. Learning by seeing is important to the extent that what is seen is congruent with what is heard. Critical aspects of learning by listening include who was speaking, the way the words were said, and in what context. This issue raises questions about the ethical and cultural incongruence of assuming the role of storyteller without training or education for that role, and without a thorough understanding of the cultural implications of storytelling for learning.

Given the realities of cultural production, the use of posters, flyers, and other pictorial learning tools in health promotion and health communication programmes may have limited, if any, impacts in many cultures. Even when such materials are culturally appropriate, there are still questions to be addressed with respect to when and how they should be used. Alternative methods of cross-cultural communication should be explored to ensure that the process does not disempower the target approach. When listening is the culturally appropriate method of learning, health professionals involved in developing, implementing, and evaluating programmes in cultures other than their own should be required to develop the requisite skills for effective and meaningful programme implementation. Furthermore, institutions of higher learning that have claimed intellectual hegemony over teaching and learning should reform their health curricula to reflect the cultural realities of the global population.

Summing Up

Health care is one of the growing industries in any country. It is a service, not a production industry, and is vital to the health and well-being of the individual, the population, and the economy. Because it employs large numbers of skilled professionals and many unskilled persons, it is often vital to the economic survival of small communities, as well as for a sense of community well-being.

Health management includes planning, leading, controlling, organizing, motivating, and decision-making. It is the application of resources and personnel toward achieving targets. Therefore, it involves the study of the use of resources, and the motivation and function of the people involved, including the producer or provider of service, and he customer, client or patient. This cannot take place in vacuum, but is based on the continuous monitoring of information and its communication to all parties involved. These functions are applicable at all levels of management, from policy to operational management of production or a service system.

Risk assessment is the process by which risks are identified and quantified and risk management is the process by which this information is used in making decisions to reduce or eliminate the risk. When there are fundamental uncertainties in a problem, there is often a tendency to resort to 'conservative estimates' which then adds up to a model that is far too conservative. Risk management in the public sector addresses economic efficiency and justice and equality. There is a lack of consistency in public decision-making in the face of risk. An essential ingredient in any risk management programme is that of risk communication. When addressing a crisis, health officials should not only consider the critical elements of risk (probability and impact) but also the outrage experienced by the population. Message mapping is an effective way to identify stakeholders early in the communication process, anticipate their questions and concerns before they are raised, and prepare key messages and supporting information within a clear, concise, transparent and accessible framework. It is also a great tool to open an internal dialogue among the professionals and to develop consensus on how to handle typical communication dilemmas.

References

Basch, P. (1990), *Textbook of International Health*, New York: Oxford University Press.

Covello, V. (2002), *Message Mapping*, WHO Workshop on Bioterrorism, Geneva: WHO.

Fiske, J. (1990), 'A Role of Communication Theory in Ethnography and Cultural Analysis', Unpublished Manuscript, University of Massachusetts.

Freire, P. (1993), *Pedagogy of the Oppressed*, New York: Continuum.

Illich, Ivan (1976), *Medical Nemesis*, New York: Pantheon.

Kunreuther, H. (2002), 'Risk Analysis and Risk Management in an Uncertain World', *Risk Analysis*, 22(4): 655–64.

Mazuri, A.A. (1986), *The Africans: A Triple Heritage*, Boston: Little Brown.

Mitroff, I.I. and G. Anagnos (2000), *Managing Crises Before They Happen: What Every Executive and Manager Needs to Know About Crisis Management*, New York: Amacom.

Pate-Cornell, M.E. (1996), 'Uncertainties in Risk Analysis: Six Levels of Treatment', *Reliability Engineering and Systems Safety*, 54: 95–111.

Rosenmoller, M. et al. (2006), 'Risk Management, Perception and Communication in Health Care', in Maggie Davies and Wendy Macdowall (eds), *Health Promotion Theory*, New Delhi: Tata McGraw-Hill.

Sandman, P.M. (2002), *Dilemmas in Emergency Communication Policy: Emergency Risk Communication CDCynergy*, Atlanta, GA: Centres for Disease Control and Prevention, UD Department of Health and Human Services (CD-RIM)

Slovic, P. et al. (1979), 'Rating the Risk', *Environment*, 2: 14–20.

Thiong'O, Ngugi wa (1993), *Moving the Centre: The Struggle for Cultural Freedom*, London: Curry.

Tulchinsky, Theodore H. and Elena A. Varavikova (2009), *The New Public Health*, London: Elsevier Academic Press.

Section III

Systems of Medicine, Hospital and Social Relationship

12

Systems of Medicine and Medical Pluralism in India

Indeed there is a great variety of knowledge, means, methods and skills that the Indian people have gained. Medical care in India also has plurality of systems of medicine which people have been using over a period of time.

Indigenous Systems of Medicine (ISM)

Ayurveda, siddha and unani are indigenous systems of medicine in India in relation to biomedicine that was introduced by the colonial state two centuries ago. Interestingly, homoeopathy and naturopathy – also entrants during the colonial rule – have found considerable support among people and have been formally grouped together with ISM in the current acronym of the government department (AYUSH). Homoeopathy in India today has the second largest number of practitioners after ayurveda and naturopathy, which was consonant with Gandhi's philosophy of life and is aligned with yoga to offer a coherent model for a healthy lifestyle in contemporary India (Sujatha and Abraham, 2012).

Indian society is regarded as a pluralistic society with different types of cultures, ethnic population and different religious categories and at the same time having rich systems of medicine which look at health, causes of disease and medicine in an all together different mode of treatment. These together are called Indian Systems of Medicine or Indigenous Systems of Medicine. Their main idea is to look at the integrated health and well-being of the society. However, in India, during the British rule the network of allopathic system of medicine started spreading its wings. It was serving the elite classes of society. The allopathic system of medicine is also called modern system of medicine or scientific system of medicine. The traditional system of medicine or indigenous systems of medicine included ayurveda, unani, siddha and naturopathy. However, these systems did not receive patronage from the government and therefore, suffered in its expansion and researches. These systems of medicine are popularly known as Indian Systems of Medicine (ISM). They received little attention for the public health discussion. Though, finally the Government of India recognized the Indian System of Medicine, which included: ayurveda, unani, siddha, naturopathy and yoga. Homoeopathy is also recognized by government of India as a system of medicine. During the colonial time, homoeopathy had also entered in India and became quite a popular system of health care.

In 1995, the Ministry of Health and Family Welfare had given an independent identity to the Indian Systems of Medicine and Homoeopathy (ISM and H). Again in 2003, these systems were renamed under the heading of Department of Ayurveda, Yoga, Naturopathy, Unani, Siddha and Homoeopathy (AYUSH). AYUSH means long life. The Ministry has given directions to the state governments to include them in the recognized systems of medicine. They also opened AYUSH centres in the respective states. Even in 2005, during the Rural Health Care Mission, AYUSH was propagated. This is precisely done to encourage these systems as the holistic systems and indigenous systems which look towards human health. These systems are entrusted with better alternatives for chronic diseases and also for prevention and promotive interventions for health. Besides AYUSH, there are other health care practices also which are vastly used by the rural and tribal people and they vary from one region to another region and are known as Local Health Traditions (LHT). Local Health Traditions are defined as health promotive, preventive and curative methods having mass acceptance and prevalence among households of different socio-economic background. Although, these systems do have some threads with the indigenous health scripts, however, they do not conform to the same ancient health systems and their scripts. They may be confined to some households as home remedies or may be some services provided by folk practitioners. They are not regarded as scientific and do not have the textual references, but they are time tested through people's usability and experiential knowledge. Other forms of health providers who are informal in the social structure are also recognized by the people in the rural structure of the Indian society. They are: Traditional Health Practitioners (THP), Folk Healers (FoH), Faith Healers (FH), *Dais* and Traditional Birth Attendants (TBAs). They also treat the people for their health problems.

Epistemologically, the codified indigenous systems of medicine like ayurveda, unani and siddha are far more compatible, but unfortunately did not receive the state patronage. The indigenous systems of medicine consist of codified and organized knowledge with sophisticated theoretical foundations, expressed in several manuscripts and covering all branches of medicine and surgery. It functions through institutions in the areas of teaching, research and manufacture. The medical practice, however, is largely non-institutionalized, and mainly carried out in clinics. Ayurveda is the main indigenous system of medicine in India. Apart from mainstream ayurveda, there are its regional manifestations like the siddha (in Tamil Nadu) and the Tibetan medical systems.

ISM and Medical Education

The early engagement of colonial powers with ISM was guided by economic and trade interests and a scientific curiosity supported by mercantile pluralism. Historical accounts of this period cites certain facts; for example, that there was an official cannon salute at Fort Williams to symbolize the triumph of modern science when Madhusudan Gupta, an ayurveda *vaidya* who joined the reconstituted medical college, dissected the first cadaver. While this act was ridden with symbolism both for the colonial state as well as for a certain variety of medical history-writing which sees the all-encompassing nature of the colonial power; what is of interest to us is the response of the ayurvedic practitioners to the introduction of modern medicine, and specifically to such symbolic acts. These historical accounts concur with the colonial portrayal of indigenous medicine as 'closed' systems and as opposed to scientific methods. The facts that anatomy and dissection as epistemic tools were neither entirely new to indigenous systems such as ayurveda and that during this period several *vaidya* and *hakims* learnt modern anatomy and surgery from Indian or British surgeons and some of them chose to incorporate it into the curriculum in the new ayurveda and unani colleges that they established are ignored when the emphasis is on symbolic acts.

Medical education in ISM has seen an enormous growth in recent years. At present, there are 219 medical colleges that offer undergraduate training in ayurveda (BAMS), 37 in unani (BUMS) and six in siddha (BSMS). The total annual turnover of ayurveda, yoga, unani, siddha and homoeopathy (AYUSH) graduates from 450 medical colleges is around 20,000. There have been some experiments in institutional arrangements for learning ayurveda. For instance, during the 1980s one of the colleges attempted to include in the modern curricula elements of the traditional *gurukula* system. Besides the regular course work students underwent extended periods of apprenticeship with well-known traditional *vaids* and some of these *vaids* also spent periods of residence in the college. The curriculum for the undergraduate degree programme of ISM includes the biomedical subjects of anatomy and physiology.

ISM before Independence

The services of *vaids* and *hakims* were employed during the 1860s and 1870s by the administration in Punjab to popularize its vaccination programme among the masses (Hume, 1977). The high success rate of these trails led to the development of a programme in 1867 under which practising *hakims* trained in the unani system were re-trained in aspects of Western medicine and were employed to provide medical relief to the rural masses. Such schemes were started in a few medical schools and in the Oriental College where allopathic lessons were conducted in Urdu and English. Little is known, however, about what the *hakims* and *vaidya* made of the western medicine imparted to them, what kind of medicine they actually practised or how they negotiated with their dual roles and identities once they returned to their rural communities. Colonial state also began supporting the training of *dais* from 1902 onwards. The requirements to join and complete the various courses were not easy for women in general; a vernacular or Anglo-vernacular lower primary certificate was needed, besides a certificate of good moral character to be able to enroll in midwifery training. The midwifery classes gradually picked up with the enrollment of Christian women, and the modern upper- and middle class women began to use the services of the newly trained midwives while continuing to opt for home births. According to *Forbes*, these new midwives 'went to homes, delivered babies like doctors and left. Cleaning up after birth and nursing the mother during the day of confinement were not a part of their duties' (Forbes, 2005: 99). The variety of functions performed by *dais* from the start of labour through the delivery and postpartum care were now reduced 'strictly' to the cleaning up, especially in upper class homes. The deskilling of *dais* by limiting their services to polluting tasks, along with the loss of upper class patronage now confined the professional domain of the *dais* to deliveries in lower caste and poor households (Sujatha and Abraham, 2012: 9).

Registration of ISM Practitioners during Colonial Time

By the turn of the 20th century, even Indians trained in Western medicine expressed their concern about repeated moves by the British to bring in Registration Acts that excluded the vast population of ISM practitioners, the withdrawal of several major land grants and allocations made to *vaids*, and stringent action against registered allopathic practitioners who associated with ISM institutions.

ISM and Medicine during Colonial Time

Ayurvedic and unani leaders such as P.S. Verma, P.S. Varier, the Azizis, Amal Khan, and others established new institutions for training and for commercial production of ISM medicines (Alvai, 2007). The *vaids* and *hakims* were shifting from households to bulk production of medicines at the same time when allopathic pharmacology in India was organizing itself against the total control of the British government over raw ingredients necessary for the allopathic pharmaceutical industry.

ISM and Training Institutions in Colonial Time

The development of ISM training institutions continued with support coming from associations of ISM practitioners, wealthy patrons and princely states such as Travancore, Cochin, Gwalior, Mysore and Hyderabad. The end result was that at the time of India's Independence there were more than 40 colleges of ayurveda, unani and siddha (Abraham, 2005). Unlike the case of Western medical education, institutional developments in ISM did not bring an end to the traditional forms of training conducted through *pathshalas* and through apprenticeships.

ISM Practitioners in Independent India

While the state in independent India inherited the functions set up by colonial forces, its approach to ISM has been ambivalent: excluding legitimacy without economic support or defining any specific role for the vast ISM resources that it recognizes (Sujatha and Abraham, 2012: 22). The establishment of various councils, national institutes, uniform curriculum, drug-testing laboratories and the publications of pharmacopoeia were direct outcomes of recommendations made by various committees set up by the government. The key, almost singular, concern of state-induced institutional development, however, has been the validation of ISM drugs in the laboratory along scientific lines and this is clearly expressed in their reports, pamphlets and website.

However, a number of institutions and arrangements have proliferated in the non-state through private trusts of *vaids,* their professional associations, community institutions and NGOs that mitigate the hegemony of the scientist model. In the West, medical pluralism is a carefully regulated state response to civic initiatives against the excesses of biomedicine. But the idea of pluralism is subverted by the fact that biomedical doctors often undertake training in CAM in order to sustain themselves in the highly competitive health care sector today (Cant and Sharma, 1999).

Currently, the AYUSH sector of the Government of India is large enough to warrant a disaggregated analysis of regional trends and variations so much so that even budgetary allocation of ISM has not been significant. First, the data suggest that the ISM facilities in the government institutions are uneven across the country (Abraham, 2005). For instance, they have a strong presence in states such as Maharashtra, UP, Karnataka and Kerala. These facilities are virtually absent in Jharkhand, Chhattisgarh, Arunachal Pradesh and Assam. Secondly, the data indicate that the popularity of ayurveda, siddha and unani varies in different parts of the country and has also waxed and waned over the years. West Bengal, which was historically a major centre of ayurveda, has fewer modern institutions in ISM. However, Bengal has emerged as a popular centre of homoeopathy. Thirdly, the data also contradict the general argument that attributes the popularity of ISM to the absence of allopathic facilities; those states with better distribution of allopathic facilities are also the ones with better ISM facilities. For example, in Kerala, Maharashtra and Karnataka, facilities in ISM and in allopathy are widespread (Sujatha and Abraham, 2012: 23).

According to recent data (GOI, 2005) there are nearly 7.1 lakh registered qualified AYUSH practitioners in India, of which about 2 lakh are not institutionally qualified. The overall trend in the growth of practitioners in the ISM since 1980 shows a doubling of the figures in the last 20 years. This may be due to the sudden growth of private ayurveda colleges during this period as a result of state policies to liberalize and privatize the education sector in the country. Between 1980 and 2000, about 186 new private ISM colleges were established (GOI, 2001). Further, the number of institutionally trained practitioners has been steadily growing while the number of non-institutionally trained practitioners shows a marginal increase up to 1995 and thereafter a decline. Thus, institutionally trained ISM practitioners are taking the place held by non-institutional practitioners, in both cases far outweighing the practitioners of biomedicine.

A programme for 'Mainstreaming Ayurveda' by integrating and collocating ayurveda, siddha, unani and yoga practitioners in primary and district health centres has been launched by the central government. It is evident that utilizing ayurveda doctors to provide allopathic services in remote areas because MBBS graduates are not willing to go there does not amount to any recognition of ayurveda's therapeutic value. On the other hand, the Tamil Nadu government's experiment in mainstreaming ISM seems to accord greater autonomy to ayurveda and siddha. The Tamil Nadu government formed a committee of ayurveda and siddha doctors and developed a kit of 50 medications for regular use that includes pasts for nutritional deficiency prescribed in ayurveda/siddha texts for pregnant mothers. These are distributed through Auxiliary Nurse and Midwife (ANMs) and Accredited Social Health Activist (ASHA) workers in interior areas.

Indian Systems of Medicine (ISM) and Medical Pluralism: The Cultural Context

Earlier, the Public Health System was not including the ISM, but now in 2005 the Rural Health Care Mission has given boost to the ISM by replacing it with AYUSH. The health culture in India is pluralistic in nature which means it negotiates with the various medical systems. People use different systems of medicine at the same time for the same illness or use different systems of medicine at different point of time for different ailments. This differential usability is based on their personal preference and also on the basis of gender, age group, or other social and economic criteria within the family. This phenomenon is universal, i.e. perhaps there are no families in India who have not used more than one system of medicine in their lifetime or may be for their family for different ailments. This is called medical pluralism. This dynamic therapeutic pluralism is supported by the philosophy of different systems of medicine and their cultural linkages which exist together. In the beginning it was thought that the traditional system of medicine will go away as science and development will grow, but it did not happen in spite of the percolation of modern education. Rather, it has given birth to the hierarchy of medical systems. Some systems got patronage from the political system and therefore, hierarchically they occupied superior position and in turn could also achieve their position at national and international levels. Allopathy has achieved its higher position as compared to other systems of medicine as it also remained privileged even after Independence. It is regarded as the most scientific system of medicine and the only legitimate system which places it at a superior position in the hierarchy. The discourse did not take place much on why a particular system has received much higher position and why the other systems of medicine has been neglected? There are a number of sociological studies that have focused on the preference of a particular system of medicine by the people. In 1960s and 1970s social scientists argued that allopathy was physically inaccessible to a large segment of the rural population and therefore, this vacuum was filled by other systems of medicine (Gould, 1965). Leslie (1980) pointed out that cultural belief systems of rural people determine their health seeking behaviour. Other anthropologists believed that it is folk classificatory model of illness that dominates the health behaviour. It can be concluded that people's health behaviour is influenced by broad cultural framework which is derived from ayurvedic system. Sociologists in their studies of use of different systems of medicine concluded that people use non-allopathic systems because they are less expensive, easily available and the interaction with practitioners takes place in a more intimate manner.

Besides that there is growing alienation from the allopathic system of medicine because of its unsatisfactory cures for many ailments and side effects. Allopathic medicine is not preferred by many because of its invasive methods of diagnosis and unethical practices. There is a greed for profits which is highly practised in the treatment by allopathic practitioners. However, the initiation taken by the government by recognizing multiple health systems has provided broader social and political context for the growth of medical pluralism.

Ayurveda, yoga and naturopathy, unani, siddha and homoeopathy (AYUSH) are Indian systems of medicine. As per the state-wise distribution provided by the Department of ISM and H, there are more practitioners of AYUSH than of allopathy in India.

Medical Pluralism in India

Medical Pluralism is the name given to the situation where a patient has a number of choices while selecting a system of treatment. The term was coined specifically to describe the treatment avenues available in the early modern age, i.e. barbershop surgeon, apothecaries, physicians or wise women/village elders. A person suffering from illness or disease could choose from these potential treatment sources or in fact choose them all that is called medical pluralism. Medical pluralism is the adoption of more than one medical system, or the simultaneous integration of indigenous and modern systems of medicine.

The term medical pluralism was introduced by the social sciences in the mid-1970s to characterize the situation in the Third World in which people were resorting to multiple options for health care outside the governmental health care system based on biomedicine. By the 1990s, however, medical pluralism became the buzzword in the West as well and came to denote the inclusion of Complementary and Alternative Medicine (CAM) within the state health administration. The ever increasing demand for cure and care for a growing range of health conditions which elude any particular system of medicine has made pluralism in therapeutic options a way of modern life. Pluralism in treatment-seeking among all sections of people is well known; among the poor and the well-off sections of both 'underdeveloped' as well as the most 'developed' countries (GOI, 2002; WHO, 2002).

In India, the colonial state and independent state did not ban or strictly regulate the indigenous systems of medicine, namely, ayurveda, siddha and unani (henceforth Indian Systems of Medicine, ISM). In India, pluralism in health care has been officially supported since the beginning of the development of planned health services in the post-Independence period, which included bio-medicine and six other systems (ayurveda, yoga, naturopathy, unani, siddha and homoeopathy).

Health care in India presents a complex scenario and that is significantly influenced by colonial and postcolonial history and politics of country. Multiple medical systems such as bio-medicine (allopathy), ayurveda, unani, siddha, homoeopathy, naturopathy, yoga and a variety of folk traditions all contribute to providing health care in present time. In the following pages we will discuss ayurveda, siddha and unani, allopathy, homoeopathy and other alternative systems of medicine in their historical, social and scientific base.

Ayurveda

Ayurveda is one of the oldest scientific medical systems in the world. The history of the origin of ayurveda starts almost from the beginning of the creation. The ayurveda, the Veda of long life, of therapeutics, was first preached by Brahma according to the tradition. From Brahma, Prajapati or Daksha received it, from him it came down to Ashwvin twins and from them to Indra. Further, according to Sushruta, Indra taught ayurveda to Dhanvantri, (i.e. the professor of surgery), the surgeons of Gods embodied as king Divodasa of Benaras. Divodasa then transmitted it to the wise men, who approached him as pupils, out of sympathy for the suffering of humanity, and also in order to prolong their own life. However, he taught ayurveda to Sushruta along with his six companions, with special reference to surgery. Ayurveda is composed of two words – 'Ayur' and 'Veda' which put together literally mean 'science of life'. As regards the definite meaning, it would be interesting to note that the 'life' which is the preview of ayurveda connotes a combination of body, perceptory organs, mind and soul. For the promotion, prolongation and maintenance of health, ayurveda prescribes the observation of certain principles of daily routine, night routine, seasonal routine and ethical routine and also stresses that one must follow a regulated diet, sleep and avoid mental and sexual intercourse without purpose. Thus, ayurveda is not only a medical science, but also a way of life.

Ayurveda takes into account the fundamental principles like the creation theory of Panchmahabhuta, the physiopathological thought of *Tridosha* (*vata*, *pitta* and *kapha*), and even the evaluation process of universe and creation, since it believes that there is no essential difference between the outside world and the human body. According to ayurveda, illness occurs if there is any derangement in the body humours such as *vata*, *pitta* and *kapha* or in the psychic factors such as satwa, rajas and tamas caused either by excessive or inadequate interactions. Ayurveda is a very old system of medicine in India and it has its unbroken history of over 3000 years. It also has its medical texts which were written in a period between 1500 BC to 1900 AD. Ayurveda has also its documentation in over 1,00,000 manuscripts. Many of its texts are in Sanskrit language. Different ayurvedic colleges engaged in teaching and research on ayurveda are transmitting the knowledge via these textbooks from one generation to another, and in turn are keeping alive the knowledge of ayurveda. The medical colleges which are teaching and doing research in ayurveda are also adding their knowledge to this system of medicine. Ayurveda is also enriched with the added clinical experience, resources and insights of the ayurvedic practitioners. Ayurveda is regarded as the most ancient system of medicines with its efficacy and its outcome of treatment with no threat of side effects. It had originated during Vedic times, and has progressed because of its experimental, perceptual orientation and intuitiveness. The main goal of ayurveda is to promote health and get rid of ailments so as to enhance humanity of all sorts of pain, i.e. physical, mental, intellectual and spiritual. Ayurveda is basically a knowledge about life and deals with humanity. It tries to find out the root cause of the disease and its treatment is based on the natural or herbal products.

Diagnosis in Ayurveda

Ayurveda diagnoses the deviation from the state of equilibrium of *doshas*. Ayurveda also emphasizes the patient's case history, physical examination and a rational approach of diagnosis. The focus of Ayurvedic diagnosis, however, is different from that of Western medicine due to difference in perception between the two systems. Since the central tenet of its theory is that illness results from imbalance of *dosh* (functions), identification of the impaired *dosh/doshas* play an important role in ayurvedic diagnosis. While this is addressed by the evaluating factors such as the patient's inherent physical and mental constitution (*prakriti*), age, occupation, the season in which the disease has manifested itself, the region in which the patient lives, the patient's food habits, and so on. This helps fine-tune the diagnosis and aids the physician in tailoring and customizing the treatment to meet the specific therapeutic needs of the individual.

To help diagnose the pathological state of *doshas,* all clinical symptoms have been classified under the three *doshas*. To illustrate this, consider swelling. While an air-filled swelling associated with pain indicates involvement of *vata,* reddishness and burning sensation denote aggravation of *pitta*. On the other hand, if it is a pitting/fluid-filled oedema associated with no pain or dull pain, *kapha* is impaired. A combination of these would indicate the derangement of more than one *dosha*. All clinical symptoms ranging from cold, cough, fever, and diarrhoea, to swelling and skin discolouration, have been classified under *vata, pitta* and *kapha*. It is to be noted that no clinical symptoms can elude the purview of this *doshic* classification.

In ayurveda, the clinical symptoms of the disease are understood in terms of imbalance of *dosha/doshas*. Aetiology is thus known for every disease in ayurveda. Moreover, the affected *doshas* are further identified with the causative factors of this imbalance such as diet and activities (physical and mental).

Treatment in Ayurveda

Ayurveda defines *cikitsa* (treatment) in the following ways: 'measures aimed at removal of disease-causing factors' and 'correction of the imbalances and restoration of the health condition'. Charaka has expanded the scope of the term treatment further. He said, 'mere removal of the causative factors may not always result in complete removal of the disease because effects of the disease may still continue to be operative. So, the treatment should aim at mitigating both the cause and effect'. Ayurvedic treatment, thus, aims not only at removal of the disease-causing factors but also at restoration of the equilibrium of *doshas* and body functions in a way which is compatible, conducive and nourishing to the patients without weakening them. Sushruta goes on to say that a proper treatment not only alleviates the disease but also cures the patient completely without causing recurrence, side effects or creating newer diseases.

A combination of medicines, medical procedures (*panchakarmas),* diet and activities (mental and physical) are adopted in treatment. Just as all clinical symptoms are classified in terms of *tridoshas*, all treatment components are also understood in terms of *doshic* classification. For example, medicines are categorized according to their action on either one/two/all the *doshas* – *rasnadi kashayam* is *vata – reducing whereas dashamulakatutrayam* is a *kapha*-reducing medicine. Food is also similarly categorized. All substances are first classified into six *rasas* (tastes) – a substance can either be a single *rasa* or a combination of *rasas,* which are then understood in terms of *doshas*. For example, while sweet and fatty items increase *kapha* (that is, certain functions and parameters in the body) and decrease *pitta* and *vata* (certain other functions and parameters), those which are hot (for example, chilli) will increase *pitta* (predominantly) and *vata* and reduce *kapha*.

The relation between physical and mental activities and *doshas are* as follows: while physical exercise will increase *vata*, mental activities such as worrying and anger will increase *vata* and *pitta,* respectively. Everything ranging from medicines and diet to mental, physical and emotional activities and even seasons are categorized and understood in terms of the changes they cause in the various functions and parameters of the body, that is, the *doshas*. Once the disease-causing *dosha* is diagnosed, the entire treatment is planned to bring back the deranged functions to balance using a variety of treatment modalities.

Siddha

Siddha system is regarded as one of the oldest systems of medicine in India. The meaning of 'siddha' is achievement. The literature of sidhha is written in Tamil language and is also practised in Tamil society. This system of medicine is believed to have evolved in Tamil Nadu, although siddha medical literature talks of the 'Siddhas of Varanasi'. The system is largely therapeutic in nature and specializes in pharmacy. It was practised by 'Siddhars', a Shaivite sect which aimed at maintaining perfect health in order to achieve 'siddhi' or heavenly bliss.

The practitioners of siddha are called Siddhars. They are saintly persons and achieved the result in medicine through yoga. They establish the intense links between man and environment. The Siddhars believe that the human body is replica of the universe, as also are food and drugs.

Unlike ayurveda, which was primarily a system of medicines, siddha medicine was an offshoot of the siddha yogi's experiments in yoga and alchemy towards the achievement of an uninterrupted lifespan and an imputrescible body in this world.

Diagnosis in Siddha

Siddha system believes that all objects in the universe are composed of five elements and these are: earth, water, fire, air and space or ether. Thus, the human body is also composed of these five elements. The food that we eat and the drugs we use are also made up of these five elements. As the earth is susceptible to natural calamities and epidemics, the human organs are influenced by food, poison, the seasons and mental stress. The siddha system views the human body as a conglomeration of three *doshas*, seven *dhatus* and three *malas*. Food is the basic building material of the body which gets processed into *doshas, dhatus and malas*. Equilibrium between the three is considered to be 'health' and its imbalance regarded as 'disease' or 'sickness'. The diagnosis of disease involves identifying its causes. This is done by examining the pulse, urine, eyes, and studying abnormal sounds, the colour of the body and the tongue and above all, the status of *agni* (the digestive system of the body).

Treatment in Siddha

The siddha system emphasizes that treatment is not directed towards disease but has to be seen in totality which includes the environmental and meteorological considerations, age, sex, race, habits, mental frame, habitat, diet, appetite, physical conditions, physiological conditions, etc. The treatment focuses on normalization of the individual and it will reduce the chances of error. Sidhhas basically use mercury and sulphur and also other metals, minerals, plant and mineral parts for the medicines.

Siddha experiments in yogic practices involve the use of herbal and mineral substances that mitigate the effects of severe yogic practices and aid yogic attainments. Their works on the processing of metal and mineral substances and the procedure for the correct use of herbal ingredients constitute the corpus of siddha medicine. Metals and minerals as ideals of imperishable substances became key ingredients in siddha medicine for two reasons: the idea that imperishable substances as nourishment would be more conducive to the siddha ideal of the imputrescible body than herbs that are perishable, and the need to ensure steady supply of medicine unfettered by the seasonal availability of herbs.

Difference in Ayruveda and Siddha

The difference between ayurveda and siddha may be discerned in terms of philosophical orientation, history, spatial spread and language of expression. But their conceptual framework for medicine is the same: the theory of panchmahabhuta and *tridoshas* form the basic edifice of siddha and ayurveda. The pharmacological preparations in ayurveda and siddha follow similar principles as applied to plant, animal and mineral ingredients but, siddha medicines have more mineral and metal ingredients in their preparations. Though the siddha corpus was laid down by siddha yogis, not all the siddha practitioners were yogis. As a system of medicine, it was also carried forward by *vaids* trained in the gurukula system, as in ayurveda. In the popular perception of clinical practice, the *vaid* and lay people do not strictly delineate between siddha and ayurveda.

The basic principles of ayurveda and siddha are quite similar in terms of its fundamental and applied aspects. The basic differences which exists in these two systems is of language rather than of doctrine. Siddha medicine is more often practices in South. Its concepts are traced back to Sangam period (500 BC–500CE) in India. Sidhha system is very close to the chemistry and auxiliary to medicine and alchemy. The plants and minerals are regarded as of very high value for medicines in the siddha system.

Unani-Tibb

The Graeco-Roman system of medicine conserved and developed by the Arabs during the 8th to 13th centuries in the classical empires of Islam travelled to India in the 12th century. It was subsequently indigenized in the Indian subcontinent through interchange with ayurveda and through the translation of Arabic medical texts into Persian and Urdu, acquiring the name *Yunani Tibb* (Kumar, 1997; Alavi, 2007; Attewell, 2007). Thus, unani medicine came from West Asia 800 years ago.

The word 'unani' (Yunani) is a corruption of the Arabic word for Ionian, (i.e. Greek). The unani system had originated in Greece and in India also it has its very strong roots. Around 11th century, it was introduced in India by Arabs and Persians. In the contemporary time it is regarded as one of the leading countries that practises unani system of medicine. It has many educational institutions, research centres and health care institutions.

This system believes that disease is a natural process and the function of the physician is to aid the natural forces to the body. Unani system is based on a humoural theory. The four humours of this system are in the form of: blood, phlegm, yellow bile and black bile. Temperament is assigned to each humour and they are as follows: blood is hot and moist; phlegm is cold and moist; yellow bile is hot and dry; and the black bile is cold and dry. The drugs in the unani system are also assigned temperaments. These temperaments are: every person has a unique humoural constitution which represents his healthy state. Any change in this brings about a change in his state of health. A person also has a power of self-preservation or adjustment which strives to restore disturbances within his constitution. Unani places great reliance on a person's power. Thus, unani treatment not only helps the person to overcome the present disturbances, but also facilitates the person to acquire additional power of resistance to further disturbances. Since humours are produced for digested food, unani practitioners attach great importance to diet and digestion both in health and disease. For diagnosis, unani relies heavily on its method of testing pulse.

In India, the unani system closely interacted with the ayurvedic and other local medical systems. After subjecting them to its own tests, it absorbed the best of the native medical systems. Special attention was paid to the medicinal herbs found in India and several books on the therapeutic qualities of these herbs were written by Arab physicians. Gradually, the system set up several schools to impart instruction in the unani system of medicine; hospitals and dispensaries were established in large and in important cities for the treatment of the sick. Unani system asserts that the body has a self-preservation power and therefore, it always tries to restore any disturbance within the parameters prescribed by the constitution or state of the individual. The practitioners of unani only help in the action of that power.

Yoga

Yoga is a scientific system which focuses on the interaction of mind, body, brain and behaviour. It is basically about using the mind which in turn will affect the physical functioning and result in promoting health. Its basic method is meditation which includes certain postures, directed attention and free mind and does not involve any distraction. People use meditation to increase their focused attention, calmness and relaxation so that they can cope with illness and are able to enhance their health and well-being. There are various types of yoga practices for various types of ailments. Yoga is a combination of physical postures, breathing techniques and meditation. Yoga is also regarded as an art of living which focuses on a person's physical, moral, mental and spiritual aspects. This is not the propriety of certain persons but it is practised across the globe by different race, class, age, sex and creed for the well-being of the society.

The medical knowledge in India has viewed health as a state of harmony and disease as a state of imbalance. More emphasis is given to remaining healthy, not getting ill and then getting treatment for cure. Yoga is not regarded as a system of medicines like ayurveda or allopathy or homoeopathy. Although, yoga carries certain principles through which a person is advised to remain healthy and mentally free from worries. The meaning of yoga is joining or yoking the individual's soul to the universal soul which means the union of the personal soul with God. The origin of the word 'yoga' is from the Sanskrit word 'yuj', meaning thereby 'to join' or 'to yoke'. The Rigveda, which is regarded as an important text, is full of hymns and it tells that supernatural power can be achieved by following yoga. The first time the term yoga occurred was in the *Taittiriva Upanishad* (*Yaittriya Upanishad: II*) and the *Katha Upanishad* (*Katha Upanishad: II*). In *Vedas* and *Upanishads* we find the literature related with yogic concepts and techniques till about 300 BC. The old writings of yoga are complied in Yoga Sutras by Patanjali.

Howerver, Patanjali did not create the yoga techniques and philosophy but he only compiled them and published. He made use of theoretical and metaphysical foundation for yoga which already existed in the Samkhya philosophy and adapted it to yoga meditation. The other important work on yoga is also done by Patanjali. Although we do not have the full proof of it, but it is assumed that this relevant work could have been written later than the 10th century. It is assumed that these works must have been written in between 4th or 5th century AD. Yoga practices are regarded as very old healthy practices. Some of the Mohenjodaro excavations show that some divine being is sitting in a yogic posture which is enough to substantiate that time yoga may have been practised then as well. Yoga *asanas* are also narrated in *Rigveda*. *Upanishads* do have a different mention of yogic exercises and procedures. Patanjali was the one who systematized the existing yoga practices around 3rd century BC. He also linked it to the Samkhya school of philosophy. Thus, Patanjali evolved the yoga philosophy and then enunciated it in his Yoga Sutras. He mentioned eight components of yoga namely: *yama, niyama, asana, pranayama, pratyahara, dharana, dhyana, and samadhi. Yama, niyama, asana, pranayama* and *pratyahara* are related with the body and they prepare the body for the *dharana, dhyana* and *samadhi* which are related to the mind. The basic tenets of yoga are: restraining of social behaviour (*yama*), good personal conduct (*niyama*), yogic exercise (*asana*), breathing exercises (*pranayama*), mediation (*dhyana*), and attainment of super-consciousness (*samadhi*). When somebody practises, then he/she is able to achieve calmness of mind. These above practices help in achieving the maximum creativity and knowledge (Udupa, 1983). Practice of yoga is not the monopoly of the Hindu religion or the propriety of Indians alone. The essential features of yoga practice are *yama* and *niyama*, not the concepts of Hindu religion only. In India and China, yogic practices are widespread and they are also common among Muslims and Christians. Udupa (1983) regarded Indian yoga as the most systematic and effective. The text of *Hatha-Yog-Pradinika* mentions that very cautiously the trained practitioner of yoga should administer the treatment and prescribed methods (Jaggi, 1973). Thus, we conclude that yoga is a science of health and philosophy which has very efficiently treated certain conditions of stress and psychosomatic illnesses. Yoga does not involve any chemical, physical or botanical agent which is administered to the body in the form of medicine. Thus, yoga is regarded as a system of health which is less time consuming and economic. Indians are quite familiar with the yoga practices and they are in great demand in other countries also. It is accepted as a global medicine for maintaining the health of the people. Baba Ramdev is regarded as a great practitioner of yoga in the country and is very popular. Along with the yogic exercises he teaches benefits of yogic exercises with minimal effort (*Dainik Jagran*, 5 September 2005).

Western Systems of Medicine

Hippocrates (460 – 377 BC), considered the father of western medicine, brought to its realm the concept of logical rather than supernatural explanations for illness. Since dissection of human cadavers was forbidden on religious grounds in those days, his followers relied primarily on logic and tangible evidence to understand the human body and explain and treat diseases. The central tenet of his theory was that illness was a result of imbalance among the four humours – blood, black bile, yellow bile and phlegm. Centuries later, Galen (130–201 AD), a Greek philosopher and physician, stressed on the importance of anatomy but studied it using animals, mainly pigs. He extrapolated human anatomy from that of pigs, whose anatomy he considered similar to humans. He also associated each humour with a personality type. Hippocratic-Galenic theories of the body-mind-personality relationship and Galen's ideas of anatomy dominated western medicine for nearly the next 1,500 years and served as its basis (Conrad et al., 1995; Nutton, 2004).

In the 16th century, the Belgian physician Andreas Vesalius corrected the mistaken notions of human anatomy proposed by Galen. Medical, social and even religious objections had prevented dissection of human cadavers all these years. In 1539 AD, following the judgment by an Italian judge, Vesalius was able to dissect the bodies of executed criminals for studying human anatomy. Although he was ridiculed by the other physicians as a 'barber', this marked a crucial step in the field of western medicine. Structures that were previously extrapolated from those of animals and only imagined were now being visualized. Simultaneously with this development, however, the body-mind-personality connection that had been fundamental to Galenic medicine was beginning to be discarded (Conrad et al., 1995; Nutton, 2004).

In addition, other developments also began to play a major role in changing perceptions in the field of biology and medicine. For example, William Harvey's discovery in 1628 AD of the circulation of blood by the heart marked the beginning of an era of viewing the human body as a mechanized assemblage of organs supplied with fuel/energy by the blood. The use of microscope by Robert Hooke in 1664 AD to view cells marked yet another stage of development in the field of western medicine by starting the use of microscopy to study disease processes. Information about microscopic pathological anatomy played a crucial role in making the transition of western medicine from philosophy to science.

Pathological anatomy as a science, however, materialized with Giovanni Battista Morgagni's publication of *De Sedibus et Causis Morborum per Anatomen Indagatis*, meaning 'On the Seats and Causes of Diseases' in 1761 AD (Ventura, 2000). This exhaustive work connecting the aetiology of diseases to specific anatomical locations started an era of experiment-based medicine that continues to date. Before this, symptoms were considered to be natural physiological responses of the disease. The industrial age brought in new diseases and to meet this challenge, the physicians discarded the classical theories of Hippocrates and Galen and adopted newer concepts such as viewing symptoms as manifestations of the disease. This also led to the concept of treating diseases by suppressing their symptoms, which continues to date (Conrad et al., 1995; Nutton, 2004).

Nowhere health delivery system or usability of health care systems is exclusively based on one system of medicine. In fact, there are varieties of systems of medicine which have evolved over a period of time in different parts of the world. These systems of medicine have a differential growth in relation to its origin and scientificness. How these different systems of medicine have survived and grew finds its answer in the social and historical conditions of the society in which they live. There is an evidence that every society uses multiple systems of medicine. They are not exclusively dependent on one system of medicine. With the forces of globalization the world is rapidly free flowing with different systems of medicine. People have varieties of systems to choose for different ailments and different systems of medicine. India has, perhaps, the world's largest community supporting tradition of its own indigenous systems of medicine.

The western systems of medicine include allopathy and homoeopathy is included in other systems of medicine. We will discuss different systems of medicine prevailing in India.

Allopathy as a System of Medicine

Allopathic medicine is an expression commonly used by homoeopaths and proponents of other forms of alternative medicine to refer to mainstream medical use of pharmacologically active agents or physical interventions to treat or suppress symptoms or pathophysiologic processes of diseases or condition. The expression was coined in 1810 by the creator of homoeopathy, Samuel Hahnemann (1755–1843). Never accepted as a mainstream scientific term, it was adopted by alternative medicine advocates to refer pejoratively to mainstream medicine. In such circles, the expression 'allopathic medicine' is still used to refer to 'the broad category of medical practice that is sometimes called Western medicine, biomedicine, evidence-based medicine, or modern medicine'.

The term allopath was used by Hahnemann and other early homoeopaths to highlight the difference they perceived between homoeopathy and the medicine of that time. Practitioners of alternative medicine have used the term 'allopathic medicine' to refer to the practice of conventional medicine in both Europe and the United States since the 19th century. The term allopathic was used throughout the 19th century as a derogatory term for the practitioners of heroic medicine, a precursor to modern medicine that did not rely on evidence.

Allopathy medicine is what most of us understand to be 'standard' or 'regular' medicine as practised and distributed by the practitioners. We recognize it as legitimated, true and credible. In broad definition, 'Allopathic medicine is that practice which combats by use of remedies producing effects different from those produced by the disease treated, including the use of all measures that have proved to be of some value in the treatment of disease' (Rosengren, 1980). Thus, from such a view, the human body in its normal state is free of disease, and therefore, any disease found must be regarded as a foreign intrusion into an otherwise healthy organism. Further, allopathic medicine is rooted in the other general idea that in as much as disease is foreign its cure can usually be brought by the application of some form of opposites to it. For example, surgery to remove the affected part, the indigestion of chemically compounded substances to 'reverse' the course of disease, the application of various physical manipulation and physical exercise to 'restrain' misused, unused, or atrophied parts; and where deemed necessary the 'temporary' reversal of the ill person's social behaviour so as to allow one's body to recover and regenerate itself (Rosengren, 1980).

Scientific medicine is characterized by the assumption that every disease is partially generated by specific etiological agents such as bacteria, viruses, parasites, genetic malformations, or internal chemical imbalances.

Scientific medicine evolved in the late 19th century primarily from French and German laboratories (Anchernect, 1968). It has based itself around the discovery of microbiological agents (bacteria) as the cause of disease and around the theory of scientific etiology as a mechanism for explaining the role of these agents. Scientific medicine was not just a new name for allopathy, although many allopaths adopted the framework and terminology of the new medicine as an attempt to appropriate the legitimacy conferred to the name scientific medicine. Scientific medicine has a different theoretical basis and epistemology than other existing modes of medicine of late 19th century, but it has an extremely limited clinical and therapeutic repertoire (Berliner, 1983).

Diagnosis in Allopathy

Diagnosis in allopathy generally begins with an assessment of the patient's case history followed by physical examination and a number of laboratory tests ranging from simple laboratory evaluations to sophisticated imaging modalities. The emphasis is on objectivity in diagnosis using high-end technologies and various laboratory techniques. What is considered normal within its conceptual framework is known through various laboratory parameters and the patient's condition is evaluated against those accepted as 'normal' parameters; any deviation from normal values is considered to indicate a disease state.

The diagnostic techniques generally measure structural abnormalities both at grass root level and subtle levels. For example, imaging techniques such as X-ray, ultrasound, computerized tomography (CT) and magnetic resonance imaging (MRI) provide information about structures and structural abnormalities such as fracture in a bone and cancerous growth in an organ. The bio medical tests also focus on structural entities, though at a subtler level. For example, anaemia is diagnosed by decreased haemoglobin and diabetes by the levels of glucose and insulin, all of which are subtler structural entities. Microbiological tests also involve identification of structures like bacteria, viruses or parasites. Although there are techniques for providing functional information such as electrocardiogram (ECG), electroencephalogram (EEG) and electromyogram (EMG), all of which measure the electrical activities of tissues, the focus is generally on structural abnormalities. Many of the diagnostic techniques are designed and fine-tuned to observe structures and structural changes which need not be the causative factors of the disease (Jayasundar, 2012).

Treatment in Allopathy

It is well-known that a substantial number of diseases in bio medicine are regarded as 'idiopathic'. In the absence of the knowledge of causation, the treatment is quite often symptomatic and interventional. Surgery plays a major role in treatment and is used to rectify or replace damaged structures. Drug interventions include supplementing deficiencies (for example, iron in anaemia, and insulin in diabetes) and manipulating the chemistry of body. Consider the example of osteoarthritis; it is diagnosed with imaging techniques such as X-ray, CT or MRI, all of which give structural information pertaining to the affected joint/joints. The clinical symptoms are generally pain and loss of movement. Although obese patients are generally advised weight reduction and exercises, the first line of treatment is suppression of pain with painkillers. Surgical intervention is advised for patients who have severe pain despite the use of painkillers (American College of Rheumatology, 2000). While symptoms are evaluated thoroughly and objectively, the aetiology of symptoms is not known. Since the root cause is not diagnosed, all treatment strategies aim at reducing the symptoms.

Homoeopathy

Homoeopathy as a system of medicine has slowly but definitely gained a foothold in India. It is based on the principle of *similia similibus curentis*, namely whatever causes the derangement of the vital force alone can cure it best. In this lies the strength of the system. The second outstanding feature of homoeopathy is that it treats each individual as a separate identity and the total personality – mental and physical – as one whole. It believes that an individual's state of mind has a direct bearing on the health of the body. The mental symptoms or how the individual feels is taken to be the most important guiding force. Weather, the time of day and night is also taken into consideration while prescribing treatment. In homoeopathy, importance is given to the part played by food and way of life in curing a disease. In India, homoeopathy is popular in all major cities; in West Bengal it receives its highest patronage. Today, there is a resurgence of interest in traditional medicine. Ironically, the inspiration for this has arisen out of desperate search for alternatives to allopathic medicine and has resulted into yoga, meditation, acupuncture, etc.

In 1810, some German physicians and missionaries arrived in India and they brought homoeopathy. They distributed their homoeopathic remedies in Bengal. The Government of India, established the Central Council of Homoeopathy. For more than a century and a half, homoeopathy is being practised in India. It is regarded as one of the important systems of medicine in providing health care to a number of people in the country. Its importance lies in viewing the person in its totality and looks at the inner balance, i.e. mental, emotional, spiritual and physical levels.

Alternative Medicine/Other Systems of Medicine

Alternative medicine is a group of diverse medical and health care systems, practices and products that are not a part of conventional medicine. While some scientific evidence exists regarding some alternative therapies, but for some there are key questions which are yet to be answered through scientific and logical studies as whether these therapies are safe and whether they work for the disease or medical conditions for which they are in use. Alternative medicine is used in place of conventional medicine. An example of an alternative therapy is using a special diet to treat cancer instead of undergoing a surgery, radiation or chemotherapy that has been recommended by a conventional doctor. Conventional medicine is medicine as practised by allopathic doctors who hold MBBS degrees and further specialization in different branches. Alternative systems are built upon complete systems of theory and practice.

The Folk Medicine

The folk medical stream is located in the villages of India, and there is no tribal or rural community without a local health tradition. This system is local resource-based, relying on locally available flora, fauna, and minerals. So intense is the dependence on local resources that an ethno-biological survey conducted by the All India Co-Ordinative Research Project on Ethnobiology, covering 80 per cent of the tribal areas, reported the use of 7,500 wild plants for medicinal purposes by tribal groups alone. This amounts to almost 50 per cent of all the higher flowering plants of India. The folk tradition represents a 'people's health culture', which provides services at the village level. The system is so pervasive that at the grassroot level, in village communities all over India, an estimated 7,00,000 traditional *dais* conduct the majority of rural deliveries, 60,000 village bone-setters treat problems ranging from simple dislocations to compound fractures, and 80,000 herbal healers handle primary health care problems and conditions ranging from common ailments to poisonings, dental problems, diseases of eyes etc. (VHAI, 1997). In addition, millions of housewives possess an impressive knowledge of home remedies, local food resources and their nutritional values.

Tibetan Medicine

Tibetan medicine in India is, in a sense, regional manifestation of ayurveda in the trans-Himalayan regions and in parts of the north-east. The Tibetan people, through long and serious effort, have imbibed and assimilated ayurveda via Buddhism and built upon its principles and resources. Tibetan medicine has its origins largely in ayurveda, in local traditions of the people living in the trans-Himalayas, and to a lesser extent in Chinese medicine. Tibetan medical literature is available today in the Tibetan language. Its main teaching institutions are in Dharamsala but clinics have been established in several parts of the country.

Naturopathy

Naturopathy is also called as nature-care treatment and basically deals with curing of the body in the natural manner. It is based on the philosophy that body needs time to heal on its own. It has five main elements of treatment, and these are: air, water, heat, mud and space.

Acupressure and Acupuncture

In the acupressure, the pressure is applied or massage is done to specific sites on the body so that symptoms of pain or nausea can be controlled. To stop the bleeding, acupressure is used. It originated in China and is regarded as one of the important forms of treatment in China. It is regarded as one of the old practices of healing in the world. Chinese people have very well integrated the allopathy and acupressure in their systems of treatment. In this form of treatment pressure is exerted on certain points which are called 'acupressure points'. It is a group of procedures involving stimulation of specific points on the body and varieties of techniques are used. These techniques are: penetrating the skin with needles and that can be handled by hand or by electrical stimulation. Acupuncture is another Chinese form of system of health care which involves the insertion of pins in certain vital points of the body. It is regarded very useful in the treatment of certain chronic diseases like arthritis, bursitis, headache, athletic injuries, and post-traumatic and post-surgical pains. Acupuncture is also regarded very useful in treating chronic pain which is associated with immune function, dysfunction such as psoriasis (skin disorders), allergies, and asthma. Lifestyle problems like alcoholism, addiction, smoking and eating disorders are also treated by acupuncture.

Why Indigenous Systems Are Not Promoted in India?

There is enough evidence to conclude that the British suppressed Indigenous Systems of Medicine (ISM) in India for political and economic reasons. The discouragement to surgery, indigenous medical schools, and practices like the indigenous smallpox inoculation during the 19th century, illustrates this point clearly. Again, by simply cutting off state financial support to indigenous systems of medicine and instead providing support only to western medicine, the British were able to effectively marginalize ISM. At an ideological level, ISMs were sought to be discredited by British policy by compelling traditional physicians to prove their indigenous medical therapies on the basis of allopathic theory and its parameters. Thus, at the time of Independence, the best medical institutions were those based on western medicine, and the entire health services of the country were manned by Indians trained in western medicine. The major government and private hospitals were managed by western-trained doctors; and drug outlets and pharmacies in the towns and cities were stocked with western medicines. The institutional infrastructure and the leadership in the health sector that India inherited in 1947 made it almost inevitable that the post-Independence government would continue to build on the edifice created by the British. There is another sociological explanation for the distorted growth of ISMs in the last century. It is a social fact that a substantial percentage of western educated Indian elite has got alienated from indigenous traditions and shares the prejudices of Europeans. The reasons for this alienation have nothing to do with the efficacy of ISMs, but are solely due to a western ethnocentric social outlook and world view that have become part of the modern social culture of westernized Indians. Although the government has the option of dismantling the health services infrastructure created by the British, it did not do so. It provided lip service to the indigenous systems and proclaimed them to be equal in policy terms to western medicine. However, only a tiny part of the national health budget was provided for their upkeep. In 1996, the Ministry of Health, Government of India, established a department for indigenous systems of medicine. This department has not benefitted the ISM in its future development, as the budget still remains a low priority. In India, science and technology policy is dominated by western science paradigm. Indian scientists often take offence when one qualifies science by the cultural and geographical term 'western', but the fact is that historically, 'science' has its origin in Europe. It is a product of philosophical schools that are based on western cultural and intellectual traditions. The view of western science is that traditional medicine systems are irrational and unscientific. In fact, there has been absolutely no attempt made or even an epistemologically valid method evolved to evaluate indigenous systems of medicine. This view is, therefore, totally without basis. As a result of prejudice of the Indian scientific establishment to traditional medicine, the Government of India's policy provides no support whatsoever to folk medicine, only 4 per cent of the national health budget is allotted to the codified systems of traditional medicine.

Integrative Medicine

The Rural Health Care Mission in 2005 included the Indian systems of medicine in health care along with homoeopathy to have a positive impact on the health of people. Integrative medicine is the model in which the synergy and deployment of the best aspects of different systems of medicine are taken in the best interest of patients and the community. Due care is taken on clinical evidence. Safety, accessibility, economic considerations and culture compatibility are the key elements of integrative medicine.

Integrative medicines are widely used for the promotion of health and prevention of disease which are chronic in nature and also in degenerative diseases. Officially we have recognized the multiple systems of medicine in our health care. However, there are still gaps between the acceptances of different systems of medicine. There are certain recommendations which are given to enrich our pluralistic health care systems. They include sanitation, hygiene, clean water and nutrition which should receive maximum attention so that infectious diseases can be minimized. Personal hygiene should be given duc importance. Healthy lifestyles should be followed by families, groups and communities so that number of incidence can be reduced for the lifestyle diseases. The private practitioners of Indian systems of medicine should be motivated to integrate the professional and social inducements.

Some case histories are presented where the integrative systems are used and they can become a model for further treatment.

Different disciplines involved in health studies, namely public health and social medicine, economics, demography, sociology and anthropology, are trying to grapple with some of the issues raised at various levels of specificity and degrees of proximity to governmental policy and initiatives. Through this we may realize the concerns raised by the visible entry of medical systems like homoeopathy, ayurveda and unani medicine that were hitherto kept out of public institutions of health care. But the compartmentalization of disciplines, such as that between sociology and anthropology, which produces dichotomies of the knowledge and experience of the richer countries and from that of poor ones, inhibits an appraisal of what systems of medicine could do or not do with regard to tackling health problems. The question as to whether the focus at the level of the population and at the level of the individual follow a similar logic and whether medical systems are capable of addressing both, requires among other things, an analysis of medical pluralism which has been somewhat muted in mainstream social science.

Summing Up

India was invaded by the Aryans around 1400 BC. It was probably during this period that the ayurveda and the siddha system of medicine came into existence. Ayurveda or the science of life developed a comprehensive concept of health. The Manusamhita prescribed rules and regulations for personal health, dietics and hygiene ritual at the time of birth and death and emphasized the unity of physical, mental and spiritual aspects of life. The next phase in Indian history (650–1850 AD) witnessed the rise and fall of Mughal empire. The Muslim rulers introduced the unani system of medicine sometime around 1000 AD. The Arabic system of medicine, popularly known as unani system of medicine is traced back to Greek medicine. With changes in the political conditions in India, the torch which was lighted thousands of years ago by the ancient sages became static, and the ancient universities and hospitals disappeared. By the middle of the 18th century, the British brought the allopathic system of medicine in India, which is based on the scientific theories of science. This system has achieved a great deal of success in curing illness.

References

Abraham, Leena (2005), 'Indian Systems of Medicine (ISM) and Public Health Care in India', in Leena V. Gangoli, A.R. Duggal and A. Shukla (eds), *Review of Health Care in India*, Mumbai: Centre for Enquiry into Health and Allied Themes.

Alavi, Seema (2007), *Islam and Healing: Loss and Recovery of an Indo-Muslim Medical Tradition, 1600–1900*, New Delhi: Permanent Black.

American College of Rheumatology (2000), 'Recommendations for the Medical Management of Osteoarthritis of the Hip and Knee', *Arthritis Rheum*, 43(9): 1905–15.

Anchernect, E.H. (1968), *A Short History of Medicine*, New York: Ronald Press.

Attewell, Guy (2007), *Refiguring Unani Tibb: Plural Healing in Late Colonial India*, New Delhi: Orient Longman.

Berliner, H.S. (1983), 'Medical Modes of Production', in A. Treacher and P. Wrights (eds), *The Social Construction of Medicine*, Edinburg: University of Edinburg Press.

Cant, Sarah and Ursula Sharma (1999), *A New Medical Pluralism? Alternative Medicine, Doctors, Patients and the State*, London: UCL Press.

Conrad, L.I. et al. (1995), *The Western Medical Traditions: 800 BC to 1800 AD*, Cambridge: Cambridge University Press.

Crawford, D.G. (1914), *A History of Indian Medical Service, 1600–1913*, Vol. 2, London: Thacker & Co.

Dainik Jagran (2005), 5 September.

Forbes, G. (2005), *Women in Colonial India: Essays on Politics, Medicine and Historiography*, New Delhi: Chronicle Books.

Gould, H.A. (1965), 'Modern Medicine and Folk Cognition in Rural India', *Human Organisation*, 24: 201–08.

Government of India (2001), *Indian Systems of Medicine and Homoeopathy in India 2001*, New Delhi: Planning and Evaluation Cell, Department of ISM and Homoeopathy, Ministry of Health and Family Welfare.

—— (2002), *National Health Policy on ISM and H-2002*, New Delhi: Planning and Evaluation Cell, Department of ISM and Homoeopathy, Ministry of Health and Family Welfare.

—— (2005), *AYUSH in India*, New Delhi: Planning and Evaluation Cell, Department of ISM and Homoeopathy, Ministry of Health and Family Welfare.

Hume, J.C. (1977), 'Rival Traditions: Western Medicine and Yunan-I-Tibb in Punjab, 1849–1889', *Bulletin of the History of Medicine*, 51: 214–31.

Jaggi, O.P. (1973a), *Folk Medicine*, Vol. III, Delhi: Atma Ram and Sons.

—— (1973b), *Yogic and Tantric Medicine*, Vol. V, Delhi: Atma Ram and Sons.

Jayasundar, Rama (2012), 'Contrasting Approaches to Health and Disease: Ayurveda and Biomedicine', in V. Sujatha and Leena Abraham (eds), *Medical Pluralism in Contemporary India*, New Delhi: Orient Blackswan.

Kumar, Deepak (1997), 'Unequal Contenders, Uneven Grounds: Medical Encounters in British India, 1820–1920', in Andrew Cunningham and Bridie Andrews (eds), *Western Medicine as Contested Knowledge*, New York: Manchester University Press.

Leslie, Charles (1968), 'The Professionalization of Ayurvedic and Unani Medicine', *Transactions of the New York Academy of Sciences*, Series II, 30(4).

—— (1980), 'Medical Pluralism in World Perspective', *Social Science and Medicine*, 14: 191–95.

Naik, J.P. (1977), *An Alternative System of Health Care Services in India*, Bombay: Allied Publishers.

Nutton, V. (2004), *Ancient Medicine*, New York: Routledge.

Rosengren, William R. (1980), *Sociology of Medicine: Diversity, Conflict and Change*, New York: Harper and Row.

Sujatha, V. and Leena Abraham (eds) (2012), *Medical Pluralism in Contemporary India*, New Delhi: Orient Blackswan.

Taittitiya Upanishad, II, Yoga Atma.

Udupa, K.N. (1983), Presidential Address on the Occasion of the Asian Congress of the Indian Association for Traditional Asian Medicine, held at Bombay, 6–9 March, London: W. Thacker.

Ventura, H.O. (2000), 'Giovanni Battista Morgagni and the Foundation of Modern Medicine', *Clinical Cardiology*, 23(10): 792–94.

Voluntary Health Association of India (1997), *Report of the Independent Commission on Health in India*, New Delhi: VHAI.

World Health Organization (2002), *Traditional Medicine Strategy 2002–2005*, Geneva: WHO.

13

Hospital as a Social System

Like all organizations providing goods or services, medical facilities exhibit the twin features of increasing complexity and increasing rationality. Their complexity stems from the great accretions of medical knowledge and technique that engender an ever-finer division of labour; also, medical institutions are subject to so many demands and expectations that they are, by definition, multiple in characters. Their rationality, in turn, is a product of the imperatives of complex organizations for planning and control as well as the heightened imperative of economic accountability. Both complexity and rationality, however, despite being pervasive in modern organizational life, may strike critics as somehow alien in spirit to the helping relationship that is the crux of medical care. If medical institutions share with other enterprises these dominant structural themes, they are probably unique in the way they blend particular features of other, less comprehensive versions of institutional life. The hospital, for example, is at once a business, a hotel, a university, a social service agency, and so on through the long list of functions it is called on to perform. Hospitals resemble a business or factory in rapid flow of work, heavily practical emphasis on speedy results, and perhaps in the tangibility of desired outcome in levels of wellness. Yet they are very similar to the university in their array of specialists, their administrative confederation in a 'collegial' bureaucracy (as distinguished from the 'hierarchical' bureaucracy of business or governmental enterprise), and above all, in fact that their product is people in a health process rather than a good or service once and finally delivered (Wilson, 1970: 48).

Historical Overview of Hospitals

The functions that have been institutionalized in the hospital have varied from time to time and from place to place. Persons specialized who perform in these hospitals have also varied. And so, too, has the physical setting in which these functions have been performed. A brief historical overview will illustrate that how crescive norms, especially customs, and enacted norms have changed with time.

The function of the treatment of the sick was first institutionalized on a religious basis and those early hospitals in Hindu, Egyptian, Greek, and Roman civilizations were built mainly under religion auspices. As early medicine was sacerdotal, the first organized institutions for the care of the sick were established in connection with temples (Lewinski-Corwin, 1932: 463). Later some of the priests associated with the temple became specialized to take care of the sick. It was, in fact, until the days of Hippocrates that hospitals came to be separated from the temples.

In Greece, by the end of the 6th century BC there were already communal physicians who took care of the sick people in cities in an *iatreion*, which became the community hospital and city dispensary. In the 5th century BC mainly cities provided large, light and airy buildings and the *iatreion* became a private sanatorium. The Roman army developed military hospitals as an intrinsic part of the military establishment. The humanitarian impulse that received great impetus with the dawn of the Christian era resulted in the establishment of many Christian hospitals both by Church leaders and emperors. These hospitals performed functions in addition to that of caring for the sick. Some special hospitals took care of the sufferers of leprosy, plague, and syphilis. Port hospitals would also quarantine travellers coming from the infected regions. John Howard exposed conditions at the end of the 18th century and the movement toward reorganization and modernization of hospitals that were started.

We have thought of the hospital, from Roman times till the present, as a segregated place for the tending of the sick (as distinguished from catering to the leisurely well). However, although the Greek spa may have been considered as a place for retreat and rejuvenation for the wealthy and propertied class, it ought not to be regarded as a hospital. Still and all, as a place for the promotion of well-being (as distinguished from a place for the tending of the sick), these precursors to the hospital were like their modern counterparts if only to the extent that they were responsive only to those members of the society so dictated by the larger social order. And it is not really important to know whether the Temples of Asclepius preceded or followed the spas, but only that their links to the prevailing religious-philosophical tenets of the time were strong. For just as Lewis Rumford persuasively argued that the first differentiated social organization in prehistory was probably the Church. It means the first health place probably had sacred connotations and priest-like proprietors. Remember that even the Hippocratic oath and the promises contained therein were offered and made to the gods and not to sick men and also that a strong body was the quintessence of Spartan values.

Even in earlier times, villagers of any size whatsoever probably possessed 'inns' where the homeless, infirm, and penniless could count on to find solace, some rest and food, and some reassurance. Health care as we know it? Surely not. But these early sick places were certainly holy places, whether Greek, Jewish, or early Christian. It seems that very early in the history of civilization, being sick was often an essential qualifier for kindness; being poor neither then or now necessarily enhanced one's position in this regard. As Eliot Freidson (1963) observed, 'in the most general sense, the hospital is a place in which ailing people sleep and receive care. Because ailing people live in it, the hospital will always have some attributes of the hotel or dormitory: some of its personnel will play domestic roles and others will supervise them. Because ailing people will receive some sort of care while they are living there, the hospital will always have some of the attributes of the school or prison: some of its personnel will assume responsibility for the inmates'. Provision of hospital care thus implies a profound division of people into those who assume responsibility, those for whom responsibility is assumed, and those who keep house. The nature of that division has varied with prevailing notions of what ails people and what must be done to help them. In all, the word 'hospital' has been applied to institutions that have on one occasion or another resembled a skid row hostel, a religious retreat, a school, a prison, a hotel, an elephant's graveyard, and a hospital. Such variation is not entirely historical.

The relatively short-lived link between hospitals and the citadel has been traced to Roman times, and especially to the pre-Christian era, in which the travelling Roman legions carried with them members whose special task was to care as best they could for their fallen comrades; a more concrete and secular expression of the service of the healers in the interest of the state than was probably true of the situation in earlier times.

It seems clear that, as medicine inched forward in its technological capabilities, the more valuable a resource it became and hence the more did it become an object of competition for 'interested parties' who might benefit from it however illusory those benefits might in fact have been. Historically, therefore, it is not inaccurate to say that the socio-political implications of medicine were more and more elaborated as the technology acquired increased utility, and the early state surely became one of the earliest manifestations of structural differentiations in early civilization to articulate and utilize that resource. Health, therefore, historically was an expression of collective rather than individual interest (that was to come much later in historical development). Health, as an expression of a higher order of service, was certainly given long-lasting impetus by early Christian teachings, in which the link between the care of the ill and benevolence becomes highly specific (Rosengren, 1980: 168–169). This continued through the long years of the medieval period and up to the Renaissance. As Lewis Mumford (1961: 267) points out: Hospitals, for the general are of the sick and ailing, were not provided on a remarkable scale. The sanatorium was no longer a health resort set apart from the city and catering mainly to those who could afford to travel, but a place in the heart of city, near at hand, open to all who needed it, under the care of men and women willing to undertake all the repulsive offers demanded by sickness, wounds, and surgical operations. Both the hospitals and the isolation ward were direct contributions of the monastery; and with them came a more general kind of hospitality for the healthy, in need of overnight rest and food. Through all the centuries when inns and hotels were lacking, when private lodging was meagre and wretched, the monastic hospice provided decent free accommodation. The provision of alms-houses was likewise a medieval municipal institution, for the care of the poor and the destitute was an obligation of Christian charity, and not the least handsome buildings in the late medieval city were in fact almshouses – though their existence shows that poverty kept pace with increasing wealth. Finally, for the first time again, institutions for the care of the aged flourished in the late medieval cities.

So widespread was the growth of this type of institution that by the end of 1400s England contained over 600 of these hospitals, some of the larger ones with the beginnings of differentiations into departments which catered to clients with differing needs – medical, the aged, and so forth. But with these early beginnings in the spiritual realm, even it could not forestall the drift in the later medieval period toward guildism, in which work in the hospital came to be more in nature of an occupation than of service in the name of God and in the interests of salvation. The growing rationalism of the hospital is evidenced also in the later Renaissance period with the increasing links of the hospitals to the national government in its civilian aspects and with the processes and structures of mercantilism and industrialization.

The Renaissance and the Age of Rationalism were undoubtedly important in affecting the importance of rational administration in hospitals as well as increasing the base of pluralistic control. And these in turn, can be readily traced to democratization and economic growth in the western world.

Motivating Factors Behind Opening of Hospitals

Originally one of the basic motives in the establishing or instituting of hospitals was charity toward the sick, particularly the sick poor. This motive was probably as early as the ancient Indian hospitals and it was predominant in the hospitals of the Middle Ages under the auspices of the Church. However, in others the nondenominational, the university, or the government (city, state or federal) hospital-charity is supplemented, if not succeeded, by a more practical type of motive. The directly charitable motive has yielded to a more impersonal recognition that the community must look after its citizens when they are sick and cannot take care of themselves. It is a kind of 20th century version of altruism, which, though it may be less personal, may be more efficient.

Along with these changes in motivation and purpose there is also a change in the patients who are taken care of in the hospital. Before hospitals had achieved present standards, they were viewed, almost with horror by many, as only the last resort. One went to hospital to die. If people could afford home care, that was far more preferable to going to hospital, for the hospital was associated not only with the extreme illness but also with poor people. Home nursing, home parturition, and some convalescence were customary and much preferred by those who could manage it. Today hospital is no longer the gloomy, frightening place. Much of this change is the result of technological and scientific advances. At first the invention of anaesthesia and aseptic techniques, then the cast accumulation of diagnostic and treatment inventions and the growth of laboratories and special departments transformed the whole concept of medical care.

Functions of Hospitals

In addition to the diagnosis, cure, treatment, care, isolation and protection of the sick persons, modern hospitals dispense services to outpatients. For there has emerged a vast proliferation of specialized kinds of hospitals for special functions, and there will undoubtedly be more. Of fairly recent date is the rehabilitative function that has been assumed to take care of those suffering from degenerative conditions arising from the aging process. For it has been found that many of those with chronic illnesses can be rehabilitated, if not cured, to live satisfactory and useful lives. Increasingly, too, the concept of prevention as a hospital function is gaining acceptance. Realizing that many diseases can be prevented, hospitals are taking an increasingly active part, along with other community agencies in programmes of prevention, including the education of the public in the recognition of preventable diseases and urging the public to use all known preventive measures.

These functions have to do directly or indirectly with the patient himself. But hospitals today have functions that take them beyond the traditional patient-centred ones. Medical and health personnel are trained in the hospitals itself. As the medical profession emerged as an organization, it found it convenient to train its personnel in institutions set up for the care of the sick; conversely, the growth of medical schools greatly stimulated the growth of hospitals. The two need each other and, as medical training of necessity became more complicated, the demands on the hospital grew until today. We find almost every outstanding hospital much concerned with the training of undergraduate and graduate doctors. Still another function performed by modern hospitals is that of clinical and epidemiological studies. A hospital is essential for the expansion of medical knowledge. Modern hospitals have facilities for carrying out investigative procedures that systematically go through large amount of data to furnish new knowledge to improve patient care and treatment.

Another function that modern hospitals perform is integrating the several health professions. No longer can the doctor be alone and sufficient unto himself and render the best services that modern science can afford.

The modern hospital plays even greater part in the complicated team work required for modern health service.

Closely allied with this intramural service-integrating function is another modern concept, that of integrating all heath facilities in the community, beginning with the rural clinic and correlating it, through the community and district hospital, to the medical colleges. This plan brings a system of hospitals and health centres planned to meet the needs of the state or region, closely integrated for hospital care and health promotion. In addition to this mobile clinics are also in practice in the remote areas to serve the patients.

The Hospital as a Social System

Social workers often confront the complex and changing systems of authority and require interacting and reporting to various departments. Social workers' success depends upon the cultivation of relationship with different functionaries in the hospital. When the relationship between the social work department and hospital administration is characterized by mutual respect then the institution is more supportive.

Now we would like to discuss the standards which the social workers follow while discharging their work.

- *Hospital Work Plan:* The a social worker maintains the contact number of patient and kins of patient.
- *The Principles:* To provide clear and reliable information to the patient which will be helpful in coordinating care.
- *Psycho-Social Support:* A social worker makes the assessment of financial and emotional strength of the patient before treatment starts.
- *Educating Patients:* A social worker is supposed to educate the patient and family regarding the outcome of treatment and treatment refusal entitlements.
- *Counselling:* A social worker gives counselling before the treatment and also tells about the coping mechanisms during illness and how to manage illness.
- *Communication:* Communication is always needed between patient, his family and social worker regarding interpretation of any information related with the treatment.
- *Discharge Planning and Continuity of Care:* After hospitalization every patient is discharged, therefore a social worker plans for the discharge of the patient and gives further information about the continuity of medical care.
- *Advocacy:* Directly representing patients and their rights in health care, championing the rights of patients through direct intervention or empowerment are also a part of a social worker's duty.

Hospital is a social organization and logical combination of the activities of a number of persons with different levels of knowledge and skills for achieving a common goal of patient care through a hierarchy of authority and personality.

Further to organize activities in the hospital, the groupings of workable units are made and they are connected by authority, communication and control. Grouping in the hospital depends on the task and function. Hospital employs people with different skills and functions. More centrally it is associated with planning, decision-making and administration. There is also peripherally implementation, monitoring and supervision.

Integration is the linking of line function to staff (group) function to make it a unified whole. However, the problem in the hospital is because of functional groups with different skills and job responsibility like doctors, nurses, technical and unskilled staff.

Hospitals are among the most complex organizations in modern society, characterized by an extremely fine division of labour and an exquisite repertory of technical skill. The major hospital embraces multiple goals, chiefly patient care, teaching and research. It is at once a hotel, a treatment centre, a laboratory and a university. Because the institution's work is so specialized, staffed by a variety of professional and technical personnel, there are very important problems of coordination and authority. Paramount in the social structure are relationships between patients and hospital staff and among staff members. The patient, both client and product of the organization, enters a therapeutic situation in which his style is largely passive. He encounters the physician – like himself, a 'guest' of the hospital – and the nurse, who is the full-time symbol of the organization's atmosphere. The physician is undergoing a shift from his older charismatic role toward a more nearly bureaucratic niche in the hospital. Staff relationships are distinguished by unclear patterns of authority and intense competition for spheres of competence and prestige. The physician is implicated as the professional least amenable to hierarchical control and the leading figure in skill and status. Although the hospital illustrates vital, unresolved issues in the organization of work, it flourishes under the impetus of professional zeal and patients' needs.

Hospital as an Institutional Extension

The present hospital system has not taken root and arisen without retaining important elements of normative systems that at one time in history may have been prominent in the structure and functioning of hospitals. Hospitals still retain some shadow of their former sacred nature conveying to patients, as they do, expectations of humanism, diffuseness of interests, and omnipotence. Second, hospitals have become a centre for the promotion of the scientific norms of empirical truth and validity, certain important self-correcting functions, the communistic sharing of ideas and information, a search for logical consistency, and, perhaps above all, a pervading organized scepticism. Third, the professional norms entered the hospital quite early in its history: guildism and its associated protectionism, the claims of autonomy, lack of accountability, expertise, elite entrepreneurism, and the enforcement of monopolistic dominance over those served. In addition, the observer may note the presence of the associated technical norms of universalism, predictability, the maintenance of affective neutrality in human relations, and objectivity sometimes bordering on disenchantment. Entering rather later are the bureaucratic rules of rationality, order, rational predictability and calculation, a tendency to expand domains, and the tendency toward insulated self-perpetuation. Finally, note must be taken of the hospital's fundamental general collectivity orientation, involving external democratization, surrounding political and social pluralism, and a continual threat of boundary permeation by others.

Only the last serves as a threat to the practice of organizational autonomy and professional dominance; all the others – sacredness, scientism, professionalism, technocracy, and bureaucracy – have at one point or other entered into hospital structure. These have historically, remained there, and presently contribute to the enormous asymmetry that now characterizes the relationships of hospitals to their internal milieus and their external environments with each other. Even though logical consistency may be absent and conflict is to be expected as the proponents of each compete for ideological, technological, organization, and resource dominance, their very liveliness and ubiquitousness contributes to the dominance that the hospital is able to exercise over those who fall into its orbit.

Hospital as a Community: The Total Institution

In mental hospitals or hospitals for long-term care, the patient remains for a long time. There is a kind of stability about such a hospital. It is like a prison, the barracks, or a boarding school, which takes on the characteristics of a 'closed community'. They are more or less isolated from the outside world. In such a situation, patients develop their own society with their own culture. Short-term hospitals pit a daily changing population, one that is temporary or transient, against a relatively fixed staff. There is little chance for 'conspiracies' to develop or protest or resisting 'organizations' or 'cultures' to arise. It differs, therefore, from hospitals with long-term patients (Bernard and Thompson, 1966). Such institutions have been called total because they encompass the total life of the patients. In them, 'two different social and cultural worlds develop; jogging alongside each other with points of official contact not little mutual penetration' (Goffman, 1961: 9). One experiment based on the accumulated research can be cited for the illustrative purpose. In the late 1950s, it occurred to one student that perhaps it would be possible to give formal recognition to the informal organization that patients autonomously formed (Brown et al., 1961). It was observed that patients developed by and for themselves some roles that were not officially recognized or required. One such role was that of welcoming and orienting newcomers to the hospital. Other roles involved planning and helping, which operated on a totally informal basis. It was felt that it might be useful to put such findings to work on the service by formalizing them and making them explicit so that such activities and roles would be planned for and continued by the succeeding generations of patients.

A Patient Planning Organization was established, composed of a social committee representing all wards and a ward committee for each floor. Each ward committee was to have five members. Two were to represent the ward on the social committee; one was to perform the welcome role, one the clarifier, and one the suggester or trouble shooter role. Staff members were to meet the committees, thus creating channels of communication. The purpose was to increase the participation and decrease isolation and boredom, to improve communication between patients as a group and the staff, and to make life more pleasant and comfortable. Although for a number of reasons – including the patient culture itself, impaired staff participation, and hospital procedures – the experiment was not considered a success at the end of three months, though it did have positive therapeutic results and the experimenters felt the programme should be continued after overcoming as many drawbacks as possible.

Hospital as a Dynamic Institution

People enter the medical establishment whether it is in doctor's office or in a hospital as whole persons whose lives are a complex of experiences, commitments, engagements, and past and future directions. Although it may occasionally appear so, they do enter as inanimate objects; however, they may sometimes be treated that way. Given the twin complexities of the human social personality and the multifaceted character of hospitals as organizations, the relations between hospitals and patients can be complex indeed.

A hospital, selectively intervenes in the present and future lives of the patients in varying scopes and in varying intensities. In fact, the delivery of any service makes an imprint upon the kind of person the patient will be, both in there and then later on in life. The fact that hospitals must be organized internally to bring about this desired change has important consequences for the kind of hospitals we experience around us.

From this point of view it must be obvious that a hospital may exhibit an interest in patients ranging from a truncated and abbreviated span of time – as in an emergency room to a nearly infinite period – as in a long-term psychiatric facility, a chronic illness or rehabilitation resources; also arrangement for work and behaviour toward patients are strongly influenced by the stake the hospital has in the patient's future, and the types of hospital that are revealed by such a view also range from those that are most compatible with a social model of illness as against a more strict medical model. There is also a second type of career interruption, that is, hospitals may have an interest in a limited aspect of highly selected facets of their patients. Still others may elect for a broader scope of interest in patients, as in the case of psychiatric services. In theses, an effort is made to incorporate the entire person into the hospital system and to work on multiple facets of human life simultaneously.

The need for additional functions by the hospital, such as outpatient service and centres for expensive diagnostic equipment, have been met by the enlargement of these facilities and education of additional persons to staff them. Sometimes the addition of new services has involved the development of new categories of employment or role systems within the institution.

Mental Hospital

Medical institutions also include the mental hospitals. Indeed, the most dramatic attention of recent decades has been focused not on the general hospital but on the mental hospital. There are several excellent reasons for this concentration, among them the most important are the ghastly condition of the hospitals, the well-publicized fact that mentally ill individuals occupy substantial beds, the immense costs of care, and perhaps, the inherent fascination that bizarre behaviour exercises on the public imagination. In addition, the winds of change have blown more strongly through our 'human warehouses' in recent years than through any other medical institutions (Wilson, 1970: 53).

The general attributes of the public mental hospital are all too well known: geographic isolation from the community of the well; overcrowding and under budgeting with attendant outrages upon sanitation, diet, and privacy; the substitution of custodial care for any serious effort to treat illness; an emphasis on prison-like conformity in an atmosphere of incarceration, accompanied at some times and places by punitive mistreatment; and abrogation of basic civil and human rights of the patient. Perhaps more damaging than the blatant horrors of the 'snakepit' has been the insidious erosion of independence and self-regard brought about by enforced passivity and isolation. Thus were developed those 'institutionalized personalities' who had learned the tasks of patienthood so thoroughly that they were forever unable to resume the normal social roles of the mentally well. Consigned by society to a limbo, the long-term patient learned to live in what amounted to a social vacuum. He came to adapt his aspirations and behaviours to the patterns most agreeable to the staff and achieved a sort of expertness in the condition of being hospitalized (Wilson, 1970: 53).

There were, of course, a set of very familiar reasons why all this should be so. Public sentiments about psychological disorders has historically stressed the dangers threatened by the floridly ill, and hence the community's urgent desire to locate mental patients out of sight and out of mind. Not only did people fear the mentally disturbed individual, but his condition was typically attended to by an air of hopelessness. In the absence of any clear-cut biological agent of disease (or at any rate, the failure to identify any such etiological villain) for most varieties of disorder, the public felt rightly that comparatively little could be done for the patient. Understanding meant that a patient's contact with any physician was minimal. Treatment was for the most part custodial rather than curative, the latter consisting of sporadic organic efforts such as shock therapy or occasional psychotherapeutic encounters.

Since World War II, however, and especially in the last three decades, two strands of truly revolutionary change in the mental hospitals have appeared. The first of these was actually a revival of certain ideas and values that had surfaced at least once before, in the moral treatment of 19th century reform. This was essentially recognition of the disturbed person as a human being who possesses a valid claim to dignity and a genuine potential for return to normalcy. Premised on the assumption that individuals who are treated as fully human and are engaged in sequences of normal interpersonal relations by those around them will indeed behave normally for the most part, this shift in orientation was accompanied by increased attention to the social structure of the mental institution. A series of fresh psychological and sociological investigations revealed the existence of a patient culture as well as staff culture and showed how the hospital constituted a total system of relationships that had meaning for each patient's chance of improvement. Erving Goffman brilliantly traced the patient's career in the hospital, and his work implied that dismal career might be altered or interrupted. All the events in the hospital system were influential on patients' states of health. In all, there arose a renewed conviction that attentive care, utilizing the full resources of staff culture and patient culture, might reclaim a major fraction of those who have been cast aside by their society. Intensive therapeutic efforts even demonstrated some signal, if partial, victories among the populations of the notorious 'backwards', the habitat of the most deteriorated long-stay patients (Wilson, 1970: 54).

The second revolutionary strand, complementing the first with an appropriateness seldom found in human affairs, was the emergence of chemotherapeutic technique. Tranquilizers and energizers provide for the first time a fever for the control of symptoms, and to some extent, of mood, that enables treatment to go forward in something approaching calm rationality. Whether or not the 'core' of the illness, the underlying conflicts and predispositions that are postulated by psychodynamic theory, is ever effectively altered, the individual is at least enabled to perform standard social roles with some efficiency. This attainment of minimal functional competence in the hospital, much more speedy discharge, and the possibility of maintaining large numbers of ill people at home in their community fits nicely into the emphasis on active therapy and on the interactive engagement of the patient. In brief, the disturbed individual can be chemotherapeutically 'fitted' for interpersonal relatedness.

Hospital Social Workers

Social workers hold primary responsibility for discharge planning and psycho-social care of the patient. In many hospitals social workers have the formidable task of providing both discharge planning and emotional support to patients and families. There is considerable variety in the types of cases seen by hospital social workers as well as in the pace of work. The amount of time social workers spend with patients is yet another variable, as is the intensity of the clinical interaction. Some patients need to be seen only once; others daily during an acute critical phase of care and then less frequently as the crisis subside.

Hospital-based social workers face unique circumstances during the assessment and treatment phase of their work. They must be comfortable dealing with unknowns, working quickly and adjusting to patient cues. For example, when they enter the patient's room they may encounter someone who is feeling ill or is in pain. Patients may be disoriented, confused or agitated. Perhaps the patient's illness has brought together family members with long-standing conflict and the atmosphere around the patient is silent but tense. As most patients do not self-refer they are sometimes puzzled by the social worker's presence. If they associate social workers with financial assistance or child protective services they might be suspicious or guarded. In addition the reason for the referral to social work is often vague and the amount for psycho-social information available about the patient is likely to be limited. Therefore, the social worker enters a room filled with unknowns. Hospital social workers must be infinitely skilled at quickly assessing all of these variables such as: the patient's mental status, emotional state, the family dynamics, the patient's needs and the staff's agenda in seeking social work consultation. They must quickly establish rapport and credibility. They need to simultaneously assess, check and re-assess the situation, developing, refining and implementing a treatment plan.

While the patient's needs are always the first and primary focus of an intervention, hospital social workers are often called upon to address more than agenda at a time. Tension between 'advocacy and collaboration' and between 'loyalty to the patient and to the organization' are a constant for a hospital social worker. Before going to see the patient it helps to have a good sense of what the treatment team hopes to accomplish by calling for the social worker. To manage the complicated task of balancing the often conflicting and competing needs of a patient, a family and a team of a hospital system require critical thinking.

Sometimes health care providers tend to view patients in a vacuum, forgetting that they exist in a world outside of the hospital. The social worker will often remind the team that the strengths and vulnerabilities of the patient's system follow them into the hospital and should be taken into consideration when developing plans for treatment or follow up care in hospital. Social workers, therefore, need to have a good understanding of baseline functioning, family system theories and a high degree of comfort intervening with family systems.

Summing Up

The function of the treatment of the sick was first institutionalized on a religious basis and those early hospitals in Hindu, Egyptian, Greek, and Roman civilizations were built mainly under religious auspices. In even earlier times, villagers of any size whatsoever probably possessed 'inns' where the homeless, infirm, and penniless could count on to find solace, some rest and food, and some reassurance. Before hospitals had achieved present standards, they were viewed, almost with horror by many, as only the last resort. Originally one of the basic motives in the establishing or instituting of hospitals was charity toward the sick, particularly the sick poor. Hospital is a social organization and logical combination of the activities of a number of persons with different levels of knowledge and skills for achieving a common goal of patient care through a hierarchy of authority and personality. Hospitals still retain some shadow of their former sacred nature conveying to patients as they do expectations of humanism, diffuseness of interests, and omnipotence. Social workers hold primary responsibility for discharge planning and psycho-social care of the patient. In many hospitals social workers have the formidable task of providing both discharge planning and emotional support to patients and families. Social workers hold primary responsibility for discharge planning and psycho-social care of the patient. In many hospitals social workers have the formidable task of providing both discharge planning and emotional support to patients and families.

References

Bernard, Jessie and Lida F. Thompson (1966), *Sociology: Nurses and their Patients in a Modern Society*, USA: Mosby.

Brown, Robert G. et al. (1961), *Experience with a Patient-planning Organisation: An Interim Analysis*, Chapel Hill: University of North Carolina Press.

Freidson, Eliot (1963), *The Hospital in Modern Society*, New York: Free Press.

Goffman, Erving (1961), *Asylums*, Chicago: Aldine Publishing Co.

Lewinski-Corwin, E.H. (1932), 'Hospitals and Sanatoria', in *Encyclopaedia of the Social Sciences*, Vol. 7, New York: The Macmillan Co.

Mumford, Lewis (1961), *The City in History*, New York: Harcourt.

Rosengren, Willam R. (1980), *Sociology of Medicine: Diversity, Conflict and Change*, New York: Harper and Row.

Wilson, Robert N. (1970), *The Sociology of Health: An Introduction*, New York: Random House.

14

Physician-Patient Relationship

The physician-patient relationship is the central focus of attention in the hospital as a social system. Though rapid advancement is occurring in the medical profession in terms of plurality of health care, in terms of health care given by government, private health care, public-private partnership of health care and non-governmental organization of health care, etc. but still the interaction between doctor-patient has always remained a constant feature in all the health care services. With the rapid advancement in the technology and changing relationships, the physician-patient relationship is also undergoing changes.

Importance of Physician-Patient Relationship

The topic of physician-patient relationship is an important theme of sociological interest. In every social system, the interaction and inter-relationship between its members in accordance with the goals and the institutional sanctions is the basis for the functioning of the system. The hospital is considered as a social system and the physicians and patients are the sole occupants who mutually interact to form relationships directed by their specific goals and the general goals of the system. The entire organization and instrumentality within this system has its concern with the social aspects of human behaviour. Thus, the forms, patterns and directions of the relationship with their bearing on the goals and the norms of this collectivity have to be ascertained in relation to the functioning of the system with reference to the physicians, patients and their satisfaction in a given situation, existing in a hospital at a particular time. From sociological point of view, we are mainly concerned with the prevalent beliefs and values, explicit and implicit, held by the members in the hospital, especially by the management which yield profound influence in shaping management philosophy and executive behaviour in the hospital. Sociological rcsearchers in the hospital include various areas, like social history of hospital, patterns of bureaucracy among medical staff, goals and authority structure, organizational support, teaching atmosphere of hospital, negotiations of order in the hospital, alienation of labour, physical environment of the mental hospital ward, ecology and obstetrical services, and the time table for treatment. Mechanic (1968) points out that sociologists have been interested in the fact that the hospital does not conform to typical bureaucratic model first formulated by Max Weber. Coser (1958) focuses primarily on patient's adaption to hospital system. Georgeopoulos and Mann compared several hospitals to ascertain the relations among internal organizational variables, such as cohesiveness, communication, coordination, and effectiveness. Physician-patient relationship is of utmost significance in medical science. In this context the first and foremost requirement is that the doctor needs to develop a good rapport with the patients, which would enable him to know about him. There are a large number of questions in the mind of the patient, which are creating problems and bad health. Physicians can remove many of the patient's doubts through communication. It is of great significance for the physician to take the patient in confidence. Physician and patients are intimately connected as the existence of one without the other is not possible. In ancient universities in India, convocation address to the medical personnel said: '... everyday you should continuously and whole-heartedly try to promote the health of the patients. Even if your own life is in danger, you should not desert your patients. You should not entertain an evil thought about the health or lives of others. Your dress should be modest not foppish. Avoid drinking; do not commit a sin, nor help one who is committing it. Your speech should be smooth, polished, truthful and to the point. Taking all facts into consideration, you should make a deliberate endeavour to increase the stock of your knowledge and instruments ... . When you enter a patient's room, all your attention should be centred on the patient, his expression, movements and medicines, to the exclusion of anything else ...'. The harmonious relationship depends upon the sincerity, earnestness and co-operation between the physician and the patient. The achievement of good relations between the physician and the patient is a matter that does not depend by any means solely on the conduct of physicians. It equally depends on the attitude of patients and thus their relations. People must behave well towards physicians. If loose and unsubstantiated allegations are made about their incompetence, dishonesty, laziness and indifference to the public interests, it is unlikely that physicians will develop or display qualities of integrity, industry and public spirit. Both the physicians and the public must exhibit harmonious relationship between them. This would promote good rapport between the two, which would prove good relationship. Physician-patient relationship means the development of cordial, equitable and therefore, mutually profitable relations between the two.

Physician as a Provider of Health Care

The role of a physician is quite in proportion to the continuum of increasingly high levels of technical competence required for the performance. Parsons (1951), indicating the collective orientation of the doctor, mentions that the profession which is entrenched with the ideology puts great emphasis on the duty of doctor for patients over the personal interest of a doctor. Professionals are regarded as away from commercial interest and self-interest. The physician is expected to treat patients as objects not having personal biasness. Objectivity is based on the scientficness. The liking or disliking of doctor for the patient is avoided. For doctor the patient is a patient, irrespective of his class, sex or any other social category. The responsibility of doctor is to treat patient and show his competence in curing the patients.

Mechanic observes that the average general practitioner has found himself with a workload, too large to fulfil the enthusiastic and idealistic expectations concerning his role in dealing with social and psychological implications of medical problems, nor is he equipped to do so by training. Loomis emphasizing the collectivity orientation of a physician observes that the profit motive is excluded and also his nature of duties cannot be encompassed within the office hours. Merton stresses the need of preventing the disease and not only curing illness, though the society largely rewards medical men for the therapy. The values governing the physician's self-image relate to his self-education, medical responsibilities, self-critical attitude, sense of autonomy, specialized education, moral character, and advancing medical knowledge.

Patient as a Receiver of Health Care

The patient is helpless and needs help, technical competence and emotional involvement. Parsons (1951) suggests that the following expectations apply to a greater or lesser degree, depending on the severity of his illness: that he avoids obligations with many exacerbating his condition; that he accepts the idea that he needs help; that he desires to get 'well'; and that he seeks technically competitive help in getting well. An adequate sociological definition of illness must go beyond the capacity in normal relationship and include all the four components listed by Parsons as necessary for a system of action – the organism, personality, social system and culture. Further, Parson's inclusion of the expectation to seek professional care as a component of the sick role is merely an indication of a possible social response to the deviant nature of illness. The legitimization of the patient status-role is itself a tension-management device for the patient. Considering the needs of the patient Loomis points out that although the relationship between physician and patient tends to be functionally specific the medical people usually must take into account factors about the patient besides his sickness like need to return to work, the kind of care he is likely to receive after discharge, and so on. The goal of the sick person is recovery – a goal to be obtained not only by the patient but by all the relevant collectivities. Implicit in his relation to the patient is the physician's goal of facilitating the latter's recovery to the best of his ability. Great physicians in every age have recognized that a patient must be seen as a whole, i.e. in terms of his interpersonal relations and his social environment. Although the conception of the patient as a person is long established and generally acknowledged in medical circles, it is also said to be a conception more honoured in the breach than observance. Many physicians continue to regard the patient as a case of sickness rather than a person.

Physician-Patient Relationship

In the social system, idea regarding the doctor-patient dyad, the reciprocity between roles is pictured with a view to economic exchange, as between producer and consumer. While the doctor is not only a producer of care but also a consumer of the patient's willingness to be treated, the patient emerges as a producer of the health service by the very token of consuming it (Parsons, 1951). However, where health is involved, the modern doctor is vastly more competent to treat than the lay person. This motivates Parsons to insist on a basically unequal structure of the two-role system. The recent trend towards more democratization in the doctor-patient relationship, epitomized as a fiduciary element, appears ill placed where health matters are at stake. Parsons quotes that 'the fiduciary responsibility ... should be regarded as shared by sick persons ... . I fail, however, to see how it is at all possible to eliminate the element of inequality. To get too far in attempting to do so would surely jeopardize the therapeutic benefits of the vast accumulation of medical knowledge and competence which culture has painfully built up over a very long period'.

Thus, the social system perspective detects the sick role and physician role structure of medical practice.

On the patient's admission to a hospital, the physician becomes the centre of the patient's universe. The physician-patient relation is central in many social systems.

There is a tendency for individuals to live up to the role expectations of those with whom they are interacting and come to perceive themselves in accordance with these expectations. The physician-patient relation is collectivity-oriented, forming a Gemeinschaft-like 'community of life' because the welfare of the patient must come ahead of the self-interest of the doctor. Parsons (1951) states: 'The classic 'doctor-patient relationship' should be considered to be minimal relevant collectivity. It is the solidarity of this collectivity which constitutes the basis of mutual 'trust' between physician and patient. The relationship can be differentiated between a private and a hospital doctor. Analytically, however, the private case of the doctor-patient relationship is an undifferentiated one in which the relationship of employer-employee and of seller-buyer is focused on each other. In clinic or hospital practice, on the other hand, they become differentiated. Then, the relevant patients, in the aggregate have transferred the role of employer not to the physician but to the hospital or clinic or collectivity. Martin (1967), while discussing the preferences for the types of patients also examines some questions pertaining to the patient's types of illness and his relationship with the doctor. Merton (1957) presents some values governing the physician-patients relationship. These values relate to physician's emotional detachment, preferences for patients' confidence, diagnosis, medical care, time, psychological and social circumstances, specific tests and reasonable fee. Others who studied physician-patient relationship suggest that ethical code to be adopted by physician in regard to their relations with patients, communication is an important aspect of the relationship.

Essential Features of Physician-Patient Relationships

Patients are demanding a more substantive, collaborative role in their own health care 'decision-making'. Collaborative health care means to apply information and communication technologies between patients, doctors and with their families. The introduction of healthware is playing an important role in enhancing the relationship between doctors and patients and also helps the patients in better understanding of their roles as patients and how the values affect decision-making. Thus, we can define collaborative health care as a process which is integrated with the people and its successful implementation will ultimately improve the patient care and be helpful in the management of health care (Safran, 2002). In the process of collaborative health care, the relationship between provider and patient is involved along with the families. The patients assume that in the collaborative health care doctors will provide them with complete information and provide all guidance based on the competence of doctors. Besides giving them full information, doctors will also educate them about illnesses, available therapies, alternative therapies, potential outcomes, and complications. This information will help a patient to make decision accordingly for the treatment and its possible outcomes (Ferguson, 1995). Patients are given opportunities so that they can actively participate in the decision-making and it will ultimately affect their lives and well-being (Ferguson, 1995). However, the patients' preferences for participation might vary with the clinical decisions (Brennan, 1999). Although, the desire for information for knowing about health and health care is very high (Brennan, 1999). Patients' anxiety is towards knowing about health and health care as it addresses their individual concerns and conditions and is also helpful work as an interactive tool in managing their health (Kaplan, 2001). The information provided to the patients is helpful in building the trust and confidence between themselves and doctors (Tang, 1998).

Framework for Physician-Patient Relationship

Supporting patient-physician collaboration with technology requires an underlying framework to facilitate participation. Goldberg et al. suggest a framework for patient empowerment and the technical realization of that framework. Such a framework is a requirement for properly designed collaborative healthware applications. This framework consists of core elements essential for facilitating patients' active access to personally relevant credible information, ongoing and facilitated communication, clinical data capture, a reporting and feedback mechanism, and community support. In addition to this framework, other issues must be considered prior to the design, implementation, and evaluation of collaborative healthware. Such considerations should include: What do patients need? What do providers want? How can the patients' view be designed into the system? How can prescribed, profile-driven knowledge be delivered? What are the best methods for information delivery? How can credible data be collected from the patients? How can the system be integrated into the current work flow? With widespread adoption of collaborative healthware applications, all patients and their families will come to expect improved access to services, greater convenience, and alternative methods of communicating with their health care providers. Since the emphasis is on the partnership between patient and provider, collaborative healthware will be used to promote informed decision-making, improve patient outcomes, increase patient satisfaction, enhance patient education, lower health care costs, and improve the coordination of care. While collaborative healthware applications have intuitive appeal to diverse groups of health care stakeholders, adoption of such systems will likely depend on their ability to demonstrate positive impact on outcomes (Goldsmith and Safran, 2004).

Elements of Physician-Patient Relationship

There are several elements of relationship between physician-patient relationships. We will discuss them: Confidentiality: The doctor must keep all the information shared by the patient with him as confidential. Patient is afraid of family and society if some adverse information about the patient is leaked. This becomes very important for stigmatized diseases like AIDS, mental illness, sex related problems, etc. These diseases have stigma attached to them. They are looked down upon in the society. The doctors should not share information with anybody until and unless it is required for the treatment purpose. Patient wants that information should only be used for the medical purpose. Privacy, credibility of medical information, and ability to correctly use that information for decision-making will be essential features of the medical internet. Effective communication: Communication is the touching of mind by mind, of person with person. It can include conversation, interview, dialogue or carefully used visual technique. Communication is an integral part of every function of health administration and that is why it is said to be the bloodstream of an organization. It is a two-way process between people. In communication, a message is transmitted and received. Transmission of message is the first half of the communication and message received and understood is the second half of the communication. Communication can be transmitted through audio, visual and audio-visual. Communication plays the same role as the nervous system in a body.

Terry has given eight factors which are helpful in making communication effective between health providers and health receivers.

- One should be fully informed.
- Have mutual trust.
- Search for a common ground of experience.
- Use common words for mutual interaction.
- One should be concerned for the context.
- One should always try to seek and hold the receiver's attention.
- Use of visual aids for communication.
- Practise long-term relationship.

In the contemporary society, where there is intense use of technology, there should be use of communication technology so that the process of communication can be made more fast and updated. The hospital system or health organizations should also play an important role in providing information and should also provide access to it. From the patients' point of view, it is extremely necessary. The acceptability of patients and doctors for this communication technology is increasing. Although, with the increasing level of communication technology, many legal issues are challenging the medical practice of doctors. But, the communication between doctors and patients has provided a platform for better understanding of patients and in turn it is helpful in managing the health (Goldsmith and Safran, 2004). Developing rapport and relationships: Building rapport with the client is the first important step so that he can divulge all his problems frankly and freely. This is also called principle of acceptance. Principle of acceptance, on the part of social worker means that he must perceive, acknowledge and establish relationship with the individual as a client. It means that no matter how much our perception of it may differ from his, we must acknowledge and accept him as if we are to help him. In health education, one begins from where the client is. Purpose is to respect, to help, to add, to comfort, therapeutic understanding, acknowledge, receiving, etc. Quality of acceptance: warmth, courtesy, listening, respect, concern, interest, consistent, maturities, fairness, willingness to enter and share life experience etc. are essential features of a physician's behaviour. Bhattarcharya (2003) has given obstacles to acceptance and these are as follows:

- Insufficient knowledge of human behaviour.
- Non-acceptance of something in self (lack of self-awareness).
- Biases and prejudices.
- Imparting to the client one's own feelings.
- Unwanted assurance.
- Confusion between acceptance and approval.
- Loss of respect for the client.
- Over identification.

The home, as a site of health care delivery, is of increasing interest to health care planners and providers. For those individuals whose access to traditional health care delivery is limited by circumstances such as distance and mobility, home-delivered services would be particularly attractive and potentially beneficial. In recent years, major advances in computing and telecommunication technologies, particularly in exponential growth of the internet have suggested possible approaches to improving health through the direct provision of services to patients (Goldsmith and Safran, 2004).

Criticism of Parsons' Image of Doctor-Patient Relationship

Finally, Parsons' image of the doctor-patient relationship has been heavily criticized. Bryan Turner (1995), in particular argues that Parsons portrays doctors as universally beneficent, competent and altruistic, and patients as compliant, passive and grateful. Neither of these images necessarily fits the reality. Instead doctors pursue their own careers and incomes as well as provide medical expertise. Patients, too, have their own needs and wishes when they attend the clinic, and these may not fit the role of unquestioning compliance, which Parsons seems to suggest. Turner suggests that the doctor-patient relationship can better be understood as a site of conflict between the differing needs and desires of doctors and patients.

Motivating the Patients

Doctors should not discourage the patient about disease. He should rather motivate the patient and create will power, which is basic for any treatment. They should be motivated to do this job as a part of their medical duties. S.S. Sooch, in his article, 'Revamping Health Care' in the *Daily Tribune* (26 January 2000), rightly remarks that health care providers in the government hospitals are mostly indifferent, apathetic and insensitive and some of them are arrogant in their behaviour. They do not have any sense of compassion, sympathy and human touch is missing. Doctors must devote time and energy to solve patient's problems in collaboration of paramedical personnel. There are some important points which every doctor must follow: that the patients are treated as close to their homes as possible in the smallest, cheapest and simply equipped unit such as a sub-centre which is capable of looking after them adequately; that the medical services should be organized and administered in such a way that the quality of medical care improves gradually; the medical care services should be organized from the bottom-up and not from the top-down; that the services planned should meet the needs of people; that all members of health and medical personnel function as a well-knit team; and that new category of health personnel such as multi-purpose health workers and community health workers should be given suitable training to provide simple medical care and preventive services to large sections of the community. In the case of virtual epidemic of behavioural disorders, modern health care must place a new emphasis on solving the human side of medicine. Health education: The most important aim of health education is to alter behaviour, which may have directly or indirectly influenced occurrence of spread of diseases in a given cultural setting. A culturally relevant health education programme can be planned only after understanding the behaviour in all its manifestations. The basic aim of health education is to make people aware about their own health so that they can take their own action in achieving the health. The effort of the health education is to improve the living conditions of the people so sense of responsibility is generated among them. The health education not only promotes the individual responsibility but also that at the level of family, community and at society level. The studies of the world have shown that fluctuations in the toll of diseases and deaths depend even more on the level of education than on the social and economic conditions in which people live. Ignorance can be just as much a killer as poverty, and these two often go hand in hand (WHO, 1995). Health education does not mean merely removal of ignorance. On the other hand, it involves three important things (WHO, 1995): It provides a person with appropriate knowledge to enjoy decent health and also the knowledge about the occurrence and spread of disease thus enabling him to adopt relevant preventive measures; it creates in him an interest for the health of other members of his family as well as of those living in his surrounding; and it creates in him a desire to support health education programmes in this area (Goel, 2008). Patient is a person: There is need of dedication and not being an earning machine on the part of doctor. To the mechanization of medicine is added the sin of commercialization. This is an age of consumerism where the lure of money which brings with it power, luxury, comfort, and enjoyment of life in all its varied physical forms is paramount. Contemporary medicine is the crippling expense an ill patient often incurs, an expense that is often ruinous to the family.

This is partly due to the fact that the physician of today has forgotten the art of medicine and remains solely preoccupied with its science. His rapport is with machines and not with patients; it is technology that dictates his course of action and not his clinical judgement. History taking is a neglected art; he forgets to use his senses – his eyes, ears and hands – but remember numbers, equations and formulae. Expensive investigations and expensive modes of treatment result are used, when simple tests and simpler measures would have sufficed. Institutionalized medicine has also led to malpractice. Expensive glittering machines and foyers resembling five star hotels are the landmarks of modern institutions. To meet the cost, and hopefully, make profit, machines have to be fed, and patients become the fodder for these machines.

Faith in Values of Medical Problems

Why there has been such a decline in the ethics of cotemporary medicine? It is almost certainly related to the decline in the sense of values in our present day world. This decline is observed in all professions and in the whole of society, perhaps even to a greater extent than that observed in medicine. A burning desire for material gain and wealth dominates life today. It is indeed difficult for a profession to remain an island of virtue when surrounded by a sea of filth and corruption. Welfare of the patient: The first is clinical iatrogenesis-diseases produced by the physicians, either by treatment or investigations, or by the hospital in which patients are treated. But then iatrogenic disease is as old as medicine; it is an inseparable comparison of medicine since antiquity. Contemporary medicine is aware of the epidemic of iatrogenesis resulting from the frequent use of potent drugs, sophisticated gadgetry and invasive procedures used in the diagnosis of management of patients. Far too often the treatment meted out to patients today may be worse than the disease. The second form of iatrogenesis is social iatrogenesis by which is meant the creation of an environment which no longer has the ability to allow people in society to look after them. People are hopelessly dependent on the medical system and the medical system operates to ensure that this remains so. Medical help is sought for trivial and unnecessary reasons, for the benefit of the medical profession and the detriment of people in society. The third form of iatrogenesis, according to Illich, is cultural iatrogenesis whereby institutionalized medicine has sapped the ability of the people to face the reality of the sufferings in life and the inevitability of death. This may be true in the West but it is not so in India and many Eastern countries. A patient's, and for that matter a doctor's attitude to suffering and pain, and death is conditioned by socio-cultural and religious factors. Most people in the East accept that life cannot be divorced from suffering and pain, and that each one is apportioned his or her share of pain and suffering in life. It is being increasingly recognized today that modern medicine with its science and technology should relieve suffering but should refrain from prolonging the act of dying. Sympathy: It is necessary to recapture the spirit of humanism and re-establish the special sympathy in doctor-patient relationship. To restore the image we need to distance from lure of money, raise the ethical standards and place the welfare and care of patients above all. It is felt that there is decline in values in medical profession. The frustration of patients and relatives is often translated into litigation demanding compensation; and to protect him the doctor falls back on defensive medicine. He over investigates not to miss even a rare disorder. There is a need for healthy interaction between medicine and society, which is a two-way reciprocal affair. Trustworthiness: Medical doctors are regarded as the pillars and builders of students' behaviour applying a standard programme. Medical doctors develop the curriculum according to the needs of the society and also according to the advancement in the science and technology. It helps in building the future medicos. The *Charka Samhita* clearly mentions that the good teacher is one who is very clear about his knowledge of the medical scriptures and uses that knowledge in his practice of the medical profession.

Doctor should have a high standard of professional and personal values in relation to patients and their care. He should be accessible and available to the patients. He should be able to communicate effectively. Doctor should not be exploitative: Doctor should treat the patients with economy and efficiency. It has been seen that a doctor prescribes a large number of tests relating to laboratory investigations and radiology, which are costly and harmful to the body. Doctor is not interested in treating the patient but exploiting this for material benefits. In this way mind of the doctor gets perverted and he loses self-respect in his own mind. This trend is on the increase, which should be curbed. Doctor must treat the patient on the basis of equity: It is well known that a doctor is highly qualified in medicine but this is not sufficient until and unless the doctor treats the patients on the basis of equality and in a dignified way. His diagnosis and treatment would depend upon the information he is able to get from the patient. If the doctor keeps himself on high pedestrian, this prevents the disclosure of information and prevents the good rapport between patient and the doctor. Involving patients in the provision of their own care offers enormous benefits to both the patients and their providers. Physicians recognize that the patient is their primary source of information regarding symptoms and perceived reactions to treatment. They would further assert that the critical factor in the effectiveness of treatments is the patient's compliance with prescribed protocols. So patients already are involved in their own care. Empowering patients simply acknowledges their shared responsibility and builds upon the trust that has historically served as the foundation of the provider-patient relationship. The empowerment comes from giving patients greater access to information and from facilitated doctor-patient communications. Empowered patients are better equipped to manage their own health, to educate them regarding their health conditions, and to play an effective part in their treatment.

Theoretical Discourse of Physician-Patient Relationship

The traditional approach to professional-patient communication was doctor-centred. This places the health professional in the role of an authority figure who instructs and directs the passive patient. It was assumed that there was a one-way transfer of knowledge from the expert health professional to the lay person. This type of approach fails to acknowledge that the client/patient will have their own areas of expertise to add to the consultation, e.g. their symptoms and lifestyle. A doctor-centred approach to communication may lead to patients feeling powerless and unable to exercise little control over their own health. An alternative model is the patient-centred or consumerist approach, where the patient makes the decisions about treatment options.

The discourse on doctor-patient relationship/interaction has been analysed by many sociological studies. With the increasing cost of treatment, the expanding domain of psychology of health, sociology discourse on doctors' professionalism and patients increasing awareness have given direction to the doctors on how to take the clinical decisions (Hughes et al., 2008; Dowie and Elstein, 1988; Schwartz and Griffin, 1986). The studies on physician-patient relationships show that doctors make high use of biomedical knowledge and beyond the scope of social influence. Doctors focus on the cognitive aspects for medical reasoning for cure of the ailment and suggest alternative therapies based on the scientific reasoning. These studies are scientific and psychologistic in nature. Many more sociological studies have taken the sociological variables like caste, class, gender, ethnic background, professional socialization and payment system in the studies of doctor-patient relationship. Duff and Hollinshead (1968) found that class background of the patients affects the interaction pattern between the doctor and the patient. Medical knowledge in the pattern of interaction between doctor-patient relationship is particularistic and socially loaded (Clark et al., 1991), instead of scientific knowledge (Freidson, 1970). Thus, the sociological studies conclude that the social factors play a very important role in the development of medical knowledge. It determines who has access to it and how people are differentially treated having gained access to it. From the Marxist point of view, the study done by Mishler (1984) finds that how doctors take the patients' information of their social context and redefine it in terms adequate to their technological framework. He also argues that the voice of medicine with its technical vocabulary and the voice of the life world, are important for the social existence of the patient. Mishler finds that during the interaction between doctor and patients the doctor dominates because of his technical expertise and does not recognize the importance of social factors which are also relevant from the patient's point of view. The patients' illnesses which have grown out of their situation are converted by doctors as diseases (Blumhagen, 1982; Helman, 1985; Kleinmann, 1980). West (1984) found that doctors structure consultation in such a way that patients' stories comply with the notion of doctors' pre-existing categories. The macro-level structures of capitalism are linked to micro-level structures in the clinical setting (Waitzkin, 1984, 1985, 1989). He argues that during the process of doctor-patient interaction macro-structures are always present. Doctors directly voice the explicit ideological messages that legitimate the class structure of society. In the process of interaction the social relations of capitalism are maintained by the doctors. Doctors reinforce the position ascribed to the women in capitalist society as unpaid domestic labour and which is responsible for nurturing the next generation of workers, and thus in this way, reproduction of labour takes place. Waitzkin uses the classical Marxist sociological model of Lukacisian concept of reification.

Luckacs framework suggests the second nature of law which is related with the social and historical forms of social life. In this context Habermas (1970) argues that the science which exists is further influenced by capitalism. According to Waitzkin doctors latently act as agents of social control and enforce the values of capitalism and are active partners of process of medicalization. C. Wright Mills (1959) pushed his argument that this task is achieved by rendering public issues into private troubles. In the process of medical encounters, technical statements given by doctors help direct patients' responses to objectified symptoms, signs and treatment. This results into shift of attention from the social relation and social issues which are the root causes of personal troubles (Waitzkin, 1989; Freidson, 1983). This analysis concludes that the ideological function is performed in organizing the society according to doctor's point of view. The social context of illness is lost over medicalization of social problems. Social problems are reduced into technical and scientific ones. The doctors control the sickness certificate, control over diagnostic categories and also the access to mood altering drugs in the daily practice and in turn it is a way of reinforcing the ideologies of capitalism. The women's depression is seen in terms of prescription of tranquilizers denying the factors of women's subordinated position in the family and exploitation of domestic labour. Doctors never question the status quo of the women rather they actively support it. The industrial labour class injuries and suffering are also treated in the mechanical manner and repaired by them. Doctors are hardly concerned about the occupational health hazards they face during the working hours. The recurrence of the same complaint is never questioned and that why this problem is occurring again and again. This social control is present because individual health practitioner is not aware of capitalistic forces in which he is living and it does not affect his standard of life in any situation. Even the doctors are aware of it, the professional socialization of doctors do not perceive social problems under their control and, therefore, they ignore it and restore to the idea that they cannot change it. The conscious or unconscious exclusion of social context from the medical practice is a feature closely related to social control and ideology. Ignoring the social issues, especially when these issues are very important from a patient's point of view, turn finger towards the inadequacy of personal training of doctors. This is a very important lacking on the part of doctors (Freidson, 1984; Waitzkin, 1989). Waitzkin is influenced by Althusser's analysis of macro level of society and micro levels of life. The macro level of society is reduced totally into micro levels. The individuals perform their assigned roles which are determined by the requirements of the system. There is no denying of the fact that medicine does not function in the modern society. However, these functions are performed according to the deterministic model of human action. Other categories of Marxists have attempted to provide somewhat more balanced view of interaction between macro and micro structures. However, the impact of sociological variables like class, gender and ethnicity keep on going in the capitalist class structure. According to Aday et al. (1980), the impact of ethnicity is particularly important. Different cultural groups explain normal behaviour in their own parameters. This is supported by Anderton et al. (1989) in his study of Canadians and Chinese that their orientation of chronic illness is reflected by their cultural background. The Chinese are not very much concerned about the returning of the sick person into normal situation but are more concerned with the secure future of the individual. On the other hand, Canadians are worried about the ways of rehabilitation of the individual into normal life. Thus, the study clearly brings out the differences of perception of illness into two different cultural communities. Anderton also argues that western medicine acts as an ideology and enforces normalization of the chronically sick and handicapped person. Those who are not the part of this system are labelled as abnormal with all the implications this has for the treatment and access to the health care system. Thus, the medial knowledge and practice are build up around political, economic and social boundaries. Anderton's analysis is centred around cultural differences by taking the idea of Schutz's phenomenology, while the Waitzking's analysis is centred around economic imperative. Anderton views that the difference between Chinese and Canadian is not-cultural differences in viewing the concept of normality but rather it is economically driven. The poor are more worried about their working class position, therefore they are much more worried about their security. Ethnicity is also rendered as ideology. Here also Anderton argues that ethic differences are also due to the material circumstances of people's lives (Anderton et al., 1989). Thus, the whole analysis of Anderton is reduced to the class explanation.

In the end, a doctor who focuses upon the patient as a human being rather than as an object must also give an increased attention to the problems of health as well as disease. Health is a very complicated matter, consisting as it does of a relative adaptation to many different influences from the physical, biological, socio-cultural and psychological environments. Still doctors should find more time to pay more attention to keeping their patients well.

Summing Up

The hospital is considered as a social system and the physicians and patients are the sole occupants who mutually interact to form relationships directed by their specific goals and the general goals of the system.

The ideology of the profession lays great emphasis on the obligation of the physician to put the welfare of the patient above his personal interest, as regards commercialism as the most serious and insidious evil in the physician's role. The goal of the sick person is to get well soon by all relevant collectivities. The physician's goal is to facilitate the recovery of patient to the best of his ability. Confidentiality, effective communication, developing rapport and relationship, motivating the patients, health education, trustworthiness, sympathy, etc. are the essential elements of a relationship between physician-patient.

References

Aday, L. et al. (1980), *Health Care in the US: Equitable for Who?* Beverly Hills, CA: Sage Publications.

Advani, Mohan (1980), *Doctor-Patient Relationship in Indian Hospitals*, Jaipur: Sanghi Prakashan.

Anderton, J. et al. (1989), 'Ideology in Clinical Context: Chronic Illness, Ethnicity, and the Discourse on Normalisation', *Sociology of Health and Illness*, 11(3): 253–78.

Bhattarcharya, Sanjay (2003), *Social Work*, New Delhi: Deep and Deep Publications.

Bloor, D. (1986), 'Some Determinants of Thought Style in Science', in R. Cohen and T. Schnelle (eds), *Cognition and Fact: Materials on Ludwik Fleck*, Holland: D. Riedel.

Blumhagen, D. (1982), 'The Meaning of Hypertension', in N. Chrisman and T. Maretzki (eds), *Clinically Applied Anthropology*, Dordrecht: D. Riedel.

Brennan, P.F. (1999), 'Health Informatics and Community Health: Support for Patients as Collaborators in Care', *Methods Inform Med*, 38(4–5): 274–78.

Brennan, P.F. and S. Ripich (1994), 'Use of a Home Care Computer Network by Persons with AIDS', *International Journal of Technology Assess Health Care*, 10(2): 258–72.

Cassell, E.J. (1985), *Talking with Patients*, Cambridge: MIT Press.

Clark, J. et al. (1991), 'Bringing Social Structure Back into Clinical Decision Making', *Social Structure and Medicine*, 32(8): 853–66.

Conrad, P. and J. Schneider (1980), *Deviance and Medicalisation: From Badness to Sickness*, St. Louis: Mosby.

Coser, R.L. (1958), 'Authority and Decision-Making in a Hospital: A Comparative Analysis', *American Sociological Review*, 23(1): 56–64.

Dowie, J. and A. Elstein (1988), *Professional Judgement: A Reader in Clinical Decision Making*, Cambridge: Cambridge University Press.

Duff, R. and A. Hollingshead (1968), *Sickness and Society*, New York: Harper and Row.

Eisenberg, J.M. (1979), 'Sociologic Influences on Decision Making by Clinicians', *Annals of Internal Medicine*, 90: 957.

Ferguson, T. (1995), 'Consumer Health Informatics', *Health Care Forum Journal*, 38(1).

Freidson, E. (1970), *Profession of Medicine: A Study of the Sociology of Applied Knowledge*, Chicago: University of Chicago Press.

—— (1983), 'Viewpoint: Sociology of Medicine: A Polemic', *Sociology of Health and Illness*, 5: 208–19.

—— (1984), 'The Changing Nature of Professional Control', *Annual Review of Sociology*, 10: 1–20.

Georegepolous, B.S. and F.C. Mann (1962), *The Community General Hospital*, New York: Macmillan.

Goel, S.L. (2008), *Rural Health Education*, New Delhi: Deep and Deep Publications.

—— (2010), *Management Techniques and Good Governance in Health Care System and Hospital Administration*, Vol. 7, New Delhi: Deep and Deep Publications.

Goldsmith, D. and C. Safran (2004), *Consumer Informatics*, New York: Springer.

Habermas, J. (1970), 'Technology and Science as Ideology', in J. Habermas (ed.), *Toward a Rational Society*, Boston: Beacon.

Helman, C. (1985), 'Pseudo Angina and Magical Illness: A Case History', in R. Hahn and A. Gaines (eds), *Physicians of Western Medicine: Anthropological Approaches to Theory and Practice*, Dordrecht: D. Riedel.

Hughes, B.P. et al. (2008), *Patient Safety and Quality: An Evidence-based Handbook for Nurses*, Vol. 3, Rockville, MD: Agency for Healthcare Research and Quality.

Kaplan, B. (2001), 'Consumer Informatics: Supporting Patients as Co-producers of Quality', *JAMIA*, 8(4): 309–16.

Katz, J. (1984), *The Silent World of Doctor and Patient*, New York: Free Press.

Kleinmann, A. (1980), *Patients and Healers in the Context of Culture*, Berkeley, CA: University of California Press.

Loomis, C.P. (1960), *Social System*, New Jersey: Nostrand.

Lopez, S.R. (1989), 'Patient Variable Biases in Clinical Judgement: Conceptual Overview and Methodological Considerations', *Psychological Bulletin*, 106(2): 184–203.

Lukacs, G. (1968), *History and Class Consciousness*, London: Merlin Press.

Mansour, Esmat (1995), *Towards a World without Polio*, Geneva: WHO.

Martin, S.A. (1967), *Nurses' Perception and Attitudes Related to Nurse-Patient Interaction*, Missouri: At. Louis University.

Mechanic, David (1968), *Medical Sociology: A Selective View*, New York: The Free Press.

Merton, R.K. (1957), 'Some Preliminaries to a Sociology of Medical Education', in R.K. Merton et al. (eds), *Student-Physician*, Cambridge: Harvard University Press.

Mills, C.W. (1959), *The Sociological Imagination*, New York: Oxford University Press.

Mishler, E.G. (1984), *The Discourse of Medicine: Dialectics of Medical Interviews*, Norwood, NJ: Ablex.

Nagla, Madhu (1988), *Medical Sociology*, Jaipur: Printwell Publications.

Parsons, T. (1951), *The Social System*, New York: Free Press.

Safran, C. (2002), 'The Collaborative Edge: Patient Empowerment for Vulnerable Populations', *International Journal of Medical Informatics*, 69(2): 185–90.

Schwartz, S. and T. Griffin (1986), *Medical Thinking: The Psychology of Medical Judgement and Decision Making*, New York: Springer.

Tang, P.C. (1998), 'Information Patients: A Guide for Providing Patient Health Information', *JAMIA*, 5(6): 563–70.

Tang, P.C. et al. (1997), 'Meeting the Information Needs of Patients Results from a Patient Focus Group', *Proc AMIA Annual Fall Symposium*, 672–76.

Turner, Bryan S. (1995), *Medical Power and Social Knowledge*, Thousand Oaks, CA: Sage Publications.

Waitzkin, H. (1984), 'Doctor-Patient Communication: Clinical Implications of Social Science Research', *Journal of the American Medical Association*, 252: 2441–46.

—— (1985), 'Information Giving in Medical Care', *Journal of Health and Social Behaviour*, 26(2): 81–101.

—— (1989), 'A Critical Theory of Medical Discourse: Ideology, Social Control, and the Processing of Social Context in Medical Encounters', *Journal of Health and Social Behaviour*, 30: 220–39.

West, C. (1984), *Routine Complications: Troubles with Talk between Doctors and Patients*, Bloomington: Indiana University Press.

Woolhandler, S. and D. Himmelstein (1989), 'Ideology in Medical Sciences: Class in the Clinic', *Social Science and Medicine*, 28(11): 1205–09.

15

Drugs, Pharmaceuticals and Health Care in India

An outstanding feature of the modern health care services all over the world is that drugs, which were earlier a small appendage to the health services, have now become almost central to their existence. In this chapter, we look into important issues related to the medicinal aspects of health care.

The Concept of Essential Medicine

People between 1.3 and 2.1 billion remain without access to medicine despite decades of effort (WHO, 2004a). Improvement is slow; the proportion of the world's population with access to essential medicines has improved from an estimated 63 per cent to only 70 per cent between 1987 and 1999. Almost 80 per cent of those without access live in low-income countries, and 20 per cent in middle-income countries. Such figures conceal major differences within countries, and do not adequately convey a sense of which medicines are lacking. Annual expenditure on medicines in 2000 varied from US$ 396 per head in high-income countries to only US$ 4 in low-income countries. At the same time, medicines accounted for a higher percentage of total health expenditure in low-income (19%) and middle-income countries (25%) than high-income per cent countries.

Essential medicines are those that satisfy the priority health care needs of the population, with due regard to evidence on efficacy and safety, and comparative cost-effectiveness. They are intended to be available at all times in the context of functioning health systems, in adequate amounts, in the appropriate dosage forms, with assured quality and adequate information, and at affordable prices (WHO, 2004b). Countries and health care systems should apply these principles to select a list of essential medicines, linking it to evidence-based treatment guidelines, for use in professional training, supervision and audit. The impact of an essential medicines list depends on how the health system is structured and governed. In most countries the ministry of health can use regulatory procedures to ensure that all public sector providers adhere to it and its accompanying rational treatment guidelines. However, this may be subverted in systems with a large and unregulated private sector. This list can be used by insurance agencies to set standards and guidelines for reimbursement or coverage of care.

History of Drugs and Pharmaceutical Companies in India

From ancient times, two systems of medicine were in vogue in India. First, there was ayurvedic medicine, which dates back to the Vedic period. Ayurvedic medicine depends largely on the combination of various herbs, minerals and metals like gold, copper, etc. Medicines for allopathy treatment were imported by the British for the use of Britons living and ruling in India. Indigenous production of these medicines was started in 1901 with the establishment of the Bengal Chemical and Pharmaceutical Works, due to the pioneering efforts of Acharya P.C. Ray. Scientists in India undertook research of tropical diseases like malaria, typhoid and cholera. Between 1904 and 1907, four research institutes were established. Yet another significant development in this period was the use of chemicals for treating various diseases. Some very important drugs like aspirin and barbiturates were made available during this period. The First World War gave a real stimulus to domestic production of pharmaceuticals. Indigenous production in 1939 was sufficient to meet only 13 per cent of medical requirements. The Second World War provided a propitious atmosphere for further expansion of production.

From a mere ₹ 10 crore (production value) in 1947 to a whopping ₹ 26,540 crore in 2002–03, the pharmaceutical industry in India has come a long way. Today, India manufactures over 400 bulk drugs and around 60,000 formulations. The number of pharmaceutical units too has increased from 1,752 in 1955 to over 23,000 in 2002. It is estimated that there are presently 1,600 firms engaged in the production of drugs and pharmaceuticals (Chaganti, 2008).

In the 1960s, the government started to encourage the growth of drug manufacturing by Indian companies, and also passed the Patents Act in 1970. The number of purely Indian pharma companies are less in number. Foreign companies dominate and control the Indian pharma industry. These have subsidiaries in India for its cheap labour. In terms of the global market, India holds a modest 1–2 per cent share, but it has been growing at approximately 10 per cent per year. India with its innovatively-engineered generic drugs and active pharmaceutical ingredients, has gained a good foothold in the global scene. And today India is seeking to become a major player in outsourced clinical research as well as contract manufacturing and research.

In India, the output of Indian pharmaceutical industry increased to ₹ 260 billion in the financial year 2002, which accounts for 1.3 per cent of the global pharmaceutical sector. The bulk drugs account for ₹ 54 billion (21%), the remaining ₹ 210 billion (79%) for formulations, imports were ₹

20 billion while exports were ₹ 87 billion in the year 2000. There has been huge expansion of domestic pharma sector with estimated US$ 11.72 billion (₹ 55,454 crore) in 2008–09 from US$ 6.88 billion (₹ 32,575 crore) in 2003–04. India exports its pharma products to various countries around the globe, including highly regulated markets of USA, Europe, Japan and Australia. The growth of Indian pharma industry has grown tremendously since 2008–09 in terms of export. The Indian pharmaceutical industry has grown from a humble ₹ 1,500 crore turnover in 1980 to ₹ 1,00,611 in 2009–10. The Indian pharmaceutical industry consists of more than 20,000 registered units which are highly fragmented. It has been expanding in a tremendous manner in the last two decades and includes 250 pharmaceutical companies which control 70 per cent of the market. The Indian pharma industry has around 70 per cent of the country's demand for bulk drugs, drug intermediates, pharmaceutical formulations, chemicals, tablets, capsules, orals and injectibles. About 250 large units and 8,000 small scale units, are from the core of the pharmaceutical industry in India. The units produced have the complete range of medicines which are ready for consumption by patients (<www.indianmirror.com> accessed on 11 December 2005).

Drug Policy in India

In 1975, the Hathi Committee was appointed by the Government of India to analyse the Indian drug industry. In 1978, the Government of India declared a drug policy and recommended the followings things:

- A restricted list of essential drugs and that measures be implemented to ensure their production.
- That a gradual shift be made from brand names to generic names.
- That price control measures be effected with the aim of making life-saving drugs and essential drugs affordable.
- That public sector play a leading role in drug production.
- And certain drugs be reserved to encourage the growth of Indian drug companies.
- Elimination of irrational drugs.
- The committee decided the role played by MNCs and recommended immediate dilution of foreign equity in drug companies up to 40 per cent and progressively to 26 per cent.
- It had also recommended the nationalization of foreign drug companies (Government of India, 1975).

The Drug Policy of 1986, which was titled 'Measures for Rationalization, Quality Control and Growth of Drugs and Pharmaceutical Industry in India' was evolved under the dynamic guidance and leadership of late Rajiv Gandhi. The main objectives of the Drug Policy are as follows:

- Ensuring abundant availability, at reasonable prices of essential life saving and prophylactic medicines of good quality.

- Strengthening the system of quality control over drug production and promoting the rational use of drugs in the country.
- Creating an environment conducive to channelizing new investment into the pharmaceutical industry to encourage cost-effective production with economic sizes and for introducing new technologies and new drugs.
- Strengthening the indigenous capability for production of drugs.

For meeting the requirements of medicines for health needs at reasonable prices and strengthening the indigenous base, the Government has, over the years been guided by the above policy. Implementation of the main policy provisions has been through the Industrial (Development and Research) Act on Industrial Licensing Aspects and through Drugs (Prices Control) Orders under the Essential Commodities Act in regard to the pricing mechanism. The drug policy has also given the policy framework in regard to Quality Control and Rational Use of Drugs. Enforcement of quality and standards in medicines is done through the provisions contained in the Drugs and Cosmetics Act, which is administered by the Ministry of Health and Family Welfare, Government of India.

The Pharmaceutical Policy (2002) calls for relaxation of production and price controls. Production controls have now mostly gone except for bulk drugs produced by the use of recombinant DNA technology, bulk drugs requiring in-vivo use of nucleic acids, and specific cell/tissue targeted formulations.

Critique of Drug Policy

In the absence of a clear, comprehensive and rational drug policy, the distorted pattern of drug production and the proliferation of non-essential, irrational and harmful drugs continues. Indian markets are flooded with over 1,00,000 formulations; there is no system of central registration of these formulations. These drugs are sold under numerous brand names rather than their generic names. There has also been a phenomenal increase in drug prices. Despite the phenomenal growth of the drug industry during the past six decades, the availability of modern drugs is still low. For example, in 1984 only 5 to 6 per cent of the population could afford the modern drugs they needed; another 25 per cent had limited access to essential drugs. A majority of the people living in rural areas and urban slums, the main victims of endemic and epidemic diseases, had little or no access to modern drugs. With the predicted increase in the cost of drugs after joining the World Trade Organization (WTO), the problems are likely to go out of control. Since 1983, the government has issued various orders banning several harmful and/or useless formulations marked in India, but to little effect. Drug and health activist organizations, under the auspices of the All Indians Drug Action Network (AIDAN), went to the Supreme Court demanding implementation of the ban. Some constituent bodies publish drug information bulletins for prescribers. In general, representatives of pharmaceutical companies are the only source of information to prescribers in remote areas. The government has taken little initiative to fulfil its statutory function to monitor manufacturers' promotional literature and has taken no steps to supply objective and unbiased drug information to prescribers. Drug and health activist organizations have intervened in a petition challenging the government's move to further curtail the number of drugs under price control (Sarkar, 2004).

Pharmaceutical Issues in Health Care

There are certain important issues related to the medicinal aspects of health care. These are: international intellectual property right system and other trade-related impediments and use of rational medicine, corrupting influence of profit-driven pharmaceutical companies on health professionals, academics and regulatory bodies and the way pharmaceutical R and D is funded and incentives offered to them.

Intellectual Property Rights, Monopolies and High Prices

The price of new medicines is largely governed by an Intellectual Property Rights (IPR) regime that grants patents to any company that registers a new medicine. Patents are granted by governments and give a company monopoly power to manufacture and sell a medicine free of competition from any other manufacturer in that particular country. This monopoly power allows the patent-holder to set a price many times greater than the cost of production. Patents are usually granted for a fixed period after which other companies are permitted to manufacture generic versions of the same medicine.

Big pharmas argue that patents are vital incentives to companies to invest in pharmaceutical research and development. It also says that the revenue from profitable products can be used to support research of new treatments for diseases, including those which particularly affect the developing world (IFPMA, 2005).

TRIPS had stipulated that by January 2005, all member states of the WTO must grant patents on all medicines for a period of 20 years. Whereas patents were previously granted by governments on a country-by-country basis, there is now a single and standard patent agreement that applies to all countries. A particular concern is the potential impact on our country which is important source of generic medicines, including antiretrovirals. There is presently a campaign against the amendment to Indian patent, the fourth WTO ministerial conference adopting the Doha declaration on the TRIPS Agreement and Public Health in 2001 (WTO, 2001). This says that TRIPS should be implemented in a manner that supports the right of countries 'to protect public health and, in particular, to promote access to medicine for all'. There is a list of policy of flexibilities that can be sued to overcome intellectual property barriers to medicines. It asserts the freedom of each member state to determine the grounds on which compulsory licences can be granted without the consent of patent-holder, and confirms that the agreement in no way limits countries' capacity to allow parallel trade in patented medicines. The Doha declaration left one issue unresolved. A country without local manufacturing capacity would not be able to make use of a compulsory or government-use licence to improve access to medicines (Correa, 2002). The WTO, therefore, decided in 2003 to allow for a temporary waiver of the requirement that medicines produced under a compulsory licence should be predominantly for the domestic market (Correa, 2004).

The TRIP agreement, despite the flexibilities permitted by the Doha declaration and the WTO 2003 decision, has harmed efforts to improve access to essential medicines. Even worse has been the development and implementation of a variety of 'TRIPS-plus' agreements and policies aimed at killing off the flexibilities and eroding further the capacity of governments to regulate the pharmaceutical sector and the price of medicines.

Bilateral trade agreements are being used to erode the power and role of national authorities for the regulation of medicines and the structures responsible for medicines selection. Regulation of medicines is one of the most important health stewardship functions of government. An effective framework should include a competent process for ensuring that medicines produced, sold and dispensed are safe and effective; that monitoring and surveillance systems exist to identify problems with safety; and that clinical trials conducted by the pharmaceutical sector are ethical, transparent, methodologically sound and free of bias.

Corruption and Funding of Pharmaceutical Companies

There is a growing concern about big pharmas' unethical behaviour and lack of transparency. It is increasingly entering into financial arrangements with academic and research institutions that threaten the objectivity and credibility of clinical research (Medawar and Hardon, 2004). In contrast with academic researchers, the companies may insist on controlling how the research is done and reported, and whether the results will be made public. Furthermore, a growing number of clinical trials are being managed by investor-owned businesses that are even more beholden to the drug companies because the companies are their only clients.

The contract between pharmaceutical companies and researchers has become pervasive, as shown by the decision by the highly respected *New England Journal of Medicine* to drop its requirement that authors of review articles of medical studies must not have financial ties to the companies whose medicines are being analysed (Drazen and Curfman, 2002). The authors of scientific studies are often funded by private drug-companies with a stake in the results.

In other cases, papers are ghost-written by pharmaceutical company's staff or contractors. Scientists at universities are often allowed to have stock options in companies benefitting from the research they are conducting. Researchers on industry payrolls may be persuaded to suppress unwanted results, and those who defy their corporate sponsors may lose their funding. Lastly, where university research was once oriented to producing independent and public knowledge, it is now increasingly locked up in patents (*An Alternative World Health Report*, 2005). This type of corruption and bias also extends to prescribing doctors and medicine regulatory authorities (Angell, 2004). Big pharmas spend lavishly to influence doctors who write the prescriptions through gifts, air tickets, sponsorship of conferences and meeting and many more incentives.

Pharmaceutical companies have also been able to purchase influence in regulatory bodies and in government circle. There is another aspect of absence of effective laws and regulation for drug companies to reveal all clinical trials. The selective and biased release of scientific data, which should be made illegal, is potentially harmful to patients and also has a potential effect on ethics and values of scientific inquiry. Regulatory bodies are also under political pressure to speed up the licensing of new medicines in order to minimize the loss of potential profits due to delays in marketing of a new drug.

Pattern of Drug Production

A careful analysis of the drug policy, which speaks mainly of self-reliance and 'abundance' of drugs that meet our health needs, shows that it does not lay special emphasis on the pattern of drug production. It is not enough to see that drugs are produced by Indians and in abundance. It is even more important to see what drugs are produced and for whom. There is now an overproduction of drugs (often very costly) meant for the rich and well-to-do while the drugs needed by the poor people (and these must be cheap) are not adequately available. This skewed pattern of drug production is in keeping with our iniquitous social structure which stresses the production of luxury goods for the rich at the cost of the basic needs of the poor. In fact, the drug industries in India are in private hands which produce mainly for profit and hence result in a situation where the drugs required by the poor are not produced on the main ground that there is not profitable market and adequate demand for them, while the country continues to be flooded by a plethora of costly and wasteful drugs meant for the minor illnesses of the rich and well-to-do. For instance, the production of INH for tuberculosis is only one-third of minimal requirement. On the other hand, tonics and vitamins most of which are alcoholic preparations and spin money, are produced in wasteful abundance (ICSSR and ICMR, 1981).

One of the most distressing aspects of the present health situation in India is the habit of doctors to over-prescribe or to prescribe glamorous and costly drugs with limited medical potential. It is also unfortunate that the drug producers always try to push doctors into using their products by all means – fair or foul. These basic facts are more responsible for distortions in drug productions and consumption than anything else. If the medical profession could not be made to be more discriminating in its prescribing habits, there would be no market for irrational and unnecessary medicines (*Health for All: An Alternative Strategy*, 1981).

Quality Control

Quality control of drugs is extremely important. It is necessary to prescribe realistic standards (not those mechanically copied from books) and to enforce them uniformly in all parts of the country. The drug control organization needs to be strengthened. It will be essential to prescribe criteria and processes for the quality control of indigenous medicines also since health programmes are dependent on adequate supply of drugs of assured quality.

Intellectual Property Rights

Intellectual property right is a legal protection for new inventions, products or processes, which are the result of an individual's ideas. India is also a signatory of GATT (General Agreement on Trade and Tariffs) including TRIPS (Trade Related Intellectual Property Rights) signed on 15 April 1994. The main impact of TRIPS on pharmaceutical patents in India has been:

- A patent term of 20 years from the date of filing.
- Recognition of product patents.
- Import of a product to be accepted as 'working' as a patent.
- Compulsory licensing to be confined to special circumstances like emergency or abuse of patent rights.
- Reversal of 'burden of proof' in infringement action relating to process patents (obliging the defendant to prove that the process is non-infringing).

Pharmaceutical Companies and Doctors in India

According to Planning Commission in India, pharmaceutical marketing and aggressive promotion contribute to irrational use of drugs and therefore, there is a need for a mandatory code to identify and penalize unethical promotion by pharma companies. The government has also made use of generic names or the International Non-Proprietary Name (INN) compulsory, instead of brand names, at all stages of government procurement, distribution, prescription and use.

A study by Planning Commission's high-level expert group said the pharmaceutical industry spent more than 25 per cent of its annual turnover on sales promotion alone as compared to a paltry 7 per cent on research and development in 2008–09 (*The Times of India*, 10 December 2014).

To deal with the reported nexus between doctors and pharma companies, the Medical Council of India (MCI) has proposed clear punishment for doctors accepting freebies in the form of gifts, cash or travel facility, etc. from pharma companies. This proposal is passed by the Ethics Committee and subsequently agreed by the Union Ministry of Health and Family Welfare, which led to the amendment to the MCI (Professional Conduct, Etiquette and Ethics) Regulations, 2002. However, a gazette notification for the same is awaited since then (*The Times of India*, 10 December 2014).

Critique of Freebies by Doctors

In January, the MCI urged all the doctors registered under the MCI Act to prescribe generic medicines 'as far as possible' and to ensure rational prescribing of drugs.

India's health care market is dominated by thousands of independent doctors who run small clinics. Even those doctors who are associated with hospitals have their own clinics. Only about 25 per cent of India's population is covered by medical insurance. This means that a vast majority of patients buy medicines with their own money. This market, estimated to be worth ₹ 60,000 crore, is what drug-makers are fighting over, and they need the doctors to prescribe medicine of their company. The budget that pharma companies have for freebies is huge. According to one estimate, the top 20 drug-makers in India spend about $ 600 million a year on only freebies.

Move to stop freebies will only be a mild step by the medical council and will not have any significant impact on the practice of doctors receiving gifts and bribes from pharma companies. It will be very difficult to prove that a doctor is taking a bribe.

'Drugs for diabetes, hypertension and chronic renal diseases are the fast-moving drugs and in large volumes. These drugs face the toughest competition in the market because of the large varieties available, and a doctor can be a big help in pushing up the sale of a favourite'. A cholesterol lowering drug Atorvastatin is believed to have nearly 150 brands. And the price ranges somewhere from ₹ 40 to ₹ 150 for 10 tablets of 10 mg each. Likewise, a gastritis drug Pantoprazole has about 250 or more brands and may vary in cost from something over ₹ 20 to about ₹ 100. Another category of drugs that face tough competition is antibiotics. Cancer drugs and psychotropic drugs are others that require long-term use, bringing more brands and competition and price ranges (*The Hindu*, 29 May 2013).

But not all doctors, including the Indian Medical Association, are in support. They say that prescribing must focus on drug quality rather than cost, and they point out that some formulations contain more than one active ingredient and do not exist in generic form (*The Times of India*, 29 April 2013).

Multinationals

There are laudable population-based approaches and interventions and the drift in policy attempts to tackle diet-related ill health should be done at the individual's level. There are good reasons for this. Governments and companies are more comfortable in offering a combination of exhortation, advice and individual appeals than in setting out to re-frame food culture. They are frightened of accusations of 'many stateism', an ethic set by the neo-liberal consensus in the face of public health evidence. There has been rapid market concentration (domination by fewer giant companies). They vie for market share and compete in the tough market where tens of thousands of food products jostle for consumer attention, and they are uncomfortable with a population approach. The prevailing logic is to appeal to consumers to choose particular products and to take responsibility for themselves. In the corporate world, health is a matter of appealing to people to change diet to make themselves more beautiful to be culturally positive, to seek sexual advantage, to follow role models, to fit into social marketing norms, to respond to advertising, to be targeted by advice leaflets and so on.

Pharmaceutical Business and Social Environment

The changing social and demographic profile of the country affects the business of pharmaceutical companies. The ultimate user of the product of pharmacy is the consumer. For example, if the children below 14 years account for about 40 per cent of population, than the demand for baby care products, primary immunization, paediatric dosage will increase over the years. By the turn of century, the present paediatric market will be changing to the 'youth market'. There are very few marketers in the pharmaceutical industry who had visualized these changes early enough and started diagnostic centres, health insurance schemes and hospitals chains as a part of their diversification plans. This is a result of increasing literacy levels and the consequent increase in awareness of health and fitness.

Expenditure on Medicines and Health Needs

There is a mismatch between expenditure on medicine and health needs in the world. About 42 per cent of the global expenditure on medicines is spent on 5 per cent of the world's population living in North America, while only 20 per cent is spent on the majority of the world's population with the highest burden of diseases in Africa, Asia, the Middle East and Latin America (McCoy, 2003).

Critics claim that the high prices of patented drugs are not a major barrier to access. Many essential medicines that are cheap and off-patent remain unavailable or inaccessible to millions of people, primarily a reflection of impoverished health care systems and communities.

Escalating levels of expenditure on medicines may reflect high volumes, high prices, inappropriate choices and irrational prescribing.

As new diseases and health threats emerge and pathogens develop resistance to medicines, and because many existing essential medicines are toxic or limited in their effectiveness, access to essential medicines is also determined by the success of the research and development (R. and D.) of new medicines.

Summing Up

The First World War gave a real stimulus to domestic production of pharmaceuticals. Indigenous production in 1939 was sufficient to meet only 13 per cent of medical requirements. The Second World War provided a propitious atmosphere for further expansion of production. The Indian pharma industry has around 70 per cent of the country's demand for bulk drugs, drug intermediates, pharmaceutical formulations, chemicals, tablets, capsules, orals and injectibles. About 250 large units and 8,000 small scale units, are from the core of the pharmaceutical industry in India. For meeting the requirements of medicines for health needs at reasonable prices and strengthening the indigenous base, the Government over the years has been guided by the drug policy of 1986. The Pharmaceutical Policy of 2002 calls for relaxation of production and price controls. Production controls have now mostly gone except for bulk drugs produced by the use of recombinant DNA technology, bulk drugs requiring in-vivo use of nucleic acids, and specific cell/tissue targeted formulations. However, in the absence of a clear, comprehensive and rational drug policy the distorted pattern of drug production and the proliferation of non-essential, irrational and harmful drugs continues. Indian markets are flooded with over 1,00,000 formulations; there is no system of central registration of these formulations. There are certain other issues related to the medicinal aspects of health care. These are: international intellectual property right system and other trade-related impediments and use of rational medicine; corrupting influence of profit-driven pharmaceutical companies on health professionals, academics and regulatory bodies and the way pharmaceutical R and D is funded and incentives offered to them.

References

An Alternative World Health Report (2005), *Global Health Watch 2005–2006*, Bangalore: People's Health Movement.

Angell, M. (2004), *The Truth About the Drug Companies: How They Deceive Us and What to Do About It*, New York: Random House.

Chaganti, Subba Rao (2008), *Pharmaceutical Marketing in India*, New Delhi: Excel Books.

Correa, C. (2002), *Implications of Doha Declaration on the TRIPS Agreement and Public Health*, Geneva: WHO.

—— (2004), 'Access to Medicine in Under-Served Markets: What are the Implications of Changes in Intellectual Property Rights, Trade and Drug Registration Policy?', *DFID/HSRC Overview Paper*, London: DFID Health Systems Resources Centre.

Drazen, Jeffery M. and Gregory M. Curfman (2002), 'Financial Association of Authors', *New England Journal of Medicine*, 346(24): 1901–02.

Global Health Watch 2: An Alternative World Health Report, London: Zed Books.

Government of India (1975), *Hathi Committee: Report of the Committee on the Drugs and Pharmaceutical Industry*, New Delhi: Ministry of Petroleum and Chemicals, April.

ICSSR and ACMR (1981), *Health for All: An Alternative Strategy*, Pune: Indian Institute of Education.

IFPMA (2005), *Intellectual Property and Patents*, Geneva: International Federation of Pharmaceutical Manufacturers and Associations, http://www.ifpma.org/issues/issues_intell.aspz accessed 16 April 2015.

McCoy, D. (2003), 'Health Sector Responses to HIV/AIDS and Treatment Access in Southern Africa: Addressing Equity', *Discussion Paper 10*, EQUINET, http://www.equinetafrica.org accessed 16 April 2015.

Medawar, C. and A. Hardon (2004), *Medicines Out of Control?* Netherlands: Aksant.

Sarkar, P.K. (2004), 'A Rational Drug Policy', *Indian Journal of Medical Ethics*, 1(1).

The Hindu (2013), 29 May.

The Times of India (2013), 29 April.

—— (2014), 10 December.

World Health Organization (2004a), *The World Medicine Situation*, WHO/EDM/PAR/2004–5, Geneva: WHO.

—— (2004b), *What are Essential Medicines?* http://www.who.int/medicines.rationale.shtml. accessed 16 April 2015.

WTO (2001), *Declaration on the TRIPS Agreement and Public Health*, Fourth WTO Ministerial Conference, Doha, Qatar, http://www.wto.org/english/thewto_e/minist_e?min01_e/mindeel_trips_e.htm accessed 16 April 2015.

www.indianmirror.com accessed 11 December 2015.

Section IV

Health Delivery Systems in India

16

Delivery of Public Health Care in India

Health care is one of the India's largest service sectors. Under the Indian Constitution, health is a state subject. Each state, therefore, has its own health care delivery system in which both public and private (for profit as well as non-profit) actors operate. While states are responsible for the functioning of their respective health care systems, certain responsibilities also fall on the Federal (Central) Government, namely aspects of policy-making, planning, guiding, assisting, evaluating and coordinating the work of various provincial health authorities and providing funding to implement national programmes.

Model of Health Care Delivery System in India

India is a union of 29 states and seven union territories. States are largely independent in matters relating to the delivery of health care to the people.

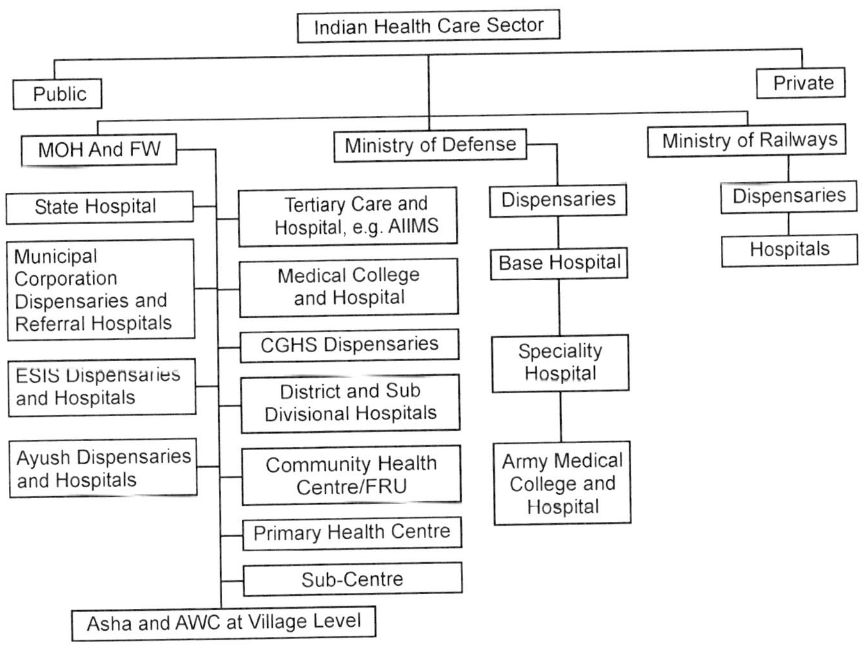

Each state has developed its own system of health care delivery, independent of Central Government.

The organization at the national level consists of the Union Ministry of Health and Family Welfare. In each state, the organization is under the State Department of Health and Family Welfare that is headed by a State Minister and with a Secretariat under the charge of the Secretary/Commissioner (Health and Family Welfare).

Health Infrastructure in Public Sector

Health Infrastructure (Public Sector)

Parameter	*Ist Plan (1951–56)*	*10th Pan (2002–07)*
Primary Health Centre	725	22,370
Sub-Centres	NA	1,45,272
Community Health Centres	0	4,045
Total Beds (2002)	1,25,000	9,14,543
Medical Colleges	42	270
Dental Colleges	7	205
Allopathic Doctors	65,000	7,67,500
Nurses	18,500	9,28,149
ANMs	1,27,800	5,26,242
Health Visitor	578	50,393
Health Workers(F)	0	1,47,439
Health Workers (M)	0	62,881
Village Health Guides (2002)	0	3,23,000
Block Extension Educators	0	4,068

India's Medical Infrastructure at a Glance

- 5,097 hospitals
- 8,70,162 hospitals beds
- 5,03,900 doctors
- 7,37,000 nurses
- 162 medical colleges

Financial Position

- Total public expenditure on health is 5.2 per cent of GDP
- Public investment, 0.9 per cent of GDP
- Budget allocation for health, 1.3 per cent of central budget
- Government expenditure, 25 per cent
- Out of pocket expenditure, 75 per cent
- Central Government contribution to state, 15 per cent
- State budgetary allocations reduced from 7 per cent to 5.5 per cent
- India's health budget has gone up nearly 4000 crore to ₹ 21,113.33 crore ($ 4.35 billion)

Organs of Health Delivery Systems

The Central Government responsibility consists mainly of policy making, planning, guiding, assisting, evaluating and coordinating the work of the State Health Ministries. The health system in India has three main links:

1. Central
2. State
3. Local and peripheral

At Central Level

The official organs of the health system at the national level consist of:

- Ministry of Health and Family Welfare
- Directorate General of Health Services
- Central Council of Health and Family Welfare

Union Ministry of Health and Family Welfare

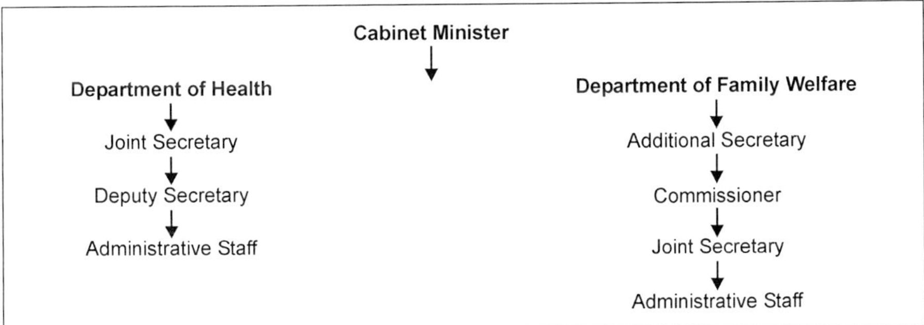

Functions

Union List

- International health relations and administration of per quarantine.
- Administration of Central Institutes such as All India Institute of Hygiene and Public Health, Kolkata
- Promotion of research through research centres
- Regulation and development of medical, pharmaceutical, dental and nursing profession
- Establishment and maintenance of drug standards
- Census and collection and publication of other statistical data
- Immigration and emigration
- Regulation of labour in the working of mines and oil fields
- Coordination with states and with other ministries for promotion of health

Concurrent List

The functions listed under the concurrent list are the responsibility of both the Union and State Governments:

- Prevention and extension of communicable diseases

- Prevention of adulteration of food stuff
- Control of drugs and poison
- Vital statistics
- Labour Welfare
- Ports other than major
- Economic and social planning
- Population control and family planning
- Preparation of health education material for creating health awareness through Central Health Education Bureau
- Collection, compilation analysis, evaluation and dissemination of information through the Central Bureau of Health Intelligence
- National Medical Library

Directorate General of Health Services

Functions

- International health relations and quarantine of all major ports in country and international airports
- Control of drug standards
- Maintain medical store depots
- Administration of post-graduate training programmes
- Administration of certain medical colleges in India
- Conducting medical research through Indian Council of Medical Research
- Central Government Health Scheme
- Implementation of national health programmes
- Preparation of health education for creating health awareness through Central Health Education Bureau
- Collection, compilation, analysis, evaluation and dissemination of information through the Central Bureau of Health Intelligence
- National Medical Library

Central Council of Health and Family Welfare

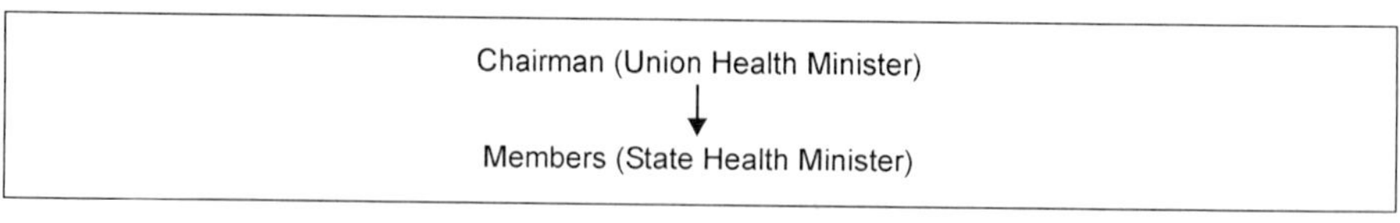

Functions

- To consider the recommended broad outlets of policy regard to matters concerning health like environment hygiene, nutrition and health education.
- To make proposals for legislation relating to medical and public health matters.
- To make recommendations to the Central Government regarding distribution of grants-in-aid.

At the State Level

The health subjects are divided into three groups: federal, concurrent and state. The state list is the responsibility of the state, including provision of medical care, preventive health services and pilgrimage within the state.

State Health Administration

At present, there are 29 states in India, each state has its own health administration.

State Health Administration

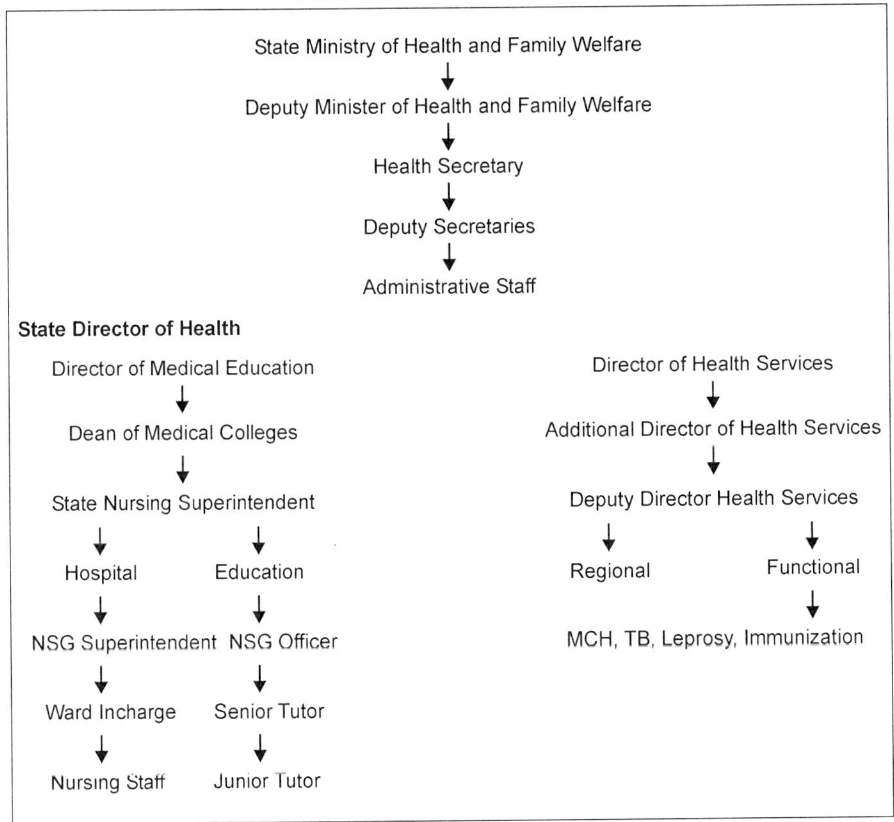

Functions of State Health Director

- Studies in depth the health problem and needs in the state and plans scheme to solve them
- Providing curative and preventive services
- Provision for control of milk and food sanitation
- Prevention of any outbreak of communicable diseases
- Promotion of health education
- Promotion of health programmes such as school health, family planning, occupational health
- Supervision of PHC.
- Establishing training outcomes for health personnel
- Coordination of all health services with other minister of state such as minister of education, central health minister and voluntary agency

At the District Level

In each district in India, there are six types of administrative areas:

1. Sub-Divisional
2. Tehsils (Taluks)
3. Community Development Blocks
4. Municipalities and corporations
5. Villages
6. Panchayats

Functions of Municipal Board

- Construction and maintenance of roads
- Sanitation and drainage
- Street lighting
- Water supply
- Maintenance of hospital and dispensaries
- Education
- Registration of births and deaths, etc.
- The corporations are headed by Mayor, elected by councillors, who are elected from different wards of the city.

Panchayati Raj

The Panchayati Raj is a three tier structure of rural local self-government linking the villages to the district includes:

- Panchayat (at the village level)
- Panchayat Samiti (at the block level)
- Zila Parishad (at the district level)

Health Care System

1. At village level
2. At the centre level
3. At PHC level

4. At CHC level

At the village level, the elementary services are rendered by:

1. *Village health guides:* A village health guide is a person with an aptitude for social service and is not full time government functionary. Village health guide scheme was introduced on 2 October 1977. The guide provides the treatment for common minor ailments; first aid during accidents and emergency; Maternal and Child Health (MCH) care; family planning and health education.
2. *Local dais:* Most deliveries in rural areas are handled by untrained *dais.* The training for *dais* is given for 30 working days. Each *dai* is paid stipend of ₹ 300 during the period of training. During her training, each *dai* is required to conduct at least two deliveries under the supervision and guidance of a health worker (female), an Auxiliary Nurse and Midwife (ANM), a health assistant (female). *Dai* performs the function of MCH cares; family planning; immunization; education about health, referral services; safe water and basic sanitation and nutrition.
3. *Anganwadi workers:* Under the ICDS scheme, there is an anganwadi worker for a population of a thousand. There are about 100 such workers with each ICDS project. The anganwadi worker is selected from the community and she undergoes training in various aspects of health, nutrition and child development for four months. She is a part-time worker and is paid an honorarium. She performs MCH care; family planning; immunization, education about health, referral services, safe water and basic sanitation, supplementary nutrition and non-formal education of children.
4. *Accredited Social Health Activist (ASHA):* One of the key components of National Rural Health Mission is to provide every village in the country with a trained female community health activist – ASHA, selected from the village itself and accountable to it. The ASHA is trained to work as interface between the community and the public health system. There is one ASHA on the population of a thousand. ASHA must be primarily a woman from the resident of the village itself. ASHA will take steps to create awareness and provide information to the community on determinants of health such as nutrition, basic sanitation and hygiene practice, healthy living and working conditions, information on existing health services and the need for timely utilization of health and family welfare services. She will counsel women on birth preparedness, importance of safe delivery, breast-feeding and complementary feeding, immunization, contraception and prevention of common infections including reproductive tract infection, sexually transmitted infections and care of the young child. ASHA will mobilize the community and facilitate them in assessing health and health-related services available at the village/sub-centre/primary health centres, such as immunization, ante-natal check-up (ANC), post natal check-up (PNC), Integrated

Child Development (ICD), sanitation and other services being provided by the government. She will arrange escort/accompany pregnant women and children requiring treatment/admission to the nearest pre-identified health facility. ASHA will provide primary medical care or minor ailments such as diarrhea, fever, and first aid for minor injuries. She will also inform about the births and deaths and any unusual health problems/disease outbreaks in the community to the sub-centre/primary health centre. She will also promote construction of household toilets under total sanitation campaigns.

Critical Evaluation of Functioning of Health Delivery

There is still a shortfall of 16 per cent of PHCs and 58 per cent of CHCs. PHCs also suffer due to non-availability of staff and weak referral system.

Problems in Public Health Care

Very low use of massive Public Health Infrastructure (PHI) poor availability and access; and unsatisfactory work of PHI.

Only 20 per cent of OPD and 45 of in-patient care is obtained from government health infrastructure while the rest is from private sector.

Primary Health Care (PHC)

It is important to emphasize that PHC is not just a descriptive term denoting the first level of health care. It is a comprehensive view of health that emerges from the most critical conceptual advances of 20th century public health. Unlike the techno-centric approaches that derive from the bio-medical sciences – such as linear campaigns against small pox and malaria – the PHC approach confronts complex socio-economic, political, and technological relationships. The emphasis of PHC is on:

- Equity in health care;
- Need-based, socially acceptable services with full participation of people;
- State responsibility for incorporating PHC into national development plans through inter-sectoral strategies;
- Affordable technologies ensuring self-sufficiency and effective basic health care with the support of secondary and tertiary care; and
- Collective, not individual efforts.

The repeated failures of technocentric approaches and researches that emphasized the link between socio-economic and demographic factors and health transitions led to the 1978 Alma-Ata Declaration. It stated that mere formal government support would not be sufficient to achieve the desired level of health and that PHC would require a reorientation of national strategies for health planning. It would imply a transfer of health resources to the under-served. The health budget might have to be increased until the total population received essential care and institutions supporting PHC were made effective.

Financial Calculation for Comprehensive Health Care in India[1]

Primary health care (Family Medical Practitioner + Epidemiological Station–PHC) consists following features:

- Staff composition for each PHC-FMP unit to include four doctors, one PHN, two nurse midwives, eight ANMs (females), four MPWs (males), one pharmacist, one clerk/assistant, one office assistant, one lab technician, one driver, one sweeper – this adds up to salaries and benefits/capitation of ₹ 6 million (salary structures across states may be different and hence this could vary). Doctors and nurses may either be salaried or contracted in on a capitation basis as in the NHS of UK. The curative care component should work as a family medical practice with families (500–2000, depending on density) being assigned to each such provider.
- There should be 10 beds per PHC.
- Average rural unit to cover 20,000 population (in the range 10–30 thousand depending on density); average urban unit to cover 50,000 population (in the range 30–70 thousand population depending on density)
- Non-salary costs separately for rural and urban units per unit cost as per Table 1:

Table 1

Primary Health Care and Its Finances

Line item	*Rate*	*Rural (20,000 population per unit)*	*Urban (50,000 population per unit)*
Medicine and other clinical consumables	₹ 40 per capita per year	₹ 8,00,000	₹ 20,00,000
Travel, POL, etc.	₹ 10,000 pm rural; and ₹ 5,000 pm urban	₹ 1,20,000	₹ 60,000
Office expenses, electricity, water, etc.	₹ 10,000 and ₹ 12,000 pm for rural and urban, respectively	₹ 1,20,000	₹ 2,00,000
Maintenance of building and equipment, etc.		₹ 1,50,000	₹ 2,50,000
Rent and/or amortization		₹ 2,00,000	₹ 3,00,000
CHW honorarium	Rural: 1 CHW per 500 population @ ₹ 1,000 pm per CHW; Urban 1 CHW per 1,500 population @ ₹ 1250 pm per CHW	₹ 4,80,000	₹ 4,95,000
Other costs		₹ 1,30,000	₹ 1,95,000
Total non-salary		₹ 20,00,000	₹ 35,00,000
Total primary care cost per unit		₹ 8,000,000 (₹ 400 per capita)	₹ 9,500,000 (₹ 190 per capita)

Cont'd...

...Cont'd

Total primary care cost for country	Rural: 750 million population needing 37,500 PHCs; and urban 350 million population needing 7000 PHCs	₹ 300 billion	₹ 66.5 billion

First Level Referral Care[2]

In rural areas, for every five PHCs, there would be one 50-bedded hospital and this would cost ₹ 4,00,000 per bed per annum or ₹ 20 million per such hospital. As per this ratio, we would need 7,500 rural hospitals and this would translate into ₹ 150 billion for the country as a whole.

In urban areas, for 10 PHCs, one 200-bedded hospital would be needed and this would cost ₹ 5,00,000 per bed per year or ₹ 100 million per hospital. As per this ratio, 700 such hospitals would be needed and this would translate into ₹ 70 billion for the country as a whole.

Secondary and Tertiary Care/Teaching Hospitals

One such hospital per 2.5 million populations, that is 440 hospitals of 500 bed each at a cost of ₹ 5,00,000 per bed per year translating into ₹ 250 million per hospital or Rs 110 billion for the country as a whole.

Primary + First Referral + Secondary/Tertiary = ₹ 696.50 billion

Other Costs

- Capital @ 10 per cent or ₹ 69.65 billion.
- Research and data systems @ 4 per cent or ₹ 27.86 billion.
- Administration costs @ 4 per cent or ₹ 27.86 billion.
- Audit costs @ 2 per cent or ₹ 13.93 billion.

Grand total would be ₹ 835.80 billion or ₹ 760 per capita and this works out to be 1.9 per cent of GDP. This calculation excludes medical education and medical research, which would be 15 per cent and 10 per cent of the total health care cost, respectively, amounting to an additional ₹ 209 billion.

Table 2
Health Care Costs

Types of Cost	*Amount in Rupees (billion)*
Primary care	366.50
First Referral Rural	150.00
First Referral Urban	70.00
Secondary/Tertiary care	110.00
SUBTOTAL	696.50
Capital @ 10 per cent	69.65
Research and data systems @ 4 per cent	27.86
Admin @ 4 per cent	27.86

Cont'd...

...Cont'd

Audit @ 2 per cent	13.93
TOTAL Health Care Cost	835.80 or 1.9 per cent of GDP
Medical Education and Research	208.95
Grand Total (₹ 950 per capita)	1044.75 or 2.4 per cent of GDP

Distribution of Costs

The above costs from the point of view of the public exchequer might seem excessive to commit to the health sector given the current level of public health spending. But this is less than 3 per cent of GDP at ₹ 950 per capita annually, including capital costs. The public exchequer's share, that is from tax and related revenues, would be about ₹ 800 billion or three-fourths of the cost. This is well within the reach of current resources of the central states and local governments put together. The remaining would come from other sources discussed earlier, mostly from employers and employees in the organized sector (social insurance), and other innovative mechanisms of financing. As things progress the share of governments should stabilize at 50 per cent and the remaining balance should come from other sources. Raising further resources will not be too difficult. Part of the organized sector today contributes to the ESIS 6.75 per cent of the salary/wage bill. If the entire organized sector contributes even 5 per cent of the employee compensation (2% by employee and 3% by employer) then that itself will raise close to ₹ 350 billion. In fact the employer share could be higher, at 5 per cent. The present initiative of expanding social insurance through a national legislation for the entire unorganized sector can help boost the social insurance contributions to the health budget. Further resources through other mechanisms suggested above will add substantially to this, which in fact may actually reduce the burden on the state exchequer and increase contributory share from those who can afford to pay. Table 3 shows is a rough projection of the share of burden by different sources:

Table 3

Projected Sharing of Health Care Costs (2007, ₹ in millions)

	Type of Source			
	Central Govt.	*State/ Muncp.*	*Social Insurance*	*Other Sources*
Primary Care	1,20,000	1,40,000	80,000	26,500
Basic Hospitals	20,000	1,00,000	85,000	15,000
Secondary/Tertiary Hospitals	30,000	50,000	25,000	5,000
Medical Educ/Research	1,50,000	50,000	7,000	1,950
Audit/Info. Mgt./Soc. Research	20,000	15,000	6,790	–
Administrative Costs	10,000	10,000	7,860	–
Capital Costs	40,000	20,000	9,650	–
ALL COSTS	3,90,000	385,000	221,300	48,450
Percentages	37	37	21	5

We are at a stage in history where political will to do something progressive is conspicuous because of its absence. We may have constitutional commitments and backing of international law but without political will nothing will happen. To reach the goals of right to health and health care discussed above, civil society will have to be involved in a very different way.

The initiative to bring health care on the political agenda will have to be a multi-pronged one and be fought on different levels. The idea here is not to develop a plan of action but to indicate the various steps and involvements that will be needed to build a consensus. Following are some suggestions:

- Policy level advocacy for creation of an organized system for universal health care.
- Research to develop a detailed framework of the organized system.
- Lobbying with the medical profession to build support for universal health care and regulation of medical practice.
- Filing a public interest litigation on right to health care to create a basis for constitutional amendment.
- Lobbying with parliamentarians to demand justiciability of directive principles.
- Holding national and regional consultations on right to health care with involvement of a wide array of civil society groups.
- Running campaigns on right to health care with networks of organizations at the national and regional level.
- Right to health care on the agenda of political parties to incorporate it in their manifestos.
- Pressurizing international bodies like WHO, Committee of ESCR, UNCHR, as well as national bodies like NHRC, NCW to effectively monitor India's state obligations and demand accountability.
- Preparing and widely circulating shadow reports on right to health care to create international pressure.

The above is not an exhaustive list. The basic idea is that there should be widespread dialogue, raising of awareness, research, documentation and legal/constitutional discourse across the board with various agencies of civil society involved like NGOs, trade unions, people's movements, academia, etc.

It is, thus, evident that the neglect of the public health system is an issue larger than government policy-making. The latter is the function of the overall political economy. Under capitalism only a well-developed welfare state can meet the basic needs of its population. Given the backwardness of India, the demand of public resources for the productive sectors of the economy (which directly benefit capital accumulation) is more urgent (from the business perspective) than the social sectors, hence the latter get only residual attention by the state. The policy route to comprehensive and universal health care has failed miserably. It is now time to change gears towards a rights-based approach. The opportunity exists in the form of constitutional provisions and discourse, international laws to which India is a party, and the potential of mobilizing civil society and creating a socio-political consensus on right to health care. There have been a lot of small efforts towards this end all over the country, for instance the People's Health Movement or the 'Jan Swasthya Abhiyan'. Synergies have to be created for these efforts to multiply so that people of India can enjoy right to health care. On the government front, the UPA Government of Manmohan Singh had promised to restructure the public health system via one of its flagship programmes, the National Rural Health Mission (NRHM).

The preamble of the NRHM document states: *Recognizing the importance of Health in the process of economic and social development and improving the quality of life of our citizens, the Government of India has resolved to launch the National Rural Health Mission to carry out necessary architectural correction in the basic health care delivery system … . The Goal of the Mission is to improve the availability of and access to quality health care by people, especially for those residing in rural areas, the poor, women and children.* (MoHFW 2005). This goal will be achieved by strengthening the three levels of rural health care – the sub-centre, PHC and CHC. At the village/hamlet level, a health worker called ASHA (Accredited Social Health Activist) will be appointed who will be the link worker for rest of the public health system in rural areas. Additional resource allocation and upgradation of the facilities at each level has been planned under the Mission. However, the budget heads for NRHM do not address the missing link in rural health care and medical care. They have mainly subsumed the erstwhile family welfare, RCH and national disease programme heads under the NRHM umbrella. In that sense the integration into comprehensive health care, which the Mission document talks about, is at least not reflected in the budget. Linked to this is the fact that allocations to rural health would become restricted to NRHM – and any other source of funds for rural health may get blocked. This is the usual consequence of verticalization of any programme, and here is the danger that NRHM may become an amalgamated vertical health programme for rural areas.

Thus, the key issue in access to health care which even the NRHM fails to address is the mechanism for allocating resources. Resources are presently distributed on the basis of what is available, what can be procured and where they can be parked in terms of infrastructure, human resources, etc. and this is often done on ad hoc basis. Thus, if the PHC is mandated to provide a package of services for which the requirements are defined and the funds needed for that are determined, the actual allocation of resources does not happen in terms of those requirements. What happens in reality is that the state, for instance, has a certain number of existing PHCs and for that it starts procuring the human resources and other inputs needed and these have to be worked out on the basis of the available budget and rationing of resources across the board rather than in terms of what the PHC as a unit requires to function optimally. The consequence of such a mechanism is allocative inefficiency in the use of resources because the PHC may have a doctor but no nurse or adequate allocation for drugs, etc. and this leads to the poor performance of the public health facility. Therefore, to address this deficiency, the mechanism of allocation of resources has to change to a system which meets the objective of the specific health care facility as discussed above. There should be no compromise on this. Unless this kind of a radical change is put in place, all efforts, even enhanced budgets, would stop at mere tinkering with what exists. The discussions on NRHM strategizing continue, especially on financial management and autonomy in decision-making at the unit/programme level, and hence options are still open for influencing change.

To conclude, the NRHM should be used as an opportunity to work out a new health financing strategy, which devolves financial resources to local governments and uses a social audit framework to monitor its implementation. Only this will lead to structural changes and improvements in the health of the Indian people. But the government will not do this unless health care becomes a political agenda and drives elections. Thus, the civil society has to exert pressure. The initiatives of the 'Jan Swasthya Abhiyan', which has set in motion a campaign on Right to Health Care, is one such move in this direction. The JSA has formulated a People's Health Charter, has mobilized groups in 18 states to support the campaign on right to health care, has collaborated with the National Human Rights Commission to conduct public hearings on denial of health care across the length and breadth of the country and is now actively engaging with the NRHM initiative to not only monitor its progress through community involvement but also use it as an opportunity to restructure health and health care in India.

Summing Up

Health care is one of the India's largest service sectors. Under the Indian Constitution, health is a state subject. Each state, therefore, has its own health care delivery system in which both public and private (for profit as well as non-profit) actors operate. While states are responsible for the functioning of their respective health care systems, certain responsibilities also fall on the federal (central) government, namely aspects of policy-making, planning, guiding, assisting, evaluating and coordinating the work of various provincial health authorities and providing funding to implement national programmes. The health subjects are divided into three groups: federal, concurrent and state. The state list is the responsibility of the state, including provision of medical care, preventive health services and pilgrimage within the state. At present, there are 29 states in

India, each state has its own health administration. At the village level, the elementary services are rendered by village health guides, local *dais*, aganwadi workers and ASHA workers. The initiative to bring health care on the political agenda will have to be a multi-pronged one and fought on different levels. The idea here is not to develop a plan of action but to indicate the various steps and involvements that will be needed to build a consensus and struggle for right to health care.

Notes

1. This is updated to 2007 prices from calculations originally done for a 'Jan Swasthya Abhiyan' discussion on the National Rural Health Mission.
2. All higher level care would be on basis of referral from primary care providers, except in the case of emergencies. This should help rationalize higher levels of care as well as make it more efficient and cost-effective.

References

Abel-Smith, B. (1977), 'Minimum Adequate Levels of Personal Health Care', in John Mckinlay (ed.), 'Issues in Health Care Policy', *A Milbank Reader* 3, New York: OECD.

Ahmed, S.U. (1980), 'Urban Problems and Government Policies: A Case Study of the City of Dacca, 1810–30', in K. Ballhatchet and J.B. Harrison (eds), *The City in South Asia*, London: Curzon Press.

Andreassen, B., A. Smith and H. Stokke (1992), 'Compliance with Economic and Social Rights: Realistic Evaluations and Monitoring in the Light of Immediate Obligations', in A. Eide and B. Hagtvet (eds), *Human Rights in Perspective: A Global Assessment*, Oxford: Blackwell.

Annual Abstract of Statistics for East India (1870).

Annual Reports of the Sanitary Commissioner with Government of India (1865).

Anstey, V. (1936), *The Economic Development of India*, London: Longmans.

Arnold, D. (1985), 'Medical Priorities and Practice in Nineteenth Century British India', *South Asia Research*, 5(2): 167–86.

Ballhatchet, K. (1980), *Race, Sex and Class under the Raj*, New Delhi: Vikas.

Bhore, J. (1946), *Report of the Health Survey and Development Committee*, Volume I to IV, New Delhi: Government of India.

BIS (1989), *Basic Requirements for Hospital Planning CIS: 12433 (Part 1) – 19,883*, New Delhi: Bureau of Indian Standards.

—— (1992), *Basic Requirements for a 100 Bedded Hospital: A Draft Report*, New Delhi: Bureau of Indian Standards.

CBHI, Various Years: Health Information of India, Central Bureau of Health Intelligence, MoHFW, Government of India, New Delhi.

Census of India (1921), Delhi: Government of India.

Chapman, A. (1993), *Exploring a Human Rights Approach to Healthcare Reform*, Washington, D.C.: American Association for the Advancement of Science.

Duggal, R. (2000), *The Private Health Sector in India: Nature, Trends and a Critique*, New Delhi: VHAI.

—— (2002), 'Resource Generation without Planned Allocation', *Economic and Political Weekly*, 5 January.

Farrell, J.S. (1973), *The Siege of Krishnapur*, London: Penguin.

Gillion, K.L. (1968), *Ahmedabad: A Study in Indian Urban History*, Berkeley, CA: University of California Press.

Gupta, R.B. et al. (1992), *Baseline Survey in Himachal Pradesh under IPP VI and VII*, 3 Vols, Jaipur: Indian Institute of Health Management Research.

Harrison, J.B. (1980), 'Allahabad: A Sanitary History', in K. Ballhatchet and J.B. Harrison (eds), *The City in South Asia*, London: Curzon Press.

Harvey, W. (1895), 'Presidential Address', in *Proceedings of the First Indian Medical Congress*, Calcutta: Indian Medical Gazette.

ICMR (1990), *A National Collaborative Study of High Risk Families*, New Delhi: ICMR Task Force.

Jaggi, O.P. (1979), *Western Medicine in India: Medical Education and Research*, Delhi: Atma Ram.

Jeffery, R. (1988), *The Politics of Health in India*, London: University of California Press.

King, M. (ed.) (1966), *Medical Care in Developing Countries*, Nairobi: Oxford University Press.

Klein, I. (1973), 'Death in India', *Journal of Asian Studies*, 32(4): 639–59.

Mahler, H. (1977), 'The Staff of Aesculapius', *World Health*, 3.

—— (1979), 'Urbanization and the Introduction of Modern Town Planning Ideas in India, 1900–1925', in K.N. Chaudhuri and C.J. Dewey (eds), *Economy and Society*, Oxford: Oxfam.

MoHFW (2005), *National Rural Health Mission*, Ministry of Health and Family Welfare, Government of India, New Delhi.

Morley, D. et al. (1984), *Practising Health for All*, New Delhi: Oxford University Press.

NICD (1988), *Combined Surveys on ARI, Diarrhoea and EPI*, National Institute of Communicable Diseases, Delhi.

NSS (1987), *Morbidity and Utilisation of Medical Services*, 42nd Round, Report No. 384, National Sample Survey Organisation, New Delhi.

OECD (1990), 'Health Care Systems in Transition: The Search for Efficiency', *Social Policy Studies*, No. 7, Paris.

Ramasubban, R. (1984), 'Public Health and Medical Research in India: Their Origins under the Impact of British Colonial Policy', *Stockholm: SAREC Report*, No. 4, Swedish Agency for Research Cooperation with Developing Countries.

Rao, K.N. (1966), *The Nation's Health*, Delhi: Publications Division.

Roemer, M.I. (1972), *Public Health Papers*, No. 48, Geneva: WHO.

Sanitary Commission (1865), *Report of the Commissioner Appointed to Inquire into the Sanitary State of the Army in India*, London: Her Majesty's Stationery Office.

Toebes, B. (1998), *The Right to Health as a Human Right in International Law*, Antwerpen: Intersentia/Hart.

UNCESCR (2000), General Comment 14 on Article 12 of ICESCR, CESCR 22nd Session 25 April – 12 May 2000, UN: Geneva.

WHO (1961), *Planning of Public Health Services*, TRS 215, Geneva: WHO.

—— (1988), *Country Profile, India*, WHO – SEARO, New Delhi.

—— (1993), *Third Monitoring of Progress, Common Framework, CFM 3, Implementation of Strategies for Health for All by the Year 2000*, Geneva: WHO.

WHO and UNICEF (1978), *Primary Health Care: Report of the International Conference on Primary Health Care, Alma-Ata USSR*, 6–12 September, Geneva: WHO.

17

Rural Health Care in India

The health care services are divided under State list and Concurrent list in India. While some items such as public health and hospitals fall in the State list, others such as population control and family welfare, medical education, and quality control of drugs are included in the Concurrent list. The Union Ministry of Health and Family Welfare (UMHFW) is the central authority responsible for implementation of various programmes and schemes in areas of family welfare, prevention, and control of major diseases. In the case of health, the term infrastructure takes on a wider role than mere physical infrastructure.

Health Infrastructure in India

The health care in rural areas has been developed as three-tier structure. The sub-centre is the most peripheral institution and the first contact point between the primary health care system and the community. Each sub-centre is manned by Auxiliary Nurse Midwife (ANM) and one male Multi-Purpose Worker (MPW). A Lady Health Worker (LHV) is incharge of sub-centres, each is provided with basic drugs for minor ailments and are expected to provide services in relation to maternal and child health, family welfare, nutrition, immunization, diarrhoea control, and control of communicable diseases. Under National Rural Health Mission (NRHM), there is a provision for one additional second ANM on contract basis. One Lady Health Visitor (LHV) is entrusted with the task of supervision of six sub-centres. There are 1,52,326 sub-centres in India in 2014. Sub-centres are also expected to use various medicines of interpersonal communication in order to keep a track of behavioural change in reproductive and hygiene practices. The sub-centres are needed for taking care of basic health, needs of men, women and children. PHC is the first contact point between village community and the medical officer. The PHCs were envisaged to provide an integrated curative and preventive health care to the rural population with emphasis on preventive and promotive aspects of health care. There were 25,020 PHCs in the year 2014. Community Health Centres (CHC) forming the uppermost tier are established and maintained by the State Government under the Minimum Needs Programme (MNP)/Basic Minimum Services(BMS) programme. Under NRHM, there is a provision for two additional staff nurses at PHCs on contract basis. It acts as a referral unit for six sub-centres and has six beds for patients. CHCs are being established and maintained by the State Government under MNP/BMS programme. Four medical specialists including surgeon, physician, gynaecologist and paediatrician supported by 21 paramedical and other staff are supposed to staff each CHC. Norms require a typical CHC to have 30 in-door beds with operation theatre, X-ray, labour room, and laboratory facilities. A CHC is a referral centre for four PHCs within its jurisdiction, providing facilities for obstetric care and specialist expertise. There were 5,363 CHCs functioning in the country in 2014.

Table 1

The Health Infrastructure in India

National Level Ministry of Health and Family Welfare	
State and UTS Department of Health Family Welfare	
Apex Hospital	
Districts District Hospital	
Rural Areas Community Health Centre Primary Health Centre Sub-Centre Village Health Guides and Trained *Dais*	Urban Areas Hospital Dispensary

Status of Health Infrastructure in Villages

The break-up by the type of health care provider is presented in Table 2. The percentage of villages with trained birth attendants is alarmingly low (37%) and almost 64 per cent of the villages do not have any doctors. The survey data reveals that absenteeism among the primary health providers in India, is the highest (40%) among the surveyed countries (Choudhury et al. 2006). Their surveys findings reveal that absence is fairly widespread. Private and government hospitals are relatively more accessible as they are typically located in areas well connected by metalled roads.

Table 2

Status of Health Infrastructure in Villages

Infrastructure/Services	*% Villages*
Connected with roads	73.9
Having any Health Provider	95.3
Having Trained Birth Attendant	37.5
Having Aganwadi Worker	74.2
Having a Doctor (Private and Visiting)	43.5
Having a Private Doctor	30.5
Having a Visiting Doctor	25.0

Note: Any Health Provider includes: Private doctor, Visiting doctor, Unani doctor, Ayurvedic doctor, Homoeopathic doctor, Sidha doctor, Traditional healer, Village Health Guide (VHG), Trained Birth Attendants, *Dai*, ICDS/Aganwadi worker and others.

Source: RCHS Round II, 2002–4.

Table 3
Health Centre Norms

Centre	Population Norm		Status 2014
	Plain Area	Hilly/Tribal/Difficult Area	
Sub-Centre	5,000	3,000	5,473
Primary Health Centre	30,000	20,000	33,323
Community Health Centre	1,20,000	80,000	1,55,463

Source: MHFW (2005), Population Norms (Census 2001), Government of India.

As on 31 March 2014, 67.2 per cent of sub-centres, 88.7 per cent of PHCs and 93.8 per cent of CHCs were located in government buildings. The rest were located either in rented building or rent free panchayat/voluntary society buildings.

Health Practices and Problems in Rural India

The majority of rural deaths, which are preventable, are due to infectious and communicable, parasitic and respiratory diseases. Infectious diseases dominate the morbidity pattern in rural areas (40% rural and 23.5% urban). Waterborne infections, which account for about 80 per cent of diseases in India. Every fourth person in the world affected by such diseases is an Indian. Annually, 1.5 million deaths and loss of 73 million workdays are attributed to waterborne diseases (Park, 2000).

Three groups of infections are widespread in rural areas, they are as follows:

1. Diseases that are carried in the gastrointestinal tract, such as diarrhoea, amoebiasis, typhoid fever, infectious hepatitis, worm infestations and poliomyelitis. About 100 million suffer from diarrhoea and cholera every year.
2. Diseases that are carried in the air through coughing, sneezing or even breathing, such as measles, tuberculosis, whooping cough and pneumonia. Today there are 12 million TB cases (an average of 70%). Over 1.2 million cases are added every year and 37,000 cases of measles are reported every year.
3. Infections, which are more difficult to deal with, include malaria, filariasis and kala-azar. About 2.3 million episodes and over 1000 malarial deaths occur every year in India. Every third person in the world suffering from leprosy is an Indian.

Malnutrition is one of the most dominant health related problems in rural areas. There is a widespread prevalence of protein-energy malnutrition (PEM), anaemia, Vitamin A deficiency and iodine deficiency. More than 85 of rural children are undernourished.

In addition, agricultural and environment related injuries and diseases are also quite common, for e.g. mechanical accidents, pesticides poisoning, snake, dog and insect bites, skin and respiratory diseases, oral health problems, etc.

Health Policy and Infrastructure in Rural Areas

Significant portion of the country's medical needs, especially in rural areas, have been attended to by the indigenous health systems such as ayurveda, homoeopathy, unani, naturopathy and folk medicine, it has been conveniently neglected by the policy makers and planners. The concept of a family physician with social accountability, which has traditional roots and acceptance from the rural masses, has diminished with the existing policies and value systems.

Table 4

The Disparity of Rural and Urban Health in India

S.N.	*Indicator*	*Rural*	*Urban*	*Combined*	*Reference Year*
1.	Population (million)	716.0	286.0	1002.0	2000
2.	Birth rate	30.0	22.6	28.3	1995
3.	Death rate	9.7	6.5	9.0	1997
4.	Infant mortality rate	80.0	42.0	72.0	1998
5.	Maternal mortality rate per lakh population	438.0	378.0	408.0	1997
6.	Still birth rate	10.8	5.3	10.5	1995
7.	% deliveries attended by untrained people	71.0	27.0	59.0	1995
8.	% deaths attended by untrained people	60.0	22.0	54.0	1995
9.	Total fertility rate	3.8	2.8	3.5	1993
10.	% children (12–13 months) who received all vaccinations	31.0	51.0	–	1992–93

Source: Sample Registration System, Government of India, 1997–98

The present westernized hospital-based medical education and training, which is supported by public funding, has proved beyond doubt that new doctors are not inclined to and capable of meeting the needs of the majority of the public (i.e. rural people), which is where their services are most required.

A recent study conducted by the Rural Medical College (unpublished data) on the involvement of general practitioners, has revealed the following facts:

1. About 80 per cent of general practitioners practice western medicine (allopathic medicine) without proper training.
2. Close to 73 per cent consider cost to be the most important factor when prescribing a drug, without considering pharmacological properties.
3. Around 75 per cent were aware of the government-run Primary Health Centre (PHC) or village sub-centres without knowing the names of the medical officer at the PHC; half (53%) do not know the health workers in their own area.
4. About 67 per cent had knowledge of various national health programmes but only 33 per cent participated.

5. Over 68 per cent received information regarding the health programmes through the media, and only 28 per cent received information through public health staff.
6. About 75 per cent provide family planning services, mainly oral contraceptives and condoms. General practitioners do provide services to pregnant women (65%), but only 35 per cent registered them.
7. Almost all general practitioners routinely handle cases of diarrhoea, but only 29 per cent know the exact composition of Oral Dehydration Solution (ORS); amazingly, none knew the right method to prepare the ORS packet.

While the current need for rural areas is medical and paramedical manpower, such as social physicians, public health nurses and midwives and paramedical workers (e.g. laboratory technicians, rural health and sanitation workers, health literacy educators, population educators, community health guides, community oral health guides), the country has been producing specialist doctors. The concept of placing a community-selected person from the village, and providing them with essential training so that the community can cope more effectively with its health problems.

Inequality and Inadequacy

It is unfortunate that while the incidence of all diseases are twice higher in rural than in urban areas, the rural people are denied access to proper health care, as the systems and structures were built up mainly to serve the better off (Table 5).

While the urban middle class in India have ready access to health services that compare with the best in the world, even minimum health facilities are not available to at least 135 million of rural and tribal people, and wherever services are provided they are inferior. While the health care of the urban population is provided by a variety of hospitals and dispensaries run by the corporate, private, voluntary and public sector organizations, rural health care services, mainly immunization and family planning are organized by ill-equipped rural hospitals, primary health centres and sub-centres.

Table 5

Health Infrastructure Rural Versus Urban

	Rural	*Urban*	*Total*	*Year*
Hospitals	3,968 (31%)	7286 (69%)	13,692	1993
Beds	95,315 (20%)	5,24,118 (80%)	6,96,203	1993
Dispensaries	12,284 (40%)	15,710 (60%)	27,403	1993
Doctors	4,40,000	66,000	11,00,000	1994
All Systems	4,40,000	66,000	11,00,000	1994
% allopathy	25%	75%	38%	

Source: Duggal, R. (1997), 'Health Care Budgets in a Changing Political Economy', *Economic and Political Weekly*, 17–24 May.

It is unfortunate that while the incidence of all diseases are twice higher in rural than in urban areas, the rural people are denied access to proper health care, as the systems and structures were built up mainly to serve the better off (Table 5).

Strengthening of Rural Health Infrastructure Under National Rural Health Mission

From 2005 the National Rural Health Mission (NRHM) seeks to provide effective health care to rural population throughout the country with special focus on 18 states, which have weak public health indicators and/or weak infrastructure. These 18 states are Arunachal Pradesh, Assam, Bihar, Chhattisgarh, Himachal Pradesh, Jharkhand, Jammu and Kashmir, Manipur, Mizoram, Meghalaya, Madhya Pradesh, Nagaland, Odisha, Rajasthan, Sikkim, Tripura, Uttarakhand and Uttar Pradesh. The mission is an articulation of the commitment of the government to raise public spending on health from 0.9 per cent of GDP to 2–3 per cent of GDP.

NRHM aims to undertake architectural correction of the health system to enable it to effectively handle increased allocations and promote policies that strengthen public health management and service delivery in the country. It has its key components: provision of a female health activist in each village; a village health plan prepared through a local team headed by the Village Health, Sanitation and Nutrition Committee (VHS and NC) of the panchayat; strengthening of the rural hospital for effective curative care and making it measurable and accountable to the community through Indian Public Health Standards (IPHS); integration of vertical health and family welfare programmes, optimum utilization of funds and infrastructure, and strengthening delivery of primary health care. It seeks to revitalize local health traditions and mainstream AYUSH into the public health system. It further aims at effective integration of health concerns with determinants of health, like sanitation and hygiene, nutrition, and safe drinking water through a District Plan for health. It seeks decentralization of programmes for district management of health and to address the inter-state and inter-district disparities, especially among the 18 high focus states, including unmet needs for public health infrastructure. It also seeks to improve access of rural people, especially poor women and children, to equitable, affordable, accountable and effective primary health care.

National Rural Health Mission

The National Rural Health Mission (2005–12) was launched in April 2005 by the Government of India. It seeks to provide effective health care to rural population throughout the country with special focus on 18 states in the first phase, which have weak public health indicators and/or weak infrastructure. These states are Arunachal Pradesh, Assam, Bihar, Chattisgarh, Himachal Pradesh, Jharkhand, Jammu and Kashmir, Manipur, Mizoram, Meghalaya, Madhya Pradesh, Nagaland, Orissa,

Rajasthan, Sikkim, Tripura, Uttaranchal and Uttar Pradesh. The NRHM will cover all the villages in these 18 states through approximately 2.5 lakh village-based 'Accredited Social Health Activists' (ASHA) who would act as a link between the health centres and the villagers. One ASHA will be raised from every village or cluster of villages, across 18 states. The ASHA would be trained to advise village populations about sanitation, hygiene, contraception, and immunization to provide primary medical care for diarrhoea, minor injuries, and fevers; and to escort patients to medical centres. They would also be expected to deliver direct observed short course therapy for tuberculosis and oral rehydration to give folic acid tablets and chloroquine to patients and to alert authorities of unusual outbreaks. ASHA will receive performance-based compensation for promoting universal immunization, referral and escort services for RCH, construction of household toilets, and other health care delivery programmes. Following are the goals of NRHM:

- Reduction in infant mortality rate and maternal mortality ratio.
- Universal access to integrated comprehensive public health services.
- Child health, water, sanitation and hygiene.
- Prevention and control of communicable and non-communicable diseases, including locally endemic diseases.
- Population stabilization, gender and demographic balance.
- Revitalize local health traditions and mainstreaming of AYUSH.
- Promotion of healthy life style.

The strategies to achieve the goals include:

- Train and enhance capacity of PRIs to own, control and manage public health services.
- Health plan for each village through village health committee of the panchayat.
- Strengthening sub-centre through a united fund to enable local planning and action (each sub-centre will have an United Fund for local action at ₹ 10,000 per annum). This fund will be deposited in a joint bank account of the ANM and Sarpanch and operated by the ANM, in consultation with the Village Health Committee, and more Multi Purpose Workers.
- Provision of 24 hour service in 50 per cent PHCs by addressing shortage of doctors, especially in high focus states, through mainstreaming AYUSH manpower.
- Preparation and implementation of an intersectoral District Health Plan prepared by the District Health Mission, including drinking water, sanitation and hygiene and nutrition.

This document has strong commitment towards crafting credible public systems by having five key approaches:

- Communitization
- Adequate and flexible financing
- Monitoring against Indian Public Health Standards

- Innovations in human resource management
- Building capacity at all levels for centralized health action (Sinha, 2009: 72)

The thrust of NRHM is public systems and its accessibility, affordability and accountability. Unlike many other programmes in the health sector in the past, the NRHM is about crafting a credible public system of health delivery at all levels starting from the village and going right up to the district level. All programmes (except HIV/AIDS, cancer and mental health) were brought under the umbrella of NRHM. Very categorically NRHM committed itself to communitization under the Panchayati Raj Institutions (PRIs). Accordingly, Village Health and Sanitation Committees are set up, joint accounts of Auxiliary Nurse-Midwife and Sarpanch are opened at the sub-centre level. Block level and district level health missions are constituted involving PRIs. Facilities specific *Rogi Kalayan Samitis* (patient welfare committees) are established in Primary Health Centres (PHCs), Community Health Centres (CHCs), sub-district and district hospitals. The village Health and Nutrition Day every month at the village Integrated Child Development Services (ICDS) centre is intended to promote greater convergence among sectors that determine health outcomes like water, sanitation, education, health and nutrition. The NRHM provided the flexibility to the states to design their own interventions for outreach of services. From the Gram Panchayat headquarter level clinics at sub-centres in West Bengal to the *Muskaan* programme at the ICDS centre in Bihar, the *Mamta Abhigyan* in Gujarat, the boat clinics and mobile medical units in Assam, all is an affirmation of flexibility available to the states.

The interventions made in the last three years are as follows:

- Cellphones to ANMs to interventions for sickle cell anaemia
- Floursis
- School Health Programmes
- Emergency Medical Transport Systems, etc. (Sinha, 2009: 73)

Involving Local Institutions

NRHM has also provided for their village level organizations like self-help groups (SHG), women's groups, *mahila samakhya* groups, water and sanitation groups to be represented on the Health and Sanitation Committees as the intention to ensure that all those who have the motivation are given authority as well. The *Rogi Kalyan Samitis* also have the representation of civil society besides the PRIs for the health facilities.

Expanding Trained Cadres

The NRHM has managed to bring in an additional 2,500 specialists, 10,000 doctors (including ayurveda, yoga, unani, siddha and homoeopathy (AYUSH) doctors and over 40,000 ANMs and staff nurses into the health system. The NRHM has added over 5,00,000 ASHAs who are at the various stages of their training. More than half of them have been provided their drug kits. The NRHM saw ASHA as a health activist who connects households to health facilities.

Funds and Accounting

For 2005–06, the mission document states that ₹ 6,713 crores have been allocated for NRHM. The total allocation for the departments of Health and Family Welfare has been hiked from ₹ 8,420 crores to ₹ 10,820 crores in the budget proposals for the year 2005–06. Nowhere do we see that NRHM budget is a separate budget.

Summing Up

The health care in rural areas has been developed as three-tier structure. The sub-centre is the most peripheral institution and the first contact point between the primary health care system and the community. The majority of rural deaths, which are preventable, are due to infectious and communicable, parasitic and respiratory diseases. Infectious diseases dominate the morbidity pattern in rural areas. Significant portion of the country's medical needs, especially in rural areas, have been attended to by the indigenous health systems such as ayurveda, homoeopathy, unani, naturopathy and folk medicine. NRHM from 2005 onwards aims to undertake architectural correction of the health system to enable it to effectively handle increased allocations and promote policies that strengthen public health management and service delivery in the country.

References

Chaudhury, N. et al. (2006), 'Missing in Action: Teacher and Health Worker Absence in Developing Countries', *Journal of Economic Perspective*, Vol. 20, 1 November, Pittsburgh.

Duggal, R. (1997), 'Health Care Budgets in a Changing Political Economy', *Economic and Political Weekly*, 17–24 May.

MoHFW (2005), *Population Norms (Census 2001)*, Government of India, New Delhi.

Park, K. (2000), *Textbook of Preventive and Social Medicine*, Jabalpur: Banarsidas Bhanot.

Patil, A.V., K.V. Somasundaram and R.C. Goyal (2002), 'Current Health Scenario in Rural India', *Australian Journal of Rural Health*, 10: 129–35.

RCHS Round II, 2002–04.

Sample Registration System, Government of India, 1997–98.

Sinha, Amarjeet (2009), 'In Defence of the National Rural Health Mission', *Economic and Political Weekly*, XLIV(14): 72–75.

18

Urban Health Care in India

As per the Census 2001, 28.6 crore people live in urban areas. The urban growth has led to rapid increase in number of urban poor population, many of who live in slums and other squatter settlements. As per Census of 2011, 37.7 crore people live in urban area, which is 31.16 per cent of the total population. About 17 per cent of people lived in slums. The increasing concentration of people and economic activities in towns and cities has brought economies of scale and proximity to infrastructure. The burgeoning 80 million urban poor in India struggle for basic services like housing, water and sanitation. Large sections of the urban population live in tenements, boarding houses and illegal settlements, slums, where conditions are very poor and health burdens very high.

Defining the Urban Environment

The urban environment is multifaceted: each aspect of the environment influences, and is influenced by, the others. The concept of driving forces that influence health and the environment is particularly appropriate in the urban situation. Rapid urbanization represents a profound transformation of human ecology ... that is generally outstripping social and political response (McMichael, 1993). Table 1 from Landon (2006: 185) gives some examples of urbanization. Urban areas are characterized by their high-density population, which are accommodated by the development of extensive road networks, housing schemes, service and production industries and recreational facilities. The changes in the environment that occur as a result of urbanization are shown in Table 1.

The largest growth in urbanization is taking place in low and middle income countries, many of which have tropical climates that exaggerate environmental changes. For example, rainfall is higher in non-tropical regions, causing greater problems with run-off and sedimentation. Many cities in low and middle income countries were colonial outposts that began life as small trading posts or administrative centres. Many were not in suitable sites for expansion, with swamps, rivers, steep slopes or otherwise unsuitable topography restricting their growth (Table 2) (Gupta and Asher, 1998).

Table 1

Aspects of Urbanization

Aspect	*Example*	*Potential Health Effect*	*Prevention*
Physical	Air pollution from transport	Respiratory and cardiovascular disease	Reduced care numbers provide better public transport
Social/cultural	Lack of education	High infant mortality	Improve access to education
Psychosocial	Over-crowding	Mental health problems	Better-quality housing
Economic	Lack of employment	General health	Encourage industry and services to relocate

Table 2

Changes in the Environment as a Result of Urbanization

Change	*Effect*
Water	Increased run-off
	Flood intensity increases
	Depletion of water sources
	Problem with waste water
Climate	Increased temperatures (heat island effect)
	Increased cloudiness and precipitation
	Reduced humidity, reduced wind speed
Air	Pollution increased including particulates
Ecology	Reduced vegetation and wildlife
	Introduction of exotic species
Physical	Changes of water channel
	Problem of solid waste disposal

Source: Gupta and Asher (1998)

Physical Aspect of Urban Environment

Physical aspects of the urban environment that have an effect upon the population's health include water supply and quality, sanitation provision, industrial and residential pollution, housing, infrastructure and the city's geographical situation (e.g. on flood plain or an earthquake belt). Road transport has two important physical influences: first, it is the major source of air pollution, and, second, motor vehicles cause accidental injuries. Indoor air pollution can cause acute respiratory infections in children and chronic lung disease in adults.

Social and Cultural Aspects of Urban Environment

Urban living has more of a socio-economic differentiation, which points to unequal access to economic resources and differing opportunities for health according to an individual's standing in the community with respect to their income or occupation. Living in urban centres can offer great potential gains, such as more employment opportunities and health care facilities. However, it also leads to over-crowding and urban poverty in low and middle income countries. The extract describes the rise in slums in Mumbai, India. However, living on the margins does not necessarily mean a breakdown of social organization; squatter settlements can be stable communities with strong community organization and the provision of cheap or informal labour to support the economy as the following extract by Lanegran (1999) illustrates:

> The City of Mumbai is based on the island of Bombay in the West of India and has one of the world's largest best natural harbours. It is India's second largest, but most modern city. Slums have always existed in Mumbai. When the original fort was developed, the native villages moved close to the centre as squatter settlements. There was no planning, construction of infrastructure or implementation of facilitates such as water, sewage, and drainage. Over the passage of time, this has led to problems for Mumbai's poor population. Mumbai has a very dense population with 16,500 people per square mile and a scarcity of housing. Before 1950, slums were predominantly found around the mills, on the western part of the island. Health care and provisions to these areas were largely ignored. In 1954 there was a slum clearance, yet despite this, the slum population has increased and today slum dwellers make up 60 per cent of Mumbai's population, approximately seven million people. The scarcity of housing has meant the slums have spread wherever they can find space, including onto roads. Conditions are difficult. Inhabitants have to deal with issues such as constant migration, lack of water, no sewage or solid waste facilities, lack of public transport, pollution and housing shortages. Infant mortality in these areas is as high as there are no amenities in rural India. General hospitals in the Greater Mumbai region are over-crowded and under-resourced. There is either too little water in the area for drinking and sanitation, or in the monsoon season too much water and flooding. There have been moves by the government to improve the slum areas. In 1985, the slum upgradation project began. The aim of the project was to offer secure, long-term, legal plot tenure to slum households if they agreed to invest in their housing. The programme managed to target only the 10–12 per cent of the slum population who were capable of upgrading their homes. It offered no incentive for those without homes. Despite the attempts to remedy the slum problem of Mumbai, the slums are still growing.

Economic Infrastructure

A viable economic infrastructure is vital if a city is to achieve sustainability, growth and provide a healthy environment. The provision of adequate water supplies, sewerage, lighting, housing and communication support is essential but there must also be employment available for workers with a diversity of skills. Manufacturing industries or the service-led economy may predominate. However, reliance on a narrow economic base such as ship building is dangerous, because a decline in that particular industry will depress the entire city.

Health and the Urban Environment

In low and middle income countries, with rapid urbanization, there are settlements on unsuitable marginal land, poor housing in settlements or shanty towns, large increases in population density, an uncontrolled increase in pollution (air, water and land) and a lack of basic infrastructure (electricity, water, sewerage, waste disposal, health care, education). These circumstances have meant a rise in these areas of communicable diseases known as the 'diseases of poverty'. These include malaria, flu, hookworm and a range of gastric and respiratory diseases, nutritional deficiency and drug-related illness. High density living is also associated with over-crowding which leads to non-communicable diseases – specifically accidents in the home and on the roads. The stresses of urban life have been linked to an increase in depression, suicide and substance abuse. It is suggested that the breakdown or lack of social relationships caused by over-crowding and migration creates a perception of loss of control which causes stress and leads to mental health problems.

Health Condition of the Urban Poor

- IMR (under 5) of urban poor is 72.7 per 1000 as against 51.9 per 1000 in urban.
- About 46 per cent are under-weight children among urban poor as against urban average of 32.8 per cent.
- Threre are around 46.8 per cent poor women with no education as against 67.5 per cent of urban average.
- An astounding 71.4 per cent are anaemic among urban poor as against 62.9 per cent of urban average.
- A meagre 18.5 per cent of urban poor have access to piped water supply as against 50 per cent of urban average.
- Approximately 60 per cent miss total immunization before completing one year.
- Poor environmental condition with high population density – lung diseases, TB, etc.
- Poor access to safe water and sanitation – water-borne diseases, diarrhoea, dysentery.
- High incidence of vector borne diseases among urban poor.

Health Challenges in Urban Areas

- Poor households not knowing where to go to meet health need.
- Weak and dysfunctional public system of health for outreach.
- Contaminated water, poor sanitation.
- Poor environmental health, poor housing.
- Unregistered practitioner: Use of irrational and unethical medical practice.
- Community organization helpless in health matters.
- Weak public health planning capacity in urban local bodies.

Urban Health Care Facilities

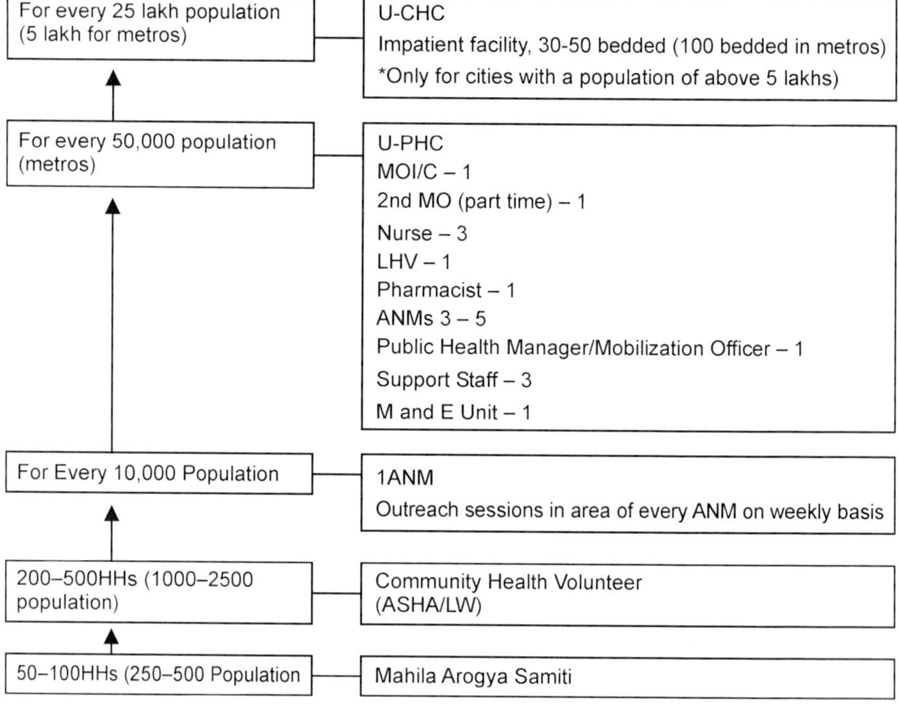

- Large private sector but poor cannot access them.
- Problems in targeting the poor on the basis of Below Poverty line (BPL) Card.
- No convergence among wider determinants of health.
- No system of counselling and care for adolescents.
- Over congested secondary and tertiary facilities and underutilized primary care facilities.
- Problem of drug abuse and alcoholism.
- Many slums do not have primary health care facility.
- High incidence of domestic violence.
- Multiplicity of local bodies, State government, etc. management of health needs of urban people.
- No norms for urban health facilities.
- No concerted campaigns for behaviour change.
- Problems of unauthorized settlements (Government of India, 2013: 31–36).

Health Care Facilities in Urban Areas

Most of the existing primary health facilities, namely, the Urban Health Posts (UHPs)/Urban Family Welfare Centres (UFWC)/Dispensaries are functioning sub-optimally due to the problems of infrastructure, human resources, referrals, diagnostics, case load, spatial distribution, and inconvenient working hours. The main functions of Urban Health Posts (UHP) are to provide outreach, primary health care and family welfare and MCH services.

National Urban Health Mission (NUHM)

The NUHM is a sub-mission of National Health Mission and has been approved by the Cabinet on 1 May 2013. The NUHM envisages to meet health care needs of the urban population with the focus on urban poor. This will be achieved by strengthening the existing health care service delivery system, targeting the people living in slums and converging with various schemes relating to wider determinants of health like drinking water, sanitation, school education, etc. implemented by the Ministries of Urban Development, Housing and Urban Poverty Alleviation, Human Resource Development and Women and Child Development.

Goals and Issues of NUHM

The NUHM would aim to improve the health status of the urban population in general, but particularly of the poor and other disadvantaged sections, by facilitating equitable access to quality health care through a revamped public health system, partnership, community-based mechanism with the active involvement of the urban local bodies. NUHM would aim to provide a system for convergence of all communicable and non-communicable disease programmes, including HIV/AIDS, through integrated planning at the city level. The objective would be to enhance the utilization of the system through the convergence mechanism, through provision of a common platform and availability of all services at one point (U-PHC) and through mechanisms of referrals. The existing IDSP structure would be leveraged for improved surveillance. The management, control and supervision systems, however, would vest within the respective divisions but urban component/within the programmes would be identified and all services will be sought to converged/located at U-PHC level. Appropriate convergences and mechanisms for co-locations and strengthening would be sought with the existing systems of AYUSH at the time of operationalization. NUHM will not provide for contractual staff of AYUSH as the case with NRHM.

NUHM will specifically address the peculiarities of urban health needs, which constitutes non-communicable diseases (NCDs) as a major proportion of the burden of disease. The primary health care system being envisaged under NRHM will screen, diagnose and refer the cases of chronic diseases to the secondary and tertiary level through a system of referral. Hence, strengthening of health care facilities in secondary and tertiary care also needs substantial upgradation.

Functioning of NUHM

- Need based by specific urban health care system to meet the diverse health care needs of the urban poor and other vulnerable groups.
- Institutional mechanism and management systems to meet the health-related challenges of a rapidly growing urban population.
- Partnership with community and local bodies for a more proactive involvement in planning, implementation, and monitoring of health activities.
- Availability of resources for providing essential primary health care to the urban poor.
- Partnership with NGOs, for profit and not for profit health service providers and other stakeholders.

Coverage in NUHM

NUHM would cover all state capitals, district headquarters and cities/towns with a population of more than 50,000. It would primarily focus on slum dwellers and other marginalized groups like rickshaw pullers, street vendors, railway and bus station coolies, homeless people, street children, construction site workers.

Financing of NUHM

The centre-state funding pattern will be 75:25 for all the states except North-Eastern states including Sikkim and other special category states of Jammu and Kashmir, Himachal Pradesh and Uttarakhand, for whom the centre-state funding pattern will be 90:10. The NUHM provides an annual grant of ₹ 5,000 to the Mahila Arogya Samitis (MAS) every year. This amount can be used for conducting fortnightly/monthly meetings of MAS, sanitation and hygiene, meeting emergency health needs, etc. To build the capacity of MAS, quarterly orientation workshops on the subjects of group organization, governance and management of the group, leadership skills, etc. would be organized in the first year, and thereafter once a year.

Operationalization of NUHM

The NUHM would encourage the effective participation of the community in planning and management of health services. It would promote a community health volunteer – Accredited Social Health Activist (ASHA) or Link Worker (LW) in urban poor settlements (one ASHA for 1,000–2,500 urban population covering about 200 to 500 households); ensure the participation by creation of community based institutions like *Mahila Argoya Samiti* (50–100 households) and *Rogi Kalyan Samitis*. However, the states will have the flexibility to take the work of motivating community from the *Mahila Arogya Samitis* (MAS) and in that case recruiting an ASHA may not be necessary. The performance-based incentives can be credited to the account of MAS in that case, which can be used to enhance the revolving fund or distributing some honorarium to the other active members. Existing women groups under the JnNURM and other like structures can be adopted for implementation of NUHM. Self-help groups of women made under programmes of urban development department, etc. can also play the role of MAS.

NUHM would proactively reach out to urban poor settlements by way of regular outreach sessions and monthly health, sanitation and nutrition day. States would be encouraged to involve NGOs to facilitate communitization process, build the capacity of ASHA and MAS and carry out IEC/BCC activities. It mandates special attention for reaching out to other vulnerable sections like construction workers, rag pickers, sex workers, brick kiln workers, rickshaw pullers and street children. This could be done through the public health care systems or through Public-Private Partnership (PPP) or other innovative models deemed suitable by the states. ANM will also be provided with mobility support to reach out the unreached area and vulnerable population with outreach session. Communication facility in the form of Closed User Group (CUG) will be made available.

The NUHM has provided flexibility to the states to choose their own model which suits their needs and capacities. Models can be decided through community led action. For strengthening the present primary public health systems, NUHM based on the key characteristics of the existing urban health delivery system proposes a broad framework rationalizing the available manpower and resources, improving access through a communitized risk pooling mechanism and enhancing participation of the community in planning and management of the health care service delivery by ensuring a community link volunteer (ASHA/Lone Workers from other programmes like JnNURM, ICDS, etc.) and establishment of Rogi Kalyan Samitis (RKS), ensuring effective participation of urban local bodies and their capacity building along with key stakeholders, and by making special provision for inclusion of the most vulnerable amongst the poor in the development of e-enabled monitoring system.

All the services delivered under the urban health delivery system through the Urban-PHCs and Urban-CHCs will be universal in nature, whereas the outreach services will be targeted to the targets groups (slum dwellers and other vulnerable groups). Outreach services will be provided through the Female Health Workers (FHWs), essentially ANMs, with an induction training of three to six months, who will be headquartered at the urban PHCs. These ANMs will report at the U-PHC and then move to their respective areas for outreach services (including school health) on designated says. They will be provided mobility support for providing outreach services. On other days, they will conduct immunization and ANC clinics, etc. at the U-PHC itself.

Urban Health Care Delivery Model

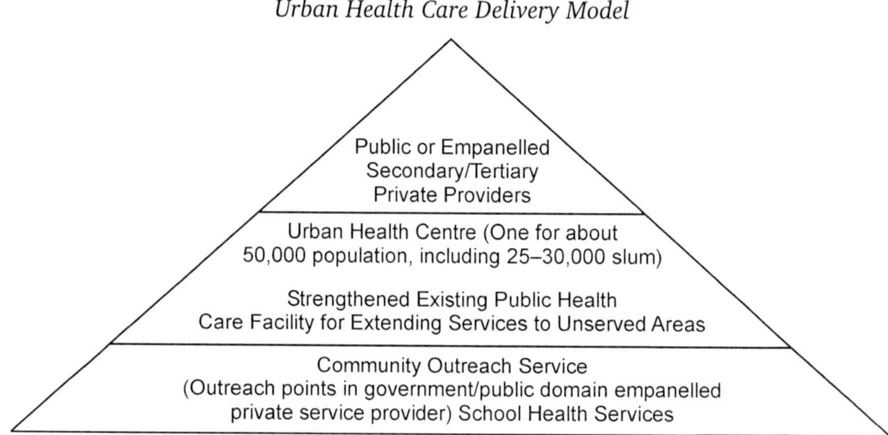

Source: Government of India (2013), *National Urban Health Mission: Framework for Implementation*, New Delhi: Ministry of Health and Family Welfare.

Indicative Norms for Operationalization of Urban PHC

Accessibility

- Preferably located near the slum to be served
- Accessed by slum dwellers

Services

- Medical care: OPD services: from 12 noon to 8 pm
- Services as prescribed under RCH II
- National Health Programmes
- Collection and reporting of vital events and IDSP
- Referral services
- Basic laboratory services
- Counselling services
- Services for Non-Communicable Diseases
- Social mobilization and community level activities

Basic Infrastructure

- Consultation room, dressing and treatment room, medicine room
- Medical equipment and instruments.

Basic Staff

- Medical Officer: Two (one regular and one part time)
- Staff Nurse: Three
- Pharmacist: One
- Lab Technician: One
- Public Health Manager/Community Mobilizer: One
- Lady Health Visitor: One-Two (Depending upon number of ANMs)

- Auxiliary Nurse and Midwife: Four-Five (Depending upon the population)
- Secretarial Staff including Account Keeping and MIS: Two
- Support Staff: One

Indicative Norms for Operationalization of Urban Community Health Centres

Accessibility

- The hospital/nursing home to be easily accessible for the served population
- Willingness to provide services at the rates negotiated

Facilities

- As per IPHS norm for hospitals locally adapted as per need
- Round the clock availability services

Availability of specialities services for which the partnership is being entered. Some of them may be:

- Obstetrics and Gynaecology
- Paediatrics
- General Surgery
- Ophthalmology
- ENT
- Orthopaedics
- Dermatology
- Endocrinology (Diabetes, Thyroid)
- Mental Health
- General Medicine
- Dental
- Any other based on epidemiological profile of the city

Diagnostic Facilities: As per the requirement

- Fully equipped laboratory for biochemistry, microbiology and haematology
- X-ray machine with minimum capacity of 60 MA
- Ultra-Sonography
- Any other based on epidemiological profile of the city

Critique of Urban Health Mission

The NUHM for the urban poor is being backed by a mere budget of ₹ 1 crore for the entire fiscal period. Attempts by the Health Ministry to use the rural health mission funds to push the new venture along is likely to impose a high cost on the already cash strapped rural programme. The sharing of allocation could also end up diminishing the freshly launched flexible pool of funds to fight specific diseases. The urban mission has been clubbed with the rural under the National Health Mission and is called a sub-mission. The 12th Five-Year Plan provided ₹ 16,995 crore as the centre's share for the urban mission, which is roughly ₹ 3,300 crore every year. But in the second part of the plan, there was only ₹ 1 crore available.

Summing Up

In 2011 Census, urban growth has led to rapid increase in number of urban poor population, many of who live in slums and other squatter settlements. Physical aspects of the urban environment that have an effect upon population health include water supply, sanitation provision, industrial and residential pollution, housing, infrastructure and the city's geographical situation. Urban living has more of a socio-economic differentiation, which points to unequal access to economic resources and differing opportunities for health according to an individual's standing in the community with respect to their income or occupation. The deliveries of health care services in urban areas are delivered through government hospitals, private hospitals, clinics and dispensaries. However, recently NUHM envisages to meet health care needs of the urban population with the focus on urban poor, by providing essential primary health care services and reducing their out of pocket expenses for treatment.

References

Government of India (2013), *National Urban Health Mission: Framework for Implementation*, New Delhi: Ministry of Health and Family Welfare.

Gupta, A. and M. Asher (1998), *Environment and the Developing World: Principles, Policies and Management*, Chichester: John Wiley and Sons Ltd.

Landon, M. (2006), *Environment, Health and Sustainable Development*, New Delhi: Tata McGraw-Hill.

Lanegran, D. (2003), *Geography of World Urbanization*, Macalester College.

McMichael, A.J. (1993), *Planetary Overload: Global Environmental Change and the Heath of the Human Species*, Cambridge: Cambridge University Press.

19

Privatization of Health Care in India

Markets in the health care are also governed by the purchasing power of the individuals in society. These are not democratic institutions which results in the marginalization of the marginal. It is evident that the private health sectors attract and treat persons who can pay more and, hence, it is selective. Quality of health care in private sector is a myth as in private sector job insecurity and poor working conditions are bound to affect the quality of care provided to the patients. Private health care professionals are essentially for the sale and making over-use of goods produced by the health care industry. User charges, misuse of high-tech diagnostic tools, irrational diagnosis, and technology for money has become a culture of practice for the doctors. Professionals in health care defend unfair and trade practices which sometimes leads to the unethical practices under the garb of professional independence. This chapter attempts to collate literature from various sources in an attempt to answer four pertinent questions related to private health care in India. First, the structure of private health sector, second how the private health care sector is delivering health in terms of its quality; third what is the structure and pattern of health care from the provider's perspective? Fourth, it looks into emerging relationship between private health care and market. Finally, the chapter tries to highlight some of the dehumanizing issues/aspects in private health care which are relevant for the consumers of health care.

Private Health Care

Health in equalities are the unjust differences in health between groups of people occupying different positions in society. Before 1930, health and illness were recognized as being appropriate topics for sociological study. It was the impact of social structure on people's health that was noted rather than how a person's physical and mental state might influence their actions (Jones, 1994: 40). The science of health has been characterized by positivism and extreme rationalism, divested from its social and economic context. Medicine is not a science but a learned profession deeply rooted in a number of sciences and charged with obligation to apply them for man's benefit (George, 1972: 9). The present chapter attempts to understand the delivery of health care in private sector. The debate on the role of private health care has primarily focused on issues of cost and quality. Studies indicate that private health care practices significantly affect both the cost and quality of available health care services in India (Uplekar, 2000; Dugal, 1989; Vishwanathan and Rohde, 1990; Yesudian, 1990; Qadeer et al., 2001). Cases of superfluous services and the high cost of services rendered by private physicians and hospitals have been reported by (Baru et al., 2000; Nandraj, 1994; Nanda and Baru, 1993; Baru, 1998). Structure and pattern of private health care have been addressed by (Bhat, 1999; Muralidheran, 1994; Patranobis, 2003; Jesani, 1989; Yesudian, 1994). The issue of consumer protection and dehumanizing aspects in private health care has been addressed and the effectiveness of legislation has been discussed (Minocha, 2011; Tulasidhar, 1994; Bhat, 1999). Gross insufficiencies in the public health care delivery system acted as a driver for the growth of private sector institutions in the country (Nadkarni, 2010; Chatterjee, 2008). Inherent factors like improved efficiency, better quality, greater reliability and transparency has aided in the growth of private health sector. Private health sector continues to explore the opportunities – a tradeoff between 'social welfare' and 'business orientation' is critical (Shah and Mohanty, 2010).

The private sector plays an important role in India's health care delivery system. Through a wide network of health care facilities, this sector caters to the needs of both urban and rural populations and has expanded widely to meet the increasing demands. The significance of the private health care sector in India can be summarized as follows:

- Total health expenditure in India is estimated to be about 6 per cent of GDP, of which private health care expenditure is 75 per cent or 4.25 per cent of GDP. About one-third of this expenditure is on secondary and tertiary in-patient care, the rest meeting the curative needs at primary level (World Bank, 1995). Insurance coverage mechanisms are negligible and most of this expenditure is out-of-pocket.
- Private health care expenditure in India has grown at the rate of 12.5 per cent per annum since 1960–61. For each 1 per cent increase in per capita income, private health care expenditure has increased by 1.47 per cent (Bhat, 1996).
- About 57 per cent of hospitals and 32 per cent of hospital beds are in the private sector. The share of the private sector investment in total health infrastructure, e.g. hospitals, investments in medical equipment and technology, is also quite significant.
- At present about 80 per cent of 3,90,000 qualified allopathic doctors registered with the Medical Council of India are working in the private sector (Jassani, 1989; Bhat, 1996). There are over 6,50,000 providers of other systems of medicine practicing in India (Planning Commission, 1998) and most of them are in private practice.

- Utilization studies show that one-third of in-patients and three-quarter of out-patients utilize private health care facilities (Duggal and Amin, 1989; Yesudian, 1990; Visaria and Gumber, 1994).

Growth of Private Sector in Health Care

- Notwithstanding its limitations, the public sector continues to be the single largest provider of in-patient services. The cutbacks in financing have affected the quality of services provided by these institutions. Individual private practitioners play an important role in providing out-patient care both in rural and urban areas. Several studies have commented on the role of private practitioners in rural areas and their high levels of utilization for out-patient care (Baru, 1994).
- The growth of private nursing homes and hospitals took place essentially during the late 1970s, mainly in urban areas and in agriculturally prosperous states. The 1980s saw the rise of the corporate sector in medical care with active support from the government. The promoters of these enterprises were only regional business groups and non-resident Indian doctors. Interestingly, the rise of corporate sector in medical care was largely confined to the southern cities of Hyderabad and Madras.
- Through the 1990s, there has been an expansion of secondary level private hospitals in several states. The private sector is no longer a mere urban phenomenon, due to intense competition within this sector, they are forced to move into peri-urban and rural areas. The real significant changes have taken place at the tertiary level. One of these is that corporate and trust hospitals at this level have started collaborating with state governments and very recently with multinational corporations (MNCs). Given the growth of the middle class, there is a market for speciality services for the middle and upper middle classes in both urban and rural areas. This demand has also fuelled the import of high technology equipment.

Investment in Private Health Sector

- Investments in tertiary care have become profitable also because of relaxation in import policies for high technology medical equipment. In the 1996–97 budgets, there has been a drastic cut on import duties on equipment i.e. from 120 per cent to 30 per cent. Further, foreign manufacturers are making inroads into the Indian market.
- With the growth of the tertiary private sector, the demand for medical equipment is on rise. According to the managing director of Philips Medical Systems India, 'The health care business is a $ 3,000 billion industry worldwide. If we attract even 1 per cent of that here, the potential for the medical equipment industry is tremendous' (*Business World*, 1997).

- Apart from high technology medical equipment, there is a tremendous demand for items like syringes and surgical instruments. Indigenous production of these items is low; there has been no public or private investment in the manufacture of medical equipment. The rate of growth of the disposable syringes market, which is about 750 million units a year at present, is 20 per cent per annum (*Business World*, 1997).

Structure of Private Health Care in India

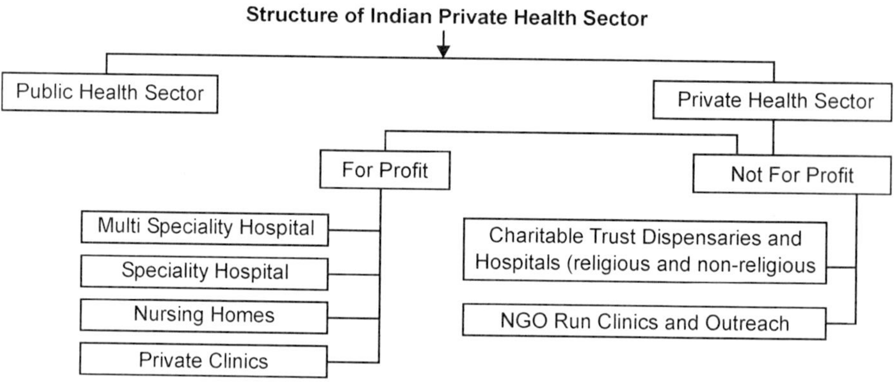

Process of Privatization of Health Care Services

The private sector is not new to Indian health services. It was predominant mode of service for the well off until the end of the colonial period. During the pre-Independence period, the private sector was restricted to individual practitioners. The Bhore Committee conducted a survey on medical institutions which revealed that 92 per cent of the institutions were maintained on public funds and the remaining 8 per cent were wholly maintained by private agencies. The proportion of allopathic doctors in private practice was as high as 73 per cent and the remaining 27 per cent were employed in government service (Government of India, 1946). When the recommendations of the committee were adopted there seemed to be reservations regarding private practice by doctors in government service. As far as individual private practitioners were concerned, the committee assured them that their interest would not be affected. Although the committee had categorically stated that private practice by government doctors must be prohibited, it did not visualize the role of independent private practitioners in government hospitals. A shift in policy could be seen as early as 1961 in the report of the Mudaliar Committee. This Committee took note of the fact that nearly 40–70 per cent of doctors in different states were private practitioners. Thus, the committee visualized a role for them in government services because of inadequate manpower. It was important that they were given opportunities to serve in government hospitals on a part-time or honorary basis, and hospital authorities could encourage them to admit their patients needing in-patient care. It further stated: Independent practitioners have to be considered as a separate entity whose legitimate right must be protected (Government of India, 1961). Thus even as early as 1961, the demarcation between the public and private sectors had become clear, especially with individual private practitioners being encouraged to use government hospitals to treat their patients.

The private sector has been expanding since the last three decades in India. Earlier during the 1950s and 1960s, the presence of private sector institutions was small but over the years this sector has grown and diversified to include commercial-based institutions like nursing home and corporate hospitals. With the increasing penetration of high-tech investigating equipment, investing in medical care has become a profitable proposition and has been an important reason for fuelling the growth of private institutions. The private sector has been largely involved in the provision of curative services while the public sector has provided both preventive and curative services. Stagnation of public expenditures during the 1970s and 1980s created space for the growth of private sector. An added reason has been the profitability of private enterprises which resulted in their proliferation. The government has also played a supportive role to the private sector by offering a number of concession and subsidies. Supportive government policies have been in the form of concessional loans, custom duty exemptions and reduction of import duties on high technology medical equipment. The indirect benefits are the accommodation of private interests in the government sector. These interests are served through liaison with the private sector for purchase of drugs and equipment. It also encourages the private sector to fill the gaps of inadequate investment by the government, allowing private practice by government doctors and handing over hospitals to the private sector. Another reason for the private medical sector in urban area is the lack of expansion of public services in urban areas. It has given rise to a peculiar situation. There are very few opportunities for medical graduates in urban areas while a large number of posts are lying vacant in rural areas. The proportion in government service has continued to decline (Nanda, 1993).

Policy of Liberalization and Business in Medical Care

The international Monetary Fund and the World Bank started applying greater economic pressures on the developing world. The period of liberalization and globalization introduced new issues. This was an opportunity for the developed nations to use and intergrate markets of the developing world and dominate them. Hence, the pressure to open up trade in agriculture and services mounted on developing countries.

Since the 1980, pressure for change has come from different quarters. As far as the public sector health services are concerned, the government has cut back the fund and promoted the medical care as industry. Private sector Practitioners, who had enjoyed the privilege of state protection since independence in India's mixed economy of service provision, aspired to influence policy and create more advantage for themselves. The private sector grew from polyclinics to nursing homes, private hospitals and finally to the development of corporate hospital. This is because the government hospital has offered a number of concessions for the growth of private sector (Qadeer, 2002: 26).

Interestingly globalization resulted in emerging of a middle class, which succeeded in acquiring a reasonably adequate standard of living and lobbied for 'high tech hospital' which conformed to their concepts of international standards of health care.

The establishment of Apollo marked the entry of non-resident Indian doctors into medical care and signalled recognition of a hospital as a corporate enterprise. Several big business groups like Tata, Hinduja, Modis, and Escorts have floated multi specialty hospitals and are mainly registered as Trusts. These enterprises have been promoted by business groups and doctor entrepreneurs, some of who are non-resident Indians based in the United States (Baru, 2000). Baru in her study of private medical institutions found that the private limited hospital is organized like any other company and does not issue public shares in the market. The public limited hospital, on the other hand, issues public shares in the market while the trusts are essentially supposed to be 'non-profit' concerns. Section–35 of the Income Tax Act offers tax exemptions in respect of expenditures on scientific research. Therefore the groups have set up many of these multi-specialty hospitals as a research centres and therefore can be registered as a non-profit enterprises (Baru, 1994).

Structure of Private Health Sector

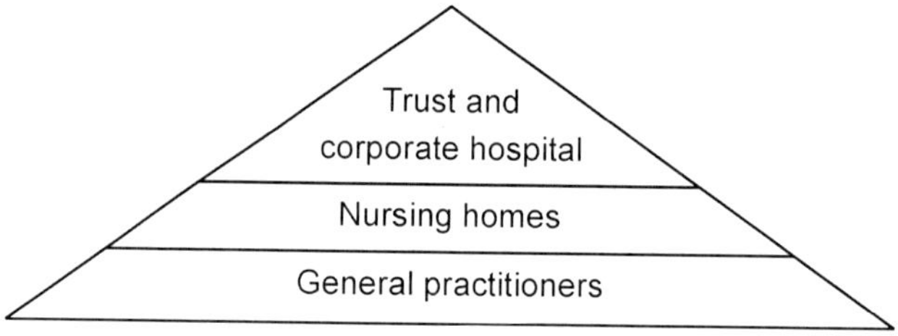

Trust and corporate hospital
Nursing homes
General practitioners

Instead of learning from past experiences and contradictions within the Indian health care system and enhancing an efficient and integrated approach to improving its working, the entire exercise was dominated by unquestioning acceptance of the prescribed reforms. The main aspects of the IMF – World Bank inspired reforms cuts in health sector investment and results in opening up of medical care to private sector. Introduction of user fees and private investments in public hospitals are the main agenda of liberalization. Public health care delivery system has suffered a lot due to the cutbacks in the welfare sector and the proposed health sector reforms.

Issues in Health Care

National Council of Applied Economic Research (NCAER) conducted a national survey in 1990 which found that 54.75 per cent people in urban areas utilize private health facilities and in rural area the number is 55.46 per cent. The average household expenditure on health is ₹ 142.60 per illness episode in urban areas and ₹ 151.81 in rural areas. State policy towards the private sector has to be addressed within a systemic perspective covering not only providers of health care services but also other related components in the health care system. Within this perspective, it is essential to delineate the structure of private health care sector and its delivery of health to the people. Following are the issues of concern:

- Structure of private health sector
- Privatization and quality of health care
- Health care provider and pattern of practice
- Privatization and market
- Dehumanizing aspects and consumer concern in health care

Structure of Private Health Sector

Insight into the health care provisioning shows that the private health sector accounts for over 70 per cent of all primary medical care and over 40 per cent of all hospital care (NSS, 1987; Duggal and Amin, 1989; Thankappan et al., 1987; NCAER, 1992; George et al., 1992). As per the National Health Policy 1983, the health care expenditure in India is 6 per cent of GDP of which 1.3 per cent is contributed by the public sector and 4.7 per cent is contributed by the private sector. The private sector health care provisioning has a pyramidal structure. The base is formed by individual practitioners; the large middle piece consists of small hospitals and nursing homes and the apex includes large super specialty research centres, public ltd., corporate and trust hospitals. Majority of the individual practitioners are usually general practitioners (GP). They are concentrated in rural areas.

The bulk of medical care in rural India is provided through the private practitioners who are untrained, non-graduates practicing allopathy and providing outpatient care. The nursing homes consists of 2 to 50 bed units, which are owned individually or in joint partnership. They generally operate as family business. These centres provide out-patient as well as in-patient care. The trust hospitals, corporate hospitals, public ltd and supers peciality research institutes constitute the tertiary care providers. The private sector hospitals have 300 to 500 bed and have well trained nursing and paraclinical support staff. These hospitals generate revenue to self-sustain and expand further. Majority of these hospitals are under private sector and located in urban areas.

Privatization and Quality of Health Care

Much of the debate on privatization of health care has been based on the assumption that the private sector provides better quality of services than the public sector. Efforts are on to restructure public institutions on market principles to promote efficiency. This assumption does not stand up to empirical scrutiny because of the difference in stated goals. Patient load and the clinical practice of spending time with each patient by private doctor will have a significant bearing on the quality and cost of health care.

In a study to understand health seeking behaviour of semi-urban population, it was observed that 62 per cent of the households preferred private health care facility. The reasons for avoiding government facility are: services are free of cost and so included waiting time, facility located at distance, inadequate facilities, unclean premises, harsh behaviour of the staff and low faith in government doctors. Interestingly, quality of medical care is not considered to be the criterion for selection of public or private sector facilities (Patel and Trivedi et al., 2010). In another study conducted in the city of Mumbai (Dilip and Duggal, 2004), reasons for the preference of private sector facility included proximity, quality of care and convenient timing. Affordability was a leading factor for selection of public health care facility. Pinto and Udwadia (2010) cited reasons like poor quality with a general lack of trust in government services, lack of attention offered to patients, long waiting time, poor hygiene, suspected poor quality of drugs and lack of privacy for non-preference of public sector hospital. Similarly, another study (Chirumle and Gupta, 1997) reiterated the role of affordability, quality of medical care and availability of medical services as critical in selection of public or private health care institutions, across five different states in India.

On an average, doctors in developing countries spend less than 60 seconds in prescribing medicines and explaining the regimen to their patients, according to the WHO *World Medicine Situations 2011* that was released on 22 April 2011. As a result, only half the patients receive any advice on how to take their medicines immediately on leaving the facility. Though around 80 per cent of all prescribed medicines are dispensed, as many as 20–50 per cent of medicines dispensed are not labelled. According to the report, 'the dispensing process greatly influences how medicines are used. The WHO database shows that, on an average, dispensing time is one minute. In such circumstances, it is not surprising that patient adherence to medicines is poor. Dr Ranjit Roy Choudhry, an eminent clinical pharmacologist, said, 'The issue of doctors taking no time to explain the drugs they give to their patients is an acute problem, especially in overcrowded hospitals in India. Adherence also improves if a doctor and a patient have a rapport between themselves which develops by giving each other time'. As per report, about 60 per cent countries train their medical students on various aspects of prescribing medicines, and about 50 per cent require continuing medical education. The basic training for nurses and paramedical staff, who often do the bulk of prescribing, was even below standard – only about 40 per cent of countries give them any basic training on how to prescribe medicines (*The Times of India*, 24 April 2011).

Most private doctors work in their chambers either in the morning or evening, and some practice at multiple locations. The timing pattern of private practice primarily addresses the convenience and needs of clients. Fifty per cent of providers have a maximum patient load of 26 or more, and about 45 per cent of doctors spend less than 15 minutes on each patient. Private doctors are spending less time on clinical diagnosis, and depend more on referrals and diagnostic tests. This will have significant cost and quality implications (Bhat, 1999). Bhat (1999) survey shows that 50 per cent of private doctors occasionally refer patients to other specialists, and in one-third of cases this referral is quite frequent. When referring to specialist, the doctor generally refers the patient to particular individuals. It is evident that the private sectors attract and treat persons who can pay more hence there is already a selecting out of patients. The public sector, on the other hand, seeks to provide universal access and, therefore, the patient load is always higher than the intended capacity. These different goals set reflected mixed social background of patients and rate of patient turnover in the private and public hospitals. These differences make comparisons of efficiencies of the public and private sectors difficult and therefore generalizations are also not possible. There are difficulties in arriving at any generalization based on studies which tend to be unit specific in their comparisons. A comparison of private and public providers in Trivandrum raises some of the methodological problems in doing such an exercise (Homan and Thankappan, 1997, cited in Baru et al., 2000).

The quality of care of any service organization highly depends on the providers' skills (qualification), working conditions, attitude and wages of staff, and other social factor which is related to providers. Hospitals are labour intensive organizations which are not only merely dependent on medical expertise but also require the coordination of different levels of staff to provide quality patient care. It is not enough to have well qualified specialist alone, it is equally important to have well trained paramedical and supportive staff for ensuring good quality patient care.

Studies on private nursing homes in Bombay (Nandraj, 1994), Delhi (Nanda and Baru, 1993) and Hyderabad (Baru, 1998) have shown that paramedical and supportive staff often work at very low wages and are not qualified for the work that they do. Hence, there is a great deal of turnover of staff at these levels and they work under abysmal conditions which is bound to have a direct impact on patient care. In any hospital, it is the paramedical and supportive staff that interacts closely with patients by attending to their physical and emotional needs while the medical personnel look after the clinical aspect of treatment. Therefore, a hospital that is responsive to patients requires well trained personnel at various levels who interact with each other as a team coordinating and complimenting each other's roles. The problem of contractualizing the support staff means that it does not generate a sense of belonging and loyalty among the workers and towards the institution in which they are employed. This is definitely not conducive for building commitment among the workers towards the hospital that employs them. In fact, over worked, ill trained and insecure workers are likely to make more mistakes and hide them too. In short, the reputation of the consultant alone supported by a shaky and overstretched staff at different levels is responsible for the quality of service that is provided (Baru et al., 2000).

Health Care Provider and Pattern of Practice

The doctor is undoubtedly a professional and this status is due to his or her acquired knowledge and special skill and the position, he or she occupies in society. Therefore, the society's dependency on doctors and that realization creates a gap for mechanical practice or a culture of practice driven by hiding information.

In the private practice the desire to earn more money is undoubtedly a significant reason for irrational practice, rising cost of health care, commercialization of health, over-medicalization, unethical practice, increasing usage of technology, etc. The health care as a commodity is sold by the health care provider in the market.

As a useful commodity producer, the doctor does own his or her skill and certain instrument for providing service. The relationship between the consumer (patient) and trade person (doctor) and the technology used for curing (drugs) is no longer of old type in the sense that the industry has almost thoroughly penetrated in this relationship. Since the doctor as a professional is essential for the sale and the use of goods produced by the health care industry, he or she while acting as a small commodity producer simultaneously works as an 'agent' (or a sales person) of the industry in the market for the realization of profit. This new role of doctor is almost universal because he or she no longer gathers herbs and chemical, and compounds drugs. The increasing technological use in diagnosis and the treatment has, therefore, changed the practice of medicine from caring to mere curing. Thus, the changes in the organizational set up of individual medical practice are not limited to the change in the doctor-doctor relationship and doctor-patient relationship but the very social position of the doctor as a health care provider has changed. The doctor has, indeed, become an essential part of the market strategy of the health care industry. The convergence of the interests of the industry and the practicing doctor takes place most visibly in the for-profit medical care.

In our country, the private sector almost exclusively works on user charges. Intensive use of hi-tech equipment, irrational diagnosis, diagnosis for money, and technology for earning has become a culture of practice. The issues of over-medicalization and iatrogenesis are assertively raised by Ivan Illich (1975) and Ian Kennedy (1981). Such issues have equal relevance in our country. Indian Council of Social Science Research, or Indian Council of Medical Research (ICSSR/ICMR) Committee (1981), expressed serious concern about 50,000 drugs and formulations available in our country which are hazardous, useless, unnecessary and irrational. Such products not only harm the interests of the consumers and inculcate irrational medical practice, but also cause waste of resource and increase the cost of medical care.

The role of increasing usage of various technologies and specifically the new hi-tech instruments in medical care is well documented. Nearly 80 per cent of private health practice is based on the nexus commission and cuts between the GP and the consultant (Muralidheran, 1999). The most dominant provider payment system in India is fee-for-service. Bhat (1999) finds that 70 per cent of providers charge on a fee-for-service basis and 30 per cent charge on a case basis in which the total charges depend upon the specific services and procedures. About 47 per cent doctors use cost as the basis for charging fee and about one-third follow what others are using and use market-based data to determine their fee structure. The providers indicate that users have little influence on medical associations in deciding the fees charged by providers.

An anti-cancer drug is not only being widely and wrongly used by doctors to treat infertility in women, but is also being tested illegally on unaware patients. Letrozole, the drug has no proven use in curing infertility anywhere in the world. At least a dozen doctors were involved in the unlawful and potentially hazardous trials in Nagpur, Jodhpur, Kolkata, Hyderabad, Kottayam and Amritsar. No one bothered to take the necessary permission for the tests from the Drugs Controller General of India, a necessary requirement for any clinical trial (Patranobis, 2003).

The doctors prior to technological revolution were independent healers. They examined, diagnosed, investigated and treated the patients under one roof. They could be compared to the artisans of medieval times. In modern times, large-scale, capital-intensive diagnostic and therapeutic centres like the CT and MR Scan units and the shock-wave lithography units have been set up by businessmen. For these centres, the doctor is just a pawn in their endeavour to increase profit margins. The doctor, consciously or unconsciously, falls prey to the industry. Studies from both developed and developing countries have shown that private hospitals often discharge patients even before they are ready for it in order to maximize patient turnover and increase interventions. According to a promoter of a corporate hospital, it makes profits on beds after which the profit margins tend to fall. It is during the first few days of hospitalization and till the procedures, both surgical and non-surgical, are completed, that there is little scope for charging patients more than bed charges. The hospital is likely to be deprived of profits during the recovery phase when the patient is on drugs and nursing care. This is an important reason why private hospitals tend to discharge patients much earlier than public hospitals (Baru et al., 2000). 'Much of a private hospital's profits are derived from the usually step charges for in-patient services and diagnostic tests. It is also extracted from exorbitant bed charges' (Workers Solidarity, 2000).

The health care insurance is also introduced in the Indian market. The insurance schemes have actually helped in the increasing usage of hi-tech cost medical care in the private sector. In her study of technology use in hospitals, Lovise Russell (1979) argues that the growth of third party payment system has also diminished cost consciousness amongst the health care providers and the patients, leading to an excessive usage of technology.

The value systems of private sector medical care have come to dominate the practice of medicine. Hence, the curative care component of public sector is also greatly influenced by this value system of the private sector. As a result, one witnesses increasing illegal or unofficial private medical practice by government doctors in PHCs and hospitals. There are even agitations by doctors to make their private practice official. Some even use PHCs' medicine for the practice while sitting in the OPD of the PHC. We also find the government doctors functioning in the same way and for the same purpose as they do for doctors in the private sector.

Some scholars have written that the public sector's malfunctioning is providing scope for the expansion of the private sector. It is also necessary to assess how the private sector oriented policies of the state and the actual existence of an unnecessarily large big private sector with its dominant value system have contributed to the malfunctioning of the public sector (Jesani and Anantharam, 1989: 59). Yesudian (1994), through an opinion-based study, observes that malpractice and medical negligence seem to be rampant in the private sector. Bhat (1999) finds that over-prescription of drugs is ranked as the first major prevalent medical practice by respondents. This is followed by fee-splitting practices and inadequate measures for disposal of waste followed by over-prescription of diagnosis.

Privatization and Market

Markets are the new buzzword. They are to be left free to operate. This means freedom for capital and labour laws that have evolved over long periods of time to check the extreme forms of exploitation by capitalists are now being diluted. Markets are an institution to exchange goods and services and governed by the purchasing power of the individuals in society. They are not democratic institution, in effect, left to themselves – they lead to the marginalization of the marginal. In that sense markets are valueless. Markets are governed by the principles of 'more is better' and 'consumer sovereignty'. Individual's welfare is supposed to increase as she/he consumes more. Consumer sovereignty means that the consumer knows her/his interest best, so whatever she/he wishes to consume should be made available in the market. There should be no interference with this from any quarter. Efficiency means achieving of the wish of the consumers. This may be iniquitous in the extreme with one person having all and the others having nothing. But as long as this is consistent with the initial endowments, it is 'efficient' and in that sense the notion of market 'efficiency' is status quo.

Since 'more is better' consuming less is not desirable as it lowers the individual's welfare. Restraint is then meaningless. The notion of 'consumer sovereignty' means that the focus is on self as opposed to the collective. So both these market principles weaken the idea of community and of working towards a common goal. The idea of the notion based on a shared common goal itself weakens. Markets do not decide which goods are socially good or bad. They have no social value. Judgment about the nature of goods is made and imposed by society from outside the markets. For instance, markets do not decide that smoking is injurious to health or that cigarette advertising should not be allowed. Society decides that children should not be targeted by advertising or that sex and violence should not be targeted at them. Penetration of the markets into the social realm is undermining social values.

In the market, there is no distinction between essential and non-essential goods. All goods are alike except that their elasticity of demand differs. Hence, in economic theory, there is no need to curb the import of luxury goods or to tax them heavily. Dominant western values are being imposed on the developing nations through the media with the help of power of money and politics but above all because of the dominance over ideas.

In such a situation, there could be only two reasons for the increasing pressure or privatization. The first could be the failure to support public sector personnel to perform their duties in the skeleton comprehensive programmes which inevitably created a very 'big market' for the private sector. This is an increasing burden on the poor who are at the receiving end of this scheme of things. Two, recent nationwide surveys (NSSO, 1992; NCAER, 1992) on the pattern of utilization of medical institutions reveal that expenditure for getting treatment for diseases is the second most cause for rural indebtedness (after dowry) among these impoverished people (Qadeer et al., 2001: 47). The second could be ideological because it is easy to play along with the popular belief that public sector health care service is inferior to that provided in the private sector.

Dehumanizing Aspects and Consumer Concerns in Health Care

Decades of unregulated growth in the health care market have led to a situation wherein a vocal and powerful section of health care professionals are shamelessly and assertively declaring that the medical profession is answerable to medical profession and not to society. They defend unfair market and trade practices under the garb of professional independence. They have interpreted the new economic policy as being one which promotes market forces without enforcing any regulations and allows private practice to continue without obligations to ethics or patients/users. On the one hand, they demand the status of an industry for financial support, including the granting of status of infrastructure, providing a level field for health care, giving nursing homes the status on medical equipment, and on the other hand, they want to retain the privileges of a welfare institution. This is the outcome of a Delhi Government Report. This committee not only takes stock of the performance of the private sector and its adherence to conditional ties but also defines the role of the state in monitoring these hospitals like other industries. Health care enterprises must also adhere to rules and regulations regarding employment conditions, minimum wages for all levels of staff, and certain minimum procedures regarding pricing, billing, maintenance of medical records, financial and medical audit which are requirements for ensuring transparency and accountability to the consumer and the state.

In this era of consumerism, free market economy and information explosion, how can one empower the consumer to utilize health care services more effectively without endangering doctor-patient relationship which is based on trust? With the consumer rights, consumer responsibility gains an equal importance. An irresponsible use of the rights may lead to a distorted and expensive health care delivery as seen in the US today. In the current Indian scenario, despite great technological advances and specialization in medicine, health care still depends greatly on trust, care and compassion. Unfortunately, in the blind practise of scientific knowledge, the human side of doctor-patient relationship is often forgotten. The doctors should find time to listen to their patients and allay their anxieties. This would humanize medicine. The piecemeal and de-humanized health care that is available today causes a lot of consumer dissatisfaction and is largely responsible for the litigations in consumer protection councils.

The Consumer Protection Act in 1986 was passed to protect the interests and rights of the consumers. But the effectiveness of COPRA is in doubt also because of the number of cases pending with the courts (Bhat, 1999).

Summing Up

The adoption of a new market economy due to liberalization has resulted in different interpretations of the role of state and its relations to social welfare services and market institutions. Against this backdrop, this paper studies the private health care services and challenges brought about by the rapid marketization and the quality of health services delivered to the masses, structure and pattern of health service from providers' perspective and resultant dehumanizing issues. On the surface, the data indicate improvement in the proliferation of private health services and increase in investment of health care. However, a closer look reveals that marketization has resulted in cost escalation of health services which has deterred the accessibility to the poor sections of society and quality of health care has also degraded. The analysis suggests that there are increasing inequalities in the access to and quality of health care services as a result of the rapid and fundamental changes within the health sector.

Universalization of health care is the heart of health policy in India since Independence in 1947. The country, since then, has experienced different models to improve access to health services and ensure universal care to entire population. During the first few decades after 1947, the government had planned and invested in the development of a national and integrated network of care facilities (primary, secondary and hospital). The private sector was later on supported through public-private partnership policies in order to develop and diversify the supply of care. Targeted programmes have been implemented for patients suffering from certain particular diseases (tuberculosis, HIV/AIDS, mother and child). Programmes for health insurance have been developed over the last decade to reduce financial barriers to care for the poor (RSBY, Aarogyasri Scheme).

Despite the proliferation of governmental and private initiatives, the majority of the Indian population still has great difficulty in obtaining appropriate health care services. The lack of health centre nearby is cited as the second reason for not using government health services after the low quality of care (NFHS–3). According to the same survey, a quarter of women placed remoteness of care services as the first barrier in access to care. Along with these problems of spatial coverage, other barriers stand between patients and health care services. Health expenditures are, for example, the second cause of indebtedness of rural families. In 2004–2005, 39 million people slipped into poverty due to health spending (NSSO 2004–2005).

References

Anthoven, Alain and Richard Kronick (1989), 'A Consumer-Choice Health Plan for the 1990: Universal Health Insurance in a System Designed to Promote Quality and Economy', *The New England Journal of Medicine*, 320(1): 29–37.

Ascher, Kate (1987), *The Politics of Privatisation: Contracting Out Public Services*, London: Macmillan Education Ltd.

Auster, Richard D. and Ronald L. Oaxaca (1981), 'Identification of Supplier Induced Demand in the Health Care Sector', *The Journal of Human Resources*, XVI(3): 327–42.

Barsky, Arthur J. (1988), 'The Paradox of Health', *The New England Journal of Medicine*, 318(7): 414–18.

Baru, R.V. (1994a), 'The Rise of Business in Medical Care', *Health for Millions*, 2(1): 19–21.

—— (1994b), 'Structure and Utilization of Health Services: An Inter-State Analysis', *Social Scientist*, 22(9–12): 105.

—— (1998), *Private Health Care in India: Social Characteristics and Trends*, New Delhi: Sage Publications.

—— (2000), 'Privatisation and Corporatisation', *Seminar*, May, New Delhi.

Baru, R.V. et al. (2000), 'Medical Industry: Illusion of Quality at What Cost', *Economic and Political Weekly*, 38(28–29).

—— (2001), 'Health Sector Reforms and Structural Adjustment: A State Level Analysis', in Imrana Qadeer, Kasturi Sen and K.R. Nayar (eds), *Public Health and the Poverty of Reforms: The South Asian Predicament*, New Delhi: Sage Publications.

Bhat, R. (1996), 'Regulation of Private Health Care in India', *International Journal of Health Planning and Management*, 11: 253–74.

—— (1999a), 'Characteristics of Private Medical Practice in India: A Provider Perspective', *Health Policy and Planning*, 14(1): 26–37.

—— (1999b), 'Regulations of Private Health Sector in India', in N.B. William (ed.), *Private Health Sector Growth in Asia: Issues and Implications*, Ahmedabad: IIM.

Bhore Committee (1946), *Report of the Health Survey and Development Committee*, Vol. IV, Summary, New Delhi: Government of India.

Brown, Michael Barratt (1971), 'The Welfare State in Britain', in Miliband Ralph and Saville John (eds), *The Socialist Register: A Survey of Movements and Ideas*, London: The Merlin Press.

Business World, 22 May 1997.

Chatterjee, P. (2008), *Factors that Faster Ate Growth of Private Health Sector in India* (retrieved from medind.nic.in/hass/t08/i1p5pdf).

Chirmule, G. (1997), *Factors Affecting Health Seeking and Utilization of Curative Health Care*, Pune: Bhartiya Agro Industries Foundation.

Dilip, T.R. and R. Duggal (2004), 'Unmet Need for Public Health Care Services in Mumbai, India', *Asia-Pacific Population Journal*, 19(2): 27–40.

Duggal, R. and S. Amin (1989), *Cost of Health Care: A Household Survey in an Indian District*, Bombay: The Foundation for Research in Community Health.

Duggal, Ravi (1994), 'Health Care Utilization in India', *Health for the Millions*, 2(1), New Delhi.

Funchs, Victor R. (1978), 'The Supply of Surgeons and Demand for Operations', *The Journal of Human Resources*, 13: 35–56.

George, R. (1972), 'The Evolution of Social Medicine', in H.E. Freeman et al. (eds), *Handbook of Medical Sociology*, New Jersey: Prentice Hall.

Green, Francis and Nore Peter (eds) (1977), *Economics: An Antitext*, London: The Macmillan Press Ltd.

Green, Jerry (1978), 'Physician-Induced Demand for Medical Care', *The Journal of Human Resources*, 13: 21–34.

Harris, David (1987), *Justifying State Welfare: The New Right Versus the Old Left*, Oxford: Basil Blackwell Ltd.

Higgins, Joan (1988), *The Business of Medicine: Private Health Care in Britain*, London: Macmillan Education Ltd.

Homan, R.K. and K.R. Thankappan (1997), *An Examination of Public and Private Sector Sources of Inpatient Care in Trivandrum District, Kerala*, UNDP/GOI/DRC Research Project Report (Unpublished), Thiruvananthapurum: Centre for Development Studies.

ICMR/ICSSR Committee (1981), *Health for All: An Alternative Strategy*, Pune: Indian Institute of Education.

Illich, Ivan (1975), *Medical Nemesis: The Exploration of Health*, London: Marion Boyans.

Iyer, Ramaswamy R. (1966), 'Red Herring of Privatization', *Economic and Political Weekly*, 7 July, 1491–92.

—— (1990), 'Privatization Debate: Alternative Framework', *Economic and Political Weekly*, 7 July, 1491–92.

Jeffery, Rogers (1988), *The Politics of Health in India*, London: University of California Press.

Jesani, A. and S. Anantharam (1989), *Private Sector and Privatization in the Health Care Studies*, Bombay: Foundation for Research in Community Health.

Jesani, Amar and Sunil Nandraj (1994), 'The Unregulated Private Health Sector', *Health for the Millions*, 2(1), New Delhi.

Jones, L. (1994), *The Social Context of Health and Health Work*, New York: Macmillan.

Kennedy, Ian (1981), *The Unmasking of Medicine*, London: Allen and Unwin.

Kinzer, David (1988), 'The Decline and Fall of Deregulation', *The New England Journal of Medicine*, 14 January, 112–16.

Lee, Philip R. and Etheredge Lynn (1989), 'Clinical Freedom: Two Lessons for the UK from the US Experience with Privatization of Health Care', *The Lancet*, 4 February, 263–65.

Minocha, Aneeta A. (2011), 'The Socio-Cultural Context of Informed Consent in Medical Practice', in B.V. Baviskar and Tulsi Patel (eds), *Understanding Indian Society: Past and Present*, New Delhi: Orient Blackswan.

Muraleedharan, V.R. (1987), 'Rural Health Care in Madras Presidency, 1919–1939', *Indian Economic and Social History Review*, 24(3): 1323–34.

—— (1994), 'Diet, Disease and Death in Colonial South India', *Economic and Political Weekly*, 29(1).

—— (1999), *Characteristics and Structure of Private Hospital Sector in Urban India: A Study of Madras City*, Massachusetts: Abt Associates Inc.

Nadkrani, S. (2010), *Healthcare System in an Industry, Management of the Sick Healthcare System*, New Delhi: Vora Medical Publications.

Nanda, P. and R. Baru (1993), *Private Nursing Homes and their Utilization: A Case Study of Delhi*, New Delhi: VHAI.

Nandraj, S. (1994), 'Beyond the Law and the Lord: Quality of Private Health Care', *Economic and Political Weekly*, 2 July.

Nandraj, S. and Ravi Duggal (1995), *Physical Standards in the Private Health Sector: A Case Study of Rural Maharashtra*, Bombay: CEHAT.

NCAER (1992), *Household Survey of Medical Care*, New Delhi: National Council of Applied Economic Research.

Patel, B.K., K.N. Trivedi, S.N. Nayak and P. Patel (2010), 'Health Seeking Behaviour of Peri-Urban Community of Chandkheda', *National Journal of Community Medicine*, 1(1): 35–36.

Patranobis, Sutirtho (2003), *The Hindustan Times*, 21 December.

Paul, Samuel (1988), 'Privatization: A Review of International Experience', *Economic and Political Weekly*, 6 February, 273–36.

Pinto, L.M. and Z.F. Udwadia (2010), 'Private Patient Perceptions about a Public Programme: What Do Private Indian Tuberculosis Patients Really Feel about Directly Observed Treatment', *BMC Public Health*, 10: 356.

Planning Commission (1998), *Approach Paper to the Ninth Five Year Plan, 1997–1998*, New Delhi.

Price, Max (1988), 'Health Care Beyond Apartheid: Economic Issues in Reorganization of South Africa's Health Services', *Radical Journal of Health*, V, 3–15 June.

Purohit, B. and T.A. Siddiqui (1994), 'Utilization of Health Services in India', *Economic and Political Weekly*, 30 April.

Qadeer, Imrana (2001), 'Impact of Structural Adjustment Programmes in Concepts of Public Health', in Imrana Qadeer et al. (eds), *Public Health and the Poverty of Reforms*, New Delhi: Sage Publications.

Reddy, Venugopal (1989a), 'State, Market and Privatization: Stalemate in State-Action in India', in T.L. Sankar and Venugopal Reddy (eds), *Privatization: Diversification of Ownership of Public Enterprises*, Hyderabad: Institute of Public Enterprises, 21–52.

—— (1989b), 'Privatization of Public Enterprises: Scope and Limits', in T.L. Sankar and Venugopal Reddy (eds), *Privatization: Diversification of Ownership of Public Enterprises*, Hyderabad: Institute of Public Enterprises, 79–115.

Relman, Arnold (1984), 'The Medical-Industrial Complex', *The New England Journal of Medicine*, 22 September, 784.

Russell, Louise B. (1979), 'Technology in Hospital: Medical Advances and Their Diffusion', *Management Review*, 4(4): 86.

Sankar, T.L. and Venugopal Reddy (eds) (1989), *Privatization: Diversification of Ownership of Public Enterprises*, Hyderabad: Institute of Public Enterprises, 21–52.

—— (1990), 'Red Herring of Privatization', *Economic and Political Weekly*, 17–24 February, 407–08.

Shah, Utkarash and Ragini Mohanty (2010), 'Private Sector in India Healthcare Delivery: Consumer Perspective and Government Policies to Promote Private Sector', *Information Management and Business Review*, 1(2): 79–87.

The Times of India, 24 April 2011.

Tualaisodher, V.B. (1993), 'Expenditure Expression and Health Sector Outlays', *Economic and Political Weekly*, 6 November.

Uplekar, M.W. (2000), 'Private Health Care', *Social Science and Medicine*, 51(16): 897–904.

Vane, Howard and Caslin Terry (1987), *Current Controversies in Economics*, Oxford: Basil Blackwell Ltd.

Visaria, P. and A. Gumber (1994), *Utilization of and Expenditure on Health Care in India: 1986–87*, Gota, Gujarat: Gujarat Institute of Development Research.

Viswanathan, H. and J.E. Rohde (1990), *Diarrhoea in Rural India: A Nationwide Survey of Mothers and Practitioners*, New Delhi: Vision Books.

—— (1994), 'The Rural Private', *Health for the Millions*, 2(1): 13–16.

Winkenwerder, William and John R. Ball (1988), 'Transformation of American Health Care', *The New England Journal of Medicine*, 318(5): 43–46.

Workers Solidarity (2000), *Critical Condition: A Report on Workers in Delhi's Private Hospitals*, New Delhi.

World Bank (1993), *World Development Report: Investing in Health*, New York: Oxford University Press.

—— (1995), *India: Policies and Finance Strategies for Strengthening Primary Health Care Services*, Report No. 13042 – IN, Population and Human Resource Division, South Asia Country Department II, Washington, D.C.

Yesudian, C.A.K. (1990), 'Utilization Pattern of Health Services and its Implications for Urban Health Policy', Draft, Takemi Programme in International Health, Harvard School of Public Health.

—— (1994), 'The Nature of Private Sector Health Services in Bombay', *Health Policy and Planning*, 9(1): 72–80.

20

NGOs and Social Work in Health Care

As per estimates, the NGOs provide health care to 5 per cent of the Indian population (Hsiao and Sen, 1995). An important part of private health finance is the service provided by the voluntary and charitable organizations of India. Such groups do not account for a large share of health care, they are often the only source or only trusted source of health service to the population. The quality of health care available to the poor population in India is unacceptable. Services available through public health care facilities, which are supposed to be free, are often charged for. Moreover, private health care services available to the population are of poor quality. Many NGOs operate in India to provide preventive and curative health care services to the people. This chapter defines the meaning of NGOs and the need of NGOs in health care. It further explains the major concerns of NGOs. The basic values of social work, from promoting an individual's right to self-determination to having an attitude of empathy for the individual, are the foundation of social work practice.

Defining NGOs

In India, active involvement and initiatives of NGOs have been occurring since late 1970s. One of the criteria for defining an NGO, as given in the Seventh Plan Document, is that the organizations should have a legal identity. The Planning Commission considers societies, associations, trusts, or companies registered under the Societies Registration Act, 1860; Indian Trust Act, 1882; The Charitable and Religious Trust Act, 1920 or Section 25 of the Companies Act, 1956 as NGOs (Planning Commission, 2002). NGOs are bound by an appeal to voluntarism. The importance given to NGOs was based on the neo-liberal assumption that governments are inefficient, corrupt, inflexible, and irresponsible to the needs of the people they serve. According to the proponents of the third sector, organizations like NGOs in those sector share distinct characteristics; they possess an internal organizational structure; they are structurally separate from government, and they do not generate profit that are distributed to members (Robinson and White, 1997). Non-profit sector is increasingly central to the health and well-being of the society. They are primarily working to improve the service delivery system and have neglected their role as catalyst for social, economic and political changes favouring the poor, marginalized, and disadvantaged (Pruthi, 2006).

History of NGOs

NGO involvement in community work in an organized manner may be traced back to Christian Missionary activity. Though missionary work was introduced early in India, it proliferated most during British rule. The missionaries approached deprived and exploited communities and offered the compassion, hope and benefits (health, education, nutrition or even finances). They were motivated workers, convinced of Christian ideals and worked sincerely with the ultimate objective of proselytization.

It was only in the 19th century that various non-Christian NGOs began to evolve, mainly as a part of the efforts of Vidysagar and Raja Ram Mohan Roy to bring reform within the Hindu society. Linked to India's freedom struggle, a large number of NGOs emerged in a wide range of activities but only Gandhian/Sarvodaya organizations, besides the religious groups, may be considered for any significant consequences in the welfare sector, especially in rural areas. Until the late sixties most NGOs, especially religious missions and Gandhian/Sarvodaya groups, were primarily charity-oriented.

Charity linked to altruism did not remain confined to religious missions but also afflicted the sensibilities of large business houses. For instance, Tata at the turn of the present century began charitable work among tribals, where the city of Jamshedpur is today.

In 1952, the government of independent India, faced with the tremendous tasks of development, especially rural uplift, launched its Community Development Programme (CDP). It is interesting to note that the basis for evolving the CDP were experiments of two NGOs, one by Albert Meyer in Etawah district of Uttar Pradesh and the other by the YMCA in Martandam, Tamil Nadu. Both these models were based on earlier American experiments.

From the very beginning, the government recognized the role of NGOs in the welfare sector. The Ist Five Year Plan, during which the CDP was launched, notes: 'A major responsibility for organising activities in different fields of social welfare, like the welfare of women and children, social education, community organization, etc. falls naturally on private voluntary agencies. These private agencies have long been working in their own humble way and without adequate aid for achievement of their objectivities with their own leadership, organization and resources'.

A change in the charity organization of NGOs became apparent in the mid-1960s, till then the Green Revolution had taken the corporate sector to the countryside. The World Bank too had become supportive of anti-poverty programmes for the rural areas of the Third World because widespread famine and drought conditions had generated a lot of unrest.

The government soon realized that most of its development efforts had failed miserably, the strategy changed from charity to self-reliance. As a consequence, area development programmes were chalked out in close collaboration with NGOs as well as with the corporate sector. NGOs working in the welfare sector also moved away from the charity approach to a community approach whereby local resources were to be used for the development of the community. It was in the health sector that this new orientation first emerged. Experiments in Narangwal (Punjab) in the late 1960s showed the way but its consolidation took place in Maharshtra with the Jamkhed, Mandwa/Uran, Miraj and Kasa projects leading the field. This new approach as contrasted with charity approach has been attributed three characteristics:

- It is against giving anything free of charge.
- It is characterized by a project-brand involvement.
- It is professional in character.

The working philosophy of his new approach thus appears to be 'not to give anything free of charge' because (i) whatever is given free is not seen by people to have a value; (ii) it creates a 'feudal' relationship of donor-recipient, reinforcing 'patriarchy'; (iii) it generates a dependency among the beneficiaries and therefore makes the latter complacent; and (iv) it acts as a barrier to people's participation.

In the field of health care, the necessity for making a special effort to take health care to the underprivileged majority was recognized as early as 1946 by the Bhore Committee. But government policies generally chose to ignore the need because health care services by themselves lack political capital; it was assumed that a proliferation of health care facilities would be sufficient in themselves. On the other hand, a few non-government agencies, both Indian and foreign, did perceive the need for evolving health projects specifically targeted at areas in primary health care that were deficient and urgently needed.

The Voluntary Health Association of India (VHAI) is one of the major national networks of more than 4,000 NGOs across the country which is an association of voluntary agencies, working in the area as of health and development. Until the mid-1960s, the health sector was hospital-based, but later expanded to include community health in developmental projects. A number of NGOs took up health eduction, as part of their community programmes. Often health was used by NGOs as the entry part to communities. Several NGOs in India work on varied issues such as, livelihood and poverty and education, improving water supply and sanitation, etc. other than those providing medical care. These wider developmental issues addressed through social mobilization are known to impact individual, family and community health. Both the National Health Policies of 1982 and 2002 also highlight the expected roles of the third sector or NGOs in the health sector. These not-for-profit organizations are presently delivering curative services ranging from faith-based to community-based organizations working at the primary and secondary levels, and also a few at the tertiary level.

Role of NGOs

India was a signatory to the Alma Ata Declaration in primary health care. The NGO report presented at Alma Ata in 1978 defines the role of NGOs more clearly and indicated the NGO could:

- Provide assistance to develop and/or strengthen local NGO capabilities and activities with particular attention to local community development groups.
- Conduct reviews and assessment of existing health and developmental programmes and assist communities in the exercise of their own role in such reviews.
- Place primary health care in the context of comprehensive human development.
- Ensure that their existing programmes and new initiatives promoted full participation by individual and communities in the planning implementation and control of these programmes.
- Expand training efforts as in training of health workers, supervisors, administrators, planners and other developmental workers.
- Extend their efforts to develop locally sustainable and appropriate health technologies, and use of resources to particular attention to energy, water, sanitation and medical care.

Need for NGOs in Health Care

In a large developing country like India, there are numerous gaps in the development process between reach and requirement of services:

- Sometimes due to ignorance.
- Sometimes due to lack of willingness.
- Sometimes due to lack of awareness.
- Sometimes just due to reluctance.
- Sometimes due to non-availability of services.

The NGOs try to bridge the above gaps. The major strengths of NGOs are – experience of working with community, integrated project approach, people's faithfulness, community acceptance, innovation encouraged, transparency, need-based planning, enabling and facilitation, working in team, learning from doing and intervision (Basu, 2009).

Charitable and voluntary organizations have been contributing significantly towards various dimensions of health care of the community. NGOs have equipped themselves adequately and come up in providing services like relief to the blind, the disabled and disadvantaged and helping the government in other and child health care, including family planning programmes. As a result, all concerned have realized the strength of NGOs and their considerable merit compared to the public/private health sectors because of their staff's motivation, dedication and sympathy for the deprived sections of the society and their personalized approach towards the solution of problems. The National Population Policy, 2000 and National Health Policy, 2002 states that there should be greater involvement of NGOs in the implementation of different health and family welfare programmes in the country. In recognition of the crucial role played by them, the Government of India started granting financial aid to NGOs for various schemes. NGOs describe and discuss the common characteristics of health system functioning in the given socio-economic, socio-cultural, political and ecological settings. Many of them try to highlight and delineate crucial factors responsible for the health sector reforms and to undertake as the most challenging endeavour, effective and efficient health management and quality health care services provisions in the community. To act as a catalyst in bringing about local initiative and community participation in overall improvement in quality of life is considered as a major concern or objective of NGOs.

Major Concern of NGOs in Health Care

In the field of health, NGOs have long helped to set standards for practice, training, and continuing education and to define the role of health workers in national programmes. Today, some of the NGOs have become large institutions in their own right, providing primary care services and strengthening community action for change. Some have concentrated on a particular disease or activity (e.g. cardiovascular diseases, leprosy, tuberculosis, programmes for the disabled, etc.). The diverse programmes and competencies of numerous organizations, not directly involved in health care, also contribute in one way or another to total human development. They include projects to improve nutrition, food production and housing; provide safe water; promote literacy; provide educational and other instructional materials; further community development; provide training in broad range of skills; and protect the environment. In short, they are helping to create conditions conducive to the protection, promotion, and maintenance of health and the prevention of illness.

Inadequate sanitation facilities are a major problem to human health, especially in the neglected low-income areas and slum settlements. NGOs are actively involved in Community Sanitation Improvement Projects.

NGOs are working diligently to educate the public about the prevention of AIDS and provide support and counselling for HIV-infected persons. The additional dangers of placing value judgements on how individuals become HIV positive is one of the toughest issues being faced by NGOs that work with the people who are HIV positive. One key in the prevention of AIDS is to eliminate negative images of HIV-infected persons as projected by the media.

NGOs run health care facilities such as hospitals and clinics, providing free or subsidized medicines. Sometimes, the government takes help from the NGOs in many social, especially health care programmes like polio eradication, poverty eradication, sanitation, child and mother care, etc. which have been proved successful. The government or the international bodies like the World Bank can provide financial sustainability to many NGOs in India.

There are innovative NGOs which have come with the concept of mobile health care. Through this concept they visit different rural areas where the government and private health care is very rare to get, and provide the basic medicines and the first aid to the poor and needy people. The major sources of funding are payment/insurance schemes, national and local government support, commercial schemes (income generating activities) fund-raising activities and private donations, endowments, contributions by employers or associations, saving through cost containment measures and efficiency improvements, and international donor support.

The earlier approach of the NGOs was to set up a hospital or dispensary at a taluka level or in a densely populated village on an accessible route, most often providing free services. But since the early 1970s, there has been an increasing trend to provide health care services at subsidized costs at the doorstep of consumers through village level workers (VLS). This has come to stay; and charity, as far as free-of-charge service is concerned, it is on the decline. From 1980s onwards, civil liberty movements towards consumer action are more prevalent which in turn lead to more efficiency, efficacy and accountability.

Bhattacharjee (1996) has completed a study on 'NGOs Approaches to Health and Development in India: Strategies and Sustainability'. He observes that, in order to achieve appreciable and sustainable results, NGOs will have to make long-term commitments to the community. During its period of function, it may encounter difficulties, such as (i) shortage of trained staff; (ii) very high turnover rate of middle level staff due to low pay and uncertain future; (iii) dependency on the donor agency; (iv) rivalry between the NGOs; and (v) too much interference at the grassroots level by political parties. Many of these problems, however can be overcome if financial stability is achieved. To do so, it has to depend upon government, donors and internal resources (generated by itself). But the NGOs cannot completely rely on the government or donor, since its activities might be controlled in the interest of the donor or the government. It would then become difficult to act as a pressure group.

Financing of NGOs

The fund for NGOs are generated from various sources. Some of the NGOs generate their own funds either by charging a fee for service; by production and marketing of gods, through voluntary local donations or by a combination of all these. Many NGOs do not depend on external funding agencies to carry out their programmes. Some other NGOs largely depend on government funds. Such institutions are generally referred to as grant-in-aid institutions; they receive such grants more or less on a permanent basis.

Christian church funds constitute an important source of funding, especially in health care, and there are a large number of Mission Hospitals in the country. Most church-funded organizations are directly run by missionaries, but a few exceptions do exist. Mission organizations from various European and American countries are the main funders.

Indian corporate funding has recently emerged as an important source for rural development and welfare activities. Corporate houses may directly run NGO projects by creating their own trusts or they fund other NGOs. Corporate houses also have their trusts which fund NGOs – for instance Dorabji Tata Trust and Pirojsha Godrej Trust.

However, it is international organizations that have emerged in the last decades as the single most important source of funds for NGOs. They include international NGOs such as OXFAM and Action Aid, bilateral agencies like USAID and DANIDA, multilateral agencies like UNICEF and WHO, and private foundations like Ford, Rockefeller, Gates. Except for bilateral and multilateral agencies (who have to channelize funds through the government), all other international organizations fund NGOs directly.

Social Workers in Public Health

Social workers have been involved in the health care field since the turn of 20th century. As the social work role expanded, social workers joined other health professionals in the delivery of high quality services. Today, social workers can be found in every component of health care system.

Social Work Guiding Principles

The basic values of social work, from promoting an individual's right of self-determination to having an attitude of empathy for the individual, are the foundations of social work practice. When confronting dilemmas or needs in health care, social workers can use the principle of client self-determination in matters where clients or their proxies are faced with such issues.

Social workers have skills in cultural awareness and cultural competence, in which social work practice respectfully responds to, and affirms, the worth and dignity of people of all cultures, languages, classes, ethnic backgrounds, abilities, religions, sexual orientation, and other diverse features found in individuals. Social workers look at the person-in-environment, including all of the factors that influence the total health care experience. Social workers practice at the macro and micro level of health care and thus have the ability to influence policy change and development at local, state, and federal levels and within systems of care. Social work research in health care benefits not only individuals and families but also the very existence, effectiveness, and validation of the profession. These standards offer a guide for social workers practicing in any health care setting.

Standards for Social Work Practice in Health Care Settings

Primary mission of the social work profession is to enhance human well-being and to meet the basic human needs of all people, with particular attention to the needs of people who are vulnerable, disenfranchised, oppressed, and are living in poverty. The mission is rooted in a set of core values. These core values are embraced by social workers throughout in the profession's history. The core values of the social work are as follows: social service, justice, dignity and worth of person, importance of human relationships, integrity and competence.

In health care system which are increasingly driven by technological advances, the ethical and moral questions and dilemmas raised for clients, families and health care providers are numerous and complex. Health care settings have designed a number of different systems to ensure ethical behaviour among health care practitioners. Ethnic committees are often used to provide 'objective' reviews to health care providers and clients and families, when there is conflict between providers and clients, and families. Institutional review boards are used to protect clients from the experimentation in research projects. Social work supervision and peer consultation can also be used for solving problems. Social workers practicing in local, state, national and international health care settings require knowledge and skills to understand the health problems and address inequalities and injustices directed towards clients, organizations, and communities related to access and provision of health services.

Social workers have an ethical obligation to address the health care needs of vulnerable groups and advocate for change to ensure access to care. The training of health care professionals to achieve a level of cultural competence in understanding of practice patterns and attributes and attributes of diverse group is an essential part of basic and continuing education for all health care professionals, including social workers. Health care social workers strive to gain knowledge about health care behaviour, expenditures, reforms, insurance, health maintenance, health protective behaviours, etc. Social workers also help clients to gain access to health care as they navigate between complex service delivery systems and entitlements.

Different entities shape public and global policies in every country. Social workers must keep abreast of policies to competently help clients and to assess physical, environmental, historical, situational, cultural, and structural factors that affect health care systems. Accessibility to preventive, palliative, and curative health care depends largely on the client's ability to pay, and often, people cannot afford existing fees. In many non-profit community-based clinics, services are provided on a 'first come-first serve' basis often with a long wait time and are limited by a shortage of supplies and equipment. Increasingly, private systems of care emerge alongside public systems and other health care providers to care for the uninsured or underinsured who need health services, yet prefer to care for those who can pay fee-for-services. When these realities exist, social workers shall act as brokers, advocates, and mediators for clients.

Qualities of Social Workers

Following are the qualities that a social worker is required to possess:

Cultural Competence

Social workers shall develop and maintain an understanding of the history, traditions, values, and family systems of client groups in relation to health care. The importance of recognizing, respecting, and understanding other cultures in terms of health beliefs lays a foundation to build therapeutic alliance with clients and families. Social workers are responsible for self-reflection regarding the impact of their own cultural beliefs on their professional and personal life. Social workers in health care shall approach each client and family interaction from a perspective of cultural aspects and its awareness. This implies reluctance to stereotype individuals based on assumed group similarities and seeks instead to ask individuals that aspects of their cultural experience are meaningful in understanding a particular health care need. Social workers recognize that ethnic, cultural, spiritual, and religious factors can have an impact on health care choices and adherence to regimens of care.

Confidentiality

Appreciation of cultural influences is especially important for clients at critical health junctures, such as birth, diagnosis of a major illness, and facing the end of life. Social workers have a responsibility to assist the client and family system in observing culturally meaningful practices wherever possible. Health care social workers are expected to maintain appropriate safeguards for the privacy and confidentiality of client information. Social workers must be familiar and comply with local, state, and federal mandates related to confidentiality. Professional judgment in the use of confidential information shall be based on best practice, ethical, and legal considerations regulations. Client, families, and other professionals should be informed of the confidentiality limitations and requirements before services are initiated and in all phases of the health care experiences.

Knowledge

Social workers in health care settings shall demonstrate a working knowledge of current theory and practice and integrate such information into practice. The social worker uses knowledge about psychosocial implications of illness, injury, and health conditions to clients and families to manage and cope with the impact of their health matters. Social workers should have expertise in communication, navigating systems of care, resources, client and family coping skills and the comprehensive impact of health conditions on the client.

Essential areas of knowledge and understanding about health care include: the roles and functions of social work in health care, physiological elements of illness and their impact on psychosocial functioning of clients and their families. The legal questions, dilemmas about laws, regulations and policies affecting clients are to be dealt by a social worker. Social workers shall provide ongoing assessment, including gathering comprehensive information to use in developing interventions and treatment strategies. Assessment is a fundamental process of social work practice. Treatment and intervention strategies require to be addressed by social workers. Social work assessments in health care settings include considering relevant biomedical, psychosocial, and spiritual factors and the needs of individual client and the family. Comprehensive assessments shall address unique needs relevant to special populations, including children, people with severe and persistent mental illness, immigrants and refugees, people with substance use disorders, victims of violence or trauma, homeless people, and people with physical or psychiatric disabilities.

Treatment and Intervention

Social workers are supposed to implement treatment plans that promote client well-being and ensure a continuum of care. Planning shall be based on a comprehensive, culturally competent assessment with interdisciplinary input. Intervention and treatment plans are steps indentified by the health social worker, in collaboration with the client and with other members of the team – to achieve objectives identified during assessment. Social workers should be able to adapt practice techniques to best meet client needs within their health care settings to work effectively with individuals across the life-span, with different ethnicities, cultures, religions, socio-economic and educational backgrounds, and across the range of mental health and disability conditions.

Intervention or treatment plans may include strategies to address needs identified in the assessment information, referral. Education to individual, family, or group, vocational, educational, and supportive counselling, financial counselling and system advocacy, etc. are the main functions of a social worker.

Empowerment and Advocacy

Social workers have a responsibility to advocate for the needs and interests of clients and client systems in health care, including advocating for larger system change to improve access to care and improved delivery of services. Social workers have a special responsibility to advocate for the needs of the disenfranchised to the most vulnerable of the population at both the micro and macro levels. Social workers will identify barriers to service and actively seek to resolve them. The responsibility to advocate for quality improvement also implies a responsibility for health workers to act as advocates to expand the role of the profession, develop leadership programmes and mentor new professionals. Social workers act as educators for client, families and community and other professionals regarding disease, prevention, impact of illness and disease progression, advocacy for benefits, health maintenance, and adherence to treatment regimens. Social workers have a formal role as educators. Social workers gain knowledge and expertise in the health practice from other professionals and from formal education, work or teaching experience. They have the knowledge and skill to implement the principles of learning theories in education programmes, activities, and resources. They communicate and collaborate with departments and other staff to foster client education. They service with other members of the health care team for programme and resource development, planning, implementation and evaluation.

Team Work Spirit

Social workers should have the team work spirit. A social worker participates in multiple care teams, which are typically interdisciplinary. These teams often provide comprehensive care and information in a client's home, inpatient health and mental health care settings. As a part of such teams and collaborations, social workers shall demonstrate the ability to understand the mission and functions of the service organization or group for which the social worker is employed. He/she should also understand the role of other relevant professions and organizations and communicate and cooperate appropriately. The size of the social work staff shall represent the scope and the complexity of the organization and the nature and number of population to be served. Both the health care organizations and the social work leader and staff have joint responsibility for establishing and maintaining a workload that allows for adequate and appropriate interventions and monitoring of services and outcomes. Workload consists of any social work function performed for the purpose of the social work position, including direct practice, administration, policy, research or education. The workload also reflects the demands of the population served and may include social work coverage outside of regular office hours. The importance of clear, concise, and organized documentation reflects the hallmark of quality social work services and often serves as the mode of communication between a social worker and other professionals and clients. There are core elements that need to be included and responsibilities to follow in record keeping.

Close Contact with Research

Social workers should understand the research planning, methodology, evidence based outcomes, and programme evaluation. Social workers have a responsibility to be familiar with the literature crucial to their area of practice. As professionals, social workers in all settings have a mandate to improve the knowledge of the field and this can best be accomplished through participation in research activities. Social workers should have sources of rich data that will permit opportunities for qualitative and quantitative research. Clinical trials (methodological assessments of the safety and efficacy of new treatments or new methods for administering existing treatments) help to answer scientific questions and in turn depend on the committed participation of social worker. Social workers may help physicians, nurses, pharmacists, and others to recruit individuals and encourage study participation and adherence to medication regimens. They can also help clients to manage problems that may hinder adherence and retention, such as challenging life circumstances and demands from family members.

Performance of Social Workers

Health care social workers shall be a part of ongoing, formal evaluation of their practice to assess quality and appropriateness of services, to improve practice and to ensure competence. Social workers are trained to facilitate improvements that alter the processes in which health care is delivered. They are ethically charged to promote process improvements that will enhance patient or consumer safety, satisfaction, efficient and effective care, and identify and promote best practices and equitable care on a multidisciplinary basis. The evaluation of social work practice is a vital part of social work service delivery. The methods to evaluate such practice include peer review, self-evaluation, supervision, and other research methods. Increasingly, social work outcomes from evaluations are used for position justification, performance review, and social work standards for practice, goal setting, and research efforts. Using appropriate tools such as clinical indicators, practice guidelines, consumer satisfaction surveys and measures, and standardized performance assessments, are used for further improving the said work practice in health care.

Access to Information and Technology

Health care social workers should have access to computer technology and the internet, as the need to communicate electronically and seek information on the Web for purposes of education, networking, and resources is essential for efficient and productive practice. Health care professionals, including social workers, communicate, learn, educate, and document using computer technology on a daily basis. Social workers need initial and ongoing training in technology applications relevant to their practice, including clinical care, research policy, education, resource funding and administration. Social workers shall continue to follow guidelines for privacy with regard to confidential information of the client, family or health care providers.

Summing Up

The Indian Constitution still does not recognize health as a basic human right. Yet, NGOs have used this rationale of social justice to target specific sub-population – the tribals, the scheduled castes, those living in slums, or those in the most poor in rural settings. NGOs have tried to achieve equity by identifying these disadvantaged and serving their health needs. The NGO sector plays a vital role in health care particularly for the poor and the areas where accessibility to health care is negligible. In order to achieve appreciable and sustainable results, the NGOs have to make long-term commitments to the community. In the functioning, the NGOs often encounter difficulties, such as shortage of trained staff, dependency on the donor agency, rivalry between the NGos and too much interference at the grassroots level by the political parties. The basic values of social work, from promoting an individual's right and self-determination to have an attitude of empathy for the individual, are the foundations of social work practice. As professionals, social workers in all settings have a mandate to improve the knowledge of the field and this can best be accomplished through participation in research activities.

References

Basu, B. (2009), *Changing Role of NGOs: From Project Implementation to Local Health System Development*, West Bengal Health Voluntary Association, India.

Bhattacharjee, S. (1996), 'NGO Approaches to Health and Development in India: Strategies and Sustainability', M.A. Dissertation, Belgium: Prins Leopold Instituut Voor Tropische Geneeskunde.

Hsiao, W.C. and P.D. Sen (1995), *Cooperative Financing for Health Care in Rural India*, International Workshop on Health Insurance, Bangladesh.

Planning Commission (2002), *The Tenth Five Year Plan*, Government of India, New Delhi.

Pruthi, R.K. (2006), *NGO in the New Millennium*, Delhi: Saad Publications.

Robinson, M. and G. White (1997), 'The Role of Civic Organizations in the Provision of Social Services', *Working Paper*, United Nations University, WIDER.

Section V

Health Policy, Planning and Development

21

History of Health Care in India

The presentation of the history of public health is especially oriented to the interests of public health practitioners in India. The history of public health can capture the attention of practitioners by playing on themes that relate the past to the present. Henry E. Sigerist believed that history is an essential discipline in training health professionals; those working in practical and policy-related positions needed perspective that could only be provided through the knowledge of the past.

Establishment of Medical Services in India

The history of western medicine in India dates back to 1600 AD, when the first medical officers arrived in India along with the British East India Company's first fleet of surgeons on board. In 1757, the East India Company established its rule in India, which led to the development of civil and military services. A medical department was established in Bengal far back in 1764, for rendering medical services to the troops and servants of the Company. At that time, it consisted of four head surgeons, eight assistant surgeons, and 28 surgeons' mates. In 1775, Hospital Boards were formed to administer European hospitals comprising of the Surgeon General and Physician General, who were in the staff of the Commander-in-Chief of the Royal Indian Army. In 1785, medical departments were set up in Bengal, Madras, and Bombay Presidencies with 234 surgeons. The medical departments involved both military and civil medical services. In 1796, hospital boards were renamed as medical boards to look after the affairs of the civil part of the medical departments. In 1857, the Indian Rebellion led to the transfer of administration of India to the Crown and different departments of civil services were developed. It was not until 1868 that a separate civil medical department was formed in Bengal. In 1869, a Public Health Commissioner and a Statistical Officer were appointed to the Government of India. In 1896, with the abolition of the presidential system, all three presidential medical departments were amalgamated to form the Indian Medical Services. Medical departments were under the control of the Central Government until 1919. The Montgomery-Chelmsford

Constitutional Reforms of 1919 led to the transfer of public health, sanitation, and vital statistics to the provinces. This was the first step towards the decentralization of health administration in India.

Health in British India

Mckeown (1988) and others, some 30 years ago argued that modern medicine had little effect on mortality before the latter half of the 20th century, and that progress before the time must be explained broadly in terms of 'profound changes in conditions of life'. More specifically, he assigned an important role to improved nutrition, rising incomes, and the beginnings of environmental sanitation. The thesis that mortality had declined because of rising living standards was initially offered as a residual explanation, after all other likely causes had been ruled out. But responding to criticisms in his published work, he also sought to support it on extensive experience of infectious disease in relation to nutrition in the Third World. The evident assumption is that conditions in present-day Third World countries are reasonably similar to those in the no longer observable pre-industrial West.

The power of modern medicine and sanitation, banished from the vital revolution in the west by McKeown, was reinstated by S.H. Preston to explain the rapid population growth in many backward countries between 1940 and 1970. He, too, proceeded by using Mckeown's process of successively excluding various causes, within the residual effect being attributed to a residual cause (Preston, 1975). It must be evident that if Preston is correct, then modern studies of the Third World cannot depend upon the understanding of early European experience, as modern medicine must have altered the epidemiological profile of the population substantially. An explanation similar to Preston was developed for the State of Kerala by Panikar and Soman in a book, *Trenchantly,* criticized by Imarana Qadeer for weaknesses in its evidence and its 'bias in favour of medical technology' (Panikar and Soman, 1987). Her review also noted that several major diseases began to decline before medical interventions could have had any effect. The technological or technocratic approach to health has been acerbically criticized by D. Banerji, who argued:

> A closer examination of the impact of services provided at various health institutions on the incidence and prevalence rates of the major health problems might reveal that it can account for only a fraction of the decline in the rates. The major impact is due to improvements in the socio-economic conditions and due to biological changes in the host and in the causative agents as part of the wider ecological changes (Banerji, 1992).

Finally, Ewbank and Preston commented on deficiencies in earlier studies, as those by Mckeown and Preston himself, and particularly criticized the unjustified application of labels to essentially explained variation: 'specific features of living standards or medical and health practices that were implicated in the mortality decline were named but never properly justified.

They went on to suggest that changes in these are capable of substantially altering mortality levels' (Ewbank and Preston, 1989).

Guha (2001) found that the nutritional status of British soldiers was relatively good and probably superior to that of the Indian soldiers and even the Indian soldiers must have mentioned a nutritional status above the average of say, the bottom half of Indian population. Although the relation between nutritional status and mortality is not a simple one – and it is possible that the link, often seen between economic distress and enhanced mortality, acted by gendering epidemics among the poorer classes that went on to affect the better fed as well. Military death rates of the healthiest period, 1910–1914, for a well-fed, well-housed, well-tended and reasonably educated population were, for both men and women, 50 per cent higher than those of the Indian population during the 1970s, and 100 per cent higher than those of 1986. This was true of the Indian soldiers also, so genetic composition or acclimatization cannot account for it. As regards infant mortality, however, the army record was much superior to India during the 1970s, somewhat better even than during the 1980s.

How is This to be Explained?

As clue is perhaps offered by Nigel Crook's (24 January 1992) that the equally striking present-day differences in morality between urban and rural India, may, in part, be attributed to the easier availability of health care and causative facilities in town. Is modern technology the answer to our conundrum as well? It would certainly be difficult to explain the differences in morality of the two populations in terms of better nutrition, housing, or sanitation. Then, has the fusillade of the magic bullets of modern science routinely and randomly loosened off at India's towns and villages struck home more often than has been thought to be possible?

Adults in their twenties are strong enough to resist infections and sufficiently important to the household to demand and receive medical care; infants, on the other hand, cannot easily make their needs felt, and in any case succumb quickly to illness. Infants, therefore, would benefit strongly from the campaign of macro and micro sanitation carried out by the army; new curative methods will have a more dramatic effect on the health of the adults. Preventive medicines have lagged behind curative medicine in independent India.

In the early period of the British rule, apart from providing health care to the army of the East India Company, its medical officers extended their services to British civilians through dispensaries, district and jail hospitals. This rudimentary Indian Medical Service (IMS) was considered after the Mutiny of 1857. Though Sanitary Commissioners were appointed in 1869, the work of sanitation remained confined to the cantonments. No investments were made for the general population on the pretext of not imposing reforms on people. It was only the threat of loss of revenue and trade caused by epidemics such as malaria, cholera, and plague that finally changed the colonial policy in favour of interventionist strategies.

A Sanitary Policy, enunciated in 1914, acknowledged the importance of proper survey and studies. Yet, the bacteriological research wing was moved out of the sanitary commissioner's charge and given to the IMS wing on the basis that it interfered with their touring and that non-separation of research and clinical work deterred men from entering the clinical departments (GOI, 1927). While the IMS administration alone was formally under military administration, the latter also used the provincial services. For example:

- It helped retain large army reserves over peace time.
- Provincial services kept the army doctors and trained them in handling large populations.
- Civil posting was a carrot offered to the European doctors, who found it remunerative as they could do private practice.
- The IMS officers ensured for the while civilian population care from physicians of their own colour and creed.

The indifference of the British Government to the plague epidemic until it threatened Bombay's trade (Catanach, 1989), and its neglect of famines conveys the nature of British concern about the problem of health in India.

Apart from the political control of the health department, there were also internal adjustments within the health services structure. After the mutiny, the amalgamation of the IMS and the Army Medical Division of Her Majesty's Service (AMD) was considered between 1860–64. It was proposed that a royal medical service be constituted with complete authority vested with the Government of India. A subordinate civil medical service was also proposed. This was not acceptable to the military department as it neither wished to give up control over AMD nor lose the provincial control through the IMS (Crawford, 1914). On the one hand, the army held the IMS captive and on the other, the newly awakened political forces pressed for expansion of services, Indianization, and rural health services. The demand for civil medical services was raised in the Legislative Assembly by professional associations and Indians (Government of India, 1921, 1991). The importance of rural services too was accepted because of the constant threat of epidemics and the inability of provincial services to reach out to the villages. The 1914 public health policy talked of travelling dispensaries, local organizations, voluntary agencies, disinfection of wells, and sanitary activities, but the paucity of funds in the provincial governments restricted the building of an effective infrastructure. The services were not only inadequate but also totally unrelated to social conditions. By 1926, only 13 per cent of the population has access to the civil hospitals (Government of India, 1949). The medical and sanitary activities for the public were, in fact, a part of the 'noble task' of civilizing the 'native' and controlling the 'untamed tropical environment.' Disease was a reflection of social and moral inferiority and biological determinism inspired by Darwin's ideas while justified the weak and the vulnerable perished (Arnold, 1989). In other words, the British rationalized both their action and inaction in the medical field.

The British adopted the strategy of legislative control and provided limited services to the masses. The vaccination against small pox, cholera and plague were inadequate in terms of coverage as well as in terms of availability and supply of quinine (GOI, 1936).

The army showed a decline in mortality rate as compared to general population in early 20th century. However, the reasons for stark contrast in mortality were never explored. Instead, the tropical climate and the unwillingness of the natives to make use of a 'superior' science were considered sufficient explanations. The differences in their living conditions, and access to and availability of food, apart from the age differences, were completely ignored. The link between famine and disease, which was repeatedly recorded, was not taken seriously and hunger was taken for granted among the general population. It was seen as an outcome of their 'lifestyles' and backwardness rather than an outcome of the British agricultural and economic policies.

The discipline of public health in early 19th century Britain was dominated by the sanitarians. Cantonments were the focus of sanitary activities. Germ theory replaced the sanitarian popularity. The causal theory of indigenous local conditions give rise to disease was, thus, never given up. Similarly, while the science of nutrition influenced British welfare policies to introduce feeding programmes for the vulnerable, in the sub-continent the idea was entertained only after the vast devastation caused by the Bengal Famine of 1942.

Critical Evaluation of Health Care during British Period

In British India, the policy for health services was not necessarily guided by the trends and principles of public health as it evolved in Britain. The military and political interests shaped the services till the 1940s. This points towards the overreaching power of economic, political, and social factors on the use of science. As a result, public health efforts that was evolved was fragmented and imbalanced. Political compromises were made through Indianization and expansion but with an eye to retaining subtle political control and reducing cost. Research was highly centralized, focused on bacteriological and clinical medicine, and controlled by the medical department. For all this, a series of structural adjustments were made. Establishment of voluntary and charitable health care institutions by the elite was encouraged to cut down state costs and enhance the philanthropic image of the government. These trends had a deep impact on the growth of public health structures and ideas after Independence.

Health Care in India before Independence

The Indian National Movement not only compelled the British Government to set up the Health Planning and Development Committee in 1944 (GOI,

1946) but it also set up its own sub-committee on health under the National Planning Committee in 1944 (National Planning Committee 1948). The Gandhian and People's Plans along with Sokhey Committee emphasized the role of agriculture and health of the people in rural areas. People's Plan held the state solely responsible for health. The Bombay Plan held it responsible for infrastructure but not for controlling the private sector in health. Both the Sokhey and Bhore Committees proposed banning private practice by public sector doctors while leaving the private sector to wither away with the growth of the public sector.

The notion of technological excellence remained common to the two ideological opponents – the Bombay Plan and People's Plan. Both visualized the best hospitals and technologies for disease control. The former through initial dependence on foreign countries for 'machines and technical skills'; the latter through equity as an incentive to generate and acquire technology. Both saw doctors and nurses as the key personnel in health care. Only the Bhore and Sokhey Committees talked of short-term training to health assistants, while the Gandhian Plan emphasized people's role in self-care.

Independent India and Health Care

Many Third World societies have experienced substantial declines of mortality since World War II, at much lower levels of living, and much more quickly, than in the historical experiences of developed countries. Mortality rates in poor countries seem more responsive to improvements in living conditions than to other changes; yet over this period, living standards, at least as measured by conventional indicators of economic growth, have not improved dramatically and sometimes have been stable or declined. The availability of powerful techniques to attack the transmission of many of the common diseases of poverty, such as malaria, cholera, and small pox may be crucial. In industrialized countries, these diseases gave way to the more general improvements in living standards, hygiene, and environmental health provisions, such as protected water supplies. However, the possibilities provided by disease-specific health policies may be limited by poverty (Ruzicka and Hansluwka, 1982). The available evidence suggests a steady decline in mortality in India since 1947 despite the slow fall in its major component, infant mortality. The expectation of life at birth has risen, but life expectancy at age five has risen more decisively still. Mortality might continue to fall in the immediate future. Yet poverty indicators show no overall decline (despite a rise in per capita national income); inequality in consumption has not noticeably fallen; unemployment has risen and so has landlessness; and indicators of nutritional status remain poor. Indicators of specific infectious diseases show dramatic declines (especially malaria and small pox, but also plague and cholera) so it is tempting to conclude that specific disease-control programmes have caused the decline in mortality. Yet this conclusion flies in the face of most assessments of Indian public health provisions, which point to their urban, curative bias and to the inadequacies of single-disease programmes in improving public health (Jeffery, 1988). Mortality has continued to decline since Independence, though it has not fallen steadily. Mortality fell relatively little, if at all, in the decade around 1970s. It has not fallen equally for all age groups, though if the official estimate of infant and child mortality before 1970 is corrected upward, the variation by age becomes less significant. Mortality has fallen more in states that already had low mortality rates than in those with higher ones. Male-female differentials seem to have worsened until 1970, perhaps because men received more of the early benefits from improved medical services up till then. These declines cannot easily be explained by reference to the increase in per capita income, since there is no evidence of this having benefitted the poorest sectors of the population.

According to Jeffery (1988), two factors might help to explain the apparent paradoxes of substantial declines in mortality, stable or declining per capita food grain availability, no change in the proportion of the population below poverty level, and little reason to believe the general health services provided by the state have been very effective. First, protection from famine has probably continued to be effective. Several measures, all flawed because they leak and leave the very poor in vulnerable and insecure positions, probably do prevent the poor from starving to death. Second, public health measures may have been more effective than they have usually been credited for, an argument that will be assessed.

Independent India started charting its own trajectory based on the liberal ideas by building infrastructure with a system of providing basic health services to the common people. In the 1st and 2nd Five Year Plans the priority was given to building infrastructure, water supply and sanitation, and maternity and child health. In both, health sector planning was visualized as a technical and managerial exercise. The central problem of poverty was left for the economic planners after recognizing the link between poverty and disease. This separation led to a disjunction between nutritional planning, agricultural policies, sanitation, control of communicable and occupational diseases, and welfare sector planning.

The health sector could not remain isolated over the 3rd and 4th Five Year Plans. Not only did the rate of expansion of infrastructure slow down, but there was also a shift from building peripheral health centres and training paramedical professionals to hospitals and specializations. Vertical technocentric programmes were accepted for disease control and maternal and child health services were kept separate from the vertical Family Planning Programme (FPP) with the fear that they may suck all the funds given their very poor status. Force and coercion became the hallmarks of FPP and the height of arrogance was reached during the Emergency when officially inflicted atrocities became the main reason for the downfall of the Congress Government in 1977.

After this experience, some adjustments were made in terms of expanding the primary health centre network in rural areas under the Minimum Needs Programme, Community Health Guide Scheme at the village level, and a move toward integrating services for nutrition, MCH, FPP, and malaria into general health services (GHS) (GOI, 1974). The last in the series of these comprehensive strategies was the acceptance of the Alma-Ata Declaration in 1978. The crunch came in the 1980s. The national debt by then was of an order that the Indian ruling class could no longer keep the common man hopeful while taking care of itself. It made its choice, no doubt at the cost of the poor. The Five Year Plans were undermined to give space to market forces, welfare sectors were drastically pruned and handed over to the private sector, and dependence replaced the goal of self-sufficiency in the name of globalization and one world.

Liberalization and Health Sector

Health sector reforms or health care system reforms are important initiatives taken in India to address national health and health care problems and priorities. Health sector reforms are the sustained economic processes and the approaches of fundamental and purposive changes in the policy of macro and micro level financing of production, consumption/utilization and distribution of health goods and services at all levels. Organizational and managerial aspects may be important, but financing is the key process of health sector economic reforms which do affect organizational and managerial aspects and also the reach of the service delivery to people.

Health sector reforms include financing of institution, organizations and also all the stakeholders responsible for and as partners of health development. Although, in this approach and process, the policy formulation and guidance have to be taken up by government at all levels, yet, in implementation of economic strategies and financing of health programmes, emanating from policy directions for reforms, all concerned partners, including various sectors, non-governmental organizations and community groups are required to play their due role.

Strategic support for financing health sector is workable, directly through capacity building, promotion of service delivery, promotion of research and development through specific allocations and also utilizing the 'out of pocket expenses' and the external finding from bilateral and international organizations and sources like WHO, World Bank, UNDP, etc. In tune with it, structural adjustment policies, in general, were introduced in 1991 by the Indian Government to seek fiscal austerity through cutting government expenditures and subsidies in social sector – reducing direct taxes, liberalizing trade through extension of incentives to foreign investments, etc. No doubt, such economic policy uses 'free market ideology' as the guiding principle and is designed to place 'market' in a central position, but, of course, it proves people-friendly nature of governance and regulation by State in the event of 'market failure' and any moral hazards (Sharma, 1999).

There are aspects of external aid, General Agreement Trade and Tariff (GATT) prices of pharmaceutical products and issues related to Intellectual Property Rights (IPRs), etc. which are also important and have relevance to financing and efficient utilization of financial resources to be analysed in the light of economic reforms and liberalization in India. Particularly the aspects of generic resources, i.e. medicinal plants, and also our traditional system of medicine, may definitely have effects on them. Health care is one of the fields in which specific advances can be made in a relatively short time. Health is a signal of development. Health care enables the people to give a concrete meaning to the ideas of equity, social justice and pursuit of a better of life through improvement in their own health status and of their kith and kin.

Growth of private medical sector became possible due to the direct sponsorship of government financing. While setting up of medical colleges and producing a large number of allopathic medical graduates over the years, government was not realizing fully well that more than 60–70 per cent doctors were likely to work for private medical sector only. This became more rapid during the years of initiating of structural adjustments and formal economic reforms in 1990s. After the economic reforms began, the process of State's supporting was further activised to enhance privatization in health by providing economic aids and recognition to private medical colleges in India. The support was provided in various forms, such as indirect financing to private medical sector, liberalizing the conditions of land subsidies, etc. to private and corporate hospitals in mega cities.

Diminishing role for the government would manifest itself in terms of its broad cuts and slashing of government expenditure in the beginning. Later, government may like to withdraw, may have to confine more on those characterized health-related efforts – mostly concerned with public and merit goods and services. State financing and expenditure will decline or remain stagnant at the earlier lower levels. This may affect proportionate meeting of the rising demand due to high rate of increase in population, in addition to the existing very large base of population and the changing age composition, adding newer and higher demands emanating from ageing population due to their chronic, serious and acute emergency health problems. These clubbed and complex situations – that is demographic and epidemiological transition; cutbacks in government financing for state-run free health-care institutions and services, etc. advances in medical technology and its promotion; and a high inflation rate – would affect the poorer sections of rural and urban population and unemployed more seriously over a period of time. The experiences of other developing countries corroborate these ground realities (Sharma, 1999).

Summing Up

The history of health care in India demonstrates the social production of health and disease, the placing of physicians and public health practitioners within their social context, shoving how their changing ideas and practices related to the larger framework of political and economic conditions. In the British period, services such as railways, roads, and postal systems become popular because common people could appreciate their value for their own welfare. In the area of public health, people's experience with health campaigns was very limited and often negative because of the use of force and coercion as in the plague epidemic and early variolation, the practice of inoculating someone with the virus of small pox and vaccination campaigns. Medical services were restricted and people's experience of public health was barely sufficient to generate confidence in it. After Independence, programmes against malaria, small pox, and tuberculosis did reach out to people, though in a limited way. However, given their curative nature, they only strengthened the hold of clinical medicine on popular imagination. The only exception was vaccination against smallpox. In spite of most disease prevention programmes being therapeutic in nature, the preventive significance of mass therapeutics never became a popular perception. Urban middle class took civic amenities for granted and pressed for better and more hospitals, the poor despite realizing the value of shelter, water, and food for health never could perceive these as part of public health facilities (Qadeer, 2001). Hence, both classes shared a mind-set where health service system was synonymous with curative services. Similarly, while the planners and politicians, in a hurry to show results, depended heavily upon technology at the cost of improving environment and living conditions of people, the poor too, saved time by seeking cures when actually sick, instead of losing wages to take preventive action.

References

Arnold, D. (1989), 'Introduction: Disease, Medicine and Empire', in D. Arnold (ed.), *Imperial Medicine and Indigenous Societies*, Delhi: Oxford University Press.

Banerji, Debabar (1992), 'Political Economy of Public Health Practice in India', paper presented at the Workshop of Health and Development in India, New Delhi, 2–4 January.

Catanach, I.J. (1989), 'Plague and the Tensions of Empire: India, 1896–1918', in D. Arnold (ed.), *Imperial Medicine and Indigenous Societies*, Delhi: Oxford University Press.

Crawford, D.G. (1914), *A History of the Indian Medical Service, 1600–1913*, Vol. 2, London: Thacker and Co., 268, 298, 301.

Ewbank, D.C. and S.H. Preston (1989), 'Personal Health Behaviour and the Decline in Infant and Child Mortality: The United States 1900–30', paper presented at the Health Transition Workshop, Canberra, 15–19 May.

Government of India (1921), Resolution in Legislative Assembly by B.S. Kamath regarding Reorganization of Medical Services in India, Department of Education (Medical), File No. 23–26, New Delhi: National Archives of India.

—— (1927), *India Sanitary Policy, 1914*, Calcutta: Central Publication Branch.

—— (1936), *Annual Report of Public Health Commissioner*, Vol. 1, 54.

—— (1946), *Report of the Health Survey and Development Committee* (Chairman Sir Joseph Bhore), Delhi: Manager of Publications.

—— (1949), *Indian Statistical Abstract.*

—— (1974), *Minimum Needs Programme*, Draft Fifth Five Year Plan, 1974–79, New Delhi: Planning Commission.

—— (1991), *Resolution of Delhi Medical Association*, Department of Home (Medical), File No. F. 48/49, New Delhi: National Archives of India.

Guha, Sumit (2001), *Health and Population in South Asia: From Earliest Time to the Present*, London: Hurst and Co.

Jeffery, Roger (1988), *The Politics of Health in India*, Berkeley, CA: University of California Press.

McKeown, Thomas (1988), *The Origin of Human Disease*, New Delhi: Oxford University Press.

National Planning Committee (1948), *Sub-Committee on National Health: Report of the Sokhey Committee*, Bombay: Vera Publications.

Panikar, P.G.K. and C.R. Soman (1984), *Health Status of Kerala: Paradox of Economic Backwardness and Health Development*, Trivandrum: Centre for Development Studies.

Preston, S.H. (1975), 'The Changing Relationship between Mortality and Level of Economic Development', *Population Studies*, 29(2): 231–48.

Qadeer, Imrana (2001), 'Impact of SAPs on Concepts in Public Health', in Imrana Qadeer, Kadturi Sen and K.R. Nayar (eds), *Public Health and the Poverty of Reforms: The South Asian Predicament*, New Delhi: Sage Publications.

Ruzicka, L.T. and H. Hansluwka (1982), 'Mortality Trends in South and East Asia: Technology Confronts Poverty', *Population and Development Review*, 8(3): 567–88.

Sharma, B.B.L. (1999), 'Financing Health Care Reforms: An Overview of Issues', *The Indian Journal of Public Administration*, XLV(4): 763–81.

22

Health Policy in India

Retrospect and Prospect

Health care planning in India has undergone substantial changes since its first comprehensive formulation in 1946 in respect of its form, structure, application and of its access to the Indian populace in general. During the post-Independence era, India has initiated, made frameworks and implemented several indigenous programmes along with entering also into global partnership with experts in the field, but so far the results have not been very encouraging. Thus, the objective of the millennium programme, combining clear theoretical thought and idealistic application which is dependent on the attainment of the previous, remained unfulfilled to a large extent. This was attempted to be overcome through adopting a multi-sectoral approach at various levels of the programme through training and employing skilled workers, but it still did not percolate to the grassroot and the health and family welfare programme still called for a lot more to be desired. The single factor of its failure lay in the fact that the available infrastructural facilities catered only to 20 per cent of the population. The remaining eighty per cent of the people's health need were being met with by private health care agencies. Restricted access to health facilities led to a higher incidence of morbidity and mortality. Furthermore, it forced people, especially in rural pockets, to incur heavy indebtedness through borrowing and their inability to pay back, and the vicious cycle caused, to a good measure, even in urban areas, for people to suffer from poverty, malnutrition and poor health.

Concept of Health Development

The concept of health development is founded on the premise that strategies of health sector reforms are important 'initiatives' in a country intended to address health care problems and priorities. Health sector reforms are a significant process in which structural and organizational changes may take place with the express intention of achieving health care objectives. In this paper, the policy formulation and guidelines suggested in different reports of the health commissions and various committees established by government at all levels have been examined. Here, our prime concern remains to discuss health care planning which is primarily related to the health policy and development with reference to India, since Independence.

Objectives of Health Care Planning

Health care planning in India has a number of objectives. Among the three most important are (a) keeping up with modern developments in the field of allopathic and other medicines, (b) making medical care and medical education relevant to India's needs, and (c) increasing the access of the masses to the modern and other medicines. Several committees appointed by the central government since Independence have periodically reviewed the progress made in health planning. We have also discussed alternative viewpoints for a health policy, which are claimed to be more relevant to the local conditions and provide a wider access to people. Various aspects of the National Health Policy of India 2002 along with recent National Rural Health Mission of 2005 have also been analysed in this unit.

Health Policy and Planning in India Just After Independence

With the advent of British Rule, every facet of Indian life – including the medical and public health services – was subordinated to commercial, political and administrative interests of the imperial state in the United Kingdom and its representatives in India. However, along with their own, the Britishers also permitted native Indian elite to avail modern health care. Keeping in view the constitutional directions aiming at elimination of poverty and ill health, the Government of India, soon after Independence, planned several approaches for health care delivery. The basis of the health development policy in India was laid in the recommendations of the Health Survey and Development Committees namely, Bhore Committee as early as in 1946, Mudaliar Committee (1961), Chadah Committee (1963), Mukherjee Committee (1965), Jungalwala Committee (1967), Jain Committee (1968), Kartar Singh Committee (1973), and Srivastava Committee (1975). Besides the Committees, inputs have been provided by some studies on health policy, which were conducted by autonomous institutions like the ICSSR and the ICMR. The important recommendations by these committees can be thematically grouped under the following: (a) for improving the existing institutional structure of health care delivery system, (b) to improve the supporting services for a proper and quick delivery of medi-care facilities, and (c) to improve the quality of the delivery system thereby improve the health standard of the masses (Nagla, 1993). Health care planning has undergone changes in its structure, personnel and in its acccss to the populace on the basis of recommendations made by different committees. Nagla (1993) has highlighted the enormous efforts made by the various committees to chart out the growth of health manpower in India. The works of these committees have, however, been subject to serious data limitations. Information on different categories of health personnel, their priorities and distribution (especially in respect with professionals outside the public sector) has been rather scanty. The various committees and even institutions like the ICSSR/ICMR study group have been focusing on providing expert opinions rather than garnering accurate statistical data. No committee has been able to take into account the contribution of non-governmental health institutions and that of professionals in rendering health care services. Perhaps, more importantly, the committees have been unable to assess the health care needs of the people through field surveys and ascertain the extent of utilization of health care institutions and practitioners (Yesudin, 1981). Introduction of economic reforms and liberalization has created space for social insurance schemes introduced by public sector Life Insurance Corporation and private insurance companies, introducing medical insurance policies, was the initiation of public-private mix for health care support in India.

Health for All by the year 2000 AD

The low access to the basic health care facilities is a common phenomenon in most of the developing countries. In order to provide minimum basic health facilities, it was resolved by the Health Assembly of the WHO to launch a movement known as 'Health for All by the year 2000 AD'. In 1978, the Alma-Ata conference reaffirmed Health for All as the major social goal of all governments. In 1981, a global strategy for this programme was adopted by the WHO, which was later endorsed by the United Nations General Assembly. India is a signatory to those declarations and has made efforts to extend health facilities to the vulnerable sections of its society.

'Health for All' has been defined as attainment of 'a level of health that will enable every individual to lead a socially and economically productive life' (Government of India, 1982). By 2000 AD, this concept implied a substantial change in basic health policies and in approaches to health care. In order to provide minimum health facilities, the government of India along with state governments increased the allocation of resources to the health sector. On the whole, it appeared that there was tremendous investment in widening the health infrastructure, which included within its purview a variety of programmes and viewed health and humans as a vital component of overall socio-economic development. A group set up jointly by the ICSSR and ICMR with Dr Ramalingaswami as the Chairman came up with an alternative strategy to achieve health for all citizens. It suggested certain steps for restructuring the health care service infrastructure based on the principle of promoting the preventive and curative aspects of health. This group felt that 'the growth of health care services in the country has been haphazard and unrelated to the needs of poor and rural people who stand most in need of health care'. The group remarked that several assumptions on which the present system is based were wrong. For instance, there was no distinction between planning for health and for health services so that, little or no attention has been paid to the social, economic, political and cultural dimensions of health. The recommendations of the study group were more practical and provided details of health services up to the village level. It emphasized that most common illnesses can be self-cured and need only symptomatic treatment with simple remedies, be it herbal, indigenous or allopathic medicine. The diseases, which are communicable, can be controlled by preventive measures and readily diagnosed and treated with the help of cheap and highly effective drugs. Therefore, the group proposed that primary health services should be extended to the community through a trained and involved community health volunteer, preferably male or female, for a population of 1,000. The study group has recommended elimination of the PHC category as it feels that it is an institution of semi-professional and paramedical personnel who deliver poor medical care and extend no preventive and promotive health care (ICSSR and ICMR, 1981). To lift the status of such aspects of medical services, the working group has suggested that greater emphasis should be given to departments of preventive and social medicine, which are currently underdeveloped. By improving the status of women we can hope to give better quality of health services to the population. Thus, the group provides details of the services and their components such as education, environmental conditions, level of nutrition and employment that are needed for improving the health of people.

Health Policy, 1983

The historical development reflected through various Plan documents and Policy directions (1982) brings out explicit actions on inter-sectoral cooperation not only of different developmental sectors, but also of various intra-sectoral efforts in the field of health, family planning education and research, drugs, pharmaceuticals, agriculture, food, water supply and drainage, housing, education, social welfare, rural development etc. NHP–1983, in a spirit of optimistic empathy for the health needs of the people, particularly the poor and under-privileged, had hoped to provide 'Health for All by the year 2000 AD', through the universal provision of comprehensive primary health care services.

Under the important aspects for the reforms directed through the process of planning and health policy (1983), the Government of India has already considered and provided for health legislation, research and its monitoring, and review of health care quantitative goals. Therefore, it can be concluded that the genesis of health sector reforms and its various dimensions is already an important part of Indian policy and its developmental framework. However, several pertinent issues in health sector reforms have a bearing on our constitutional provisions like equity, accessibility of poor, efficiency in using resources and inadequacy of resources, gender bias, quality of health care, impact of liberalization etc. The changed circumstances relating to the health sector of the country since 1983 have created such circumstances which led to the formulation of the National Health Policy-2002 (NHP). It has been observed, after analysing the health policy, that financial resources and public health administration have proved inadequate in their capacity and therefore, the set goals for the policy could not be achieved. As a result, the National Health Policy-2002 was formulated to meet realistic expectations and focusing more on financial resources. It was also envisaged that over a period of time there would be a growth in financial resources also. The main recommendation of the NHP is to raise the availability of health services to the masses, considering the realistic aspects of the policy.

National Health Policy, 2002

The main objective of the NHP is to achieve an acceptable standard of good health amongst people, especially the poor people. To facilitate the availability of health services to the people, it becomes necessary to decentralize the system of public health services. It can be done by setting new infrastructure in deficient areas and upgrading the existing infrastructure in different institutions. Importance would be given to equitable access to the health services across all sections of society, and particularly the poor people and to those living in remote areas. It was also emphasized that aggregate public health spending would be increased by the central government. In turn, this initiative would strengthen the capacity of the public health administration at the State level to render effective delivery of health services. Since the country has accepted the policy of liberalization, the interference of private sector in health policies is also equally encouraged. It is primarily done with the help of those people who can afford to pay for the health services. In the NHP, importance is given to the preventive and first-line curative initiatives at primary level through increased sectoral share of allocation. The rational use of drugs within the allopathic system is also preferred. Recently, increasing use of generic drugs over branded drugs is also given high preference, particularly in the health facilities provided by government. The govenment also ensures that people have an easy access to the tried and tested systems of traditional medicine. Public health investment in the country is very low as compared to many other countries of the world. It has declined from 1.3 per cent in 1990 to 0.9 per cent in 1999, and it has slightly increased to 1.37 per cent in 2009. The total expenditure in health facilities is around 5.2 per cent of Gross Domestic Product (GDP). However, between 2012 and 2013, aggregate health expenditure is expected to reach a rate of 5.5 per cent by 2013. Nonetheless, there is not much increase in the health expenses over a period of different budgets for health planning and policies (National Health Policy, 2002). After looking at these figures, it is concluded that the expenditure on public health services is very meagre and below the expected standard. After all, under the constitutional structure, public health is the responsibility of the states. Under the federal structure it is the state that provides the health services to their population and central government helps it in certain National programmes and Health initiatives. The contribution of central resources to overall public health funding has been limited to about 15 per cent (National Health Policy, 2002). Whereas the fiscal resources of the State Government are inelastic, as reflected in the declining percentage of the state resources which are allocated to the health sector out of the total health budget. If we really want to improve the decentralization of public health services, we have to increase the health budget of the state government as well as the budget of the central government on the formation of health policies. The NHP-2002 was formulated against this backdrop, taking into consideration availability of major resources. However, this is also a reality that there is a paucity of public heath investment. It can be increased only when State Governments and central governments would play a key role in reducing the fiscal deficit to augmenting public health investments. It was also proposed in the NHP that central government will spend 6 per cent of GDP, with 2 per cent of GDP being contributed to public health investment by the year 2010. However, it is the failure of the government that it has not done what it envisaged in the NHP-2002 (National Health Policy, 2002). To keep a higher budget for increased public health investment is also contingent upon the increasing capacity of the public health, expenditure to ensure that the funds can be utilized in a profitable manner. Central planning is the key feature and equitable regional distribution is the major objective in the sphere of the country's development. However, the deliberate focus on development proves, that attainment of health indices has remained uneven across the states, expecially in rural-urban division, e.g. infant mortality is much higher in rural areas as compared to urban areas. To reduce this inequality and disparity at inter-regional level and rural-urban level between different economic classes and caste groups, the primary health sector is targeted. This approach will provide access to vast number of people and in turn will facilitate preventive and curative initiatives at early stage which are much more cost-effective. This public health principle has set an objective in the NHP-2002 by increasing an allocation of 55 per cent of the total public health investment for the primary health sector which has always been given importance over tertiary and secondary health sector. Secondary health sector has been allotted 35 per cent of total health investment, whereas tertiary sector is given only 10 per cent from the total resources. The NHP-2002 also projected that the increased aggregate outlay for primary health sector will boost the existing facilities, and also open avenues for new primary health centres and sub-centres according to the norms of such facilities. India is a country with pluralistic society, therefore, there are different socio-economic and ethnic settings which require differential programmes to cater to the health needs of its diverse population. Therefore, national health porgrammes should be designed with enough flexibility to allow State Governments to design their own programmes according to the needs of their people. These programmes can be carried out by the State Governments through decentralized system of public health machinery. In the past decade, the government has focused more on the vertical structure for the implementation of major disease control programmes. With the help of this substantial achievements have been made in government's efforts to reduce diseases. However, it was realized that such an organizational structure requires independent manpower for each disease control programme. Thus, it becomes very expensive and difficult to sustain these vertical programmes for a long period of time. It can be possible only in the case of certain diseases whose elimination or eradication is seen as foreseeable in a time-span. The central government, alongwith the active participation of the state governments, plays a major role in the execution of these policies, which are framed for the eradication and elimination of diseases. In the area of public health facilities, the outdoor funding is also insufficient. The appointment of medical and para-medical personnel is also much lower than prescribed norms. The availability of consumable items is also every negligible. The equipment used in many public health facilities are also outdated or obsolescent and the buildings in use are in dilapidated condition. Some facilities are provided in the rented accommodations. In the indoor facilities, there are insufficient beds and obsolescent equipment. The availability of essential drugs is minimal and the capacity of facilities is grossly inadequate. The problem of over-crowding also results in the steep deterioration of the quality of health services delivered to people. This leads to the decreasing use of public health facilities, i.e. around 20 per cent. Only less than 20 per cent seek outdoor services and less than 45 per cent avail indoor facilities in the public health facilities. The situation is getting worse in spite of peoples' inability to pay for the private services, which results in out-of-pocket payments.

Darryl D. Monte (1992), after the initiation of the process of economic reforms in India, emphasized that it would be a tragedy if under the pretext of economic liberalization, the government would allow health policies to get short shrift. In the same way, according to a nation-wide survey of household expenditure on health care, it was known that nearly 55 per cent was spent on private doctors and it was only 39 per cent that was spent on public health care organization (National Council of Applied Economic Research, 1992). Researchers and scholors on the subject of health have also noted that at least 8 per cent of poor family's income gets spent on the expenses of injections. It is estimated that personal health expenditurc, i.c. about more than ₹ 20,000 crore, works out to be three times to that of government's expenditure, including its expenditure on health, providing the facilities of water and sanitation. In the current situation, independent practitioners are also contributing to the private health care organizations. Private employees are also providing services by treating large number of patients at the primary level for the major diseases. However, the treatment that is given by them is diverse and not scientifically optimal, which leads to an increase in the incidence of drug resistance. In principle, this policy welcomes the participation of private sector in all areas related to health activities – primary, secondary or tertiary. The policy encourages private insurance companies to increase the coverage of secondary and tertiary sector under health insurance packages. In the National Health Framework, the alternative systems of medicine like ayurveda, unani, siddha and homoeopathy are also put under one umbrella to make use of their substantial roles in health care. There is a distinct advantage of these alternative systems of health care as they have a diverse, modest, cost-effective, and low level of technology input, based on the treatment obtained from natural products. These advantages attract the underserved, remote and tribal people as they find themselves closer to nature. There is substantial untapped potential of the alternative systems of medicine as India is one of the important global centres of plant diversity in medicinal and aromatic plants.

National Rural Health Mission (NRHM), 2005

National Rural Health Mission was launched in April 2005 in 18 states to provide health care to the rural people, particularly to the vulnerable section, i.e. children and women. It aims to provide a comprehensive and integrated health care system to the rural masses. In this mission, there is a provision to provide every village with trained female community health activist known as Accredited Social Health Activist (ASHA). ASHA would be selected from the village community itself and would be accountable to the panchayat. She would work as a mediator between the community and public health system. These ASHA workers would not get any remuneration, rather they would be provided only performance-incentives for promoting universal immunization, referral and escort services for reproductive and child care and other health programmes. On an average, they get ₹ 1,100 in a month and are provided with a drug kit which contains drugs for certain common ailments. P.K. Hota, Union Health Secretary, remarked that ‘it is a massive project aimed at providing basic health care to the villagers’. The central government has framed this Rural Health Care Mission at the policy level, but it is the responsibility of the state governments to execute and support it. There might be few problems in its implementation, but it has to be regularly monitored to remove the bottlenecks. In 2006–2007, for NRHM, ₹ 120 crore has been spent out of the total fund of Rs, 6,714 crore. Still, the recruitment of many voluntary health workers which is mandatory for the NRHM, remains pending till date.

Delivery of National Public Health Programmes

Over the last decade or so, the Indian Government has relied upon a ‘vertical’ structure for the implementation of major disease control programmes. Through this system, it has been able to make a substantial mark in reducing the burden of specific diseases. However, such an organizational structure, which requires independent manpower for each disease programme, is extremely expensive and difficult to sustain. Over a long time, 'vertical' structures may only be affordable for those diseases which offer a reasonable possibility of elimination or eradication in a foreseeable span of time.

It is a widespread perception that over the last decade and a half, the rural health staff has become a vertical structure exclusively for the implementation of family welfare activities that are beneficial for families. As a result, for those public health programmes where there is no separate vertical structure, there is also no identifiable service delivery system at all. The NHP will also address this distortion in the public health system.

This policy envisages a key role for the central government in designing national programmes with active participation of the State Governments. Also, the policy ensures the provisioning of financial resources, in addition to technical support, monitoring and evaluation at national level by the centre. However, to optimize the utilization of public health infrastructure at the primary level, NHP-2002 envisages the gradual convergence of all health programmes under single administration. Vertical programmes for the control of major diseases like TB, Malaria, HIV/AIDS, as also the RCH and Universal Immunization Programmes, need to be continued till the moderate levels of prevalence are reached. The integration of these programmes will bring about a desirable optimization of results through a convergence of all public health inputs. The policy also envisages that the implementation of these programmes must be effected through autonomous bodies at state and district levels. The interventions of State Health Departments may be limited to overall monitoring of the achievement of the targets and other technical aspects of the programme.

The policy envisages that apart from the exclusive staff in a vertical structure for the disease control programmes, all rural health staff should be available for the entire gamut of public health activities at the decentralized level, irrespective of whether these activities relate to the national programmes or to the other public health initiatives.

Present State of the Health Services

The provision of health under the Indian Constitution falls under the jurisdiction of state. Today, every state is free to formulate its health programmes and strategies. In fact, India was the first country in the world to introduce the Family Planning Programme in 1952. Since Independence, we have invested a lot in the infrastructure for health facilities and created 1,45,000 sub-centres, 23,000 Public Health Centres (PHCs) and 3,222 Community Health Centres (CHCs). However, this infrastructure is still insufficient for the vast population as approximately, 80 per cent of the population is still receiving health care facilities from the private sector. Poor access to public health facilities heads to higher incidences of morbidity and mortality. Poor people have out-of-pocket expenses which often results in indebtedness. This vicious circle of indebtedness further leads to poverty, malnutrition and poor health. In India, the contribution of private households to health care is 75 per cent. Most of these costs are out-of-pocket costs. State governments contribute 15.2, the central government 5.2, and third party insurance and employers put in 3.3 per cent whereas, local governments and foreign donors contribute 1.3 per cent of the total costs. Out of this amount, 58.7 per cent is spent on primary health care (curative, preventive and promotive); 38.8 per cent on secondary and tertiary inpatient care and the rest is spent on non-service costs (World Bank, 1997). Private Expenditure on Health (PHE), as a per cent of per capita income, has almost doubled since 1961. It has increased from 2.71 during 1961–70 to 5.53 during 2001–03 (Government of India, 1997). The raise is at a much higher rate as compared to the per capita income over a period of time. D. Banerji (1977) has commented that the partition of the department of Health and Family Planning is not going to solve the problem of health care. Basically, the principle behind Alma Ata Declaration was not understood properly and, nor was it executed effectively in letter and spirit. The responsibility of public health should be given in people's hands, which means that primary health care should be given priority over secondary and tertiary health care planning (Walsh and Warren, 1979). Rich countries mobilized organizations such as the WHO, UNICEF and the World Bank to promote their agenda of Selective Primary Health Care (SPHC). This led to an opening of virtual barrage of what the international agencies called International Initiatives (Grant, 1985). The vertical or categorical programmes were technocentric programmes which were imposed by western countries over the poor developing countries without understanding their specificity. When these programmes were launched, prediction was done for the success of these programmes, despite massive investment in billions of US dollars. However, it has still not helped in the attainment of goals (Banerji, 1999). Even the Government of India had admitted in its National Health Policy Document of 2002 that the system of health services suffered due to its agreement to the donor driven vertical programmes which include immunization for tuberculosis and AIDS. The International Monetary Fund (IMF), while giving loans, has imposed certain conditions in the form of imposition of international initiative in the early phase of 1990s. The Structural Adjustment Programme (SAP) has enabled the entry into the health sector of country in the form of influencing budgetary allocations in the country. The government was also forced to make certain unimaginative regime of 'cost-recovery' from small allocations made for the government funded health services (Banerji, 1994; World Bank, 1992, 1997). SAP has also given a breakthrough to the market of private health sector rapidly. There is a sharp decline in the government's commitment to public health services which is reflected in various plans laid out. India's public health expenditure, in terms of its percentage from the GDP, is the fifth lowest in the world. It is even less in comparison to some sub-Saharan African countries. Although private sector has been provided many subsidies and rebate in the import of medical instruments and drugs, yet India has the largest and the least regulated private health care industry in the world (Rao: *The Times of India*, 2006).

The government's initiatives towards globalization has further extenuated this trend of commodification of the medical services. There has been a mushrooming growth of numerous unregulated profiteering private hospitals, nursing homes, diagnostic centres and other ancillaries of the medical industry. With an unabashed political support, unregulated institutions for education of physicians and other health personnel such as dentists, nurses, homoeopaths and *vaids* have rapidly expanded in the private sector as health care became a lucrative field for making profits at the expense of the suffering of people. All these trends point to what Ivan Illich had long ago mentioned as 'medicalization of life' (Illich, 1977). Producing dependence, almost addiction to medicine and generation of iatrogenesis of various kinds, were mentioned by him as maladies of the market driven 'modern' medicine. Systematization of medicine, when healers become a cog of the wider 'system' and it's even more awesome manifestation in the form of a still bigger conglomerates – conglamoratization – have been the more advanced manifestation of this malignant trend in the 'developed countries' (Illich, 1977). The imposition of the TRIPS (Trade Related Intellectual Property System) by the World Trade Organization (WTO) has led to a sharp rise in the prices of drugs. The National Rural Health Mission seeks to provide effective and integrated health care to the poor, needy, vulnerable and marginalized sections of the society throughout the country (Government of India, 2005). The basic mission of health care is to provide universal access to health care facilities to all sections of the society, that is why ₹ 6,713 crore has been marked for NRHM in the budget. However, in the 2005–2006 budget, the central government did not provide separate budget for NRHM. In fact, NRHM is asked to use its funds from the budget of Reproductive and Child Health Care (RCH-2), Integrated Disease Surveillance project and the AYUSH programme. The critique of NRHM mentions that with the exception of small states like Nagaland and Haryana, there has been zero per cent growth in the setting up of primary health care centres. The performance of Community Health Centres is also pathetic. Only 11 CHCs were set up during April 2994 and January 2005 as against the countrywide target of 103. The mission document-2005 also draws a gloomy picture of the results as people on an average spend 58 per cent of their income on hospital expenses. They borrow heavily or sell their assets to cover the expenses. Another 25 per cent of hospitalized Indians fall below poverty line because of the hospital expenses (*The Pioneer*,

2005). Another study by Nandraj and Duggal (1997) finds that private hospitals and clinics do not confirm to the minimum standards of medical care. They are not only providing poor quality medical care, but even the measures taken by them are circumventing and in turn prove dangerous to the safety and well-being of patients. In 1993, a committee was appointed by Mumbai High Court to assess the quality of health care given by private nursing homes and hospitals in Mumbai, which found that the quality of health care given by these hospitals and nursing homes was very low in standards. Although the rural and urban areas have abundant health infrastructure, the quality of health care has not improved in private sectors. India is a highly populous country. Therefore, its health needs are also enormous and the financial resources and managerial capacity of the country to meet the optimistic projection of the health goals fall short. The NHP-2002 has had to prioritize certain plans and operations in this direction. At no point of time the NHP-2002 claimed to be a road map for meeting all health needs of the population of the country. Like any other unit or element of society which is in a dynamic state, the state of health is also dynamic. The threats and priorities related to the issue of health keep on changing over time. Keeping a scope for dynamic changes in its various elements. The health policy is holistic and undertakes necessary risks for emphasis on different components of the policy. The NHP-2002 focuses on the need for enhanced funding and organizational restructuring of the national public health initiatives in order to facilitate more equitable access to the health facilities. The burden of historical diseases like tuberculosis, malaria, blindness, etc. is taken care under the framework of this policy. At the same time the newly emerging diseases like HIV/AIDS, lifestyle diseases, and diabetes are also noticed in the NHP-2002. By identifying various core and other supplementary areas, various priorities are accorded in the policy framework. Under the umbrella of this macro-policy document, various government and private sector planners have designed separate schemes according to the health needs of women, children, old age people, tribals and other socio-economically disadvantaged people. Many times, there are certain calamities and disasters for which various robust management plans are made to cope with the situations in an effective manner. The most important aspect of the policy document which influences health planning at every level is the equity dimension. It is obligatory to evaluate the health policy on its equity front irrespective of the evaluation made after the NHP–2002. The success or failure of the policy is mainly judged on the basis of its equity component. In the framework of equity dimension, a marked emphasis has been given to the expansion and improvement of primary health facilities, including the new concept of provisioning of essential drugs through central funding. The policy document has also made a commitment to the central government for increased over-writing of the resources for meeting the minimum health needs of its people. Thus, the NHP-2002 attempts to provide guidance for prioritizing expenditure, thereby facilitating the equal allocation of resources. The improvement in the health status of people depends upon the quality of health services. Increase in financial and material input is not sufficient for the improvement in health status but it also depends on more empathetic and committed attitude of the service providers in the private and public sectors. In this backdrop, it needs to be recognized that any policy in the social sector is critically dependent on the service providers who should not treat their responsibility as a commercial activity, but as a service, albeit a paid one. In the public health sector, it is an enhanced standard of governance which is a prerequisite for the success of any health policy.

Retrospect and Prospect

The most important aspect of the National Committee (Sokhey Committee) was to have one Community Health Worker (CHW) for every 1000 population in the village. This CHW should be from the village, and should be trained in personal hygiene, first aid and simple medical treatment with more emphasis on social aspects and implications of medical and public health work. The committee also recommended that the practitioners of indigenous systems of medicine like ayurveda and unani should also be incorporated in the state health systems. These practitioners should be given a scientific training as and when necessary. The most important committee till date is Bhore Committee (1946), not because of its distinguished authorship, but because of its many proposals and recommendations that continue to be valid even today. The genuine principle that 'nobody should be denied access to health services for his inability to pay' is still relevant for the recommendatons made by the committee. The committee focused on the rural areas as it found that the vast majority of population is living in the rural areas. It also focused on the preventive measures to be undertaken under this policy. It also believed in the manner that each individual should be trained as a 'social physician'. The political soil was not adequate to nurture the seeds of hope that took shape during the freedom struggle. There were many challenges soon after the Independence of the country. However, at the political level, it was very clear that democratic ideas will be the foundation for all planning processes. Taken as a whole, these democratic decisions gave a perspective to the public health principles and practices in the country, which was markedly different from those preached in the conventional school of public health in western countries elsewhere (Naik, 1977). There were many hurdles and difficulties in developing the nation, but India could develop an endogenous and alternative body of knowledge that suited more to the social, cultural, economic and epidemiological conditions prevailing in the country. This has led to the emergence of an alternative approach to education, training, practice and research in public health (Banerji, 1988). There were many major decisions that were taken for the poor people, which lasted only during the early years of

Independence. The independent India accepted the report of Bhore Committee, beginning the process of the setting up of primary health centres (Dutt, 1965). These primary health centres are encouraged to provide integrated preventive, curative and rehabilitative services to the entire population as an integral component of a wider Community Development Programme (Bhattarcharya, 1972). Later on, the same has been further promoted in the Alma Ata Declaration on primary health care (World Health Organization, 1978).

The increasing role of the state in delivering health care services and the consequent bureaucratization of health care delivery has created a divergence between governmental goals and targets for collective health status and the individual's efforts to maintain its health and well-being. While the lack of governmental health care is found to adversely affect the health status of a population, greater interference of medical services through the government bureaucracy and a rapid diffusion of privatized medical care leads to the inequality of health status.

Universalization of health care is at the heart of health policy in India since Independence in 1947. Since then, the country has experienced different models to improve access to health services and ensure universal care to the entire population. Despite the proliferation of governmental and private initiatives, the majority of Indian population still has great difficulty in obtaining appropriate health services. Along with the problems of spatial distribution of health services, there are several other barriers which stand between patients and their access to the health care services.

Summing up

This chapter briefly summarizes the health policy and its planning in India since Independence. Health care planning has undergone changes in its structure, personnel and in its access to the populace on the basis of recommendations made by different committees. After Independence, India has initiated several policies and programmes and global partnership has been introduced, but expected results have been not shown. Therefore, without the realization of the goals of the programme of action of the millennium development which combines clear theoretical thinking with realistic application. Though multi-sectoral approach has been adopted at various stages, there is a need to percolate these aspects to the grassroot level through trained and well-skilled workers for the sustainable impact of health and family welfare programmes. The infrastructure of health facilities is still insufficient for the vast population because approximately 80 per cent of the population is receiving health care from the private sector. Such poor access to the public health facilities heads to the higher incidence of morbidity and mortality. The poor people have an out-of-pocket expense which often leads to the state of indebtedness. This vicious circle of indebtedness leads to poverty, malnutrition and poor health. In India, the contribution of private households to health care sector is 75 per cent and most of these costs are out-of-pocket expenses incurred by the poor people of our country.

References

Banerji, D. (1973), 'Social Orientation of Medical Education in India', *Economic and Political Weekly*, 8: 485–88.

—— (1977), 'Community Response to Intensified Family Planning Programme', *Economic and Political Weekly*, 12: 261–66.

—— (1986), 'Technocentric Approach to Health: Western Response to Alma Ata', *Economic and Political Weekly*, 28: 1233–34.

—— (1988), 'New Public Health', *Journal of Sociological Studies*, 7: 160–67.

—— (1994), 'A Simplistic Approach to Health Policy Analysis: The World Bank Team on the Indian Health Sector', *International Journal of Health Services*, 24(1): 151–59.

—— (1999), 'A Fundamental Shift in the Approach to International Health by WHO, UNICEF and the World Bank: Instances of the Practice of "Intellectual Fascism" and Totalitarianism in Some Asian Countries', *International Journal of Health Services*, 29(2): 227–59.

Bhattarcharya, S.N. (1972), *Community Development: An Analysis of the Programme in India*, Calcutta: Academic Publishers.

Dutt, P.R. (1965), *Rural Health Services in India: Primary Health Centres*, New Delhi: Central Health Education Bureau.

Government of India (1946), *Report of the Health Survey and Development Committee (Bhore Committee)*, Vol. 2, Delhi: Manager of Publications.

—— (1961), *Report of the Survey and Planning Committee (Mudaliar Committee)*, Vol. 1, New Delhi: Ministry of Health.

—— (1963), *Report of the Survey and Planning Committee (Chadah Committee)*, New Delhi: Ministry of Health.

—— (1965), *Report of the Health Survey and Planning Committee (Mukherjee Committee)*, New Delhi: Ministry of Health.

—— (1972), *Report of the Health Survey and Planning Committee*, New Delhi: Ministry of Health.

—— (1973), *Report of the Committee on Multi Purpose Workers under Health and Family Planning Programme*, Vol. 21, New Delhi: Ministry of Health and Family Planning, 13–16.

—— (1975), *Health Services and Medical Education: A Programme for Immediate Action Report (Srivastava Committee)*, New Delhi: Ministry of Health and Family Welfare.

—— (1983), *Statement on National Health Policy 1982*, New Delhi: Ministry of Health and Family Welfare.

—— (1985), *National Health Policy*, New Delhi: Lok Sabha Secretariat.

—— (1997), *Planning Commission: Evaluation of Community Health Centres*, New Delhi: Programme Evaluation Organisation.

—— (2002), *National Health Policy 2002*, New Delhi: Ministry of Health and Family Welfare, 1–39.

—— (2005), *National Rural Health Mission: Indian Public Health Standards for Community Health Centres*, New Delhi: Ministry of Health and Family Welfare.

Grant, J.P. (1985), *The State of World's Children*, New York: UNICEF.

ICSSR and ICMR (1981), *Health for All: An Alternative Strategy*, Pune: Indian Institute of Education.

Illich, Ivan (1977), *Limits to Medicine-Medical Nemesis: The Expropriation of Health*, Bombay: Rupa.

Independent Commission on Health in India (1997), *Report*, New Delhi: Voluntary Health Association of India.

Monte, Darryle D. (1992), 'Privatised Health Care', *The Times of India*, 9 November.

Nagla, Madhu (1993), 'Health Policy and Planning in India', in B.K. Nagla (ed.), *Development and Transformation: Themes and Variations in Indian Society*, Jaipur: Rawat Publications.

Naik, J.P. (1977), *An Alternative System of Health Services in India: Some Proposals*, Bombay: Allied Publishers.

Nandraj, Sunil and Ravi Duggal (1997), *Physical Standards in the Private Health Sector*, Mumbai: CHEAT, 23.

National Council for Applied Economic Research (1992), *Household Utilization of Medical Care*, New Delhi: NCAER.

National Planning Committee, Sub-Committee on National Health (Sokhey Committee) (1948), *Report*, Bombay: Vora.

Rao, Mohan (2006), *The Times of India*, 27 March, New Delhi.

The Pioneer (2005), 23 April, New Delhi.

The Times of India (2006), 8 January, New Delhi.

Walsh, J.A. and K.A. Warren (1979), 'Selective Primary Health Care: An Interim Strategy for Disease Control for Developing Countries', *New England Journal of Medicine*, 301: 967–74.

World Bank (1992), *Indian Health Sector Financing*, Washington, D.C.

—— (1993), *World Development Report, 1993: Investing in Health*, New York: Oxford University Press.

—— (1997), *India New Sectors in Health Sector Development at the State Level: An Operational Perspective*, New Delhi: Population and Human Resource Division, South Asia Country Department II.

World Health Organization (2001), *Report of the Commission on Macroeconomics and Health: Investing in Health for Economic Development*, Geneva: WHO.

Yesudin, C.A.K. (1981), 'Health Manpower Planning in India', *The Indian Journal of Social Work*, XLV(11).

23

Health Inequalities in Social Groups

Illness and health are generally attributed to genetic inheritance and chance. All that an individual can do is to lead healthy lifestyle in order to maintain a healthy body. However, sociologists argue that social factors are the main causes of diseases. There is a close relationship between health, disease and social divisions. Standards of health and longevity of life are clearly distributed along the divisions of caste, class, ethnicity, geography and gender. Chance plays a small part in our health; far more important are the social factors which create the context in which people live their lives.

A research in social sciences was conducted on the topic of health to analyse the transformation of societies and their environment alongwith examining the vulnerabilities and inequities that these transformations may produce on health and well-being of populations.

Health Inequalities and Inequities

Health inequality is an enduring and notable feature of a modern global society. The chances and opportunities to lead a healthy, active and a life free of illness and pain are not evenly distributed across societies. There is a clear class gradient even in the causes of morbidity and mortality; those at the lower end of the society exhibit higher levels of ill-health and premature death than those at higher end of the society. These existing distinct social patterns demonstrate that experiencing good or bad health does not necessarily relate to the choice of lifestyle or engaging in risk behaviours such as, smoking, drinking and eating fatty foods. It is rather where one is located by gender, ethnicity and social class, and in which country one lives that exert the greatest influences on one's health. Over the years, numerous reports and evidences have explored and confirmed that gender, ethnicity, caste and class influence morbidity, mortality and self-perceived health. Reports such as *The Black Report* and *The Acheson Inquiry* and more recently the World Health Organization's (CSDH, 2008) *Closing the Gap in a Generation,* share the similar conclusion that health inequalities are a real and demonstrable feature of health in society, and the reason for their continued existence is social, and not individual in origin.

Improvement in the health of poor and reduction in health inequalities has become the central goal of many international organizations including the World Bank, and World Health Organization and government within the context of domestic policies and development assistance programmes.

The expression 'health inequalities' is used to refer to a broad range of differences between different groups of people, belonging to different countries, regions, socio-economic groups, ethnic groups, caste groups, and gender. It generally reflects the population differences in circumstances and behaviours that are in the most case determined socially (Leon, Walt and Gislon, 2001). The expression, 'health inequities', represents unfair inequalities that, at least in theory, could be remediable. The term is often used to describe unjust access to health services, that is a major concern in the developing countries and those in transition (if access to health care was the same for everyone in a region or country, then access inequities would not exist). The health inequalities and inequities are not understood in the same way everywhere.

However, in general terms, health inequalities are looked in the following manner:

- Morality rates are higher in poorer people as compared to richer people.
- Individuals living in a certain part (like slums, rural area) more often suffer more from certain types of diseases.
- People from a rich class background have a higher risk of dying from a cardiovascular disease.
- Poor people suffering from chronic diseases cannot afford to see a doctor regularly.

Assessment of Health Outcomes

Health Inequality: A Case of Class Division

Difference of class in a society causes variations in health status, rather than vice versa. Ways of living are also presumed to vary between different social positions. It is seen that people in lower social classes indulge more frequently in unhealthy behaviours such as smoking, drinking alcohol, eating more fat and sugar and taking less exercise. At one extreme, these factors are seen to be in the control of an individual, and so it is up to the individual to alter his or her behaviour and nurture more healthy attitudes (Sutton, 2011). Modern studies of the differences in mortality and morbidity can be traced back to *The Black Report* (1980) and Townsend and Davidson (1982).

The Black Report gathered evidences of differences in the Standardized Morality Ratio (SMR) of different social classes in Britain by using the official registry of deaths and then categorizing the SMRs by the Registrar General's classification. This involves the division of occupations into five groups or classes according to the official classification of social classes used by the government. The study also drew a wide range of morbidity statistics, taken largely from the official sources.

The conclusions of the study were unambiguous:

> In case of adults between the ages of 15 and 64, for virtually all causes of death there is consistent inverse relationship between social class and mortality. That is, the higher the social class group, the lower its SMR, and conversely the lower the social class group, the higher its SMR. (Black Report, 1980)

It further argues:

> Over time ... the position of social class groups has remained stable ... . So while mortality has been improving for the population as a whole, the gap between the social class grouping has remained wide.

The Black Report suggests that possible explanations for the differences in social class could be categorized under four headings:

1. Artefact: The differences are a reflection of the methodologies used to measure mortality and social class.
2. Social selection: The differences in social class reflect the fact that healthier people are able to work their ways as per the social class structure.
3. Cultural differences: The people of working-class are more likely to engage in unhealthy lifestyles.
4. Material differences: The economic differences in Britain lead directly and indirectly to poorer health for the less well-off people, increasing their chances of early death.

The Black Report has been extremely influential, and these categories of explanation are used even today. A more recent attempt to provide statistics on health inequalities was *The Acheson Report* (1998) which provided an evidence of continuing inequalities and suggested that the relative differences between the social classes were actually increasing at extremes of the division of social classes. In the 1970s, the mortality rate among men in social class V was twice as for those in social class I, but by the 1990s it had increased to three times a high. The increased differential occurred because death rates declined for all social classes, but declined more slowly for the lower social classes. Looking at life expectancy, those in the two highest social classes increased their life expectancy by 2.0 years in the 30 years between 1970 and 2000, while those in the lower social classes experienced a smaller increase of 1.4 years. The infant mortality rate is higher for routine and manual occupational groups. The research also shows that although mortality rates have fallen overall, the gap between classes had grown between the times of the two reports. The situation seems even worse in terms of morbidity. According to *The Acheson Report,* there has been a slight increase in the overall long-standing illness, showing a significant increase in the gap between the two classes.

Health Inequality: A Case of Race Division

Of all the inequalities in the distribution of health and life chances in American society, the most striking are those that accompany the general inequality between racial groups. Although Negroes have been benefitted from the overall decline in mortality, they continue to be at disadvantage in every category of death and illness. Negro health deficits begin early and continue at all ages up to seventy-five; prenatal and infant mortality are substantially higher for Negroes (Wilson, 1970: 78). The roots of this maldistribution of illness are apparent in bold outline but unquestionably complex in causal detail. Like those of the poor, the annals of the racially disfavoured are neither short nor simple. They are lifelong configurations of hazards and are incredibly tangled and snarled in a capricious social fate. Broadly speaking, the Negro suffers from lack of access to the conditions that are thought to promote good health, that correspond to the lack of access to the facilities that might cushion and alleviate ill-health. Pearson argues that collecting data on race and health is problematic, as definitions of 'race' and ethnicity vary between studies. For example, the term 'Asian' can include a range of different groups of people varying in nationality, place of birth, religion and language.

However, some patterns emerge, however, with people from the Indian sub-continent having the highest levels of heart disease and those from Caribbean backgrounds suffering particularly from high levels of strokes. The explanations for such health variations focus on genetic, cultural and socio-economic factors. According to Nettleton (2006), although genetic differences may have some influence, they are unable to account for the wider 'racial' patterning of health status.

Cultural accounts of different health and lifestyle have been particularly common and influential on government policy. These differences include higher levels of rickets among 'Asian' children because of the dietary deficiency of vitamin D.

The problem with the cultural explanation is that when it is imposed upon differences of social class in matters of health, it tends to place the blame upon individuals and regard improvements in health as a matter of choice of the persons themselves. Positive cultural health practices such as, the low rates of smoking and alcohol consumption among many Asian groups may be easily ignored.

Racialized inequalities in both health and access to health care are explained as resulting from cultural differences and deficits. Institutional racism and racial discrimination have no part in this equation. If we turn to wider socio-cultural factors, particularly associated with 'race', rather different reasons emerge for health variations between ethnic groups. The first piece of evidence is (as for women) the higher rate of poverty and deprivation among minority ethnic groups in Britain. This includes poorer housing conditions, concentration in some of the most deprived neighbourhoods, employment in more hazardous areas of work and higher unemployment and lower wages.

Health Inequality: A Case of Living Place

Social class, gender and ethnicity are key factors in understanding health inequalities, but sociologists have also given recognition to the element of living place. Using data from the Census, Shaw et al. (1999) identified the parliamentary constituencies which had the highest number of people (the mortality rate) and the lowest number of people who are dying before the retirement age. They constructed two lists – one containing all the constituencies with 1 million people with the highest mortality race and the other with the constituencies with 1 million people with lower rate. Shaw et al. (1999) argue that differences in chances of death are linked by a mixture of spatial, social and economic factors, which combine over a person's lifetime to affect the age of death. There should be a distinction between the social composition and social context in understanding these health inequalities.

The issue of geographic distance is important in a large country like India with limited means of communication. The direct effect of distance of a given population from primary health care centre on the childhood mortality is well documented (Bimal, 1991: 43–49). Those who live in remote areas with poor transportation facilities are often removed from the reach of health systems. Incentives for doctors and nurses to move to the rural locations are generally insufficient and ineffective. Poor housing conditions, exposure to excessive heat or cold, diseases, air, soil and water pollution along with industrial and commercial occupational risks, exacerbate the already high environmental health risks for the poor.

Health Inequality: A Case of Caste Division

The caste system, with its societal stratification and social restrictions, continues to have a major impact on the Indian society. The data from the National Family Health Survey-III (2005–06) clearly highlight the caste differentials in relation to health status. The survey documents the low levels of contraceptive used among the scheduled castes and scheduled tribes as compared to the people of upper classes. Reduced access to maternal and child health care is evident with reduced levels of antenatal care, institutional deliveries and complete vaccination coverage among the lower castes. Health problems like stunting, wasting, underweight and anaemia are higher among the lower castes. Similarly, neonatal, postnatal, infant and child, and under-five statistics clearly show a higher mortality among the scheduled casts and scheduled tribes.

It is widely recognized that the determinants of health are social and economic rather than purely medical. The poor health of people from the lower castes, their social exclusion and steep social gradient is due to the unequal distribution of power, income, goods and services. Caste is inextricably linked to and is a proxy for socio-economic status in India. The restricted access of those from the lower castes to clean water, sanitation, nutrition, housing, education, health care and employment is due to a toxic combination of poor social policies and programmes, unfair economic arrangement and bad politics.

The structural determinants of daily life contribute to the social determinant of health and fuel the inequities in health between the caste groups. Viewing health in general as an individual or medical issue, reducing the population of health to a biomedical perspective and suggesting individual medical interventions reflect poor understanding of issues. Caste-based inequality in household health expenditure reflects an unequal access to quality health care by different caste groups. Households with needs of high health care and chronic health care are most affected by the caste inequality. Also, households in the most marginalized castes and with high health care need require protection against impoverishing health expenditures (Mukherjee et al.: 2011)

Boorah (2007) compared the average death rate in India to that of the forward castes among Hindus, and found that even after imposing all controls, it was 4.9 years lower for the tribal people and 7.1 years lower for the scheduled castes.

Kopparty (1994) found that the low caste group has higher prevalence of morbidity than the high caste groups.

Health Inequality: A Case of Gender

Although there has been an overall improvement in the health condition of both males and females, women are still differentiated from men when it comes to providing medical care, which implies a comparative low status of care to women in our society. According to UNICEF, 12 million girls are born in India every year, out of which 25 per cent do not survive the 15th year due to the fact that the mortality rate of 0–5 years age group is about 20 times greater than any other age group to 5 years. Female mortality rate up to the age of 40 years is higher than the normal rate of mortality. Although an increase in the life expectancy for women has been recorded in absolute numbers, it is still lower in comparison to the life expectancy of males. It is striking to note that in comparison to this, maternal mortality rates are particularly high (Padmanabha, 1982). The sex-ratio at birth among the most population in the world favours a female-child, but at younger age-group a male-child is favoured more and therefore, the sex ratio at birth varies between 102 to 107 boys per 100 girls for biological reasons. However, this gets neutralized by the age of twenty because the rate of mortality is higher among boys than girls (Premi, 2001). If we see the Child Sex Ratio (CSR) in the population between 0–6 years of age-group, we will find that it has declined from 962 to 945 from 1981 to 1991. Further, in 2001, the child sex-ratio has declined by 18 points from 945 in 1991 to 927. After becoming alert from the 2001 data, the sex-ratio has further gone down by 13 points, i.e. 914 from 927 in 2001 (Census of India, 2011). It is due to pathological causes, high morbidity and low nutritional status. Girls are brought for their treatment at more critical stages of illness or taken to less qualified doctors that causes their mortality likely to be greater even when they are under treatment. The higher mortality of girls under 0–6 years is largely responsible for the skewed sex ratio. Mathur (1995) opined that at birth, chances of survival for a male child are less than those for a female child, but after the neo-natal stage, social factors such as care, immunization, nutrition of the mother and child and sanitation come into force and govern the survival prospects of an infant. Ghosh (1985) accords adverse sex-ratio because of high risk of female deaths from infancy to the end of the reproductive period; traditionally inculcated attitude of self effacement among women and infant mortality rate is higher for females than males. The same neglect is evident in exceedingly high maternal mortality rates, because the number of cases attended by health care workers are fewer than half the births.

A woman often derives power and authority from her association with the male head of the family. However, this association is not in the correlation and therefore, her access to resources for care and sustenance is reduced to make her vulnerable. It is further aggravated among women who are poor and do not have any assets for survival such as education, social status and gainful employment. This pathetic condition gets compounded resulting into failing health and disability. Worst is the case for widows as they become vulnerable at all levels (Chen and Dreze, 1995). The elder women not only suffer from certain specific ailments of ageing process but also from ill-health accumulated over the life cycle, which may be manifested in an aggravated form in old age. Many women have also reported that 'problem of joints' is higher than that among men. This is expected, as after menopause women are particularly prone to the development of osteoarthritis, a painful degenerative joint disease (Tinker et al., 2000). Conditions of disability also affect the health of elderly people. It is well known that the prevalence of blindness in India varies not only by geographical location and degree of urbanization, but also by gender (World Bank, 1994).

Several health conditions like skeletal, cardiovascular, nervous, skim, genitourinary and gastro-intestinal systems affect women in the older age group. It is due to the decline in ovarian hormonal levels that is triggered by menopause. The absence of ovarian steroids, chronic diseases like osteoporosis, coronary heart diseases and cerbovascular also develop (Tinker et al., 2000). Gynaecological cancers, prolapse and fistulae are some other conditions afflicting elderly women, which are caused as the result of high fertility rate and child bearing at an early age. These women may find it difficult to disclose the nature of their illness to the younger members of their family, especially if there are gynaecological problems.

It cannot be denied that poverty is a major cause of malnutrition and undernourishment of women. Moreover, it is more due to the unfavourable socio-cultural values operating against women in the case of distribution of food. Optimum standards of nutrition is determined on the basis of body weight, sex, climate, and nature of the work performed. More than half of the women in India do not get the recommended dietary intake of nutrients (Roy, Kulkarni, and Vaidehi, 2004). Generally undernutrition among women and girls in India is a part of vicious circle in terms of its devastating consequences for pregnant and lactating women and their infants. Undernourished women give birth to low-birth-weight babies. If the underweight baby is female, than she further remains undernourished throughout her childhood, adolescence and adult life. This lack of nourishment in her life affects her reproductive and lactating capacities.

Anaemia is a major health problem among Indian women. Studies carried out by the Indian Council of Medical Research found that over 65 per cent of girls from 1–14 years of age in the cities of Hyderabad, New Delhi and Calcutta were anaemic (ICMR, 1982). Anaemia is particularly widespread among women during pregnancy, when iron requirements increases nearly fivefold (Hallberg, 1988).

There is enough ethnographic literature which suggests that females are not fed well in comparison to males, particularly in northern India (Harriss, 1986; Miller, 1981). Other studies like Khan and others (1982) in Uttar Pradesh and Bidinger, Nag and Babu (1986) in Andhra Pradesh and Devadas and Kamalanthan (1985) in Tamil Nadu indicate that there is a lot of discrimination in the allocation of food within the household against females. There is a marked difference between the food that is fed to boys and girls. The discrepancy increases with age. According to the figures obtained from the National Nutrition Monitoring Bureau, in the age group of 10–15 years, boys are fed 31 gm of pulses a day whereas, girls get only 25 gm a day. Boys get more leafy vegetables, fruits and calcium. As children grow up and take up a sedentary or active job, the gap in the degrees of nutrition widens even more. For instance, women in a sedentary job gets 403 gm of cereals a day, whereas a man in a similar job gets 475 gm. (NNMB, 1980). Indian women may be malnourished because of the poor nutritive quality of what is available even when they are provided the required quantity of food.

Access to health care is determined by 'need', 'permission', 'ability', and 'availability' (Chatterjee, 1990). The use of health system is determined by perceived need and often this 'need' is limited to the child-bearing years. Even in the child-bearing years the use of health care system tends to be limited. For example, the NFHS reported that out of the births which occurred in the previous four years, 62 per cent of mothers had received anti-natal care while 26 per cent had delivered in medical institutions, and 34 per cent were delivered by trained medical persons (IIPS, 1995). The reason for such low levels of use is that women often perceive the services to be unnecessary. Social and economic norms determine 'permission' and 'ability'. Women often need permission to seek health care. When there is dependence, either physical or financial on care givers, access is determined by the willingness and ability of the care givers to provide the needed treatment, for example, in the case of those women who needed treatment for visual disability if they had no sons or could not find alternative escorts (World Bank, 1994). The availability also depends upon the geographical proximity and on ones purchasing capacity. There is a considerable evidence that male children receive more and better health care at an earlier age than female children do. At the All India Institute of Medical Sciences, of all the surgeries which are conducted on children and infants, 70 per cent are on boys and only 30 per cent are on girls.

Summing Up

Excess mortality rate of female child after birth continues to be the dominant practice in reducing the number of female children. Sex-selective abortion is also accounted to gender-bias to make sex-ratio unfavourable to women. Early marriage and more number of pregnancies result in higher maternal mortality rates. Nutrition is also an important element in preserving health but, within households, women and girls are often discriminated in matters of food allocation. This type of discrimination starts from child birth, with the male child being nursed for longer duration than the female child, and continues over lifetime. Adolescence is the period of the growth spurt and girls get less than the required daily allowance of nutrients. As a result, they do not achieve their potential growth, causing risks during the critical years of child bearing. In the old age also, women bear the burden of malnutrition that started at an early period in their life. Also, in times of food shortages, elderly women are most likely to be more affected. Women of all ages have not only poor access to the health care system but are also less likely to use it. The number of boys who are brought to clinics for treatment is higher as compared to girls. Girls are even provided with poorer medical care in comparison to boys. This type of gender discrimination continues in later life as well, where women may downplay their morbidities, attempt home remedies and seek traditional medical treatment before reaching the hospital. Further, the blatant targeting of women in family planning programmes has also adversely affected their health. Lack of information and availability of different family planning methods have its bearing on women's health. The methods of family planning are limited and women cannot avail them, but have to depend on the medical staff. Such a disproportionate emphasis on female sterilization, in conjunction with a lack of concern about health outcomes for women, is a manifestation of gender inequality built in the state government programmes as well as into Indian society.

References

Acheson, Donald (1998), *Acheson Report: Independent Inquiry into Inequalities in Health Report*, UK: Government of UK.

Bidinger, Patricia, M. Nag and P. Babu (1986), *Factors Affecting Intra-Family Food Distribution in a South Indian Village*, New York: Ford Foundation.

Bimal, K.P. (1991), 'Health Services Resource as a Determinant of Infant Death in Rural Bangladesh: An Empirical Review', *Social Science Medicine*, 32(1): 43–49.

Black, Douglas (1980), *Black Report*, UK: Department of Health and Social Security.

Blackburn, C. (1991), *Poverty and Health: Working with Families*, Buckingham: Open University Press.

Borooah, Vani K. (2007), 'Inequality in Health Outcomes in India: The Role of Caste and Religion', *Munich Personal RePEc Archive*, Paper No. 19832.

Census of India (2001), *SRS Bulletin*, 35(1), New Delhi: Registrar General.

—— (2011), New Delhi: Government of India.

Chen, Martha Alter and Jean Dreze (1995), 'Widowhood and Well-being in Rural North-India,' in Monica Das Gupta, Lincoln C. Chen and T.N. Krishnan (eds), *Women's Health in India: Risk and Vulnerability*, Bombay: Oxford University Press.

Devadas, R. and G. Kamalanathan (1985), 'A Woman's First Decade', paper presented at the Women's NGO Consultation for Equality, Development, and Peace, New Delhi: UNICEF.

Ghosh, Shanti (1985), 'Discrimination Begins at Birth', paper presented for UNICEF Journalist's Workshop on the Female Child, New Delhi: UNICEF.

Hallberg, L (1988), *Iron Balance in Pregnancy*, Nestle Nutrition Workshop Series 16, New York: Raven Press.

Harriss, Barbara (1986), *Intra-family Distribution of Hunger in South Asia*, London: School of Hygiene and Tropical Medicine.

ICMR (Indian Council of Medical Research) (1982), 'Report of ICMR Working Group', *American Journal of Clinical Nutrition*, 35: 1442.

IIPS (International Institute for Population Sciences) (1995), *National Family Health Survey: India, 1992–93*, Bombay: IIPS.

Khan, M.E., Richard Anker, S.K. Ghosh Dastidar and S. Bairathi (1989), 'Inequalities between Men and Women in Nutrition and Family Welfare Services: An In-Depth Enquiry in an Indian Village', in J. Caldwell and M.G. Santow (eds), *Selected Readings in the Cultural, Social and Behavioural Determinants of Health*, Canberra: Australian National University.

Kopparty, S.N.M. (1994), *Social Inequality and Health Care*, New Delhi: Northern Book Centre.

Leon, D.A., G. Walt and L. Gislon (2001), 'International Perspectives on Health Inequalities and Policy', *British Medical Journal*, 322: 591–94.

Mathur, Deepa (1995), 'Gender Dimension of Health in India', in Indu Mathur (ed.), *Health, Hazards, Gender and Society*, Jaipur: Rawat Publications.

Miller, B. (1981), *The Endangered Sex: Neglect of Female Children in Rural North India*, New York, Ithaca: Cornell University Press.

Mukherjee, Subrata et al. (2011), 'Social Class-related Inequalities in Household Health Expenditure and Economic Burden: Evidence from Kerala, South India', *International Journal for Equity in Health*, 10(1).

Nagla, Madhu (1999), *Sociology of Medical Profession*, Jaipur: Rawat Publications.

National Family and Heath Survey (NFHS–3) (2005–06), IIPS, Mumbai.

Nettleton, Sarah (2006), *Sociology of Health and Illness*, UK: Polity Press.

NNMB (National Nutrition Monitoring Bureau) (1980), *Report for the Year 1980*, Hyderabad: National Institute of Nutrition.

NSSO (National Sample Survey Organization) (1991), *Sarvekshana*, 15(2), Department of Statistics, Ministry of Planning, Government of India, October–December.

Padmanabha, P. (1982), 'Mortality in India: A Note on Trends and Implications', *Economic and Political Weekly*, XVII(32): 1285–90.

Premi, M.K. (2001), 'The Missing Girl Child', *Economic and Political Weekly*, 36(21): 1875–80.

Roy, T.K., Sumati Kulkarni and Y. Vaidehi (2004), 'Social Inequalities in Health and Nutrition in Selected States', *Economic and Political Weekly*, 39(7): 677–83.

Shaw, M. et al. (1999), *The Widening Gap: Health Inequalities and Policy in Britain*, Bristol: The Policy Press.

Sutton, Philip W. (2011), 'Health, Illness and Disability', in Anthony Giddens (ed.), *Sociology*, London: Polity Press.

Tinker, Anne et al. (2000), *Improving Women's Health: Issues and Interventions*, Health, Nutrition and Population (HNP) Discussion Paper, World Bank.

Townsend, Peter and Nick Davidson (1982), *Inequality in Health: The Black Report*, London: Penguin.

Wilson, Robert N. (1970), *The Sociology of Health: An Introduction*, New York: Random House.

World Bank (1994), *Averting the Old Age Crisis: Documents and Reports*, Washington, D.C.: World Bank.

24

Globalization and Health Care

In this chapter we will learn about the health implications of globalization. First, we will look into why globalization has intensified the need for states and other national level policy actors to cooperate internationally, and then indentify the actors who seek to develop health policies at the global level and those who operate internationally to influence policy at the national health level.

Defining Globalization

There is more and more agreement on the fact that globalization is an extremely complex phenomenon; it is the interactive co-evolution of multiple technological, cultural, economic, institutional, social and environmental trends at all conceivable spatiotemporal scales. Hence, Rennen and Martens (2003) define contemporary globalization as an intensification of cross-national cultural, economic, political, social and technological interactions that lead to the establishment of transnational structures and the global integration of cultural, economic, environmental, political and social processes on global, supranational, national, regional and local levels. Although complex, this definition is in line with the view of globalization in terms of deterritorialization and explicitly acknowledges the involvement of multiple dimensions. However, the identification of all possible health effects of the globalization process goes far beyond the current capacity of our mental ability to capture the dynamics of our global system; due to our ignorance and inter determinacy of global system that may be out of reach forever (Martens and Rotmans, 2002).

Globalization and Health

Health, as so much of all aspects of 21st century life, is inextricably bound up in global relationships. Global health therefore refers to perceiving health as the outcome of global processes, with solutions to improving the health of the global population as being the responsibility of an alliance of global organizations, national governments and non-governmental organizations.

The concept of global health, therefore, seeks to explore how health is increasingly conditioned and modulated by global processes and relationships. A global health perspective conceives health as referring to the health of all the people on the planet. By adopting this perspective, which embraces the entire world, a radical break from the past was made when the health initiatives were mainly focused on the health of people in one particular geographic region or specific population. It is also not just different groups of people around the world that global health brings under its auspices but the global approach to health, of bringing together different groups of people, is also apparent in other ways.

Conceptual Model of Global Health

It is identified that global governance structures, global markets, global communications and the diffusion of information, global mobility, cross-cultural interaction and global environmental changes are important features of globalization. Figure 1 shows that features of globalization operate at the contextual level of health determination and influence distal factors such as health related policies, economic development, trade, social interactions, knowledge and the provision of ecosystem goods and services. In turn, these changes in distal factors have the potential to affect proximal health determinants and consequently, health. The conceptual framework for globalization and health links the features of globalization process with the identified health determinants.

Figure 1

Globalization and Health

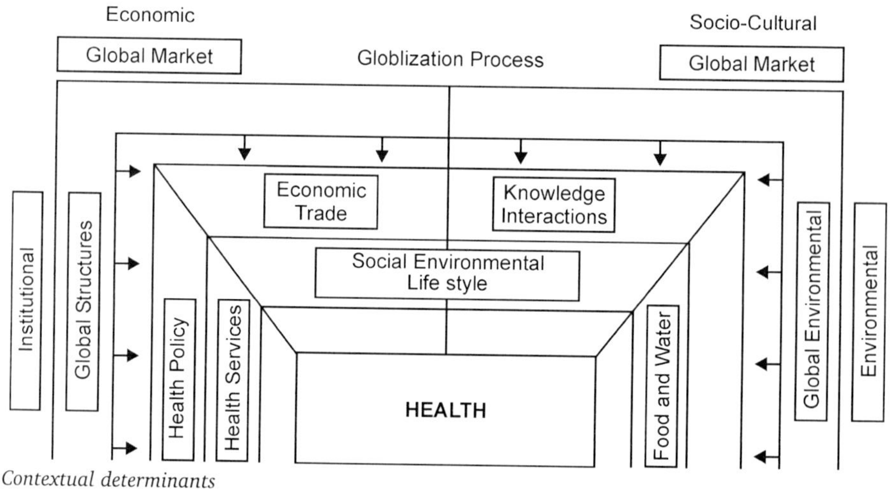

Contextual determinants

Distal determinants

Proximal determinants

Source: Huymen et al. 2005, 'The Health Impact of Globalization: A Conceptual Framework', *Globalization and Health,* 1:14.

Challenges to Health across the Globe

The WHO (2008) has identified the following challenges to health across the globe:

- One in five of the 58.8 million deaths that occurred in 2004 were children. Under the age of five, malnutrition is one of the main reasons for those deaths.
- Lung cancer, as a consequence of smoking is now the leading cause of cancer-related mortality among men.
- Ischemic heart diseases and cardiovascular diseases are the leading causes of death.
- HIV/AIDS is the main cause of death for 15–59 year old in the African region accounting for 40 per cent of all female deaths.
- Depression and other instances of mental distress are among the leading causes of disability. Other causes of disability arise from vision and hearing impairments.
- Road traffic accidents are increasing globally due to increasing urbanization. Quite simply, more and more people are now living in built environments with greater proximity to cars, with all the advantages and disadvantages that entails.

Impact of Globalization on Health Care

The implications of the globalization on distal determinants are discussed:

Health Related Policies

High income countries adopt global health polices to control and combat infectious diseases at international borders, while in low income countries they are subject to external pressures. Policy conditions may be set by the donor organizations on ministries of health in return for access to loans. These policies may also be established in response to the pressure from global social movements. Moreover, implementation of policies such as childhood immunization programmes, may be dependent on support from global public-partnership such as the Global Alliance for Vaccines and Immunizations. While national policies have always been subject to external influences, globalization has amplified and multiplied them.

For health care analysis at the global level, we have to understand how globalization affects the process of making policy. This can be broken down into three parts: (1) How do global interactions facilitate the transfer of polices among countries and organizations? (2) Who influences the transfer of policies? (3) How has globalization shaped the content of health policy?

Economic Development

Optimists argue that global market facilitate the economic growth and economic security, which would benefit health. It is argued that although other nations or households become richer, absolute poverty is reduced and this is beneficial for the health of the poor. On the other side, pessimists are worried about effects of the exclusion of nations and persons from the global market on health. They argue that the risk of exclusion from the growth dynamics of economic globalization is significant in developing countries.

Trade

Due to the establishment of global markets and a global trading system, there has been a continuing increase in the world trade. According to WTO, the total trade multiplied by a factor of 14 between 1950 and 1997. Today, all countries trade internationally and they trade significant proportions of their national income which is around 20 per cent of the total world output. The array of products being traded is wide-ranging from primary commodities to manufactured goods. Besides goods, services are increasingly traded as well.

Social Interactions: Migration

Due to changes in the infrastructures of transportation and communication, human migration has increased at unprecedented rates. Tourism is one of the most obvious forms of cultural globalization and it illustrates the increasing compression of current societies in time and space. However, travel for business and pleasure constitutes only a fraction of total human movement.

Knowledge

The capital of knowledge within a population is increasingly affected by developments in global communication and global mobility. It is expected that the development in knowledge and communication will also improve health training and health education.

Ecosystem Goods and Services

Global environment changes can have profound effects on the provision of ecosystem and goods and services to mankind. It is expected that climate change can result in significant disruptions in ecosystem and threatens substantial changes to earth's natural system. There is also a link between biodiversity and ecosystem. Ecosystem provides us with the basic human needs like food, clean air, water and soil. They prevent the spread of diseases through biological control. Ecosystem provides us with medical and genetic resources, which are necessary to prevent or cure diseases.

Health Services

Health services are increasingly influenced not only by globalization-induced changes in health care policy, economic development and trade and knowledge, but also by migration. Population of many economies are no longer protected by a centralized health sector that provides universal access to everyone, and some are even denied the most basic medical services. The increasing trade in health services can have profound implications on the provision of proper health care. Although it is perceived as to improve the consumer's choice, some of the developments are believed to have long-term dangers such as, establishing a two-tier health system, movement of health professionals from the public sector to the private sector, inequitable access to health care and the undermining of national health systems. The illegal trading of drugs and the provision of access to controlled drugs via the internet are potential risks in matters of health. In addition, the globalization process can also result in a brain-drain in the health sector as a result of the migration of labour from developing to developed nations. However, increased economic growth is generally believed to enhance improvements in health care. The increased technological knowledge resulting from the diffusion of information can further improve the treatment and prevention of all kinds of illness and diseases.

Social Environment

The central mechanism that links personal affiliations to health is social support and the transfer from one person to another of instrumental, emotional and informational assistance. Social networks and social integration are closely related to social support and, as a result, globalization-induced changes in social cohesion, integration, and interaction can influence the degree of social support in a population. Another important factor in the social environment is violence, which often is the result of the complex interplay of many factors. The WHO argues that globalization gives rise to obstacles as well as benefits for the prevention of violence. It induces changes in protective factors like social cohesion and solidarity, knowledge and eduction levels, and global violence-prevention activities such as the implementation of international law and treaties designed to reduce violence (e.g. social protection). On the other hand, it also influences important risk factors associated with violence such as social cohesion, income inequality, collective conflict, and trade in alcohol, drugs or firearms.

Lifestyle

Due to the widespread flow of people, information and ideas, lifestyle has also changed throughout the world. It is already widely recognized that several modern behavioural factors such as unhealthy diet, physical inactivity, smoking, alcohol misuse and the use of illicit drugs have a profound impact on human health. Individuals respond to the range of healthy as well as unhealthy lifestyle options and choices available in a community which are in turn determined by global trade, economic development and social interactions. Although the major chronic disease are not transmitted via infectious agent, yet the behaviour that predisposes to these diseases can be communicated by advertising, product marketing and social interactions. Global trade and marketing developments drive the nutrition transition towards diets with high proportions of salt, saturated fat and sugars. However, health education can play a key role in promoting healthy lifestyles by improving an individual's knowledge about the health effects of different lifestyles. Besides health education, global policies can also directly discourage unhealthy behaviour by means of economic incentives or other legislations.

Physical Environment: Infectious Diseases Pathogens

The spread of infectious diseases is probably one of the most mentioned health effects of globalization and the past disease outbreaks have been linked to factors that are related to the globalization process. The recent outbreak of the Severe Acute Respiratory Syndrome (SARS) demonstrates the potential of new infectious diseases to spread rapidly in today's world by increasing the risk of global panic. The combination of the movement of goods and people and profound changes affecting ecosystem goods and services together contribute to increased risks of the spread of disease. Enhanced knowledge and new technologies will improve the surveillance of infectious disease and monitoring of antibiotic resistance.

Food

Food trade has become an increasingly important factor with regard to the worldwide matters of food security. At present, however, the developed countries usually subsidise their agricultural sectors. Current liberalization policies are expected to have profound implications on food trade and subsequently food security. Some argue that the resulting free trade will create access to better and cheaper food supplies via food imports, and can stimulate more efficient use of the world's resources as well as the production of food in regions that are more suitable to do so. Free trade permits food consumption to grow faster than domestic food production in countries where there are constraints in increasing the latter. Accelerated economic growth can also contribute to food security. For many countries, increasing dependence on import of food goes hand in hand with a higher vulnerability to shocks arising in global markets, which can affect the capacity of and access to import of food.

Water

The effects of globalization are also raising concerns over water security. The current globalization process is accompanied by privatization policies affecting the provision of water. The virtual trade of water is also believed to be of increasing importance. The water that is used in the production process of commodity is called 'virtual water' contained in that commodity. Therefore, the increasing global trade of commodities is accompanied by an increasing global trade in 'virtual water'. The global volume of this water embedded in crop and livestock products traded between nations is estimated to have increased too much. In addition, the globalization process can increase water security by facilitating the worldwide implementation of better technologies and improved knowledge. At the same time, the actual resource base is increasingly threatened as, for example, global climate change and deforestation profoundly affect the ability of our ecosystem to provide us with sufficient and adequate fresh water.

Globalization and Health

The impact of globalization on health is most evident in the area of infectious diseases. Microbes can now find their way to multiply destinations across the world in less than 24 hours. The SARS outbreak in 2003 had spread rapidly from China to the neighbouring countries and on to places such as Canada. Not only did the virus cause illness and death, it was estimated to have cost Asian economies US$ 30 billion and economy of Toronto US$ 30 million per day at its peak. In 1990, a ship pumping its bilge in a Peruvian harbour had spread cholera throughout Latin America causing 4,000 deaths infections in the first year and considerable costs in terms of its trade and travel. This was a part of the seventh cholera epidemic which spread more quickly than the preceding six. In 2003 and 2004, polio spread from Nigeria to 12 polio-free countries in Central, West and Southern Africa. These outbreaks demonstrate that if an epidemic is not detected by a national health system, it can rapidly become a health threat in other parts of the world because of globalization (Buse, Mays and Walt, 2005: 140).

It is not that only infectious diseases are benefitted from globalization. The global production, distribution and marketing of foods, for example, carry, with them health risks linked to unhealthy diets. Individual behaviour is also prone to globalization in relation to road accidents, sedentarism, smoking, use of alcohol, sex trade and so on. Globalization can also affect the ability of health care system to respond to health threats. Due to globalization, the health professionals also have free flow from one country to another to meet the demands where there is a shortage of professionals are in short.

Global Agencies in Health Care

Global governance structures are gaining more and more importance in formulating health related policies. According to Dodgson et al. (2002), the most important organizations in global health governance are the World Health Organization (WHO) and World Bank (WB). The latter plays an important role in the field of global health governance as it acknowledges the importance of good health for economic development and focuses on reaching the Millennium Development Goals. The global agencies like United Nations (UN), World Trade Organizations(WTO) and United States Agency for International Development (USAID) are also established to facilitate cooperation at global level.

The United Nations

The UN system was established at the end of the Second World War to maintain peace and security and to save further generations from the scourge of war. Within this system, the World Health Organization (WHO), United Nations International Children' Emergency Fund (UNICEF), UN programme on HIV/AIDS(UNAIDS) and world Bank (WB) have been established to share common problems. The WHO was founded in 1948 as the UN's specialized health agency with a mandate to lead and coordinate international health activities. Presently, most nation-states (192) belong to WHO and non-voting 'associate membership' allows 193 NGOs in 'officials relations' to participate in the governance of the organizations (Buse, Mays and Walt, 2005: 141).

The WHO is governed through the World Health Assembly (WHA). The WHA meets annually to approve their organization's programme and budget and to make international health policy decisions. Its constitution grants to the WHA the authority 'to adopt conventions or agreements with respect to any matter within the competence of the organization'. The WHO collectively performs the following functions:

- Articulating consistent, ethical and evidence-based policy and advocacy positions.
- Managing information by assessing trends and comparing performance and setting the agenda for, and stimulating research and development.
- Catalyzing change through technical and policy support, in ways that simulate cooperation and action and help to build sustainable national and inter-country capacity.
- Negotiating and sustaining national and global partnership.
- Setting, validating, monitoring and pursuing the proper implementation of norms and standards.
- Stimulating the development and testing of new technologies, tools and guidelines for disease control, risk reduction, health care management and service delivery.

Among these functions, the WHO is best respected for technical norms and standards developed by its extensive network of experts and technical advice to its members. While the WHO may provide technical basis for health policies around the world, it has virtually no ability to impose these policies on sovereign states; its influence rests on its technical authority.

World Bank

The World Bank has a mandate to provide financial capital to assist in the reconstruction and development of member states. The Bank entered the health field through lending for population programmes in the 1960s, for health services in the 1980s and by the late 1980s, to an international health policy focusing on financing reforms. By the end of the century, it was the largest external financier of health development in low and middle income countries. Its influence was derived not just from the loans it disbursed, but also from the perceived neutrality and authority of its economic analysis and its relationships with powerful finance ministries in borrowing countries. In effect, the acceptance of policy conditions associated with health sector loans (which may have been resisted by health officials) could be linked to the Bank's support for projects in energy or industrial sectors, cared deeply by the other ministeries. Although the Bank's policies have been contested, most donors, industry and governments have supported them in general.

The World Trade Organizations

The WTO administers and enforces a series of international trade agreements with the goals of facilitating trade. These global rules for trade can impact health directly through access to medicines, trade in health services or flow of health workers, and indirectly through exposure to consumption and environmental risks that arise from trade. The domestic policies dealing with these issues have become more constrained as a result of the WTO agreements because, by joining the organization, states commit themselves (with no reservations allowed) to alter their policies and statues to conform with the principles and procedures established in all the WTO agreements.

A number of WTO agreements have implications on health policy. Trade Related Intellectual Property Rights (TRIPS) has had the highest profile among the treaties in international health policy circles because of its impact on the policies concerned with the generic drug production and trade. Yet, the agreement on Technical Barriers to Trade, the Agreement on the Application of Sanitary and Phytosanitary Measures and the General Agreement on Trade in Services have all been invoked to challenge the health policies of member states when other governments fear that they serve to protect domestic industries instead of protecting health.

Bilateral Cooperation

Bilateral relationships (between government of one country to another country) includes cooperation and assistance by USAID and Swedish International Development Agency (SIDA). They play major roles at the international, regional and national levels. They are often the major financiers of health programmes in low income countries and of the health programmes of the UN organizations.

Global Civil Society

There has been a spectacular proliferation of global civil society groups over the past 50 years; from 1,117 international associations registered with the Union of International Associations in 1956 to over 16,500 in 1998 (UIA, 1998). Global associational revolution is underway that will be as significant to the later 20th century as the rise of the nation-state was to the later 19th century Global Civil Society. It encompasses a diverse set of actors targeting a diverse set of issues. For example, there are Global Civil Society Organizations active in:

- Reproductive health – such as the International Women's Health Coalition
- Trade agreements – such as Health Action International (a coalition of 150 NGOs from 70 countries)
- Rights of people with AIDS – for example, the International Community of Women living with HIV/AIDS which claim to represent 19 million HIV positive women
- Ethical standards in humanitarian relief – for example, the SPHERE Project
- Landmines – for example, the International Campaign to ban Landmines is coordinated by a Committee of 13 organizations by bringing together over 1,300 groups from over 90 countries.

The Global Civil Society constitutes a heterogeneous lot from a group of people linked together via the internet to communicate a shared vision across national frontiers to organizations which have vast amounts of political assets. It is the one civil society that eclipsed the World Bank in many important respects as the epicentre of global health.

The Bill and Melinda Gates Foundation was established in 2000 and is now a central actor in international health. The Foundation, with an endowment of over US$ 27 billion (in 2005), disburses over US$ 500 million per year on health in the developing countries. The foundation has played a catalytic role in changing the organizational landscape in international health. The other major financer of health development, the World Bank, largely provides loans to governments; the Foundation has mainly supported non-governmental organization, with grants particularly the public-private partnerships.

The growth of global civil society has been embraced for a number of reasons. For some, it is welcomed due to the declining capacity of some states to manage policy domains such as health. For others, it is a means to improve the policy process by beginning new ideas and expertise into the process by reducing conflict and improving communication or transparency. For others, the involvement of civil society provides the means to democratize the international system to give voice to those who are affected by policy decisions thereby making these policies more responsive.

Intellectual Property Rights

According to the WTO, Trade Related Intellectual Property Rights (TRIPS) has a particularly powerful enforcement mechanism and is likely to have profound implications on public health. The Agreement obliges countries that had hitherto failed to protect product or process patents to make provisions for doing so, and in particular, to set the patent period at 20 years. The industry argues that monopoly protection is required to encourage investment in Research and Development. Critics are concerned that this will place unnecessary restrictions on the use of generic products, inevitably increase drug costs and erect barriers to scientific innovation.

Globalization and Health Care in India

India is a mixed economy and has one of the most privatized health systems in the world. India is being exhorted by international banks to reduce public expenditure in health through increasing privatization. It only has 23 per cent of the public health expenditure of total health expenditure as compared to the United Kingdom which has 96 per cent and Japan with 80 per cent of its public health expenditure. Even in the United State of America, it is over 50 per cent (Sengupta, 1994). However, in 1990 India has agreed for health care reforms under the ambit of the globalization of health care. It has provided following logic for the health care reforms:

- India needs more finance for health care.
- Health care safety net for poor people in the form of social insurance.
- More consumer choices will be available after reforms.
- It will bring more competition among providers of health care in public and private sectors.
- Non-competitive public provision of health services is likely to be inefficient or of low quality.

The government has looked towards the scarcity of resources in health care for equity, efficiency and affordability turned towards the health sector reforms. The International Monetary Fund (IMF) and World Bank have dictated certain policies for reforms such as:

- Cut government spending in health care, education and subsidies to the farmers and poor.
- State owned industries and services must be sold off to private corporations.
- More export to increase the repayment rate of loans to lead to commercial farming.
- Open the door to foreign multinational companies.
- Reduce duties and tariffs on imports that facilitates the accessibility of Multi National Corporations (MNCs) and prevents local companies to compete with MNCs.

Impact of Globalization on Health Care

There are multiple sides through which health care is affected because of globalization. These are as follows:

User Charges

User charges have been introduced in the public sector for curative aspect of health care and not for preventive and promotive health care. At tertiary levels, fee will be charged for services and medicine and not for consultation of doctors. Government servants have been given access to high technology and other tertiary health care services in private health sector through reimbursement policy.

Cut in Budget

There is a continuous fall of expenditure in health care budget at the centre and state level. Within that budget, 70 to 80 per cent budget goes for salaries of health care professional and therefore, it affects the budget for supplies and material goods. With a fall in gross demostic product, health expenditure is declining from 1990 onwards, leading to stagnancy in central budget and a fall in the funds for public sector.

Resurgence of Communicable Diseases

Rapid migration from one place to another is leading towards more spread of communicable diseases. It has more effect on the health of poor people because they have less immunity and reduced accessibility to the health care facilities. Tuberculosis (TB), plague, dengue and malaria are some common rampant diseases.

No Medicine for Poor

Patent, i.e. TRIPS has a monopoly in the sense that these rights are given to persons over the creation of minds. They usually give the creator an exclusive right over the use of his/her creation for a certain period of time. TRIPS protects the interests of big biotechnology, pharmaceutical companies and others to impose the cost of policing on cash strapped government, while slowing down or preventing altogether the transfer of useful technology. India opposed the patent of medicine as it is a non-trade issue. At domestic front, India did not favour strong protection to patents before the WTO agreement was signed. It is illogical to trust a single patent structure on all countries of the globe, irrespective of their stage of development. The WTO did not allow countries with domestic laws that enabled domestic companies to manufacture drugs invented elsewhere at prices that were anything between 1/20 and 1/100 of the global prices. Research and patenting in pharmaceutical are driven not so much by actual therapeutic needs, but by the needs of manufacturing companies to maintain their super profits at present levels. The kinds of drugs to be sold to the people are also decided by the companies, keeping in mind the purchasing power of people. Lifestyle drugs like Viagra and slim diet drugs are expanding their markets. Whereas, orphan drugs which cure life threatening diseases are not encouraged for production. Around 4 per cent of money allocated for research in drugs is going for the manufacture of new drugs for diseases spreading in developing countries.

International Migration of Doctors and Collaboration with Private Sector

Our country has a shortage of health care professionals. However, continuous migration of doctors at international level is also affecting the health care at domestic level. More and more doctors are also encouraged to enter the private health sector which further creates the shortage of health professionals in public health sector.

Making of Corporate Hospitals

Health care is regarded as an industry like other industries. With the advent of globalization, the investment in health sector is encouraging and resulting into more proliferation of corporate hospitals. The aim of corporation is to draw benefit out of their investment. Corporate hospitals are exempted from custom duty towards the cost of import of medical equipment and technologies. They are also given land at lesser prices for establishing the hospital.

Opportunity Costs

Government facilities are still not available at the door steps of people, therefore it increases the opportunity costs and force them to go to private health care facilities. The NSS data shows that the share of persons who do not take treatment due to financial reasons in the rural areas has risen from 15 per cent in 1986–87 to 25 per cent in 1995–96, and 10 per cent to 20 per cent in the urban areas over the same period (Duggal, 2005).

Differentials in Health Status Among Different States

There is a differential in the availability of sub centres, primary health centres and community health centres in different-states.

Differentials in Health Status among Socio-Economic Groups

It is evident that there has been a widespread adoption of market-led policies reinforcing the ideology of capital accumulation. A symptom of this is that the most marginalized groups are most likely to suffer ill health and are least able to improve their health. There is a differential in health status among different socio-economic groups like scheduled castes, scheduled tribes and other groups.

Vertical Programmes for Diseases

Vertical programmes for prevention of diseases have miserably failed.

Public Health Infrastructure

Public health infrastructures are inadequate in terms of hospitals, dispensaries, beds, health professionals, etc.

Inter-Sector Contribution to Health

Adequate nutrition, safe drinking water, basic sanitation, clean environment and primary education are not linked together.

Changing Lifestyle

Due to the widespread flow of people, information and ideas, varied forms of lifestyle also spread throughout the world. It is already widely acknowledged and demonstrated that several modern behavioural factors such as an unhealthy diet, physical inactivity, smoking, misuse of alcohol and the use of illicit drugs have a profound impact on human health. Individuals respond to the range of healthy as well as unhealthy lifestyle options and choices available in the community, which are in turn determined by global trade, economic development and social interactions.

Summing Up

The emergence of a global economy has led to the erosion of sovereignty and local autonomy. An important consequence of the free market economy has led to a great divide between those who have benefitted and those who have lost. This is also reflected in divergent patterns of health and well-being. Increasingly, development aims such as meeting basic needs are subsumed by a reliance on market forces as the key determinant in policy formation. In India, welfare provision is a stated objective; the prescription tends to emphasize economic growth in the belief that such growth will benefit the whole community.

Although technological progress has brought the means to control infectious disease, some aspects of globalization have contributed to an increased risk of unhealthy lifestyles. All people are at risk, but the marginalized groups are more likely to experience inferior living conditions and limited purchasing power. It results in the adoption of unhealthy lifestyles. These include stress, alienation and the aggressive marketing of fast foods, cigarettes and alcohol.

References

Ashton, S. and R. Stepney (1982), *Smoking*, London: Tavistock.

Bailey, K.V. and A.H. Ferro-Luzzi (1995), 'Use of Body Mass Index of Adults in Assessing Individual and Community Nutritional Status', *Bulletin of the World Health Organization*, 73(5): 673–80.

Beck, U. (1994), *Reflexive Modernization: Politics, Tradition and Aesthetics in the Modern Social Order*, Cambridge: Polity Press.

Becker, M.H. et al. (1977), 'The Health Belief Model and Prediction of Dietary Compliance: A Field Experiment', *Journal of Health and Social Behaviour*, 18: 348–66.

Buchanan, K. (1985), 'Centre and Periphery: Reflections on the Irrelevance of a Billion Human Beings', *Monthly Review*, New York, July/August, 86–97.

Buse, Kent, Nicolas Mays and Gill Walt (2005), *Making Health Policy*, New Delhi: Tata McGraw-Hill.

Chomsky, N. (1993), *The Prosperous Few and the Restless Many: Noam Chomsky Interviewed by D. Barsamian*, Berkeley, CA: Odonian Press.

Cohen, S. et al. (1986), *Behaviour, Health and Environmental Stress*, New York: Plenum.

De Garine, I. and N. Pollock (eds) (1995), *Social Aspects of Obesity*, South Australia: Gordon and Breach.

Department of Environment, Sport and Territories (1995), *Active and Inactive Australians: Assessing and Understanding Levels of Physical Activity*, Canberra: Commonwealth of Australia.

Dodgson, R., K. Lee and N. Drager (2002), *Global Health Governance: A Conceptual Review*, Centre on Global Change and Health, London School of Hygiene and Tropical Medicine.

Duggal, Ravi (2005), 'Public Health Expenditures, Investment and Financing under the Shadow of Growing Private Sector', in Leena V. Gangoli, R. Duggal and Abhay Shukla (eds), *Review of Health Care in India*, Mumbai: CEHAT, 107–16.

Ender, N.S. (2012), 'Hassles, Health and Happiness', in M.P. Janisse (ed.), *Individual Differences, Stress, and Health Psychology*, New York: Springer-Verlag, 24–56.

Frank, A.G. (1978), *Dependent Accumulation and Underdevelopment*, London: Macmillan.

Harpham, T. (1994), 'Urbanization and Mental Health in Developing Countries: A Research Role for Social Scientists, Public Health Professionals and Social Psychiatrists', *Social Science and Medicine*, 39(2): 233–45.

Hart, R.H. et al. (1990), *Integrating Maternal and Child Health Services with Primary Health Care*, Geneva: WHO.

Hodge, A. et al. (1996), 'Obesity in Pacific Populations', *Pacific Health Dialog*, 3(1): 77–86.

Huymen, Martens P. et al. (2005), *The Health Impacts of Globalization: A Conceptual Framework*, Bilthoven: Netherlands Environmental Assessment Agency.

Khan, M. et al. (1987), 'Inequalities between Men and Women in Nutrition and Family Welfare Services: An In-Depth Enquiry in an Indian Village', in J.C. Caldwell and G. Santo (eds), *Selected Readings in the Cultural, Social and Behavioural Determinants of Health*, Health Transition Series No. 1, Health Transition Centre, Australian National University, Canberra, 175–99.

Manning, W. et al. (1991), *The Costs of Poor Health Habits*, Massachusetts: Harvard University Press.

Martens, P. and L. Rotmans (2002), 'Transition in a Globalising World', *Futures*, 37(10): 1133–44.

McMurray, C. (1995), *Report on the Republic of the Marshall Islands Fertility and Family Planning Survey, November–December*, Unpublished Report, Majuro: Office of Planning and Statistics, Republic of the Marshall Islands.

Mills, S. (ed.) (1988), *Alternatives in Healing: An Open-Minded Approach to Finding the Best Treatment for Your Health Problems*, London: Macmillan.

Mull, D.S. (1991), 'Traditional Perceptions of Marasmus in Pakistan', *Social Science and Medicine*, 32(2): 175–91.

Myrdal, G. (1953), *The Political Element in the Development of Economic Theory*, London: Routledge and Kegan Paul.

Rennen, W. and P. Martens (2003), 'The Globalisation Timeline', *Integrated Assessment*, 4: 137–44.

Robertson, R. (1992), *Globalization, Social Theory and Global Culture*, London: Sage Publications.

Royston, E. and S. Anderson (1989), *Preventing Maternal Deaths*, Geneva: WHO.

Salamon, L.M. (1994), 'The Rise of Non-Profit Sector', *Foreign Affairs*, 73(4): 109–22.

Sengupta, A. (1994), 'World Development Report: Implications for Infrastructure Development in Health Care and Pharmaceutical Industry', *Social Scientist*, 22: 112–28.

Shukla, Abhay (2001), *Review of Health Care in India*, New Delhi: Indian Council for Research on International Economic Relations.

Simons, J. (1989), 'Cultural Dimensions of the Mother's Contribution to Child Survival', in J.C. Caldwell and G. Santow (eds) *Selected Readings in the Cultural Social and Behavioural Determinants of Health*, Health Transition Series No. 1, Health Transition Centre, Australian National University, Canberra, 132–46.

Spielberger, C.D. et al. (1988), 'The Experience, Expression and Control of Anger', in M.P. Janisse (ed.), *Individual Differences, Stress, and Health Psychology*, New York: Springer-Verlag, 89–108.

UIA (1998), *Yearbook of International Associations, Vol. I: Organizational Descriptions*, London: Union of International Associations.

Wallerstein, I. and T. Hopkins (1996), *The Age of Transition: Trajectory of the World System, 1945–2025*, London: Zed Books.

World Health Organization (2008), *The World Health Report 2008: Primary Health Care Now More than Ever*, Geneva: WHO.

Zuckerman, M. (1988), 'Sensation Seeking, Risk Taking, and Health', in M.P. Janisse (ed.), *Individual Differences, Stress, and Health Psychology*, New York: Springer-Verlag, 72–88.

25

Indian Constitution and Health Rights

Human life is precious and every person has a fundamental right to live with dignity. It is the duty of a welfare state to protect and develop the life of every citizen and to promote his rights to health and medical care. Right to medical care is important because it relates to the very existence of human life. Medical care is as essential as the other basic needs of a person like food, water, shelter and clothing. Every nation has evolved its own system of laws to ensure the health rights of its citizens. These laws aim to establish a humane system of health care based on the principles of equity, justice and efficiency. By emphasizing the rights of citizens for proper health and care, every good government tries to enhance the welfare of its people so that they can live healthy and productive lives.

Today, privatization of health care has created manifold sufferings and problems for poor patients. Medical profession, which is a noble profession, has become a business in the hands of those whose only aim in life is to accumulate wealth by any means, fair or foul. Medical personnel often forget their responsibilities towards their patients and conduct their professional work without observing the code of ethics and thereby violate the rights of patients. A patient's trust in a doctor is often exploited by him for his personal gains.

Defining Health Rights

The concept of right to health as a human right has recently emerged as a result of ever growing consciousness about the dignity of human life all over the world. Health care is considered as a socio-medical concept which implies that whatever is medically possible to promote the physical, mental and well-being of the patient must be done.

Right to health and health care is also a fundamental right under Article 21 of the Constitution of India. This has also been emphasized by the Supreme Court of India in several obligations on state to protect citizen's life from medical and other forms of negligence.

The Indian Constitution is based on the policy of welfare and democratic and socialistic framework of development. Civil and political rights in our Constitution are given as fundamental rights whereas social and economic rights, which include health, livelihood etc. are provided within the framework of directive principles for the State and are not justifiable. Fundamental rights are justiciable under which, Right to Primary Education has also been made a fundamental right. Health, livelihood and higher education comes under the domain of planning and hence, they are rooted through Five Year Plans and other policy initiatives. Various meanings are attached to a right. So, right is a permission to do something that is secured and protected by law. Still, other definitions associate a right with a conditional duty that binds only on the condition that the beneficiary chooses to have it exercised. There is something to recommend in each of these interpretations of the meaning of right to health care. Patients have a right to be informed about the benefits and risks of medical procedure, but they are not required to exercise the right. Right is protected by society or secured by law to the individual (Barry, 1982). According to CESCER (2000), the Right to Health is defined as the enjoyment of different facilities, goods and services which are utmost necessary for the experiencing of the highest attainable standard of health.

Historical Perspective of Right to Health

Historically speaking, the right to health has roots in the 19th century public health movement in Europe and the US, which produced sanitation reforms designed to reduce the burden of infectious disease. These efforts helped to solidify the belief that governments had a fundamental duty to provide for and protect the public health. In the Human Right Revolution, the government's duty in the health fields was translated into the right to health (David, 1999). The concept of right to health as a human right has recently emerged as a result of ever growing consciousness about the dignity of human life all over the world. Health care is considered as a socio-medical concept which implies that whatever is medically possible to promote the physical, mental and well-being of the patient, must be done.

Right to health and health care is also a fundamental right under Article 21 of the Constitution of India. This has also been emphasized by the Supreme Court of India in several obligations on state to protect citizen's life from medical and other forms of negligence. The right to health is one of the economic, social and cultural Human Rights that requires affirmative government action to create better conditions for people rather than just governmental restraint vis-à-vis citizens.

Relationship between Health Rights and Health

Health and human rights are intrinsically related with one another. When we talk about human rights, we can talk about them in the absence of health. However, over a period of time, there is unregulated growth of private health sector which has a restricted access to health care to the common and poor masses. At the same time there is weakening of public health system. Thus, there is restricted access to universal and comprehensive health care. The International Human Right Treaties and norms hold the government responsible for providing health to its people. The right-based approach asserts that health is a fundamental right of every human being as it implies the enjoyment of the highest attainable standard of health. The right to health care can only be achieved through the provision of adequate social and health measures. These health and social measures are integrated into research strategies and then monitored. They are further mobilized through community actions, education and policy formulation. In Article 12 of the International Covenant on Economic, Social and Cultural Rights, the right to the highest standard is encapsulated. It mentions the underlying preconditions necessary for health and also the provisions of different medical care. The most important thing in the philosophy of right to health is its realization. With the impact of globalization in the world as a whole, there is weakening of public health system and expansion of private sector of health. Globally, the health sector is still dominated by vertical and ethnocentric approaches, which are often supported by public partnership at different levels. There is an urgent need to replace this dominant paradigm shift of public-private partnership in health to the universally achieving public health care system of achieving the right to health and to health care objectives. Ethics of doctors are not good as per their duty or humanity. Very few doctors pay adequate attention towards patient's problem in their duty time. If anyone needs medical help after their duty, very few of them provide their services to them; some of them may ignore or demand to pay. All these show lack of moral values or ethics. Health and health care is viewed under the perspective of human right and these are also mentioned in Article 12 of the right to highest attainable standard of health under the heading of International Covenant on Economic, Social and Cultural Rights. In the Committee on Economic, Social and Cultural Rights, it is clearly mentioned that realization of right to health and the availability, accessibility and quality of health care is the precondition for good health. Further, the Article 12.1 subscribes the Right to Health as an inclusive right, not only related with time and appropriate health care but also with underlying determinants of health like access to potable water, sanitation facilities, safe and adequate food, housing and nutrition. Health occupational environment and ecological conditions are also necessary. Health education, health information and education about sexual and reproductive health is most important and necessary. The right to health is reflected in its diverse forms at different levels, and has some essential elements as discussed below:

- *Availability:* There should be availability of health and health care facilities through a provision of goods and services as well as through various health programmes.

- *Nature of facilities:* It depends upon the state's commitment to the health of people. The facilities are in the form of potable drinking water, adequate sanitation facilities, hospitals, clinics and other health related infrastructure, trained medical and health personnel and also the supply of essential medicines. These health facilities should be accessible to everyone, irrespective of their caste, class, race, gender and other discriminatory variables.

Dimensions Related with Health Accessibility

There are five overlapping dimensions related with accessibility:

(i) *Non-Discriminational:* Health facilities in terms of provision of goods and services are desired to be accessible to all and specifically to the weaker sections, marginalized, and the most deprived sections of the society.

(ii) *Physical Accessibility:* When the health services and goods are within the reach of common masses or to all sections of the society, we call it physical accessibility of health services. Most deprived sections of population like marginalized groups, minority groups, women, children, person with disabilities or persons with HIV/AIDS have lack of adequate means. Therefore, for them, physical accessibility is the prime requirement. Accessibility also means the physical accessibility of potable and safe drinking water and sanitation facilities particularly to the rural people.

(iii) *Affordability:* Health facilities and health services should be affordable to all. Payment for health services should be based on the principles of equity so that all get the benefits of health care services. Principle of equity ensures that poor people should not be disproportionately burdened with health expenses as compared to rich people.

(iv) *Information Accessibility:* Information accessibility means the right to seek, receive and impart education related to health care issues. This accessibility of information should not be applied in the case of confidential and personal information.

(v) *Acceptability:* Health facilities provided by state and different agencies should be acceptable to people. People should also respect medical ethics and are expected to be cultural specific. In sum, health services should be culturally specific in relation to the people of different communities. Provision of health services should be gender sensitive and according to the requirements of life cycle.

(vi) *Quality:* Good quality of health services are also needed for good health of citizens. Quality of services also means skilful manpower and scientifically approved drugs within their time framework including manufacturing date under the framework of quality. Hygienic hospital, safe and potable water and adequate sanitation are also the part of quality services. Thus, to conclude, it can be said that for the protection of right to health care, universal access of good quality health care along with equitable distribution is also a necessary element. To make it possible, the state governments and central government are obliged to respect, protect and fulfil the above criteria in a progressive manner.

Government and Levels of Obligations

There are three types or three levels of obligations on the part of State Government for the health rights:

(i) The obligation to respect, protect and fulfil the right to health, which means that to facilitate right to health the government must facilitate, provide and promote health care among people.

(ii) The obligation on the part of government is to refrain from interfering, directly or indirectly, with the enjoyment of the right to health. The States are expected to take measures that prevent third parties from interfering with Article 12.

(iii) Under the obligation to fulfil health right, the states are required to adopt appropriate legislative, administrative and other measures towards the full realization of the right to health (Committee on Economic, Social and Cultural Rights Twenty Second session, 25 April, 12 May 2000). The Alma Ata Declaration, in which India was also a signatory, proclaims that the existing inequalities in health status of people between developed and developing nations, as well as within the countries, are unacceptable and therefore, all efforts will be done to remove social and economic inequalities. It is a common concern of all nations. The countries or state parties are under the obligation to ensure the health rights enunciated in the Covenant including essential primary health care. Great emphasis was given in the Alma Ata Declaration on the Health to All. Following are the core areas of concern:

   1. Non-discriminatory basis for ensuring the right to access of health facilities, goods and services. Accessibility to the essential food requirement and nutritional adequacy is the key component of right to access to health services. No one should die because of hunger. Basic shelter, housing and sanitation is the right of each individual. For keeping good heath, adequate supply of safe and potable water is must. Equity in distribution of health facilities, goods and services is the most important framework for the realization of health rights.

To address the health concern of the whole population, there are other obligations on the basis of priority which are to be taken for the health concerns of the people:

- To ensure reproductive facilities which include maternal and child health care; to make arrangements for immunization against major infectious diseases in the community; have preventive measures to control and treat endemic and epidemic diseases; access to education and information related with health problems for controlling the health problems in the community; and to arrange required training for health personnel and updating of their education in relation to health and human rights.

Health Care and Health Rights

Health is a State subject which comes under the directive principles of the state charter. However, there is enough scope for the centre where large number of items are mentioned in the Concurrent List of the Constitution. The central government has enough scope of its manoeuvrability in relation to providing a major health policy and also through various national health programmes. Various such programmes are already pushed by the central government and are still in force with several other programmes. There are certain vertical programmes like National Programme for Leprosy, Tuberculosis, Blindness, Malaria, Small-Pox, Filarial, Diarrhoea, Goitre, Polio and HIV/AIDS, etc. They are completely sponsored by the central government however, State Government is obliged to cooperate in its implementation in making them successful. These national programmes are uniformly implemented throughout the country along with the required funds. Besides that, there are other programmes which are also of national concern and include Family Planning Programme, Immunization programme and other *Aganwadi* programmes. The states are obligatory to implement these national programmes in their respective states. Thus, the central government and state government are together responsible for the provision of health care services and goods. The right to health requires comprehensive systems of health care delivery along with health insurance policy for the country. The country is supposed to promote individual and community health care at preventive and promotive level. Prevention of diseases actually reduces the burden of morbidity and decreases the mortality. The elimination of the causes of health inequalities brings the realization of the health right more closely to people. This will help in improving the health of people. Health right is never seen in isolation, it is actually dependent on other human rights. The human right to health is inclusive of physical and mental, and reproductive and sexual health. It is the right to equal and adequate health care and health related services irrespective of one's caste, class, gender, ethnicity, etc. The basic human right is related with an adequate standard of living and shelter. There is also another human right to access to safe drinking water and sanitation alongwith the right to safe and healthy environment. There should be safe and healthy workplace and adequate protection for pregnant women so that no harm is done to them. Access to information related to health, which includes reproductive health and family planning, is also a part of the human right charter. Couples can decide with full freedom and responsibilities about all matters related with reproduction and sexuality. Although, health sector is the responsibility of state, local and central government, in terms of service delivery, it is the state government which is accountable for health of its people. The central government is accountable for its services in terms of developing and monitoring national standards and regulations elated with health care. Centre provides linkages with the funding agencies at various levels and also sponsors certain schemes and programmes for implementation of the same by state governments. The government at state, local and central level provides publicly financed and managed curative and preventive services from primary to tertiary level throughout the country so that they can reach to the masses. In terms of its financial liability, it accounts for approximately 18 per cent of the overall health expenditure and 0.9 per cent of the Gross Domestic Product. Roughly, 82 per cent of the overall health expenditure and 4.4 per cent of GDP is incurred by private sector through ambulatory services.

The Central Council for Health and Family Welfare Department looks after the goal and strategies for public health sector which are the outcome of several discussions at various levels related to health. Public health and sanitation and hospitals and dispensaries are listed under the State List in the Seventh Schedule to the Constitution. Health services in India are mainly a state subject. That probably explains why there is no All India Health Service on the lines of erstwhile IMS (Indian Medical Service) before Independence, which was next in status to the coveted ICS. However, Population Control and Family Planning figures in the Concurrent List. By and large, health services in the whole of India follow the same general pattern, especially in rural areas. Each State has a State Health Directorate with Director Health Services as the head. Each district in the State has the Chief Medical Officer as the head at district level. Within the district, each block has a Community Health Centre (CHC) at the block level which has a 30 bedded hospital attached to it. It serves a population of one lakh on an average. Within the block there are three Primary Health Centres (PHC), each for a population of 30,000. The CHC itself continues to act as a PHC for its 30,000 population. There is a provision of six beds in PHC. Each PHC has one or more medical officers. Health services in PHC area are provided through six sub-centres. The health sub-centre has one male and one female health worker and is the primary point of contact between the community and health system. The female health worker is commonly known as Auxiliary Nurse Midwife (ANM). One ANM provides services to about 5,000 population spread over one-five villages. In most villages in India, there is also another female functionary called *Anganwadi* Worker (AW), who provides health and nutrition support to women and children. The AW is not a government employee. She is a part-time voluntary worker under the national ICDS (Integrated Child Development Services) scheme which is run by the Ministry of Human Resource Development rather than the Ministry of Health. At the central level, there is a Central Ministry of Health and Family Welfare which has three departments under it, viz., Department of

Health, Department of Family Welfare and Department of ISM and H (Indian Systems of Medicine and Homoeopathy).

Some national institutions are directly financed and controlled by the central Ministry of Health and Family Welfare. They are All India Institute of Medical Sciences, Indian Council of Medical Research and National Institute of Health and Family Welfare. In addition to the above, there are government dispensaries and hospitals in urban areas. The railways and defence services have their own network of health services. The corporate sector has also made a notable entry during the last two decades. The Appolo group of hospitals may be mentioned as an example in the same line.

The Indian Constitution and Right to Health

The actual base of right to health lies with the fundamental rights and Article 21 (related with life and dignity). Article 21 of the Indian Constitution clearly spells out that no person shall be deprived of his/her life or personal liberty except only in cases of procedures established by law. Further, the Supreme Court has expanded its meaning of the term 'life' with the meaningful and healthy life. Over the years, life-term is accepted in terms of dignified life with concomitant attributes and not like animal existence. It means that life is extensively related with the healthy environment and proper health care facilities. Therefore, the fundamental right to life is interpreted in a broader context.

As we all know that fundamental rights are by and large enforceable by the state. In the various chapters of the fundamental rights, it is mentioned that there are certain duties and obligations of state and its citizens. As and when we talk about the right to health and health care as a fundamental right, we simply mean the obligation of the Sate towards its citizens and not the obligation of private health care sector of health which includes individual practitioner, private nursing homes, private hospitals or corporate hospitals. At no point of time, does it exempt private health care practitioners from an obligation towards their patients in a negligent manner. They abide by certain rules and regulations framed by the Medical Council of India or Sate Medical Council, and also keep on informing about the new guidelines as and when they are framed. These private practitioners are under no obligation to provide free or subsidized treatment to the people. However, the corporate hospitals that have taken subsidized lands for hospitals and have asked for the exemption of import duty for certain equipment are liable to provide free and subsidized treatment to certain percentage of their total strength of patients. The right to health cannot be separated from right to life. Further, right to medical facilities is dependent on right to health which is an essential component of right to life. In India, which works on the philosophy of welfarism of its people, the onus lies on the state to have the provision of health care facilities for its people. The health rights are enforced against the states in various courts of law. In our Constitution, Part–3 prescribes the fundamental rights of citizens. Nowhere, we have directly stated that right to health and health care is a fundamental right. However, it has been mentioned that right to life is a fundamental right. At various points of time, the courts have also interpreted that the expanded meaning of right to health and health care is a fundamental right. Part-4 of the Constitution lists the directive principles of State Policy. These principles are meant for the state to follow and move further in terms of guiding principles which enables them to enact laws and frame policies. Traditionally they were never challenged in the court of law. However, with the passage of time, people are moving in the court of law to challenge them. A citizen can go to the court for the enforcement of different provisions of health care which comes under the directive principles. As and when the need arises, the fundamental rights are interpreted by taking the help of the directive principles. The court also cites certain relevant provision of the directive principles which enforce the state to ensure good health to its citizens. It gives the reference of Article-38 which clearly mentions that sate should provide order for the welfare of its people and strive to promote the security and protection in an efficient and effective manner. State shall also strive to reduce the inequalities of income and bring social order of justice in social, economic and political spheres. It shall also try to eliminate inequalities of status, facilities and opportunities between different sections of society and amongst individuals, irrespective of their socio-economic background. The essence of this is that no person of the country will be deprived of a healthy life just because he/she cannot pay for it. The state must ensure health facilities to the poor people so that they do not have to spend from their pocket as better-off persons can even afford to spend out of their pocket for health care facilities.

Article 39

There are certain principles of policy which are to be followed by the state. The state shall direct the policy framers and implementers to secure the health of men, women and children. They should not be forced to spend on health care beyond their capacity so that they do not enter into the situation of debt. Foremost, children should be provided all health facilities so that they may develop in healthy conditions of freedom and dignity. Young children and youth should be protected against any type of exploitation like child labour. In Article 47, it has been mentioned that the state is bound to raise the level of nutrition and standard of living to improve public health care services. It should make all efforts to reduce the cases of drug addiction and prohibition of intoxicating drinks and drugs which are injurious to health.

Some Examples of Judicial Pronouncements on Health Care

There are many incidents when the right to health care is debated in various courts of law between government and users of health care. In this context, the court has made certain relevant observation by giving importance to health rights. At various times health rights are denied or restricted by the state and public health care agencies, which in turn has resulted in judicial pronouncements on health care. Below we are presenting certain cases which in turn will help in understanding the right to health and health care as a fundamental right.

Right to Health and Health Care as a Fundamental Right

Right to health is a fundamental right which we have already discussed in our preceding pages. Here we will cite a case which has been fought in the court of law in 1991 by a company CESC Ltd. Vs Subhash Chandra in Fir No. 1992, Section 573, 585 in the Supreme Court. The court reiterated that health is a fundamental right. The court has taken a broad meaning of health as not only the condition of the absence of sickness, but emphasized that medical care and health facilities should protect sickness and ensure stability of manpower for economic development. Medical facilities should not be only for curative purpose, but also for healthy development of workers which increases the devotion and dedication of workers for economic development. Best physical and mental environment is necessary for the healthy development of society. Good health of workers increases the productivity and, in turn, helps him in leading a good economic, social and cultural life. Thus, the judgment advocates for the availability of good medical facilities which are a part of medical security and helps in immediate return of out-of-health productive activity. Thus, this judgment ensures that good health also includes healthy physical, social, mental and economic activity. Socio-economic justice is assured under the Universal Declaration of Human Rights, in Article 22 to 25 under the banner of International Covenant on Economic, Social and Cultural Rights, in our Constitution. Thus, it automatically becomes a fundamental right. The goal of our Constitution is to maintain the health of its people, and its implementation requires the interaction of social and economic factors.

Right of the Government Employee to Receive Health Care

This case is related with the policy for reimbursement of medical expenses. There is a policy for the reimbursement of medical expenditure during the service or after service. This has been done to uphold that adequate medical care is an employee's right to live with dignity. The below mentioned case is of the State of Punjab Vs Mohinder Singh Chawla (1997: 2: SCC 83). Mohinder Singh Chawla was suffering from heart ailment. He was seeking treatment, but it was beyond the capability of the state hospital and, therefore, they referred the case to All India Institute of Medical Sciences, New Delhi. The State Medical Board granted permission for the heart treatment of Mr Chawla at AIIMs, New Delhi, and he went to AIIMS for his heart treatment. After his treatment he approached the authorities for reimbursement of his medical expenditure and his expenses on rented accommodation. His expenditure on medical reimbursement were made but the expenses on accommodation were rejected. The Punjab Government has taken the plea for rejecting the accommodation expenses that the changed State Health policy does not reimburse the expenses incurred on diet, stay and stay of attendant. Further, Mr Chawla went to the Supreme Court and asked for the reimbursement of his expenditure on accommodation. The issue before the Supreme Court was the extent of state's responsibility to provide medical facilities to its employees. At one level, the state was justifying its denial of the expenses incurred on accommodation and on the other hand, it is the state's responsibility to provide medical facilities to its employees. Mr Chawla's claim was that medical treatment is inclusive of room-rent for treatment. In the judgment it was upheld that rent of room is an integral part of the expenses incurred on medical treatment and therefore it cannot be excluded. The state is obligatory to bear the expenses of the government servant while in service or after retirement.

Obligation of Private Sector

With the rapid expansion of private sector in the health care delivery services, the gradual withdrawal of public sector, i.e. state is increasing. In this context, it is necessary to understand the rights of citizens in relation to the private health sector. There are certain crucial issues which appeared both in Mumbai and Delhi concerning the obligation of the private sector to provide free and subsidized treatment to poor patients. The overwhelming majority of private hospitals, nursing homes or corporate hospitals are registered under the banner of public trusts. Such registration entitles them for income-tax rebate or exemption as well as certain other subsidies. These subsidies are in the form of rebate in the import duty for purchasing certain drugs, medical equipments etc. Land for building hospitals is also provided on concessional rates. It is a well-known fact that these medical care facilities charge exorbitant fees which is difficult for the poor to afford and therefore, they are debarred by using medical facilities in these medical care centres. However, these institutions are charitable institutions and registered under Charitable Act. These institutions get income tax rebate and subsidized land from the government and various other subsidies and are bound to serve the people in turn. These trusts are obligatory to treat certain number of patients free. Various empirical studies have found that these hospitals are not complying with the requirements and are evading their responsibility. Various court cases against charitable trusts are filed in Bombay and Delhi Courts. The Court has directed state governments to prepare certain guidelines for treatment so that even poor people can have an easy access to these charitable and private hospitals.

Examples of Right to Health explained by Empirical Studies

The medical profession by its very definition is for the service of humanity. Its main principle is to render service with full respect to the dignity of profession and man. A physician should have altruistic orientation and merit the confidence of patients entrusted to their care. He is expected to devote his service with full devotion. These physicians and other health personnel are expected to upgrade and improve their medical skills and knowledge for the benefit of patients so that these benefits can be shared by the medical community at large. A doctor is always expected to practice his art of healing based on certain scientific principles and not on the basis of his own predispositions based on certain non-rational beliefs. At no point of time, he is expected to indulge in violation of scientific principles of medical practice. The ideals of medical profession or for that matter of medical fraternity are obligatory to the masses and not to the individual (Medical Council of India, 2002). This shift of public sector doctors to the private sector is losing the ideals of medical profession. Other personnel, however, are fleeced and exploited by private hospitals through long hours, low pay scales and an almost complete denial of benefits and lack of any rational system of work monitoring. Inevitably, this drastically affects their performance and overall levels of care (Baru et al.: 2000). Banerji (1982) points out in his study that a doctor's behaviour is not same towards all patients in medical check-ups. Patients with resistance and those who need new drug may not get it. This also denies the right of individuals to quality treatment. The debate related with the implementation of human right to health is new and full of possibility for the developing world. Still, India is in a nascent state, particularly for the health right. However, it could be able to develop a mechanism whereby the right to health can be protected and achieved. In 1997, watershed in human rights litigation was witnessed with the *Keshavanand Bharti Vs. State of Kerala* ushering in an unprecedented judgement that the directive principles of the state policy should enjoy the same status as 'traditional' fundamental rights. With this judgement, the standing rules were relaxed in order to promote public interest in litigation and access to justice. This has led to increase in health related litigations (Khan, 1995). Hasan (1979), in a study, finds out that a doctor treated the villagers with sympathy, talked to them very mildly, paid enough attention to each patient, made queries from the patient or his relative and examined his body with hand or stethoscope. Among the qualities which the people attributed to the doctor, was his quality of paying equal attention to all without any discrimination. The doctor was devoid of casteism or communalism, made no distinction between men, women or children and did not show any favour to the rich. He paid more attention to the poor and did not charge any fees for home visits from them. Sometimes he himself brought costly medicines to the poor patients and did not charge even the actual cost. Private health care provision is an important element of the health care delivery system in India and its continuous expansion over a period of time. There are many studies on the access and usability of the health care system, and they conclude that not only rich people are using private health care facilities, but even poor people are forced to use these facilities for their health problems. The fast growth of private health sector raises many issues for poor people who cannot afford the expenses. Therefore, state is supposed to play an important role in regulating private health sector. So far, the government's role in regulating the health sector has remained passive (Bhat, 1993). Today, privatization of health care has created manifold sufferings and problems for poor patients. Medical profession, which is a noble profession has become a business in the hands of those whose only aim in life is to accumulate wealth by any means, fair or foul. Medical personnel often forget their responsibilities towards their patients and conduct their professional work without observing the code of ethics and thereby violate the rights of patients. A patient's trust in a doctor is often exploited by him for his personal gains. Growing incidences of malpractices and medical negligence are keeping poor patients out of hospitals and clinics. In some cases the Supreme Court and High Court uphold the decision of right to health. The right to health is applicable even in case of emergency, criminal and non-paying capacity. Providing a first-aid in cases of emergency is also must for the private health practitioners. They cannot deny a person for its emergency medical aid situation. The court also mentions clearly that in certain cases, access to medical care is a right in certain life threatening situations. The workers' right for safe working environment and a suitable arrangement for medical care is also essential. However, these rights are pronounced by courts in various cases but they are hardly respected by the people who engage workers in their organizations. Further, many times the state has also failed to respect, protect and fulfil the health rights of individuals and one is forced to go to courts of law.

In India, approximately 27 per cent of the population which is below poverty line are not expected to go to court for seeking justice. Mere constitutional provisions are not enough to guarantee a right, and particularly in the case of health and health care, they are required to have extensive health services and infra-structural health resources. The provisions related to health care are not adequate, but still, it is very important to have right to health in the Constitution. It becomes a guiding principle in the provision of health care services. Although the prime function of the Constitution for mentioning the right to health is in its symbolic form, but it sets guidelines for state government to protect the health of its people. Health rights are taken care of in the formulation of various health policies and programmes. It is not only sufficient to make health policies and programmes, but at the application level also, the state has to ensure the entitlement of health care services to its masses by developing certain specific statutes, programmes and services. By mentioning the right to health in our Constitution, we aim to inform people that protection of their health is the official policy and efforts are made for the provision of health services.

Magnitude of Right to Health

In India, there is a very small proportion of population in the organized sector who are either working in the government sector or in private organized sector and have some sort of health coverage. This health insurance is done through community insurance, family insurance or by the individual. There are certain insurance mechanisms, such as social security legislation like Employee State Insurance Scheme, Central Government Health Scheme, Maternity Benefit Scheme, etc. There are other specific sections of the society like mine workers, plantation workers, *beedi* workers, cinema workers and artisans who are also protected under some form of health insurance scheme. Railway employees and armed forces are protected under the provision of health care services or through reimbursements. This population is approximately 12 per cent of the total population. Another one per cent of the population is covered under private health agencies like Prudent, Max, Aviva, Medi-Claim etc. (Ellis et al.: 2000). These private insurance agencies have different layers of coverage of diseases with differential level of premiums. The private insurance agencies provide coverage to only those who can pay, therefore it does not cover the general population. Health insurance is a positive provision but, it does not cover the whole population and thus it becomes discriminatory in the sense that it becomes a selective right instead of a universal right.

Summing up

The right to health is defined as the enjoyment of different facilities, goods and services which are utmost necessary for the experiencing of the highest attainable standard of health. In the rights-based approach, health is viewed as the responsibility of government and places the government accountable. This approach also recognizes that the right to health is a fundamental right of every human being and it implies the enjoyment of the highest attainable standard of health. In India, health care infrastructure is grossly inadequate in relation to its population, therefore in that context it becomes very important to provide basic health facilities to its people, particularly to those who are very poor. Various committees have given certain recommendations to put health right in the proper direction. There are concerns of accessibility, affordability, quality, etc. which become obstacles for the proper attainment of health rights in the society. In various judgments, the fundamental right to health and health care has been recognized by the Supreme Court. The court has also guided the State to enforce the fundamental rights, however, subject to availability. Negative fundamental rights are those fundamental rights which cast an obligation on the state not to act in a manner that would deprive a citizen of his/her fundamental rights. As a developed nation, the courts have also realized that right to health and health care is a promotive and positive right. Simply, it should not be denied because of the poor financial capacity of the country.

References

Barry, Norman (1982), 'The Tradition of Spontaneous Order', *Literature of Liberty*, 5: 1–58.

Baru, R.V., I. Qadeer and R. Priya (2000), 'Medical Industry: Illusion of Quality at What Cost?', *Economic and Political Weekly*, 35(28–29): 2509–11.

Bhat, R. (1993), 'Public-Private Mix in Health Care in India', *Health Policy and Planning*, 8(1): 43–56.

Ellis, Randall P. et al. (2000), 'Health Insurance in India: Prognosis and Prospectus', *Economic and Political Weekly*, 35(4): 207–17.

Hasan, K.A. (1979), *Medical Sociology of Rural India: The Cultural Frontier of Health in Village India*, Ajmer: Sachin Publications.

26

Ethics in Health Care

Health care is very much related with ethical issues for more acceptance and effectiveness. These ethics include issues linked to the relationship between individuals and society, and the basis on which health care is justified. In the present chapter, we will look at some theoretical approaches for considering ethical issues in political and ethical philosophy and how they are resolved in practice.

Numerous indicators reflect a growing interest in ethical issues in medical and health care. Increasingly, media coverage includes discussion of ethical issues surrounding such developments as has been the case with reproductive technologies such as surrogate motherhood, cloning of human beings, etc. Moreover, professional organizations are devoting more time at their meetings and more space in their publications to discussion of ethical issues (Gottlieb, Burdine and McLeory, 1987). Against this background, one might suspect an equivalent development of sociological interest in medical ethics. This is so because many issues in medical ethics are sociological topics of major interest. For example, work in the area of medical care ethics, particularly work focusing on the rights and duties of medical professionals and patients, bears directly on the evolving nature of the doctor-patient relationship (Stacey, 1985). Ethical analysis of medical and health care public policy has significant implication for such macro sociological issues as equality in access to care and the role of the professions in determining the availability of medical and health care services (Mechanic, 1979).

A review of recent medical sociology works reveals some coverage of an array of ethical issues in medical and health care (Mechanic, 1983; Susser, Watson and Hopper, 1985; Mechanic and Atken, 1986; Simmons and Canio, 1979). Much of this has focused on micro-ethical issues, such as the doctor-patient relationship and treatment decisions for critically ill patients (Crane, 1975). More recently there has been an extension to societally focused issues, such as the rationing of medical care (Mechanic, 1979). Lesser attention has been devoted to exploring ethical issues in the interactions between institutions and professionals to studying the dynamic relationships between the professions and society (Freidson, 1970). Some sociological attention also has been given to the rise and current interest in bioethics (Fox, 1974). The number of specific medical and health issues that have received ethical analysis is very large; they include such topics as death and dying, kidney dialysis, organ transplantation, clinical research, genetic counselling and screening, decision to extend or terminate life support system, allocation of scarce medical resources, cost containment, and ethical issues in the development of profit hospitals.

In India, not much work has been done on medical ethics. However, Desai (1988) tries to see medical ethics in the continuity of indigenous and classical folk traditions. Wig (1985) discusses the forced population control measures as a medical and ethical issue. Desai and Chand (2007) lamented on the lacunae and absence of laws specifically with the duties of health facilities and personnel to provide medical treatment in emergency cases. Sriram et al. (1991) and Minocha (2010) have studied the discourse of informed consent in medical ethics along with field study. There is not much work at the theoretical and empirical level which has been done on the medical ethics, particularly in the Indian context.

History of Medical Ethics

Since the beginning of human history, concern for medical ethics has been expressed in the form of laws, decrees, assumptions and 'oaths' prepared for or by physicians. Among the oldest of these are the Code of Hammurabi in Babylonia (approximately 1750 BC), Egyptian papyri, Indian and Chinese writings, and early Greek writers, mostly Hippocrates (lived between 460 and 377 BC). Early medical ethical codes were written by individuals or by small groups of people, usually physicians. The oath of Hippocrates is considered historically to be the first such code written in an organized and logical way which describes proper relationship between physician and patient. During the Middle ages, other medical codes were written. In recent times, Thomas Precival's writings, disseminated in 1803, represent one of the first ethical codes in the United States and the Western World (Lustig et al., 1993).

Beginning in the second-half of the 19th century, medical organization began writing codes of medical ethics. The first ethical code of the American Medical Association (AMA) was published in 1847 which was the first ethical code of a professional organization outlining the rights of patients and caregivers. In the 19th century, medicine along with university teaching, law and ministry underwent professionalization. The medical profession succeeded, after prolonged agitation, in getting recognition for their status and prestige in 1858 when the Act creating the General Medical Council was passed in the UK. Initially, the Medical Councils of developed countries paid almost exclusive attention to reducing competition from outside and within. Thus, traditional practitioners and quacks were forcibly eliminated in the later part of the 19th century. Elaborate codes were made to restrict or eliminate unhealthy competition within the profession. Entry to the profession was restricted by getting control over medical education and registration of doctors. To these were gradually added the internal regulations or disciplinary procedures to curb the misuse of power detrimental to patients' well-being.

The World Health Organization (WHO) issued the Declaration of Geneva in 1948. This is the first world-wide ethical code, modelled after the oath of Hippocrates. Many other medical organizations throughout the world have also issued medical ethical codes.

Defining Ethics

Ethics involve normative questions, reasoning, and decision, for example, how one should act or ought to, both as a moral ideal and in an actual situation? Normative ethics, as a discipline, is not synonymous with law or social sciences.

Ethics is the branch of philosophy that has traditionally concerned itself with examining the worth or value of conduct with developing and defending views on what might be meant by 'worthwhile' and understanding how life could be led with it.

Ethical Traditions

Different ethical traditions have developed with conflicting views on the purpose of ethics (metaethical views) and the on the kind of ethics in which we should actually engage (normative views). In particular, western philosophy has been profoundly shaped by the three theories of ethics: Aristotelianism, Deontology and Utilitarianism. Each of these theories can in turn be seen as essentially a product of the times in which it was originally born. These theories are based on trying to determine:

- What is meant by leading a good or virtuous life? (Aristotelianism)
- What kind of duty or obligation we owe to each other? (Deontology)
- How we might take account of consequences while deciding a particular course of action? (Utilitarianism).

Aristotelianism

Aristotle's ethics is representative of ethical theories that aim to work out what a good (moral) life might mean and how the development of such life can be encouraged. He attempted to do this by looking at the nature of world and individuals within it in order to assess what it means by being virtuous. For this reason, Aristotle is frequently thought of as an empiricist. In viewing the world, he argued that we become virtuous by performing virtuous actions. What is most important is not simply the identification of means (the virtuous) in all aspects of human actions. It is the idea that through reflection and contemplation we should develop our lives so that we know how to act according to the means; in other words, how to act virtuously (or morally). We, thus, become morally expert, reflecting the consequent performance of virtuous action and determining, what it means to lead the worthwhile (good) life.

Deontology

Immanuel Kant developed the ideas representative of Deontology. It is a thinking based on the notion that we owe to each other particular duties or obligations. Kant claimed the existence of a reality independent of our experience. Part of his justification for his claim lay in his analysis of our experience as humans. We live in a world subject to scientific laws of causation, yet we retain the freedom of will, with the capacity to act morally or otherwise. Out moral choices must therefore be framed within an independent reality. Kant argued that reasons exist independently of experience and that the right use of reason is directed towards moral ends. Reasons move us to act out of duty for its own sake and independent of any thought about the consequences. How then, is the difficulty overcome? One way (which of course the strict deontologist could not accept) is to allow the consideration of consequences to play an important part in making moral decisions, which leads to the third ethical tradition of Utilitarianism.

Utilitarianism

According to J.S. Mill, careful thought needs to be given to the consequences of any action, and if those consequences are likely to be adverse for some, the reason for the action must be robust. Utility, or the greatest happiness principle, holds that actions are right in proportion if they tend to promote happiness and wrong if they tend to produce the reverse of happiness. By happiness is intended pleasure, and the absence of pain; by unhappiness, pain, and the privation of pleasure (Mill, 1962). Utilitarianism and consequentialist ethical theory in general corresponds with a belief held by many that whereas there are important moral duties, action simply for the sake of duty, whatever the consequences, is problematic. In addition, a deliberation about consequences may well include thoughts about the level of 'happiness' or 'unhappiness' likely to accrue from a particular course of action.

Ethical and Moral Discourse

In the ethnographic terms, moral processes differ in a fundamental way from ethical discourse. Whereas moral experience is always about practical engagements in a particular local world, in a cultural space that carries political, economic, and psychological specificity, ethical discourse is a globally elaborated abstract articulation of and debate over translocal values. It strives for an acontextual universality and objectivity; a view from nowhere. Ethical discourse is generated out of and applied in local worlds, so that it gets taken up in moral processes that are inseparable from local elations and conditions. The institutions, relationships and lived experiences that serve ethical deliberations are themselves grounded, in the oral processes of local worlds so that in actual practice, the distinction has blurred boundaries with overlapping components. But for heuristic purposes it is still useful to draw the distinction between local and moral processes that are inseparable from local relations and conditions and ethical discourse that brings, or at least aspires to, a translocal perspective (Kleinman, 2004).

The other side of duality is that ethics can be (and all-too-frequently are) irrelevant to local moral worlds. Thus, structural positioning of poverty and wealth systematically distributes health and health care resources inequitably as part of what defines the moral reality of a local world. To talk about universal ethical formulations of justice and equity, without beginning with the local moral condition of real people who experience the systematic injustices of higher rates of ill health and fewer health care resources owing to their positioning in local social structures of power, is to make those formulations utopian and irrelevant to the local world (Daniels et al.: 1999). When, for example, informed consent in bioethics is made into the overriding ethical condition of international health research in case of vaccine trials of HIV. In impoverished African villages where few people are literate and there is no equivalent in local knowledge of ideas of randomized controlled trials, placebo controls or perhaps even individual autonomy in deciding about participation of community becomes important.

Theoretical and Methodological Perspectives on Ethics

The territory of ethics and the examination and discussion of the values underpinning conduct is largely conceptual, and in the case of many concepts discussed in ethics, there is a large degree of dispute or contestedness. Some philosophers have attempted to suggest that value ('ought') judgements have a status roughly equivalent to those concerning empirical fact. For example, someone has suggested that 'killing is wrong' is an undeniable truth. Aristotle, Kant and Mill are very important representatives of philosophers attempting normative moral projects. In more recent times, contemporary thinkers viewing health care have tried to suggest that there are important principles that should underlie work in this field of activity. Among others, Beauchamp and Childress (1994) and Gillon (1994) have suggested that the following principles are particularly important for health care workers:

- *Autonomy:* It is the capacity to be incharge of your actions and your destiny. The principle of respect for autonomy asserts that we have a moral obligation to allow this capacity to individuals to the extent that it does not infringe on the equal rights of others. The obligation to respect the autonomy of others, for example, patients or clients, lies to the extent that this is compatible with the autonomy of all who are likely to be affected by the action being considered.
- *Beneficence:* This is frequently regarded as a moral obligation that ought to be held by health care workers and clearly connects with beneficence. The ethical commitment in health care is to produce benefits for patients or clients.
- *Non-Maleficence:* The obligation not to harm patients or clients is closely linked to the previous principles, because any given action has the potential to result in both benefit and harm. The obligation on health care professionals is to ensure that the balance is always in favour of benefits in any given situation.
- *Justice:* The obligation to act fairly when dealing with competing claims to do with, for example, resources or rights.

Importantly, the four principles are prima facie, which means that each is binding unless it conflicts with another, in which case a choice must be made between the competing principles as to which one should be followed. Those who support the four principles argue that whereas they cannot yield a definitive ethical judgment in all health care situations, they do provide a framework for considering, and reasoning about obligations.

Medical ethics is an area of applied ethics concerned with health and illness and health care and medical care. Ethics applied to health care and medicine has a number of roles to play and a number of limitations (Beauchamp and Childress, 1994). Most people involved in medical ethics would agree that it is a useful but rather imprecise 'diagnostic' and 'prescriptive' tool when brought to bear on real-life situations. 'Moral action guides', but seldom offers ready solutions to the hard choices that confront providers, patients or policy-makers. This is so, in part, because medical ethics most often deal with dilemmas in which no set of moral reasons for a given view or action is obviously the correct one.

History of Medical Ethics in India

The beginning of recorded medical practice in India date back to the advent of Aryan invaders. Much useful information is also found in the seminal Ayurvedic classics – *Caraka Samhita, Susruta Samhita* and *Bhela Samhita* (around 600 BC). In these classics, ethical principles were enunciated and steps taken to ensure that they were followed. Teacher and student were reminded that the profession existed for the welfare of the patient. Whilst fair compensation was not frowned upon, the physician was constantly reminded that the primary goal was not a fortune for the self and family, but the care of the sick. A healthy human body is essential to the realization of life's tasks, including the ethical. Health-seeking was a religious obligation. Ayurveda was created before the creation of the world so that the potential for protection of health and removal of disease was built into the act of creation. Ethical laws were natural laws and the Ayurvedic worldview was a part of the Hindu conception of humanity and its place in the universe.

The advent of the Portuguese, French and, most significantly, the British into India witnessed the system of medicine that continue to dominate the sub-continent. The officers of the Indian Medical Service introduced the principles of medicine and western concept of medical ethics. To this day, discussion on ethics in India start with the enumeration of the principles of beneficence, non-malevolence, autonomy and justice (Pandya, 2000). Questions about medical ethics in India interact with local customs and tradition in everyday practice. Unusual occurrences may be resolved by a reference to mythology or folklore. This is not to suggest that Indian medicine does not address the problems of ethics. They are intertwined in medical texts, and mythical figures are seen as models of exemplary ethical behaviour. Ethical solutions may be inferred and derived from scriptural texts. This is particularly so in the context of modern and recent medical technologies, with which medicine in India has no prior contact (Desai, 1988).

In India, the formal process of medical profession began in 1912 when the Bombay Medical Act was passed. This was followed in 1914 by the Madras Medical Registration Act, Bengal Medical Act and so on. In 1933, the Indian Medical Council Act brought higher education in medicine under the purview of a national level medical council. After Independence, separate National level and State level Councils were created for allopathy, homoeopathy and the Indian System of Medicine (ISM). The Medical Council of India under its Medical Council Act, 1956 has recently, i.e. in 2002, made regulations relating to the professional conduct, etiquette and ethics for registered medical practitioners.

Functioning of Medical Council

The national level council have controlled and supervised medical education whereas, the state council maintains the registers of doctors and exercises powers to discipline doctors whose conduct is found to be unethical. In the MMC Act, the Medical Council is empowered to hold an enquiry of any registered doctor suo moto (on its own) or any complaint made to it. This is properly codified in the Chapter VI, rules 62-75 of the Rules of the MMC Act. Thus, the Medial Council can act against the erring doctor even if no complaint is filed by the patient(s).

Further, the Council has the power to punish those who are found guilty of much misconduct in a properly held enquiry. Accordingly, the Council can warn a doctor, or can temporarily or permanently remove the name of the doctor from the register. But the Council has no power to award compensation to the patient of the complaint. When there are persistent reports of unethical practices in the profession (e.g. organ trade, cut practices), the Council cannot advance a pretext that there is no specific complaint filed. The Council has *suo moto* power to investigate. This also provides scope to patients' organizations and social organisations in filing complaints and in pressurising the Councils to play a more active role.

Importance of Medical Ethics

Medical ethics are not merely a moral code but a legally sanctioned code of conduct acceptable and normal within the medical profession. This does not mean that morality or moral theories do not influence medical ethics, but medical ethics must be understood, analysed and practised from a rational standpoint. This rational component of professional conduct is legally codified under the code of medical ethics of the legally constituted medical council with which all qualified medical practitioners must be registered.

The registrations as well as the conduct as per the code of ethics are essential because, 'Doctors use technical skills and expertise which the untrained person does not possess. Possessing these skills gives him great power over his patients who by the very fact of being patients are dependent, ill and vulnerable. In caring for his patients, a doctor makes a series of judgements and decisions which patients have the right to expect are made fairly in the light of the doctor's knowledge and experience' (British Medical Association, 1988). Thus, although the code of medical ethics is for the self-regulation of the profession, it is there in order to fulfil certain rights and expectations of the patient. In a nutshell, the code describes the doctor's duties towards the patient. If these rights are not fulfilled or duties are not performed, then the doctor in question loses his or her right to be a part of the profession.

Code of Medical Ethics

The Medical Council of India under its Medical Council Act, 1956 has recently, i.e. in 2002 made the regulations relating to the professional conduct, etiquette and ethics for registered medical practitioners as discussed below:

(a) *Declaration:* Each applicant at the time of making an application for registration under the provisions of the Act, shall be provided a copy of the declaration and shall submit a duly signed Declaration. The applicant shall also certify that he/she has read and agreed to abide by the same.

(b) *Duties and Responsibilities of the Physician in General:* Doctors with the qualification of MBBS or MBBS with post graduate degree/diploma or with equivalent qualification in any medical discipline shall uphold the dignity and honour of medical profession. The prime objective of medical profession is to render service to humanity, reward or financial gain is a subordinate consideration. Whosoever chooses his profession, assumes the obligation to conduct himself in accordance with its ideals. He shall keep himself pure in character and be diligent in caring for the sick; he should be modest, sober, patient, prompt in discharging his duty without anxiety, conducting himself with propriety in his profession and in all the actions of his life.

No person other than a doctor having qualification recognized by the Medical Council of India and registered with Medical Council of India/State Medical Council(s) is allowed to practice modern system of medicine or surgery. A person obtaining qualification in any other system of medicine is not allowed to practice modern system of medicine in any form.

(c) *Maintaining Good Medical Practice:* The principal objective of medical profession is to render service to humanity with full respect for the dignity of profession and man. Physicians should merit the confidence of patients entrusted to their care, rendering to each a full measure of service and devotion. They should continuously try to improve medical knowledge and skills and should make available to their patients and colleagues the benefits of their professional attainments. The physician should practice methods of healing founded on scientific basis and should not associate professionally with anyone who violates this principle.

(d) *Maintenance of Medical Records:* Every physician shall maintain the medical records pertaining to his/her indoor patients for a period of three years from the date of commencement of the treatment in a standard pro forma laid down by the Medical Council of India. If any request is made of medical records either by the patients/authorized attendant or legal authorities involved, the same may be duly acknowledged and documents shall be issued within the period of 72 hours. Registered Medical Practitioner shall maintain a register of medical certificates giving full details of the certificates issued. When issuing a certificate, he/she shall always enter the identification marks of the patient and keep a copy of the certificate.

(e) *Display of Registration Numbers:* Every physician shall display the registration number accorded to him by the State Medical Council/Medical Council of India in his/her clinic and in all his prescriptions, certificates or money receipts given to his/her patients. Physicians shall display as suffix to their only recognized medical degrees or such certificates/diplomas and memberships/honours which confer professional knowledge or recognize any exemplary qualification/achievements.

(f) *Use of Generic Names of Drugs:* Every physician should, as far as possible, prescribe drugs with generic names and he/she shall ensure that there is a rational prescription and use of drugs.

(g) *Highest Quality Assurance in Patient Care:* Every physician should aid in safeguarding the profession against admission to it of those who are deficient in moral character of education. A physician shall not employ, in connection with his professional practice, any attendant who is neither registered nor enlisted under the Medical Acts in force, and shall not permit such persons to attend, treat or perform operations upon patients in whose case professional discretion is required.

(h) *Payment of Professional Services:* The personal financial interests of the physician should not conflict with the medical interests of his patients. A physician should announce his fees before rendering service and not after the operation or treatment has begun. Remuneration received for such services should be in the form and amount should be specifically announced to the patient at the time when the service is rendered. It is unethical to enter into a contract of 'no cure no payment'.

(i) *Obligation to the Sick:* Though physician is not bound to treat each and every person asking his services, he should not only be always ready to respond to the calls of sick and injured, but should be mindful of the high character of his mission and the responsibility that he discharges in the course of his professional duties. In his treatment, he should never forget that health and the lives of those entrusted to his care depend on his skill and attention. No physician shall arbitrarily refuse treatment to a patient. However, for good reason, when a patient is suffering from an ailment which is not within the range of experience of the treating physician, he may refuse treatment and refer the patient to another physician.

(j) *Patience, Delicacy and Secrecy:* Patience and delicacy should characterize the physician. Confidences concerning individual or domestic life entrusted by patients to a physician and defects in the disposition or character of patients observed during medical attendance should never be revealed unless their revelation is required by the laws of the state.

(k) *Prognosis:* The physician should neither exaggerate nor minimize the gravity of a patient's condition. He should ensure himself that the patient, his relatives or his responsible friends have such knowledge of the patient's condition as will serve the best interests of the patient and the family.

(l) *Avoid Unnecessary Consultation:* However, in case of serious illness and in doubtful or difficult conditions, the physician should request consultation, but under any circumstances such consultation should be justifiable and in the interest of the patient only and not for any consideration. Consulting pathologists, radiologists or asking for any other diagnostic lab investigation should be done judiciously and not in a routine manner. Differences of opinion should not be divulged unnecessarily but when there is irreconcilable difference of opinion, the circumstances should be frankly and impartially explained to the patient of his relatives or friends. It would be opened to them to seek further advice as they so desire.

(m) *Treatment after Consultation:* No decision should restrain the attending physician from making such subsequent variations in the treatment if any unexpected change occurs, but at the next consultation, reasons for variations should be discussed/explained. The same privilege, with its obligations, belongs to the consultant when sent for in an emergency during the absence of attending physician. The attending physician may prescribe medicine at any time for the patient, whereas the consultant may prescribe only in case of emergency or as an expert when called for.

(n) *Patients Referred to Specialists:* When a patient is referred to a specialist by the attending physician, a summary of the case of the patient should be given to the specialist, who should communicate his opinion in writing to the attending physician.

(o) *Fee and Other Charges:* A physician shall clearly display his fees and other charges on the board of his chamber and/or the hospitals he is visiting. The prescription should also make clear if the physician himself has dispensed any medicine. A physician shall write his name and designation in full along with registration if he has himself dispensed any medicine. A physician shall write his name and designation in full along with the registration particulars on his prescription letter-head. However, in government hospital where the patient-load is heavy, the name of the prescribing doctor must be written below his/her signature.

(p) *Advertising:* Soliciting of patients directly or indirectly by a physician, by a group of physicians or by institutions or organizations is unethical. A physician shall not make use of him/her (or his/her name) as subject of any form or manner of advertising or publicity through any mode either alone, or in conjunction with others which is of such a character as to invite attention to him or to his professional position, skill, qualification, achievements, attainments, specialities, appointments, associations, affiliations or honours or of such character as would ordinarily result in his self-aggrandizement. A physician shall not give, to any person, whether for compensation or otherwise, any approval, recommendation, endorsement, certificate, report or statement with respect of any drug, medicine, nostrum remedy, surgical or therapeutic article, apparatus or appliance or any commercial product or article with respect of any property, quality or use thereof or any test, demonstration or trial thereof, for use in connection with his name, signature or photograph in any form or manner of advertising through any mode, nor shall he boast of cases, operations, cures or remedies or permit the publication of report thereof through any mode.

(q) *Running an Open Shop (Dispensing of Drugs and Appliances by Physicians):* A physician should not run an open shop for the sale of medicine for dispensing prescriptions prescribed by other doctors, or for the sale of medical or surgical appliances. It is not unethical for a physician to prescribe or supply drugs, remedies or appliances as long as there is no exploitation of the patient. Drugs prescribed by a physician or brought from the market for a patient should explicitly state the proprietary formulae as well as generic name of the drug.

(r) *Rebates and Commission:* A physician shall not give, solicit or receive nor shall he offer to give solicit or receive any gift, gratuity, commission or bonus in consideration of or return for referring, recommending or procuring of any patient for medical, surgical or other treatment. A physician shall not directly or indirectly, participate in or be a party to act of division, transference, assignment, subordination, rebating, splitting or refunding of any fee for medical, surgical or other treatment.

(s) *Euthanasia:* Practicing euthanasia shall constitute unethical conduct. However, on specific occasion, the question of withdrawing supporting devices to sustain cardio-pulmonary function even after brain death shall be decided only by a team of doctors and not merely by the treating physician alone. A team of doctors shall declare the withdrawal of support system. Such team shall consist of the doctor in-charge of the patient, Chief Medical Officer/Medical Officer in-charge of the hospital and a doctor nominated by the incharge of the hospital from the hospital staff, or in accordance with the provisions of the Transplantation of Human Organ Act, 1994.

Summing Up

Ethical analysis of medical and health care policy has a significant implication on the distribution of health care and the role of medical professional in determining the availability of health care services over a period of time. There are some studies done outside India on ethical issues. However, there are very few studies in India which are directly related to medical ethics. Beginning of human history is witnessed by concern for medical ethics in Babylonian, Egyptian, Indian, Chinese and Greek writings. The oath of Hippocrates is considered the first such code written in an organized and logical way. The WHO issued the first world-wide ethical code and is modelled after the oath of Hippocrates.

Ethics are concerned with normative questions reasoning and decisions. Different ethical traditions have developed over a period of time based on western philosophy. Each tradition is a product of times in which they were born. Morals are related with practical engagements in a particular local world and cultural specificity. Ethics are globally elaborated abstract articulation over translocal values. However, to talk about universal ethical formulation of justice and equity, without beginning with the local moral condition is useless and irrelevant. Therefore, in the real sense, the distinction has blurred boundaries between moral and ethics and overlaps with its components.

There is a large degree of dispute over the discourse of values and conduct related with the ethics. Aristotle, Kant and Mill represent philosophies of normative moral projects whereas, Beauchamp and Childress and Gillon view that autonomy, beneficence, non-maleficence and justice are binding unless they conflict with each other.

India has a long history of medical ethics enunciated in Ayurvedic classics around 600 BC. Recently, in 2000, the Medical Council of India has made the regulation relating to the professional conduct and ethics for Registered Medical Practitioners.

Medical profession is controlled and supervised by the national and state level medical councils. Medical council is empowered to hold an enquiry against a doctor suo moto, however, the council cannot advance its investigation against unethical practices like organ trade, and rebate-commission practices unless the complaint is made.

The codes of medical ethics are for the self-regulation of medical profession and in turn, to prescribe doctors' duties towards patients. If the duties are not performed by the doctor, his right to be a part of medical profession is questioned.

The Medical Council Act of 1956 has made some insertions in 2002 relating to the professional conduct, etiquettes and ethics for Registered Medical Practitioners. Every doctor has to sign the declaration of code of conduct. The doctor is expected to uphold the dignity and honour of medical profession and render service to humanity. Every doctor shall maintain medical records of indoor patients under their treatment. The display of registration number given by the Medical Council is mandatory. The doctor shall also ensure that there is a rational prescription and use of drugs. The personal financial interests of the physician should not conflict with medical interest of the patient. No physician shall refuse treatment to a patient. The doctor should neither exaggerate nor minimize the gravity of patient's condition. Soliciting of patient directly or indirectly by a physician is unethical.

The modern concept of health care reform through privatization is putting poor people under debt as they are not able to pay the costs of private care and insurance. Globalization accompanied by changing life-style and food habits is sweeping the world, but people are not simultaneously aware of adverse impacts of this changed life-style and food-habits on their health.

Advances in bio-medical field are putting challenges on ethics in terms of parenthood, genetic ordering, cloning and organ transplantation. Informed consent should be obtained from each volunteer/patient prior to his/her treatment or clinical trial. However, clinical trials are silent about contraceptive research and they do not address the concerns arising out of their specificities and ensure adequate safeguards. The concept of patient autonomy and freedom of choice is silent as most of the patients are illiterate and dependent on others or on family members.

References

Aristotle (1955), *Ethics*, Harmondsworth: Penguin.

Asai, Arushi (1996), 'Barriers to Informed Consent in Japan', *Eubios Journal of Asian and International Bioethics*, 6 (4): 91–93.

Beauchamp, T. and J.E. Childress (1994), *Principles of Biomedical Ethics*, Oxford: Oxford University Press.

Chapman, Carleton B. (1984), *Physicians, Law and Ethics*, New York: New York University Press.

Code of Ethics Regulations, 2002 (2009), Medical Council of India, Amendment Notification, New Delhi, 10 December.

Cohen, L. (1999), 'Where it Hurts: Indian Material for an Ethics of Organ Transplantation', *Daedalus*, 128(4): 135–66.

Crane, Diana (1975), *The Sanctity of Social Life: Physicians' Treatment of Critically Ill Patients*, New York: Russell Sage.

Daniels, N. et al. (1999), 'Why Justice is Good for Our Health: The Social Determinants of Health Inequalities', *Daedalus*, 128(4): 215–52.

Dasgupta, Rajashri (2004), 'Quick-fix Medical Ethics: Quinacrine Sterilization and the Ethics of Contraceptive Trials', in Mohan Rao (ed.), *The Unheard Scream: Reproductive Health and Women's Lives in India*, New Delhi: Zubaan, 279–308.

Desai, Mihir and Dipti Chand (2007), 'Right to Emergency Health Care', in Mihir Desai and Kamayani Bali Mahabal (eds), *Health Care Case Law in India: A Reader*, Mumbai: CEHAT.

Desai, Prakash N. (1988), 'Medical Ethics in India', *The Journal of Medicine and Philosophy*, 13: 231–55.

Farmer, P. (1999), *Infections and Inequalities*, Berkeley, CA: University of California Press.

Fox, Renee C. (1976), 'Ethical and Existential Developments in Contemporaneous American Medicine: Their Implications for Culture and Society', in M. Sokolowska et al. (eds), *Health, Medicine, Society*, Netherlands: Springer, 131–58.

Gillon, R. (1994), 'Medical Ethics: Four Principles Plus Attention to Scope', *British Medical Journal*, 309: 184–88.

Gottlieb, N., J. Burdine and K. McLeroy (1987), 'Ethical Dilemmas in Health Promotion', *Health Education Quarterly*, 14: 1–109.

Gupta, Jyotsna Agnihotri (2000), *New Reproductive Technologies, Women's Health and Autonomy: Freedom or Dependency?* New Delhi: Sage Publications.

Jayshri, K. (2011), 'Organ Transplantation: Legal, Social and Ethical Issues', 5 April, www.legalserviceindia.com.

Kleinman, Arthur (2004), 'Ethics and Experience: An Anthropological Approach to Health Equity', in Sudhir Anand, Fabienne Peter and Amartya Sen (eds), *Public Health, Ethics and Equity*, New York: Oxford University Press.

Lustig, B.A. et al. (1993), *Bioethics Yearbook*, Vol. 2, Dordrecht: Kluwer Academic Publishing.

Mathiharan, Karunakaran (2011), 'Ethical and Legal Issues in Organ Transplantation: Indian Scenario', *Medicine, Science and Law*, 51(3): 134–40.

Mechanic, David (1979), *Further Issues in Health Care: Social Policy and the Rationing of Medical Services*, New York: Free Press.

Mechanic, David (ed.) (1983), *Handbook of Health, Health Care and the Health Professors*, New York: Free Press.

Mechanic, David and I. Aiken (1986), *Application of Social Science to Clinical Medicine and Health Policy*, New Brunswick, NJ: Rutgers University Press.

Mills, J.S. (1962), *Utilitarianism and Other Writings*, Glasgow: Fontana.

Minocha, Anita (2010), 'Informed Consent in Medical Practice', in B.S. Baviskar and Tulsi Patel (eds), *Understanding Indian Society: Past and Present*, New Delhi: Orient Blackswan.

Nagla, Madhu (1997), *Sociology of Medical Profession*, Jaipur: Rawat Publications.

Pandya, Sunil (2000), 'History of Medical Ethics in India', *Eubios Journal of Asian and International Bioethics*, 10: 40–44.

Saheli Women's Resource Centre (1999), *The Consultative Document on Ethical Guidelines on Biomedical Research Involving Human Trials: A Critique and Some Recommendations*, September.

Simmons, R. and M. DiCanio (1979), 'Biology, Technology and Health', in H. Freeman, S. Levine and L. Reeder (eds), *Handbook of Medical Sociology*, Englewood Cliffs, NJ: Prentice-Hall, 150–73.

Srinivasan, Sandhya (2001), 'Discussion on Biomedical Research on Human in India: A Short Review', paper presented at the Workshop on Research Ethics in South Asia, Achutha Menon Centre for Health Science Studies, Thiruvananthapuram.

Sriram, T.G. et al. (1991), 'Informed Consent: A Study of Experiences and Opinion of Utilizers of Health Services from India', *Social Science and Medicine*, 32(12): 1389–92.

Stacey, Margaret (1985), 'Medical Ethics and Medical Practice: A Social Science View', *Journal of Medicine Ethics*, 11: 14–18.

Susser, M.W. Watson and K. Hopper (1985), *Sociology in Medicine*, New York: Oxford University Press.

The Times of India (2012), 'Shaming the Hippocratic Oath', 4 June.

Vashistha, Vipin M. (2010), 'MCIs New Code of Ethics for Medical Professionals: An Exercise in Vain or a Welcome Move', *Indian Paediatrics*, 47: 329–30.

Wig, K.L. (1985), ' Medical and Ethical Issues of Population: Reflection of a Physician', a keynote address in the Plenary Session on 23 February 1985 in World Congress of Law and Medicine, New Delhi.

Section VI

Emerging Issues in Health Care

27

Reproductive Health Care

Men and women have the right to be informed and have access to safe, effective, affordable and acceptable methods of their choice for the regulation of fertility. They must have the right of access to appropriate health care services for safe pregnancy and childbirth which provide couples with the best chance of having a healthy baby. Reproduction is life-long, beginning even before women and men attain sexual maturity and continuing beyond a woman's child-bearing years. Reproductive health implies that people are able to have a responsible, satisfying and safe sex life and that they have the capability to reproduce and the freedom to decide if, when and how often to do so. Individuals do face inequalities in reproductive health services. Inequalities vary based on socio-economic status, eduction level, age, ethnicity, religion and resources available in their environment. Unmet needs for sexual and reproductive health deprive women the right to make crucial choices about their own bodies and futures, affecting family welfare. This chapter will spell out the meaning of reproductive health along with its episteme. It will also look into the economic and political debates regarding reproductive health and right. It reviews the Cairo Consensus as the global normative rights framework

History of Reproductive Health

The term 'reproductive rights' was introduced in the 1980s during the second wave of feminism largely generated by the women's movements in North America, Europe, Australia and Latin America. The consensus focused on women's liberation and autonomy, violence against women, the fight for abortion. Women expanded the concept to embrace maternal health and morbidity, child bearing and child raising.

This historical, legal and ethical evolution of reproductive health could be traced back in the human rights conference, Tehran (1968), which emphasized the importance of free and informed choice in contraception. These were later elaborated in the subsequent world conferences. The Bucharest Conference (1974) and Mexico Conference (1984) made specific reference to reproductive rights. The Bucharest conference stated the reproductive right of 'individuals and couples' and not merely of parents. The 1984 Mexico Conference went further in declaring that women's right to control their own fertility forms an important basis for the enjoyment of other rights.

The formation of the Cairo Consensus was complex, bringing together the North and South agendas developed through regional and international meetings led by networks of southern-based women such as the Women's Global Network for Reproductive Rights (WGNRR), Development Alternatives with Women for New Era (DAWN) and the international Women's Health Coalition (Correa, 1994; Petchesky, 2003; Antrobus, 2004).

The Fourth World Conference in Beijing (1995) adopted the exact language of the International Conference on Population and Development (ICPD) Programme of Action on reproductive health. The Beijing Platform for Action highlighted the need to promote and protect the reproductive life cycle. The discrimination against women begins at the earliest stages of life and must be addressed from then onwards. Thus, reproductive health emphasizes on the rights to health, to have children by choice, and to have a safe and satisfying life. It is now recognized that women have the right to the fullest enjoyment of health throughout their life cycle.

These movements have different emphasis but many shared concerns, and the global reproductive health and rights movement managed with the support of UN agencies (particularly UNFPA) and some governments to establish a consensual women-centred rights-based framework. In Latin America, women's health movements emphasized quality reproductive and sexual health services in the face of religious and state oppression and in the context of citizenship needs. In Asia, women were concerned with population control and coercion, maternal mortality, the health of the girl child and all forms of violence against women. Activists in Africa were concerned with poverty and survival issues, maternal mortality and morbidity, sexually transmitted diseases along with HIV/AIDS. European and North American women focused on autonomy and expression, the medicalization of reproductive health and the rising cost of services. Middle Eastern women were concerned with access and rights to holistic reproductive health care throughout the life cycle. Central and Eastern European women focused on public health, gender equality and women's rights issues (Bandarage, 1997; IRRAG, 1998).

Cairo presented a rights-based framework for population stabilization, discrediting old population control programmes. Its goal is to make reproductive health care services universally accessible through primary health care no later than 2015. The new consensus discredits the targeted approach to population control, rejects incentives and targets in family planning and underlines the need for comprehensive reproductive health services. It also defines health services as encompassing family planning care during pregnancy, prevention and screening of sexually transmitted diseases, basic gynaecological care, sexuality and gender education and referral systems for other health problems. It adopts a life cycle approach with services for all aspects of reproductive health rights. Although it fell short of demanding universally safe and legal abortion, it asked countries to deal with the public health consequences of unsafe abortion and to ensure that where abortion is legal, it is also safe (The Corner House and WGNRR, 2004).

The Cairo Programme of Action is not binding but has proved a useful lobbying and advocacy tool. It has also been used more broadly as a platform for women's rights because of its emphasis on gender equality and public health and development, and its links to the Beijing platform of action (Fourth World Congress on Women, 1995). It was used to push for women's inclusion in decision-making in Brazil; to fight for changes in property rights in Kenya; and to lobby for human-centred health and development in the Philippines. It persuaded the Government of India to abandon targets and overt forms of coercion. Governments now speak of reproductive rights, men's responsibility, women's empowerment and women's rights instead of population control, family planning methods and mother child programmes. However, despite indications of success in reproductive health eduction, access to contraception, infant mortality and skilled care during childbirth, five and 10 year reviews show that the programme is still far from being implemented.

Definition of Reproductive Health

The first global agenda for sexual and reproductive health and rights was agreed at the UN International Conference on Population and Development in Cairo in 1994. It marked a paradigm shift from a narrow, technical, medical approach based on delivery of services and numbers rather than well-being – placing rights at the centre of population and development, and defining reproductive health as 'a state of complete physical, mental and social well-being ... in all matters relating to the reproductive system and to its functions and processes ... . Reproductive health implies that people are able to have a safe and satisfying sex life and have the capacity to reproduce and to have the freedom to decide if, when and how often to do so' (UNICPD, 1994). Reproductive health, therefore, implies that people are able to have a satisfying and safe sex life and that they have the capability to reproduce and the freedom to decide if, when and how often to do so. Reproductive rights rests on the recognition of the basic right of all couples and individuals to decide freely and responsibly the number spacing and timing of their children and to have the information and means to do so, and the highest standard of sexual and reproductive health. It also includes their right to make decision concerning reproduction free of discrimination, coercion and violence as expressed in human rights documents. Sexual health aims to enhance life and personal relations and not merely counselling and care related to reproduction and sexually transmitted diseases (IPCD, 1995: 31).

Reproductive Health as an Episteme

Episteme means the body of ideas that determine the knowledge that is intellectually certain at any particular time. The medico-juridical (related to the medical justice) and scientific fields of knowledge are discursive (conclusion by reasoning) formation of these episteme. According to Foucault, modernity does not place power in 'juridical' establishments, neither it depends on the forceful means and violent coercion. Power resides on the contrary in and through discourses and episteme that determine the prevalent norms in any society and eventually lead to the formation of a collective consensual common sense (Foucault, 1980: 121).

In this light reproductive health is viewed as construction of new discourse and episteme and a sophisticated method to control the utmost personal spaces of people's lives which does not rely on coercion but through proliferation of information and knowledge it functions the same. This proliferation of information and knowledge created a ubiquitous idea of reproductive health, a common sense/norm that trusses different people together on the issue of reproduction. Consequently, giving reproductive health a totalizing effect, a universal norm one that flattens out deviations and glosses over fissures and cracks to portray it as a continuous and singular development and existence of thought. The definition of reproductive health put forward by IPCD might be considered as the holistic representation of the concept. However, it may not exactly be visible through the subjective experiences of masses. It regards and holds the perspective of activists and actors whose 'worldview' may, in some cases, not belong to the populations that they seek to represent. Ironically, the programme and policies use the same definition, local communities can, therefore, find themselves as passive recipients of programme oriented definitions coined their social world and realm of understanding (Castle et al.: 2002).

The antiquity of reproductive health can be traced to the origin of population control, fertility behaviour, birth control, family planning or family welfare. These earlier terminologies were criticized, but the may the new terminologies kept on coming one after another with merely shift in approaches and paradigm evidently suggests that there is nexus between knowledge and power. Knowledge is, thus, constitutive in which there is dynamic interaction between knowledge and power. Power creates knowledge and maintains it. Thus, it is realized that coercive power: proscription and other forceful and violent means is unsuited for modernity. Within the realm of knowledge and power, the question is how reproductive health is projected as a paradigm shift from the earlier Malthusian and Neo-Malthusian view of population and later became a normative ground for the countries.

The History of Sexuality traces Foucault's extension beyond sexuality and develops a notion of biopower, which embraces all the forms of modern power directed toward us as living beings, that is, as subject to standards of not just sexual but biological normality. Biopower is concerned with the 'task of administering life', a process that operates on two levels. On the level of individuals, there is an 'anatomo-politics of the human body, on the level of social groups, there is a 'bio-politics of populations' (Foucault, 1976: 139). The 'bio-politics of populations' concerns the modern focus on a nation's entire population as a resource that must be protected, supervised, and improved. Thus, capitalism requires universal medical care and education to ensure an adequate workforce; racist ideologies call for eugenic measures to protect the purity of the population 'stock', and military planners develop the concept of 'total war', as a battle between not just armies but entire populations (Foucault, 1973: 34).

Foucault views modern society as a disciplinary society where coercion neither has any relevance nor any scope but it does not mean that people are not controlled. The modern society is continuously scrutinizing people's lives, even the most intimate part of human life is under constant surveillance. The disciplinary society which ensued was a consequence of the distribution of people within social spaces which individualize them and place them under constant surveillance. As such, the realignment of the medical gaze was associated with shifts within other social institutions. These transformations created an arrangement of power, for which the 'Panopticon' (an area where everything is visible), is metaphorically used (Anderson, 1995: 69). This 'panoptic scheme' was destined to spread throughout the social body; its vocation was to become a generalized function (Foucault, 1973: 207). Within this panoptic gaze the information related to reproductive and sexual health and available technology related to it is propagated and proliferated through various apparatuses as a means to control very personal aspect of people's lives. Qadeer (2010: 20) has rightly pointed out that reproduction is efficiently being pushed out of the personal domain to the industrial one. The extensive interpersonal communication activities and the information, education and communication strategy too could be seen in terms of producing normative idea of sexual and reproductive health.

Interaction occurs in this disciplinary society, through a process in which the gaze of technocrats create the docile body useful for modern society. Power makes its presence everywhere, to the point that it is decisive in moulding our view at every level from global to local from macro to micro. The configuration of this power is such that it creates new spaces and new systems of power within its macrostructures (Anderson, 1995). Rao (2004) quoting Hartman argued that this paradigm shift of reproductive health is nothing but a new strategy to obscure class, gender and race inequalities in grand consensus in which everyone's interests are apparently served. Women, population and the environment have become formally linked, a holy trinity in the consensus cosmology. This perspective has given reproductive health an omnipresence status which is seen everywhere and probably with every possible angle and multiple stance. The scope of the concept is so much broadened that now it occupies new social spaces hitherto uncharted.

The Birth of the Clinic (1973: 207) by Foucault analyses how powerful entities establish and enforce new ways of thinking about health. The discourse on a certain issue can be controlled by these entities, which in turn dictates, and limits, how the issue is conceptualized by the general population. It is interesting to observe that how the masses contemplate on this issue, how somebody has more than two or three children, how somebody not opting for institutional delivery is looked down on.

It is significantly important to analyse how the concept of reproductive health encompasses and vehemently promotes the idea of reproductive choice and how technology is crucial and decisive for reproductive choice where plethora of technologies invented to facilitate freedom to exercise reproductive choice. On this issue, Rao (2004: 188) questions whether 'reproductive health is a way to make contraceptives more acceptable'. It needs to be examined how the new assortment of contraceptives – injectables, implants, etc. – is frenziedly waiting to infiltrate the women's bodies and markets of the Third World countries. He asserts that reproductive choice is referred to the plethora of contraceptive devices that a 'free' women is supposed to be empowered to choose from. Reproductive health created and justified the presence of contraceptive market engendered by reproductive expertise. In this environment, the concept of choice is reduced to consumption that fosters a private enterprise in women's bodies (Raymond, 1996). It needs to be understood that even these technologies are not value neutral but are deeply embedded in society and culture. Hence, it demands closer understanding of the individual vis-à-vis the society. Qadeer (1998) holds the view that reproductive health has derived heavily from the notions of biological vulnerability of women and the concept of life cycle. This has brought about a subtle shift, transforming the social processes of bearing and rearing children into essentially biological events. The notion of life cycle compartmentalizes women's lives, creates artificial disjuncture and places bio-demographic aspects above class and gender differences on health. Worse, it imbues women with instinctive and mindless existence of vertebrates, de-emphasizing their power to intelligently act upon and transform their own environment.

Economic and Political Debate for Reproductive and Health Right

The reproductive health moved the Cairo agenda into political and economic debates over access and right to knowledge, resources and appropriate services, making it highly contested (Lohmann, 2003; Petchesky, 2003; Sen and Barroso, 1996).

Many macroeconomic factors undermine Cairo, linked to growingly conservative environment and the predominance of the World Bank policies. For example, the Millennium Development Goals (MDG) do not include the sexual and reproductive rights agenda (Barton, 2004; Harcourt, 2004), a telling indication of how much ground the Cairo agenda has lost. The goals exclude sexuality, reproductive rights and health as determinants of gender equality, and focus on education for girls and maternal health and morbidity. This places women and children's rights to health within a purely biological framework.

The universal rise of fundamentalism has fired a 'morality' debate with many examples of how these conservative approaches are undermining the sexual and reproductive health and rights agenda. One is the rule imposed by President Bush in 2001 prohibiting overseas NGOs from receiving US Government aid if they promote or provide referrals for abortion. In 2002, the US Government withheld US$ 34 million promised to UNEPA because it said it funded abortion in China. Meanwhile it is funding the anti-abortion lobby and promotion of abstinence overseas (using the ABC approach: Abstinence until marriage, Be faithful, and Condoms where appropriate; Jacobson, 2003). The Vatican and conservative states consistently attack the sexual and reproductive and rights agenda. Such strategies threaten many sexual and reproductive health and rights projects in the global South and are leading to increased unsafe abortion, closure of family planning clinics and shortages of contraceptive supplies.

Lack of donor funding is not the only obstacle. Broader underlying economic and political conditions are undermining women's health and their control over safe sex and child bearing. Health services are in decline and economically poor women in particular have little or no access to reproductive or other health services. Global inequalities in income and health have been growing and hunger has increased despite falling population growth (Desai, 2004; Rao, 2004).

Many activists are developing an alternative vision far more critical of the development establishment and globalization that goes beyond the Cairo consensus. They believe Cairo went along too readily with the neo-liberal agenda that is providing so disastrous for the poor, the vast majority of whom are rural women and children. Structural adjustment and trade policies are leading to greater exploitation of women's time/work and sexuality (Rao, 2004).

Cairo took a passive line and as a result could not guarantee women the basics they need to make reproductive health choices. It failed to take into account the power imbalances in economic and social structures among countries, and between man and women. Some say its tendency to focus on abortion and reproductive rights marginalized the basic issues of primary health care, social security and investment in health systems. In reality, women's health is largely determined by economic and social constraints – it is difficult to separate reproductive rights and health from other economic and political rights and needs (such as land rights, food security and communal harmony) that impact on economically poor women's lives.

Reproductive Health in India

It is well recognized that in patriarchal settings such as India, hierarchical gender relations and unequal gender norms impact women's sexual and reproductive health and choice and act as significant obstacles to access services and facilities. Equally, the achievement of good sexual and reproductive health may be inhibited by such structural factors as:

- poverty and malnutrition
- early marriage
- inadequate educational and health systems

Although there are regional variations, with women in south India facing somewhat fewer constraints than those in the north, undoubtedly women in both regions are far lesser empowered than men to have a say in their own lives. From an early age, gender role differentials persist: compared to adolescent boys, female share limited autonomy and face huge constraints on decision-making, mobility and access to resources. Double standards ensure that young females are closely supervised as their chastity is inextricably linked to the family's honour (both natal and marital). At the same time daughters are viewed as a 'source of misery' and a drain, through dowry, on the family's resources, while a son is the 'saviour of the family'. After marriage, a young woman is expected to remain largely invisible and under the authority of her husband's family. She has little say in domestic decisions and little freedom of movement. Almost the only avenue available to enhance her prestige and even security in her husband's home is through her fertility, and particularly the number of sons she bears. Women who have borne only daughters can be subjected to harassment, and childlessness can be grounds for divorce or abandonment (Jejeebhoy et al., 2004).

Gender roles have significant implications for sexual and reproductive health and choice. Gender norms condone early onset of sexual activity and sex worker contacts among young males, while severely prescribing even the hint of sexual misconduct among young females. Lack of awareness, lack of spousal intimacy and communications on sexual matters, and widespread gender-based violence compound women's ability to negotiate safe sex, seek appropriate health care or experience a healthy pregnancy. Finally, gender roles that perpetuate the 'culture of silence' inhibit women from communicating a health problem or seeking prompt treatment unless it inhibits them from carrying out their daily chores. This 'culture of silence' is even more pronounced for gynaecological and reproductive morbidity that are so closely linked with sexuality (Jejeebhoy et al., 2004).

Policies and Programmes Related with Reproductive Health in India

Over the course of the 1990s, existing policies and programmes in the area of reproductive health have undergone significant changes, and new policies and programmes to address underserved population groups and neglected issues have been introduced. These include, notably, the National Population Policy 2000, the Reproductive and Child Health Programme, The National AIDS Prevention and Control Policy, 2002. Additionally, legislative measures in the area of reproductive health have been introduced such as amended Medical Termination of Pregnancy (MTP) Act, 2001 and the Pre-natal Diagnostic Techniques (Regulation and Prevention of Misuse) (PNDT) Act, 1994. These programmes have been implemented in practice and have succeeded to gain access to care and exercise reproductive rights. We provide here a broad overview of the main policies and programmes.

National Family Planning Programme

During the first decade of existence, family planning programme was considered more of a mechanism to improve the health of mothers and children than a method of population control (Visaria, 2000; Visaria and Chari, 1998). Clinic-centred family planning service delivery, along with health education activities, were promoted during this period. The 3rd Five-Year Plan period (1961–66) marked a subtle shift in programme emphasis, from the welfare of women and children to the macro objective of population stabilization. During 1965–75, the programme was integrated with the maternal and child health programme, and at the same time, time-bound, method-specific targets for population control were introduced. The 1990s witnessed dramatic changes in the family welfare policy and programme in the country. The organized pressure from multiple constituencies on family planning programme regarding choice and quality issue has led to the changes in policy approach. An additional catalyst was provided by the International Conference on Population and Development (ICPD) in 1994 and Beijing Women's Conference in 1995. Target-free approach was introduced where goals are set at the community level. Again in 1997, the target-free approach was recast as the Community Needs Assessment approach, and a decentralized participatory planning system was put in place.

Reproductive and Child Health (RCH) Programme

The Reproductive and Child Health Programme, which was launched in 1997, focuses on the principle of client satisfaction and utilizing and upgrading the existing health infrastructure to deliver high quality health services. It seeks to integrate services for the prevention and management of unwanted pregnancy, promotion of safe motherhood and child survival, and the prevention and management of RTIs and STIs. The programme aims to expand services to meet the needs of underserved and neglected population groups; including adolescents, economically and socially disadvantaged groups such as urban slum dwellers and tribal populations. To make the programme a people's programme, the new approach champions local need-based, decentralized, participatory planning and monitoring, and seeks to involve several stakeholders in more meaningful ways to move the new agenda forward (MOHFW, 1997).

The new approach represents a dramatic change in the culture of the family planning welfare programme (Pauchauri, 1999), and for the first time, the programme has focused attention on gender concerns. It seeks to address gender issues impinging on women's health by improving quality of care, including the interaction between providers and clients, increasing the availability of female health care providers at the primary health care level, addressing neglected concerns of women such as RTIs, addressing the needs of neglected population sub-groups like adolescents, organizing gender sensitization training for stakeholders, encouraging male involvement in reproductive health; and facilitating women's and men's involvement in monitoring reproductive and child health through client feedback (World Bank, 1997).

National Population Policy (NPP), 2000

The National Population Policy, adopted in February 2000, further legitimized the paradigm shift. The National Population Policy provides a policy framework for achieving the twin objectives of population stabilization and promoting reproductive health within the wider context of sustainable development. The NPP addresses the unmet need for contraception and health system personnel, and to provide integrated service delivery for basic reproductive, and child health care. NPP affirms the government's commitment to the provision of quality services, information and counselling, and expanding contraceptive method options in order to enable people to make voluntary and informed choices. Disincentives have not been included in the NPP.

National STD and AIDS Control Programme and Policy

The National STD Control Programme was initiated in 1946 and remained operational until 1991. Recognizing the synergy between STIs and HIV/AIDS, in 1992, the national STD Control Programme was integrated with the National AIDS Control Organization (NACO) (NACO, 1998). The thrust of the project has been on changing behaviour through interventions, particularly among high-risk groups, supporting decentralized service delivery and protecting human rights by encouraging voluntary counselling and testing, and discouraging mandatory testing (NACO, 2003). The National AIDS Prevention and Control Policy 2002 envisages effective containment of the infection levels of HIV/AIDS in the general population in order to achieve zero-level of new infections. To meet these objectives, the policy has delineated various strategies for the safety of blood and blood products, improving services for the care and support of people living with HIV/AIDS, and creating an enabling socio-economic environment.

National Plans

The 10th Five-Year Plan has identified a number of targets that have implications for reproductive health. It outlines efforts in three broad areas: (a) meeting the unmet need for contraception; (b) reducing infant and maternal mortality; and (c) enabling families to achieve their reproductive goals.

National Youth Policy

National Youth Policy 2000 addresses the needs of those aged between 13 to 35, and stresses the need for multisectoral approach to youth, with a thrust on 'youth empowerment', notably education, skill building and leadership as well as nutrition, and equality of opportunity. While it discusses the need for access to health services among young people, especially women, and refer the need for reproductive health 'guidance' population and family life education, it's obvious focus lies on nutrition and education, rather than on sexual and reproductive health matters.

Medical Termination of Pregnancy (MTP) and Pre-Natal Diagnostic Techniques (Regulation and Prevention of Misuse) (PNDT) Acts

The Medical Termination of Pregnancy (MTP) Act was passed in 1971 and came into effect in 1972. The Act enables trained practitioners to terminate a pregnancy of less than 20 weeks duration in several conditions, including risk to the life of the pregnant woman or grave injury to her physical or mental health, contraceptive failure, rape, and risk to the child. The Act was amended in 2002 to decentralize the approval process for registration of MTP centres and increase access to MTP services at the primary health care level.

In order to curb the trend towards sex-selective abortion following pre-natal diagnostic technique, the Pre-Natal Diagnostic Techniques (Regulation and Prevention of Misuse) Act was passed in 1996. This Act attempts to regulate the administration of pre-natal diagnostic techniques (including sonography) and the conditions under which these can be sued, and prohibits communication of the sex of the foetus should the investigations be conducted. As the Act was ineffective in preventing sex-selective abortions, it was amended in 2003 to incorporate regulation of pre-conception and pre-implantation procedures for sex-selection, regular recording of procedures and empowering local authorities to ensure compliance.

Reproductive Health Outcomes in India

Pregnancy and child bearing characterize the experiences of a number of young women in India. Adolescent fertility rates in India during the last three decades has declined. In 1971, the rate in India was 101, and in 2008 it declined to 41.6 in 2008 (Registrar General, 2009). The total marital fertility rates for India in 2008 indicates that married women bear around four (4.3) children by the end of their reproductive period. The annual age-specific marital fertility rate for adolescent women aged 15–19 years is 252 births per 1000 married women which accounts for about 29 per cent of the overall total marital fertility rate suggesting that about three-tenth of the fertility level could be reduced in India by increasing female age at marriage to 20 years (India Registrar General, 2009). Little over two-fifth of currently married adolescent women in India have given birth to at least one child. Out of these, eight per cent of them have reportedly parity two. It suggests that significant proportions of women undergo pregnancy at ages below which obstetric risks are particularly elevated. Not only does child bearing occur early among married adolescents, but subsequent pregnancies also tend to be more closely spaced than among adults (Santhya and Jeejeebhoy, 2003). The experience of early and closely spaced childbearing is particularly risky for adolescents because large proportions are anaemic and may not have reached physical maturity. Early child bearing has resulted in adverse health consequences, including damage to the reproductive tract, maternal mortality, pregnancy complications, peri-natal and neonatal mortality and low birth weight. Evidence from community and facility based studies reiterate that maternal deaths are considerably higher among adolescents than older women (Kulkarni, 2003).

Induced Abortion

Abortion is such a sensitive topic and greatly underestimated. However, the national-level estimate suggests 6.4 million abortions, or a rate of 26 abortions per 1,000 women of reproductive age – which comes from a 2002 facility-based study by the Abortion Assessment Project-India (AAPI). About 4.8 million induced abortions were estimated to have been performed annually in formal facilities (2.4 million of which were performed in abortion certified facilities), and another 1.6 million abortions were performed by informal providers. Unsafe abortions in India is commonly carried out by women self-administering unapproved and typically infective drugs or taking approved drugs incorrectly; these types of abortion attempts often result in incomplete abortion and further complications (Banerjee and Andersen, 2012). Providers who have medical training but lack specific training in abortion procedures are another source of unsafe abortions. Additionally, traditional providers without any medical training may use sticks, roots, herbal medicines or other unsafe and ineffective means for terminating a pregnancy, but the prevalence of these methods seems to have declined considerably in recent years (Banerjee and Andersen, 2012). A few studies specific to unsafe abortion and its consequences have been conducted in recent years. Unintended pregnancies and subsequent abortions may be indicative of women's inadequate access to and ineffective use of modern contraceptives, as well as gender inequities that often compromise women's ability to negotiate contraceptive use when they do not desire a pregnancy. Across quantitative and qualitative studies conducted in India, the most common cause for having an abortion is to limit family size. Other common reasons are to increase the spacing between births or to protect their health in cases where underlying medical conditions would be worsened by pregnancy or childbirth. Poverty and economic constraints also emerged as an important reason in some of the qualitative studies. For many women, beginning child bearing soon after marriage is a way of providing fertility and achieving status within the martial family, but for some of them becoming pregnant soon after marriage is also a cause of abortion. Health problems with the foetus and having a female foetus are also mentioned as reasons for abortion.

Reproductive Tract and Sexually Transmitted Infections

Reproductive Tract Infections (RTIs) and Sexually Transmitted Diseases (STDs) represent a major public health problem is quite significant from the point of being the reproductive problem among women. The National Behavioural Surveillance Survey of the national AIDS Control organization indicates that approximately 3 per cent of young males and 5 per cent of females reported the experience of symptoms of infections (STIs or RTIs more generally) such as discharge, ulcers or sores (NACO and UINICEF, 2002). A significant finding is that husband's behaviour may transmit infection to their wives, which could have serious implications given that many infected women are asymptomatic and are unlikely to seek care even when symptoms appear (Joseph, Prasad and Abraham, 2003).

Risk and Protective Factors for Reproductive Health

A host of factors many inhibit young people from achieving good sexual and reproductive health. Many are structural, such as poverty and malnutrition, patriarchy, early marriage and inadequate educational and health systems, and, in turn, influence risk and protective factors at the individual level. The range of obstacles observed to prevent young people from achieving good health and exercising informed choices are outlined below:

Limited Awareness of Health Promoting Behaviours

While awareness of contraception and infection may be almost universal at a superficial level, in-depth awareness of sexual health issues, health promoting actions and risky sexual behaviours is limited among young people. The NACO National Behavioural Surveillance Survey discloses that although 90 per cent of young men and 80 per cent of young women aged 15–19 years had heard of HIV/AIDS, yet this awareness did not translate into in-depth knowledge of symptoms, modes of transmission or methods of prevention. The unmarried are more likely to be aware of HIV than the married, suggesting that married women may be particularly poorly aware and vulnerable (NACO and UNICEF, 2002). Misconceptions are common. Many young people believe that women cannot become pregnant at sexual debut; that symptoms of infections go away on their own; that one can clearly identify an infected person by their appearance; that pregnancy can occur through physical embrace; or that infection is transmitted through everyday activities or can be prevented by proper personal hygiene (Brown et al., 2001). Adolescents are poorly informed about the physiological changes associated with maturation (UNESCO, 2000). In school settings, where programmes on population, family life, and sex education exist, they focus more on biological and scientific information than broader issues of sexuality (Chakrabarti, 2003).

Limited Self-Efficacy, Negotiation, Life and Livelihood Skills

Double standards in gender and power imbalances shape adolescents' lives and often undermine their ability to make informed reproductive choices both in marital and premarital partnerships. The high priority place on preserving young women's chastity before marriage can constrain girls' eduction, access to services, age at marriage, autonomy and mobility. Young females have a limited voice in matters relating to their own lives – whether to continue schooling, decisions on when and whom to marry, physical mobility and sexual relations. Young men are affected by a different set of gender-based expectations, including social pressure to have sex at an early age, often under conditions that place them at the risk of infection. Gender power imbalances are observed in both marital and premarital partnership. In many cases, male partners, parents or in-laws play a leading role as decision-makers (Jejeebhoy and Sebastian, 2004: 152).

Limited Communication, Interaction and Support on Sexual and Reproductive Health Matters

A lack of communication, interaction and support characterizes relationships between parents and their adolescent children in matters relating to sex and reproduction. Sex and reproductive issues are taboo subjects within families. In many cases, parents believe that talking to adolescents about these matters would imply approval of sexual activity (Masilamani, 2003). Concern for the sexual security and chastity of daughters appears to dominate parental relationships with adolescent girls. While parents closely supervise the activities of adolescent daughters in an attempt to inhibit sexual activity, they often condone the sexual activity of their sons. However, relationships in which parents take on a policing role may not always safeguard against risky sexual behaviour: intimate non-sexual and even sexual relation does indeed occur, unwanted pregnancy and resort to abortion are not unknown, notwithstanding parental perceptions (Mehra, Savithri and Coutinho, 2002).

Lack of Youth-centred Programmes on Sexual and Reproductive Health

Though there is a law stipulating the minimum age at marriage, it is not strictly enforced. Large proportions of young women continue to marry and bear children in adolescence and can exercise little autonomy over their sexual and reproductive lives. There are limited programmes that make concentrated efforts to delay early marriage or address married adolescents as a distinct group. Hence, while the adverse consequences of pregnancy in adolescents are well known, adolescents are not more likely to receive antenatal or intra-partum care than adult women (Santhya and Jejeebhoy, 2003).

Summing Up

The term reproductive health is most often equated with one aspect of women's lives; motherhood. Complications associated with various maternal issues are indeed major contributors to poor reproductive health among millions of women worldwide. The term 'reproductive rights' in the 1980s on the second wave of feminism largely generated by the women's movements in North America, Europe, Australia and Latin America. Reproductive rights rests on the recognition of the basic right of all couples and individual to decide freely and responsibly the number spacing and timing of their children and to have the information and means to do so, and the highest standard of sexual and reproductive health. It also includes their right to make decisions concerning reproduction free of discrimination, coercion and violence as expressed in human rights documents. The women, who are in the reproductive age group, are highly vulnerable to problems related to sexual intercourse, pregnancy, contraceptive side effects, etc. Death and illnesses from reproductive causes are the highest among poor women everywhere. In India, women who are disproportionately poor, illiterate, and politically powerless, have higher rates of reproductive illness, and death is normal.

References

Anderson, I. (1995), 'Bodies, Disease and the Problem of Foucault', *Social Analysis*, 37: 67–81.

Antrobus, P. (2004), *The Global Women's Movement*, London: Zed Books.

Bandarage, A. (1997), *Women, Population and Global Crisis: A Political-Economic Analysis*, London: Zed Books.

Banerjee, S.K. and K. Andersen (2012), 'Exploring the Pathways of Unsafe Abortion in Madhya Pradesh, India', *Global Public Health*, 7(8): 882–96.

Barton, C. (ed.) (2004), *Seeking Accountability on Women's Human Rights: Women Debate the Millennium Development Goals*, New York: Women's Coalition for Economic Justice.

Brown, A. et al. (2001), 'Sexual Relations among Young People in Developing Countries: Evidence from WHO Cases Studies', *Occasional Papers of the Department of Reproductive Health and Research*, World Health Organization, No. 4 (WHO/RHR/01.8).

Castle, S. et al. (2002), 'Re-Defining Reproductive Health with and for the Community: An Example of Participatory Research from Mali', *African Journal of Reproductive Health*, 6(1): 20–31.

Chakrabarti, V. (2003), 'Population Education in Formal and Non-Formal Sectors in India', in S. Bott et al. (eds), *Towards Adulthood: Exploring the Sexual and Reproductive Health of Adolescents in South Asia*, Geneva: WHO, 165–67.

Correa, S. (1994), *Population and Reproductive Rights: Feminist Perspectives from the South*, London: Zed Books.

DAWN (2004), *Mumbai on the Many Faces of Fundamentalism*, Special Supplement for the World Social Forum, Mumbai.

Desai, M. (2004), 'Gender, Health and Globalization: A Critical Social Movement Perspective', *Development*, 47(2): 36–42.

Foucault, M. (1973), *The Birth of the Clinic*, Translated by Alan Sheridan, New York: Vintage.

—— (1976), *History of Sexuality: The Will to Knowledge*, Vol. I, Translated by Robert Hurley, New York: Pantheon Books.

—— (1980), *Power/Knowledge: Selected Interviews and Other Writings, 1972–1977*, New York: Pantheon Books.

Harcourt, W. (2004), *The Road to the UN Millennium Development Goals: Some Insights into the International Debate*, Amsterdam: NCDO.

India Registrar General (2009), *Compendium of India's Fertility and Mortality Indictors 1971–2007 based on SRS*, New Delhi: Registrar General of India.

IRRAG (1998), *Negotiating Reproductive Rights: Women' Perspectives across Countries and Cultures*, London: Zed Books.

Jacobson, J. (2003), 'First Global Women's Scorecard on Bush Administration', *Women's Global Network for Reproductive Rights Newsletter*, 80: 12–19.

Jejeebhoy, S.J. and M.P. Sebastian (2004), 'Young People's Sexual and Reproductive Health', in Shireen J. Jejeebhoy (ed.), *Looking Back, Looking Forward: A Profile of Sexual and Reproductive Health in India*, Jaipur: Rawat Publications.

Jejeebhoy, Shireen J. (ed.) (2004), *Looking Back, Looking Forward: A Profile of Sexual and Reproductive Health in India*, Jaipur: Rawat Publications.

Joseph, A.R., J. Prasad and S. Abraham (2003), 'Gynaecological Problems among Young Married Women in Tamil Nadu, India', in S. Bott et al. (eds), *Towards Adulthood: Exploring the Sexual and Reproductive Health of Adolescents in South Asia*, Geneva: WHO, 138–41.

Kulkarni, S. (2003), 'The Reproductive Health Status of Married Adolescents as Assessed by NFHS–2, India', in S. Bott et al. (eds), *Towards Adulthood: Exploring the Sexual and Reproductive Health of Adolescents in South Asia*, Geneva: WHO, 55–58.

Lohmann, L. (2003), 'Re-Imagining the Population Debate', *The Corner House Briefing*, 28 March.

Masilamani, R. (2003), 'Building a Supportive Environment for Adolescent Reproductive Health Programmes in India: Essential Programme Components', in S. Bott et al. (eds), *Towards Adulthood: Exploring the Sexual and Reproductive Health of Adolescents in South Asia*, Geneva: WHO, 156–58.

Mehra, S., R. Savuthri and L. Coutinho (2002), 'Sexual Behaviour among Unmarried Adolescents in Delhi, India: Opportunities Despite Parental Controls', paper presented at the 002 IUSSP Regional Population Conference, Bangkok, June.

Ministry of Health and Family Welfare (MoHFW) (1997), *Reproductive and Child Health Programme: Schemes for Implementation*, New Delhi: Government of India.

NACO and UNICEF (2002), *Knowledge, Attitudes and Practices of Young Adults (15–24 years)*, New Delhi: NACO and UNICEF.

National AIDS Control Organisation (NACO) (1998), *Country Scenario 1997–98*, New Delhi: Government of India and NACO.

—— (2003), http://www.naco.nic.in

Pachauri, S. (1999), 'Moving Towards Reproductive Health: Issues and Evidence', in S. Pauchauri (ed.), *Implementing a Reproductive Health Agenda in India: The Beginning*, New Delhi: Population Council, xiii-xvii.

Petchesky, R. (2003), *Global Prescriptions: Gendering Health and Human Rights*, London: Zed Books.

Qadeer, Imrana (1998), 'Reproductive Health: A Public Health Perspective', *Economic and Political Weekly*, 33(4): 2675–84.

—— (2010), *New Reproductive Technologies and Health Care in Neo-Liberal India: Essays*, New Delhi: Centre for Women's Development Studies.

Rao, M. (2004), *Malthusian Arithmetic: From Population Control to Reproductive Health*, New Delhi: Sage Publications.

Santhya, K.G. and S.J. Jejeebhoy (2003), 'Sexual and Reproductive Health Needs of Married Adolescent Girls', *Economic and Political Weekly*, 38(41): 4370–77.

Sen, C. and C. Barroso (1996), 'After Cairo: Challenges to Women's Organizations', paper presented at the Workshop on Reproductive Health, Rights and Women's Empowerment, New Delhi: Centre for Development Studies, September.

UNESCO (2000), 'Cultural Settings Affect Adolescent Needs', *Adolescent Education Newsletter*, 3(2): 6.

UNICPD (1994), *Programme of Action of the UN International Conference on Population and Development.*

Visaria, L. (2000), 'From Contraceptive Targets to Informed Choice: The Indian Experience', in R. Ramassubban and S.J. Jejeebhoy (eds), *Women's Reproductive Health in India*, Jaipur: Rawat Publications, 331–82.

Visaria, L. and V. Chari (1998), 'India's Population Policy and Family Planning Programme: Yesterday, Today and Tomorrow', in A. Jain (ed.), *Do Population Policies Matter? Fertility and Politics in Egypt, India, Kenya and Mexico*, New York: Population Council, 53–112.

WGNRR (2004), 'A Decade After Cairo: Women's Health in a Free Market Economy', *Corner House Briefing*, 31 June.

World Bank (1997), *Project Document: India, Reproductive and Child Health Project*, World Bank Population and Human Resources Division, South Asia Country Department II, Report# 16393 – IN. Washington, D.C.: World Bank.

28

Environment and Health

Environment health is part of public health concerned with assessing and understanding the impact of environment on people and of people on the environment. Wherever people live and work, it is called their environment. The environment encompasses people's surroundings and the circumstances relating to their surroundings; so it includes physical, biological, social and cultural factors. People constantly interact with their environment; it helps shape their lives, and it affects their health.

Health, Environment and Development

The quality of the environment and the nature of any economic development taking place are major determinants of the health of people in that environment. However, environmental health issues have not traditionally been seen as a priority in policy making, or in developmental planning. This is despite the fact that biological agents in the environment such as mosquitoes, parasites and water-borne bacterial pathogens are involved in the world's most significant health problems. These factors are responsible for deadly diseases leading to premature fatality of millions. (often infants and children). In addition, chemical agents such as pesticides and, cleaning agents, and physical hazards in the home, the workplace and the natural environment are responsible for millions of other illnesses, injuries, and deaths. Health and the environment are not independent entities; they are influenced by external driving forces such as population pressure and poverty.

If the world's people are to achieve good health, then governments and other agencies must learn to balance the interaction between human activities and the environment. In order to achieve this, two important criteria must be met:

- Economic development must meet people's needs.
- Ecological sustainability must be achieved; this means ensuring that natural resources can be sustained for present and future use without being irreparably damaged or destroyed.

To achieve these goals, action is required on the local, national and global level by individuals and through cooperation between governmental and non-governmental agencies.

Environmental Health

WHO defines environmental health as those aspects of human health, including quality of life, that are determined by physical, biological, social and psycho-social factors in the environment. It also refers to the theory and practice of assessing, correcting, controlling, and preventing these factors in the environment which can have an adverse effect on the health of present and future generations (WHO, 1993). We will give the example of the relationship between human activities, health and the physical and biological environment. The environment can be improved by human activity, for instance, by draining mosquito breeding sites in marshland or by improving housing. Human activity can just as easily impair health, by releasing toxic chemicals into the atmosphere and changing the physical environment. Some environmental agents are responsible for damage to health without human intervention, for instance, ultraviolet light from sun, leading to the development of skin cancers, or a lack of minerals such as iodine or selenium in soil and foodstuffs, arsenic in water, leading to nutritional disorders. In these instances, human activity can mitigate the effects of the environmental agents through the use of technology, nutritional supplements or education.

Figure 1

Interaction Between Human Activities and the Physical and Biological Environment

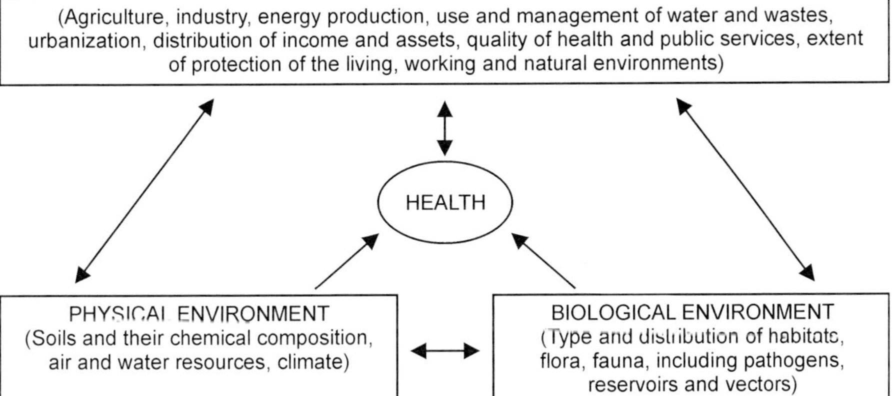

Source: Adapted from WHO (1992). *World Development Report 1992: Development and Environment,* Oxford: Oxford University Press.

Sustainable Development

The World Commission on Environment and Development define sustainable development as 'meeting the needs of the present generation without compromising the ability of future generations to meet their needs' (World Commission on Environment and Development: 1987). These include food, work, shelter, and health care for all the population and they must be provided in a manner that prejudices none of them and preserves the environment and its resources.

Throughout our history, humans have interacted with the environment and freely used natural resources. Sustainable development is also about addressing equity within the present generation. It is often the poorest groups in society who are most exposed to environmental hazards, including dangerous working conditions and restricted access to adequate and safe food and water. In addition, low-quality housing is often found in the most populated areas, which mostly are near industrial plants. The importance of this has been enshrined as part of the United Nations Universal Declaration of Human Rights: 'all people have the right to a standard of living adequate for the health and well-being of themselves and their family, including food, clothing, housing, health care and the necessary social services' (UN, 1948). It is only recently, however, that this declaration has been translated into action that will ensure these rights for present and future generations. A number of international meetings have been held to discuss the way forward. At the 1992 Earth Summit in Rio de Janerio, Brazil, a number of principles relating to an integrated approach to the environment, health and sustainable development were agreed upon, along with a plan for future action. The first principle is that 'human beings are at the centre of concerns for sustainable development. They are entitled to a healthy and productive life in harmony with nature' (UNCED, 1992).

Hazards and Risks in the Environment

A hazard is defined as 'a factor or exposure that may adversely affect health' (Last, 1995). This is basically a source of danger; it is a qualitative term used to express the potential of an environment agent to harm particular individuals if the exposure is above a certain level. A risk is defined as 'the probability that an event will occur, e.g. that an individual will become ill or die within a stated period of time or age; the probability of a (generally) unfavourable outcome' (Last, 1955). Table 1 illustrates some of the hazards. Traditional hazards have been linked with lack of development, while modern hazards are associated with unsustainable development – in other words, development that lacks adequate mechanisms to protect human health or the environment.

Table 1

Examples of Traditional and Modern Health Hazards

Traditional Hazards	*Modern Hazards*
Lack of access to safe drinking water	Water pollution from populated areas or intensive agriculture
Inadequate or poor quality housing and shelter	
Inadequate basic sanitation (household and community)	Urban air pollution from motor cars; coal power stations and industry, traffic accidents

Cont'd...

...Cont'd

Food contamination with pathogens, dietary deficiency	Food contamination with pesticides; poor diet leading to obesity
Indoor pollution from cooking and heating using biomass fuel (wood, animal dung and crop residues)	Tobacco smoke
Disease vectors, mainly insects and rodents	Emerging and re-emerging infectious disease hazards
Inadequate solid waste disposal	Solid and hazardous waste accumulation
Occupational injury hazards in agriculture and cottage industries	Chemical and radiation hazards following introduction of industrial and agricultural technologies
Natural disasters, including floods, droughts and earthquakes	Deforestation, land degradation and other ecological changes at local and regional levels
	Climate change, ozone depletion in the stratosphere and trans-boundary pollution

Source: Landon, Megan(2006), *Environment, Health and Sustainable Development*, New Delhi: Tata McGraw-Hill.

The Risk Transition

Risk transition is the process by which societies change exposure from traditional to modern hazards and is associated with economic development. This can be a problem if the transition is not well managed as there can be an overlap, of traditional and modern hazards, leading to an extra health burden on society (Landon, 2006). The following extract from the WHO (1997) explains:

> Traditional environmental health risks relating to unsafe food and drinking water; inadequate sanitation; infections from animals and vectors, and poor housing have a major influence on health when countries are at early stages of development. Industrial development introduces 'modern' environmental health risks relating to air pollution, chemical exposures and traffic accidents. The term 'risk transition' is used to describe the reduction in 'traditional risks' and increase in 'modern risks' that take place as economic development progresses. However, when environmental health risks are poorly managed, the 'traditional risks' are not eliminated in all parts of society and remain important health threats among the poor and disadvantaged, while the 'modern risks' continue unabated. If environmental health risks are well managed, the 'traditional risks' can be eliminated almost completely and 'modern risk' can be reduced through effective prevention programmes.

Favourable completion of the environmental health risk transition can be threatened by the emergence of new infectious diseases; the occurrence of old disease in geographic areas where they had not previously appeared, and the resurgence of old diseases that had once appeared to be under control. In some countries, the revival of traditional health risks of this type is the result of poverty and inequitable development. Associated factors are wide-ranging and include destruction of pristine areas, add use changes, resource extraction and agricultural exploitation, introduction of new agricultural and animal husbandry methods, increasing spreads of drug-resistant pathogens and pesticides resistance in vectors, increased mobility of people and foodstuffs and changing lifestyles and eating habits.

Managing the risk transition also involves preventing or minimizing modern environmental health risks. These can arise from the very modernization activities that help lower traditional risks.

Eco-System and Human Health

A change in the environmental conditions in one part of the world can lead to a reaction in another part of the world (this is called the butterfly effect). Environmental problems do not necessarily stop at regional or national boundaries but frequently have consequences elsewhere. One of the results of this is global climate change, of which there are other consequences which include stratospheric ozone depletion, acidic precipitation, and loss of diversity. We will discuss these:

Ozone Depletion and Utlraviolet (UV) Radiation

High in stratosphere, there is a layer of ozone molecules, formed by the action of ultraviolet (UV) radiation on oxygen molecules. Ozone accumulated over a great deal of time; it acts as a screen which absorbs some of the ultraviolet radiation and prevents it from reaching the Earth's surface. Damage caused to the ozone layer by some chemicals during the past century has thinned it, allowing more UV radiation to pass through. There is a hole in the ozone layer above America from September to December each year, and a small hole in the Arctic region.

The health effects of ozone depletion are both direct and indirect. Direct effects include skin cancer, eye damage and damage to the immune system. Indirect effects include damage to terrestrial and aquatic systems, which themselves generate further consequences for the environment and human health. There are some crops which are vulnerable to UV effects and will show a drop in yield. The natural ecosystem has a mixture of resistant plants and some of these areas may be under threat.

Acidic Precipitation

The effect of acidic chemicals dissolved in the rainwater, snow and other forms of precipitation can damage delicate aquatic systems as well as some species of plants and trees. These acidic chemicals, mainly oxides of sulphur and nitrogen, originate from industrial sources. This effect was first observed in 1850 around Manchester in England. This was a heavily industrialized area with significant use of coal, a rich source of sulphur dioxide emissions. These emissions may reach the clouds and ultimately fall as acid precipitation, hundreds or thousands of kilometres from their original source. Small bodies of water in particular are unable to compensate for the changes in acidity and there is a follow-on effect on the biota such as plants, bacteria, fish and amphibians, leading to a simplification of the ecosystem.

Direct effects on humans are more difficult to assess; there may be increased airway reactivity and asthma although this is likely to be a small effect. The presence of negative health effects from the toxic metals in groundwater is suggested, but as yet is unproven. There may also be a bio-accumulation of toxic metals such as mercury in fish which can then enter the human food chain.

Acid rain can also cause damage to food crops. This can occur in three ways: (1) direct damage to the crop; (2) acidification of the soil leading to diminished fertility; and (3) the leaching of heavy metals such as cadmium into the crop. The possible beneficial effect of acid rain in some areas must be acknowledged; this occurs in regions with sulphur-deficient soil; the depositing of sulphate ions in the soil may lead to a fertilizing effect (McMichael, 1993).

The pollutants that are responsible for acidification also play a role in other changes to the environment, including climate change and eutrophication. They are also a precursor for the production of ground-level ozone. Nitrogen oxides, together with volatile organic compounds, forms ground-level ozone in the presence of sunlight. Ozone causes damage to agricultural crops, trees and humans, including eye irritation and respiratory tract irritation, exacerbation of respiratory disease and reduced exercise capacity. The concentration of ground-level ozone regularly reaches harmful levels all over Europe.

Human Health and Biodiversity

Humans have been cultivating and collecting plants and animals for their own purposes for thousands of years. The identification of edible plants as well as plant substances that can treat diseases, act as pesticides, or have industrial uses has been ongoing, and we still have not identified them all. Loss of diversity may threaten this source of nutrition and innovation.

Many pharmaceutical products originate from natural sources, including the antibiotic penicillin, which is a natural toxin that kills bacteria, released by particular fungal moulds. WHO has estimated that three-quarter of all primary health care is by traditional medicine (90% in low and middle income countries) (McMichael, 1993). Half of all prescription drugs originate from substances extracted from natural organisms. There are plant substances both from the tropics and temperate areas that have been identified as useful in the treatment of cancer.

Once a plant has been identified as useful to humans, there is danger that it may become extinct due to overuse. The Cinchona tree was harvested almost to the point of extinction before the Dutch made a very successful plantation in Java that supplied 90 per cent of all quinine until 1940s. Taxol is a potent anti-cancer drug found in the Pacific yew; which is being felled as part of commercial forestry and is rapidly being depleted. It is not only plants but also animals that are a source of medicinal drugs, in particular, *bufo* toxins from various amphibians, and yet their habitats are under threat in many parts of the world.

Food and Diversity

Biodiversity allows plant species to grow in unproductive or degraded land. The careful breeding of wild strains with domesticated stock has meant that agricultural practices can spread into new areas. Wheat, maize and rice provided half of the world's food, and new ways have been found to substantially increase yields. In some areas this has meant vast areas planted in single varieties; while this has meant increases in yield and ease of harvesting, it also points to the potential loss of some cultivars, as well as the opportunity for pest or disease outbreaks to devastate whole areas. To ensure food security, we need to preserve genetic diversity. There are now seed banks throughout the world collecting as many different cultivars as possible and storing them.

Genetic Modification

There has always been selective breeding of plants to obtain desired traits such as high yield, and resistance to pest or drought. The genetic modification of organisms using genes from other species is used to alter crop characteristics, e.g. their yield, pest resistance or herbicide tolerance. The technology is not without controversy. The arguments against genetic modification focus on the unknown health, environmental and economic risks. For example, consumers may have allergic reactions to new substances, pest resistance or herbicide tolerance could spread into wild plants, and there could be toxicity to wildlife. Opponents are also wary of repercussions of increasing the control of agriculture by large biotechnology corporations. Arguments in favour of genetic modification include the solving of some food production problems due to the production of greater crop yields. Proponents argue that genetic modification of crops can, therefore, help to alleviate food shortages in low income countries.

Deforestation

Currently, about 30 per cent of the earth's land surface is forested; less than half of this is primary, undisturbed forest. The rate of destruction is increasing, particularly in the rainforests where two-third of the clearance is for agricultural purposes secondary to the needs of growing populations. The Millennium Goals aimed at ensuring sustainable development, include preference being given to land covered by forest. Deforestation results in a loss of natural habitat and of biodiversity. The effects of biodiversity in tropical areas have some immediate local effects; there is increased soil erosion and resultant sedimentation of rivers with loss of plants and animals. The tropical forests have the richest ecosystems on Earth. Forests have a critical role in the removal and storage of carbon dioxide from the atmosphere, identified as being important for the regulation of global climate change. If there is increasing deforestation, then the ability to hold carbon dioxide is reduced. Forests are being cleared for agriculture by people who have little other access to alternative economic activities strategies. In short term, this provides jobs and some economic security, but this practice is difficult to regulate by governments and is not sustainable in the long term. There are a number of innovative programmes designed to reduce deforestation and preserve the forests for the future; not all of these are successful, as they rely on input and the cooperation of local and national agencies and logging companies.

Health and Environmental Sanitation in India

Environmental sanitation envisages promotion of health of the community by providing clean environment and breaking the cycle of disease. It depends upon various factors that include status of the people, types of resources available, innovative and appropriate technologies according to the requirement of community, socio-economic development of country, cultural factors related to environmental sanitation, political commitment, capacity building of the concerned sectors, social factors including behavioural pattern of the community, legislative measures adopted, and others.

Nature and Extent of Health and Sanitation in India

As per estimates, inadequate sanitation costs India almost $ 54 billion or 6.4 per cent of the country's GDP in 2006. Over 70 per cent of this economic impact or about $ 38.5 billion was health-related, with diarrhoea followed by acute lower respiratory infections accounting for 12 per cent of the health-related impacts (OWSA: 2011). Evidence suggests that all water and sanitation improvements are cost-beneficial in all developing sub-regions (Hutton et al., 2007). Sectoral demands for water are growing rapidly in India owing mainly to urbanization and it is estimated that by 2025, more than 50 per cent of the country's population will live in cities and towns. Population increase, rising incomes, and industrial growth are also responsible for this dramatic shift. National Urban Sanitation Policy 2008 was the recent development in order to rapidly promote sanitation in urban areas of the country. India's Ministry of Urban Development commissioned the survey as part of its National Urban Sanitation Policy in November 2008 (Water Supply and Sanitation in India, 2011). In rural areas, local government institutions in charge of operating and maintaining the infrastructure are seen as weak and lack the financial resources to carry out their functions. In addition, no major city in India is known to have a continuous water supply and an estimated 72 per cent of Indians still lack access to improved sanitation facilities (Kumar et al.: 2011). Percentage of urban population without proper sanitation in India is 63 per cent. The 11th Five Year Plan envisages 100 per cent coverage of urban water and urban sewage, and rural sanitation by 2012. Although investment in water supply and sanitation is likely to jump by 221 per cent in the 11th Five Year Plan over the 10th Plan, the targets do not take into account both the quality of water being provided into account, or the sustainability of systems being put in place (The Water and Sanitation Sector in India, April 2011).

Water and Sanitation: Retrospect and Prospect

A number of innovative approaches to improve water supply and sanitation have been tested in India, in particular in the early 2000s. These include demand-driven approaches in rural water supply since 1999, community-led total sanitation, public-private partnership to improve the continuity of urban water supply in Karnataka, the use of microcredit to women in order to improve access to water (Sustainable Sanitation in India, April 2011). Total sanitation campaigns gives strong emphasis on Information, Education, and Communication (IEC), capacity building and hygiene education for effective behaviour change with involvement of panchayati raj institutions, community-based organizations and non-governmental organizations (NGOs), etc. The key intervention areas are Individual Household Latrines (IHL), School Sanitation and Hygiene Education (SSHE), Community Sanitary Complex, Anganwadi toilets supported by Rural Sanitary Marts (RSMs), and Production Centres (PCs) (Kumar et al., 2011). The main goal of the Government of India is to eradicate the practice of open defecation. To give fillip to this endeavour, the government has launched Nirmal Gram Puraskar to recognize the efforts in terms of cash rewards for fully covered PRIs and those individuals and institutions who have contributed significantly in ensuring full sanitation coverage in their area of operation.

Most of the interventions (including multiple interventions, hygiene, and water quality) were found to significantly reduce the levels of diarrhoea illness, with the greatest impact being seen for hygiene and household treatment intervention (Fewtrell et al., 2005). Interventions to improve water quality at the household level are more effective than those at the source (Clasen et al., 2006). Unfortunately, in developing countries, public health concerns are usually raised in the institutional setting, such as municipal services, hospitals, and environmental sanitation. There is a reluctance to acknowledge the home as a setting of equal importance along with the public institutions in chain of disease transmission in the community. When sanitation conditions are poor, water quality improvements may have minimal impact regardless of amount of water contamination. If each transmission pathway is sufficient to maintain diarrhoeal disease, single-pathway interventions will have minimal benefit, and ultimately an intervention will be successful only if all sufficient pathways are eliminated. However, when one pathway is critical to maintaining the disease, public health efforts should focus on this critical pathway (Water Supply and Sanitation in India, 2011). The positive impact of improved water quality is greatest for families living under good sanitary conditions, with the effect statistically significant when sanitation is measured at the community level but not significant when sanitation is measured at the household level. Improving drinking water quality would have no effect in neighbourhoods with very poor environmental sanitation; however, in areas with better community sanitation, reducing the concentration of fecal coliforms by two orders of magnitude would lead to 40 per cent reduction in diarrhoea. Providing private excreta disposal would be expected to reduce diarrhoea by 42 per cent, while eliminating excreta around the house would lead to a 30 per cent reduction in diarrhoea. The findings suggest that improvements in both water and sanitation are necessary if infant health in developing countries is to be improved. They also imply that it is not epidemiological but behavioural, institutional, and economic factors that should correctly determine the priority of interventions (Sustainable Sanitation in India, 2011). Another study highlighted the water quality interventions to the point-of-use water treatment was found to be more effective than previously thought, and multiple interventions (consisting of combined water, sanitation, and hygiene measures) were not more effective than interventions with a single focus (Fewtrell et al., 2005).

Lack of water supply, poor environmental sanitation, improper disposal of human excreta, and poor personal hygiene add to perpetuate and spread diarrhoea diseases in India. Since diarrhoea diseases are caused by 20–25 pathogens, vaccination, an active disease prevention strategy is not feasible.

Summing Up

The quality of the environment and the nature of any economic development taking place are major determinants of the health of people in that environment. In order to have a healthy environment, economic development must meet people's needs and ecological sustainability must be achieved. WHO defines environmental health as those aspects of human health, including quality of life, that are determined by physical, biological, social and psycho-social factors in the environment. Throughout our history, humans have interacted with the environment and freely used natural resources. Sustainable development is also about addressing equity within the present generation. It is often the poorest groups in society who are most exposed to environmental hazards, including dangerous working conditions and restricted access to adequate and safe food and water. A change in the environmental conditions in one part of the world can lead to a reaction in another part of the world. The result of this is a global climate change and there are other consequences which include stratospheric ozone depletion, acidic precipitation and loss of diversity. In India, the public health system is not well equipped to deal with the health probelms. There is a poor quality of potable water and sanitation facilities.

References

Cairncross, S., D. O'Neill, A. McCoy and D. Sethi (2003), *Health, Environment and the Burden of Diseases: A Guidance Note*, London: DFID.

Clasen, T. et al. (2006), 'Interventions to Improve Water Quality for Preventing Diarrhoea', *Cochrane Database System Review*, 3: CD004794.

Fewtrell, L. et al. (2005a), 'Water, Sanitation and Hygiene Interventions to Reduce Diarrhoea in Less Developed Countries: A Systematic Review and Data Analysis', *Lancet Infectious Diseases*, 5: 42–52.

—— (2005b), 'Water, Sanitation and Hygiene in Developing Countries: Interventions and Diarrhoea – A Review', *Water Science and Technology*, 52: 133–42.

Hutton, G. et al. (2007), 'Global Cost-benefit Analysis of Water Supply and Sanitation Interventions', *Journal of Water Health*, 5: 481–502.

Inadequate Sanitation Costs India $54 Billion Yearly (April 2011), http://southasia.pneworld.net/todaysheadlines/inadequatesanitationcosts-india-54-billion-yearly.

Kumar, Ganes S. et al. (2011), 'Health and Environmental Sanitation in India: Issues for Prioritizing Control Strategies', *Indian Journal of Occupational and Environmental Medicine*, 15(3): 93–96.

Landon, Megan (2006), *Environment, Health and Sustainable Development*, New Delhi: Tata McGraw-Hill.

Last, A. (1955), *A Dictionary of Epidemiology*, New York: Oxford University Press.

McMichael, A.J. (1993), *Planetary Overload*, Cambridge: Cambridge University Press.

—— (2001), *Human Frontiers, Environments and Disease*, Cambridge: Cambridge University Press.

OWSA: One World South Asia (2011), *One World Net*, New Delhi.

Total Sanitation Campaigns (2011), http://www.ddws.nic.in/tsc_index.htm.

UNCED (1992), United Nations Conference on Environment and Development, Rio de Janeiro, htpp://www.un.org/esa/sustdev/documents/unced_dics.htm

UNDP (2003), *Human Development Report 2003: Millennium Development Goals: A Compact among Nations to End Human Poverty*, New York: Oxford University Press.

United Nations (1948), *Universal Declaration of Human Rights*, New York: United Nations.

—— (2004), *Implementation of the United Nations Millennium Declaration: Report of the Secretary-General*, New York: United Nations.

Water Supply and Sanitation in India (2011), http://www.gtz.de/en/dokumente/encosan-sustainablesanitation-india-2008.pdf.

WHO (1992a), *World Development Report 1992: Development and the Environment*, Oxford: Oxford University Press.

—— (1992b), *Our Planet, Our Health*, Geneva: WHO.

—— (1993), *Global Strategy: Health, Environment and Development: Approaches to Drafting Country-wide Strategies for Human Well-being under Agenda 21*, Geneva: WHO.

—— (1997), *Environment, Health and Sustainable Development*, Geneva: WHO.

World Commission on Environment and Development (1987), *Report to United Nations General Assembly (A/RES/42/187)*, 11 December.

29

Food, Nutrition and Health

There is a complex relationship between food, nutrition and health. The differential pattern of eating, consumption and shopping behaviour results in differential health and nutritional outcomes.

Why then is the sociology of food and eating emerging as a more substantial area of research in sociology today? Such trends often have multiple causes. One influence may be the increasing awareness of nutritional problems both as a malnutrition and deprivation of nutrition. The incidence of eating disorders including anorexia nervosa, bulimia and obesity is attracting more and more attention. A second influence may be the people are becoming ill because of deprivation of sufficient nutrition. The new interest in sociology of food and eating also stems from some quite different sources. In particular, its upsurge seems to be connected with the rise of interest in 'the sociology of culture', a popular catchall category encompassing a great deal that has been neglected as perhaps being 'too trivial' by sociologists in the past. This particular rise is probably bolstered by social respectability afforded by a shift in analytic and empirical attention from the sociologies of industrialized production to those of industrialized consumption. In turn, this has reflected a greater openness to other neighbouring disciplines, notably history and anthropology.

Current Status of Food Security in India

Nutrition, Food Security and Safety

The greatest burden of disease over the last half century was premature death from hunger and malnutrition. But epidemiological evidence also suggests that the toll from inappropriate nutrition also results in many more diseases and health problems. Specifically, from the 1950s, the issue of diet related degenerative diseases emerged. At the end of the 20th century, the environmental aspects of food production such as pesticides and genetic modification attracted considerable global attention from the public and from policy makers, it was safety that had greater impact on the architecture of governance. New food agencies and laws were framed through the parliaments of many developed nations. Developing countries rushed towards seizing the opportunities for export markets.

Developed countries focused more on the food processing industries and prided themselves on being modern, clean and run to meet high technical standards. However, the monitoring of food-borne illness suggested that existing controls were not sufficient. Explanations included new varieties of existing diseases due to production changes; changing food handling in the home; poor skills in food service industries; and so on. Outbreaks of comparatively rare diseases such as *E coli* or listeriosis became world news, with the emergence of new types, in case of Ecoli 0157, and new opportunities, in the case of *listeria monocytogenes.* The emergence of food-borne health problems in rich societies followed the emergence of new systems of food handling, associated with changes in women's role. New technologies such as packaging, cook-chills (pre made tc dinners) and changes in cooking technology (microwaves) gave greater choice to affluent consumers. Cook-chills/TV dinners, for instance, are preserved at 0–3 degrees Celsius, but provided opportunities for *listeria* (which survives in this temperature range) to survive.

Further, UN Development Programme has calculated that the richest 20 per cent of the World's populations already account for:

- About 86 per cent of all total private consumption
- Around 58 per cent of the world's energy
- Close to 45 per cent of all meat and fish
- Nearly 84 per cent of all paper
- About 87 of all cars
- And, 74 per cent of all telephones

Conversely, the poorest 20 per cent of the world consume 5 per cent or less of all of the above goods and services (UNDP, 1998).

Proponents of maintaining current policies argue that such questions are defeatist or anti-progress or fail to take account of human ingenuity or are immoral in that the poor are being denied opportunities from which the affluent already benefit. The critics of the existing system are not arguing a position of 'less for all' but that if health gains are to be won for everyone, policies and structures need to be different (McMichael, 2000).

To meet projected population growth and consumer demand, for example, global food production must double by 2020. The Food and Agricultural Organization (FAO) is optimistic that food supplies can and will grow faster than the world population (FAO, 2000). This optimism is welcome, but a note of caution is due. It is based on total food supplies, and takes little account of distribution or of ecological constraints.

Food Security

Food security exists when all people, at all times, have physical and economic access to sufficient, safe and nutritious food to meet their dietary needs and food preferences of active and healthy life (Food and Agriculture Organization, 1996). In the post World War II period, food security was deemed to be the national concern. Countries aimed for self-reliance, that is, to feed themselves from their own resources. The over-arching policy goal of under consuming countries was to increase production. By the end of the 20th century, the goal of food insecurity had been redefined – to mean not necessarily producing food within the borders but to produce enough economic output to be able to afford to buy food in world or regional markets. This shift of definition represented the triumph of neo-liberal approaches to managing economies. Global institutions such as World Bank and FAO had encouraged developing countries to build export markets and to abandon the autarkist tendencies of the post-colonial movement for self-reliance. Economic strategies such as structural adjustment programmes enabled this new approach to take root, but ironically, the environmental critique of current 'efficient' food supply systems is reawakening interest in reducing unnecessary trade. Transporting food long-distance to earn export currencies is a fragile policy; it depends on commodities retaining their value when, as many export-dependent developing countries have found, they may not. Although the majority of food is still produced regionally, if not locally, food trade has been encouraged by liberalization measures. An estimated 90 per cent of the world's food consumption occurs where it is produced (McMichael, 2000).

Food Security in India

The Green Revolution Strategy adopted by India since the mid-1960s to reduce food insecurity, has paid rich dividends. The most significant change has been the increase in the domestic output of foodgrains, particularly cereals.

Owing to the increase recorded in the output of foodgrains, the dependence on imports for meeting the food needs of the population went down considerably. The increase in output of cereals has kept pace with the increase in population. Per capita net output of cereals which had increased at the rate of 2.51 per cent per annum. During the 1990s, though the growth rate has decelerated compared to that during the 1980s, it continues to be higher than the growth of population.

Another important development contributing to the food security has been the increase in economic access of masses to cereals. With the retail prices of rice and wheat increasing at a rate lower than the increase in average per capita income in the country, the proportion of average per capita per day income required to buy a kg of wheat declined from 57 per cent in 1973–745 to 20 per cent in 1994–95 and that of rice from 75 per cent to 30 per cent during this period (Acharya, 1997).

Utsa Patnaik in her analysis of *The Republic of Hunger* (2004) tries to analyse the rural poverty responsible for the declining level of absorption of foodgrains. In the course of the last five years, the population of India has been sliding down towards sharply lowered levels of per capita foodgrains absorption, levels so low in particular years that they have not been seen for the last half-century. Between the early 1990s when economic reforms began, and now taking three-year averages, the annual absorption of foodgrains per head has come down from 178 kg to 155 kg. There was a slow decline in the absorption of foodgrains per head of the country's population between 1991–92 and 1997–98, after which it has fallen very sharply. Thus, in 2000–01, the average Indian family of four members was absorbing 93 kg less of foodgrains compared to a mere four years earlier – an unprecedented drop, entailing a fall in average daily intake by 64 gms per head, or a fall in caloric intake by 250 calories from foodgrains which accounts for 65–70 per cent of the food budget of the poor. Since the richest one-sixth to one-fifth of the population, mainly urban, has been improving and diversifying diets, the nutritional decline for the poorer three-fifth of the population, mainly rural, has been much greater than the average fall indicates. The recent trend in this country of sharply declining foodgrains absorption per head while average per capita income has been rising is, thus, highly abnormal. This is not only in the light of international experience, but also in comparison with our own past experience.

Diet and Health

From the 1950s, evidence from epidemiological studies shows that dietary composition is a key factor in patterns of disease. As a result in the last quarter of the 20th century, food became the subject of heated policy debate in many countries. The emerging consensuses from such studies have been summarized in numerous reports. The 1990 document of the World Health Organization (WHO) entitled *Diet, Nutrition, and the Prevention of Chronic Diseases,* is a good assessment of the consensus towards the turn of the century. In 2000, the Sub-Committee on Nutrition of the United Nations (UN) produced another major statement with the IVth Report on the *World Nutrition Sanitation: Nutrition throughout the Life Cycle.* These reports proposed that a trend in global diet focuses on the emergence of chronic diseases particularly: cardio-vascular disease (coronary heart disease, high blood pressure, cerebrovascular disease); some cancers (stomach, colorectal, breast, prostate, and so on); diabetes; obesity. They proposed that the world was experiencing these effects as the result of a nutrition transition, a shift from a restricted diet to one with more choices. By the turn of the new millennium, although global policy [for example from WHO and the Food and Agriculture Organization (FAO)] was still largely concerned about huger and population growth, the new evidence about the co-existence of underconsumption, overconsumption and malconsumption required policy responses. The WHO and FAO worked together and in 2004, the WHO produced a new *Global Strategy on Diet, Physical Activity and Health,* approved at the World Health Assembly in May 2004.

Nutrition Policy in India

Around one-third of new born infants are underweight; half of the children in low income groups show stunted growth while 50 per cent of pregnant women are anaemic. What more, there has been no significant improvement in the quality of household diet, in the country, latest researches show.

India is in a phase of transition, wherein diseases of developing countries still affect thousands while lifestyle diseases are hitting in a big way. Gopalan (1990) reports that 'we will have to fight at two ends of development spectrum for next 20 years. On one hand, we need to achieve complete elimination of under nutrition. On the other hand, we need to prevent chronic degenerative diseases among the affluent sections.'

Nutrition policy has been in existence since 1993, but hardly 10 per cent of its recommendations are being followed. Some programmes for tackling malnutrition exist, but there is no programme for tackling lifestyle diseases. It is just heart centres which are coming up all over, but there is no programme to educate people.

However, at the same time we should not turn back to the western nutrition model as perfect, especially since many of them are making dramatic U-turns such as return to breast feeding, doing away with high saturated fat diets and recognizing the importance of vegetables and fresh fruits.

'Whereas the production of cereals has soared, the production of pulses has actually declined in per capita terms, which to a large extent is to blame for not very good quality of household diet.' (Gopalan, 1990).

In the present health policy thrust is on the child survival and not on child health. This has led to an expanding pool of children with some or the other problem. The nutritional status of women is also questioned especially that of pregnant women in terms of the various programmes launched for women and particularly for mothers.

The traditional focus on undernutrition has to be widened to encompass all aspects of malnutrition, which includes overnutrition. Rather than separate issues of deficit and excess, we need to create health and nutrition messages that broadly address the concerns of unbalanced nutrition in the community – both under and overnutrition. It is important to emphasize the need for primary prevention of diet and lifestyle – determined health problems such as obesity in countries where resources are scarce and limited. The need of a nutrition-driven policy that encompasses the cooperation of all sectors that influence dietary and food practices and lifestyles related to physical activity is essential to generate changes in health-related behaviour that will address both the problems of dietary deficiency and dietary excess.

Nutritional Security in India

An important development related to the improvement in the nutritional security is that with improved availability of staple cereals at declining real prices, the subsistence and small farmers in several regions diverted the resources from low yielding coarse cereals to other crops which inter *alia* helped in increasing the output of oilseeds/edible oils, sugarcane, vegetables, fruits, spices and condiments, thereby stepping up the availability of other food items.

Another important development relating to food security is the buffer stocks of foodgrains with the public agencies and the public distribution system created in the country which helped in not only reducing the inter-year fluctuations in supply but also in checking the starvation deaths during the periods of severe droughts or floods.

Apart from these positive developments on the food production front there were some failures as well. These relate mainly to the output of pulses and nutritional levels of the masses in the country.

- Another area of concern relates to the number of hungry people. According to NSS Survey, during 1993–94, 6.45 million people were starkly hungry (without two square meals a day) and 44.8 million were partially hungry in the country (NSSO, 1997). In percentage, the figure may be small, yet the number is substantial.
- In regard to the level of nutrition, the average per capita calorie intake is closer to the accepted norm, food intake of even the poorest sections has improved somewhat (Kumar, 1996).

Food Safety

According to WHO, health could be defined as what sustains the physical and mental well-being of people. Once this concept is applied to food, two ways to address the health issue are to be distinguished.

The negative approach: Food must not compromise the health of consumers by any chemical, biological, or microbiological element or substance that it might contain.

The positive approach: Food is perceived as per its nutritional qualities, and as far as it helps to be in form, sustains physical performance, slows down ageing, prevents sickness, and, more generally, obstructs the misdeed of life.

The first approach alone refers to food safety, and defines the field of the standard studies of risks related to food additives, pesticides residues, veterinary medicines, microbial germs and their toxins, and other contaminants.

The world over, the production of the consumers' safety is an integral part of the major duties of public authorities, which elaborate in this regard regulations and officials controls. This is not such an easy task, and FAO and WHO have decided to set up in 1962, a body able to guide the national governments in this field: the Codex Alimentarius Commission.

Any safety regulation enacted by any government was supposed to be scientifically based, on acknowledged procedures of risk analysis. First of all, the parameters should be identified for the risk of food safety. It can be microbial germ, chemical element, biological substance. This can be helpful in analyzing the level of contamination by any type of residue and contaminant, or the presence of any additive in a given food category.

The public discourse around food – security, nutrition, safety – had come together and in a political and civil society. The range of potential tactics within public health strategies to reduce food-related ill health is considerable. Tactics include: (Lang, Pomerleau and McKee, 2005)

- Prevention – on an individual and/or population basis
- Health education and promotion
- Composition regulation
- Labelling and product information
- Production controls and monitoring
- Product traceability
- Product development and specification of niche markets such as low-fat spreads, fortification or other technological change
- Genetic screening (if and where possible)

In practice, all of these tactics are drawn upon one reason that food safety is consumer's responsibility. No label warns consumers that food is or may be contaminated. Food is presumed to be safe at source. In case of nutrition, however, there has been a fierce debate about the level of consumer choice and information. In the case of obesity, for instance, where scientific evidence is strong on the decline of physical activity, are consumers ignoring information about fat contents of processed foods or are unable to act on it? Nestle and others have shown how, if agriculture is producing a high level of fat, somehow it will end up down consumers' throats. Producers' invention of 'low fat' products is accompanied by a plethora of other products replete with hidden fats.

Ensuring Food Quality and Food Safety: Emerging Challenges

Ensuring food quality and food safety is equally significant for the welfare of an individual, a community and a nation. Many human illnesses are food related. Nutritional status and economic well-being are affected by food carrying pathogenic organisms and their toxins, and by poisonous chemicals. It is estimated that approximately 3 million children below the age of five die of diarrhoea every year. About 70 per cent of these deaths are said to be food-borne in origin (Esrey, 1990).

In developing countries, people spend almost 50 per cent of their income on food; among poor income groups this figure may go up to 70 per cent (Malik, 1981). At the national level, food and agriculture form a major sector of almost all national economies in terms of GDP, employment and foreign exchange earnings. About $ 500 billion worth of food enters international trade each year. In the USA alone, over 30,000 consignments of food valued at over $ 1 billion were detained in 1992 due to unsatisfactory quality and safety requirements (US Food and Drug Administration, 1992).

Many foods are highly perishable. They are easily contaminated when produced in an unhealthy and unclean environment. In fact, food is a very good indicator of environmental contamination and spoilage of food needs to be prevented through safe handling practices (Microbiological Aspects of Biological Contamination and Chemicals in Food, 1976). With the introduction of intensive agricultural and animal husbandry practices, there is a simultaneous need to control the use of pesticides, fungicides, animal drugs, etc. as they otherwise leave undesirable residues. The use of food additives during food processing and marketing requires careful control.

Food can easily be adulterated to defraud consumers and deprive them of their money's worth. Adulteration adversely affects the nutritional quality of food.

Types of Food Hazards

The main causes for such potential problems in food lie in the fact that before reaching the consumer, it usually passes through a complex, and quite often lengthy, food production, processing and distribution chain. Until recently, many foods were locally produced. Now, with the dynamism of the food sector and the lengthening of the food distribution chain, there is also an increase in potential hazards to the consumer.

The range of food systems can be gauged from the fact that while on the one hand, there is the organized food industry producing and distributing pre-packaged foods, utilizing the latest and mostly safe technologies, on the other we have street foods, where food is often handled and prepared under primitive conditions. There are, in addition, any number of situations in between. The types of food hazards which may endanger the quality and safety of foods have been listed in Table 1.

Table 1

Types of Food Hazards

Physical	Foreign matter, for example, glass, metal, wood paint, insects and their fragments, insect and rodent excreta, human air, rodent hair, dirt hides, rubber, paper, plastics, etc.
Microbiological	Related with microbes and viruses
Chemical	Pesticides; environmental contaminations and toxins; trace metals; lubricants; solvents, sanitising agents; veterinary drugs; vitamins and minerals.

Risk Perception

While it is recognized that risk should be kept to the minimum, very few countries have reliable data on food-borne illnesses. In industrialized countries alone, only 10 per cent of such cases are reported. In developing countries, the figure is not more than 1 per cent (Health consequences of biological contamination and chemicals in Food, 1992). In spite of such underreporting, food control and health officials, toxicologists and food scientists have attempted to prioritize health hazards (Wodicka, 1982). The ranking appears to be valid for developed and developing countries, and is as follows:

- Microbiological hazards
- Nutritional deficiencies
- Natural toxicants and environmental contaminants
- Hazards from improper use of pesticides and veterinary drugs
- Hazards from improper use of food additives

As against the above, it is interesting to notice consumer concerns and the order in which they are perceived (Knauer, 1984). They include:

- Chemicals in food
- Adulteration, particularly in developing countries
- Environmental pollution
- Microbiological quality

Mass media has a big role to play in this respect. It formulates and gives expression to consumer concerns.

Ensuring Food Quality

To ensure that quality and safety are built into the product, quality control must be carried out throughout the food chain – production, processing, storage and distribution up to the point of sale. For this purpose, three stages can be identified:

Food Production

The environment under which the food is produced; control on the use of pesticides, veterinary drugs and fertilisers; quality control at the time of harvesting; post-harvest handling, particularly during storage (temperature, humidity/water activity and time control); grading and segregation of sub-standard or spoiled produce are the important dimensions of food production.

How much of this is carried out in developing countries? The type of monitoring done by governmental authorities and the opportunities available to the producers to upgrade their technical skills are moot points. An ICMR report on 'Surveillance of Food Contaminants in India, 1993' indicates that considerably more work needs to be done in this direction in order to determine the scope and extent of the problems and to identify measures and strategies to control them. Post-harvest handling of food requires skills and facilities not commonly available in rural areas. The food industry, which has a vital stake in the quality and safety of the raw materials procured by it, should be able to play a crucial role. The industry can and should impart the necessary know-how and physical inputs to increase the producers' awareness and assist them in introducing good agricultural and animal husbandry practices as well as good food handling practices.

Food Processing

The food industry plays a pivotal role here. With increasing quantities of food being processed every year, the industry has a unique opportunity to ensure the quality and safety of food and maintain or enhance its nutritional value. This calls for proper hygiene; sanitation and cleaning schedules of plants and machinery; hygienic employee practices; appropriate processing technology; the proper use of additives; appropriate packaging to ensure product integrity and long life; correct labelling giving the necessary information to the consumer, not only about product use but also about its composition, nutritional properties, shelf-life, conformity to national food standards and other requirements.

The most important means available to the industry to achieve the above objectives include:

- The use of good manufacturing practices.
- The application of the HACCP approach to achieve optimum results with regard to the quality and safety of the product.
- The application of the ISO 9000 series of standards to establish quality control regimens.

Food Distribution and Sale

The food needs to be kept under conditions which will prevent spoilage until it reaches the consumer. Some of the important areas calling for quality control are:

- The ambient conditions under which food is stored or transported, for example time, temperature, and humidity.
- The application of the 'first-in, first-out' principle to see that food is not held beyond its shelf-life.
- Protection against insects, rodents and extraneous matter.
- Preparation of food, particularly street foods under hygienic conditions in food service establishments.

Ensuring the quality and safety of food is a multi-disciplinary subject and can be looked at from various angles. Several issues are being currently debated, which are:

Risk Assessment

Advances in science has enabled us to measure the minutest quantity of toxic substances in air, water and food. Even in industrialized countries, while the risks may be smaller than ever, they seem quite big because they can be measured in quantitative terms. It must be realized that there is no such thing as 'zero risk' or 'absolute safety'. Risk assessment does not lend itself to the clear-cut 'yes' or 'no' answers demanded by the public. Food control authorities determine compliance policies depending upon 'risk analysis', which includes risk assessment, risk management, and risk communication. Risk assessment is the most important of these, and the main responsibility of the scientific community. It includes:

- Hazard identification: Qualitative indication that a hazard can be present in a particular food.
- Exposure characterization: Quantitative evaluation of the nature of adverse effects; it may include dose-response assessment.
- Risk characterization: Integration of the above steps into the estimation of effects likely to occur in a given population, including potential uncertainties.

In the above exercise, the extrapolation from the high-dose biological response of animals, to the low-dose exposure of the human population is the single most important source of uncertainty. The most important challenge for the scientific community is either to remove this uncertainty or to reduce it to the minimum. The question is whether the mathematical model used to derive a quantitative risk assessment is biologically valid. This calls for more information on, and a better understanding of, what occurs at biochemical, cellular and molecular levels within the organism. Data needs to be available on toxicity mechanisms, pharmacokinetics and exposure; not only in the magnitude of the exposure but also in the exposure frequency, duration and route, and in the period of life covered.

Biotechnological Revolution

While the assessment of the safety and efficiency of newer technologies will always be a challenge to scientists, the immediate need for safety evaluation of products from the present-day 'biotechnological revolution' is paramount. It is a forceful emerging challenge as several foods have already started entering the market. Contemporary techniques of genetic modification have made it possible to speed up traditional processes of plant and animal breeding, and enable interspecies gene transfer which are not possible by traditional methods. Besides safety considerations, nutritional concerns, particularly in novel food plants, are going to be major issues, especially where important nutrients are modified or eliminated. In addition, the lost, reduced (or increased) bio-availability of micronutrients and the increase in anti-nutritional factors are concerns that would need to be addressed. Besides the scientific issues, there are ethical issues, consumer perception, and labelling, which will need to be taken up by the food control authorities.

New Regulatory Concepts

The increasing complexity of the food chain due to advances in food sciences and technology, innovations in storage and distribution systems, and the growing demands of consumers – radically altered by aggressive publicity – have also prompted the industry and food control authorities to further intensify their efforts to better protect the consumer. With newer foods entering the markets every day, and exotic and ethnic foods becoming available throughout the year, opinion at the international level is shifting towards newer approaches, such as:

- Greater emphasis on horizontal standards covering all foods: examples include food hygiene requirements; food additives and other chemicals including pesticides residues in food through positive lists; and labelling, including nutritional labelling.
- Better utilization of the available technical and financial resources: limiting the preparation and use of individual food standards (often called recipe standards) to those absolutely necessary. Simultaneously, greater use of labelling standards to provide consumer information.
- Food quality control: to be more strictly applied during the stages of production and processing by the food industry – that is, vigorous application of the GMP and HACCP approach and the ISO 9000 series requirements. This means that the onus of ensuring conformity to national regulations shall lie squarely with the industry. This method will necessitate the involvement of approved private inspection, monitoring and certification agencies.
- Reviewing the role of governmental food control authorities: to lay greater emphasis on the overall monitoring of in-process quality control procedures of the industry, rather than spending disproportionate resources on sampling and inspection at the retail end. As the resources shrink, greater stress should be placed on the scientific calibre of the inspection stag and their training, rather than on increasing manpower. The introduction of computerization and other modern means for the collection and dissemination of vital data should improve the efficiency of the food control system.

Governmental Credibility

There has been an ever-increasing demand from consumer groups for greater transparency in food control decision-making processes, and for them to play a more active role in determining the regulatory policy. Such a demand has now been further strengthened and, in fact, made obligatory (although for different reasons) for governments through the recent GATT agreements, that is, the agreement on sanitary and phyto-sanitary measures and the agreement on Technical Barriers to Trade. The three basic elements of these agreements concern:

- *Equivalence:* The members shall accept the sanitary and phyto-sanitary measures of other countries as an equivalent, provided that the exporting country can objectively demonstrate that it can achieve the appropriate level of consumer protection. Other countries can ask for access to national inspectional systems.
- *Risk Assessment:* Shall be based on scientific evidence and any arbitrary or unjustifiable distinction in the levels of protection shall be avoided.

- *Transparency:* The members shall notify changes in their sanitary/phyto-sanitary measures (read regulations and inspection procedures) and provide information to other countries and the WTO.

No government can act in isolation, as the world food system has become quite interdependent. As domestic food production goes up, so does the import and export of food. This calls for strengthening the scientific core of food safety decision-making processes, increasing the role of advisory bodies, appropriate reorganization of food control agencies, reviewing compliance policies and lastly, bringing about greater measures should not become an unnecessary stumbling block in the healthy development of the food industry and trade. Considerable action is called for, especially in developing countries, in the near future.

Involvement of Consumers and the Industry

One of the important causes that militate against the effective integration of consumer interests in food control relates to the lack of awareness and knowledge among consumers about food quality and safety issues vis-à-vis the inherent constraints of the food system and the need for the maintenance of food supplies at an optimum level. While it is the responsibility of government and the industry to provide such information, it is equally necessary that consumer organizations work towards increasing their credibility. This calls for improved scientific literacy among consumer groups. The first step is for industry, academia and the government to understand and deal with the public's emotional reactions. It is no use calling them irrational or unscientific. What is required is to understand how public opinion is shaped, and which communication methods are the most effective. This calls for a continuous, frank and honest dialogue between the consumers, the government and the industry. It is an emerging high-priority issue and deserves serious attention.

Street Food

Street food plays a very important role in providing inexpensive and nutritious food, particularly for millions in the middle and lower income groups. Such food is easily available, especially to those who have no opportunity to go home for their mid-day meal. Many itinerant workers who do not have proper housing and cooking facilities have no option but to depend upon street foods. While it is an age-old phenomenon, rapid urbanization and industrialization have brought about a sudden spurt in street food vending throughout the world, particularly in developing countries.

There has been quite a bit of concern about street foods at the international level. The FAO and the WHO have carried out several studies on street foods in countries in Asia, Africa and Latin America. Besides their convenience and employment potential, the greatest factor in their favour is the fact that they can provide per capita calorie and protein requirements within a cost of around $ 1 (Winarao, 1993). There are, however, serious problems. More often than not, the microbiological quality of street foods, especially that of prepared dishes and drinks, is below standards, indicating inappropriate sanitary and hygienic practices preparation and handling. There are also problems with the use of unauthorized food colours and some other additives, as well as chemical contamination from the environment. The consumer has, therefore, a high potential risk of serious health problems from streets foods. However, because of the many socio-economic issues involved, any attempt to ban street food vending is bound to fail.

Keeping in mind the scale of operation of such enterprises, it is quite a challenge to bring about improvements in the street food scenario. Policing action has to be coupled with training. Local bodies have also to provide facilities for safe water supply, garbage disposal, etc. Codes on 'Practice for Street Foods' are being prepared by the joint FAO/WHO Codex Alimentarius Commission. These would call for appropriate implementation. The HACCP approach can be applied to reduce hazards to consumers. What is required is the recognition of the problem and full cognizance of this informal sector of the food system. It is only then that strategies can be determined to meet local socio-economic situations.

Marketing and Advertising of Food

From the last decade the percentage of people who eat food outside, e.g. restaurants and canteens, have increased remarkably. Fast food consumption has also increased substantially. These trends have been driven, in part, by enormous advertising and marketing expenditure by the food industry. It is also due to massive migration of the people to software industry which means people are moving away from their native homeplace, and so have no option but to eat outside. Marketing campaigns links brand names and other discounts. Furthermore, even school canteens serve fast-food and soft drinks which attract children which in turn results in overconsumption of saturated fat, and underconsumption of fruits, non-starchy vegetables, fibres, and some other micronutrients.

Sedentary Lifestyle

Availability of sedentary pursuits, including television, video games, computers, and the internet, has risen greatly. Walking hours have drastically reduced. Opportunities for physical activity have decreased for various reasons. Physical education, is typically considered less important than academic disciplines. Parks, side paths, bike paths, safe play grounds are not given importance. Moreover, our culture places a premium on convenience: the car is preferred to walking, the lift to stairs, and the remote control to manual adjustments. These cultural forces arguably culminate in the drive-through window of fast-food restaurants, where a maximum of energy can be obtained with a minimum of exertion.

Obesity and Health

Eating and physical activity are two critical behaviours with the potential to influence energy balance in the body. It is now widely accepted that changes in lifestyle and patterns of consumption have followed wider social, economic and cultural change within modern societies and have resulted in systematic reductions in human energy expenditure. These include changes in employment patterns that have led to a reduction in manual labour and an increase in sedentary non-manual jobs, longer working hours (which have resulted in more limited opportunities for other forms of activity during the working day), widespread car ownership, and the rise of labour-saving devices for use at home and work. Nevertheless, the impact of these changes in the physical activity of children is less clear, this is despite evidence of reductions in walking and cycling to school. For children, other factors may also be relevant, such as the increased fears of parents about unsupervized outdoor play for children.

Obesity has reached epidemic proportions in India in 21st century, with morbid obesity affecting 5 per cent of the country's population (Agarwal, 2002). Obesity among the females is 16 per cent and among the males is 12.1 per cent (NFHS Survey of 2007). India is following a trend of other developing countries that are steadily becoming more obese. Unhealthy, processed food has become more accessible following India's continued integration in global food markets. This combined with rising middle class incomes, is increasing the average caloric intake per individual among the middle class and above income households.

The concept of a 'family of obesities' is a useful way of recognizing the complexity of the causes of obesity within society and, as a consequence, research is increasingly turning to an examination of the social and cultural context within which these food and activity-related habits and beliefs develop (*Foresight Report,* 2007: 43). Some of the social and cultural contexts of obesity that have been identified would include (among many others) the following factors:

- Social pressure to consume: An increasing exposure to food advertising combined with the greater affordability of processed food.
- Increasing social acceptability of 'fatness': This development, however, is complicated by the promotion of an ideal 'slim' body image within the media.
- Changing socio-cultural valuation of food: This in part reflects the growth in working hours for both men and women with a commensurate reduction in time available for food preparation. As a consequence, less value may now be placed on family mealtimes with the result that there has been a diminishing of parental control over children's diet.
- Great availability of 'passive entertainment': Television, computer games, and internet. Passive lifestyle contributes to obesity.

- Greater urbanization with opportunities for physical activity reduced: In relation to children the lack of availability for outdoor play in many urban schools has led to a diminishing of the importance of physical sports in the curriculum.
- Greater reliance on car use and ownership for transport.

Rather than seeing individual health lifestyles as a distinct set of choices made between possible actions and as potentially remedial by increasing health knowledge, health behaviour can be alternatively be seen as a routinized feature of everyday life guided by a practical or implicit logic. These daily practices or individual 'dispositions' (following the work of Bourdieu, 1984) are formed in different ways reflecting an individual's particular social position and their socialization into an associated set of 'worldviews' (described by Bourdieu as an individual's 'habitus'). Thus, in a very practical way, food choices can be conceived of as being a social attribute of an individual reflecting shared social attitudes and cultural conventions. Bourdieu conceptualizes these choices as reflecting individual 'taste' (referring to consumption behaviour and of lifestyle preferences rather than the physical sensation of tasting). Important social class differences in 'taste' or preferences have been found to exist in relation to dietary intake as well as the manner in which food is consumed. These social differences can be seen as manifested in terms of a preference for heavy filling fatty foods seen as sustaining the body, versus health-giving, light and non-fattening foods; and also in terms of having regular family meals around the table versus the acceptability of irregular 'grazing' of food in front of television.

Summing Up

When considering the new public agenda on food, it can be helpful to recognize that arguments about food are not new. Modern food policy might have to juggle quality, production efficiencies, prices, ownership, education, public health, food security, food safety, cultural tastes, and much more. Nevertheless, we can note some important policy shifts over the last century. For instance, the mid-20th century concern with quantity has now shifted to quality; similarly, attention has moved from macronutrients to micronutrients, fertilizer food to organic produced food, etc. Unravelling this history can be illuminating, and reminds us how public health is socially constructed.

References

Acharya, K.T. (1994), *Indian Food: A Historical Companion*, Bombay: Oxford University Press.

Acharya, S.S. (1997), 'Agricultural Price Policy and Development: Emerging Issues and Challenges', *Indian Journal of Agricultural Marketing*, 8(2): 149–73.

Agrawal, P. Kumar (2002), 'Emerging Obesity in Northern Indian States: A Serious Threat for Health', IUSSP Conference in Bangkok.

Anon (1985), 'Foods', *Eve's Weekly*, Bombay, 11–17 May, 17.

Blaxter, M. (1990), *Health and Lifestyles*, London: Routledge.

Bourdieu, P. (1984), *Distinction: A Social Critique of the Judgement of Taste*, London: Routledge.

Brown, L.R. (1996), *Tough Choices: Facing the Challenge of Food Scarcity*, London: Earthscan.

Charles, N. and M. Kerr (1988), *Women, Food and Families*, Manchester: Manchester University Press.

Dyson, T. (1996), *Population and Food: Global Trends and Future Prospects*, London: Routledge.

Esrey, S.A. (1990), 'Food Contamination and Diarrhoea, 1990', *World Health*, 19–20.

Food and Agriculture Organization (1996), *Rome Declaration of Food Security and World Food Summit Plan of Action*, Rome: Food and Agriculture Organization, Economic and Social Department.

—— (2000), *Agriculture Towards 2015/2030: Technical Interim Report*, Rome: Food and Agriculture Organization, Economic and Social Department.

Foresight Report (2007), *Tackling Obesities: Future Choices*, London: Government Office for Science.

Gopalan, C. (1998), 'Obesity in the Indian Urban Middle Class', *NFI Bulletin*, 19(1): 1–4.

—— (1990), 'Science and Nutrition in the Future', *Current Science*, 59(1): 18–25.

Graham, H. (1984), *Women, Health and the Family*, Brighton: Harvester/Wheatsheaf.

—— (1992), 'Budgeting for Health: Mothers in Low-Income Households', in C. Glendinning and J. Millar (eds), *Women and Poverty in Britain in the 1990s*, London: Harvester/Wheatsheaf.

Knauer, V.H. (1984), Keynote Address to the Second National Conference for Food Protection, US Department of Health and Human Services.

Kumar, P. (1996), 'Agricultural Productivity and Food Security in India', *Agricultural Economics Research Review*, 9(2): 128–41.

Lang, Tim, Joceline Pomerleau and Martin McKee (2005), 'Food, Trade and Health', in Joceline Pomerleau and Martin McKee (eds), *Issues in Public Health*, New Delhi: Tata McGraw-Hill.

Malik, R.K. (1981), 'Food: A Priority for Consumer Protection in Asia and the Pacific Region', *Food and Nutrition*, 7(2): 18–23.

Malik, Raj K. (1996), 'Ensuring Food Quality and Food Safety: Emerging Challenges', *NFI Bulletin*, 17: 5–8.

McMichael, P. (2001), 'The Impact of Globalization, Free Trade and Technology on Food and Nutrition in the New Millennium', *Proc Nutr Soc*, 60: 215–20.

Microbiological Aspects of Biological Contamination and Chemicals in Food (1976), *Report of a WHO Committee with Participation of FAO*, Geneva: WHO, Annex 1, 92–93.

National Family Health Survey 2005–06 (2007), Mumbai: International Institute of Population Sciences.

National Sample Survey Organization (NSSO) (1997), Reported Adequacy of Food Intake in India: 1993–94, 50th Quinquennial Survey of Consumer Expenditure, NSS 50th Round, Department of Statistics, Government of India, Report No. 415, September.

Patnaik, Utsa (2004), 'The Republic of Hunger', *Social Scientist*, 32(9–10): 9–35.

Ramanamurthy, P.S.V. (1969), 'Physiological Effects of "Hot" and "Cold" Food in Human Subjects', *Indian Journal of Nutrition and Dietetics*, 6: 187.

Sharma, B.N. (1972), *Social and Cultural History of North India about 1000–1200 AD*, New Delhi: Abhinav Publications.

Shastri, R.P. (1986), 'The Acid Test', *The Times of India*, Bombay, 22 June.

Storer, Jenny (1977), 'Hot and Cold Food Beliefs in an Indian Community and their Significance', *Journal of Human Nutrition*, 31: 33–40.

US Food and Drug Administration (1992), *Worldwide Import Summary*, Fiscal Year.

Winarno, F.G. (1993), 'Street Foods in Developing Countries: Lessons from Asia', sponsored by the Chinese Academy of Preventive Medicine, International Life Sciences Institute in Cooperation with FAO and WHO.

Wodicka, V. (1982), *An Overview of Food Risk/Hazards*, presented at the Food and Drug Officials Sponsored Symposium on Food Toxicology, Spring Workshop, New Orleans, Louisiana, USA.

World Health Organization (2003), *Diet, Nutrition and the Prevention of Chronic Diseases*, WHO Technical Report Series No. 916, Geneva: WHO.

30

Technology in Medicine and Health Care

Medical technology as well as medical care can be understood to be a social science par excellence in the sense that definitions of illness, inventions of medical technologies, differential diagnosis, types of medical care organization, and their varied and differential application to populations is a function not of the technology itself, but of social and cultural forces that play upon the medical establishment itself.

Development of modern medicine related much to the technological progress after the industrial revolution. Modern medicine which was primarily based on the rationality totally eclipsed the traditional knowledge of healing which was largely based on traditional learning and use of natural remedies as well as religious methods. Incorporating various technological advancements into its intervention, bio medicine has gone into the hands of 'experts' who decides the course of treatment (Lane, 2001). The expertise has been gained through various ways: the industrial revolution, development of technological artifacts, scientific discoveries and institutional arrangements. The scientific and technological advancements in the medical field assimilated into medical practice, where it has become one of the main factors to decide the course of health care services. Apart from this wider social, economical political considerations also played a role. Medical care institutions changed continuously in response to the scientific events.

The introduction of X-ray was seen as the hope to alleviate disease and bring happiness to lives. This has changed with the introduction of new-technologies like ultrasounds, CAT scan, MRI, etc. Applications of all these technologies in the field were done mainly by medical practitioners. Medical practitioners who are part of society have been influenced by the promises of technology along with economic interest. Thus, the medical practitioners started playing a vital role in controlling and executing technological artifacts in medical practice. That is why one should note that in public health comprehending the prevalence of medical technology is not only important it is also equally essential to know about the medical practitioners and their understanding of medical technology.

Evolution of Medical Practice and Medical Technology

The use of technology in treatment started with the use of curves and roots. Evidences discovered in parts of Europe, Asia and South America suggest that various surgical procedures were tried. For example, skulls with holes, suggesting crude surgical attempts, were found. Earlier, physicians were treated as Gods of healing. Hippocrates installed a scientific spirit by changing the nature and nomenclature of physicians and viewed them as scientists rather than priests. Diagnostic observations and clinical treatment began to replace superstition under this regime. According to him, body has the potential to recover naturally and the role of a physician was to aid these natural processes. In Renaissance period, sickness and pain were seen as processes which provide genuine insight into the working of heart, lung, brain and muscle structures. Body temperature and pulse rates became measures that could relate to other symptoms.

Hospital medicine shifted from a belief in disease as a disturbance of the total system to what is called 'localized pathology', i.e. ill health could be caused by malfunctioning of one particular part of the body. Doctors correlate the external symptoms with those internal malfunctions that they could discover using various instruments which were developed during this period. The public health field which was developed during this period used preventive and environmental strategies but it was of little interest to most practitioners of curative medicine. With the development of germ theory in the late 19th century, the emphasis of medical practice swung more towards individual care. This was the period of 'laboratory medicine' where doctors probed deeper into the bodies of human. Mechanistic world view body as different parts without harmonizing with other parts of the body and with wider social, economic and environmental factors.

In the industrial revolution, machines were put in place of animals and human muscles. The second industrial revolution initiated the use of machinery for functions that was hither to be performed by the senses and human mind. After World War II, technological improvement was mainly in pursuits of military objectives which also brought nuclear medicine and medical imaging and this has made great impact on the medical care till 1970s. Improvements in clinical chemistry, computing, clinical microbiology, etc. in recent years brought specialized medical care.

Technological Improvements in the 20th Century Medicine

From physics, biochemistry, astronomy, and neuroscience to molecular genetics; technological imaging is changing the way we see ourselves and also the world around us. It tells us what we are and how we really look. Wilhelm Roentengen's discovery of X-rays in 1895 led us to see the human body. But over the last three decades, the wide spread use of high-resolution electron microscopy had provided powerful micrographic images on a molecule level.

The technical advances in 20th century related to enhanced visualization, includeing TI (Thermal Imaging), MRI (Magnetic Resonance Imaging), CT (Computed Tomography X-ray Imaging) and PET (Positron Emission Tomography), contributed to a radical shift in the ways of viewing the body and the view of medical practitioners. On the one hand, the body can be seen in a quantifiable, voluminous fashion. Now it is a mass of various readings, each one giving a different character to the whole. On the other hand, the new technologies have produced a dimensional multiplication of how the human body is conceptually and visually recognized (Czegledy and Czegledy, 2000). The body is also seen in plural ways: via electronic pulses, magnetic cadences, thermal signatures, etc. The intervention of medical imaging created opportunities to have different qualitative understanding. The following table gives account of the health related technological progress over the last four centuries (Table 1).

Table 1

Health Care Innovations from the 17th to 21st Centuries

Period	*Examples of Scientific, Technologic and Organizational Innovations*
17th century	Biological basis of disease (Descartes), circulation of blood (Harvey), microscope (Leeuwenhock)
18th century	Thermometer, vaccination (Jenner), surgical anatomy (Hunter), clinical sciences (Sydenham)
19th century	Stethoscope, anaesthesia, laryngoscope, opthalmoscope, blood pressure cuff, sanitation, antisepsis, Braille printing, hygiene in obstetrics, nursing, microscopic pathology, pathological chemistry, microbiology, vaccines, X-ray, syringes
1900–1930	Penicillin, randomized clinical trials, anti-material and vector control
1946–1960	Vaccines, anti-hypertensive, psychotropic drugs, cancer chemotherapy, prepaid group practice
1961–1980	DNA, oral dehydration therapy, vaccines, open heart surgery, pacemakers, organ transplantation, computerized tomography (CT), eradication of small pox
1981–2000	Magnetic resonance imaging (MRI), position emission tomography (PET), endoscopc surgery

Definition of Medical Technology

Medical technology in broader terms could include techniques, drugs, equipment and procedures used by health care professionals to deliver medical care to individuals, and the system within which such care is delivered. Techniques here means, as Mechanic (2000) puts, 'organized inputs to get the desired output'. Drugs of various kinds are developed to administer thorough use of technological artefact. Equipment, for example, can vary from simple instrument such as syringe to highly sophisticated complex systems such as MRI scan. Procedures here mean the application of organized knowledge to minimize human sufferings. This medical technology works through a network, including hospitals, pharmacies, insurance companies, government departments, university facilities and the multinational pharmaceutical industry and of course, through professionals. All put together, medical technology is much more than science.

Socio-economic and political factors, all help to shape its evolution. Medical technology influences, changes and shapes the programme, policy, health seeking behaviour, providers' behaviour and cost. These influences promote a particular kind of culture in which values, attitudes and belief become a force which brings change (Johnson, 1995). It applies both to a patient, who is the beneficiary and a doctor, who applies the technology. In addition to that patients' trust on medical technology and confidence of doctors are also important factors for development of the medical technology.

Type of Medical Technology

Table 2 summarizes different types of medical technologies and their application.

Table 2

Types of Medical Technology (MT)

Types of MT	*Forms of Development in MT*	*Application of MT*
Drugs	Process innovation	Screening
Devices	Product innovation	Prevention
Medical and surgical procedures		Diagnosis
Support systems		Treatment
Organizational systems		Rehabilitation

Use of Body as Technology

How does technology use body in its intervention can be traced back from the Galileo period in medicine. But profound changes have happened over the past two centuries in understanding and viewing the human body due to the advancement of science and technology. In the medical world, since the 17th century till recently, the body was solely viewed through the naked eye or via elementary mechanical magnification with the help of compound lensed microscopy. With the development of advanced bio medical technologies, bodily imaging: techniques have become the centre of diagnostic medicine. Today, we consider our bodies through scientific fact. The Cartesian idea of philosophical introspection, a simultaneous separation of mind from lived-in body, becomes dominant. The sacred and numerous qualities of body, viewed by the Church and religion changed body into being as secular. The body is no longer seen as analogous to the divine but rather as similar to the engines of industry. Thus, body is equated with machine.

Bacon, Kepler and Newton separated all non-mechanical aspects of nature and humankind and held them as incapable of analysis. In doing so they treated nature with mathematical and mechanical terms, by taking clock for their analysis. The discovery of the 'pump' like circulation of the blood by the English physician William Harvey, in 1628, bolstered the growing 17th century view that the body was machine (Kimbrell, 1993). On the other hand, Descartes in his work *Discourse on Method* (1637) argued that virtually all body movement and processes could be understood in terms of machine-like activity. He gave mechanical analysis of living bodies. He dismissed the whole theology of church that human beings have an immortal soul inseparable from the body and believes that the theology was not in accord with observable fact. By 20th century, the human body and the development of medical technology made advancement in computing the body through genetic engineering. In this way bio-medicine has been emphasized and its authority is stressed. Most of the diagnostic and therapeutic techniques are of course experimental upon the body. And these technologies are overvalued for its usefulness and believed that it results in alleviating and curing diseases (Towers, 1971). By and large, man tends to seize uncritically on new medical facilities, always in the hope that somehow they will prevent the ever-flowing stream of disease and death (ibid.). The gullibility is not of the general public alone but of scientists and doctors who believed the efficacy of technology is totem, whether it is of iatro-mechanical or iatro-chemical. Mankind is scared of suffering and death and this fear makes them an easy prey to the optimism of medical technology. The same enthusiasm provides money for the advancement of medical technology. This results in viewing human into a narrowly mechanical analysis with the application of mechanical and chemical techniques (ibid.).

Technological Influences in Medical Practice

The modern medicine which started examining patients through clinical examination went through a sea change after medical imaging was introduced for the diagnosis of patients. Doctors are sometimes being given status based on their knowledge about the disease, and the frequent use of technology. This section deals with various aspects of clinical examination in diagnosing the patient, role of technology in medical practice, whether it changed the clinical examination or not, the impact of medical imaging on the medicine in general and medical practice in particular. This will also give an account of how medical imaging brought changes in the medical services and hospitals.

Importance of Physical Examination and Use of Clinical Skills

The importance of physical examination has a long history. It helped practitioners to know the status of the patient and to decide what action is needed. Clinical skills such as observation, examination and interpretation are considered important and required for physical examination through the use of skills (Phoon, 2000). The rest in medicine which includes counselling, prognosis, medical and surgical treatment is wholly based on the physical examination. Along with medical history, physical examination is and has been the frontline tool for diagnosis.

Physical examination, the oldest technique is mainly based on observation. A patient's colouring, the condition of the tongue, and other detailed clinical observations, including auscultation, were important to Chinese diagnostics (Wallnofer, 1965). Egyptians also studied the pulse and made several observations on cardiac disease and circulatory insufficiency (Chalioungui, 1984) so did the ancient civilizations of Mesopotamia and India (Ackerknecht, 1982). Clinical medicine reached new heights in the 4th century BC with Hippocrates, the 'Father of Medicine', who used physical examination skills in addition to careful history-taking. In the late 19th and early 20th centuries, the need for clinical examination was felt. During this time, with the birth of bio medicine, William Osler, one of the great clinicians of all time, felt that a thorough physical examination, along with a careful history, was among the 'principles of practice' of medicine (Harvey, 1989). But then advancement in medical technology especially in early part of the 20th century loosened the physician's control over patient. This was due to the subjective nature of diagnostic judgement. The diagnosis tools that readily provided the data claimed itself as 'objective'. So the strength of physical examination findings which are subjective and somewhat mysterious became less important. In order to know about the use of technology and the changes it had brought, it may be necessary to briefly look at the role of medical technology in medical practice.

Technological Web in Medicine and its Impact

The advancement in technology not only helped to see the body in plural ways but also transformed the medical care to be more dependent on increasingly sophisticated technologies which had been drawn from bioscience, engineering and information technology. It redefined and deconstructed the physical body in relation to health and disease. Increase of techno-science intervention had impact on dismantling the traditional practices and expertise. The increasing reliance on technologies is a move from 'biographical medicine' to 'techno – medicine' (Pickstone, 2000). This obsession with 'miracle technology' made a fundamental shift from public health approach into technological oriented intervention (Webster, 2002).

No doubt that advancement in health status and increasing life expectancy as well as public health measures were not only because of social economic improvement but also due to technology-based public health interventions in the West (Lupton, 1994). But as Ehrenreich (1978) pointed out, through the use of technology, the nature of biomedicine exerted' social control in two ways, exclusionary and co-optative'. The first, i.e. the exclusionary kind of social control fits in with the traditional political economic approach – the exclusion of certain groups from medical services and denial of access by various means, geographical inaccessibility and social status. The second type of social control, i.e. co-optation attempts to expand the jurisdiction of bio medicine to more and more aspects of human life. This is achieved through the treatment of those who enter the sick role and a further encouragement to seek medical treatment for a variety of 'non-sick' situation. Through this '... medical practitioners bring large number of people into the fold of professional management of various aspects of their lives' (Ehrenreich, 1978).

Medical Imaging: Impact on Medical Practice and Treatment

The influence of medical imaging on clinical practice can be traced from the introduction of X-ray in the last decade of 19th century and perhaps the ultrasound sonogram made profound changes in the later part of 20th century. However, the use of advanced and complex machinery has become a central feature of modern medical practice nowadays and the more complex and advanced the machine is, the more professional the physician is thought to be (Cowan, 1997). Advanced diagnostic imaging has altered for example the practice of neurology by providing new ways of seeing into the human brain and body (Kevles, 1997). The new technologies affect the clinical decision-making process. Techno-science intervention created risk society. It deconstructs the intervention of disease and legitimizes monoculture when technology can alleviate disease. Understanding medical technology in relation to work of body is important in analysing the power of 'the medical gaze' that took over the human body for its so-called objective analysis that moved deeper and deeper into body structures – from the surface anatomy, through X-rays to intra-body physiology and now to genetics. At another level it is also taken position to rule out the abnormalities by trying to find the disease at very early stage (Prior, 2001). As a result 'everyone lives under the medical regime, a light regime for those who are not yet patients, stricter according to how dependent on doctors one becomes' in the process (deSwaan, 1990). Patients were treated without symptoms and the intervention determines the normality and abnormality – illness and disease – which led to medical intervention. Powerful medical gaze works not only at the individual level (diet, body regulation, sports medicine) but also at public level by the state and its public health agencies through the various intervention programmes.

Some of the new technologies not only demand new diagnosis by replacing the existing screening, procedures, structures and manpower but also transform ideas about health, illness and disease, and thereby redefine health, medicine and body (Webster, 2002). Hi-tech medicine does not rely upon causality but rather depends upon the language of risk and probabilities which underpins the scientific 'destiny' by increasing the level of complex, integrated, specialist knowledge. The risk and probabilities made patients psychologically distressed at various levels (Peterson, 1996). They are, at first; false negatives where individual is assured of not having disease, and lose hope in the medical system if further tests proved that the earlier tests were incorrect. Secondly, false positive results, where the individual is said to have the disease which made him sick psychologically (Nelkin and Tan Credi, 1989), and lastly, those who were told the need of further investigation to confirm. This dependence on the ever-sophisticated technology would weaken the epistemological and professional authority of medical science and practice and more importantly, the interpersonal relationship that exists between the doctor and the patient.

Medical technology at one level helps physician to arrive at the correct diagnosis and subsequently prescribing the appropriate medicines and procedures. Especially the diagnostic technologies such as CAT and MRI are important tools for supplementing the physical exam but then in the right setting to help and guide life-saving therapies. On the other side, it influences the practice and makes the physician handicapped due to total reliance on it. Commercial benefits to medical imaging also shaped the medical practice. The MRI technology, which is highly dependent upon digitization technology, gives minute details of the body where it has been fast becoming star performers for profit-minded institutions and enterprises. Various studies have shown that medical imaging changes the course of medicine, from 'clinical' into 'techno'; a move towards evidence based medicine; doctors' role in the medical services; increase of cost; and unrestricted presence of diagnostic facilities.

We will take up some of the specifics of medical imaging and its impact upon the medical services and medical practice, which are:

Medical Care Services: Role of Doctors

Improvements in medical technology made half of the doctors in the United States to be employed by health plans, a setting in which the doctor is increasingly an employee of an administrative unit that ultimately mediates the doctor-patient relationship. This effect, according to Larson (1980), made the doctors lose their autonomy in economic, organizational, and technical areas. Economic alienation in terms of doctors being a salaried employee should place hospital interest above theirs. Organizational structure, within which the doctors have to play their role, such as the hospital managers who also coordinate work. Alford (1975) even went further and said doctors are increasingly becoming physician administrators who can be termed as "corporate rationalizers'. These corporate rationalizers, being full time administrators, pay full attention to fiscal side of the medical rather than patient's benefit. In this way they serve their loyalty more for the hospitals than patients.

Move towards Evidence-Based Medicine

Objective analysis of human body made the medical practice more towards evidence-based medicine (EBM) which has been defined as 'the process of systematically finding, appraising and using contemporaneous research findings as the basis for clinical decision'. Clinicians can incorporate evidence into their practices in three ways (Guyatt, 1991). First is the 'doing' mode, in which there are steps carried out before an intervention is offered. Steps are used in terms of diagnosing the patient using various technological interventions. Second is the 'using' mode, in which searches are restricted to evidence sources that have already undergone critical appraisal by others, such as evidence-based guidelines serve as a vital technique adopted in EBM to obtain relevant evidence. Third is the 'replicating' mode, in which the decisions are taken for individual patients.

The impact of EBM on clinical side is both positive and negative. Clinicians can have access to powerful, precise and up-to-date information on diagnosis and treatment (Schattner and Fletcher, 2003). But it also leaves behind the possible risk. The patients are being treated as mere machines comprising various parts and of course assembled into a body. Apart from this, there are other problems like the data collected through RCT or under the care of the physician or on hospital ward, are often different. As a result, even data collected from carefully conducted and controlled studies may not be directly applicable to an individual patient. Applying average results derived from groups of patients to a unique patient is bound to be problematic. As Mant (1999) says: 'a clinical trial is the best way to access whether an intervention works, but it is arguably the worst way to access who will benefit from it'. In addition, there are too many differences related to the population (cultural, environmental, health care facilities) and individual differences (age, co-morbidity, past or current treatments, non-biological variables) which may affect the translation of evidence from study sample to individual patient. Also how far will the clinicians be able to get the reliable information and how is he going to analyse the available in relation to diagnosis, prognosis, treatment, iatrogeneic harm, quality of care, or health economics which are all highly complex. Moreover, EBM's main focus is on the disease symptoms which will further divide the body and view it a purely mechanical part rather than considering the social determinants and structural constraints of health.

Practice of Defensive Medicine

Due to increased consumer movement and folding the medical services into consumer act, medical practitioners nowadays practice what is called 'defensive' medicine. The medical practitioners at one level assert their supremacy through EBM and at another level go in for more tests to confirm the clinical diagnosis in order to evade the possible law suit. This pushed the patients to pay more for the diagnostic tests which are otherwise unnecessary. Another consequence of defensive medicine is overuse of technology.

Economic Aspect

CAT scan which falls under medical imaging brings rapid diagnosis of lesions and it also brings cost along with it. Analysis in different countries shows that almost 40 to 70 per cent of total expenditure in hospital goes to increase in staffing managing medical technology (Tulchrisky, Elena and Varavi, 2000). The grand alliance between professionals, medical industries and medical organizations inflate the diagnostic cost. Sukanya's study on investment in the hospitals in Chennai, has revealed that medical equipment alone constitutes about 50 to 60 per cent of their total investment (quoted in Muraleedharan, 1999).

Based on the discussion above it should be noted that medical imaging starting from ultra-sound to MRI has proven cost effective and life-saving, replacing less efficient and dangerous invasive. But then it will create further divide among people if rational use of technology in terms of equitable distribution is based on the need rather than just economic benefits, while the socio-political assessment of technology in its usage is not taken into account. On the other hand, one should have critical understanding about this 'non-invasive' technology which refers not to the elimination but to the minimization of physical intervention. Question should be raised: are these non-invasive technologies truly non-invasive? Through these technologies it seems our bodies are increasingly scrutinized, recorded, evaluated, penetrated and ruthlessly appraised (by other than traditional means). MRI, PET, and similar technique have revealed our bodies in terms of hitherto unseen detail, by going further down to 'rule out' the disease at early stage in which people are being constantly kept under its surveillance by professionals. On the whole, health technologies have powerful, determining effects when introduced first; but nonetheless they do not simply arrive at the health market whose needs are to be created in the society. They also produce varied effects in multicultural, multireligious and multiethnic groups. So care should be taken in applying particular technology in the society which is already heterogenic in its character; heterogeneity in terms of regional variation, class, caste, culture, language and religion.

Public Health and Technological Influence in India

Soon after the Independence, August Comte's vision of applying principles of rationality, empiricism, and enlightenment to society got refreshed in political independence of the Third World countries with the assurance in upliftment of standards of material well-being (Alvares, 1977). Nehru in *Discovery of India* said, 'it was science and science alone that could solve the problems of hunger and poverty, of insanitation and illiteracy of superstition and deadening custom and tradition'. The science policy that India adopted in 1958 gave importance to science in eliminating poverty and set standard of living. Science was so much embedded in the planning that it becomes important in designing in Five Year Plans. Health programmes of the government focused mainly on technological intervention leaving out social, cultural and economic aspect and were implemented by top-down approach. The WHO defines appropriate technology as the 'level of medical technology needed to improve health conditions in keeping with the epidemiologic, demographic and financial situation of each country'. In this direction, Alma Ata Declaration of 1978, recognizes public health as social control over the health services that are meant to serve population, covering entire population; providing services in an integrated form; use of appropriate technology; use of relevant elements from the traditional systems of medicine; use of only essential drugs and so on. WHO estimates that 80 per cent of diagnostic radiology (i.e. basic Radiological Units BRU which is low cost, effective, diagnostic X-rays) can be performed by simple, safe and low cost equipment, supported by training of local people to operate and maintain the equipment. National Health Policy of 1983 advocated the promotion of private sector in providing health care. This is in clear contrast to the recommendation of Bhore Committee before Independence which emphasized government involvement for comprehensive health care. It states 'inability to pay should not be allowed to come in the way of seeking health services by all citizens of the country. The promotion of private sector increased medical cost and accumulation of clinic and hospitals in urban areas with introduction of latest technology from screening to diagnosis. The proliferation of medical technology has played very important role in promoting the growth of this sector which targets individual focus in diagnosis, treatment, biophysical and psychological status, physical examination and laboratory test. Medical care nowadays becomes an important aspect in private sector in terms of offering medical facilities, varying complexity and sophistication. At one hand, the urban area is concentrated much with tertiary hospital care, medical research units, and super speciality hospitals both by public and private sector. On the other hand, rural population is totally neglected where non-availability of basic instruments is pretty much evident for this scenario.

Summing Up

By stating the above issues the aim is not to demonize the use of science and technology in medicine. Rather to understand socially how technology is used in bio medicine influencing the medical practice. This deconstruction of 'the technical' to reveal its 'socially congealed' properties does not mean that the technical, which has a materiality and functionality, has no value. To analyse this, conceptual understanding of technology is discussed and then historically how technology understood the body.

References

Ackernecht, E.H. (1982), *A Short History of Medicine*, Baltimore: John Hopkins University Press.

Alford, R. (1975), *Health Care Politics: Ideological and Interest Group Barriers to Reform*, Chicago: University of Chicago Press.

Alvares, C. (1997), 'Science', in W. Sachs (ed.), *The Development Dictionary: A Guide to Knowledge as Power*, New Delhi: Orient Longman.

Cowan, R.S. (1997), *A Social History of Medical Technology*, New York: Oxford University Press.

Czegledy, Nina (1992), 'A New Approach to Teaching the Practice of Medicine', *JAMA*, 268(17): 2420–25.

Czegledy, Nina and Andre P. Czegledy (2000), 'Digitized Bodies, Virtual Spectacles', *Futures*, 32(2): 103–20.

De Swaan, A. (1990), *The Management of Normality: Critical Essays in Health and Welfare*, London: Routledge and Kegan Paul.

Ehrenreich, J. (ed.) (1978), 'The Cultural Crisis of Modern Medicine', *Monthly Review Press*, New York.

Frontline, 9 February 2002.

Ghalioungui, P. (1984), 'Four Landmarks in Egyptian Cardiology', *Journal of Royal College Physics*, 18: 182–86.

Guyatt, G.H. (1991), 'Evidence-Based Medicine', *ACP J Club*, 114: A16.

Harvey, A.M. et al. (1989), *A Model of its Kind: A Centennial History of Medicine at John Hopkins*, Vol. 1, Baltimore: John Hopkins University Press.

http://gisd.tn.nic.in

http://www.tn.gov.in/policynotes/health2003-04-3.htm

http://www:aace.com/members/leg/liability/tortreform.pdf.

Johnson, D.L. (1995), *Indian Thought between Tradition and the Culture of Technology*, New Delhi: D.K. Printworld.

Kelves, B.H. (1997), *Naked to the Bone: Medical Imaging in the Twentieth Century*, New Brunswick: Rutgers University Press.

Kimbrell, A. (1993), *The Human Body Shop: The Engineering and Marketing of Life*, Penang: Third World Network.

Lane, Joan (2001), *A Social History of Medicine: Health, Healing and Disease in England*, London: Routledge.

Larson, M.S. (1980), 'Proletarianizattion and Educated Labour', *Theory and Society*, 9: 131–75.

Mant, D. (1999), 'Evidence and Primary Care: Can Randomized Trials Inform Clinical Decisions About Individual Patients?', *Lancet*, 353: 743–46.

Mechanic, David (2000), 'Socio-Cultural Implications of Changing Organizational Technologies in the Provision of Care', *Social Science and Medicine*, 54: 459–67.

Muraleedharan, V.R. (1999), 'Technology and Costs of Medical Care: Some Emerging Issues and Policy Imperatives', in Barbara Harris-White and S. Subramanian (eds), *Illfare in Biology and Medicine*, 44(1): 99–107.

Nelkin, D. and L. Tancredi (1989), *Dangerous Diagnostics: The Social Power of Biological Information*, New York: Basic Books.

Peterson, A. and Deborah Lupton (1996), *The New Public Health: Health and the Self in the Age of Risk*, New Delhi: Sage Publications.

Phoon, C.K.L. (2000), 'Must Doctors Still Examine Patients?', *Perspectives in Biology and Medicine*, 43(4): 548–61.

Pickstone, J.V. (2000), *Ways of Knowing a New History of Science, Technology and Medicine,* Manchester: Manchester University Press.

Prior, L. (2001), 'Sociology of Health and Illness', *Review Article*, 23(2): 251–52.

Schattner, A. and R.H. Fletcher (2003), 'Research Evidence and the Individual Patient', *Quarterly Journal of Medicine*, 96: 1–5.

Towers, Bernard (1971), 'The Influence of Medical Technology on Medical Services', in G. Mclachlon and Thomas Mckeown (eds), *Medical History and Medical Care: A Symposium of Perspectives*, London: Oxford University Press.

Tulchrisky, T.H. and Elena A. Varavi Kova (2000), *The New Public Health*, London: Academic Press.

Wallnofer, H. and A. Von Rottauscher (1965), *Chinese Folk Medicine*, translated by M. Palmedo, New York: Crown.

Webster, Andrew (2002), 'Innovative Health Technologies and the Social: Redefining Health, Medicine and the Body', *Current Sociology*, 50(3): 443–57.

31

Health Insurance

Before World War II, inflationary pressures in medical care were held in check by two forces: the fact that many people could not afford to pay the doctor enough, and the norms of medical professionalism. Until the Great Depression and the War, health insurance was not generally available. Most doctors were only moderately affluent, compared with their earnings' growth during and post World War II boom. Medical doctors did not become seriously self-regulated and licensed by states as a learned profession until a generation or two earlier, in the late 19th century.

What is Health Insurance?

Health insurance connotes a form of insurance that pays for medical expenses. It is a kind of financial protection that provides payment of benefits in case of sickness or injury (Chahal, 2006). This has been defined variously as 'a mechanism whereby the risks of incurring health care costs are spread over a group of individuals households' (Arhin-Tenkorang, 2001). Under a health insurance programme, people who have the risk of a certain event contribute a small amount (premium) towards health insurance fund which is subsequently paid for treatment (Devdasan and Nandraj, 2006). The Insurance Regulatory and Development Authority (IRDA) defines 'Health Insurance Business' or 'Health Cover' as effecting of contacts which provide sickness benefits or medical, surgical or hospital expenses benefits, whether in-patient or out-patient, on an indemnity, reimbursement, pre-paid or otherwise, including assured benefits and long term-health care (Bishnoi and Saharan, 2007).

Philosophy behind Health Insurance

The idea behind health insurance is simple. In a given population, there will be at any time a certain number of people who are ill. This figure has been fairly stable for populations over long periods of time. But one cannot predict who exactly in that population will be ill; this is uncertain. It is therefore, possible to get large numbers of people to pay a defined fee that covers those in the paying population who fall ill against the risk of population for a period of time, usually a year. If everyone covers himself or herself against the risk of illness, the amount collected will be large enough to meet the health costs of those who actually fall ill. This is the opportunity that companies have converted into a business – the insurance industry. In many parts of the world, it is huge.

Health Insurance in India: Context and Historical Development

The extent and efficiency of health financing arrangements, the reach and performance of service delivery, and the evolution of risk-protection mechanisms in India have profoundly shaped the development of Government Sponsored Health Insurance Schemes (GSHISs). The GSHISs date to the late 1940s when the central government introduced the Employee's State Insurance Scheme (ESIS) for blue-collar workers employed in the private sector. This was followed in the mid-1950s by the Central Government Health Scheme (CGHS) for Central Government employees and for their families. Both schemes provided comprehensive medical coverage and followed a traditional social insurance risk-pooling model in which funds are pooled through employer and employee payroll contributions, supplemented, in these schemes, by government subsidies. Other government schemes for employees in railways and defense, and other civil servants, also emerged shortly after Independence.

The practice of health insurance evolved in the 19th century when, many friendly or benefit societies were founded to ensure good living and health of its members. Health insurance was launched in 1986 in India. The Medi-Claim Policy was launched in November in 1986 by the General Insurance Corporation. Thereafter several kinds of policies have been floated mainly through wage-based contributions and related to level of income. The Social Health Insurance (SHI) schemes are statutory programmes financed mainly through wage-based contributions and related to a level of income. An SHI Scheme is an earmarked fund set up by government with explicit benefits in return for payment. The Social Health Insurance includes the Central Government Health Schemes (CGHS) and Employee's State Insurance Scheme (ESIS) (Devadasan and Nandraj, 2006). Private health insurance is voluntary. The insurer usually collects the premium from the individuals who can afford to pay and then invests this to supplement the insurance fund. Community Health Insurance Scheme is any non-profit insurance scheme aiming primarily at the informal sector and formed on the basis of a collective pooling of health risks and payment therefore. Community Health Insurance Schemes involve pre-payment and pooling of resources to cover the costs of health-related mishaps (Devadasan et al., 2004). Government Health Insurance Schemes (GHISs) are usually for the poorest and vulnerable sections of the community. Under these schemes, the premium is totally subsidized by the government from tax-based revenues and is paid directly to the insurer. The major GHIs schemes are the Universal Health Insurance Scheme (UHIS), Rajiv Arogya Shri Scheme (RAS), Rashtriya Swasthya Bima Yojana (RSBY), Vajpayee Argogyasri Scheme, Karanataka and Chief Minister Kalaingnar Health Insurance Scheme, Tamil Nadu.

Context and capacities have played an important role in the development of the wave of GSHISs, launched in 2007. ESIS and CGHS benefitted from the earlier development of the health insurance industry over a 20-year period. Among the early attempts by the central government to introduce health insurance for the informal sector was the Universal Health Insurance Scheme (UHIS). Introduced in 2003, UHIS was a hospitalization indemnity product that could be voluntarily purchased from any state-owned insurer at a heavily subsidized price (e.g. ₹ 165, less than US$ 4 a year). Despite its name, the scheme remained far from 'universal' and covered only 3.7 million lives by 2008–09 (Forgia and Nagpal, 2012). Another scheme launched in the same year was Yeshasvini, a contributory scheme introduced by the Department of Cooperation in Karnataka for the members of rural cooperative societies in that state. Both schemes provided valuable lessons and possessed a number of common structural features that were adopted by the new generation of GSHISs. Features introduced by at least one of these schemes include: premium partially or largely subsidized by the government on the demand side; cashless inpatient coverage; service provision by the networked public and private hospitals; provider payment through prospective, case-based 'package' rates; a bottom-up coverage design consisting of targeting the informal and Below Poverty Line (BPL) populations; and the use of health insurance companies or third-party administrators as intermediaries for risk underwriting or administrative functions or both. These structural features are a departure from more traditional contributory social insurance models, such as ESIS and CGHS. These later schemes are financed mainly through payroll taxes and, unlike the recently established GSHISs, provide coverage for a comprehensive benefit package, including in-patient and out-patient care. ESIS beneficiaries receive most care through scheme-owned and operated facilities. Specialty in-patient care, however, is contracted to private hospitals. CGHS outsources in-patient care to both public and private facilities, but mainly the latter (Forgia and Nagpal, 2012). Benefit designs of UHIS and Yeshasvini were also modelled on standardized insurance products sold in the private market since the mid-1980s.

The rapid growth in the health insurance industry after 2001 can be attributed to the introduction of a new regulatory structure for the insurance industry in the late 1990s. Privately-owned insurance companies were once again permitted to operate, which led to more efforts to increase public awareness of health insurance products. The other regulatory change was the introduction of third-party administrator (TPA) regulations in 2001, which provided a quicker market entry for newer health insurers that could use already organized hospital networks and established claim processing capacities created by TPAs. The health insurance industry has grown significantly due to liberalization of economy and general awareness. According to the World Bank, by 2010, more than 25 per cent of India's population had access to some form of health insurance.

Growth Pattern and Trends in Health Insurance

During early years of development of health insurance, the private insurance industry's influence on hospital was minimal. At the turn of the century, the private health insurance system was small and insignificant in comparison to total hospital revenues (about 2 per cent of India's total spending on hospitalization). Like uninsured patients, the insured paid their bills in cash but subsequently sought reimbursement from their insurers. This meant that patients not only had to arrange substantial funds upfront, but also suffer losses due to deductions and delays during claim processing by the insurer.

By 2008–09, however, health insurance companies were paying claims amounting to about 10 per cent of all hospitalization expenditure in the country. This proportion was much higher for hospitals located in larger cities where insurers and third-party administrators (TPAs) were contributing 30 per cent or more to total hospital revenues. In 2000s, the number of 'networked hospitals' rapidly expanded, and is currently estimated at about 10,000 hospitals across the country. By the late 2000s GSHISs were able to tap into this large hospital network for access to treatment for their beneficiaries which facilitated GSHIS expansion (Forgia and Nagpal, 2012).

With the rapid growth of private insurance and the introduction of TPAs in 2000, the concept of 'cashless' hospitalization emerged, and was subsequently adapted by all GSHISs. TPAs (and insurers) entered into agreements with networked hospitals to treat the beneficiaries. Claims were settled between the TPA or insurer and the hospital, and patients were charged only for copayments or services not covered by insurance. This is a far cry from the early days of the system, when hospitals were wary of joining the cashless networks – a new, untested concept for most hospitals before the mid-2000s. Based on discussion with TPAs and insurers, the share of cashless hospitalization is currently estimated at more than 60 per cent of the private voluntary health insurance market. The remainder of the market still relies on paper-based reimbursement (Forgia and Nagpal, 2012).

The operational capacities of the private voluntary health insurance industry to process authorizations for cashless claims and the claim payment processes also grew, accounting for several million transactions annually. The information technology capabilities of insurers, TPAs, and hospitals – an essential prerequisite to the success of most new GSHISs – also witnessed consistent development across the industry.

By 2008–09, however, health insurance companies were paying claims amounting to about 10 per cent of all hospitalization expenditure in the country.

Increasing awareness about health insurance, rising health care costs and also the recent de-tariffing of the general insurance industry has increased emphasis on health insurance and other personal lines of business. Already, health insurance has become the fastest growing segment in the non-life insurance sector in India during the recent years, with the growth rate of 34.56 per cent during 2011–12. It has emerged as an increasingly significant line of business for non-life insurance companies, and many prominent life insurance companies now have health insurance products, the conspicuous ones among these having been launched in the previous decade itself. During this period, the health insurance premium grew from ₹ 1,002.18 crore in 2002–03 to ₹ 13,344.99 crore in 2011–12. When compared with 2011–1012, the health insurance premium rise was 16 per cent. The number of persons covered under health insurance has been also steadily increasing over the years. Considering the vast potential for health insurance, any increase in this segment appears to be inadequate. In the absence of health protection, the financial impact of hospitalization can be very pronounced more so on low income group which reported to be the leading cause of impoverishment in the country. Many states have recently initiated large scale health insurance programmes in association with non-life insurers to protect these vulnerable groups from such health-related financial hazards.

The share of private and public health insurance sector in health portfolio had been 6.15 per cent and 93.85 per cent in year 2002–03, which has increased to 40.01 per cent and 60 per cent, respectively, in 2011–12 showing the increase in market share of private health insurance sector by 35 per cent and decrease in public sector by 34 per cent. The total gross premium has shown an upward trend continuously from ₹ 1002.18 crore to ₹ 12,908.85 crore in years 2002–03 to 2011–12. The gross premium of public and private sector health insurance has increased from ₹ 940.51 crore to ₹ 8,006.02 and ₹ 61.67 crore to ₹ 4,902.83 crore during the 2011–12 (Shahi and Gill, 2013). It has been found that the level of gross premium has been rising in health insurance sector. However, private sector has evinced interest in non-life insurance sector as compared to public health insurers.

The health insurance business in India is growing rapidly. Given the huge population, this can be a huge business. The monopoly of the public sector has been broken, and a regulatory system has been set up. A number of private companies, with multinational partners, are becoming active. There are also non-governmental organizations (NGOs) promoting health insurance for poor people in various regions – this is called micro-insurance.

Health Insurance Model

The insurance sector has experienced significant development during last 15 years. With the liberalization of the sector, entry of private providers in health sector has given entry to insurance sector. The government has set up Insurance Regulatory and Development Authority to develop and regulate it and also safeguard the interest of policy holders. We would like to see the logic of health insurance along with the model for providing the health insurance.

Figure 1 provides the description of key stakeholders in private health insurance and their inter-relationships. From the diagram, we can see that there are three main stakeholders in the health insurance system. These are insurance companies, health care providers and customers. Other than these two, more parties which are important and involved in the process are Third Party Administrators (TPA) and regulator. Important differences between health insurance and any other kind of insurance is that in the case of health insurance, there are more stakeholders than in other types of insurance and this makes the whole process more complex and difficult to regulate. Insurance schemes are of different kinds and they differ on the basis of their ownership and profit orientation. However, the basic premise of risk pooling is the same. The ways in which insurance systems are implemented across countries vary in terms of how the money is collected, who pays and who buys the services and from whom. For example, in Canada the financing is through taxation: people pay an income on payroll tax, and the proceeds are used by the government to purchase or provide health insurance. In other nations financing is through private insurance; individuals or their employers contribute to health insurance companies, which then provide insurance for the population. While the payment of any individual may differ in these two systems, a tax financed system generally imposes relatively more on rich, the implications for provision of health insurance are generally slight. The government in both systems are intimately involved in determining what services are covered, the cost sharing that patients face and the restrictions imposed on providers.

Logic for Health Insurance

India has a 'single-payer' health system (at least in principle) that was intended to be financed by tax revenues and available free for all at government facilities (Gupta and Muraleedharan, 2014: 29).

Health risks and resulting catastrophic financial losses are probably significant threats to the people, particularly persons belonging to lower income groups as these people will be excluded from private health insurance. A health shock leads to direct expenditure on medicine, transport and treatment, and also indirect costs related to loss of wages. Several studies have found a strong link between health and income for the low-income levels. Poor are the most susceptible to a health shock. For low-income people in rural areas and informal sector market based

Figure 1
Standard Health Insurance Model

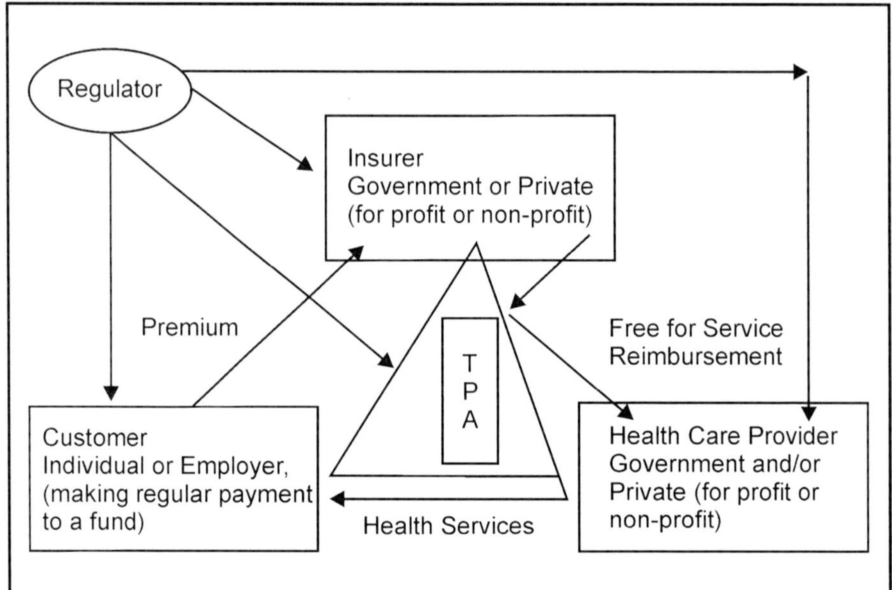

insurance such as Medi-Claim cannot meet the requirements because of its high cost. Insurance companies and health care providers face high transaction costs and also they do not have local information available with them. This makes their job of providing health insurance to this segment very difficult and schemes which are of local origin have more chance of being successful.

Private health sector constituted 87 per cent of total health expenditure in 2004–2005 (Ministry of Health and Family Welfare, 2009). The Health Policy of 2000 placed emphasis on expansion of insurance coverage to protect people against the high costs of health care which is pushing people into debt and poverty.

Types of Health Insurance in India

Several community-based organizations in India have focused on developing community-based insurance schemes during the last decade. Most of these are Community-Based Insurance Schemes (CBHI). These are aimed at poor sections of the population and designed to help them cover themselves collectively against risks, hence 'insurance'.

In India, Community Health Insurance started way back in Kolkata in 1952 as a part of student's movement. The scheme, which is called the Student's Health Home (SHH), caters to the scholars and universities students of West Bengal. Currently there are more than 20 documented CHI programmes, of which five were initiated in the past three years (Sundar, 2012). The mechanism for providing health insurance in community-based health insurance schemes is different than normal market-based schemes like Medi-Claim. Though the basic principle of covering future risks by paying premium in advance is same in all health insurance schemes, CBHI schemes are tailored for local needs and provide health insurance at low cost.

CBHI schemes in India can be divided into three broad categories based on who is the insurer. Table 1 indicates these three categories by specifying health care provider, health insurer and health care intermediary. An agency here can be an NGO, Trust, Hospital or Cooperative, etc. Their role can vary from performing as intermediary where both treatment and insurance are provided by intermediary itself or where the treatment and insurance are provided by third party.

Table 1

Types of CBHI Schemes in India

Types of CBHI	*Health Care Intermediary*	*Health Insurer*	*Health Care Provider*
Examples	SEWA, BAIF, Karuan Trust	Tribhuvandas Foundation; DHAN; Yeshaswini	Sewagram, MGIMS, VHS, RAHA
Role	Plays role of agent	Plays role of insurer	Plays role of both insurer and provider
	Purchase care from providers	Provide insurance	Running insurance scheme
	Purchase insurance from insurance companies	Provide health care	
		Purchase care from independent provider	
Transaction Costs	Less important	Less	Less
Membership Size (Size of risk pool)	Not important	important	important
In-patient, Out patient Care	Is an issue	Is an issue	Is not an issue
Benefit on Provision Side	Negligible	Low	Significant
Informational Problems	Is an issue	May be an issue	Not an issue
Payment Mechanism	Mostly fixed Indemnity	Mostly fixed indemnity	Cashless system mostly
Nature of Pool	Membership/geography based	Membership/geogra phy based	Geography based

Source: Adapted from Devadasan, Ransion et al. 2004.

The success of these schemes depends upon the reasonable coverage, low premium and local needs. However, there are many problems of CBHI schemes like non-availability of good providers, lack of professional management, financial sustainability, etc.

Middle Class and Health Insurance in India

Insurance manages risk in large population. The middle class is opting for insurance in order to access the corporate hospitals when the need arises. The more the number of people do this, the more viable the insurance industry will be. It means the important segment of the population is opting out of state system of health care. The tax concessions that the government is providing – both to encourage buying health insurance, and for investing in hospitals – suggests that it is ready to abdicate responsibility for health care provision (Vyasulu, 2008: 15). This model is based on the experience of countries that have relied on private health care financed via insurance. The best example is the United States which believes that individuals not only have the right to make their own decisions, but also that they must be encouraged to do so without state intervention. The result is a system in which the private sector provides health care as a business: doctors practice as professionals who provide their expertise for a fee. Hospitals provide institutional care on the same basis. And since this may be costly, insurance steps in to take advantage of the law of large numbers to protect those who join a scheme for a fee. It sounds perfect, however, millions in the US have no access to health care as they are not covered health insurance.

Failure of Government Sector

There are innumerable studies showing dissatisfaction with long waiting times, staff absenteeism, lack of drugs, and many other problems. India performed nearly at the bottom of 39 low and low-middle income countries in the share of use of government health facilities in 2003 (Saksena et al., 2010).

Government financing of health is extremely low, e.g. in 2012 it was only 1.3 per cent of GDP (equivalent to $ 19 per capita), one of the lowest allocations of national income in the world.

To cut the health care cost, the Health Policy has taken following steps:

1. Collecting 'partial user charges' for many health services in government hospitals.
2. Promoting health insurance.

Despite all these, the poor still in many states are seeking health care from the government health facilities. Introduction of NRHM in the states with poor health indicators accelerated the reduction of infant mortality and fertility, as well as raising the proportion of institutional deliveries. The Tamil Nadu Medical Services Corporation offers an effective model for streamlining drug supply (Singh et al., 2012). The state also ensures relatively good infrastructure in its facilities (Rao and Choudhury, 2012).

Critique of Health Insurance

Thus, just copying the health insurance model of US for India would be dangerous because of the many difficulties in regulating the insurance system. Following are the problems:

- In US, health facilities and doctors are accredited and registered, but in India, this task is difficult and enormous. There is also a very large number of non-registered medical practitioners, whose numbers are difficult to estimate (Ministry of Health and Family Welfare, 2009).
- The government has had difficulty even with the relatively simple task of ensuring that large private sector hospital groups offer a certain proportion of their services free to poor people, as promised in exchange for paying very low rates for substantial tracts of prime urban land to construct their hospitals (JSA, 2006).
- Clients face a lot of difficulty in effective health seeking. People anywhere, however well-educated, have difficulty in evaluating their doctor. It becomes graver with the poor patients to distinguish between the world class doctors to 'jhola chaap' doctor. In some cases even if the qualification is displayed on the signboard, poor patients face a problem in ensuring that health insurers provide them the coverage they are supposed to receive?
- Another important consideration is that private sector has no incentive to provide services aimed primarily at reducing population exposure to disease (e.g. communicable diseases), as opposed to treating a patient.

Summing Up

Health insurance connotes a form of insurance that pays for medical expenses. It is a financial protection that provides a payment in case of illness on sickness. The idea behind health insurance is that it covers the risk of illness at a given period of time.

Health insurance through government scheme was started in 1940s, however in private sector the health insurance was lunched in 1986. Government health schemes are mainly for the poorer sections of the society. The rapid growth of health insurance industry after 2001 can be attributed to the new-regulatory structure of industry. However, only 25 per cent of population had access to some form of health insurance. The network of hospitals is rapidly, expanding for the health insurance. The concept of 'cashless' hospitalization also emerged in 2000. The growth rate of health insurance was around 35 per cent during 2011–12. The share of private and public health insurance sector was around 40 per cent and 60 per cent respectively in 2011–12.

The government has set up Insurance Regulatory and Development Authority to safeguard the interest of policy holders. The health policy of 2000 has laid more emphasis on expansion of insurance coverage to protect people against the high cost of health care which pushes them into clout and poverty. The rapid expansion of the health insurance is viewed as dangerous move because people in India are still illiterate or less educated, therefore they face difficulty in evaluating the doctor. Private sector insurance companies do not feel comfortable in treating the public health problems like epidemics, communicable diereses, etc.

References

Arhin-Tenkorang, D. (2000), 'Health Insurance for the Informal Sector in Africa: Design Features, Risk Protection and Resource Mobilization', paper prepared for Working Group 3 Commission on Macroeconomics and Health, Geneva.

Bishnoi, V. and R. Saharan (2007), 'Health Insurance in India: Introspects and Prospects', *The Icfai Journal of Risk and Insurance*, 4(3): 58–68.

Chahal, H.S. (2006), 'Feasibility of Separate Health Insurance Company in India', *IRDA Journal*, 32: 53–62.

Devadasan, N. and S. Nandraj (2006), *Planning and Implementing Health Insurance Programmes in India*, New Delhi: Institute of Public Health.

Devadasan, N. et al. (2004), 'Community Insurance in India', *Economic and Political Weekly*, 39: 3179–83.

Forgia, Gerard La and Somil Nagpal (2012), *Government-Sponsored Health Insurance in India: Are You Covered?*, Washington, D.C.: World Bank.

Gupta, Das Monica and V.R. Muraleedharan (2014), 'Universal Health Coverage: Reform of the Government System Better than Quality Health Insurance', *Economic and Political Weekly*, XLIX(35): 29–32.

Jan Swasthya Abhiyan (JSA) (2006), *Health Systems in India: Crisis and Alternatives*, Delhi: National Coordination Committee.

Ministry of Health and Family Welfare (2009), *Regulation of Medical Practitioners in India*, New Delhi: MoHFW.

Prasad, Amit et al. (2013), 'The Effect of the National Rural Health Mission on Health Services and Outcomes of Childbirth in India: A Retrospective Analysis of Survey Data', *The Lancet*, 382: 11.

Rao, M. Govinda and Mita Choudhury (2012), 'Healthcare Financing Reforms in India', *Working Paper No. 2012–100*, National Institute of Public Finance and Policy, Delhi.

Saksena, Priyanka et al. (2010), 'Health Services Utilization and Out-of-Pocket Expenditure in Public Private Facilities in Low-Income Countries', *World Health Report (2010)*, Background Paper, No. 20, Geneva: WHO.

Shahi, Amandeep Kaur and Harinder Singh Gill (2013), 'Origin, Growth Pattern and Trends: A Study of Indian Health Insurance Sector', *IOSR Journal of Humanities and Social Science*, 12(3): 1–9.

Singh, Prabal Vikram et al. (2012), 'Replicating Tamil Nadu's Drug Procurement Model', *Economic and Political Weekly*, XLVII(39): 26–29.

Sundar, I. (2012), *Health Economics and Health Care Management*, New Delhi: Serial Publications.

Vyasulu, Vinod (2008), 'The Case Against Health Insurance', *Economic and Political Weekly*, XLIII(39).

32

Medical and Health Tourism in India

The global growth in the flow of patients and health professionals as well as medical technology, capital funding and regulatory regimes across national borders has given rise to new patterns of consumption and production of health care services over recent decades. A significant new element of a growing trade in health care has involved the movement of patients across borders in the pursuit of medical treatment and health; a phenomenon commonly termed 'medical tourism'. Medical tourism occurs when consumers elect to travel across international borders with the intention of receiving some form of medical treatment. This treatment may span full range of medical services, but most commonly includes dental, cosmetic surgery, elective surgery, and fertility treatment. There has been a shift towards patients from richer, more developed nations travelling to less developed countries to access health services, largely driven by low-cost treatments available in the latter and helped by cheap flights and internet sources of information.

History of Medical Tourism

Medical tourism is years old. In ancient Greece, pilgrims and patients came from all over the Mediterranean to the sanctuary of the Healing God, Asklepios, at Epidaurus. In Roman Britain, patients took the waters at a shrine for bath, a practice that continued for 2,000 years. In the 18th century, wealthy Europeans travelled to spas from Germany to the Nile. In the 21st century, relatively low-cost jet travel has taken the industry beyond the wealthy and desperate. Countries that actively promote medical tourism include Cuba, Costa Rica, Hungary, India, Israel, Jordan, Lithuania, Malaysia, and Thailand. Belgium, Poland, and Singapore are now entering the field. South Africa specializes in surgery.

A classic example of people travelling to India for spiritual health is that of Beatles. India was seen as a very backward country and it was thought as of a storehouse of various tropical diseases. Proper health care in India was thought to be virtually non-existent. But with health care in India improving at a rapid rate, this outdated view regarding India is also changing at a rapid steady rate. India, with its improving infrastructure and living conditions, is becoming another favourite for tourists after places in South East Asia such as Sumatra and Bali. And as health care in India is now much improved, this has given rise to medical tourism.

During the 20th century, wealthy people from less developed areas of the world travelled to developed nations to access better facilities and highly trained medics. However, the shifts that are currently underway with regard to medical tourism are quantitatively and qualitatively different from earlier forms of health-related travel. The key differences are a reversal of this flow from developed to less developed nations, more regional movements, and the emergence of an 'international market' for patients. The key features of the 21st century style of medical tourism are as follows:

- Large number of people travelling for treatment.
- The shift of patients from richer, more developed nations travelling to less developed countries to access health services, largely driven by the low-cost treatments along with cheap flights and the internet for sourcing of information.
- 'New' enabling infrastructure – affordable, accessible travel and readily available information over the internet.
- Industrial development of both the private business sector and national governments in developed and developing nations have been instrumental in promoting tourism as a potentially lucrative source of foreign revenue.

Definition of Health and Medical Tourism

Medical tourism is related to the broader notion of health tourism which, in some countries, has longstanding historical antecedents of spa towns and coastal localities, and other therapeutic landscapes. Some commentators have considered health and medical tourism as a combined phenomenon but with different emphases. Carrera and Bridges (2006), for example, define health tourism as 'the organized travel outside one's local environment for the maintenance, enhancement or restoration of an individual's well-being in mind and body'. This definition encompasses medical tourism which is delimited to 'organized travel outside one's natural health care jurisdiction for the enhancement or restoration of the individual's health through medical intervention'.

Medical tourism, as its name suggest, is about tourists who travel to get themselves cured. Medical tourism can be defined as a provision of 'cost effective' personal health care in association with tourism industry for patients needing surgical health care and other forms of dedicated treatment. This process is being facilitated by the corporate sector concerned with health care as well as the tourism industry – both personal and public.

Medical or health treatment package has become a recurrent form of vacationing, and covers a broad range of medical services. It mingles free time, amusement and recreation together with wellness and health care packages. The package of the health holiday is to offer a chance to get away from your daily routine and come into a different calm neigbouring landscape. Here one can take pleasure in being close to the beach and mountains. It is like reconstruction and cleans up process on all levels – physical, psychological and expressive.

Pattern and Growth of Medical Tourism in India

India is considered a leading country promoting medical tourism and now it is moving into a new area of 'medical outsourcing', where sub-contractors provide services to the overburdened medical care systems in western countries.

India's National Health Policy declares that treatment of foreign patients is legally an 'export' and 'deemed eligible for all fiscal incentives extended to export earnings'. Government and private sectors studies in India estimate that medical tourism to India is growing by 30 per cent a year. According to the CII-Mckinsey Study (2007), conducted by the Confederation of Indian Industry and McKinsey consultants, reported that in 2007 some 1,50,000 foreigners visited India for treatment, with the number rising by 15 per cent a year.

A nice blend of top-class medical expertise at attractive prices is helping a growing number of Indian hospitals lure foreign patients, including from developed nations such as the UK and the US. If a liver transplant costs in the range of ₹ 60 lakh to ₹ 70 lakh in Europe and double of that in the US, a few Indian hospitals, such as Global in Hyderabad, have the wherewithal to do it in around ₹ 15 lakh to ₹ 20 lakh. Similarly, if a heart surgery in the US costs about ₹ 20 lakh, the Chennai-headquartered Apollo Hospitals Group does it in roughly ₹ 2 lakh (*The Business Line*, Chennai, 11 May 2004).

Many hospitals are coming together to improve the quality of health care, boost first impression and aiming for $ 2.3 billion in annual revenue by 2012 (McKinsey Study, 2007).

Instead of paying $ 2,00,000 for a mitral valve surgery in the US, a patient could travel to India and receive the same treatment for US$ 6,700. Similarly, rather than paying 15,000 pounds for hip resurfacing in the UK, a patient can get the same procedure for 5,000 pounds in India, including surgery, airfare and hotel stay.

A number of private hospitals also offer packages designed to attract wealthy foreign patients, with airport-to-hospital bed care service, in a room with internet access and private chefs. Another trend is to combine surgery in India with a yoga holiday or trip to the world famous Taj Mahal.

Kerala has pioneered health and medical tourism in India. But low-cost treatment is the ultimate factor weighing in favour of the treatment. Medical care costs only one-fifth of the costs in the West. So if a particular surgery costs US $ 30,000 in the West, it would cost only US $ 6,000 in India.

The value addition of certain industries actually grows with the exclusion of people from the market. The private sector in health has surged in the period of liberalization. A study by the international consultancy firm Ernst and Young and FICCI estimates private hospitals revenue at Rs 62,000 crore in 2005–06, and projects it to exceed Rs 1,30,000 crore in 2012 (Goswami, 2008). Of this investment, 80 per cent is to come from the private sector. The study expects that the private sector's current share of revenues, about 80 per cent, would rise with the rich and middle class buying health insurance. Coupled with the expected growth of the pharmaceutical sector, it projects that the total health care market in the country could reach as much as 8.5 per cent of GDP (*Business Standard*, 2007).

One major opportunity for the corporate sector is the outsourcing of health care by the developed world: an earlier CII-McKinsey study projected that medical tourism could account for Rs 10,000 crore by 2012. The trend is already pronounced, with 1,50,000 medical tourists visiting India in 2004, a figure which is growing at an annual rate of 15 per cent (*Business Standaard*, 2007).

India has gained acceptance in areas of medical care such as organ transplant, knee replacement, open-heart surgery among others because of the efforts of the corporate sector in the medical as well as tourism industry. It is estimated that foreigners account for about 12 per cent of all patients in top hospitals of Mumbai, like Lilavati, Jaslok, Breach Candy, Bombay Hospital, Hinduja Hospital, Apollo and Wockhardt.

Looking at the rapid expansion of medical tourism in India and backing from the government in its Health Policy of 2002 where it has impressed upon the idea of Public-Private Partnership and giving lot of subsidy in form of import duty, etc. to the private corporate health care sector.

Renuka Chaudhary, the Union Minister (2004–2009), said that health tourism can emerge as a foreign exchange earner for the country given its advantage (*The Hindu*, Chennai, 8 June 2004). A former Finance Minister, called for India to become a 'global health destination' (*The Financial Times*, 2 July 2003). The urge for promoting medical tourism received further impetus from the Prime Minister's Council for Trade and Industry led by the Kumaramanglam Birla and Mukesh Ambani which identified it as a potential 'sunshine industry'. The National Health Policy 2002 also unambiguously legitimizes the concept when it reads 'to capiatlise on the comparative cost advantage enjoyed by domestic health facilities in the secondary and tertiary sector, the policy will encourage the supply of services to patients of foreign origin on payment. The rendering of such services on payment in foreign exchange will be treated as 'deemed exports' and will be made eligible for all fiscal incentives extended to export earnings' (as quoted in Gupta, 2004).

Since the profit-making capacity of the corporate hospitals is limited by the relatively small size of domestic consumers who have a very high purchasing power, attracting foreign patients has become an essay tool for them to expand the domestic market. The slogan has been highlighted as 'First World Treatment at Third World Prices' if you seek medical treatment in India. (Gupta, 2004).

Impact of Medical Tourism on Domestic Population

Looking to the rapid expansion of medical tourism in India, it is pertinent to understand the critical issues of medical tourism and its bearing on health care of its domestic population.

The argument that Indian corporate hospital prices are lower is a relative truth. But for a domestic patient, the cost of treatment in a five-star hospital is beyond reach, affordable only to a minority. A comparison of prices among different grades of hospitals for doing the same procedure in the cities of Chennai and Hyderabad reveals that the prices charged in corporate hospitals are three to four times higher than ordinary private hospitals (Baru, 2000). Above and beyond the arguments of comparative cost advantage, the inequities built within the rules of the international monetary system by way of the huge differences in the nominal exchange rate value make the highest amount of difference in costs. The huge difference between the exchange rate of the domestic and foreign currency is also a major pull factor for the so-called external 'brain drain' in which the developed countries are the major beneficiaries, because generally they have a higher priced currency than the third world countries (Godwin, 2004). The same anomaly is true within India as well with the nominal exchange rate between urban and rural areas being skewed in favour of the former. The urban-centric corporate hospitals are drawing away the best-qualified personnel from the public sector. This absorption by private corporates imposes huge costs on the public health services by deteriorating the quality of public health services.

Another casualty of corporatized health system is its ability to change the preference of individuals through what is called 'demonstration effect'. In a market oriented economy, quality is usually equated with cost. The rise in number of corporate hospitals influences the perception of consumers regarding quality through fancy buildings, plush surroundings and hi-tech equipments (Baru, 2000) which a resource-starved public sector institution cannot afford. The redefinition about the perception of the population regarding 'what constitutes quality care?' has implications for utilization of public health care institutions. The establishment of a corporate hospital in a given medical market also leads to higher costs in the entire market, because in the context of quality competition the rest of the competing hospitals in the market may try to emulate the quality leader which further contributes to increased cost of care.

Secondly, the concept of a heavily medicalized and hi-tech curative medical interventions with huge inequality in access to care for the majority is against the fundamental principles of historic declaration likes Alma Atta, to which India is a signatory, set out a holistic socio-economic and epidemiological view of population (public) health catering to the needs of developing countries. The document favoured a vision of 'Health for All' with a need-based approach and helping achieve the goal through universally accessible health care with a tolerable level of quality determined by the affordability of a community. If the cornerstone of Alma Atta Declaration has been primary health care with least cost, affordable and acceptable technology, currently the emphasis under corporatized health care is fully on heavy capital-intensive medical technologies. For example, studies show that medical technology constitutes around 60 per cent of a corporate hospital's investment (Bhat, 1994). Further, in majority of the medical technology assessments safety and efficacy are included and equity aspect of technology is ignored. If the required emphasis is not given to the diffusion and use of medical technologies in India, the national health care system may get into a perpetual zone of ineffectiveness, inefficiency and inequity. Since the use of technology is an important determinant of improvement in health outcomes, costly technologies act as a great barrier and leads to fundamental inequities of income and wealth in population. Medical technology is not only the single most factor which has changed the cost structure of medical care, but also the predominant component that has altered the concept of quality of care. Thus, it, in turn, has become capable enough to shift the price competition to non-price competition belittling many of the hard assumptions of mainstream economics. Hospitals in the country made use of technology to get an edge over their competitors through use of state-of-the-art technologies (Bhat, 1994). Unlike in majority of the simple technological interventions and other services in which public sector health services have been acting as an invisible regulator-cum-competitor, the financial crunch faced by public hospitals helped the private sector march ahead in the use of high-cost medical technology without any competition. Many scholars attribute India's failure to reduce the disease burden primarily to its emphasis on urban-oriented curative medical model (Antia, 1989). The unregulated growth of curative medical care without adequate financial protection against the cost of illness has been accentuating the gaps in equity health care seeking. This is exactly contrary to the very notions of equity in which poverty is the greatest disability and possessing adequate purchasing power being a chief privilege.

Thirdly, the corporate sector's entry into medical care is usually accompanied by a heavy rise in the price of medical care due to increased use of costly medical technologies, increased marketing expenditures and huge investment in the hotel aspects of care. And cost escalation has been a feature of the medical sector in a majority of the national health systems and especially so where private competition is dominant. For example, competition has been the bedrock of the US health system and the major problem facing it is cost escalation where the best care in the world is available on the one hand and an estimated 44 million population is unserved or under-served on the other due to lack of adequate coverage of protection mechanisms. Contrary to many other sectors in an economy, competition has promoted price escalation in the medical sector because it is mostly quality based and less price oriented. Further, a large number of hi-tech medical technologies possess a high degree of indivisibility in provision (e.g. R&D, operation theatre, scanners, etc.) conductive for the creation of a monopoly. Owing to the existence of a high degree of imperfections in the relationship between the principal (patient) and agency (physician) in the medical market, the physician can take advantage of the ignorance of the consumer by 'inducing' demand which finally increases the cost and financial burden on patients. High indivisibility in provision means the firm will experience increasing returns to scale for quite some time and there exists a minimum level, below which it is not viable to operate and simple competition fails to reduce prices. Even if profit is not the prime objective, the vast untapped economies of scale in specialty and multispecialty hospitals leads to the setting of prices far higher than economically efficient levels of production adding to the financial burden of patients.

However, medical tourism and the corporate health care industry divert scarce domestic medical manpower and resources from the requirements of the vast majority of people. This is in a situation where the dominance of the private sector has already made health care unbearably expensive for the vast majority. In India, 80 per cent of expenditure on health is out-of-pocket spending by patients; public health spending is among the world's lowest as a proportion of GDP (0.9%, falling from 1.3% in 1991). Remarkably, the share of the health sector in India's GDP, at 5–6 per cent, is double than that of comparable countries such as China, Sri Lanka, and Malaysia (2.4–3%); yet the these countries have much better health indicators than India (Duggal, 2005). Internationally, countries with a smaller public sector in health wind up devoting a larger share of GDP to health care than comparable countries, and yet experience worse health indicators; the classic case among developed countries is the United States. In a sense, then, the very growth of the private sector in health care both leads to the growth of the sector's share in GDP and the worsening health of the people.

The trend towards corporate health care in India would accelerate the shift of medical resources to the private sector and further prevent the poor from getting medical care. Further, salaries of public sector medical staff would have to be raised in order to prevent them from leaving for the private sector; this would reduce the amount left for other heads of expenditure. Even before the large-scale entry of the private corporate sector, the overall direction of neo-liberal policies has led to increasing exclusion of the poor from health care: NSS data show the share of persons 'not taking treatment due to financial reasons' in the rural areas rising from 15 per cent in 1986–87 to 25 per cent in 1995–96, and from 10 per cent to 20 per cent in the urban areas over the same period (Duggal, 2005). Since 1991, and particularly since the mid-1990s, there has been a steep growth in the share of 'medical care and health services' in total consumption expenditure (private final consumption expenditure from national accounts data and cited from *India's Runway Growth*, 2008); yet in the same period, the rates of decline in infant mortality ratio and under-five mortality have stagnated or slowed (Duggal, 2005).

The growing number of Joint Commission International (JCI) accreditations being awarded to Indian hospitals. The JCI is an international body which awards accreditations to hospitals all over the world. Foreign patients now will be doubly assured that they will get quality health care in India. However, for the majority of the public and private hospitals in India for the domestic population, there is no accreditation which is equally important for the domestic population.

Economic Aspect of Medical Tourism in India

Third World countries like Cuba, Argentina, Mexico, Hungry, South Africa, Thailand, Singapore and India are the chief players in the world. People from the developed nations to save money, reach out to the Third World developing countries for undertaking medical treatments. India's health market in the past few years has witnessed a high. India, in the recent past, has emerged as the major health destination. It offers treatments at half and one-third the costs of medical tourism spots such as Singapore and Thailand. Thus, among the third world countries India has emerged as a major hub since there is scarcity of medical facilities and expertise in other developing countries such as Oman and Africa.

According to Tattara, a Professor of Economic Policy, India is the second Asian country to provide the medical tourism with an inflow of about 4,50,000 tourists in 2007. Further, as reported by a Joint Report by Confederation of Indian Industry and McKinsey Consultants, there is about 30 per cent growth annually in medical tourism in India. Around 1,50,000 foreigners have visited India for treatment and the number has been rising by 15 per cent each year. In efforts to further boost this type of tourism, India has to be made a global health destination and should have improvements in airports infrastructures. Another measure taken by the government is the issuing of 'M-Visa' (Medical Visa) and MX visas for the spouse accompanying which is valid for a year (Sama Resource Group for Women and Health, 2010).

In addition, with low cost medical facilities, qualified medical professionals and availability of world class and latest technology, standing at par with those in USA, UK and Europe, India has emerged to be one of the favourable destinations for medical tourism. The trend is picking up especially among the poor people of rich countries and among the rich people of the poor countries.

It is estimated that the cost of a treatment in India starts at around a tenth of the price of comparable treatment in America or Britain. For example, as reported, a complex heart operation on an 87-year-old American patient cost around $ 8,000 inclusive of the airfare and a month's stay in a hospital in Chennai, while a less operation in America had cost him US $ 40,000. Apart from the cost savings, another attraction is the time involved in the procedure. Getting a treatment done in India does not require people to wait and people who require urgent medical attention benefit from medical tourism as one is catered to on an urgent basis as well (Lenin and Garg, 2011).

Medical tourism is believed to benefit the country in several ways, to name a few, medical tourism is one of the means of generating good revenue for foreign exchange. It will also help generate a lot of employment opportunities for the natives in India. In this process, medical professionals will develop expertise with foreign patients which will help in establishing training centres for training medical professionals. Medical tourism will also help boost pharmaceutical industries in the country for further development, training and employment opportunities (Badwe, Giri and Latti, 2012). A large part of the increase in medical tourism can be submitted to government's efforts on promoting this industry. Some of the efforts made by the government include the decreased rates for loans to help establish hospitals, making drugs available at lower prices, providing with the land for establishment of the clinic and so on. Also in the wake of boosting this industry, India legalized surrogacy as fertility tourism contributes to the economy of the country. Fertility tourism is, thus, on the rise in India, it has experienced 30 per cent growth in 2000 and 15 per cent growth between 2005–2010 (Sarojini, Marwah and Shenoi, 2011). The growth of the medical tourism in the private sector at the cost of the public sector is reflected in a rise in the GDP share of that service – even as it may mean the worsening of conditions for the majority of people.

Medical Tourism: A Case of Commercial Surrogacy in India

India has emerged as an already established, easily accessible and an international market in commercial surrogacy. Highly qualified English speaking doctors and the staff along with well-equipped hospitals are some of the factors that contribute in making India a host to majority of surrogacy treatments. India, thus, provides First World treatment at the cost of the Third World countries. The cost of surrogacy in India is around US$ 2000–3000 while the same procedure would cost about US$ 45,000 in the US. India's reproductive tourism is estimated to be worth from US$ 500 million to US$ 2.3 billion (Palattiyil et al., 2010). Thus, increased globalization and advances in artificial reproductive techniques help this business to flourish, opening the market and options across the globe. Though the first successful transnational surrogacy arrangement did not come about till 2004, Vora (2009) argued that the ground for the same was set much earlier with the establishment of neo-liberal discourse which emphasized outsourcing and the availability of cheap labour in India.

India a Booming Surrogacy Market

Durga Agarwal was India's first and the world's second test tube baby born on 3 October 1978. However, her claim of birth through IVF was highly disputed which led to suicide by the man responsible for bringing her into the world, Dr Subhas Mukherjee. Until the mid-1980s treatments to curb infertility consisted of diagnosis of its cause rather than providing the solution for it. After this came the corrective treatments like that of tuboplasty and microscopic tuboplasty. By and large, the procedure ended with very little positive results and the patients were left either to accept childlessness as a matter of their fate or seek adoption. However, today patients have a variety of options to choose from ranging from artificial insemination to in-vitro and its varied forms like GIFT and ZIFT.

Not only do the clinics in India manage surrogacy without the state's intrusion but they also benefit from the governmental policies encouraging medical tourism in India. Even though other countries in Latin America and Asia, including India, Cuba, Jordan, Malaysia, Singapore and Thailand, actively promote medical tourism, a form of travel for medical purpose, India is still considered to be the leading country after Thailand. Additionally, there are no laws that regulate the surrogate-client relationship in India akin to be the liberal model of surrogacy in California, where surrogacy comes under the arrangement of private commercial agencies that regulates agreements as per their criteria without much of state interference. As a result, the clients are able to take advantage of the user-friendly policies of the private hospitals and clinics that tare otherwise banned or heavily regulated in other countries (Pande, 2010).

Glenn Cohen, a Harvard Law professor, in the book *Patients with Passports: Medical Tourism, Ethics and Law*, estimated that about 2,000 foreign babies are born to Indian surrogates each year. Also Sama, a Delhi-based resource group for women and health in India, in its recent research, concluded that about 3,000 clinics in India provide surrogacy services to foreigners generating more than US$ 4,000 million per year. Since 2002, when India legalized commercial surrogacy, it has emerged as a hotspot, owing primarily to possibility of undergoing the procedure at a low cost. While in the US, surrogacy can cost from US$ 80,000 to US$ 1,50,000 the same procedure on the other hand in India ranges from US$ 20,000 to US$ 60,000 depending on the clinic and services provided (Kirby, 2013).

It is the affordability along with the lenient and loose legal restrictions in India that makes it an ideal choice for many intending parents. In addition to this, the high rates of compensation for surrogates have led to the creation of surplus surrogates in India that contributes to the tourism. Also, the fact that there is an increasing number of Indians who can speak English along with the advancement in medical technology has made the nation stand out in the midst of other potential countries. On the other hand, it is also a good opportunity for women from lower-socio levels to work as a surrogate; as the compensation (about US$ 6,000) is the equivalent to about 15 years of salary for some. But it also raises questions of ethics as many see these only as 'wombs for rent' and debate whether commercial surrogacy is oppression or an opportunity (Chang, 2009).

In the Indian context, Anand city of Gujarat is the leading player in the country. When one argues about the booming surrogacy market one is naturally confronted with the number and types of clinics spread throughout. Clinics cater to the wider population, with special emphasis on the foreign clientele. Thus, along with the government, the clinics and the advertisements on their websites, media – all contribute significantly in sustaining the booming market. The clinics with the help of attractive pictures and taglines try to lure the clients. An important thing to consider is how the print media as a medium of communication has widely resorted to enhance medical tourism and surrogacy as well.

Thus, one could argue that Indian medical tourism is on the rise, and regarding lack of government laws on the subject along with cheaply available surrogates in the country as the major cause of the rise. But one cannot possibly ignore the role of clinics, their manipulation of the statistics where focus is only on the positive aspect and the role of internet, media and advertisements in promoting surrogacy in India.

Issues of the Global Surrogacy Market

Transnational surrogacy can be placed in the ambit of multifaceted concerns and issues raised by feminists regarding technology, the consequences they have on women, globalization, reproductive choice and labour. Underneath the assumption that with these technologies women from all over the world are coming together to help each other lies the truth that these technologies rather help in maintaining long held class and race inequalities especially among the First World and the Third World. Another emerging issue is that of citizenship as to what happened to a child born to an Indian surrogate commissioned by a foreign couple.

Many nations, laws on parentage are rooted in traditional notions of conception and birth whereby she who carried is the child's legal mother. According to this, the surrogate by default is identified to be the mother of the child that would further aggravate the child's citizenship status. Here one could take into account citizenship laws based on birth, which takes place under two principles: *jus soil*, refers to the right of the soil and *jus sanguinis* that stands for right of blood. The countries that follow right of the soil accord citizenship rights to those who are born in their country and those who follow right of the blood grant citizenship based upon the nationality of the child's parents. These two principles could operate simultaneously and mutually, therefore a country could have both the laws functional to determine citizenship.

However, no matter how sorted these laws appear, they also pose serious issues when confronted with transnational surrogacy arrangements. If one considers a surrogacy arrangement in which a couple hires a surrogate from a country where right of the soil prevails then the child is certainly not born stateless and by virtue of the law would become a citizen of the country where he or she is born. But consider the situation of the couple that hires a surrogate where right of the blood exists, then the child is not accorded citizenship rights of any country. This leads to a situation whereby establishing parental rights could be almost impossible since the couple is strangled between the two countries that acquire different positions on surrogacy (Lin, 2012). A lot of it also depends on the country's law on surrogacy as well. The situation is best explained in the case of Baby Manji (Mohapatra, 2012) and that of the Balaz twins.

Globalization and Medical Tourism

Health policies and health delivery have traditionally been bounded by the nation state or between federal tiers of government. In recent decades, significant economic, social, and political changes have encouraged a more transnational and international role for health policy development. These national interconnections (political, economic, social and technical) include the movement of people, products, capital and ideas and this has offered new opportunities and challenges for health care delivery and regulation. A number of developments support this growth in medical travel:

- Regulatory regimes (such as the General Agreement on Trade in Services and other World Trade Organization Agreements).
- Recognition of transnational disease patterns.
- Growing patient mobility (low cost airlines, advancements in information-communication technology, and shifting cultural attitudes among the public about overseas destinations).

Summing Up

In contemporary time a large numbers of people are travelling for treatment. There is a shift towards patients from richer, more developed nations travelling to less developed countries to access health services, largely driven by the low-cost treatments and helped by cheap flights and internet sources of information. Both the private business sector and national governments in both developed and developing nations have been instrumental in promoting tourism as a potentially lucrative source of foreign revenue. We define medical tourism as, when consumers elect to travel across international borders with the intention of receiving some form of medical treatment. Medical tourism is related to the broader notion of health tourism. India has emerged as an already established, easily accessible, and an international market in commercial surrogacy. In India, the medical tourism industry has been on the rise and within this, India is fast emerging as a strong player in the reproductive tourism industry.

References

Antia, N.H. (1989), 'Poor Health Services: Who is to Blame?', *Economic and Political Weekly*, 24(39): 2214–15.

Badwe, A.N., P.A. Giri and R.G. Latti (2012), 'Medical Tourism in India: A New Avenue', *International Journal of Biomedical and Advance Research*, 3(3): 144–48.

Baru, Rama (2000), 'Privatization and Corporatization', *Seminar*, V(489), May.

BBC (20 June 2014), 'Passport Delay Leaves Surrogate Babies Stranded in India', Retrieved 18 July 2014, from Centre for Genetic and Society, http://www.geneticsandsociety.org/article.php?id=7846

Bhat, Ramesh (1994), *Private Investment in Medical Technology: The Need for Policy in India*, Policy Formulation Case Study, Ahmedabad: IIM.

Business Standard (2007), 'India's Healthcare Spending to Cross Rs 200,000 Crore by 2012', 6 March.

Carrera, P. and J. Bridges (2006), 'Globalization and Healthcare: Understanding Health and Medical Tourism', *Expert Review of Pharmacoeconomics and Outcomes Research*, 6(4): 447–54.

Centre for Social Research (2008), 'Surrogate Motherhood: Ethical or Commercial', CSR.

Chang, M. (2009), 'Womb for Rent: India's Commercial Surrogacy', *Harvard International Review*, 31(1): 11–12.

Deomampo, D. (2003), 'Transnational Surrogacy in India: Interrogating Power and Women Agency Frontier', *A Journal of Women Studies*, 34(3): 169.

Duggal, Ravi (2005), 'Public Health Expenditures, Investment and Financing under the Shadow of a Growing Private Sector', in Leena Gangolli, Ravi Duggal and Abhay Shukla (eds), *Review of Healthcare in India, 2005*, Mumbai: CEHAT.

Godwin, S.K. (2004), 'Medical Tourism: Subsidizing the Rich', *Economic and Political Weekly*, 39(36). 3981–83.

Goswami, Rahul (2008), 'Outpatient Impatient', *Hindu*, 27 January.

Gupta, A.S. (2004), 'Medical Tourism and Public Health', *People's Democracy*, 28(19): 24–25.

Gupta, J.A. (2000), *New Reproductive Technologies: Women's Health and Autonomy*, New Delhi: Sage Publications.

India's Runway Growth: Distortion, Disarticulation, and Exclusion, Part-II, Aspects of India's Economy, No. 45, Research Unit for Political Economy.

Kirby, J. (2013), 'These Two American Want Babies Through India Surrogates: It's Not been Easy', Retrieved 6 June 2014, from New Republic, http://wwwnewrepublic.com/article/115873/fertility-tourism-seeking-surrogacy-india-thailand-mexico.

Law Commission of India, Report No. 228 (2009), *Need for Legislation to Regulate Assisted Reproductive Technology Clinics as Well as Rights and Obligations of Parties to a Surrogacy*, Government of India.

Lenin, B.K. and R. Garg (2011), 'India: A Hot Place for Medical Tourism', *Medico-Legal Update: An International Journal*, 11(2).

Lin, Y. (2012), 'Born Lost: Stateless Children in International Surrogacy Arrangements', *Cardoz Journal of International and Comparative Law*, 21(1): 545–87.

Marwah, V. and N. Sarojini (2011), 'Reinventing Reproduction, Re-conceiving Challenges: An Examination of Assisted Reproductive Technologies in India', *Economic and Political Weekly*, XLVI(43): 104–11.

Mckinsey (2005), 'The Medical Tourist', *Slate*, 6 December.

Mckinsey Study (2007), 'Bedside India', *National Journal*, 5 May.

Ministry of Health and Family Welfare, Government of India, New Delhi and Indian Council of Medical Research, *The Assisted Reproductive Technology (Regulation) Bill–2010*.

Mohapatra, S. (2012), 'Stateless Babies and Adoption Scams: A Bioethical Analysis of International Commercial Surrogacy', *Berkeley Journal of International Law*, 30(2): 412–50.

Palattiyil, G. et al. (2010), 'Globalization and Cross-border Reproductive Services: Ethical Implications of Surrogacy in India for Social Work', *International Social Work*, 53(5): 686–700.

Pande, A. (2009), 'Not an Angel, Not a Whore: Surrogates as Dirty Workers in India', *Indian Journal of Gender Studies*, 16(141): 144.

—— (2010), 'Commercial Surrogacy in India: Manufacturing a Perfect Mother-Worker', Signs: *Journal of Women in Culture and Society*, 35(4): 969–94.

Panitch, V. (2913), 'Global Surrogacy: Exploitation to Empowerment', *Journal of Global Ethics*, 8(3): 329–43.

Reymond, J.G. (1989), 'The International Traffic in Women: Women Used in Systems of Surrogacy and Reproduction', *Reproductive and Genetic Engineering*, 2(1): 51–57.

Sama-Resource Group for Women and Health (2010), *Constructing Conceptions: The Mapping of Assisted Reproductive Technologies in India*, New Delhi.

Sarojini, N., V. Marwah and A. Shenoi (2011), 'Globalization of Birth Markets: A Case Study of Assisted Reproductive Technologies in India', *Globalization and Health*, 7(27): 1–9.

The Times of India (2005), 'Medical Tourism: Heatburn in the US', 18 December.

Vora, K. (2009), 'Indian Transnational Surrogacy and the Commodification of Vital Energy', *Subjectivity*, 28(274): 316–33.

—— (2010), 'Medicine, Markets and the Pregnant Body: Indian Commercial Surrogacy and Reproductive Labour in a Transnational Frame', Critical Conceptions: Technology, Justice and the Global Reproductive Market.

—— (2013), 'Potential Risk and Return in Transnational Indian Gestational Surrogacy', *Current Anthropology, Potentiality and Humanness: Revisiting the Anthropological Object in Contemporary Biomedicine*, 54(S7): 77–86.

Index

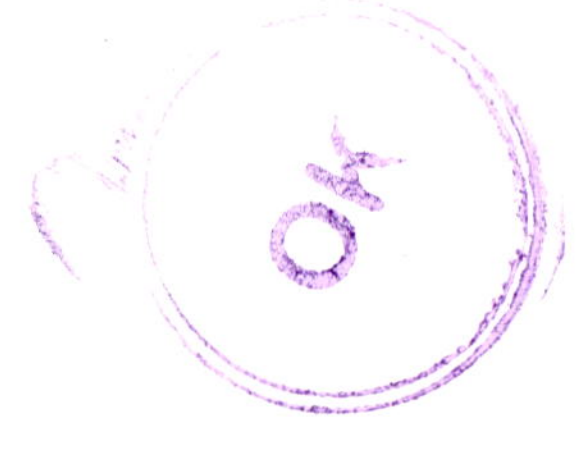